Anarchism
A Documentary History of Libertarian Ideas

dedicated to the memory of

Juils Comeault

Robert
Graham

Anarchism
A Documentary History of Libertarian Ideas

Volume One

From Anarchy to Anarchism (300 CE To 1939)

Montreal/New York/London

Black Rose Books No. II332

National Library of Canada Cataloguing in Publication Data
Graham, Robert
Anarchism: a documentary history of libertarian ideas / Robert Graham, editor
Includes bibliographical references and index.
Contents: v. 1. From anarchy to anarchism (300 CE to 1939)
ISBN: 978-1-55164-251-2 (hardcover)
ISBN: 978-1-55164-250-5 (paperback)
ISBN: 978-1-55164-576-6 (ebook)
1. Anarchism – History – Sources. 2. Libertarianism – History – Sources.
I. Graham, Robert
HX826.A53 2004 335'.83 C2004-905033-8

We wish to thank the Writer's Trust of Canada, on behalf of the Woodcock estate, for permission to reprint from The Anarchist Reader *by George Woodcock (see sections 23 & 60).*

Cover design: Associés libres

C.P. 35788 Succ. Léo Pariseau
Montreal, QC H2X 0A4
CANADA
Explore our books and subscribe to our newsletter.
www.blackrosebooks.com

ORDERING INFORMATION:

North America:
1(800) 565-9523 (Toll Free)
or +1 (416) 667-7791
utpbooks@utpress.utoronto.ca

Europe:
+44 (0)20 8525 8800
order@centralbooks.co.uk

Table of Contents

Acknowledgments

MY THANKS IN PREPARING THIS VOLUME first go to the many translators who have assisted me: Paul Sharkey, John P. Clark, Camille Martin, Robert Ludlow, the late George Woodcock, John Turner, the late Nicolas Walter, the late Vernon Richards, Hsiao-Pei Yen, Guannan Li, Edward S. Krebs, Shuping Wan, Yoshiharu Hashimoto, Dongyoun Hwang, John Crump, Yasuko Sato, Robert Cutler, and Richard Cleminson. Special thanks to those who provided me with material, assistance or suggestions of material for inclusion in this volume: John Rapp, Martha Acklesberg, Don Stewart, Gottfried Heuer, Barry Pateman and the Kate Sharpley Library, Wayne Thorpe, David Goodway, Allan Antliff, Stuart Christie, Pascal Bedos, Paddy Tsurumi, Arif Dirlik, Phil Billingsley, J.M. Adams, Andre Eisenstein, Toby Crowe and Freedom Press, Larry Gambone, Chuck Morse, Davide Turcato, Marianne Enckell and CIRA, Carl Rosenberg, Helene Bowen Raddeker, Sharif Gemie, and Charlatan Stew. I also wish to acknowledge and thank the Institute for Anarchist Studies for providing me with a grant to assist with the publication of this book. Lastly, many thanks and much gratitude to my family for putting up with all of my work on this project.

Preface

ANARCHY, A SOCIETY WITHOUT GOVERNMENT, has existed since time immemorial. Anarchism, the doctrine that such a society is desirable, is a much more recent development.

For tens of thousands of years, human beings lived in societies without any formal political institutions or constituted authority. About 6,000 years ago, around the time of the so-called dawn of civilization, the first societies with formal structures of hierarchy, command, control and obedience began to develop. At first, these hierarchical societies were relatively rare and isolated primarily to what is now Asia and the Middle East. Slowly they increased in size and influence, encroaching upon, sometimes conquering and enslaving, the surrounding anarchic tribal societies in which most humans continued to live. Sometimes independently, sometimes in response to pressures from without, other tribal societies also developed hierarchical forms of social and political organization. Still, before the era of European colonization, much of the world remained essentially anarchic, with people in various parts of the world continuing to live without formal institutions of government well into the 19th century. It was only in the 20th century that the globe was definitively divided up between competing nation states which now claim sovereignty over virtually the entire planet.

The rise and triumph of hierarchical society was a far from peaceful one. War and civilization have always marched forward arm in arm, leaving behind a swath of destruction scarcely conceivable to their many victims, most of whom had little or no understanding of the forces arrayed against them and their so-called primitive ways of life. It was a contest as unequal as it was merciless.

Innocent of government, having lived without it for thousands of years, people in anarchic societies had no conception of anarchy as a distinct way of life. Living without rulers was just something they did. Consequently, anarchism, the idea that living without government is a superior way of life, would never have even occurred to them, lacking anything to compare anarchy with until it was too late.

It was only after hierarchical societies arose that people within them began to conceive of anarchy as a positive alternative. Some, such as the early Daoist philosophers in China (Selection 1), looked back to an age without government, when people lived in peace with themselves and the world. Various Christian sects looked forward to the second coming, when the egalitarian brotherly love of Christ and his disciples would triumph over evil (Selection 3). Rationalists, such as Zeno, the founder of Stoicism in ancient Greece, and later Renaissance (Selection 2) and Enlightenment (Selection 4) thinkers, envisaged a new era of enlightenment, when reason would replace coercion as the guiding force in human affairs.

Although none of these early advocates of anarchy described themselves as anarchists, what they all share is opposition to coercive authority and hierarchical relationships based on power, wealth or privilege. In contrast to other radicals, they also reject any authoritarian or privileged role for themselves in the struggle against authority and in the creation of a free society.

We find similar attitudes among some of the revolutionaries in the modern era. During the French Revolution, the *enragés* (Selection 5) and the radical egalitarians (Selection 6) opposed revolutionary dictatorship and government as a contradiction in terms, and sought to abolish all hierarchical distinctions, including that between the governed and the governors.

But it was not until around the time of the 1848 Revolutions in Europe that anarchism began to emerge as a distinct doctrine (Chapter 4). It was Pierre-Joseph Proudhon in France who was the first to describe himself as an anarchist in 1840 (Selection 8). Anarchist ideas soon spread to Germany (Selection 11), Spain (Selection 15) and Italy (Selection 16). Following the failure of the 1848 Revolutions some expatriates, disillusioned by politics, adopted an anarchist position (Selection 14).

As the political reaction in Europe began to ebb in the 1860s, anarchist ideas re-emerged, ultimately leading to the creation of an avowedly anarchist movement from out of the anti-authoritarian sections of the socialist First International (Chapters 5 and 6). The Paris Commune, despite being drowned in blood, gave renewed inspiration to the anarchists and helped persuade many of them to adopt an anarchist communist position (Chapters 7 and 8). The anarchist communists championed the Commune, but insisted that within the revolutionary commune there should be no ruling authority and no private property, but rather free federation and distribution according to need.

Although anarchist communism was perhaps the most influential anarchist doctrine, soon spreading throughout Europe, Latin America and later Asia, the First International had bequeathed to the anarchist movement another doctrine of comparable significance, anarcho-syndicalism (Chapter 12), a combination of anarchism and revolutionary trade unionism based on direct action (Chapter 10) and anti-parliamentarianism.

Of lesser significance were anarchist collectivism (Selections 36 and 55), where distribution of wealth was to be based on labour, and individualist anarchism (Selections 42 and 61), which for the most part was but a footnote to Max Stirner (Selection 11).

At the beginning of the 20th century, a new era of revolutions began, first in Mexico (Chapter 16), then in Russia (Chapter 18), culminating, at least for the anarchists, in Spain (Chapter 23). At the same time, anarchists had to deal with a devastating war in Europe and the rise of totalitarianism (Chapters 17 and 22).

Anarchist ideas spread throughout Latin America (Chapter 19), China (Chapter 20), and Japan and Korea (Chapter 21). I was fortunate to obtain for this volume translations of considerable material from these areas and from Europe that has never before appeared in English. I have also included several translations from now out of print sources that would otherwise be unavailable. Generally, I have organized the selections chronologically, but with a specific theme for each chapter, to try to convey the scope of anarchist ideas, as well as their historical development.

This is the first of a two volume documentary history of anarchist ideas. The final chapter of this volume, with selections from Emma Goldman, Herbert Read and Errico Malatesta, constitutes both an epilogue to volume one, and a prologue to volume two, which will cover the period from 1939 to the present day. I regard all three as important figures in the transition from "classical anarchism," covering the period from Proudhon to the Spanish Revolution, to modern anarchism as it developed after the Second World War.

A review of the material in this volume alone demonstrates how remarkable was the breadth and depth of anarchist thinking for its time. Anarchists and their precursors, such as Fourier, were among the first to criticize the combined effects of the organization of work, the division of labour and technological innovation under capitalism. Anarchists recognized the importance of education as both a means of social control and as a potential means of liberation. They had important things to say about art and free expression, law and morality. They championed sexual freedom but also criticized the commodification of sex under capitalism. They were critical of all hierarchical relationships, whether between father and children, husband and wife, teacher and student, professionals and workers, or leaders and led, throughout society and even within their own organizations. They emphasized the importance of maintaining consistency between means and ends, and in acting in accordance with their ideals now, in the process of transforming society, not in the distant future. They opposed war and militarism in the face of widespread repression, and did not hesitate to criticize the orthodox Left for its authoritarianism and opportunism. They developed an original conception of an all-encompassing social revolution, rejecting state terrorism and seeking to reduce violence to a minimum.

And they paid dearly for it. Several of the contributors to this volume were executed, murdered or killed fighting for their ideals (Pisacane, Landauer, the Haymarket Martyrs, Ferrer, Guerrero, Kôtoku Shûsui, Ôsugi Sakae, Itô Noe, Arshinov, Isaac Puente), as were countless of their comrades. Others died in prison or prematurely as a result of imprisonment (Bakunin, Most, Wilde, Flores Magón, Makhno, Shin Chaeho). Others were the objects of attempted assassinations (Michel, de Cleyre, Malatesta). Still others died in tragic circumstances (Déjacque, Gross, Berkman). Virtually every one of them was imprisoned at various times for advocating anarchy. Anyone honestly assessing the impact of anarchist ideas, or the lack thereof, cannot fail to take this pervasive repression into account. The "competition of ideas" has never been a fair one.

Chapter 1
Early Texts On Servitude And Freedom

1. Bao Jingyan: Neither Lord Nor Subject (300 CE)

This first selection is from one of the earliest surviving texts to set forth an identifiably anarchist position, written by the Daoist philosopher, Bao Jingyan, circa 300 CE. Daoism originated in ancient China around 400 BCE near the end of the Zhou dynasty. It is generally associated with Lao Zi (or Tzu), a semi-mythical figure said to have lived in the 6th Century BCE, and the text Daode Jing *(or* Tao Te Ching*). Unlike the selection that follows, the* Daode Jing, *despite setting forth a philosophy of "nongovernment," is addressed to rulers, advising them that the best way to rule is by "non-rule." Whether it can be described as an anarchist text remains controversial (see John A. Rapp, "Daoism and Anarchism Reconsidered," in* Anarchist Studies, *Vol.6, No.2). A later Daoist philosopher, Ruan Ji (or Juan Chi, 210-263 CE), moved closer to an explicitly anarchist position, writing that when "rulers are set up, tyranny arises; when officials are established, thieves are born. You idly ordain rites and laws only to bind the lowly common people" (as quoted in Rapp, page 137). Bao Jingyan, whose motto was "Neither Lord Nor Subject," wrote during the Wei-Jin period, or Period of Disunity, when China was divided into several warring states. This translation is taken from Etienne Balazs'* Chinese Civilization and Bureaucracy: Variations on a Theme *(New Haven: Yale University Press, 1964), and is reprinted with the kind permission of the publisher.*

THE CONFUCIAN LITERATI SAY: "Heaven gave birth to the people and then set rulers over them." But how can High Heaven have said this in so many words? Is it not rather that interested parties make this their pretext? The fact is that the strong oppressed the weak and the weak submitted to them; the cunning tricked the innocent and the innocent served them. It was because there was submission that the relation of lord and subject arose, and because there was servitude that the people, being powerless, could be kept under control. Thus servitude and mastery result from the struggle between the strong and the weak and the contrast between the cunning and the innocent, and Blue Heaven has nothing whatsoever to do with it.

When the world was in its original undifferentiated state, the Nameless (*wu-ming*, i.e., the Tao) was what was valued, and all creatures found happiness in self-fulfillment. Now when the cinnamon-tree has its bark stripped or the varnish-tree is cut, it is not done at the wish of the tree; when the pheasant's feathers are plucked or the kingfisher's torn out, it is not done by desire of the bird. To be bitted and bridled is not in accordance with the nature of the horse; to be put under the yoke and bear burdens does not give pleasure to the ox. Cunning has its origin in the use of force that goes against the true nature of things, and the real reason for harming creatures is to provide useless adornments. Thus catching the birds of the air in order to supply frivolous adornments, making holes in noses where no holes should be, tying beasts by the leg when nature meant them to be free, is not in accord with the destiny of the myriad creatures, all born to live out their lives unharmed. And so the people are compelled to labour so that those in office may be nourished; and while their superiors enjoy fat salaries, they are reduced to the direst poverty.

It is all very well to enjoy the infinite bliss of life after death, but it is preferable not to have died in the first place; and rather than acquire an empty reputation for integrity by resigning office and foregoing one's salary, it is better that there should be no office to resign. Loyalty and righteousness only appear when rebellion breaks out in the empire, filial obedience and parental love are only displayed when there is discord among kindred.

In the earliest times, there was neither lord nor subjects. Wells were dug for drinking-water, the fields were plowed for food, work began at sunrise and ceased at sunset; everyone was free and at ease, neither competing with each other nor scheming against each other, and no one was either glorified or humiliated. The waste lands had no paths or roads and the waterways no boats or bridges, and because there were no means of communication by land or water, people did not appropriate each other's property; no armies could be formed, and so people did not attack one another. Indeed since no one climbed up to seek out nests nor dived down to sift the waters of the deep, the phoenix nested under the eaves of the house and dragons disported in the garden pool. The ravening tiger could be trodden on, the poisonous snake handled. Men could wade through swamps without raising the waterfowl, and enter the woodlands without startling the fox or the hare. Since no one even began to think of gaining power or seeking profit, no dire events or rebellions occurred; and as spears and shields were not in use, moats and ramparts did not have to be built. All creatures lived together in mystic unity, all of them merged in the Way (*Tao*). Since they were not visited by plague or pestilence, they could live out their lives and die a natural death. Their hearts being pure, they were devoid of cunning. Enjoying plentiful supplies of food, they strolled about with full bellies. Their speech was not flowery, their behavior not ostentatious. How, then, could there have been accumulation of property such as to rob the people of their wealth, or severe punishments to trap and ensnare them? When this age entered on decadence, knowledge and cunning came into use. The Way and its Virtue (*Tao te*) having fallen into decay, a hierarchy was established. Customary regulations for promotion and degradation and for profit and loss proliferated, ceremonial garments such as the [gentry's] sash and sacrificial cap and the imperial blue and yellow [robes for worshiping Heaven and Earth] were elaborated. Buildings of earth and wood were raised high into the sky, with the beams and rafters painted red and green. The heights were overturned in quest of gems, the depths dived into in search of pearls; but however vast a collection of precious stones people might have assembled, it still would not have sufficed to satisfy their whims, and a whole mountain of gold would not have been enough to meet their expenditure, so sunk were they in depravity and vice, having transgressed against the fundamental principles of the Great Beginning. Daily they became further removed from the ways of their ancestors, and turned their back more and more upon man's original simplicity. Because they promoted the "worthy" to office, ordinary people strove for reputation, and because they prized material wealth, thieves and robbers appeared. The sight of desirable objects tempted true and honest hearts, and the display of arbitrary power and love of gain opened the road to robbery. So they made weapons with points and with sharp edges, and after that there was no end to usurpations and acts of aggression, and they were only afraid lest crossbows should not be strong enough, shields stout enough, lances sharp enough, and defences solid enough. Yet all this could have been dispensed with if there had been no oppression and violence from the start.

Therefore it has been said: "Who could make scepters without spoiling the unblemished jade? And how could altruism and righteousness (*jen* and *i*) be extolled unless the Way and its Virtue had perished?" Although tyrants such as Chieh and Chou were able to burn men to death, massacre their advisers, make mince-meat of the feudal lords, cut the barons into strips, tear out men's hearts and break their bones, and go to the furthest extremes of tyrannical crime down to the use of torture by roasting and grilling, however cruel they may by nature have been, how could they have done such things if they had had to remain among the ranks of the common people? If they gave way to their cruelty and lust and butchered the whole empire, it was because, as rulers, they could do as they pleased. As soon as the relationship between lord and subject is established, hearts become daily more filled with evil designs, until the manacled criminals sullenly doing forced labour in the mud and the dust are full of mutinous thoughts, the Sovereign trembles with anxious fear in his ancestral temple, and the people simmer with revolt in the midst of their poverty and distress; and to try to stop them revolting by means of rules and regulations, or control them by means of penalties and punishments, is like trying to dam a river in full flood with a handful of earth, or keeping the torrents of water back with one finger.

2. Etienne de la Boetie: On Voluntary Servitude (1552)

Etienne de la Boetie (1530-1563), the friend of the famous essayist, Michel de Montaigne, wrote his Discourse on Voluntary Servitude *around the age of 22, when a law student at the University of Orleans in France. The essay remained unpublished until after his death, by which time he had established himself as a royal official with much more conservative views, advocating the suppression of Protestantism, by forceful conversion or exile, in favour of the Catholic Church. Ironically, his essay was first published as part of a radical Huguenot pamphlet in 1574. Since then it has resurfaced at various times of intellectual and political ferment, during the Enlightenment, the French Revolution and in the aftermath of the failed 1848 Revolution in France, after Napoleon III's coup d'etat, only to be rediscovered by the 19th Century anarchist and pacifist movements, influencing a variety of writers, including Gustav Landauer and Leo Tolstoy. These excerpts are taken from the Black Rose Books edition, using the 1942 translation by Harry Kurz.*

I SHOULD LIKE MERELY TO understand how it happens that so many men, so many villages, so many cities, so many nations, sometimes suffer under a single tyrant who has no other power than the power they give him; who is able to harm them only to the extent to which they have the willingness to bear with him; who could do them absolutely no injury unless they preferred to put up with him rather than contradict him. Surely a striking situation! Yet it is so common that one must grieve the more and wonder the less at the spectacle of a million men serving in wretchedness, their necks under the yoke, not constrained by a greater multitude than they, but simply, it would seem, delighted and charmed by the name of one man alone whose power they need not fear, for he is evidently the one person whose qualities they cannot admire because of his inhumanity and brutality toward them.

A weakness characteristic of human kind is that we often have to obey force; we have to make concessions; we ourselves cannot always be the stronger. Therefore, when a nation is constrained by the fortune of war to serve a single clique...one should not be amazed that the nation obeys, but simply be grieved by the situation;

or rather, instead of being amazed or saddened, consider patiently the evil and look forward hopefully toward a happier future...

But O good Lord! What strange phenomenon is this? What name shall we give it? What is the nature of this misfortune? What vice is it, or, rather, what degradation? To see an endless multitude of people not merely obeying, but driven to servility? Not ruled, but tyrannized over? These wretches have no wealth, no kin, nor wife nor children, not even life itself that they can call their own. They suffer plundering, wantonness, cruelty, not from an army, not from a barbarian horde, on account of whom they must shed their blood and sacrifice their lives, but from a single man; not from a Hercules nor from a Samson, but from a single little man...Shall we call subjection to such a leader cowardice? Shall we say that those who serve him are cowardly and faint-hearted? If two, if three, if four, do not defend themselves from the one, we might call that circumstance surprising but nevertheless conceivable. In such a case one might be justified in suspecting a lack of courage. But if a hundred, if a thousand endure the caprice of a single man, should we not rather say that they lack not the courage but the desire to rise against him, and that such an attitude indicates indifference rather than cowardice? When not a hundred, not a thousand men, but a hundred provinces, a thousand cities, a million men, refuse to assail a single man from whom the kindest treatment received is the infliction of serfdom and slavery, what shall we call that? Is it cowardice? Of course there is in every vice inevitably some limit beyond which one cannot go. Two, possibly ten, may fear one; but when a thousand, a million men, a thousand cities, fail to protect themselves against the domination of one man, this cannot be called cowardly, for cowardice does not sink to such a depth, any more than valor can be termed the effort of one individual to scale a fortress, to attack an army, or to conquer a kingdom. What monstrous vice, then, is this which does not even deserve to be called cowardice, a vice for which no term can be found vile enough, which nature herself disavows and our tongues refuse to name?

...It amazes us to hear accounts of the valor that liberty arouses in the hearts of those who defend it; but who could believe reports of what goes on every day among the inhabitants of some countries, who could really believe that one man alone may mistreat a hundred thousand and deprive them of their liberty? Who would credit such a report if he merely heard it, without being present to witness the event? And if this condition occurred only in distant lands and were reported to us, which one among us would not assume the tale to be imagined or invented, and not really true? Obviously there is no need of fighting to overcome this single tyrant, for he is automatically defeated if the country refuses consent to its own enslavement: it is not necessary to deprive him of anything, but simply to give him nothing; there is no need that the country make an effort to do anything for itself provided it does nothing against itself. It is therefore the inhabitants themselves who permit, or, rather, bring about, their own subjection, since by ceasing to submit they would put an end to their servitude. A people enslaves itself, cuts its own throat, when, having a choice between being vassals and being free men, it deserts its liberties and takes on the yoke, gives consent to its own misery, or, rather, apparently welcomes it. If it cost the people anything to recover its freedom, I should not urge action to this end, although there is nothing a human should hold more dear than the restoration of his own natural right, to change himself from a beast of burden back to a man, so to speak. I do not demand of him so much boldness; let him prefer the doubtful security of living wretchedly to the uncertain hope of living as he pleases. What then? If in order to have liberty nothing more is needed than to long for it, if only a simple act of the will is necessary, is there any nation in the world that considers a single wish too high a price to pay in order to recover rights which it ought to be ready to redeem at the cost of its blood, rights such that their loss must bring all men of honor to the point of feeling life to be unendurable and death itself a deliverance?

Everyone knows that the fire from a little spark will increase and blaze ever higher as long as it finds wood to burn; yet without being quenched by water, but merely by finding no more fuel to feed on, it consumes itself, dies down, and is no longer a flame. Similarly, the more tyrants pillage, the more they crave, the more they ruin and destroy; the more one yields to them, and obeys them, by that much do they become mightier and more formidable, the readier to annihilate and destroy. But if not one thing is yielded to them, if, without any violence they are simply not obeyed, they become naked and undone and as nothing, just as, when the root receives no nourishment, the branch withers and dies…

Poor, wretched, and stupid peoples, nations determined on your own misfortune and blind to your own good! You let yourselves be deprived before your own eyes of the best part of your revenues; your fields are plundered, your homes robbed, your family heirlooms taken away. You live in such a way that you cannot claim a single thing as your own; and it would seem that you consider yourselves lucky to be loaned your property, your families, and your very lives. All this havoc, this misfortune, this ruin, descends upon you not from alien foes, but from the one enemy whom you yourselves render as powerful as he is, for whom you go bravely to war, for whose greatness you do not refuse to offer your own bodies unto death. He who thus domineers over you has only two eyes, only two hands, only one body, no more than is possessed by the least man among the infinite numbers dwelling in your cities; he has indeed nothing more than the power that you confer upon him to destroy you. Where has he acquired enough eyes to spy upon you, if you do not provide them yourselves? How can he have so many arms to beat you with, if he does not borrow them from you? The feet that trample down your cities, where does he get them if they are not your own? How does he have any power over you except through you? How would he dare assail you if he had no cooperation from you? What could he do to you if you yourselves did not connive with the thief who plunders you, if you were not accomplices of the murderer who kills you, if you were not traitors to yourselves? You sow your crops in order that he may ravage them, you install and furnish your homes to give him goods to pillage; you rear your daughters that he may gratify his lust; you bring up your children in order that he may confer upon them the greatest privilege he knows—to be led into his battles, to be delivered to butchery, to be made the servants of his greed and the instruments of his vengeance; you yield your bodies unto hard labour in order that he may indulge in his delights and wallow in his filthy pleasures; you weaken yourselves in order to make him the stronger and the mightier to hold you in check. From all these indignities, such as the very beasts of the field would not endure, you can deliver yourselves if you try, not by taking action, but merely by willing to be free. Resolve to serve no more, and you are at once freed. I do not ask that you place hands upon the tyrant to topple him over, but simply that you support him no longer; then you will behold him, like a great Colossus whose pedestal has been pulled away, fall of his own weight and break into pieces?

3. Gerrard Winstanley: The New Law of Righteousness (1649)

Gerrard Winstanley (1609-1676) was part of a group of radical Christian egalitarians, the Diggers, active in the English Revolution and Civil War between 1649 and 1650, when they attempted to establish a colony on waste lands at St. George's Hill. As a result of continuing harassment from the local property owners and authorities, they moved to nearby Cobham Heath, where the lords of the manor had their houses and furniture destroyed, threatening them with death should they return. The following selections are taken from one of Winstanley's most anarchistic pamphlets, The New Law of Righteousness, *written a couple of months before Winstanley and a small group of Diggers began their attempt to cultivate the common lands at St. George's Hill. The Biblical references are from the original text (reprinted in* The Writings of Gerrard Winstanley, *Ithaca: Cornell University Press, 1941, ed. G.H. Sabine).*

EXPERIENCE SHEWS US THAT every beast doth act in oppression and cruelty, towards such creatures, as he can master at advantage. And thus doth the flesh of man, which is the King of beasts: For when the wisdome and power of the flesh raigns, which in deed is Adam, that man that appeared first to rule the earth, man-kinde, and by his un-righteousnesse makes it a land of barrennesse: For this first Adam is such a selfish power, that he seeks to compasse all the creatures of the earth into his own covetous hands, to make himself a Lord, and all other his slaves. (Rev. 13.4)

And though he gets lands, moneys, honours, government into his hands, yet he gives the King of righteousnesse, but a company of fawning words of love and obedience; for he makes unrighteousnesse to dwell in heaven and earth, that is, in the whole Creation, by his unrighteous government, and so he becomes the chief Rebell, the Serpent, the Devil, the Murderer, oppressing the Creation, setting himself above all in tyranny: And this power is the curse which the whole Creation groans under, waiting for a restoration by Christ the King and law of righteousnesse, who is the restorer of all things. (*Rom*. 8.21, 22)

And here first I shall declare what *Adam* the first man is, who to me appears to be the wisdome and power of the flesh, carrying along the Creation, man, to live upon creature objects, and to loath and despise the Spirit that made all, and that dwels in all things according to the capacity of every single creature: and all that *Adam* doth is to advance himself to be, The one power; he gets riches and government into his hands, that he may lift up himself, and suppresse the universall liberty, which is Christ. And if he preach, or pray, or performe any service relating to the Spirit, it is for this end, that he may get peace thereby, and so seeks to honour flesh by procuring his own peace, by his own wit and pollicy if that would doe.

So that this *Adam* appears first in every man and woman; but he sits down in the chair of Magistracy, in some above others; for though this climbing power of self-love be in all, yet it rises not to its height in all; but every one that gets an authority into his hands tyrannizes over others; as many husbands, parents, masters, magistrates, that lives after the flesh, doe carry themselves like oppressing Lords over such as are under them; not knowing that their wives, children, servants, subjects are their fellow creatures, and hath an equall priviledge to share with them in the blessing of liberty. And this first *Adam* is to be seen and known in a two fold sense.

First, He is the wisdome and power of the flesh in every man, who indeed is the beast, and he spreads himself within the Creation, man, into divers branches; As into ignorance of the Creatour of all things, into covetousnesse after objects, into pride and envy, lifting up himself above others, and seeking revenge upon all that crosses his selfish honours; and into hypocrisie, subtilty, lying imagination, self-love; from whence proceeds all unrighteous outward acting. This is the first *Adam* lying, ruling and dwelling within man-kinde. And this is he within every man and woman, which makes whole man-kinde, being a prisoner to him, to wonder after the beast, which is no other but self, or upon every thing whereupon self is stamped.

Secondly, The first *Adam* is the wisdome and power of flesh broke out and sate down in the chair of rule and dominion, in one part of man-kinde over another. And this is the beginner of particular interest, buying and selling the earth from one particular hand to another, saying, *This is mine*, upholding this particular propriety by a law of government of his own making, and thereby restraining other fellow creatures from seeking nourishment from their mother earth. So that though a man was bred up in a Land, yet he must not worke for himself where he would sit down. But from *Adam*; that is, for such a one that had bought part of the Land, or came to it by inheritance of his deceased parents, and called it his own Land: So that he that had no Land, was to work for those for small wages, that called the Land theirs; and thereby some are lifted up into the chair of tyranny, and others trod under the foot-stool of misery, as if the earth were made for a few, not for all men.

For truly the common-people by their labours, from the first rise of *Adam*, this particular interest upheld by the fleshes law to this day, they have lifted up their Land-lords and others to rule in tyranny and oppression over them. And let all men say what they will, so long as such are Rulers as cals the Land theirs, upholding this particular propriety of *Mine and Thine*; the common-people shall never have their liberty, nor the Land ever freed from troubles, oppressions and complainings; by reason whereof the Creatour of all things is continually provoked. O thou proud selfish governing *Adam*, in this Land called England! Know that the cries of the poor, whom thou laieth heavy oppressions upon, is heard.

This is unrighteous *Adam*, that dammed up the water springs of universall liberty, and brought the Creation under the curse of bondage, sorrow and tears: But when the earth becomes a common treasury as it was in the beginning, and the King of Righteousnesse comes to rule in every ones heart, then he kils the first *Adam*; for covetousnesse thereby is killed. A man shall have meat, and drinke and clothes by his labour in freedome, and what can be desired more in earth. Pride and envy likewise is killed thereby, for every one shall look upon each other as equall in the Creation; every man indeed being a parfect Creation of himself. And so this second *Adam* Christ, the restorer, stops or dammes up the runnings of those stinking waters of self-interest, and causes the waters of life and liberty to run plentifully in and through the Creation, making the earth one store-house, and every man and woman to live in the law of Righteousnesse and peace as members of one houshold...

The man of the flesh, judges it a righteous thing, That some men that are cloathed with the objects of the earth, and so called rich men, whether it be got by right or wrong, should be Magistrates to rule over the poor; and that the poor should be servants nay rather slaves to the rich. But the spiritual man, which is Christ, doth judge according to the light of equity and reason, That al man-kinde ought to have a quiet substance and freedome, to live upon earth; and that there shal be no bond-man nor beggar in all his holy mountaine...

When every son and daughter shall be made comfortable to that one body, of Jesus the anointed, and the same power rules in them, as in him, every one according to their measure, the oppression shall cease, and the rising up of this universal power, shal destroy and subdue the selfish power. (*Phil*. 3. 21)

But this is not done by the hands of a few, or by unrighteous men, that would pul the tyrannical government out of other mens hands, and keep it in their own heart [hands], as we feel this to be a burden of our age. But it is done by the universall spreading of the divine power, which is Christ in mankind making them all to act in one spirit, and in and after one law of reason and equity...

In the first enterance into the Creation, every man had an equall freedom given him of his Maker to till the earth, and to have dominion over the beasts of the field, the fowls of heaven, and fish in the Seas. But this freedom is broke to pieces by the power of covetousnesse, and pride, and self-love, not by the law of Righteousnesse. And this freedom will not be restored, till the spreading power of Righteousnesse and peace rise up in the earth, making all men and women to be of *one heart, and one mind*, which must come to passe, for that Scripture was never fulfilled yet. (*Gen*. 1. 28, *Rom*. 8. 22, &c)

...There shall be no need of Lawyers, prisons, or engines of punishment one over another, for all shall walk and act righteously in the Creation, and there shall be no beggar, nor cause of complaining in all this holy Mountain. (*Heb*. 8. 10, *Act*. 4. 32, *Jam*. 2. 13, *Ioh*. 3. 17, *Hos*. 3. 18)

...When this universall law of equity rises up in every man and woman, then none shall lay claim to any creature, and say, *This is mine, and that is yours, This is my work, that is yours*; but every one shall put to their hands to till the earth, and bring up cattle, and the blessing of the earth shall be common to all; when a man hath need of any corn for cattle, take from the next store-house he meets with. (*Act*. 4. 32)

There shall be no buying nor selling, no fairs nor markets, but the whole earth shall be a common treasury for every man, for the earth is the Lords. And man kind thus drawn up to live and act in the Law of love, equity and onenesse, is but the great house wherein the Lord himself dwels, and every particular one a severall mansion: and as one spirit of righteousnesse is common to all, so the earth and the blessings of the earth shall be common to all; for now all is but the Lord, and the Lord is all in all. (*Eph*. 4. 5, 6)

When a man hath meat, and drink, and doathes he hath enough, and all shall cheerfully put to their hands to make these things that are needfull, one helping another; there shall be none Lord over others, but every one shall be a Lord of him self, subject to the law of righteousnesse, reason and equity, which shall dwell and rule in him, which is the Lord; *For now the Lord is one, and his name and power one, in all and among all. (Zech*.14. 9)

...The manifestation of a righteous heart shall be known, not by his words, but by his actions; for this multitude of talk, and heaping up of words amongst professours shall die and cease, this way of preaching shall cease, and verbal worship shall cease, and they that do worship the Father, shall worship him by walking righteously in the Creation, in the strength of the Law of Love and equity one to another. And the time is now coming on, that men shall not talk of righteousnesse, but act righteousnesse. *(Ier*. 31. 34. *Joh*. 4. 23)

...Covetous proud flesh wil kil a Tyrant, but hold fast the same Tyrannie and slaverie over others in his own hand; he wil kil the Traitor, but liks wel the Treason, when he may be honoured or lifted up by it. (*Rev*. 12. 4. 2, *King*. 20. 16)

Look upon the mountaines and little hils of the earth, and see if these prickling thorns and briars, the bitter curse, does not grow there: Truly Tyrannie is Tyrannie in one as wel as in another; in a poor man lifted up by his valour, as in a rich man lifted up by his lands: And where Tyrannie sits, he is an enemy to Christ, the spreading spirit of righteousnesse: He wil use the bare name, Christ, that he may the more secretly persecute, and kil his power.

Tyrannie is a subtile, proud and envious Beast; his nature is selfish, and ful of murder, he promises fair things for the publique; but all must be made to center within self, or self interest not the universal libertie...

Leave off dominion and Lordship one over another, for the whole bulk of man-kinde are but one living earth. Leave off imprisoning, whiping and killing; which are but the actings of the curse: And let those that hitherto have had no Land and have been forced to rob and steal through povertie; hereafter let them quietly enjoy Land to work upon, that every one may enjoy the benefit of his Creation, and eat his own bread with the sweat of his own brows: For surely this particular propriety of mine and thine, hath brought in all miserie upon people. For first, it hath occasioned people to steal one from another. Secondly, it hath made Laws to hang those that did steal: It tempts people to doe an evil action, and then kils them for doing of it: Let all judge if this be not a great devil.

Chapter 2
Enlightenment And Revolution

4. William Godwin: Enquiry Concerning Political Justice (1793-97)

William Godwin (1756-1836) is the author of the first comprehensive argument for philosophical anarchism. Godwin began writing his work, An Enquiry Concerning Political Justice, and its Influence on General Virtue and Happiness, *in 1791 during the initial phase of the French Revolution. By the time* An Enquiry Concerning Political Justice *came out in 1793, France had become a republic, and King Louis XVI had lost his head along with his crown. Although Godwin's book was initially well received, within a few years both Godwin and his book were roundly vilified. In 1794, he wrote his groundbreaking novel,* Things as They Are; or, the Adventures of Caleb Williams, *a vivid illustration of his ideas imaginatively applied to English society. In 1796 he became the lover and later husband of the early feminist writer, Mary Wollstonecraft (1759-1797), author of* A Vindication of the Rights of Men *(1790) and* A Vindication of the Rights of Woman *(1792), who died after giving birth to their daughter Mary. Mary Godwin went on to marry her father's youthful disciple, the poet Shelley, who put Godwin's philosophical anarchism to verse, and she wrote the classic novel* Frankenstein *(1818).*

Godwin revised An Enquiry Concerning Political Justice *in 1795 and 1797, reissuing it under the title of* An Enquiry Concerning Political Justice and its Influence on Morals and Happiness. *The following excerpts are from the third, 1797, edition (dated 1798), with the exception of the section on property, which is from the first, 1793, edition. As Kropotkin argued in his article on "Anarchism" in the* Encyclopedia Britannica *(11th edition), Godwin's views on property in the first edition are more radical, hence their inclusion here. Unlike Gerrard Winstanley, who advocated and practiced a form of nonviolent direct action, Godwin's anarchism was almost entirely philosophical, seeing the eventual dissolution of government as the result of a gradual and patient process of enlightenment.*

NOTWITHSTANDING THE ENCROACHMENTS that have been made upon the equality of mankind, a great and substantial equality remains. There is no such disparity among the human race as to enable one man to hold several other men in subjection, except so far as they are willing to be subject. All government is founded in opinion. Men at present live under any particular form because they conceive it their interest to do so. One part indeed of a community or empire may be held in subjection by force; but this cannot be the personal force of their despot; it must be the force of another part of the community, who are of opinion that it is their interest to support his authority. Destroy this opinion, and the fabric which is built upon it falls to the ground...

Positive [governmental] institutions do not content themselves with requiring my assent to certain propositions, in consideration of the testimony by which they are enforced. This would amount to no more than advice flowing from a respectable quarter, which, after all, I might reject if it did not accord with the mature judgement of my own understanding. But in the very nature of these institutions there is included a sanction, a motive either of punishment or reward, to induce me to obedience.

"I have deeply reflected," suppose, "upon the nature of virtue, and am convinced that a certain proceeding is incumbent on me. But the hangman, supported by an act of parliament, assures me I am mistaken." If I yield my opinion to his dictum, my action becomes modified, and my character also. An influence like this is inconsistent with all generous magnanimity of spirit, all ardent impartiality in the discovery of truth, and all inflexible perseverance in its assertion. Countries, exposed to the perpetual interference of decrees, instead of arguments, exhibit within their boundaries the mere phantoms of men. We can never judge from an observation of their inhabitants what men would be if they knew of no appeal from the tribunal of conscience, and if, whatever they thought, they dared to speak, and dared to act...

Punishment inevitably excites in the sufferer, and ought to excite, a sense of injustice. Let its purpose be, to convince me of the truth of a position which I at present believe to be false. It is not, abstractedly considered, of the nature of an argument, and therefore it cannot begin with producing conviction. Punishment is a comparatively specious name; but is in reality nothing more than force put upon one being by another who happens to be stronger. But strength apparently does not constitute justice. The case of punishment, in the view in which we now consider it, is the case of you and me differing in opinion, and your telling me that you must be right, since you have a more brawny arm, or have applied your mind more to the acquiring skill in your weapons than I have...

An appeal to force must appear to both parties, in proportion to the soundness of their understanding, to be a confession of imbecility. He that has recourse to it would have no occasion for this expedient if he were sufficiently acquainted with the powers of that truth it is his office to communicate. If there be any man who, in suffering punishment, is not conscious of injury, he must have had his mind previously debased by slavery, and his sense of moral right and wrong blunted by a series of oppressions.

If there be any truth more unquestionable than the rest, it is that every man is bound to the exertion of his faculties in the discovery of right, and to the carrying into effect all the right with which he is acquainted. It may be granted that an infallible standard, if it could be discovered, would be considerably beneficial. But this infallible standard itself would be of little use in human affairs, unless it had the property of reasoning as well as deciding, of enlightening the mind as well as constraining the body. If a man be in some cases obliged to prefer his own judgement, he is in all cases obliged to consult that judgement, before he can determine whether the matter in question be of the sort provided for or no. So that from this reasoning it ultimately appears that the conviction of a man's individual understanding is the only legitimate principle imposing on him the duty of adopting any species of conduct…

No government can subsist in a nation the individuals of which shall merely abstain from tumultuous resistance, while in their genuine sentiments they censure and despise its institution. In other words, government cannot proceed but upon confidence, as confidence on the other hand cannot exist without ignorance. The true supporters of government are the weak and uninformed, and not the wise. In proportion as weakness and ignorance shall diminish, the basis of government will also decay. This however is an event which ought not to be contemplated with alarm. A catastrophe of this description would be the true euthanasia of government. If the annihilation of blind confidence and implicit opinion can at any time be effected, there will necessarily succeed in their place an unforced concurrence of all in promoting the general welfare.

…[N]othing can be more indefensible than a project for introducing by violence that state of society which our judgements may happen to approve. In the first place, no persons are ripe for the participation of a benefit the advantage of which they do not understand. No people are competent to enjoy a state of freedom who are not already imbued with a love of freedom. The most dreadful tragedies will infallibly result from an attempt to goad mankind prematurely into a position, however abstractedly excellent, for which they are in no degree prepared. Secondly, to endeavour to impose our sentiments by force is the most detestable species of persecution. Others are as much entitled to deem themselves in the right as we are. The most sacred of all privileges is that by which each man has a certain sphere, relative to the government of his own actions, and the exercise of his discretion, not liable to be trenched upon by the intemperate zeal or dictatorial temper of his neighbour. To dragoon men into the adoption of what we think right is an intolerable tyranny. It leads to unlimited disorder and injustice. Every man thinks himself in the right; and, if such a proceeding were universally introduced, the destiny of mankind would be no longer a question of argument, but of strength, presumption or intrigue...

Force is an expedient the use of which is much to be deplored. It is contrary to the nature of intellect, which cannot be improved but by conviction and persuasion. It corrupts the man that employs it, and the man upon whom it is employed. But it seems that there are certain cases so urgent as to oblige us to have recourse to this injurious expedient: in other words, there are cases where the mischief to accrue from not violently counteracting the perverseness of the individual is greater than the mischief which the violence necessarily draws along with it. Hence it appears that the ground justifying resistance, in every case where it can be justified, is that of the good likely to result from such interference being greater than the good to result from omitting it...

Revolution is engendered by an indignation against tyranny, yet is itself ever more pregnant with tyranny. The tyranny which excites its indignation can scarcely be without its partisans; and, the greater is the indignation excited, and the more sudden and vast the fall of the oppressors, the deeper will be the resentment which fills the minds of the losing party...

There is no period more at war with the existence of liberty. The unrestrained communication of opinions has always been subjected to mischievous counteraction, but upon such occasions it is trebly fettered. At other times men are not so much alarmed for its effects. But in a moment of revolution, when everything is in crisis, the influence even of a word is dreaded, and the consequent slavery is complete. Where was there a revolution in which a strong vindication of what it was intended to abolish was permitted, or indeed almost any species of writing or argument, that was not, for the most part, in harmony with the opinions which happened to prevail? An attempt to scrutinize men's thoughts, and punish their opinions, is of all kinds of despotism the most odious; yet this attempt is peculiarly characteristic of a period of revolution.

The advocates of revolution usually remark "that there is no way to rid ourselves of our oppressors, and prevent new ones from starting up in their room, but by inflicting on them some severe and memorable retribution." Upon this statement it is particularly to be observed that there will be oppressors as long as there are individuals inclined, either from perverseness, or rooted and obstinate prejudice, to take party with the oppressor. We have therefore to terrify not only the man of crooked ambition but all those who would support him, either from a corrupt motive, or a well-intended error. Thus, we propose to make men free; and the method we adopt is to influence them, more rigorously than ever, by the fear of punishment. We say that government has usurped too much, and we organize a government tenfold more encroaching in its principles and terrible in its proceedings. Is slavery the best project that can be devised for making men free? Is a display of terror the readiest mode for rendering them fearless, independent and enterprising?

During a period of revolution, enquiry, and all those patient speculations to which mankind are indebted for their greatest improvements, are suspended. Such speculations demand a period of security and permanence; they can scarcely be pursued when men cannot foresee what shall happen tomorrow, and the most astonishing vicissitudes are affairs of perpetual recurrence. Such speculations demand leisure, and a tranquil and dispassionate temper; they can scarcely be pursued when all the passions of man are afloat, and we are hourly under the strongest impressions of fear and hope, apprehension and desire, dejection and triumph...

The only method according to which social improvements can be carried on, with sufficient prospect of an auspicious event, is when the improvement of our institutions advances in a just proportion to the illumination of the public understanding. There is a condition of political society best adapted to every different stage of individual improvement. The more nearly this condition is successively realized, the more advantageously will the general interest be consulted. There is a sort of provision in the nature of the human mind for this species of progress. Imperfect institutions, as has already been shown, cannot long support themselves when they are generally disapproved of, and their effects truly understood. There is a period at which they may be expected to decline and expire, almost without an effort. Reform, under this meaning of the term, can scarcely be considered as of the nature of action. Men feel their situation; and the restraints that shackled them before vanish like a deception. When such a crisis has arrived, not a sword will need to be drawn, not a finger to be lifted up in purposes of violence. The adversaries will be too few and too feeble to be able to entertain a serious thought of resistance against the universal sense of mankind.

Under this view of the subject then it appears that revolutions, instead of being truly beneficial to mankind, answer no other purpose than that of marring the salutary and uninterrupted progress which might be expected to attend upon political truth and social improvement. They disturb the harmony of intellectual nature. They propose to give us something for which we are not prepared, and which we cannot effectually use. They suspend the wholesome advancement of science, and confound the process of nature and reason.

We have hitherto argued upon the supposition that the attempt which shall be made to effect a revolution shall be crowned with success. But this supposition must by no means be suffered to pass without notice. Every attempt of this sort, even if menaced only, and not carried into act, tends to excite a resistance which otherwise would never be consolidated. The enemies of innovation become alarmed by the intemperance of its friends. The storm gradually thickens, and each party arms itself in silence with the weapons of violence and stratagem. Let us observe the consequence of this. So long as the contest is merely between truth and sophistry, we may look with tolerable assurance to the progress and result. But, when we lay aside arguments, and have recourse to the sword, the case is altered. Amidst the barbarous rage of war, and the clamorous din of civil contention, who shall tell whether the event will be prosperous or adverse? The consequence may be the riveting on us anew the chains of despotism, and ensuring, through a considerable period, the triumph of oppression, even if it should fail to carry us back to a state of torpor, and obliterate the memory of all our improvements...

It has perhaps sufficiently appeared, from the preceding discussion, that revolutions are necessarily attended with many circumstances worthy of our disapprobation, and that they are by no means essential to the political improvement of mankind. Yet, after all, it ought not to be forgotten that, though the connection be not essential or requisite, revolutions and violence have too often been coeval with important changes of the social system. What has so often happened in time past is not unlikely occasionally to happen in future...The friend of human happiness will endeavour to prevent violence; but it would be the mark of a weak and valetudinarian temper to turn away our eyes from human affairs in disgust, and refuse to contribute our labours and attention to the general weal, because perhaps, at last, violence may forcibly intrude itself. It is our duty to make a proper advantage of circumstances as they arise, and not to withdraw ourselves because everything is not conducted according to our ideas of propriety.

...[R]epresentative government is necessarily imperfect. It is...a point to be regretted, in the abstract notion of civil society, that a majority should overbear a minority, and that the minority, after having opposed and remonstrated, should be obliged practically to submit to that which was the subject of their remonstrance. But this evil, inseparable from political government, is aggravated by representation, which removes the power of making regulations one step further from the people whose lot it is to obey them...

Whatever evils are included in the abstract idea of government, they are all of them extremely aggravated by the extensiveness of its jurisdiction, and softened under circumstances of an opposite nature. Ambition, which may be no less formidable than a pestilence in the former, has no room to unfold itself in the latter. Popular commotion is like the waters of the earth, capable where the surface is large, of producing the most tragical effects, but mild and innocuous when confined within the circuit of a humble lake. Sobriety and equity are the obvious characteristics of a limited circle...

Ambition and tumult are evils that arise out of government, in an indirect manner, in consequence of the habits, which government introduces, of concert and combination extending themselves over multitudes of men. There are other evils inseparable from its existence. The object of government is the suppression of such violence, as well external as internal, as might destroy, or bring into jeopardy, the well being of the community or its members; and the means it employs are constraint and violence of a more regulated kind. For this purpose the concentration of individual forces becomes necessary, and the method in which this concentration is usually obtained is also constraint...Constraint employed against delinquents, or persons to whom delinquency is imputed, is by no means without its mischiefs. Constraint employed by the majority of a society against the minority, who may differ from them upon some question of public good, is calculated, at first sight at least, to excite a still greater disapprobation.

...[T]he existence of a national assembly introduces the evils of a fictitious unanimity. The public, guided by such an assembly, must act with concert, or the assembly is a nugatory excrescence. But it is impossible that this unanimity can really exist. The individuals who constitute a nation cannot take into consideration a variety of important questions without forming different sentiments respecting them. In reality, all questions that are brought before such an assembly are decided by a majority of votes, and the minority, after having exposed, with all the power of eloquence, and force of reasoning, of which they are capable, the injustice and folly of the measures adopted, are obliged, in a certain sense, to assist in carrying them into execution. Nothing can more directly contribute to the depravation of the human understanding and character.

...[T]he debates of a national assembly are distorted from their reasonable tenour by the necessity of their being uniformly terminated by a vote. Debate and discussion are, in their own nature, highly conducive to intellectual improvement; but they lose this salutary character, the moment they are subjected to this unfortunate condition. What can be more unreasonable than to demand that argument, the usual quality of which is gradually and imperceptibly to enlighten the mind, should declare its effect in the close of a single conversation? No sooner does this circumstance occur than the whole scene changes its character. The orator no longer enquires after permanent conviction, but transitory effect. He seeks rather to take advantage of our prejudices than to enlighten our judgement. That which might otherwise have been a scene of patient and beneficent enquiry is changed into wrangling, tumult and precipitation...

The true reason why the mass of mankind has so often been made the dupe of knaves has been the mysterious and complicated nature of the social system. Once annihilate the quackery of government, and the most homebred understanding might be strong enough to detect the artifices of the state juggler that would mislead him...

Man is not originally vicious. He would not refuse to listen to, or to be convinced by, the expostulations that are addressed to him, had he not been accustomed to regard them as hypocritical, and to conceive that, while his neighbour, his parent, and his political governor pretended to be actuated by a pure regard to his interest or pleasure, they were, in reality, at the expense of his, promoting their own. Such are the fatal effects of mysteriousness and complexity. Simplify the social system in the manner which every motive but those of usurpation and ambition powerfully recommends; render the plain dictates of justice level to every capacity; remove the necessity of implicit faith; and we may expect the whole species to become reasonable and virtuous...

This is one of the most memorable stages of human improvement. With what delight must every well informed friend of mankind look forward to the auspicious period, the dissolution of political government, of that brute engine which has been the only perennial cause of the vices of mankind, and which, as has abundantly appeared in the progress of the present work, has mischiefs of various sorts incorporated with its substance, and no otherwise removable than by its utter annihilation!

...The direct tendency of coercion is to set our understanding and our fears, our duty and our weakness, at variance with each other. Coercion first annihilates the understanding of the subject upon whom it is exercised, and then of him who employs it. Dressed in the supine prerogatives of a master, he is excused from cultivating the faculties of a man. What would not man have been, long before this, if the proudest of us had no hopes but in argument, if he knew of no resort beyond, if he were obliged to sharpen his faculties, and collect his powers, as the only means of effecting his purposes?

Let us reflect a little upon the species of influence that coercion employs. It avers to its victim that he must necessarily be in the wrong, because I am more vigorous or more cunning than he. Will vigour and cunning be always on the side of truth? It appeals to force, and represents superior strength as the standard of justice. Every such exertion implies in its nature a species of contest. The contest is often decided before it is brought to open trial, by the despair of one of the parties. The ardour and paroxysm of passion being over, the offender surrenders himself into the hands of his superiors, and calmly awaits the declaration of their pleasure. But it is not always so. The depredator that by main force surmounts the strength of his pursuers, or by stratagem and ingenuity escapes their toils, so far as this argument is valid, proves the justice of his cause. Who can refrain from indignation when he sees justice thus miserably prostituted? Who does not feel, the moment the contest begins, the full extent of the absurdity that the appeal includes? The magistracy, the representative of the social system, that declares war against one of its members, in behalf of justice, or in behalf of oppression, appears almost equally, in both cases, entitled to our censure. In the first case, we see truth throwing aside her native arms and her intrinsic advantage, and putting herself upon a level with falsehood. In the second, we see falsehood confident in the casual advantage she possesses, artfully extinguishing the new born light that would shame her in the midst of her usurped authority. The exhibition in both is that of an infant crushed in the merciless grasp of a giant...

The argument against political coercion is equally strong against the infliction of private penalties, between master and slave, and between parent and child...The right of the parent over his offspring lies either in his superior strength, or his superior reason. If in his strength, we have only to apply this right universally in order to drive all morality out of the world. If in his reason, in that reason let him confide. It is a poor argument of my superior reason that I am unable to make justice be apprehended and felt, in the most necessary cases, without the intervention of blows.

Let us consider the effect that coercion produces upon the mind of him against whom it is employed. It cannot begin with convincing; it is no argument. It begins with producing the sensation of pain, and the sentiment of distaste. It begins with violently alienating the mind from the truth with which we wish it to be impressed. It includes in it a tacit confession of imbecility. If he who employs coercion against me could mold me to his purposes by argument, no doubt he would. He pretends to punish me because his argument is strong; but he really punishes me because his argument is weak...

The subject of property is the keystone that completes the fabric of political justice. According as our ideas respecting it are crude or correct, they will enlighten us as to the consequences of *a simple form of society without government*, and remove the prejudices that attach us to complexity. There is nothing that more powerfully tends to distort our *judgment* and *opinions*, than erroneous notions concerning the goods of fortune. Finally, the period that shall put an end to the system of *coercion* and *punishment* is intimately connected with the circumstance of property's being placed upon an equitable basis...

To whom does any article of property, suppose a loaf of bread, justly belong? To him who most wants it, or to whom the possession of it will be most beneficial...Our animal wants have long since been defined, and are stated to consist of food, clothing and shelter. If justice have any meaning, nothing can be more iniquitous, than for one man to possess superfluities, while there is a human being in existence that is not adequately supplied with these.

Justice does not stop here. Every man is entitled, so far as the general stock will suffice, not only to the means of being, but of well being. It is unjust, if one man labour to the destruction of his health or his life, that another man may abound in luxuries. It is unjust, if one man be deprived of leisure to cultivate his rational powers, while another man contributes not a single effort to add to the common stock. The faculties of one man are like the faculties of another. Justice directs that each man, unless perhaps he be employed more beneficially to the public, should contribute to the cultivation of the common harvest, of which man consumes a share. This reciprocity indeed...is of the very essence of justice...

The fruitful source of crimes consists in this circumstance, one man's possessing in abundance that of which another man is destitute. We must change the nature of mind, before we can prevent it from being powerfully influenced by this circumstance, when brought strongly home to its perceptions by the nature of its situation. Man must cease to have senses, the pleasures of appetite and vanity must cease to gratify, before he can look on tamely at the monopoly of these pleasures. He must cease to have a sense of justice, before he can clearly and fully approve this mixed scene of superfluity and distress. It is true that the proper method of curing this inequality is by reason and not by violence. But the immediate tendency of the established system is to persuade men that reason is impotent. The injustice of which they complain is upheld by force, and they are too easily induced by force to attempt its correction. All they endeavour is the partial correction of an injustice, which education tells them is necessary, but more powerful reason affirms to be tyrannical.

Force grew out of monopoly. It might accidentally have occurred among savages whose appetites exceeded their supply, or whose passions were inflamed by the presence of the object of their desire; but it would gradually have died away, as reason and civilization advanced. Accumulated property has fixed its empire; and henceforth all is an open contention of the strength and cunning of one party against the strength and cunning of the other. In this case, the violent and premature struggles of the necessitous are undoubtedly an evil. They tend to defeat the very cause in the success of which they are most deeply interested; they tend to procrastinate the triumph of truth. But the true crime is in the malevolent and partial propensities of men, thinking only of themselves, and despising the emolument of others; and of these the rich have their share.

The spirit of oppression, the spirit of servility, and the spirit of fraud, these are the immediate growth of the established system of property. They are alike hostile to intellectual and moral improvement. The other vices of envy, malice and revenge are their inseparable companions. In a state of society where men lived in the midst of plenty, and where all shared alike the bounties of nature, these sentiments would inevitably expire. The narrow principle of selfishness would vanish. No man being obliged to guard his little store, or provide with anxiety and pain for his restless wants, each would lose his own individual existence in the thought of the general good. No man would be an enemy to his neighbour, for they would have nothing for which to contend; and of consequence philanthropy would resume the empire which reason assigns her. Mind would be delivered from her perpetual anxiety about corporal support, and free to expatiate in the field of thought which is congenial to her. Each would assist the enquiries of all.

5. Jean Varlet: The Explosion (1794)

Jean Varlet (1764–1837) was part of the Enragés, a revolutionary group active during the French Revolution that fought for the establishment of a direct democracy, where power would reside in the people and their assemblies. As an opponent of both the bourgeois republicanism of the Girondists, and the revolutionary dictatorship of the Jacobins, Varlet suffered imprisonment on several occasions. The following excerpts are from his pamphlet, "The Ex-

plosion," published in October 1794, after the overthrow of Robespierre on the 9th of Thermidor (July 27, 1794), while Varlet was in the Le Plessis prison for his revolutionary activities. It is considered by some as one of the first anarchist manifestos, with its oft-quoted passage regarding the counter-revolutionary nature of all "revolutionary" governments. The translation is by Paul Sharkey.

I STAND ACCUSED OF COUNTER-REVOLUTION. Let me anticipate my appearance before the magistrates; the charge is a valid one...I consider myself convicted, if by counter-revolutionary is meant opposition to revolutionary government...

Republicans, let us not look elsewhere than the revolutionary government for the source of the oppression under which the Republic has groaned since the unforgettable events of May 31, June 1 and June 2 [1793—an uprising against the Girondins in the National Convention, resulting in the Jacobins and Robespierre's ascendancy to power]. Your confidence at that time nominated me to the insurrection committee; and as it might be concluded from this that I have served the most odious of tyrannies, I owe a frank explanation to the people and to myself.

Among the citizens elected to rescue the motherland in the revolution of May 31, there were unleashed patriots chosen by the people, patriots who had risen with it in defence of principle and to establish a republican constitution. There were also intriguers, the most destructive emissaries of factionalism. That band of Caligulas looked upon the downfall of the Brissotins [followers of Brissot, a Girondin leader] simply as opening a wider vista to their own ambitions. The insurrection committee contained the seeds of revolutionary government, devised in secrecy beforehand. Unknown to me, the sham insurgents replaced Brissot with Robespierre; and federalism with a disgusting dictatorship dressed up with the title of Public Safety. As for myself, I was too unassuming to be an initiate; I was by-passed.

I was an insurgent, and nothing more. When I saw deputies accosted in the public thoroughfares and clapped in irons, I backed off; I resigned from every post and retreated back into the ranks of the people and completely shunned the revolutionary government, except that from time to time I did my duty by fighting it...My distancing of myself from the committees and from the revolutionary tribunal, my utter insignificance and my time served in Les Madelonnettes [another prison] after May 31 are evidence enough, I reckon, to show that I wanted to be a revolutionary, pure and simple. Oh my fellow-citizens, do not accuse me of having had a hand in your misfortunes; I did nothing to deserve such a harsh reproach. Robespierre's ghastly dictatorship is scarcely a justification of Brissot's dictatorship...

Despotism has passed from the palace of the kings to the precincts of the committees. It is neither the royal robes, nor the crown, nor the scepter that have made kings hated; but rather ambition and tyranny. In my homeland there has merely been a change in costume. Frivolous, fickle nation! How much longer will you remain in thrall to names instead of things? I believe that I see clearly: I will not extend the respect owed to the National Convention to disloyal delegates if, at their instigation, a lawfully constituted authority hands down decrees that subvert all social harmony. Am I to touch a slavish forelock to a revolutionary code, palladium or tyranny? Am I to yield to hastening fear? Am I to give obedience to this despotic order? *Silence or death?* I will not be so craven. The principles enshrined in the declaration of our rights over-ride all decrees; they scream to me that above all else we must be free, to make our stand between the respect due to the bulk of the people's delegates and the respect that is even more legitimately due its sovereignty.

Before my eyes I keep this motto:

> Long live the rights of the sovereign people! Respect to the National Convention! Down with the usurpers! Perish revolutionary government rather than a principle!

What a social monstrosity, what a masterpiece of Machiavellianism is this revolutionary government! To any rational being, *government* and *revolution* are incompatible, unless the people wishes to set its constituted authorities in permanent insurrection against itself, which would be absurd.

Slaves subjected to the law of might; old courtiers bound to the chariot of all tyranny; two-legged species of the egotistical and apathetic; hack scribblers for whose daily poison the people pays dearly; fanatics, idolaters of error; bigots who see crime where there is difference of opinion, you are the advocates or dupes of revolutionary government. Its authors require some pretext on which they can legitimize dictatorship. In the name of public safety, they conjure an infinity of subsidiary dictatorships answering to the Committee of Public Safety.

In the darkness of night, in silence, in secret, without further ado, caprice and personal rancour clap citizens by the thousands in their Bastilles. The revolutionary kings can reign only if they corrupt: they must make money; the sword of Themis becomes a dagger; the laws of blood are enforced retrospectively; those with the greatest title, charged with phoney conspiracies, are hauled before a murderous tribunal, the pitiless prosecution, deaf to all defence stratagems; the criminal consciences of the panel-members are easily swayed; their ears hear a single cry: *Death! Death!* The palace of justice becomes the lair of cannibals, and these ogres prattle about humanity.

We have plumbed the depths of degradation of the rights of the people. In the state we see the oppressive and terrifying authority of a few ambitious men, overruling the legitimate authority of the *National Convention*. We see citizens stripped of their rights, wretched, quaking and mute before their tyrants; and at this sight we wonder whether France is populated by subjects or republicans.

Citizens, eager to know the laws by which you are governed, do not ask its supporters for a precise description of revolutionary government; licentious without being free, ferocious without vigour; that is how they describe that fine invention.

> Two thirds of citizens are mischievous enemies of freedom: they must be stamped out. *Terror* is the supreme law; the instrument of torture an object of veneration. If destruction is not constantly on the agenda, if the sword should cease to slaughter; if the executioners are no longer the fathers of the nation, freedom is in jeopardy. [Terror] aims to rule over heaps of corpses and wade through the blood of its enemies...

Patriots, stand firm in your attachment to principle and support the true citizen against money, usurpation and the abuse of power; he trusts and surrenders himself to the justice of your cause. But such placidity! Such stupor! Such lethargy! Silence and oblivion hang over you. Republicans, you sleep! And the counter-revolution sleeps not. Only the tyrant has been banished from Robespierre's tyranny; his ghastly system has survived him; ever since the monstrous decree that outlawed the innocent and the guilty alike, in order to draw a veil over the most deep-seated conspiracy, the delegates who carry on the tyrant's work, these brazen conspirators, despised and feared, letting their masks fall, stand exposed as *counter-revolutionaries*. You sleep! And, though the ambitious may seem to deal severely with the priests, with the nobles, the priests and nobles hold in their hands the security of a state that they have sworn to overthrow. You sleep! And there was no dagger of Brutus to drive Bourdon-de-l'Oise from the rostrum after he announced in the middle of the Senate that *'What is required is not a dictator, but a dictatorship'*...You sleep! And misery stabs you in the back and you make no effort to discover which demon has rendered sterile a soil rich in nature's gifts...Republicans, you sleep! And the murderous Vendee rises from the ruins, more formidable than before; that corner of the earth, soaked in the purest blood, still threatens to engulf new defenders. You sleep! And the sovereign voice of the people is supplanted by lying speeches, tissues of vile sycophancy, all of them ending with these words: *War, terror, revolutionary government, stand by your posts*. You sleep! And the society of Jacobins, perverted by the ringleaders, is at the mercy of the ambitious who, from there, rule the entire populace...This society serves as a mainstay of the conspiratorial government, feeding factionalism and acting as a stepping-stone for intriguers. Its inherent vice is having two peoples in its assembly: the people who pay, speaking inside the hall; and the people that does not pay, the real people, the public, is silent in the tribunals. A no less fundamental vice is the admission of deputies into this society. The people is no longer left to its own devices; the predominant delegates come to the Jacobins to be made party leaders; they go there to plot yet another 9th of Thermidor against the National Convention. Republicans, you sleep! And the eighty five departments, overrun by revolutionary tyranny reaching into every nook and cranny, are unaware of what is going on here and do not report to you the oppression beneath which they groan.

You sleep! The Republic is in irons…Citizens! Citizens! Shake off your slumbers! Wake up! Our tearful motherland looks to you patriots who have escaped the *flames* of the revolutionary tribunal to TAKE ENERGETIC ACTION for the love of liberty and in self-defence. The aristocracy back-stabs and a price is put upon your heads. Shoulder arms! Take up your pens! Close ranks! Audacity against audacity! This is where we must attack, harry and bring severe pressure to bear on the enemy, giving him no respite. Let us hold tyranny up to ridicule and publicize its misdeeds; let us thwart its sinister designs and not wait until it launches a surprise attack on us… LET US DARE! …And the danger is no more; forgetting about ourselves can save the motherland; dangers and obstacles scatter in the face of courage, devotion eludes them. Tremble! tyrants in your masks of popularity, for thought is coming into its own after lengthy suppression, it will hit you like saltpetre packed into a pipe. The free man unleashes his hatred of oppressors and the press fires its guns…And where are the ringleaders of the conspiracy?…Ashen-faced and undone, they lie in the dust, breathing their last…*And are no more.*

The French nation breathes again as its many battalions rally around her freely elected authority, forming an impregnable bulwark outside the National Convention: the sordid remnants of its would-be assassins are dispatched. Spirits are lifted and at ease. Joy and enthusiasm are universal; on the ramparts of the temple of the law, waves the tricolour flag, bearing this legend, that ten thousand free men chant in unison to the breeze:

> *Long live the rights of the sovereign people! Respect the National Convention! Down with the usurpers!* BETTER THAT THE REVOLUTIONARY GOVERNMENT SHOULD PERISH THAN A PRINCIPLE.

6. *Sylvain Maréchal: Manifesto of the Equals (1796)*

Sylvain Maréchal (1750-1803) was a materialist and atheist whose secular calendar formed the basis for the French Revolutionary calendar adopted in 1793. Prior to the French Revolution he wrote some fables and satires with an anarchist slant. His "Manifesto of the Equals" was written for the Conspiracy of Equals, a revolutionary group led by François-Noël "Gracchus" Babeuf (1760-1797). The Conspiracy advocated economic as well as political equality, and sought to overthrow the Directory, the group that came to power after the fall of Robespierre. Betrayed to the authorities, Babeuf was arrested and executed before the uprising could begin. This translation is from Charles George's 500 Years of Revolution *(Chicago: Charles H. Kerr, 1998), and is reprinted with the kind permission of the publisher.*

PEOPLE OF FRANCE! DURING FIFTEEN centuries you have lived as slaves, and in consequence unhappily. It is scarcely six years that you have begun to breathe, in the expectation of independence, happiness, equality! The first demand of nature, the first need of man, and the chief knot binding together all legitimate association! People of France! You have not been more favoured than other nations who vegetate on this unfortunate globe! Always and everywhere the poor human race, delivered over to more or less adroit cannibals, has served as a plaything for all ambitions, as a pasture for all tyrannies. Always and everywhere men have been lulled by fine words; never and nowhere have they obtained the thing with the word. From time immemorial it has been repeated, with hypocrisy, that men are equal; and from time immemorial the most degrading and the most monstrous inequality ceaselessly weighs on the human race. Since the dawn of civil society this noblest birthright of man has been recognized without contradiction, but has on no single occasion been realized; equality has never been anything but a beautiful and sterile fiction of the law. Today, when it is demanded with a stronger voice, they reply to us "Be silent, wretches! Equality of fact is nought but a chimera; be contented with conditional equality; you are equal before the law. Canaille, what more do you want?" What more do we want? Legislators, governors, rich proprietors, listen in your turn! We are all equal, are we not? This principle remains uncontested. For, unless attacked by madness, no one could seriously say that it was night when it was day.

Well! We demand henceforth to live and to die equal, as we have been born equal. We demand real equality or death; that is what we want.

And we shall have it, this real equality, it matters not at what price! Woe betide those who place themselves between us and it! Woe betide him who offers resistance to a vow thus pronounced!

The French Revolution is but the precursor of another...greater and more solemn revolution, which will be the last.

The People has marched over the bodies of kings and priests who allied against it: it will be the same with the new tyrants, with the new political hypocrites, seated in the place of the old ones! What do we want more than equality of rights? We want not only the equality transcribed in the *Declaration of the Rights of Man and Citizen*; we will have it in the midst of us, under the roofs of our houses. We consent to everything for its sake; to make a clean start, that we may hold to it alone. Perish, if must be, all the arts, provided real equality be left us!

...No more individual property in land: the land belongs to no one. We demand...the communal enjoyment of the fruits of the earth, fruits which are for everyone!

We declare we can no longer suffer, with the enormous majority of men, labour and sweat in the service and for the good pleasure of a small minority! Enough and too long have less than a million individuals disposed of that which belongs to more than twenty million of their kind!

Let this great scandal, that our grandchildren will hardly be willing to believe, cease! Let disappear, once and for all, the revolting distinction of rich and poor, of great and small, of masters and valets, of governors and governed!

Let there be no other difference between human beings than those of age and sex. Since all have the same needs and the same faculties, let there be one education for all, one [supply of] food for all. We are contented with one sun and one [supply of] air for all. Why should the same portion and the same quality of nourishment not suffice for each of us? But already the enemies of an order of things the most natural that can be imagined, declaim against us. Disorganizers and factious persons say...you only seek massacre and plunder. People of France! we shall not waste our time in replying to them, but we shall tell you: the holy enterprise which we organize has no other aim than to put an end to civil dissensions and...public misery...

The moment for great measures has come. Evil is at its height. It covers the face of the earth. Chaos, under the name of politics, has reigned there throughout too many centuries. Let everything return once more to order, and reassume its just place!

At the voice of equality, let the elements of justice and well-being organize themselves. The moment has arrived for founding the Republic of the Equals, that grand refuge open for all men. The days of general restitution have come. Families groaning in misery, come and seat yourselves at the common table prepared by nature for all her children! People of France! the purest form of all glory has been reserved for thee! Yes, it is you who may first offer to the world this touching spectacle!

Ancient customs, antiquated conventions, would anew raise an obstacle to the establishment of the Republic of the Equals. The organization of real equality, the only kind that answers all needs without making victims, without costing sacrifices, will not perhaps please everybody at first. The egoist, the ambitious man, will tremble with rage. Those who possess unjustly will cry aloud against its injustice. Exclusive enjoyments, solitary pleasures, personal ease, will cause sharp regrets on the part of individuals who have fattened on the labour of others. The lovers of absolute power, the vile supporters of arbitrary authority, will scarcely bend their arrogant chiefs to the level of real equality. Their narrow view will penetrate with difficulty, it may be, the near future of common well-being. But what can a few thousand malcontents do against a mass of men, all of them happy, and surprised to have sought so long for a happiness which they had beneath their hand?

The day after this veritable revolution they will say, with astonishment, What! the common well-being was to be had for so little? We had only to will it. Ah! Why did we not will it sooner? Why had we to be told about it so many times? Yes, doubtless, with one man on earth richer, more powerful than his neighbours, than his equals, the equilibrium is broken, crime and misery are already in the world. People of France! by what sign ought you henceforward to recognize the excellence of a constitution? That which rests entirely on an equality of fact is the only one that can benefit you and satisfy all your wants…

People of France! open your eyes and your heart to the fullness of happiness. Recognize and proclaim with us "The Republic of the Equals!"

Chapter 3
Industrialization And The Emergence Of Socialism

7. Charles Fourier: Attractive Labour (1822-1837)

Charles Fourier (1772-1837) is considered one of the first socialist theorists. He began publishing his ideas regarding the reorganization of society during the Napoleonic era, but was only many years later able to attract any adherents to his ideas. He never was able to attract a financial benefactor to fund their implementation, but some of his adherents did attempt to create Fourierist colonies or "phalanxes," the model of which Fourier called "Harmony." Although not an anarchist per se, Fourier did insist that "no coercive measures" would be tolerated in his ideal society, where work would be "indicated but not ordered" (as quoted in The Utopian Vision of Charles Fourier, *ed. J. Beecher and R. Bienvenu, Boston: Beacon Press, 1972, page 252). His ideas were influential in the burgeoning anarchist movement, particularly his notion that work should be made attractive, and society should be organized to provide for the free expression of people's natural passions, rather than people being reformed or remolded to fit someone's preconceived ideas (a flaw that permeates Fourier's own writings). The following extracts are taken from* Selections from the Works of Fourier *(London: Swan Sonnenschein & Co., 1901), translated by Julia Franklin.*

IN THE CIVILIZED MECHANISM we find everywhere composite unhappiness instead of composite charm. Let us judge of it by the case of labour. It is, says the Scripture very justly, a punishment of man: Adam and his issue are condemned to earn their bread by the sweat of their brow. That, already, is an affliction; but this labour, this ungrateful labour upon which depends the earning of our miserable bread, we cannot even get it! A labourer lacks the labour upon which his maintenance depends—he asks in vain for a tribulation! He suffers a second, that of obtaining work at times whose fruit is his master's and not his, or of being employed in duties to which he is entirely unaccustomed...

The civilized labourer suffers a third affliction through the maladies with which he is generally stricken by the excess of labour demanded by his master...He suffers a fifth affliction, that of being despised and treated as a beggar because he lacks those necessaries which he consents to purchase by the anguish of repugnant labour. He suffers, finally, a sixth affliction, in that he will obtain neither advancement nor sufficient wages, and that to the vexation of present suffering is added the perspective of future suffering, and of being sent to the gallows should he demand that labour which he may lack tomorrow...

Labour, nevertheless, forms the delight of various creatures, such as beavers, bees, wasps, ants, which are entirely at liberty to prefer inertia: but God has provided them with a social mechanism which attracts to industry, and causes happiness to be found in industry. Why should he not have accorded us the same favour as these animals? What a difference between their industrial condition and ours! A Russian, an Algerian, work from fear of the lash or the bastinado; an Englishman, a Frenchman, from fear of the famine which stalks close to his poor household; the Greeks and the Romans, whose freedom has been vaunted to us, worked as slaves, and from fear of punishment, like the negroes in the colonies today.

Associative labour, in order to exert a strong attraction upon people, will have to differ in every particular from the repulsive conditions which render it so odious in the existing state of things.

It is necessary, in order that it become attractive, that associative labour fulfil the following seven conditions:

1. That every labourer be a partner, remunerated by dividends and not by wages.

2. That every one, man, woman, or child, be remunerated in proportion to the three faculties, *capital*, *labour*, and *talent*.

3. That the industrial sessions be varied about eight times a day, it being impossible to sustain enthusiasm longer than an hour and a half or two hours in the exercise of agricultural or manufacturing labour.

4. That they be carried on by bands of friends, united spontaneously, interested and stimulated by very active rivalries.

5. That the workshops and husbandry offer the labourer the allurements of elegance and cleanliness.

6. That the division of labour be carried to the last degree, so that each sex and age may devote itself to duties that are suited to it.

> 7. That in this distribution, each one, man, woman, or child, be in full enjoyment of the right to labour or the right to engage in such branch of labour as they may please to select, provided they give proof of integrity and ability.
>
> 8. Finally, that, in this new order, people possess a guarantee of well-being, of a minimum sufficient for the present and the future, and that this guarantee free them from all uneasiness concerning themselves and their families...

In order to attain happiness, it is necessary to introduce it into the labours which engage the greater part of our lives. Life is a long torment to one who pursues occupations without attraction.

Morality teaches us to love work: let it know, then, how to render work lovable, and, first of all, let it introduce luxury into husbandry and the workshop. If the arrangements are poor, repulsive, how arouse industrial attraction?

In work, as in pleasure, variety is evidently the desire of nature. Any enjoyment prolonged, without interruption, beyond two hours, conduces to satiety, to abuse, blunts our faculties, and exhausts pleasure. A repast of four hours will not pass off without excess; an opera of four hours will end by cloying the spectator. Periodical variety is a necessity of the body and of the soul, a necessity in all nature; even the soil requires alteration of seeds, and seed alteration of soil. The stomach will soon reject the best dish if it be offered every day, and the soul will be blunted in the exercise of any virtue if it be not relieved by some other virtue.

If there is need of variety in pleasure after indulging in it for two hours, so much the more does labour require this diversity, which is continual in the associative state, and is guaranteed to the poor as well as the rich.

The first right is the right to sustain life, to eat when one is hungry. This right is denied in civilization by the philosophers, and conceded by Jesus Christ in these words:

> Have ye never read what David did, when he had need, and was an hungered, he, and they that were with him? How he went into the house of God, and did eat the show-bread, which is not lawful to eat but for the priests, and gave also to them which were with him?

Jesus by these words consecrates the right of taking, WHEN ONE IS HUNGRY, what is necessary, where it may be found; and this right imposes the duty upon the social body of securing to the people a minimum for maintenance—since civilization deprives it of the first [four] natural right[s], that of *the chase, fishing, gathering, pasturage*, it owes it an indemnity. As long as this duty is not recognized, there exists no social compact reciprocally agreed to; there is nothing but a league of oppression, a league of the minority which possesses, against the majority which does not possess the necessaries of life, and which, for that reason, tends to resume the fifth right, to form clubs or internal leagues to despoil the possessors...

If the poor, the labouring class, are not happy in the associative, state, they will disturb it by malevolence, robbery, rebellion; such an order will fail in its object, which is to unite the passional with the material, to conciliate characters, tastes, instincts, and inequalities of every description.

Having charge of the accounts, the Administration advances to every poor member clothing, food, housing, for a year. They run no risk by this advance, because they know that the work the poor man will accomplish, *through attraction and as a scheme of pleasure*, will exceed in amount the sum of the advances made him; and that, after the inventory is taken, the Phalanx will, in settling its accounts, find itself a debtor of the entire poor class to whom it shall have given this advance of the minimum...

But the first condition is *to invent and organize a regime of industrial attraction*. Without this precaution, how can we think of guaranteeing the poor man a minimum? It would be accustoming him to slothfulness: he readily persuades himself that the minimum is a debt rather than an assistance, and he therefore concludes to remain in idleness. That is what one remarks in England, where the tax of 150 millions for the needy serves only to increase their number; so true is it that Civilization is but a vicious circle, even in its most laudable actions. What the people need is not alms, but work, attractive enough for the multitude to wish to devote to it even the days and hours reserved for idleness.

If political science knew the secret of bringing this lever into play, the minimum could *really be secured* by the absolute cessation of idleness. The only ones remaining to be provided for would be the infirm; a very light burden, and one not felt by the social body, if it became opulent and, through attraction, were relieved of slothfulness, and of indifferent labour, which is almost as sterile as slothfulness.

8. Pierre-Joseph Proudhon: What is Property (1840)

Pierre-Joseph Proudhon (1809-1865), the first self-proclaimed anarchist, was from the same area of France as Fourier, Franche-Comté. Proudhon apprenticed as a printer, and was involved in typesetting Fourier's Le nouveau monde industriel et sociétaire *(1829). He later recounted that "for six whole weeks I was the captive of this bizarre genius" (as quoted by George Woodcock,* Pierre-Joseph Proudhon: A Biography, *Montreal: Black Rose Books,*

1987, page 13). Proudhon's early socialism was more egalitarian than Fourier's, and explicitly, if not consistently, anarchist (see my introduction to the 1989 Pluto Press edition of Proudhon's The General Idea of the Revolution in the Nineteenth Century*). What is* Property *was his first major publication, a ground-breaking critique of property rights and the principle of government. In* The Holy Family *(1845), Marx, later Proudhon's hostile opponent, described the book as "the first resolute, pitiless and at the same time scientific" critique of property. Both Proudhon and his book became notorious for the startling phrase, "Property is theft!" by which Proudhon meant the appropriation by capitalists of the benefit of the workers' combined labour. The following excerpts, which can only give a flavour of the book, are taken from Benjamin Tucker's 1876 translation, with some minor modifications.*

IF I WERE ASKED TO ANSWER the following question: What is slavery? and I should answer in one word, It is murder, my meaning would be understood at once. No extended argument would be required to show that the power to take from a man his thought, his will, his personality, is a power of life and death; and that to enslave a man is to kill him. Why, then, to this other question: What is property? may I not likewise answer, It is theft, without the certainty of being misunderstood; the second proposition being no other than a transformation of the first?

..."The capitalist," they say, "has paid the labourers their daily wages." To be accurate, it must be said that the capitalist has paid as many times one day's wage as he has employed labourers each day—which is not at all the same thing. For he has paid nothing for that immense power which results from the union and harmony of labourers, and the convergence and simultaneousness of their efforts. Two hundred grenadiers stood the obelisk of Luxor upon its base in a few hours; do you suppose that one man could have accomplished the same task in two hundred days? Nevertheless, on the books of the capitalist, the amount of wages paid would have been the same. Well, a desert to prepare for cultivation, a house to build, a factory to run—all these are obelisks to erect, mountains to move. The smallest fortune, the most insignificant establishment, the setting in motion of the lowest industry, demand the concurrence of so many different kinds of labour and skill, that one man could not possibly execute the whole of them...

Labour leads us to equality. Every step that we take brings us nearer to it; and if labourers had equal strength, diligence, and industry, clearly their fortunes would be equal also. Indeed, if, as is pretended—and as we have admitted—the labourer is proprietor of the value which he creates, it follows:

1. That the labourer acquires at the expense of the idle proprietor;

2. That all production being necessarily collective, the labourer is entitled to a share of the products and profits commensurate with his labour;

3. That all accumulated capital being social property, no one can be its exclusive proprietor.

These inferences are unavoidable; these alone would suffice to revolutionize our whole economical system, and change our institutions and our laws...

Just as the creation of every instrument of production is the result of collective force, so also are a man's talent and knowledge the product of universal intelligence and of general knowledge slowly accumulated by a number of masters, and through the aid of many inferior industries. When the physician has paid for his teachers, his books, his diplomas, and all the other items of his educational expenses, he has no more paid for his talent than the capitalist pays for his house and land when he gives his employees their wages...

The labouring people can buy neither the cloth which they weave, nor the furniture which they manufacture, nor the metal which they forge, nor the jewels which they cut, nor the prints which they engrave. They can procure neither the wheat which they plant, nor the wine which they grow, nor the flesh of the animals which they raise. They are allowed neither to dwell in the houses which they build, nor to attend the plays which their labour supports, nor to enjoy the rest which their body requires. And why? Because the right of increase does not permit these things to be sold at the cost-price, which is all that labourers can afford to pay. On the signs of those magnificent warehouses which he in his poverty admires, the labourer reads in large letters: "This is thy work, and thou shalt not have it."

...[I]ndustry, under the influence of property...endeavors to produce a great deal in a short time, because the greater the amount of products, and the shorter the time of production, the less each product costs. As soon as a demand begins to be felt, the factories fill up, and everybody goes to work. Then business is lively, and both governors and governed rejoice. But the more they work today, the more idle will they be hereafter; the more they laugh, the more they shall weep. Under the rule of property, the flowers of industry are woven into none but funeral wreaths. The labourer digs his own grave.

If the factory stops running, the manufacturer has to pay interest on his capital the same as before. He naturally tries, then, to continue production by lessening expenses. Then comes the lowering of wages; the introduction of machinery; the employment of women and children to do the work of men; bad workmen, and wretched work. They still produce, because the decreased cost creates a larger market; but they do not produce long, because, the cheapness being due to the quantity and rapidity of production, the productive power tends more than ever to outstrip consumption. It is when labourers, whose wages are scarcely sufficient to support them from one day to another, are thrown out of work, that the consequences of the principle of property become most frightful. They have not been able to economize, they have made no savings, they have accumulated no capital whatever to support them even one day more. Today the factory is closed. Tomorrow the people starve in the streets. Day after tomorrow they will either die in the hospital, or eat in the jail...

What is to be the form of government in the future? I hear some of my younger readers reply: "Why, how can you ask such a question? You are a republican." "A republican!" "Yes; but that word specifies nothing. *Res publica*; that is, the public thing. Now, whoever is interested in public affairs—no matter under what form of government—may call himself a republican. Even kings are republicans." "Well! you are a democrat?" "No." "What! you would have a monarchy." "No." "A constitutionalist?" "God forbid!" "You are then an aristocrat?" "Not at all." "You want a mixed government?" "Still less." "What are you, then?" "I am an anarchist."

"Oh! I understand you; you speak satirically. This is a hit at the government." "By no means. I have just given you my serious and well-considered profession of faith. Although a firm friend of order, I am (in the full force of the term) an anarchist. Listen to me."

...Man, in order to procure as speedily as possible the most thorough satisfaction of his wants, seeks rule. In the beginning, this rule is to him living, visible, and tangible. It is his father, his master, his king. The more ignorant man is, the more obedient he is, and the more absolute is his confidence in his guide. But, it being a law of man's nature to conform to rule—that is, to discover it by his powers of reflection and reason—man reasons upon the commands of his chiefs. Now, such reasoning as that is a protest against authority—a beginning of disobedience. At the moment that man inquires into the motives which govern the will of his sovereign—at that moment man revolts. If he obeys no longer because the king commands, but because the king demonstrates the wisdom of his commands, it may be said that henceforth he will recognize no authority, and that he has become his own king. Unhappy he who shall dare to command him, and shall offer, as his authority, only the vote of the majority; for, sooner or later, the minority will become the majority, and this imprudent despot will be overthrown, and all his laws annihilated...

Thus, in a given society, the authority of man over man is inversely proportional to the stage of intellectual development which that society has reached; and the probable duration of that authority can be calculated from the more or less general desire for a true government—that is, for a scientific government. And just as the right of force and the right of artifice retreat before the steady advance of justice, and must finally be extinguished in equality, so the sovereignty of the will yields to the sovereignty of reason, and must at last be lost in scientific socialism. Property and royalty have been crumbling to pieces ever since the world began. As man seeks justice in equality, so society seeks order in anarchy.

Anarchy—the absence of a master, of a sovereign—such is the form of government to which we are every day approximating, and which our accustomed habit of taking man for our rule, and his will for law, leads us to regard as the height of disorder and the expression of chaos...

Wherever this work is read and discussed, there will be deposited the germ of death to property; there, sooner or later, privilege and servitude will disappear, and the despotism of the will will give place to the reign of reason. What sophisms, indeed, what prejudices (however obstinate) can stand before the simplicity of the following propositions:

1. Individual possession is the condition of social life; five thousand years of property demonstrate it. Property is the suicide of society. Possession is a right; property is against right. Suppress property while maintaining possession, and, by this simple modification of the principle, you will revolutionize law, government, economy, and institutions; you will drive evil from the face of the earth.

2. All having an equal right of occupancy, possession varies with the number of possessors; property cannot establish itself.

3. The effect of labour being the same for all, property is lost in the common prosperity.

4. All human labour being the result of collective force, all property becomes, in consequence, collective and unitary. To speak more exactly, labour destroys property.

5. Every capacity for labour being, like every instrument of labour, an accumulated capital, and a collective property, inequality of wages and fortunes (on the ground of inequality of capacities) is, therefore, injustice and robbery.

6. The necessary conditions of commerce are the liberty of the contracting parties and the equivalence of the products exchanged. Now, value being expressed by the amount of time and outlay which each product costs, and liberty

being inviolable, the wages of labourers (like their rights and duties) should be equal.

7. Products are bought only by products. Now, the condition of all exchange being equivalence of products, profit is impossible and unjust. Observe this elementary principle of economy, and pauperism, luxury, oppression, vice, crime, and hunger will disappear from our midst.

8. Men are associated by the physical and mathematical law of production, before they are voluntarily associated by choice. Therefore, equality of conditions is demanded by justice; that is, by strict social law: esteem, friendship, gratitude, admiration, all fall within the domain of equitable or proportional law only.

9. Free association, liberty—whose sole function is to maintain equality in the means of production and equivalence in exchanges—is the only possible, the only just, the only true form of society.

10. Politics is the science of liberty. The government of man by man (under whatever name it be disguised) is oppression. Society finds its highest perfection in the union of order with anarchy.

9. Proudhon: The System of Economic Contradictions (1846)

After the publication of What is Property, *Proudhon published two more "memoirs" on property, and narrowly avoided going to jail for his subversive ideas. He immersed himself in political economy, publishing in 1846 a massive two volume critique of bourgeois political economy and socialist utopianism entitled,* The System of Economic Contradictions, or, The Philosophy of Misery. *Karl Marx (1818-1883) responded the following year with his sarcastic and unfair rejoinder,* The Poverty of Philosophy, *by which Marx hoped to establish his reputation on the intended ruins of Proudhon's. Of particular note is Proudhon's critical view of machinery, which Marx lampooned as the reactionary musings of a retrograde who wished to return to a preindustrial utopia. The following selections are taken from Benjamin Tucker's 1888 translation, with minor modifications.*

FROM THE VERY FACT THAT machinery diminishes the workman's toil, it abridges and diminishes labour, the supply of which thus grows greater from day to day and the demand less. Little by little, it is true, the reduction in prices causing an increase in consumption, the proportion is restored and the labourer set at work again: but as industrial improvements steadily succeed each other and continually tend to substitute mechanical operations for the labour of man, it follows that there is a constant tendency to cut off a portion of the service and consequently to eliminate labourers from production. Now, it is with the economic order as with the spiritual order: outside of the church there is no salvation; outside of labour there is no subsistence. Society and nature, equally pitiless, are in accord in the execution of this new decree.

...[N]o one denies that machines have contributed to the general welfare; but I affirm, in regard to this incontestable fact, that the economists fall short of the truth when they advance the absolute statement that the simplification of processes has nowhere resulted in a diminution of the number of hands employed in any industry whatever. What the economists ought to say is that machinery, like the division of labour, in the present system of social economy is at once a source of wealth and a permanent and fatal cause of misery...

An English manufacturer: "The insubordination of our workmen has given us the idea of dispensing with them. We have made and stimulated every imaginable effort of the mind to replace the service of men by tools more docile, and we have achieved our object. Machinery has delivered capital from the oppression of labour. Wherever we still employ a man, we do so only temporarily, pending the invention for us of some means of accomplishing his work without him."

What a system is that which leads a business man to think with delight that society will soon be able to dispense with men! Machinery has delivered capital from the oppression of labour! That is exactly as if the Cabinet should undertake to deliver the Treasury from the oppression of the taxpayers. Fool! though the workmen cost you something, they are your customers: what will you do with your products, when, driven away by you, they shall consume them no longer? Thus machinery, after crushing the workmen, is not slow in dealing employers a counter-blow; for, if production excludes consumption, it is soon obliged to stop itself.

...What a pity that machinery cannot also deliver capital from the oppression of consumers! What a misfortune that machines do not buy the fabrics which they weave! The ideal society will be reached when commerce, agriculture, and manufactures can proceed without a man upon earth!

...Machines! The adult workman becomes an apprentice, a child, again: this result was foreseen from the phase of the division of labour, during which we saw the quality of the workman degenerate in the ratio in which industry was perfected...

Machines promised us an increase of wealth; they have kept their word, but at the same time endowing us with an increase of poverty. They promised us liberty; I am going to prove that they have brought us slavery...

The first, the simplest, the most powerful of machines is the workshop.

Division simply separates the various parts of labour, leaving each to devote himself to the specialty best suited to his tastes: the workshop groups the labourers according to the relation of each part to the whole...Now, through the workshop, production is going to increase, and at the same time the deficit.

...[W]hoever says reduction of expenses says reduction of services, not, it is true, in the new shop, but for the workers at the same trade who are left outside, as well as for many others whose accessory services will be less needed in future. Therefore every establishment of a workshop corresponds to an eviction of workers: this assertion, utterly contradictory though it may appear, is as true of the workshop as of a machine.

The economists admit it: but here they repeat their eternal refrain that, after a lapse of time, the demand for the product having increased in proportion to the reduction of price, labour in turn will come finally to be in greater demand than ever. Undoubtedly, WITH TIME, the equilibrium will be restored; but, I must add again, the equilibrium will be no sooner restored at this point than it will be disturbed at another, because the spirit of invention never stops, any more than labour. Now, what theory could justify these perpetual hecatombs? "When we have reduced the number of toilers," wrote Sismondi, "to a fourth or a fifth of what it is at present, we shall need only a fourth or a fifth as many priests, physicians, etc. When we have cut them off altogether, we shall be in a position to dispense with the human race." And that is what really would happen if, in order to put the labour of each machine in proportion to the needs of consumption—that is, to restore the balance of values continually destroyed—it were not necessary to continually create new machines, open other markets, and consequently multiply services and displace other arms. So that on the one hand industry and wealth, on the other population and misery, advance, so to speak, in procession, one always dragging the other after it.

The machine, or the workshop, after having degraded the worker by giving him a master, completes his degeneracy by reducing him from the rank of artisan to that of common labourer...

If not misery, then degradation: such is the last alternative which machinery offers to the workman. For it is with a machine as with a piece of artillery: the captain excepted, those whom it occupies are servants, slaves...

With machinery and the workshop, divine right—that is, the principle of authority—makes its entrance into political economy. Capital, Mastership, Privilege, Monopoly, Loaning, Credit, Property, etc.—such are, in economic language, the various names of I know not what, but which is otherwise called Power, Authority, Sovereignty, Written Law, Revelation, Religion, God in short, cause and principle of all our miseries and all our crimes, and who, the more we try to define him, the more he eludes us…

The concentration of forces in the workshop and the intervention of capital in production, under the name of machinery, engender at the same time overproduction and destitution; and everybody has witnessed these two scourges, more to be feared than incendiarism and plague, develop in our day on the vastest scale and with devouring intensity. Nevertheless it is impossible for us to retreat: it is necessary to produce, produce always, produce cheaply; otherwise, the existence of society is compromised. The labourer, who, to escape the degradation with which the principle of division threatened him, had created so many marvellous machines, now finds himself either prohibited or subjugated by his own works…

Whatever the pace of mechanical progress; though machines should be invented a hundred times more marvellous than the mule-jenny, the knitting-machine, or the cylinder press; though forces should be discovered a hundred times more powerful than steam—very far from freeing humanity, securing its leisure, and making the production of everything gratuitous, these things would have no other effect than to multiply labour, induce an increase of population, make the chains of serfdom heavier, render life more and more expensive, and deepen the abyss which separates the class that commands and enjoys from the class that obeys and suffers.

…[W]hat embarrasses society's march and makes it go from Charybdis to Scylla is precisely the fact that it is not organized. We have reached as yet only the second phase of its evolution, and already we have met upon our road two chasms that seem insuperable—division of labour and machinery. How save the *parcellaire* workman, if he is a man of intelligence, from degradation, or, if he is degraded already, lift him to intellectual life? How, in the second place, give birth among labourers to that solidarity of interest without which industrial progress counts its steps by its catastrophes, when these same labourers are radically divided by labour, wages, intelligence, and liberty—that is, by egoism? How, in short, reconcile what the progress already accomplished has had the effect of rendering irreconcilable? To appeal to communism and fraternity would be to anticipate dates: there is nothing in common, there can exist no fraternity, between such creatures as the division of labour and the service of machinery have made. It is not in that direction—at least for the present—that we must seek a solution. Well! it will be said, since the evil lies still more in the minds than in the system, let us come back to instruction, let us labour for the education of the people.

In order that instruction may be useful, in order that it may even be received, it is necessary, first of all, that the pupil should be free, just as, before planting a piece of ground, we clear it of thorns and dog-grass. Moreover, the best system of education, even so far as philosophy and morality are concerned, would be that of professional education: once more, how reconcile such education with *parcellaire* division and the service of machinery? How shall the man who, by the effect of his labour, has become a slave—that is, a chattel, a thing—again become a person by the same labour, or in continuing the same exercise? Why is it not seen that these ideas are mutually repellent, and that, if, by some impossibility, the worker could reach a certain degree of intelligence, he would make use of it in the first place to revolutionize society and change all civil and industrial relations? And what I say is no vain exaggeration. The working class, in Paris and the large cities, is vastly superior in point of ideas to what it was twenty-five years ago; now, let them tell me if this class is not decidedly, energetically revolutionary! And it will become more and more so in proportion as it shall acquire the ideas of justice and order, in proportion especially as it shall reach an understanding of the mechanism of property.

To properly exploit the mule-jenny, engineers, builders, clerks, brigades of workingmen and workingwomen of all sorts, have been needed. In the name of their liberty, of their security, of their future, and of the future of their children, these workmen, on engaging to work in the mill, had to make reserves; where are the letters of credit which they have delivered to the employers? Where are the guarantees which they have received? What! millions of men have sold their arms and parted with their liberty without knowing the import of the contract; they have engaged themselves upon the promise of continuous work and adequate reward; they have executed with their hands what the thought of the employers had conceived; they have become, by this collaboration, associates in the enterprise: and when monopoly, unable or unwilling to make further exchanges, suspends its manufacture and leaves these millions of labourers without bread, they are told to be resigned! By the new processes they have lost nine days of their labour out of ten; and for reward they are pointed to the lash of necessity flourished over them! Then, if they refuse to work for lower wages, they are shown that they punish themselves. If they accept the rate offered them, they lose that noble pride, that taste for decent conveniences which constitute the happiness and dignity of the workingman and entitle him to the sympathies of the rich. If they combine to secure an increase of wages, they are thrown into prison! Whereas they ought to prosecute their exploiters in the courts, on them the courts will avenge the violations of liberty of commerce! Victims of monopoly, they will suffer the penalty due to the monopolists! O justice of men, stupid courtesan, how long, under your goddess's tinsel, will you drink the blood of the slaughtered worker?

Chapter 4
Revolutionary Ideas And Action

10. Michael Bakunin, The Reaction in Germany (1842)

Michael Bakunin (1814-1876) was a Russian revolutionary who, after the death of Proudhon, went on to play a significant role in the creation of an avowedly anarchist movement. In the 1840's, he was involved in the revolutionary ferment throughout Europe, in the realms of both ideas and action. In Germany, he became associated with the revolution in ideas instigated by the radical students of the German philosopher, Hegel (1770-1831), known as the Young or Left Hegelians. At various times this group included such intellectual luminaries as Ludwig Feuerbach (1804-1872), Karl Marx and Max Stirner. The following excerpts are taken from Bakunin's 1842 essay, "The Reaction in Germany: A Fragment from a Frenchman," written under the pseudonym Jules Elysard, reprinted in Sam Dolgoff's Bakunin on Anarchism *(Montreal: Black Rose Books, 1980). In it he affirms the revolutionary role of negation, summed up by his now notorious phrase, "the passion for destruction is a creative passion."*

FREEDOM, THE REALIZATION OF FREEDOM: who can deny that this is what today heads the agenda of history?...Revolutionary propaganda is...in its deepest sense the negation of the existing conditions of the State; for, with respect to its innermost nature, it has no other program than the destruction of whatever order prevails at the time...

To the Compromisers we can apply what was said in a French journal..."The Left says, two times two are four; the Right [the "Positivists"], two times two are six; and the middle-of-the-road Compromisers say two times two are five." They never answer yes or no; they say: "To a certain extent you are right, but on the other hand." And if they have nothing left to say, they say: "Yes, it is a curious thing." And as it is said of the Polish Jews that in the last Polish war they wanted to serve both warring parties simultaneously, the Poles as well as the Russians, and consequently were hanged by both sides impartially, so these poor souls vex themselves with the impossible business of the outward reconciliation of opposites, and are despised by both parties for their pains...

No...the spirit of revolution is not subdued, it has only sunk into itself in order soon to reveal itself again as an affirmative, creative principle, and right now it is burrowing—if I may avail myself of this expression of Hegel's—like a mole under the earth.

Nevertheless, visible manifestations are stirring around us, hinting that the spirit, that old mole, has brought its underground work to completion and that it will soon come again to pass judgment. Everywhere, especially in France and England, social and religious societies are being formed which are wholly alien to the world of present-day politics, societies that derive their life from new sources quite unknown to us and that grow and diffuse themselves without fanfare. The people, the poor class, which without doubt constitutes the greatest part of humanity; the class whose rights have already been recognized in theory but which is nevertheless still despised for its birth, for its ties with poverty and ignorance, as well as indeed with actual slavery—this class, which constitutes the true people, is everywhere assuming a threatening attitude and is beginning to count the ranks of its enemy, far weaker in numbers than itself, and to demand the actualization of the right already conceded to it by everyone. All people and all men are filled with a kind of premonition, and everyone whose vital organs are not paralyzed faces with shuddering expectation the approaching future which will utter the redeeming word. Even in Russia, the boundless snow-covered kingdom so little known, and which perhaps also has a great future in store, even in Russia dark clouds are gathering, heralding storm. Oh, the air is sultry and pregnant with lightning.

And therefore we call to our deluded brothers: Repent, repent, the Kingdom of the Lord is at hand!

To the Positivists we say: "Open the eyes of your mind; let the dead bury the dead, and convince yourselves at last that the Spirit, ever young, ever newborn, is not to be sought in fallen ruins!" And we exhort the Compromisers to open their hearts to truth, to free themselves of their wretched and blind circumspection, of their intellectual arrogance, and of the servile fear which dries up their souls and paralyzes their movements.

Let us therefore trust the eternal Spirit which destroys and annihilates only because it is the unfathomable and eternal source of all life. The passion for destruction is a creative passion, too!

11. Max Stirner: The Ego and Its Own (1844)

*Max Stirner (Johann Caspar Schmidt, 1806-1856) was part of a group of Young Hegelians who called themselves "The Free Ones." Bakunin later described them as far surpassing "the most frenzied Russian nihilists with their cynical logic" (*Statism and Anarchy*, Cambridge: Cambridge University Press, 1990, originally published 1873, page 142). Stirner's major philosophical work,* The Ego and Its Own, *was very much a critique not only of Hegelian orthodoxy but also the humanitarian, liberal presuppositions of the Young Hegelians themselves. Not even Proudhon escaped Stirner's criticism. Stirner's argument in favour of a kind of nihilistic egoism became an inspiration for later anarchist individualists, and provoked Marx and Engels into writing a lengthy retort of their own, forming a significant part of* The German Ideology *(1845, unpublished until 1932). The following excerpts are taken from the 1907 translation by Steven Tracy Byington, with some minor modifications.*

THE SAME PEOPLE WHO OPPOSE Christianity as the basis of the State, i.e., oppose the so-called Christian State, do not tire of repeating that morality is "the fundamental pillar of social life and of the State." As if the dominion of morality were not a complete dominion of the sacred, a "hierarchy."

...[O]ne must carry in himself the law, the statute; and he who is most legally disposed is the most moral. Even the last vestige of cheerfulness in Catholic life must perish in this Protestant legality. Here at last the domination of the law is for the first time complete. "Not I live, but the law lives in me." Thus I have really come so far to be only the "vessel of its glory." "Every Prussian carries his gendarme in his breast," says a high Prussian officer.

Protestantism has actually put a man in the position of a country governed by secret police. The spy and eavesdropper, "conscience," watches over every motion of the mind, and all thought and action is for it a "matter of conscience," i.e., police business...

Political liberty means that the *polis*, the State, is free; freedom of religion that religion is free, as freedom of conscience signifies that conscience is free; not, therefore, that I am free from the State, from religion, from conscience, or that I am *rid* of them. It does not mean *my* liberty, but the liberty of a power that rules and subjugates me; it means that one of my *despots*, like State, religion, conscience, is free. State, religion, conscience, these despots, make me a slave, and *their* liberty is *my* slavery. That in this they necessarily follow the principle, "the end hallows the means," is self-evident. If the welfare of the State is the end, war is a hallowed means; if justice is the State's end, homicide is a hallowed means, and is called by its sacred name, "execution"; the sacred State *hallows* everything that is serviceable to it...

To this day the revolutionary principle has gone no farther than to assail only *one or another* particular establishment, i.e., be *reformatory*. Much as may be *improved*, strongly as "discreet progress" may be adhered to, always there is only a *new master* set in the old one's place, and the overturning is a—building up...

Under the regime of the commonalty the labourers always fall into the hands of the possessors, of those who have at their disposal some bit of the State domains (and everything possessible in State domain, belongs to the State, and is only a fief of the individual), especially money and land; of the capitalists, therefore. The labourer cannot realize on his labour to the extent of the value that it has for the consumer. "Labour is badly paid!" The capitalist has the greatest profit from it. Well paid, and more than well paid, are only the labours of those who heighten the splendor and *dominion* of the State, the labours of high State *servants*. The State pays well that its "good citizens," the possessors, may be able to pay badly without danger; it secures to itself by good payment its servants, out of whom it forms a protecting power, a "police" (to the police belong soldiers, officials of all kinds, e.g., those of justice, education, etc.—in short, the whole "machinery of the State") for the "good citizens," and the "good citizens" gladly pay high tax-rates to it in order to pay so much lower rates to their labourers.

But the class of labourers, because unprotected in what they essentially are (for they do not enjoy the protection of the State as labourers, but as its subjects they have a share in the enjoyment of the police, a so-called protection of the law), remains a power hostile to this State, this State of possessors, this "citizen kingship." Its principle, labour, is not recognized as to its *value*; it is exploited, a spoil of the possessors, the enemy.

The labourers have the most enormous power in their hands, and, if they once became thoroughly conscious of it and used it, nothing would withstand them; they would only have to stop labour, regard the product of labour as theirs, and enjoy it. This is the sense of the labour disturbances which show themselves here and there.

The State rests on the—*slavery of labour*. If *labour* becomes *free*, the State is lost...

I secure my freedom with regard to the world in the degree that I make the world my own, i.e., "gain it and take possession of it" for myself, by whatever might, by that of persuasion, of petition, of categorical demand, yes, even by hypocrisy, cheating, etc.; for the means that I use for it are determined by what I am. If I am weak, I have only weak means, like the aforesaid, which yet are good enough for a considerable part of the world. Besides, cheating, hypocrisy, lying, look worse than they are. Who has not cheated the police, the law? Who has not quickly taken on an air of honourable loyalty before the sheriff's officer who meets him, in order to conceal an illegality that may have been committed, etc.? He who has not done it has simply let violence be done to him; he was a *weakling* from—conscience. I know that my freedom is diminished even by my not being able to carry out my will on another object, be this other something without will, like a rock, or something with will, like a government, an individual; I deny my ownness when—in the presence of another—I give myself up, i.e., give way, desist, submit; therefore by *loyalty, submission*. For it is one thing when I give up my previous course because it does not lead to the goal, and therefore turn out of a wrong road; it is another when I yield myself a prisoner. I get around a rock that stands in my way, till I have powder enough to blast it; I get around the laws of a people, till I have gathered strength to overthrow them…

I do not demand any right, therefore I need not recognize any either. What I can get by force I get by force, and what I do not get by force I have no right to, nor do I give myself airs, or consolation, with my imprescriptible right.

With absolute right, right itself passes away; the dominion of the "concept of right" is cancelled at the same time. For it is not to be forgotten that hitherto concepts, ideas, or principles ruled us, and that among these rulers the concept of right, or of justice, played one of the most important parts.

Entitled or unentitled—that does not concern me, if I am only *powerful*, I am of myself *empowered*, and need no other empowering or entitling.

Right—is a wheel in the head, put there by a spook; power—that am I myself, I am the powerful one and owner of power. Right is above me, is absolute, and exists in one higher, as whose grace it flows to me: right is a gift of grace from the judge; power and might exist only in me the powerful and mighty…

The fight of the world today is, as it is said, directed against the "established." Yet people are wont to misunderstand this as if it were only that what is now established was to be exchanged for another, a better, established system. But war might rather be declared against establishment itself, the *State*, not a particular State, not any such thing as the mere condition of the State at the time; it is not another State (e.g., a "people's State") that men aim at, but their *union*, uniting, this ever-fluid uniting of everything standing.—A State exists even without my co-operation: I am born in it, brought up in it, under obligations to it, and must "do it homage." It takes me up into its "favour," and I live by its "grace." Thus the independent establishment of the State founds my lack of independence; its condition as a "natural growth," its organism, demands that my nature not grow freely, but be cut to fit it. That *it* may be able to unfold in natural growth, it applies to me the shears of "civilization"; it gives me an education and culture adapted to it, not to me, and teaches me e.g., to respect the laws, to refrain from injury to State property (i.e., private property), to reverence divine and earthly highness, etc.; in short, it teaches me to be—*unpunishable*, "sacrificing" my ownness to "sacredness" (everything possible is sacred; e.g., property, others' lives, etc.,). In this consists the sort of civilization and culture that the State is able to give me: it brings me up to be a "serviceable instrument," a "serviceable member of society."

...The State always has the sole purpose to limit, tame, subordinate, the individual—to make him subject to some *generality* or other; it lasts only so long as the individual is not all in all, and it is only the clearly marked *restriction of me*, my limitation, my slavery. Never does a State aim to bring in the free activity of individuals, but always that which is bound to the *purpose of the State*. Through the State nothing *in common* comes to pass either, as little as one can call a piece of cloth the common work of all the individual parts of a machine; it is rather the work of the whole machine as a unit, *machine work*. In the same style everything is done by the *State machine* too; for it moves the clockwork of the individual minds, none of which follow their own impulse. The State seeks to hinder every free activity by its censorship, its supervision, its police, and holds this hindering to be its duty, because it is in truth a duty of self-preservation. The State wants to make something out of man, therefore there live in it only *made* men; every one who wants to be his own self is its opponent and is nothing. "He is nothing" means as much as, the State does not make use of him, grants him no position, no office, no trade, etc.

...The best State will clearly be that which has the most loyal citizens, and the more the devoted mind for *legality* is lost, so much the more will the State, this system of morality, this moral life itself, be diminished in force and quality. With the "good citizens" the good State too perishes and dissolves into anarchy and lawlessness. "Respect for the law!" By this cement the totality of the State is held together. "The law is *sacred*, and he who affronts it a *criminal*." Without crime no State: the moral world—[which] the State is—is crammed full of scamps, cheats, liars, thieves, etc. Since the State is the "lordship of law," its hierarchy, it follows that the egoist, in all cases where *his* advantage runs against the State's, can satisfy himself only by crime...

Proudhon wants not the *propriétaire* but the *possesseur* or *usufruitier*. What does that mean? He wants no one to own the land; but the benefit of it—even though one were allowed only the hundredth part of this benefit, this fruit—is at any rate one's property, which he can dispose of at will. He who has only the benefit of a field is assuredly not the proprietor of it; still less he who, as Proudhon would have it, must give up so much of this benefit as is not required for his wants; but he is the proprietor of the share that is left him. Proudhon, therefore, denies only such and such property, not *property* itself. If we want no longer to leave the land to the landed proprietors, but to appropriate it to *ourselves*, we unite ourselves to this end, form a union, a *société*, that makes *itself* proprietor; if we have good luck in this, then those persons cease to be landed proprietors. And, as from the land, so we can drive them out of many another property yet, in order to make it *our* property, the property of the—*conquerors*. The conquerors form a society which one may imagine so great that it by degrees embraces all humanity; but so-called humanity too is as such only a thought (spook); the individuals are its reality. And these individuals as a collective (mass) will treat land and earth not less arbitrarily than an isolated individual or so-called *propriétaire*. Even so, therefore, *property* remains standing, and that as "exclusive" too, in that *humanity*, this great society, excludes the *individual* from its property (perhaps only leases to him, gives his as a fief, a piece of it) as it besides excludes everything that is not humanity, e.g., does not allow animals to have property. So too it will remain, and will grow to be. That in which *all* want to have a *share* will be withdrawn from that individual who wants to have it for himself alone: it is made a *common estate*. As a common estate every one has his share in it, and this share is his property. Why, so in our old relations a house which belongs to five heirs is their common estate; but the fifth part of the revenue is each one's property. Proudhon might spare his prolix pathos if he said: "There are some things that belong only to a few, and to which we others will from now on lay claim or—siege. Let us take them, because one comes to property by taking, and the property of which for the present we are still deprived came to the proprietors likewise only by taking. It can be utilized better if it is in the hands of us *all* than if the few control it. Let us therefore associate ourselves for the purpose of this robbery (*vol*)." Instead of this, he tries to get us to believe that society is the original possessor and the sole proprietor, of imprescriptible right; against it the so-called proprietors have become thieves (*La propriété c'est le vol*); if it now deprives the present proprietor of his property, it robs him of nothing, as it is only availing itself of its imprescriptible right. —So far one comes with the spook of society as a *moral person*. On the contrary, what man can obtain belongs to him: the world belongs to me. Do you say anything else by your opposite proposition? "The world belongs to *all*?" All are I and again I, etc. But you make out of the "all" a spook, and make it sacred, so that then the "all" become the individual's fearful master. Then the ghost of "right" places itself on their side.

What then is *my* property? Nothing but what is in my *power*! To what property am I entitled? To every property to which I—empower myself. I give myself the right of property in taking property to myself, or giving myself the proprietor's power, full power, empowerment...

Not isolation or being alone, but society, is man's original state. Our existence begins with the most intimate conjunction, as we are already living with our mother before we breathe; when we see the light of the world, we at once lie on a human being's breast again, her love cradles us in the lap, leads us in the push cart, and chains us to her person with a thousand ties. Society is our *state of nature*. And this is why, the more we learn to feel ourselves, the connection that was formerly most intimate becomes ever looser and the dissolution of the original society more unmistakable. To have once again for herself the child that once lay under her heart, the mother must fetch it from the street and from the midst of its playmates. The child prefers the intercourse that it enters into with its fellows to the society that it has not entered into, but only been born in.

But the dissolution of *society* is *intercourse* or *union*. A society does assuredly arise by union too, but only as a fixed idea arises by a thought...If a union has crystallized into a society, it has ceased to be a coalition; for coalition is an incessant self-uniting; it has become a unitedness, come to a standstill, degenerated into a fixity; it is—dead as a union, it is the corpse of the union or the coalition, i.e., it is—society, community. A striking example of this kind is furnished by the *party*...

Revolution and insurrection must not be looked upon as synonymous. The former consists in an overturning of conditions, of the established condition or status, the State or society, and is accordingly a *political* or *social* act; the latter has indeed for its unavoidable consequence a transformation of circumstances, yet does not start from it but from men's discontent with themselves, is not an armed rising, but a rising of individuals, a getting up, without regard to the arrangements that spring from it. The Revolution aimed at new *arrangements*; insurrection leads us no longer to *let* ourselves be arranged, but to arrange ourselves, and sets no glittering hopes on "institutions." It is not a fight against the established, since, if it prospers, the established collapses of itself; it is only a working forth of me out of the established. If I leave the established, it is dead and passes into decay. Now, as my object is not the overthrow of an established order but my elevation above it, my purpose and deed are not a political or social but (as directed toward myself and my ownness alone) an *egoistic* purpose and deed.

The revolution commands one to make *arrangements,* the insurrection demands that he *rise or exalt himself.* What *constitution* was to be chosen, this question busied the revolutionary heads, and the whole political period foams with constitutional fights and constitutional questions, as the social talents too were uncommonly inventive in societary arrangements (phalansteries, etc.). The insurgent strives to become constitutionless...

I am *owner* of my might, and I am so when I know myself as *unique*. In the *unique one* the owner himself returns into his creative nothing, of which he is born. Every higher essence above me, be it God, be it man, weakens the feeling of my uniqueness, and pales only before the sun of this consciousness. If I concern myself for myself, the unique one, then my concern rests on its transitory, mortal creator, who consumes himself, and I may say:

All things are nothing to me.

12. Proudhon: The General Idea of the Revolution (1851)

In February 1848 there was a popular revolution in France, overthrowing the monarchy and instituting a republic. Although Proudhon lamented that they had "made a revolution without an idea," he helped set up street barricades and became the editor of a series of mass-circulation newspapers through which he did his best to impart some ideas to the revolution. Despite his opposition to government, and his view of universal suffrage as counter-revolution, he managed to get himself elected to the National Assembly as a representative of working class districts in Paris. He was shouted down in the Assembly as an advocate of class warfare when he proposed a general "social liquidation," with or without the help of the bourgeoisie, following the brutal suppression of the working class uprising in June of 1848. Disillusioned by his isolation and powerlessness in the Assembly, Proudhon advocated a "permanent revolution" by the direct action of the people. However, he came to the support of the Republican Constitution in the face of Louis Napoleon's seemingly inexorable rise to power, all to no avail, and was subjected to repeated prosecutions and the suppression of his newspapers. Eventually, he was stripped of his parliamentary immunity and sentenced to three years in prison, from where he wrote the following selections taken from his book, The General Idea of the Revolution in the Nineteenth Century *(1851; translated by John Beverley Robinson, Freedom Press, 1923; republished 1989, Pluto Press, with a new introduction by Robert Graham).*

THE FORM UNDER WHICH MEN first conceived of Order in Society is the patriarchal or hierarchical; that is to say, in principle, Authority; in action, Government. Justice, which afterwards was divided into distributive and commutative justice, appeared at first under the former heading only: a SUPERIOR granting to INFERIORS what is coming to each one.

The governmental idea sprang from family customs and domestic experience: no protest arose then: Government seemed as natural to Society as the subordination of children to their father. That is why M. de Bonald was able to say, and rightly, that the family is the embryo of the State, of which it reproduces the essential classes: the king in the father, the minister in the mother, the subject in the child...

The prejudice in favor of government having sunk into our deepest consciousness, stamping even reason in its mould, every other conception has been for a long time rendered impossible, and the boldest thinkers could but say that Government was no doubt a scourge, a chastisement for humanity; but that it was a necessary evil!

That is why, up to our own days, the most emancipating revolutions and all the eruptions of liberty have always ended in a reiteration of faith in and submission to power; why all revolutions have served only to re-establish tyranny: I make no exception of the Constitution of 1793, any more than of that of 1848, the two most advanced expressions nevertheless of French democracy.

What has maintained this mental predisposition and made its fascination invincible for so long a time, is that, through the supposed analogy between Society and the family, the Government has always presented itself to the mind as the natural organ of justice, the protector of the weak, the preserver of the peace. By the attribution to it of provident care and of full guarantee, the Government took root in the hearts, as well as in the minds of men; it formed a part of the universal soul, it was the faith, the intimate, invincible superstition of the citizens! If this confidence weakened, they said of Government, as they said of Religion and Property, it is not the institution which is bad, but the abuse of it; it is not the king who is wicked but his ministers; Ah, if the king knew!

Thus to the hierarchical and absolutist view of a governing authority, is added an ideal which appeals to the soul, and conspires incessantly against the desire for equality and independence. The people at each revolution think to reform the faults of their government according to the inspiration of their hearts; but they are deceived by their own ideas. While they think that they will secure Power in their own interest, they really have it always against them: in place of a protector, they give themselves a tyrant.

Experience, in fact, shows that everywhere and always the Government, however much it may have been for the people at its origin, has placed itself on the side of the richest and most educated class against the more numerous and poorer class; it has little by little become narrow and exclusive; and, instead of maintaining liberty and equality among all, it works persistently to destroy them, by virtue of its natural inclination towards privilege...

The idea of contract excludes that of government...What characterizes the contract is the agreement for equal exchange; and it is by virtue of this agreement that liberty and well-being increase; while by the establishment of authority, both of these necessarily diminish. This will be evident if we reflect that contract is the act whereby two or several individuals agree to organize among themselves, for a definite purpose and time, that industrial power which we have called *exchange*; and in consequence have obligated themselves to each other, and reciprocally guaranteed a certain amount of services, products, advantages, duties, etc., which they are in a position to obtain and give to each other; recognizing that they are otherwise perfectly independent, whether for consumption or production.

Between contracting parties there is necessarily for each one a real personal interest; it implies that a man bargains with the aim of securing his liberty and his revenue at the same time, without any possible loss. Between governing and governed, on the contrary, no matter how the system of representation or of delegation of the governmental function is arranged, there is *necessarily* alienation of a part of the liberty and of the means of the citizen...

The contract therefore is essentially reciprocal: it imposes no obligation upon the parties, except that which results from their personal promise of reciprocal delivery: it is not subject to any external authority: it alone forms the law between the parties: it awaits their initiative for its execution...

The social contract should increase the well-being and liberty of every citizen—If any one sided conditions should slip in; if one part of the citizens should find themselves, by the contract, subordinated and exploited by the others, it would no longer be a contract; it would be a fraud, against which annulment might at any time be invoked justly.

The social contract should be freely discussed, individually accepted, signed with their own hands, by all the participants. If the discussion of it were forbidden, cut short or juggled, if consent were obtained by fraud; if signature were made in blank, by proxy, or without reading the document and the preliminary explanation; or even if, like the military oath, consent were a matter of course and compulsory; the social contract would then be no more than a conspiracy against the liberty and well-being of the most ignorant, the weakest and the most numerous, a systematic spoliation, against which every means of resistance, and even of reprisal, would be a right and a duty...

The idea of Anarchy had hardly been implanted in the mind of the people when it found so-called gardeners who watered it with their calumnies, fertilized it with their misrepresentations, warmed it in the hothouse of their hatred, supported it by their stupid opposition. Today, thanks to them, it has borne the anti-governmental idea, the idea of Labour, the idea of Contract, which is growing, mounting, seizing with its tendrils the workingmen's societies, and soon, like the grain of mustard seed of the Gospel, it will form a great tree, with branches which cover the earth.

The sovereignty of Reason having been substituted for that of Revelation,

The notion of Contract succeeding that of Government,

Historic evolution leading Humanity inevitably to a new system,

Economic criticism having shown that political institutions must be lost in industrial organization,

We may conclude without fear that the revolutionary formula cannot be *Direct Legislation*, nor *Direct Government*, nor *Simplified Government*, that it is NO GOVERNMENT.

Neither monarchy, nor aristocracy, nor even democracy itself, in so far as it may imply any government at all, even though acting in the name of the people, and calling itself the people. No authority, no government, not even popular, that is the Revolution.

Rousseau teaches in unmistakable terms, that in a government really democratic and free the citizen, in obeying the law, obeys only his own will. But the law has been made without my participation, despite my absolute disapproval, despite the injury which it inflicts upon me. The State does not bargain with me: it gives me nothing in exchange: it simply practices extortion upon me. Where then is the bond of conscience, reason, passion or interest which binds me?

But what do I say? Laws for one who thinks for himself, and who ought to answer only for his own actions; laws for one who wants to be free, and feels himself worthy of liberty? I am ready to bargain, but I want no laws. I recognize none of them: I protest against every order which it may please some power, from pretended necessity, to impose upon my free will. Laws! We know what they are, and what they are worth! Spider webs for the rich and powerful, steel chains for the weak and poor, fishing nets in the hands of the Government…

With suffrage, or the universal vote, it is evident that the law is neither direct nor personal, any more than collective. The law of the majority is not my law, it is the law of force; hence the government based upon it is not my government; it is government by force.

That I may remain free; that I may not have to submit to any law but my own, and that I may govern myself, the authority of the suffrage must be renounced: we must give up the vote, as well as representation and monarchy. In a word, everything in the government of society which rests on the divine must be suppressed, and the whole rebuilt upon the human idea of CONTRACT...

The *system of contracts*, substituted for the *system of laws*, would constitute the true government of the man and of the citizen; the true sovereignty of the people, the REPUBLIC.

For the contract is Liberty, the first term of the republican motto...I am not free when I depend upon another for my work, my wages, or the measure of my rights and duties; whether that other be called the Majority or Society. No more am I free, either in my sovereignty or in my action, when I am compelled by another to revise my law, were that other the most skilful and most just of arbiters. I am no more at all free when I am forced to give myself a representative to govern me, even if he were my most devoted servant.

The Contract is Equality, in its profound and spiritual essence. Does this man believe himself my equal; does he not take the attitude of my master and exploiter, who demands from me more than it suits me to furnish, and has no intention of returning it to me; who says that I am incapable of making my own law, and expects me to submit to his?

The contract is Fraternity, because it identifies all interests, unifies all divergences, resolves all contradictions, and in consequence, gives wings to the feelings of goodwill and kindness, which are crushed by economic chaos, the government of representatives, alien law.

The contract, finally, is order, since it is the organization of economic forces, instead of the alienation of liberties, the sacrifice of rights, the subordination of wills...

In cases in which production requires great division of labour, and a considerable collective force, it is necessary to form an ASSOCIATION among the workers in this industry; because without that, they would remain related as subordinates and superiors, and there would ensue two industrial castes of masters and wage-workers, which is repugnant to a free and democratic society.

Such therefore is the rule that we must lay down, if we wish to conduct the Revolution intelligently.

Every industry, operation or enterprise, which by its nature requires the employment of a large number of workmen of different specialties, is destined to become a society or company of workers...

Large scale industry may be likened to a new land, discovered or suddenly created out of the air, by the social genius; to which society sends a colony to take possession of it and to work it, for the advantage of all.

This colony will be ruled by a double contract, that which gives it title, establishes its Property, and fixes its rights and obligations toward the mother country; and the contract which unites the different members among themselves, and determines their rights and duties.

Toward Society, of which it is a creation and a dependence, this working company promises to furnish always the products and services which are asked of it, at a price as nearly as possible that of cost, and to give the public the advantage of all desirable betterments and improvements.

To this end, the working company abjures all combinations, submits itself to the law of competition, and holds its books and records at the disposition of Society, which, upon its part, reserves the power of dissolving the working company, as the sanction of its right of control.

Toward the individuals and families whose labour is the subject of the association, the company makes the following rules:

> That every individual employed in the association, whether man, woman, child, old man, head of department, assistant head, workman or apprentice, has an undivided share in the property of the company;
>
> That he has a right to fill any position, of any grade, in the company, according to suitability of sex, age, skill, and length of employment;
>
> That his education, instruction, and apprenticeship should therefore be so directed that, while permitting him to do his share of unpleasant and disagreeable tasks, they may also give variety of work and knowledge, and may assure him, from the period of maturity, an encyclopedic aptitude and a sufficient income;
>
> That all positions are elective, and the bylaws subject to the approval of the members;
>
> That pay is to be proportional to the nature of the position, the importance of the talents, and the extent of responsibility;
>
> That each member shall participate in the gains and in the losses of the company, in proportion to his services;
>
> That each member is free to leave the company, upon settling his account, and paying what he may owe; and reciprocally, the company may take in new members at any time.

These general principles are enough to explain the spirit and scope of this institution, that has no precedent and no model. They furnish the solution of two important problems of social economy, that of *collective force*, and that of the division of labour.

By participation in losses and gains, by the graded scale of pay and the successive promotion to all grades and positions, the collective force, which is a product of the community, ceases to be a source of profit to a small number of managers and speculators: it becomes the property of all the workers. At the same time, by a broad education, by the obligation of apprenticeship, and by the co-operation of all who take part in the collective work, the division of labour can no longer be a cause of degradation for the workman: it is, on the contrary, the means of his education and the pledge of his security...

Unless democracy is a fraud, and the sovereignty of the People a joke, it must be admitted that each citizen in the sphere of his industry, each municipal, district or provincial council within its own territory, is the only natural and legitimate representative of the Sovereign, and that therefore each locality should act directly and by itself in administering the interests which it includes, and should exercise full sovereignty in relation to them. The People is nothing but the organic union of wills that are individually free, that can and should voluntarily work together, but abdicate never. Such a union must be sought in the harmony of their interests, not in an artificial centralization, which, far from expressing the collective will, expresses only the antagonisms of individual wills...

It is the governments who, pretending to establish order among men, arrange them forthwith in hostile camps, and as their only occupation is to produce servitude at home, their art lies in maintaining war abroad, war in fact or war in prospect.

The oppression of peoples and their mutual hatred are two correlative, inseparable facts, which reproduce each other, and which cannot come to an end except simultaneously, by the destruction of their common cause, government...

The fundamental, decisive idea of this Revolution, is it not this: NO MORE AUTHORITY, neither in the Church, nor in the State, nor in land, nor in money?

No more Authority! That means something we have never seen, something we have never understood: the harmony of the interest of one with the interest of all; the identity of collective sovereignty and individual Sovereignty.

No more Authority! That means debts paid, servitude abolished, mortgages lifted, rents reimbursed, the expense of worship, justice, and the State suppressed; free credit, equal exchange, free association, regulated value, education, work, property, domicile, low price, guaranteed: no more antagonism, no more war, no more centralization, no more governments, no more priests…

No more Authority! That is to say further: free contract in place of arbitrary law; voluntary transactions in place of the control of the State; equitable and reciprocal justice in place of sovereign and distributive justice; rational instead of revealed morals; equilibrium of forces instead of equilibrium of powers; economic unity in place of political centralization.

13. Anselme Bellegarrigue: Anarchy is Order (1850)

Proudhon was not alone during the 1848 Revolution in France in advocating anarchist ideas. Anselme Bellegarrigue, a young journalist from Toulouse, published L'Anarchie, Journal de l'Ordre, *in Paris in 1850, having previously edited one of the most popular social democratic dailies in Toulouse,* La Civilisation. *As with many others, Bellegarrigue left France after Louis Napoleon's December 1851 coup d'etat, eventually settling in El Salvador. The following excerpts, translated by Paul Sharkey, are taken from the Kate Sharpley Library edition (London, 2002) entitled* Anarchist Manifesto, *and are reprinted with the kind permission of the publisher.*

ANARCHY IS THE NEGATION OF GOVERNMENTS. Governments, whose pupils we are, have naturally found nothing better to devise than to school us in fear and horror of their destruction. But as governments in turn are the negations of individuals or of the people, it is reasonable that the latter, waking up to essential truths, should gradually come to feel a greater horror at its own annihilation than that of its masters.

Anarchy is an ancient word, but for us that word articulates a modern notion, or rather, a modern interest, the idea being daughter to the interest. History has described as "anarchic" the condition of a people wherein there are several governments in contention one with another; but the condition of a people desirous of being governed but bereft of government precisely because it has too many is one thing and the condition of a people desirous of governing itself and bereft of government precisely because it wishes none quite another. In ancient times, indeed, anarchy was civil war, not because it meant absence of governments but, rather, because it meant a multiplicity of them and competition and strife among the governing classes. The modern notion of absolute social truth or pure democracy has ushered in an entire series of discoveries or interests which have turned the terms of the traditional equation upside down. Thus anarchy, which, when contrasted with the term monarchy, means civil war, is, from the vantage point of absolute or democratic truth, nothing less than the true expression of social order.

Indeed:

Who says anarchy, says negation of government;

Who says negation of government says affirmation of the people;

Who says affirmation of the people, says individual liberty;

Who says individual liberty, says sovereignty of each;

Who says sovereignty of each, says equality;

Who says equality, says solidarity or fraternity;

Who says fraternity, says social order.

By contrast:

Who says government, says negation of the people;

Who says negation of the people, says affirmation of political authority;

Who says affirmation of political authority, says individual dependency;

Who says individual dependency, says class supremacy;

Who says class supremacy, says inequality;

Who says inequality, says antagonism;

Who says antagonism, says civil war;

From which it follows that who says government, says civil war.

Yes, anarchy is order, whereas government is civil war.

When my intellect looks past the wretched details underpinning the day to day dialectic, I discover that the intestinal strife which, throughout the ages, has decimated humankind, is bound up with a single cause, to wit: the destruction or preservation of government.

In the realm of politics, sacrifice of self for the purpose of the maintenance or installation of a government has always meant having one's throat cut and one's entrails torn out. Point me to a place where men openly slaughter one another and I will show you a government behind all the carnage. If you try to explain civil war away as other than the manner of a government's trying to ensconce itself or a government's refusal to quit the stage, you are wasting your time; you will not be able to come up with anything.

And the reason is simple.

A government is set up. In the very instant of its creation, it has its servants and, as a result, its supporters; and the moment that it has its supporters it has its adversaries too. That very fact alone quickens the seed of civil war, because the government, resplendent in its authority, cannot possibly act with regard to its adversaries the way it does with regard to its supporters. There is no possibility of the former not feeling its favour, nor of the latter not being persecuted. From which it follows that there is likewise no possibility of conflict between the favoured faction and the oppressed faction not arising from this disparity, sooner or later. In other words, once the government is in place, the favouritism that is the basis of privilege and which provokes division, spawns antagonism and civil strife becomes inevitable.

From which it follows that government is civil war.

There need only be a government supporter on the one hand and an adversary of the government on the other for strife to erupt among the citizenry: it is plain that, outside of the love or hatred borne towards the government, civil war has no *raison d'être*, which means to say that for peace to be established, the citizenry need merely refrain from being, on the one hand, supporters and, on the other, adversaries of the government.

But refraining from attacking or defending the government so as to render civil war impossible is nothing short of paying it no heed, tossing it on to the dungheap and dispensing with it in order to lay the foundations of social order.

Now, if dispensing with government is, on the one hand, the establishment of order, and, on the other, the enshrinement of anarchy, then order and anarchy go hand in hand. From which it follows that anarchy is order.

14. Joseph Déjacque: The Revolutionary Question (1854)

Joseph Déjacque (1821-1864) was also active in the 1848 Revolution in France. Imprisoned in June 1848 and June 1849, he eventually escaped into exile around the time of Louis Napoleon's December 1851 coup d'etat. He spent several years living in poverty in the United States, where he nevertheless was able to publish an anarchist periodical, Le Libertaire, making him the first person to use the word "libertarian" as synonymous with "anarchist." The following excerpts, translated by Paul Sharkey, are taken from his 1854 pamphlet, La Question révolutionnaire *(*The Revolutionary Question*).*

Of Revolution

Principles: *Liberty, Equality, Fraternity.*

Consequences: Abolition of government in all its guises, be they monarchist or republican, the supremacy of an individual or of a majority;

Rather, anarchy, individual sovereignty, complete, boundless, utter freedom to do anything and everything that is in human nature.

Abolition of Religion, be it Catholic or Jewish, Protestant or other. Abolition of clergy and altar, of priest—be he curate or pope, minister or rabbi—of Divinity, be it an idol with one person or with three, autocracy or universal oligarchy;

Rather man—at once creature and creator—with no God now but Nature, no priest but Science, no altar but Humanity.

Abolition of personal property, ownership of the soil, buildings, workshops, stores and of anything that is an instrument of labour, production or consumption;

Rather, collective property, one and indivisible, held in common.

Abolition of the family, the family based on marriage, the authority of father and spouse and on inheritance;

Rather the great family of man, a family as one and indivisible as property.

The liberation of woman, the emancipation of the child.

At last, the abolition of authority, privilege and strife.

Rather, liberty, equality and fraternity embodied in humanity;

Instead, all of the implications of the triple formula transplanted from theoretical abstraction to practical reality, to positivism.

Which is to say Harmony, the oasis of our dreams, no longer fleeing like a mirage before the caravan of generations but delivering to each and every one of us, under its fraternal auspices and in universal unity, the sources of happiness, the fruits of liberty: a life of delights at last after more than eighteen centuries' worth of agony in the desert wastes of civilization!

Of Government

No more government, that machine press, that fulcrum for the lever of reaction.

All government—and by government I mean all delegation and all authority beyond the people—is essentially conservative—narrow-mindedly conservative, backward-looking conservative—just as selfishness is a part of human nature. In the case of man, the selfishness of one is tempered by the selfishness of the others, by the solidarity that nature has established between him and his fellows, no matter what he may do. But, government being singular and therefore bereft of counter-balance, it follows that it arrogates everything to itself, that anyone who fails to prostrate himself before its image, everyone who contradicts its oracles, everything that poses a threat to its survival, in short, everything that represents progress, is necessarily its enemy. Thus, a government emerges—initially as an improvement upon a predecessor government—and soon, simply to survive the new thinking that poses a threat to it, it will summon the reaction to its aid; from the arsenal of the arbitrary it will draw the measures most inimical to the needs of the age; emergency law follows upon emergency law, spreading like fire-damp until the mine caves in and the fuse of revolution is ignited and it is blown asunder along with its whole array of defensive measures. Could it have done otherwise and surrendered a single one of its bastions? The enemy, to wit, the revolution, would only have overrun it and turned it into a gun emplacement. Surrender? It was called upon to sue for mercy: and it knew that the enemy sought the ruination of its interests, its enslavement and finally its death.

It is not the men but rather the thing itself that is evil. Depending on their surroundings, and the circumstances in which they operate, men are useful or harmful to those about them.

What is required is that they should not be set apart from the common herd, so that they will have no need to do harm. What is required is that we dispense with shepherds if we would not become a flock and dispense with rulers if we would not be slaves.

No more government, so no more of these malignant ambitions that merely clamber on to the shoulders of an ignorant, credulous people in order to make it a stepping-stone for their cravings. No more acrobatic candidates walking the tightrope of professions of faith, right foot this side, left foot that side. No more of these political sleight-of-hand merchants juggling with the three words from the Republic's motto, Liberty, Equality and Fraternity, like three cups brandished before the eyes of the onlooker, only to be palmed into the recesses of their conscience, that other poacher's pocket. No more of these charlatans of public life who, from the balcony of the Tuileries or the Hôtel de Ville, or the floor of the Convention or Constituent Assembly, have spent so many years regaling us with the same parade, the same sham *finest of republics*, for which we must all finish up paying with our sweat and our blood—poor ninnies that we are.

No more government, so no more army to oppress the people in the people's own name. No more University to crush young intelligence beneath the yoke of cretinism, tinkering with hearts and minds, kneading and molding them in the image of an obsolete world. No more magistrate-inquisitors to torture on the rack of indictment and to sentence the voices of the press and the clubs, the stirring of consciousness and thought, to the silence of imprisonment or exile. No more hangmen, no more jailers, no more gendarmes, no more town sergeants, no more snitches to spy upon, knife, arrest and put to death anyone less than devoted to the authorities. No more prescriptive centralization, no more prefects, no more ordinary or extraordinary envoys to carry the state of siege to every department in the land. No more budgets for regimentation, arming and equipping, for buttering the potatoes or truffles and for intoxicating grog or champagne for liveried retainers, ranging from trooper to general, from prefect to town sergeant and from hangman to judge.

No more government, freeing up a million men and two million strong arms for work and for production.

Toothless crone, light-fingered Shrew, snake-haired Medusa, away with you, Authority! Make way for Freedom!

Make way for the people in direct possession of its sovereignty, make way for the organized commune.

15. Francisco Pi y Margall: Reaction and Revolution (1854)

In the wake of the 1848-1849 Revolutions in Europe, anarchist ideas began to spread not only in the French expatriate community, but in other parts of Europe. Anarchist ideas were introduced into Spain by Francisco Pi y Margall (1824-1901), a writer and politician influenced by Proudhon, whom he translated into Spanish. In the 1850's he was an anti-authoritarian federalist associated with the nascent workers' movement. The following excerpts are taken from his Reaction or Revolution: Political and Social Studies *(1854), translated by Paul Sharkey.*

HOMO SIBI DEUS, ONE GERMAN philosopher said [Feuerbach]: man his own reality, his own right, his world, his purpose, his God, his all. The eternal idea made flesh and become conscious of itself: he is the being of beings, law and law-giver, monarch and subject. Is he searching for a starting-point for science? He finds it, in reflection and in the abstraction of his thinking self. Is he searching for a moral principle? He finds one in his reason which aspires to determine his actions. Is he searching for a universe? He finds one in his ideas. Is he searching for a godhead? He finds one, in himself.

A being that encompasses everything is undoubtedly sovereign. Man, therefore, all men, are ungovernable. All power an absurdity. Every man who lays hands upon another man is a tyrant. More than that: he commits sacrilege.

Between two sovereign entities there is room only for pacts. Authority and sovereignty are contradictions. Society based upon *authority* ought, therefore, to give way to society based upon *contract*. Logic demands it.

Democracy, a curious phenomenon, starts to accept the absolute sovereignty of man, its only possible foundation; but it still fights shy of the anarchy which is its inevitable consequence. Like other factions, it sacrifices logic to the interests of the moment.

I, who back down before no consequence, say: *Man is sovereign*, that is my principle; *power is the negation of his sovereignty*, this is my revolutionary justification; *I must destroy that power*, this is my goal. Thus I know from where I start and where I am bound and I do not falter.

Let me continue. Am I sovereign? Then I am free. But sovereignty does not consist solely of my intellect; when do I exercise it positively? Only when I cease in my obedience to every subjective influence and order all of my actions in accordance with the determinations of reason. Is my freedom anything other than this, my actions' independence of all external determinants?

Let me press on with my observations: my sovereignty cannot have boundaries, because the notions of sovereignty and boundary are mutually contradictory; consequently, if my freedom is merely my sovereignty exercised, my freedom cannot be conditional: *it is absolute*.

But, I answer myself, I do not live in isolation from the rest of the species; how, in the midst of my associates, should I hang on to the full measure of my freedom and of my sovereignty? ...My answer is that the absolute, by virtue of its being such, is indivisible; I must not even think of partial sacrifices of my sovereignty, nor of my freedom. Moreover, for what reason could I have joined with my fellows? ...Between two sovereignties in contention, left to their own devices, there can be only one arbiter, might; political society could not have been established with any other purpose than preventing the violation of one of the two sovereignties or breaches of their contracts, which is to say, the replacement of might by right, by the very laws of reason, by sovereignty *per se*. A society between men, it must be obvious, is scarcely conceivable on the basis of the moral destruction of man. *My freedom*, consequently, *even within society, is unconditional and irreducible.*

Yet was there ever a society that did not set a boundary to it? To date, no society has ever been founded upon right; they have striven to outdo one another with their irregularity and, forgive the paradox, anti-social characters...In essence their forms have not altered their principle and on that basis *I persist in condemning as tyrannical and absurd all forms of government, or, which amounts to the same thing, all societies as presently constituted...My conclusion, therefore, is that either society is not society, or, if it is, it is such by virtue of my consent....*

The constitution of a society without power is the ultimate of my revolutionary aspirations; with that final objective in mind, I must determine all manner of reforms...

Power, currently, should be reduced to its smallest possible expression. *I shall divide and sub-divide power, I shall mobilize it and, rest assured, I shall destroy it.*

16. Carlo Pisacane: On Revolution (1857)

The first European revolution of 1848 broke out in Sicily. It quickly spread throughout the Italian peninsula, then divided into a patchwork of kingdoms, principalities and Austrian protectorates. Carlo Pisacane (1818–1857) fought for the short lived republic in Rome and led republican troops in its defence when French troops lay siege to the city in 1849 to restore the Pope to his Holy See. Pisacane then went into exile, returning to Calabria in 1857 as part of a revolutionary expedition against the kingdom of Naples, where he was killed in action. He was an anti-authoritarian socialist and an early advocate of "propaganda by the deed." The first excerpt that follows is from his work, On Revolution *(posthumously published in 1858). The second is from his "Political Testament," written shortly before his death. Both selections have been translated by Paul Sharkey.*

NATURE, HAVING BESTOWED ALL men with the same organs, the same sensations and the same needs, has declared them equal and thereby granted them equal title to the enjoyment of the goods that she produces. Likewise, having made every man capable of making provision for his own livelihood, she has declared him independent and free.

Needs are the only natural limits upon freedom and independence, so, if men are furnished with the means of supplying those needs, their freedom and independence are all the more complete. Man enters into association wherever he can readily meet his needs, or extend the realm in which his talents can be exercised and where he may secure greater freedom and independence; any social tie that tends to trespass against those two human attributes has not been willingly embraced because it flies in the face of nature and of the purpose that society has set itself, and has only been endured perforce; it cannot be the effect of free association, but is rather of conquest or of error. It follows that any contract which one of the parties is obliged to accept or uphold through hunger or force is a blatant trespass against the laws of Nature: any contract ought in fact to be declared null and void unless it enjoys the most free consensus of the two contracting parties. From these eternal, irresistible laws which ought to underpin the social contract, the following principles follow, which encapsulate the entire economic revolution.

1. Every individual has a right to enjoy all of the material assets available to society and thereby to the full exercise of his physical and moral faculties.

2. The chief object of the social contract is to guarantee absolute freedom to every individual.

3. Absolute independence of life, or complete self-ownership:

   a) Abolition of man's exploitation of his fellow-man.

b) Any contract not enjoying the whole-hearted consensus of the contracting parties is null and void.

c) Access to the material wherewithal essential for work, by means of which each man can look to his own livelihood.

d) The fruits of one's own labours are sacred and inviolable...

On pain of the most grave evils, the laws of nature prohibit us from commanding obedience from our equal. A people which, for the sake of an easier life, delegates its own sovereignty, is akin to someone who ties up his legs and arms in order to run faster. From these truths the following principles emerge which follow from the ones established earlier:

4. Hierarchy, authority and blatant trespasses against the laws of nature, are abolished. The pyramid—God, king, their betters and the plebs—must be broadened at the base.

5. Since every Italian must be free and independent, each and every one of his fellows must be so too. Since hierarchy between individuals is nonsense, the same goes for hierarchy between communes. The individual commune cannot but be a free association of individuals and the nation a free association of communes...

The nation... does not have the right to confer the power to impose laws upon one man or a small number of men; that act is an act of sovereignty and sovereignty may not be delegated...On the very same grounds upon which sovereignty may not be abdicated or transferred, so the law-maker's and congress's term of office will be indeterminable; they are to step down as soon as the nation so decides; since it is the wishes of the mandator that should be binding upon the mandatory, it follows that every deputy must be subject to recall by his electors at every moment. It is nonsense for a government or an assembly to be imposed for a set term, just as it is nonsense for an individual to be hog-tied by one vote. That would be tantamount to declaring the wishes and determinations of a single instance the arbiter and tyrant over any wishes that may progressively emerge in future. Hence the principles which follow:

6. Laws cannot be *imposed*, but may be *proposed* to the nation.

7. Mandatories are at all times subject to recall by their mandators...

Two conditions must be met if the nation's sovereignty is to be undiminished, should some of the citizenry have to shoulder an undertaking affecting the whole of society, namely: that the task to be undertaken and the ranks to be adopted are the result of the national will, which in fact follows from principles 6 and 7 above; and that the distribution of the various functions among the group of citizen operatives should be handled by the citizens themselves. For the nation to nominate the leaders who should oversee things would be a manifest trespass against free association. From which the following principles follow:

8. No official may be appointed other than by the people and will at all times be subject to recall by the people.

9. Any band of citizens… assigned to carry out some special mission, is entitled to divvy up the various roles among themselves and choose their own leaders…

Written laws are norms and nothing more; the decisions of the people take precedence over any law. The people can elect some citizens from among its number and appoint them as judges, but the latter's verdicts will always be overruled by the collective will, the last say of which in every dispute must be acknowledged as an inalienable right inherent in its very nature, its very sovereignty. Thus it will never again be the case that punishments are inflicted which are at odds with public opinion and with the times; and it will come to pass that laws will reflect the changes and shifts in mores. The latter will never be locked in bitter and bloody struggle with the former. Therefore:

10. The people's verdict overrules any law, any magistrate. Anybody who feels that he has been misjudged can appeal to the people.

And so, on the basis of two very simple and incontrovertible truths: Man was created free and independent and his needs are the only limitations set upon those attributes; in order to break free of these limitations and achieve ever wider scope for his activities, man enters into association, but society cannot, without failing in its mission, make the slightest trespass against man's attributes—we are led to the enunciation of ten fundamental principles, the failure to scrupulously observe a single one of which would constitute an infringement of freedom and independence.

Political Testament (1857)

My political principles are sufficiently well known; I believe in socialism, but a socialism different from the French systems, which are all pretty much based on the monarchist, despotic idea which prevails in that nation…The socialism of which I speak can be summed up in these two words: freedom and association…

I am convinced that railroads, electrical telegraphs, machinery, industrial advances, in short, everything that expands and smooths the way for trade, is destined inevitably to impoverish the masses...All of these means increase output, but accumulate it in a small number of hands, from which it follows that much trumpeted progress ends up being nothing but decadence. If such supposed advances are to be regarded as a step forward, it will be in the sense that the poor man's wretchedness is increased until inevitably he is provoked into a terrible revolution, which, by altering the social order, will place in the service of all that which currently profits only some...

Ideas spring from deeds and not the other way around; the people will not be free until it is educated but it will be well educated once free. The only thing for a citizen to do to be of service to his country is to patiently wait for the day when he can cooperate in a material revolution; as I see it, conspiracies, plots and attempted uprisings are the succession of deeds whereby Italy proceeds towards her goal of unity. The use of the bayonet in Milan has produced a more effective propaganda than a thousand books penned by doctrinarians who are the real blight upon our country and the entire world.

There are some who say: the revolution must be made by the country. This there is no denying. But the country is made up of individuals and if we were quietly to wait for the day of revolution to come instead of plotting to bring it about, revolution would never break out. On the other hand, if everybody were to say: the revolution must be made by the country and I, being an infinitesimal part of the country, have my infinitesimal portion of duty to do and were to do it, the revolution would be carried out immediately and would be invincible because of its scale.

17. Joseph Déjacque: On Being Human (1857)

This section concludes with excerpts from an open letter from Joseph Déjacque to Proudhon in 1857, attacking him for his reactionary anti-feminism, which Déjacque rightly saw as inconsistent with anarchist ideals, and advocating a kind of anarchist communism. In his article, "Exchange," from Le Libertaire, *Issue No. 6, Dejacque also directed these comments to Proudhon:*

> Be frankly and wholly anarchist and not one quarter anarchist, one eighth anarchist, one sixteenth part anarchist, the way one is a quarter, an eighth, one sixteenth part an agent of change. Press on to the abolition of contract, the abolition not merely of the sword and of capital, but also of property and authority in every guise. Thereby reaching the anarchistic community, which is to say the social setting wherein every individual

> might be free to produce and to consume at will and in accordance with his dreams, without having to exercise or endure oversight from anyone or over anyone; where the balance between output and consumption would be struck naturally rather than through preventive or arbitrary distraint by this group or that, but rather through the free play of individual exertions and needs.

The translations are by Paul Sharkey.

THE EMANCIPATION OR NON-EMANCIPATION of woman or the non-emancipation of man: what are we to say about these? Can there—naturally—be rights for the one that do not extend to the other? Is the human being not equally human in the plural as much as in the singular, the feminine as much as in the masculine? Does one alter nature by separating the sexes? And the rain droplets that fall from the clouds, are they any less raindrops just because those droplets fall through the air in smaller or larger numbers, are of this or that dimension, this male or female configuration?

Placing the issue of woman's emancipation on the same footing as the issue of emancipation of the proletarian, this man-woman, or, to put it another way, this man-slave—harem fodder or factory fodder—is understandable and revolutionary; but oh! from the vantage point of social progress, it is nonsensical and reactionary to look upon her as less than the privileged man. In order to avert any misunderstanding, we should talk about emancipation of the human being. In which terms, the issue is complete; to pose it in those terms is to resolve it; the human being, in his daily rounds, gravitates from revolution to revolution towards his ideal of perfectibility, Liberty.

But man and woman striding with the same step and heart, united and fortified by love, towards their natural destiny, the anarchic community; with all despotism annihilated, all social inequalities banished; man and woman entering—arm in arm and head to head—into the social garden of Harmony: this band of humans, its dream of happiness achieved, a living portrait of the future; all these egalitarian mumblings and inklings are jarring to your ears and make you screw up your eyes. Your chastened grasp of small vanities has you looking to posterity for the male statue set atop the female pedestal, just as in preceding ages the patriarch towered over the serving-woman...

The human flood need only serve as your dykes; let the unfettered tides be: do they not find their proper levels again each day? Do I, for instance, need to have a sun of my own, an atmosphere of my own, a river of my own, a forest of my own or ownership of all the houses and streets in a town? Am I within my rights to set myself up as their exclusive owner, their proprietor, and deprive others of them, even though my own needs may not be served? And if I have no such entitlement, have I any more right to seek, through a system of contracts, to dole out to every person—according to his accidental capacity to produce—his allotted measure of all these things? How many sunbeams, cubic measurements of air or water, or square feet of forest floor he should be consuming? How many houses or parts of houses he will be entitled to occupy? The number of streets or paving stones in the streets upon which he will be allowed to tread and how many streets and paving stones from which he will be banned from setting foot?—Contract or no contract, am I going to use up more of these things than my nature or temperament requires? Can I as an individual soak up all the sunbeams, all the air in the atmosphere, all the river water? Can I invade and intrude my person into all the shade of the forests, all the streets of the town and all the paving stones in the street, all the houses in the town and all the rooms of the house? And does the same not hold for every consumer good, whether it be a raw material like air or sunshine, or a finished product, like a street or house? So what is the good of a contract that can add nothing to my freedom and which may and assuredly would infringe it?...But what of the idlers, you say? Idlers are a feature of our abnormal societies, which is to say that, idleness being feted and labour scorned, it is scarcely surprising if men weary of toil that brings them only bitter fruits. But in the context of an anarchistic community with science as developed as it is in our day, there could be nothing of the sort. There might well be, just as there are today, beings who are slower to produce than others are, but as a result, there would also be beings slower to consume, and beings quicker than others to produce and thus quicker to consume: there is a natural balance there...How can one imagine that the human being, whose organism is made up of so many precious tools, the exercise of which brings him such a range of delights, tools of the limbs, tools of the heart, tools of the intellect...is it conceivable that he would willingly allow them to be consumed by rust? What! In a state of unfettered nature and of industrial and scientific wonders, a state of anarchistic exuberance wherein everything would be a reminder of activity and every activity of life. What! Could a human being seek happiness only through imbecilic inactivity? Come on now! The contrary is the only possibility.

In the context of genuine anarchy and absolute freedom, there would undoubtedly be as much diversity between beings as there would be individuals in society, diversity in terms of age, gender and aptitudes: equality does not mean uniformity. And that diversity in all beings and at all times is the very thing that renders all government, constitutions or contract impossible. How can one commit oneself for a year, a day, an hour when within the hour, the day, the year one might very well have other thoughts than one held at the moment that commitment was given?—With radical anarchy, therefore, there would be women, just as there would be men, of greater or lesser relative worth; there would be children and old folk alike; but all of them...would be none the less human beings for all that, and they would be equally and absolutely free to move in circles to which they feel a natural attraction, free to consume and to produce as they see fit, without any paternal, marital or governmental authority, without any legal or coercive constraints to hinder them.

Taking this view of Society—and you too as an anarchist ought to see it in these terms, you who brag about your powers of reason—what have you to say now about the *sexual infirmity* of the female or male human being?

Listen, master Proudhon, do not speak about woman, or, before you do, study her; take lessons. Do not describe yourself as an anarchist, or be an anarchist through and through...

Instead, speak out against man's exploitation of woman. Tell the world, with that vigorous force of argument that has made you an athletic agitator, tell it that man cannot free the Revolution from the morass, and release it from its filthy, bleeding rut, except with woman's assistance; that, on his own, he is powerless; that he needs the support of woman's heart and head; that they must all stride in step along the path of Social Progress, side by side and hand in hand; that man could not achieve his aim and bear the weariness of the journey had he not the support and encouragement of woman's glances and caresses. Tell man and tell woman that their fates are linked and that they should get along better; that they have one and the same name just as they are one and the same being, the human being; that they are, alternately and simultaneously, one the right arm and the other the left arm, and that, in their human identity, their hearts cannot but be one heart and their thoughts one single collection of thoughts. Tell them too that only then can they cast a light upon each other and, in their phosphorescent trek, pierce the shadows that separate the present from the future and civilized society from harmonious society. Tell them, finally, that the human being—whatever his relative proportions and appearances—the human being is like the glow-worm: he shines only through love and for love!

Say that: Be stronger than your weaknesses, more generous than your rancour: proclaim freedom, equality, fraternity and the indivisibility of the human being. Say this: That it is the public's salvation. Declare Humanity endangered: summon men and women *en masse* to banish invasive prejudices beyond the frontiers of society: whip up a Second or a Third of September against this masculine high nobility, this gender aristocracy that would bind us to the old regime. Say this: You must! And say it with passion, with inspiration, cast it in bronze and make it thunder...and then you will have done well both by others and by yourself. (*Economies et Sociétés*, Vol. VI, No. 12, Dec. 1972)

Chapter 5
The Origins Of The Anarchist Movement And The International

18. Proudhon: On Federalism (1863/65)

By the 1860's, when Proudhon wrote the following selections, he had considerably moderated his political views. "Anarchy," a society without government, was for him to remain a perpetual desideratum. He attempted to develop a democratic, anti-authoritarian conception of the state as a voluntary federation of autonomous political groupings. In Proudhon's theory of federalism, power was to remain firmly based in the constitutive units of society, with the role of any central authority being strictly defined and limited to the express purposes agreed to by the contracting parties. Later anarchists accepted the idea of voluntary federation as a basis for organization, but rejected any role for a central authority, seeing it as unnecessary, authoritarian and counter-revolutionary. The first selection is taken from Proudhon's The Principle of Federation *(Toronto: University of Toronto Press, 1979; originally published 1863), translated by Richard Vernon, and reprinted with the kind permission of the publisher. The second selection is from Proudhon's political testament,* On the Political Capacity of the Working Classes, *in which he emphasizes the voluntary nature of genuine federalism, and mutualism as its necessary corollary (for more on Proudhon's mutualist conception of socialism, see Selection 12). It was originally published in 1865, shortly after Proudhon's death. The translation is by Paul Sharkey.*

The Principle of Federation (1863)

FEDERATION, FROM THE LATIN *foedus*, genitive *foederis*, which means pact, contract, treaty, agreement, alliance, and so on, is an agreement by which one or more heads of family, one or more towns, one or more groups of towns or states, assume reciprocal and equal commitments to perform one or more specific tasks, the responsibility for which rests exclusively with the officers of the federation. (In J-J. Rousseau's theory, which was also that of Robespierre and the Jacobins, the social contract is a legal *fiction*, imagined as an alternative to divine right, paternal authority, or social necessity, in explaining the origins of the state and the relations between government and individual...In the federal system, the social contract is more than a fiction; it is a positive and effective compact, which has actually been proposed, discussed, voted upon, and adopted, and which can properly be amended at the contracting parties' will. Between the federal contract and that of Rousseau and 1793 there is all the difference between a reality and a hypothesis.)

Let us consider this definition more closely. What is essential to and characteristic of the federal contract, and what I most wish the reader to notice, is that in this system the contracting parties, whether heads of family, towns, cantons, provinces, or states, not only undertake bilateral and commutative obligations, but in making the pact reserve for themselves more rights, more liberty, more authority, more property than they abandon.

According to these principles the contract of federation has the purpose, in general terms, of guaranteeing to the federated states their sovereignty, their territory, the liberty of their subjects; of settling their disputes; of providing by common means for all matters of security and mutual prosperity; thus, despite the scale of the interests involved, it is essentially limited. The authority responsible for its execution can never overwhelm the constituent members; that is, the federal powers can never exceed in number and significance those of local or provincial authorities, just as the latter can never outweigh the rights and prerogatives of man and citizen. If it were otherwise, the community would become communistic; the federation would revert to centralized monarchy; the federal authority, instead of being a mere delegate and subordinate function as it should be, will be seen as dominant; instead of being confined to a specific task, it will tend to absorb all activity and all initiative; the confederated states will be reduced to administrative districts, branches, or local offices. Thus transformed, the body politic may be termed republican, democratic, or what you will; it will no longer be a state constituted by a plenitude of autonomies, it will no longer be a confederation. The same will hold, with even greater force, if for reasons of false economy, as a result of deference, or for any other reason the federated towns, cantons or states charge one among their number with the administration and government of the rest. The republic will become unitary, not federal, and will be on the road to despotism. (...Thus a confederation is not exactly a state; it is a group of sovereign and independent states, associated by a pact of mutual guarantees. Nor is a federal constitution the same as what is understood in France by a charter or constitution, an abridged statement of public law; the pact contains the conditions of association, that is, the rights and reciprocal obligations of the states. What is called federal authority, finally, is no longer a government; it is an agency created by the states for the joint execution of certain functions which the states abandon, and which thus become federal powers…Thus the federal power is in the full sense of the word an agent, under the strict control of his principals, whose power varies at their pleasure.)

In summary, the federal system is the contrary of hierarchy or administrative and governmental centralization which characterizes, to an equal extent, democratic empires, constitutional monarchies, and unitary republics. Its basic and essential law is this: in a federation, the powers of central authority are specialized and limited and diminish in number, in directness, and in what I may call intensity as the confederation grows by the adhesion of new states. In centralized governments, on the contrary, the powers of the supreme authority multiply, extend, and become more direct, bringing the business of provinces, towns, corporations, and individuals under the jurisdiction of the prince, as a direct function of territorial scale and the size of the population. Hence arises that suppression of all liberties, communal and provincial, and even individual and national.

On the Political Capacity of the Working Classes (1865)

What, then, is mutualism's intention and what are the consequences of that doctrine in terms of Government? It is to found an order of things wherein the principle of the sovereignty of the people, of man and of the citizen, would be implemented to the letter: where every member of the State, retaining his independence and continuing to act as sovereign, would be self-governing, while a higher authority would concern itself solely with collective matters; where, as a consequence, there would be certain common matters but no centralization: and, to take things to their conclusion, a State the acknowledged sovereign parts of which would be free to quit the group and withdraw from the compact, *at will*. For there is no disguising it: if it is to be logical and true to its principle, the federation has to take things to these extremes. Otherwise it is merely an illusion, empty boasting, a lie…

What must be done in order to render confederation indestructible is at last to furnish it with the sanction for which it is still waiting, by proclaiming economic Right as the basis of the right of federation and all political order…

Thus, under the democratic constitution…the political and the economic are one and the same order, one and the same system, based upon a single principle, mutuality. As we have seen, through a series of mutualist transactions, the great economic institutions free themselves one after another, and form this vast humanitarian organism of which nothing previously could give the idea; similarly, the resulting governmental apparatus is based in its turn, no longer on some unfathomable fictional convention, imagined as being for the good of the republic and withdrawn as soon as it is posited, but on a genuine contract wherein the sovereignty of the contracting parties, instead of being swallowed up by some central majesty…serves as a positive guarantee of the liberty of States, communes and individuals. So, no longer do we have the abstraction of people's sovereignty…but an effective sovereignty of the labouring masses which rule and govern initially in the benevolent associations, chambers of commerce, craft and trades bodies, and workers' companies; in the stock exchanges, the markets, the academies, the schools, agricultural fairs and finally in election meetings, parliamentary assemblies and councils of State, in the national guards, and even the churches and temples. It is still universally the same collective strength that is brought forth in the name of and by virtue of the principle of mutuality: the final affirmation of the rights of Man and the Citizen.

I declare here and now that the labouring masses are actually, positively and effectively sovereign: how could they not be when the economic organism—labour, capital, property and assets—belongs to them entirely; as utter masters of the organic functions, how could they not be all the more emphatically masters of the functions of relation? Subordination to the productive might of what was hitherto, to the exclusion of anything else, the Government, the Powers-that-be, the State, is blown apart by the way in which the political organism is constituted:

a. An ELECTORAL BODY, spontaneously coming together, laying down policy on operations and reviewing and sanctioning its own acts;

b. A delegated LEGISLATIVE body or Council of State, appointed by the federal groups and subject to re-election;

c. An executive commission selected by the people's representatives from among their own number, and subject to recall;

d. Finally, a chairman for that commission, appointed by it and subject to recall.

Tell me, is this not the system of the old society turned upside down; a system in which the country is decidedly all; where what once was described as the head of State, the sovereign, autocrat, monarch, despot, king, emperor, czar, khan, sultan, majesty, highness, etc., etc., definitively appears as a *gentleman*, the first among his fellow-citizens, perhaps, in terms of honorific distinction, but assuredly the least dangerous of all public officials? You may brag this time that the issue of political guarantee, the issue of making the government subservient to the country, and the prince to the sovereign, is resolved. Never again will you see usurpation or *coup d'etat*; power rising against the people, the coalition of authority and the bourgeoisie against the plebs, becomes impossible.

...[U]nder federative law, how can the State retain its stability? How might a system that enshrines as its underlying thought the right of secession, enjoyed by every federated component, then act coherently and maintain itself?

To be honest, that question went unanswered as long as confederated States had no basis in economic rights and the law of mutuality: divergent interests sooner or later were fated to lead to disastrous splits and imperial unity to replace republican error. Now everything is different: the economic order is founded upon entirely different factors: the *ethos* of the States is no longer what it was; in terms of the truth of its principle, the confederation is indissoluble. Democracy, once so hostile to all thoughts of schism, especially in France, has nothing to fear.

None of the sources of division between men, cities, corporations and individuals obtains among mutualist groups: not sovereign power, not political coalition, not dynastic rights, nor civil lists, honours, pensions, capitalist exploitation, dogmatism, sectarian mentality, party rivalry, racial prejudice or rivalry between corporations, towns or provinces. There may be differences of opinion, belief, interests, mores, industries, cultures, etc. But these differences are the very basis and the object of mutualism: so they cannot, ever, degenerate into Church intolerance, papal supremacy, overbearing locality or city, industrial or agricultural preponderance. Conflicts are impossible: one would have to destroy the mutuality before they could resurface.

From where would the rebellion come? On what pretext would discontent rely? In a mutualist confederation, the citizen gives up none of his freedom, as Rousseau requires him to do for the governance of his republic! Public authority lies in the hands of the citizen: he himself yields and profits from it: if he has a grievance, it is that neither he nor anyone else can any longer usurp it and stake a claim to the exclusive enjoyment of it. There are no more hostages to fortune to be given: the State asks nothing of him by way of taxation beyond what is strictly required for the public services which, being essentially reproductive, when fairly distributed, makes a *trade* out of an imposition. Now, trade amounts to an increase in wealth: so, from that angle too, there need be no fear of disintegration. Might the confederates scatter in the face of a civil or foreign war? But in a confederation founded upon economic Right and the law of mutuality, there could be only one source of civil warfare—religion. Now, setting to one side the fact that the spiritual counts for very little once other interests are reconciled and mutually assured, who can fail to see that the corollary of mutuality is mutual tolerance: which rules out the likelihood of such conflict? As for foreign aggression, from where might that spring? The confederation, which acknowledges that every one of its confederated States enjoys a right of secession, is scarcely likely to want to bully the foreigner. The idea of conquest is incompatible with its very principle. So there can be only one foreseeable possibility of war emanating from without, namely, the possibility of a war of principle: should the surrounding States, greatly exploitative and greatly centralized, determine that the existence of a mutualist confederation cannot be reconciled with their own principle, just as, in 1792 the Brunswick manifesto declared that the French Revolution was incompatible with the principles governing the other States! To which my response is that the outlawing of a confederation rooted in economic right and the law of mutuality would be the very thing that...would incite federative, mutualist republican sentiment to settle its accounts once and for all with the world of monopoly and bring about the victory of Worker Democracy right around the world.

19. Statutes of the First International (1864-1866)

In his On the Political Capacity of the Working Classes, *Proudhon had advocated that the workers should create their own mutualist institutions outside of and in opposition to the existing political system. In 1864, workers from various countries, including some of Proudhon's supporters from France, created the International Association of Workingmen, later known as the First International. The First International began as a loosely knit federation of workers' organizations, based on the following statutes, which tried to take into account the often diverging views of its members regarding such issues as political versus economic action, and the relationship between trade unions, national political parties and the state. The following translation by Paul Sharkey is taken from the French versions of the statutes, which differed from the English versions on at least one crucial point, namely whether all political activity was to be subordinate to economic emancipation, or whether political activity was to be subordinate to economic emancipation only as a means. The anti-authoritarian federalist faction insisted on the former interpretation, while Marx and his supporters insisted on the latter, ultimately leading to the split between the two factions following the Hague Congress in 1872, and the creation of an explicitly anti-authoritarian International.*

1864 Paris Text, Adopted By The 1866 Geneva Congress

CONSIDERING: THAT THE EMANCIPATION of the workers must be the workers' own doing: that the workers' efforts to achieve their emancipation should not be geared towards the establishment of fresh privileges, but rather to establishing the same rights and the same duties for all;

That the worker's subjugation to capital is the root of all slavery; political, moral and material;

That, on that basis, the workers' economic emancipation is the great goal to which all political activity should be subordinated;

That all of the efforts made thus far have failed for want of solidarity between the workers of the various trades within each country, and of a fraternal union between the workers of various countries;

That the workers' emancipation is not simply a local or national issue, but rather that this issue is of concern to all civilized nations, its resolution being, of necessity, dependent upon their theoretical and practical collaboration;

That the mobilization under way among the workers of the most industrialized countries in Europe, by raising new expectations, has issued a solemn warning against lapsing back into old errors and recommends that all as of yet isolated efforts should be combined;

On these grounds:

The under-signed members of the Council elected by the gathering held in St Martin's Hall, London, on 28 September 1864...declare that this International Association, as well as all its affiliated societies or individuals will acknowledge that their conduct towards all men should be founded upon Truth, Justice and Morality, without regard to colour, creed or nationality.

They hold it a duty to claim the rights of man and of the citizen not just for themselves but indeed for any who live up to their obligations. No duties without rights, no rights without duties.

Statutes

Art. 1.—An association is hereby established to serve as a central clearing-house for communications and co-operation between the workers of various lands aspiring to the same end, namely: mutual assistance, progress and the complete emancipation of the labouring class...

Art. 3.—A general Congress is to be held in Belgium in 1865.

It will be incumbent upon this Congress to make Europe aware of the workers' shared aspirations: to lay down the definitive regulations of the International Association; to look into the best means of ensuring the success of its efforts and to elect the General Council of the Association...

Art. 6.—The General Council is to establish relations with the various workers' associations so that workers in each country may be continually informed regarding the movements of their class in other countries; that an investigation may be mounted simultaneously and in the same spirit into social conditions; that the issues raised by one society which may be of general interest can be examined by all; and that whenever a practical suggestion or international difficulty might require action by the Association, the latter may act in a uniform fashion. Whensoever it may deem it necessary, the General Council will take the initiative in drafting suggestions to be put to local or national societies.

Art. 7.—Since the success of the workers' movement in each country can only be ensured through the strength that springs from union and association; and, on the other hand, the usefulness of the General Council is dependent upon its relations with workers' societies both national and local, members of the International Association will have to make every effort, each of them in his home country, to marshal the various existing workers' associations into one national association...

Art. 9.—Each member of the International Association, should he move from one country to another, shall receive fraternal support from Association members.

Article 10.—Although united by fraternal ties of solidarity and cooperation, the workers' societies will nevertheless continue to exist in their own particular right.

20. Bakunin: Socialism and the State (1867)

Bakunin took an active part in the 1848 revolutions in Europe, first in France, then in Germany and Austria. In the fall of 1848 he issued his "Appeal to the Slavs," in which he advocated a general uprising against the Austrian, Prussian and Russian empires. He was one of the leaders of the unsuccessful Dresden rebellion in May 1849. Arrested and sentenced to death, he was eventually extradited to Russia, where he was kept in various Czarist dungeons and came close to death. In 1857 he was exiled to Siberia, from where he made a spectacular escape, via Japan and North America, arriving back in Europe in December 1861. By the mid-1860's, Bakunin had begun to clarify his own political ideas, ultimately adopting an anarchist stance, and helping to found the international anarchist movement. As Kropotkin noted in Modern Science and Anarchism *(reprinted in* Evolution and Environment, *Montreal: Black Rose Books, 1995, ed. G. Woodcock), "Bakunin established in a series of powerful pamphlets and letters the leading principles of modern Anarchism" (page 76). The following selections are taken from his 1867 essay,* Federalism, Socialism and Anti-Theologism, *based on a speech Bakunin delivered to the Geneva Congress of the League for Peace and Freedom, reprinted from Sam Dolgoff's* Bakunin on Anarchism.

SINCE THE REVOLUTION HAS confronted the masses with its own gospel, a revelation not mystical but rational, not of heaven but of earth, not divine but human—the gospel of the Rights of Man; since it has proclaimed that all men are equal and equally entitled to liberty and to a humane life—ever since then, the masses of people in all Europe, in the entire civilized world, slowly awakening from the slumber in which Christianity's incantations had held them enthralled, are beginning to wonder whether they, too, are not entitled to equality, to liberty, and to their humanity.

From the moment this question was asked, the people everywhere, led by their admirable good sense as well as by their instinct, have realized that the first condition for their real emancipation or, if I may be permitted to use the term, their *humanization*, was, above all, a radical reform of their economic condition. The question of daily bread is for them the principal question, and rightly so, for, as Aristotle has said: "Man, in order to think, to feel freely, to become a man, must be free from worry about his material sustenance." Furthermore, the bourgeois who so loudly protest against the materialism of the common people, and who continually preach to them of abstinence and idealism, know this very well; they preach by word and not by example.

The second question for the people is that of leisure after labour, a condition *sine qua non* for humanity. But bread and leisure can never be made secure for the masses except through a radical transformation of society as presently constituted. That is why the Revolution, impelled by its own logical insistency, has given birth to *socialism*...

Socialism, we have said, was the latest offspring of the Great Revolution; but before producing it, the revolution had already brought forth a more direct heir, its eldest, the beloved child of Robespierre and the followers of Saint-Just—*pure republicanism*, without any admixture of socialist ideas, resuscitated from antiquity and inspired by the heroic traditions of the great citizens of Greece and Rome. As it was far less humanitarian than socialism, it hardly knew man, and recognized the citizen only. And while socialism seeks to found a *republic of men*, all that republicanism wants is a *republic of citizens*, even though the citizens...by virtue of being *active citizens*, to borrow an expression from the Constituent Assembly, were to base their civic privilege upon the exploitation of the labour of *passive citizens*. Besides, the political republican is not at all egotistic in his own behalf, or at least is not supposed to be so; he must be an egotist on behalf of his fatherland which he must value above himself, above all other individuals, all nations, all humanity. Consequently, he will always ignore international justice; in all debates, whether his country be right or wrong, he will always give it first place. He will want it always to dominate and to crush all the foreign nations by its power and glory. Through natural inclination he will become fond of conquest, in spite of the fact that the experience of centuries may have proved to him that military triumphs must inevitably lead to Caesarism.

The socialist republican detests the grandeur, the power, and the military glory of the State. He sets liberty and the general welfare above them. A federalist in the internal affairs of the country, he desires an international confederation, first of all in the spirit of justice, and second because he is convinced that the economic and social revolution, transcending all the artificial and pernicious barriers between states, can only be brought about, in part at least, by the solidarity in action, if not of all, then at least of the majority of the nations constituting the civilized world today, so that sooner or later all the nations must join together.

The strictly political republican is a stoic; he recognizes no rights for himself but only duties; or, as in Mazzini's republic, he claims one right only for himself, that of eternal devotion to his country, of living only to serve it, and of joyfully sacrificing himself and even dying for it...

The socialist, on the contrary, insists upon his positive rights to life and to all of its intellectual, moral, and physical joys. He loves life, and he wants to enjoy it in all its abundance. Since his convictions are part of himself, and his duties to society are indissolubly linked with his rights, he will, in order to remain faithful to both, manage to live in accordance with justice like Proudhon and, if necessary, die like Babeuf. But he will never say that the life of humanity should be a sacrifice or that death is the sweetest fate.

Liberty, to the political republican, is an empty word; it is the liberty of a willing slave, a devoted victim of the State. Being always ready to sacrifice his own liberty, he will willingly sacrifice the liberty of others. Political republicanism, therefore, necessarily leads to despotism. For the socialist republican, liberty linked with the general welfare, producing a humanity of all through the humanity of each, is everything, while the State, in his eyes, is a mere instrument, a servant of his well-being and of everyone's liberty. The socialist is distinguished from the bourgeois by *justice*, since he demands for himself nothing but the real fruit of his own labour. He is distinguished from the strict republican by his *frank and human egotism*; he lives for himself, openly and without fine-sounding phrases. He knows that in so living his life, *in accordance with justice*, he serves the entire society, and, in so serving it, he also finds his own welfare. The republican is rigid; often, in consequence of his patriotism, he is cruel, as the priest is often made cruel by his religion. The socialist is natural; he is moderately patriotic, but nevertheless always very human. In a word, between the political republican and the socialist republican there is an abyss; the one, as a *quasi-religious phenomenon*, belongs to the past; the other, whether *positivist* or *atheist*, belongs to the future.

We hasten to add that we energetically reject any attempt at a social organization devoid of the most complete liberty for individuals as well as associations, and one that would call for the establishment of a ruling authority of any nature whatsoever, and that, in the name of this liberty—which we recognize as the only basis for, and the only legitimate creator of, any organization, economic or political—we shall always protest against anything that may in any way resemble communism or state socialism...

We shall now examine what the State...should be in relation to other states, its peers, as well as in relation to its own subject populations. This examination appears to us all the more interesting and useful because the State, as it is here defined, is precisely the modern State insofar as it has separated itself from the religious idea—the *secular* or *atheist State* proclaimed by modern publicists. Let us see, then: of what does its morality consist?...The interest of the State, and nothing else. From this point of view, which, incidentally, with very few exceptions, has been that of the statesmen, the *strong men* of all times and of all countries—from this point of view, I say, whatever conduces to the preservation, the grandeur and the power of the State, no matter how sacrilegious or morally revolting it may seem, *that is the good*. And conversely, whatever opposes the State's interests, no matter how holy or just otherwise, *that is evil*. Such is the secular morality and practice of every State.

It is the same with the State founded upon the theory of the social contract. According to this principle, the good and the just commence only with the contract; they are, in fact, nothing but the very contents and the purpose of the contract; that is, *the common interest* and *the public right* of all the individuals who have formed the contract among themselves, *with the exclusion of all those who remain outside the contract*. It is, consequently, *nothing but the greatest satisfaction given to the collective egotism of a special and restricted association*, which, being founded upon the partial sacrifice of the individual egotism of each of its members, rejects from its midst, as strangers and natural enemies, the immense majority of the human species, whether or not it may be organized into analogous associations.

The existence of one sovereign, exclusionary State necessarily supposes the existence and, if need be, provokes the formation of other such States, since it is quite natural that individuals who find themselves outside it and are threatened by it in their existence and in their liberty, should, in their turn, associate themselves against it. We thus have humanity divided into an indefinite number of foreign states, all hostile and threatened by each other. There is no common right, no social contract of any kind between them; otherwise they would cease to be independent states and become the federated members of one great state. But unless this great state were to embrace all of humanity, it would be confronted with other great states, each federated within, each maintaining the same posture of inevitable hostility.

War would still remain the supreme law, an unavoidable condition of human survival. Every state, federated or not, would therefore seek to become the most powerful. It must devour lest it be devoured, conquer lest it be conquered, enslave lest it be enslaved, since two powers, similar and yet alien to each other, could not coexist without mutual destruction.

The State, therefore, is the most flagrant, the most cynical, and the most complete negation of humanity. It shatters the universal solidarity of all men on the earth, and brings some of them into association only for the purpose of destroying, conquering, and enslaving all the rest. It protects its own citizens only; it recognizes human rights, humanity, civilization within its own confines alone. Since it recognizes no rights outside itself, it logically arrogates to itself the right to exercise the most ferocious inhumanity toward all foreign populations, which it can plunder, exterminate, or enslave at will. If it does show itself generous and humane toward them, it is never through a sense of duty, for it has no duties except to itself in the first place, and then to those of its members who have freely formed it, who freely continue to constitute it or even, as always happens in the long run, those who have become its subjects. As there is no international law in existence, *and as it could never exist in a meaningful and realistic way without undermining to its foundations the very principle of the absolute sovereignty of the State*, the State can have no duties toward foreign populations. Hence, if it treats a conquered people in a humane fashion, if it plunders or exterminates it halfway only, if it does not reduce it to the lowest degree of slavery, this may be a political act inspired by prudence, or even by pure magnanimity, but it is never done from a sense of duty, for the State has an absolute right to dispose of a conquered people at will.

This flagrant negation of humanity which constitutes the very essence of the State is, from the standpoint of the State, its supreme duty and its greatest virtue. It bears the name *patriotism*, and it constitutes the entire *transcendent morality* of the State. We call it transcendent morality because it usually goes beyond the level of human morality and justice, either of the community or of the private individual, and by that same token often finds itself in contradiction with these. Thus, to offend, to oppress, to despoil, to plunder, to assassinate or enslave one's fellowman is ordinarily regarded as a crime. In public life, on the other hand, from the standpoint of patriotism, when these things are done for the greater glory of the State, for the preservation or the extension of its power, it is all transformed into duty and virtue. And this virtue, this duty, are obligatory for each patriotic citizen; everyone is supposed to exercise them not against foreigners only but against one's own fellow citizens, members or subjects of the State like himself, whenever the welfare of the State demands it.

This explains why, since the birth of the State, the world of politics has always been and continues to be the stage for unlimited rascality and brigandage, brigandage and rascality which, by the way, are held in high esteem, since they are sanctified by patriotism, by the transcendent morality and the supreme interest of the State. This explains why the entire history of ancient and modern states is merely a series of revolting crimes; why kings and ministers, past and present, of all times and all countries—statesmen, diplomats, bureaucrats, and warriors—if judged from the standpoint of simple morality and human justice, have a hundred, a thousand times over earned their sentence to hard labour or to the gallows. There is no horror, no cruelty, sacrilege, or perjury, no imposture, no infamous transaction, no cynical robbery, no bold plunder or shabby betrayal that has not been or is not daily being perpetrated by the representatives of the states, under no other pretext than those elastic words, so convenient and yet so terrible: "*for reasons of state*."

21. Bakunin: Program of the International Brotherhood (1868)

In this passage, Bakunin emphasizes the counter-revolutionary nature of terrorism and dictatorship. Auguste Blanqui (1805-1881) was a French revolutionary who tried to institute a revolutionary dictatorship on several occasions. He spent much of his adult life imprisoned for his revolutionary activities. Towards the end of his life, well after this was written, Blanqui finally proclaimed "Neither God, nor master!" which was to become the battle cry of the anarchist movement. The translation is taken from Bakunin on Anarchism.

EVERY HUMAN INDIVIDUAL IS the involuntary product of a natural and social environment within which he is born, and to the influence of which he continues to submit as he develops. The three great causes of all human immorality are: political, economic, and social inequality; the ignorance resulting naturally from all this; and the necessary consequence of these, slavery.

Since the social organization is always and everywhere the only cause of crimes committed by men, the punishing by society of criminals who can never be guilty is an act of hypocrisy or a patent absurdity. The theory of guilt and punishment is the offspring of theology, that is, of the union of absurdity and religious hypocrisy...All the revolutionaries, the oppressed, the sufferers, victims of the existing social organization, whose hearts are naturally filled with hatred and a desire for vengeance, should bear in mind that the kings, the oppressors, exploiters of all kinds, are as guilty as the criminals who have emerged from the masses; like them, they are evildoers who are not guilty, since they, too, are involuntary products of the present social order. It will not be surprising if the rebellious people kill a great many of them at first. This will be a misfortune, as unavoidable as the ravages caused by a sudden tempest, and as quickly over; but this natural act will be neither moral nor even useful.

History has much to teach us on this subject. The dreadful guillotine of 1793, which cannot be reproached with having been idle or slow, nevertheless did not succeed in destroying the French aristocracy. The nobility was indeed shaken to its roots, though not completely destroyed, but this was not the work of the guillotine; it was achieved by the confiscation of its properties. In general, we can say that carnage was never an effective means to exterminate political parties; it was proved particularly ineffective against the privileged classes, since power resides less in men themselves than in the circumstances created for men of privilege by the organization of material goods, that is, the institution of the State and its natural basis, *individual property*.

Therefore, to make a successful revolution, it is necessary to attack conditions and material goods, to destroy property and the State. It will then become unnecessary to destroy men and be condemned to suffer the sure and inevitable reaction which no massacre has ever failed and ever will fail to produce in every society.

It is not surprising that the Jacobins and the Blanquists—who became socialists by necessity rather than by conviction, who view socialism as a means and not as the goal of the revolution, since they desire dictatorship and the centralization of the State, hoping that the State will lead them necessarily to the reinstatement of property—dream of a bloody revolution against men, inasmuch as they do not desire the revolution against property. But such a bloody revolution, based on the construction of a powerfully centralized revolutionary State, would inevitably result in military dictatorship and a new master. Hence the triumph of the Jacobins or the Blanquists would be the death of the revolution.

We are the natural enemies of such revolutionaries—the would-be dictators, regulators, and trustees of the revolution—who even before the existing monarchical, aristocratic, and bourgeois states have been destroyed, already dream of creating new revolutionary states, as fully centralized and even more despotic than the states we now have. These men are so accustomed to the order created by an authority, and feel so great a horror of what seems to them to be disorder but is simply the frank and natural expression of the life of the people, that even before a good, salutary disorder has been produced by the revolution they dream of muzzling it by the act of some authority that will be revolutionary in name only, and will only be a new reaction in that it will again condemn the masses to being governed by decrees, to obedience, to immobility, to death; in other words, to slavery and exploitation by a new pseudo-revolutionary aristocracy…

We do not fear anarchy, we invoke it. For we are convinced that anarchy, meaning the unrestricted manifestation of the liberated life of the people, must spring from liberty, equality, the new social order, and the force of the revolution itself against the reaction. There is no doubt that this new life—the popular revolution—will in good time organize itself, but it will create its revolutionary organization from the bottom up, from the circumference to the center, in accordance with the principle of liberty, and not from the top down or from the center to the circumference in the manner of all authority. It matters little to us if that authority is called Church, Monarchy, constitutional State, bourgeois Republic, or even revolutionary Dictatorship. We detest and reject all of them equally as the unfailing sources of exploitation and despotism.

22. Bakunin: What is the State (1869)

By 1868 Bakunin had joined the First International. He helped organize sections of the International in Italy and Spain and took an active role at the 1869 Basle Congress. The following passage is taken from a series of letters to his Swiss comrades in the International, originally published in 1869. The translation is reprinted with the kind permission of Robert M. Cutler from his collection of Bakunin's writings, The Basic Bakunin: Writings 1869-1871 *(New York: Prometheus, 1992).*

LET US ANALYZE FIRST THE VERY IDEA of the State, as it is portrayed by its enthusiasts. It is the sacrifice of the natural freedom and interests not only of each individual but also of every relatively small collectivity—associations, communes, and provinces—to the interests and the freedom of everyone, to the well-being of the great whole. But what, in reality, is this everyone, this great whole? It is the agglomeration of all these individuals and of all those more limited human collectivities which they compose. But what does that whole, which is supposed to represent them, actually represent as soon as all individual and local interests are sacrificed in order to create it and coordinate themselves into it? Not the living whole wherein each person can breathe freely, becoming more productive, stronger, and freer as the full freedom and well-being of individuals develops in its midst; nor natural human society, in which every individual's life is reinforced and broadened through the life of every other: on the contrary, it is the ritual sacrifice of each individual and of every local association, an abstraction which destroys living society. It is the limitation, or rather the complete negation, of the so-called good of everyone, of the life and the rights of every individual who is party to this "everyone." It is the State, the altar of political religion on which natural society has always been immolated: a universality which subsists on and devours human sacrifices, just like the Church...

The State...is the altar on which the real freedom and welfare of peoples are immolated for the sake of political grandeur; and the more complete this immolation, the more perfect the State...

As I have said, the State is an abstraction which consumes the life of the people. But for an abstraction to be born, develop, and continue to exist in the real world, there must be a real collective body interested in its existence. This collective cannot be the great masses of the people, for they are precisely its victims: it must be a privileged body, the sacerdotal body of the State, the governing and property-owning class, which is to the State what the sacerdotal class of religion, the priests, is to the Church.

And indeed, what do we see throughout all history? The State has always been the patrimony of some privileged class: the priesthood, the nobility, the bourgeoisie, and finally, after every other class has been exhausted, the bureaucratic class, when the State falls or rises—whichever you wish—into the condition of a machine.

23. Bakunin: The Illusion of Universal Suffrage (1870)

In the 19th century, many on the left saw universal suffrage as the key to social change. As the workers outnumbered the capitalists, whose numbers were supposed to be shrinking, once they received the right to vote it was naturally expected that they would soon elect working class parties that would legislate socialism into existence. Bakunin wrote the following piece in 1870 to disabuse everyone of this misconception. The translation is by George Woodcock and is reprinted from his collection, The Anarchist Reader *(London: Fontana, 1977), with the kind permission of the Writers' Trust of Canada on behalf of the Woodcock estate.*

THE WHOLE DECEPTION OF THE representative system lies in the fiction that a government and a legislature emerging out of a popular election must or even can represent the real will of the people. Instinctively and inevitably the people expect two things: the greatest possible material prosperity combined with the greatest freedom of movement and action: that means the best organization of popular economic interests, and the complete absence of any kind of power or political organization—since all political organization is destined to end in the negation of freedom. Such are the basic longings of the people.

The instincts of the rulers, whether they legislate or execute the laws, are—by the very fact of their exceptional position—diametrically opposite. However democratic may be their feelings and their intentions, once they achieve the elevation of office they can only view society in the same way as a schoolmaster views his pupils, and between pupils and masters equality cannot exist. On one side there is the feeling of superiority that is inevitably provoked by a position of superiority; on the other side, there is the sense of inferiority which follows from the superiority of the teacher, whether he is exercising an executive or a legislative power. Whoever talks of political power talks of domination; but where domination exists there is inevitably a somewhat large section of society that is dominated, and those who are dominated quite naturally detest their dominators, while the dominators have no choice but to subdue and oppress those they dominate.

That is the eternal history of political power, ever since that power has appeared in the world. That is what also explains why and how the most extreme of democrats, the most raging rebels, become the most cautious of conservatives as soon as they attain to power. Such recantations are usually regarded as acts of treason, but that is an error; their main cause is simply the change of position and hence of perspective...

In Switzerland...as everywhere, no matter how egalitarian our political constitution may be, it is the bourgeoisie who rule, and it is the people—workers and peasants—who obey their laws. The people have neither the leisure nor the necessary education to occupy themselves with government. Since the bourgeoisie have both, they have, in fact if not by right, exclusive privilege...

But how, separated as they are from the people by all the economic and social circumstances of their existence, can the bourgeoisie express, in laws and in government, the feelings, ideas, and wishes of the people? It is impossible, and daily experience in fact proves that, in legislation as well as government, the bourgeoisie is mainly directed by its own interests and prejudices, without any great concern for those of the people.

It is true that all our legislators...are elected, directly or indirectly, by the people. It is true that on election day even the proudest of the bourgeoisie, if they have any political ambitions, are obliged to pay court to Her Majesty, The Sovereign People...But once the elections are over, the people return to their work and the bourgeoisie to their profitable businesses and political intrigues. They neither meet nor recognize each other again. And how can one expect the people, burdened by their work and ignorant for the most part of current problems, to supervise the political actions of their representatives? In reality, the control exercised by voters on their elected representatives is a pure fiction. But since, in the representative system, popular control is the only guarantee of the people's freedom, it is quite evident that such freedom in its turn is no more than a fiction.

24. Bakunin: On Science and Authority (1871)

The following excerpts are from Bakunin's essay, God and the State, *one of his most widely published and translated writings. Written in 1871, it was posthumously published by Bakunin's comrades, Carlo Cafiero and Élisée Reclus, in 1882. The text has been taken from the 1916 English edition published by Emma Goldman's Mother Earth press.*

SUPPOSE A LEARNED ACADEMY, composed of the most illustrious representatives of science; suppose this academy charged with legislation for and the organization of society, and that, inspired only by the purest love of truth, it frames none but laws in absolute harmony with the latest discoveries of science. Well, I maintain, for my part, that such legislation and such organization would be a monstrosity, and that for two reasons: first, that human science is always and necessarily imperfect, and that, comparing what it has discovered with what remains to be discovered, we may say that it is still in its cradle. So that were we to try to force the practical life of men, collective as well as individual, into strict and exclusive conformity with the latest data of science, we should condemn society as well as individuals to suffer martyrdom on a bed of Procrustes, which would soon end by dislocating and stifling them, life ever remaining an infinitely greater thing than science.

The second reason is this: a society which should obey legislation emanating from a scientific academy, not because it understood itself the rational character of this legislation (in which case the existence of the academy would become useless), but because this legislation, emanating from the academy, was imposed in the name of a science which it venerated without comprehending—such a society would be a society, not of men, but of brutes...

But there is still a third reason which would render such a government impossible—namely that a scientific academy invested with a sovereignty, so to speak, absolute, even if it were composed of the most illustrious men, would infallibly and soon end in its own moral and intellectual corruption...

It is the characteristic of privilege and of every privileged position to kill the mind and heart of men. The privileged man, whether politically or economically, is a man depraved in mind and heart...

A scientific body to which had been confided the government of society would soon end by devoting itself no longer to science at all, but to quite another affair; and that affair, as in the case of all established powers, would be its own eternal perpetuation by rendering the society confided to its care ever more stupid and consequently more in need of its government and direction.

But that which is true of scientific academies is also true of all constituent and legislative assemblies, even those chosen by universal suffrage. In the latter case they may renew their composition, it is true, but this does not prevent the formation in a few years' time of a body of politicians, privileged in fact though not in law, who, devoting themselves exclusively to the direction of the public affairs of a country, finally form a sort of political aristocracy or oligarchy. Witness the United States of America and Switzerland.

Consequently, no external legislation and no authority—one, for that matter, being inseparable from the other, and both tending to the servitude of society and the degradation of the legislators themselves.

Does it follow that I reject all authority? Far from me such a thought. In the matter of boots, I refer to the authority of the bootmaker; concerning houses, canals, or railroads, I consult that of the architect or engineer. For such or such special knowledge I apply to such or such a *savant*. But I allow neither the bootmaker nor the architect nor the *savant* to impose his authority upon me. I listen to them freely and with all the respect merited by their intelligence, their character, their knowledge, reserving always my incontestable right of criticism and censure. I do not content myself with consulting authority in any special branch; I consult several; I compare their opinions, and choose that which seems to me the soundest. But I recognize no infallible authority, even in special questions; consequently, whatever respect I may have for the honesty and the sincerity of such or such an individual, I have no absolute faith in any person. Such a faith would be fatal to my reason, to my liberty, and even to the success of my undertakings; it would immediately transform me into a stupid slave, an instrument of the will and interests of others…

The mission of science is, by observation of the general relations of passing and real facts, to establish the general laws inherent in the development of the phenomena of the physical and social world; it fixes, so to speak, the unchangeable landmarks of humanity's progressive march by indicating the general conditions which it is necessary to rigorously observe and always fatal to ignore or forget. In a word, science is the compass of life; but it is not life itself. Science is unchangeable, impersonal, general, abstract, insensible, like the laws of which it is but the ideal reproduction...Life is wholly fugitive and temporary, but also wholly palpitating with reality and individuality, sensibility, sufferings, joys, aspirations, needs, and passions. It alone spontaneously creates real things and beings. Science creates nothing; it establishes and recognizes only the creations of life...

Science cannot go outside of the sphere of abstractions. In this respect it is infinitely inferior to art, which, in its turn, is peculiarly concerned also with general types and general situations, but which incarnates them by an artifice of its own in forms which, if they are not living in the sense of real life none the less excite in our imagination the memory and sentiment of life; art in a certain sense individualizes the types and situations which it conceives; by means of the individualities without flesh and bone, and consequently permanent and immortal, which it has the power to create, it recalls to our minds the living, real individualities which appear and disappear under our eyes. Art, then, is as it were the return of abstraction to life; science, on the contrary, is the perpetual immolation of life, fugitive, temporary, but real, on the altar of eternal abstractions.

Science is as incapable of grasping the individuality of a man as that of a rabbit, being equally indifferent to both. Not that it is ignorant of the principle of individuality: it conceives it perfectly as a principle, but not as a fact. It knows very well that all the animal species, including the human species, have no real existence outside of an indefinite number of individuals, born and dying to make room for new individuals equally fugitive. It knows that in rising from the animal species to the superior species the principle of individuality becomes more pronounced; the individuals appear freer and more complete. It knows that man, the last and most perfect animal of earth, presents the most complete and most remarkable individuality, because of his power to conceive, concrete, personify, as it were, in his social and private existence, the universal law. It knows, finally, when it is not vitiated by theological or metaphysical, political or judicial *doctrinairisme*, or even by a narrow scientific pride, when it is not deaf to the instincts and spontaneous aspirations of life—it knows (and this is its last word) that respect for man is the supreme law of Humanity, and that the great, the real object of history, its only legitimate object is the humanization and emancipation, the real liberty, the prosperity and happiness of each individual living in society...

Science knows all these things, but it does not and cannot go beyond them. Abstraction being its very nature, it can well enough conceive the principle of real and living individuality, but it can have no dealings with real and living individuals; it concerns itself with individuals in general, but not with Peter or James, not with such or such a one, who, so far as it is concerned, does not, cannot, have any existence...Since its own nature forces it to ignore the existence of Peter and James, it must never be permitted, nor must anybody be permitted in its name, to govern Peter and James. For it were capable of treating them almost as it treats rabbits. Or rather, it would continue to ignore them; but its licensed representatives, men not at all abstract, but on the contrary in very active life and having very substantial interests, yielding to the pernicious influence which privilege inevitably exercises upon men, would finally fleece other men in the name of science, just as they have been fleeced hitherto by priests, politicians of all shades, and lawyers, in the name of God, of the State, of judicial Right.

What I preach then is, to a certain extent, *the revolt of life* against science, or rather against the *government* of science, not to destroy science—that would be high treason to humanity—but to remand it to its place so that it can never leave it again...

On the one hand, science is indispensable to the rational organization of society; on the other, being incapable of interesting itself in that which is real and living, it must not interfere with the real or practical organization of society.

This contradiction can be solved only in one way: by the liquidation of science as a moral being existing outside the life of all, and represented by a body of breveted *savants*; it must spread among the masses. Science, being called upon to henceforth represent society's collective consciousness, must really become the property of everybody. Thereby, without losing anything of its universal character, of which it can never divest itself without ceasing to be science, and while continuing to concern itself exclusively with general causes, the conditions and fixed relations of individuals and things, it will become one in fact with the immediate and real life of all individuals...The world of scientific abstractions is not revealed; it is inherent in the real world, of which it is only the general or abstract expression and representation. As long as it forms a separate region, specially represented by the *savants* as a body, this ideal world threatens to take the place of a good God to the real world, reserving for its licensed representatives the office of priests. That is the reason why it is necessary to dissolve the special social organization of the *savants* by general instruction, equal for all in all things, in order that the masses, ceasing to be flocks led and shorn by privileged priests, may take into their own hands the direction of their destinies.

Chapter 6
The Conflict In The First International

25. Bakunin: The Organization of the International (1871)

By 1871, when Bakunin wrote this article, it had become clear that within the International there existed fundamental disagreements over its proper role and structure. Marx and his followers emphasized the importance of creating socialist political parties with a central executive authority as part of their strategy for social change. The anti-authoritarian, federalist and anarchist sections of the International advocated social revolution through the direct action of the trade union sections. In this selection, Bakunin emphasizes that the International, as an international association of workers, must necessarily take an anti-statist position, and that its internal organization must be consistent with its ideals, lest it replicate the authoritarian institutions it is seeking to overthrow. The first part of this translation is taken from Sam Dolgoff's Bakunin on Anarchism; *the concluding portion is taken from Robert M. Cutler's collection,* The Basic Bakunin: Writings 1869-1871 *(New York: Prometheus, 1992), and is reprinted with his kind permission.*

THE ORGANIZATION OF THE INTERNATIONAL, having for its objective not the creation of new despotisms but the uprooting of all domination, will take on an essentially different character from the organization of the State. Just as the State is authoritarian, artificial, violent, foreign, and hostile to the natural development of the popular instincts, so must the organization of the International conform in all respects to these instincts and these interests. But what is the organization of the masses? It is an organization based on the various functions of daily life and of the different kinds of labour. It is the organization by professions and trades. Once all the different industries are represented in the International, including the cultivation of the land, its organization, the organization of the mass of the people, will have been achieved.

The organization of the trade sections and their representation in the Chambers of Labour creates a great academy in which all the workers can and must study economic science; these sections also bear in themselves the living seeds of the new society which is to replace the old world. They are creating not only the ideas, but also the facts of the future itself.

...[T]he essential difference between the organized action of the International and the action of all states, is that the International is not vested with any official authority or political power whatever. It will always be the natural organization of action, of a greater or lesser number of individuals, inspired and united by the general aim of influencing [by example] the opinion, the will, and the action of the masses. Governments, by contrast, impose themselves upon the masses and force them to obey their decrees, without for the most part taking into consideration their feelings, their needs, and their will. There exists between the power of the State and that of the International the same difference that exists between the official power of the State and the natural activity of a club...

The State is the organized authority, domination, and power of the possessing classes over the masses...the International wants only their complete freedom, and calls for their revolt. But in order that this rebellion be powerful and capable enough to overthrow the domination of the State and the privileged classes, the International has to organize itself. To attain its objective, it employs only two means, which, if not always legal, are completely legitimate from the standpoint of human rights. These two means are the dissemination of the ideas of the International and the natural influence of its members over the masses.

Whoever contends that such action, being a move to create a new authoritarian power, threatens the freedom of the masses must be a sophist or a fool. All social life is nothing but the incessant mutual interdependence of individuals and of masses. All individuals, even the strongest and the most intelligent, are at every moment of their lives both the producers and the products of the will and action of the masses.

The freedom of each individual is the ever-renewing result of numerous material, intellectual, and moral influences of the surrounding individuals and of the society into which he is born, and in which he grows up and dies. To wish to escape this influence in the name of a transcendental, divine, absolutely self-sufficient freedom is to condemn oneself to non-existence; to forgo the exercise of this freedom upon others is to renounce all social action and all expression of one's thoughts and sentiments, and to end in nothingness...

And when we demand the freedom of the masses, we do not even dream of obliterating any of the natural influences that any individual or group of individuals exercise upon each other. We want only the abolition of artificial, privileged, legal, and official impositions. If the Church and the State were private institutions, we would, no doubt, be against them, but we would not contest their right to exist. We fight them because they are organized to exploit the collective power of the masses by official and violent superimposition. If the International were to become a State we, its most zealous champions, would become its most implacable enemies.

But the point is precisely that the International cannot organize itself into a State. It cannot do so because the International, as its name implies, means the abolition of all frontiers, and there can be no State without frontiers, without sovereignty...

The International Workingmen's Association would be totally devoid of meaning if it did not aim at the abolition of the State. It organizes the masses only to facilitate the destruction of the State. And how does it organize them? Not from the top down, not by constricting the manifold functions of society which reflect the diversity of labour, not by forcing the natural life of the masses into the straitjacket of the State, not by imposing upon them a fictitious unity. On the contrary, it organizes them from the bottom up, beginning with the social life of the masses and their real aspirations, and inducing them to group, harmonize, and balance their forces in accordance with the natural diversity of their occupations and circumstances...

But, someone will say, even though every worker may become a member of the International, they cannot all have learning. And is it not enough for the International to contain a group of men who possess the knowledge, the philosophy, and the policy of Socialism...in order for the majority, the people of the International, faithfully obeying [the former's] *fraternal command*...to be sure of following the path leading to the full emancipation of the proletariat?

That is the argument which the...authoritarian party within the International has often expressed, not openly—they are neither sincere nor courageous enough—but clandestinely, developed with all kinds of rather clever qualifications and demagogic compliments addressed to the supreme wisdom and omnipotence of the sovereign people. We have always fought this view passionately, for we are convinced that the moment the International...is divided into two groups—one comprising the vast majority and composed of members whose only knowledge will be a blind faith in the theoretical and practical wisdom of their commanders, and the other composed only of a few score individual directors—from that moment this institution which should emancipate humanity would turn into a type of *oligarchic State*, the worst of all States. What is more, this learned, clairvoyant, and cunning minority, carefully hiding its despotism behind the appearance of obsequious respect for the will of the sovereign people and for its resolutions, would yield to the necessities and requirements of its privileged position, thus assuming along with all its responsibilities, all the rights of government, a government all the more absolute because it would urge those resolutions itself upon the so-called will of the people, thereby very soon becoming increasingly despotic, malevolent, and reactionary.

The International...will become an instrument of humanity's emancipation only when it is first itself freed, and that will happen only when it ceases to be divided into two groups, the majority blind tools and the minority skilled manipulators: when each of its members has considered, reflected on, and been penetrated by the knowledge, the philosophy, and the policy of socialism.

26. The Sonvillier Circular (1871)

The anti-authoritarian elements in the First International were particularly prominent in Spain, Italy and the Swiss Jura. In 1871, Marx and his supporters, through the General Council in London, which was supposed to be an administrative, not governing body, held a secret conference, to which most of the anti-authoritarian sections were not invited, at which they gave the General Council the power to expel dissident sections of the International. The Jura Federation responded with the following circular, translated by Paul Sharkey.

IF THERE IS ONE INCONTROVERTIBLE FACT, borne out a thousand times by experience, it is that authority has a corrupting effect on those in whose hands it is placed. It is absolutely impossible for a man with power over his neighbours to remain a moral man.

The General Council was no exception to this inescapable law. Made up for five years running of the same personnel, re-elected time after time, and endowed by the Basle resolutions with very great power over the Sections, it ended up looking upon itself as the legitimate leader of the International. In the hands of a few individuals, the mandate of General Council members has turned into something akin to a personal possession and they have come to see London as our Association's immovable capital. Little by little, these men, who are not our mandatories—and most of them are not even regularly mandated by us, not having been elected by a Congress—these men, we say, accustomed to walking in front of us and speaking on our behalf, have, by the natural flow of things and the very force of this situation, been induced to try to foist their own special program, their own personal doctrine upon the International. Having, in their own eyes, become a sort of government, it was natural that their own particular ideas should have come to appear to them as the official theory enjoying exclusive rights within the Association; whereas divergent ideas issuing from other groups struck them, not as the legitimate manifestation of an opinion every bit as tenable as their own, but rather as out and out heresy. And so, gradually, a London-based orthodoxy has evolved, its representatives the members of the General Council; and soon the Council's correspondents for each country set themselves the task, not of serving as neutral and disinterested intermediaries between the various Federations, but of performing as apostles of the orthodox doctrine, seeking out disciples for it and serving sectional interests to the detriment of the overall interests of the Association.

What was the inevitable outcome of all this? The General Council naturally ran into opposition along the new course upon which it had embarked. Irresistible logic forced it into trying to break that opposition. Hence the wrangles that have begun and, with them, the personal intimacies and factional manoeuvres. The General Council becomes a hot bed of intrigue; opponents are shouted down and vilified: in the end, warfare, open warfare, erupts within the ranks of our Association...

We are not accusing the General Council of criminal intent. The personalities who make it up have found themselves succumbing to fatal necessity; in good faith and to ensure the success of their own particular doctrine, they have sought to introduce the authority principle into the International; circumstances appeared to abet this tendency and it strikes us as quite natural that that school, whose ideal is the conquest of political power by the working class, in the wake of recent developments, should have thought that the International should amend its original organization and become a hierarchical organization directed and governed by a Committee.

But while we can understand such tendencies and such actions we are nonetheless impelled to combat them, on behalf of the Social Revolution, which we pursue, and its program: "Emancipation of the workers by the workers themselves," free of all directing authority, even should that authority be elected and endorsed by the workers.

We ask for the retention within the International of that principle of autonomy of the Sections which has been the basis of our Association thus far; we ask that the General Council, whose powers have been rendered unnatural by the Basle Congress' administrative resolutions, should revert to its natural function, which is the function of a simple correspondence and statistical bureau; and we seek to found the unity some aim to build upon centralization and dictatorship, upon a free federation of autonomous groups.

The society of the future should be nothing other than the universalization of the organization with which the International will have endowed itself. We must, therefore, have a care to ensure that that organization comes as close as we may to our ideal. How can we expect an egalitarian and free society to emerge from an authoritarian organization? Impossible. The International, as the embryo of the human society of the future, is required in the here and now to faithfully mirror our principles of freedom and federation and shun any principle leaning towards authority and dictatorship.

Our conclusion is that a General Congress of the Association must be summoned without delay. Long live the International Working Men's Association! (Sonvillier, 12 November 1871; reprinted in James Guillaume, *L'Internationale: Documents et Souvenirs, 1864-1878,* Paris: Société Nouvelle, 1905)

27. The St. Imier Congress (1872)

A General Congress of the International was held at the Hague in 1872, but instead of dealing with the concerns of the anti-authoritarian, federalist Sections, Marx and his supporters had Bakunin and James Guillaume, one of the most active members of the Jura Federation, expelled from the International on trumped up charges, and then had the seat of the International transferred to New York rather than risk losing control of the organization. The anti-authoritarians responded by holding their own Congress at St. Imier in Switzerland, where they reconstituted the International along anti-authoritarian lines. Ironically, despite Marx and Engel's claims that the anti-authoritarians wanted to replace the organization of the International with anarchy and chaos, or worse, the personal dictatorship of Bakunin, the anti-authoritarian International outlived by several years the one transferred at Marx and Engel's instigation to New York, where it soon expired. Needless to say, Bakunin never assumed personal control of the anti-authoritarian International, from which he withdrew in 1873, and it had no difficulty continuing on without him. The following resolutions from the St. Imier Congress have been translated by Paul Sharkey.

Nature Of The Political Action Of The Proletariat

CONSIDERING: THAT SEEKING TO FOIST a line of conduct or uniform political program upon the proletariat as the only avenue that can lead to its social emancipation is a pretension as nonsensical as it is reactionary;

> That nobody has the right to deprive autonomous federations and sections of their incontrovertible right to decide for themselves and to follow whatever line of political conduct they deem best, and that any such attempt would inevitably lead to the most revolting dogmatism;

> That the aspirations of the proletariat can have no purpose other than the establishment of an absolutely free economic organization and federation, founded upon the labour and equality of all and absolutely independent of all political government, and that this organization and this federation can only be the outcome of the spontaneous action of the proletariat itself, its trades bodies and the autonomous communes;

Considering that all political organization cannot help but be the organization of domination to the benefit of one class and to the detriment of the masses, and that the proletariat, if it wishes to take power, would itself become a ruling, exploiter class; the Congress assembled in Saint-Imier declares:

1. That the destruction of all political power is the first duty of the proletariat.
2. That any organization whatsoever of a self-styled provisional and revolutionary political authority for the purpose of ensuring such destruction can be nothing but another fraud, and would be as dangerous to the proletariat as any government now in existence;
3. That, shunning all compromise in the attainment of the Social Revolution, the proletarians of every land should establish solidarity of revolutionary action outside of all bourgeois politicking.

Organization Of Labour Resistance

Freedom and labour are the basis of the morality, strength, life and wealth of the future. But, unless freely organized, labour becomes oppressive and unproductive as far as the worker is concerned; on which basis the organization of labour is the essential precondition for the authentic, complete emancipation of the worker.

However, labour cannot proceed freely without access to raw materials and the entire capital of society, and cannot be organized unless the worker, struggling free of political and economic tyranny, gains the right to the complete development of all his faculties. Every State, which is to say, every top-down government and every administration of the masses of the populace, being of necessity founded upon bureaucracy, upon armies, upon espionage, upon the clergy, can never bring about a society organized on a basis of labour and justice, since, by the very nature of its organism, it is inevitably impelled to oppress the former and deny the latter.

As we see it, the worker will never be able to free himself of the age-old oppression, unless he replaces that insatiable, demoralizing body with a free federation of all producer groups on a footing of solidarity and equality.

In fact, in several places, an attempt has already been made to organize labour in such a way as to better the conditions of the proletariat, but the slightest improvement has soon been gobbled up by the privileged class which is forever trying, unrestrained and unlimited, to exploit the working class. However, such are the advantages offered by [labour] organization that, even as things presently stand, it could not be foresworn. More and more it integrates the proletariat into a community of interests, trains it in collective living and prepares it for the supreme struggle. Furthermore, since the free and spontaneous organization of labour is what should replace the privilege and authority of the State, it will, once in place, offer a permanent guarantee of the maintenance of the economic organism over the political organism.

Consequently, by leaving the details of positive organization to be worked out by the Social Revolution, we intend to organize and marshal resistance on a broad scale. We regard the strike as a precious weapon in the struggle, but we have no illusions about its economic results. We embrace it as a product of the antagonism between labour and capital, the necessary consequence of which is to make workers more and more alive to the gulf that exists between the bourgeoisie and the proletariat, to bolster the toilers' organization, and, by dint of ordinary economic struggles, to prepare the proletariat for the great and final revolutionary contest which, destroying all privilege and all class difference, will bestow upon the worker a right to the enjoyment of the gross product of his labours and thereby the means of developing his full intellectual, material and moral powers in a collective setting (reprinted in James Guillaume, *L'Internationale: Documents et Souvenirs, 1864-1878,* Paris: Société Nouvelle, 1905).

Chapter 7
The Franco-Prussian War And The Paris Commune

28. Bakunin: Letters to a Frenchman on the Present Crisis (1870)

Bakunin's Letters to a Frenchman on the Present Crisis *was written during the Franco- Prussian war in 1870. In contrast to Marx and Engels, who looked forward to a Prussian victory as a means of securing the triumph of their ideas over Proudhon's, Bakunin openly called for social revolution and participated in an abortive uprising in Lyons, seeking to transform an imperialist conflict into a revolutionary insurrection. This translation is taken from Sam Dolgoff's* Bakunin on Anarchism.

THERE ARE MEN, MANY OF THEM AMONG the so-called revolutionary bourgeoisie, who by mouthing revolutionary slogans think that they are making the Revolution. Feeling that they have thus adequately fulfilled their revolutionary obligations, they now proceed to be careless in action and, in flagrant contradiction to principles, commit what are in effect wholly reactionary acts. We who are truly revolutionary must behave in an altogether different manner. Let us talk less about revolution and do a great deal more. Let others concern themselves with the theoretical development of the principles of the Social Revolution, while we content ourselves with spreading these principles everywhere, incarnating them into facts...All of us must now embark on stormy revolutionary seas, and from this very moment we must spread our principles, not with words but with deeds, for this is the most popular, the most potent, and the most irresistible form of propaganda...

Throughout the world the authoritarian revolutionists have done very little to promote revolutionary activity, primarily because *they always wanted to make the Revolution by themselves, by their own authority and their own power*. This could not fail to severely constrict the scope of revolutionary action because it is impossible, even for the most energetic and enterprising authoritarian revolutionary, to understand and deal effectively with all the manifold problems generated by the Revolution. For every dictatorship, be it exercised by an individual or collectively by relatively few individuals, is necessarily very circumscribed, very shortsighted, and its limited perception cannot, therefore, penetrate the depth and encompass the whole complex range of popular life...

What should the revolutionary authorities—and there should be as few of them as possible—do to organize and spread the Revolution? They must promote the Revolution not by issuing decrees but by stirring the masses to action. They must under no circumstances foist any artificial organization whatsoever upon the masses. On the contrary, they should foster the self-organization of the masses into autonomous bodies, federated from the bottom upward...

I regard the Prussian invasion as a piece of good fortune for France and for world revolution. If this invasion had not taken place, and if the revolution in France had been made without it, the French socialists themselves would have attempted once again—and this time on their own account—to stage a state revolution [coup d'état]. This would be absolutely illogical, it would be fatal for socialism; but they certainly would have tried to do it, so deeply have they been influenced by the principles of Jacobinism. Consequently, among other measures of public safety decreed by a convention of delegates from the cities, they would no doubt try to *impose* communism or collectivism on the peasants. This would spark an armed rebellion, which would be obliged to depend upon an immense, well-disciplined, and well-organized army. As a result, the socialist rulers would not only give another army of rebellious peasants to the reaction, they would also beget the formation of a reactionary militarist caste of power-hungry generals within their own ranks. Thus replenished, the machinery of the State would soon have to have a leader, a dictator, an emperor, to direct this machine. All this would be inevitable, for it springs not from the caprice of an individual but from the logic of the situation, a logic that never errs.

Fortunately, events themselves will now force the urban workers to open their eyes and reject this fatal procedure copied from the Jacobins. Under the prevailing circumstances, only madmen would even dream of unleashing a reign of terror against the countryside. If the countryside should rise up against the cities, the cities, and France with them, would be lost...

But my dear friends, we are not lost. *France can be saved by anarchy.*

Let loose this mass anarchy in the countryside as well as in the cities, aggravate it until it swells like a furious avalanche destroying and devouring everything in its path, both internal enemies and Prussians. This is a bold and desperate measure, I know. But it is the only feasible alternative. Without it, there is no salvation for France. All the ordinary means having failed, there is left only the primitive ferocious energy of the French people who must now choose between the slavery of bourgeois civilization and the political and primitive ferocity of the proletariat.

I have never believed that the workers in the cities, even under the most favourable conditions, will ever be able to impose communism or collectivism on the peasants; and I have never believed in this method of bringing about socialism, because I abhor every imposed system and because I am a sincere and passionate lover of freedom. This false idea and this ill-conceived hope are destructive of liberty and constitute the fundamental fallacy of authoritarian communism. For the imposition of violence, systematically organized, leads to the reinstitution of the principle of authority and makes necessary the State and its privileged ranks. Collectivism could be imposed only on slaves, and this kind of collectivism would then be the negation of humanity. In a free community, collectivism can come about only through the pressure of circumstances, not by imposition from above but by a free spontaneous movement from below, and only when the conditions of privileged individualism, the politics of the State, criminal and civil codes, the juridical family, and the law of inheritance will have been swept away by the revolution.

Since the revolution cannot be *imposed* upon the rural areas, *it must be germinated within the agricultural communities, by stirring up a revolutionary movement of the peasants themselves, inciting them to destroy, by direct action, every political, judicial, civil, and military institution, and to establish and organize anarchy through the whole countryside*.

This can be done in only one way, by speaking to the peasants in a manner which *will impel them in the direction of their own interests*. They love the land? Let them take the land and throw out those landlords who live by the labour of others!! They do not like paying mortgages, taxes, rents, and private debts? Let them stop paying!! And lastly, they hate conscription? Don't force them to join the army!!

And who will fight the Prussians? You need not worry about that. Once the peasants are aroused and actually see the advantages of the Revolution, they will voluntarily give more money and more men to defend the Revolution than it would be possible to extract from them by compulsory official measures. The peasants will, as they did in 1792, again repel the Prussian invaders. It is necessary only that they have the opportunity to raise hell, and only the anarchist revolution can inspire them to do it.

29. Bakunin: The Paris Commune and the Idea of the State (1871)

After failed attempts at insurrection in Lyons and Marseilles, the people of Paris arose in March 1871, overthrowing the central state government and instituting a revolutionary commune. In this piece, written shortly after the suppression of the Commune, Bakunin sets forth an anarchist conception of the social revolution, taking the Commune as his inspiration. The translation is from Sam Dolgoff's Bakunin on Anarchism.

ALL THAT INDIVIDUALS CAN DO IS FORMULATE, clarify, and propagate ideas expressing the instinctive desires of the people, and contribute their constant efforts to the revolutionary organization of the natural powers of the masses. This and nothing more; all the rest can be accomplished only by the people themselves. Otherwise we would end up with a political dictatorship—the reconstitution of the State, with all its privileges, inequalities, and oppressions; by taking a devious but inevitable path we would come to reestablish the political, social, and economic slavery of the masses…

Contrary to the belief of authoritarian communists—which I deem completely wrong—that a social revolution must be decreed and organized either by a dictatorship or by a constituent assembly emerging from a political revolution, our friends, the Paris socialists, believed that revolution could neither be made nor brought to its full development except by the spontaneous and continued action of the masses, the groups and the associations of the people.

Our Paris friends were right a thousand times over. In fact, where is the mind, brilliant as it may be, or—if we speak of a collective dictatorship, even if it were formed of several hundred individuals endowed with superior mentalities—where are the intellects powerful enough to embrace the infinite multiplicity and diversity of real interests, aspirations, wishes, and needs which sum up the collective will of the people? And to invent a social organization that will not be a Procrustean bed upon which the violence of the State will more or less overtly force unhappy society to stretch out? It has always been thus, and it is exactly this old system of organization by force that the Social Revolution should end by granting full liberty to the masses, the groups, the communes, the associations and to the individuals as well; by destroying once and for all the historic cause of all violence, which is the power and indeed the mere existence of the State. Its fall will bring down with it all the inequities of the law and all the lies of the various religions, since both law and religion have never been anything but the compulsory consecration, ideal and real, of all violence represented, guaranteed, and protected by the State…

The future social organization should be carried out from the bottom up, by the free association or federation of workers, starting with the associations, then going on to the communes, the regions, the nations, and, finally, culminating in a great international and universal federation. It is only then that the true, life-giving social order of liberty and general welfare will come into being, a social order which, far from restricting, will affirm and reconcile the interests of individuals and of society.

30. Louise Michel: In Defence of the Commune (1871)

Louise Michel (1830-1905), school teacher, poet and protégée of Victor Hugo (1802-1885), was at the time of the Commune a revolutionary socialist. She organized the Union of Women for the Defence of Paris and the Care of the Wounded, which issued a manifesto calling for "the annihilation of all existing social and legal relations, the suppression of all special privileges, the end of all exploitation, the substitution of the reign of work for the reign of capital." She fought on the barricades for the social revolution alongside her comrades, such as Théophile Ferré, most of whom were killed or, as in the case of Ferré, summarily executed. Some 30,000 Communards were massacred, with many more imprisoned and forced into exile. The following excerpts from her defiant defence before the military tribunal are taken from The Red Virgin: Memoirs of Louise Michel *(Tuscaloosa: University of Alabama Press, 1981), ed. and trans. B. Lowry and E. E. Gunter, and are reprinted with the kind permission of the publisher.*

The Testimony of Louise Michel

PRESIDENT OF THE COURT: YOU HAVE HEARD the acts you are accused of. What do you have to say in your defence?

THE ACCUSED: I don't want to defend myself, nor do I want to be defended. I belong completely to the Social Revolution, and I declare that I accept responsibility for all my actions. I accept it entirely and without reservations.

You accuse me of having participated in the assassination of Generals Clément Thomas and Lecomte. To that charge, I would answer yes—if I had been at Montmartre when those generals wanted to fire on the people. I would have had no hesitation about shooting people who gave orders like those. But once they were prisoners, I do not understand why they were shot, and I look at that act as a villainous one.

As for the burning of Paris, yes, I participated in it. I wanted to block the Versailles invaders with a barrier of flames. I had no accomplices in that. I acted on my own.

I am also charged with being an accomplice of the Commune. That is quite true, since above everything else the Commune wanted to bring about the Social Revolution, and Social Revolution is my dearest wish. Moreover, I am honoured to be singled out as one of the promoters of the Commune. It had absolutely nothing to do with assassinations or burning. I attended all the sessions at the Hôtel de Ville, and I affirm that there never was any talk of assassinations or burnings.

Do you want to know who the real guilty parties are? The police. Later, perhaps, the light of truth will fall on all those events. Now people naturally place responsibility on the partisans of Social Revolution.

One day I did propose to Théophile Ferré that I go to Versailles. I wanted two victims: M. Thiers [reactionary political leader] and myself, for I had already sacrificed my life, and I had decided to kill him.

Question: Did you say in a proclamation that a hostage should be shot every twenty-four hours?

Answer: No, I only wanted to threaten. But why should I defend myself? I have already told you I refuse to do it. You are the men who are going to judge me. You are in front of me publicly. You are men, and I, I am only a woman. Nevertheless, I am looking you straight in the face. I know quite well that anything I tell you will not change my sentence in the slightest. Thus I have only one last word before I sit down.

We never wanted anything but the triumph of the great principles of Revolution. I swear it by our martyrs who fell on the field of Satory [where Ferré and many others were shot], by our martyrs I still acclaim here, by our martyrs who some day will find their avenger.

I am in your power. Do whatever you please with me. Take my life if you want it. I am not a woman who would dispute your wishes for a moment...

What I demand from you, you who claim you are a court-martial, you who pass yourselves off as my judges, you who don't hide the way the Board of Pardons behaves, you who are from the military and who judge me publicly—what I call for is the field of Satory, where our revolutionary brothers have already fallen.

I must be cut off from society. You have been told that, and the prosecutor is right. Since it seems that any heart which beats for liberty has the right only to a small lump of lead, I demand my share. If you let me live, I will not stop crying for vengeance, and I will denounce the assassins on the Board of Pardons to the vengeance of my brothers.

PRESIDENT OF THE COURT: I cannot allow you to continue speaking if you continue in this tone.

LOUISE MICHEL: I have finished...If you are not cowards, kill me.

31. Peter Kropotkin: The Paris Commune (1881)

Peter Kropotkin (1842-1921) was one of the foremost exponents of anarchist communism. The following excerpts are taken from a lecture he gave on the 10th anniversary of the Commune, translated by Nicolas Walter and reprinted with the kind permission of Christine Walter.

THE REVOLUTION OF 1871 WAS ABOVE ALL a popular one. It was made by the people themselves, it sprang spontaneously from within the masses, and it was among the great mass of the people that it found its defenders, its heroes, its martyrs—and it is exactly for this "mob" character that the bourgeoisie will never forgive it. And at the same time the moving idea of this revolution—vague, it is true, unconscious perhaps, but nevertheless pronounced and running through all its actions—is the idea of the social revolution, trying at last to establish after so many centuries of struggle real liberty and real equality for all...

To find a clear and precise idea, comprehensible to everyone and summing up in a few words what had to be done to bring about the revolution—such was indeed the preoccupation of the people of Paris from the earliest days of their independence. But a great Idea does not germinate in a day, however rapid the elaboration and propagation of Ideas during revolutionary periods. It always needs a certain time to develop, to spread throughout the masses, and to translate itself into action, and the Paris Commune lacked this time...

Minds were undecided, and the socialists themselves didn't feel bold enough to begin the demolition of individual property...They tried to consolidate the Commune first and put off the social revolution until later, whereas the only way to proceed was *to consolidate the Commune by means of the social revolution!*

The same thing happened with the principle of government. By proclaiming the free commune, the people of Paris were proclaiming an essentially anarchist principle; but, since the idea of anarchism had at that time only faintly dawned in men's minds, it was checked half-way, and within the Commune people decided in favour of the old principle of authority, giving themselves a Commune Council, copied from the municipal councils.

If indeed we admit that a central government is absolutely useless to regulate the relations of communes between themselves, why should we admit its necessity to regulate the mutual relations of the groups which make up the commune? And if we leave to the free initiative of the communes the business of coming to a common understanding with regard to enterprises concerning several cities at once, why refuse this same initiative to the groups composing a commune? There is no more reason for a government inside a commune than for a government above the commune.

But in 1871 the people of Paris…let themselves be carried away by governmental fetishism and gave themselves a government. The consequences of that are known. The people sent their devoted sons to the town hall. There, immobilized, in the midst of paperwork, forced to rule when their instincts prompted them to be and to move among the people, forced to discuss when it was necessary to act, and losing the inspiration which comes from continual contact with the masses, they found themselves reduced to impotence. Paralyzed by their removal from the revolutionary source, the people, they themselves paralyzed the popular initiative.

Born during a period of transition, at a time when the ideas of socialism and authority were undergoing a profound modification; emerging from a war, in an isolated centre, under the guns of the Prussians, the Paris Commune was bound to perish.

But by its eminently popular character it began a new era in the series of revolutions, and through its ideas it was the precursor of a great social revolution…At the time of the next revolution, the people will know what has to be done; they will know what awaits them if they don't gain a decisive victory, and they will act accordingly.

Indeed we now know that on the day when France bristles with insurgent communes, the people must no longer give themselves a government and expect that government to initiate revolutionary measures. When they have made a clean sweep of the parasites who devour them, they will themselves take possession of all social wealth so as to put it into common according to the principles of anarchist communism. And when they have entirely abolished property, government, and the state, they will form themselves freely according to the necessities dictated to them by life itself. Breaking its chains and overthrowing its idols, mankind will march then towards a better future, no longer knowing either masters or slaves, keeping its veneration only for the noble martyrs who paid with their blood and sufferings for those first attempts at emancipation which have lighted our way in our march towards the conquest of freedom.

Chapter 8
Anarchist Communism

32. Carlo Cafiero: Anarchy and Communism (1880)

In 1876, various anarchists, such as Élisée Reclus, then a refugee from the Paris Commune, François Dumartheray and L'Avenir section of French refugees in Switzerland, and the Italian Federation of the anti-authoritarian International, began to advocate "anarchist communism," the revolutionary abolition of the state and wage labour, voluntary association and distribution according to need. Carlo Cafiero (1846-1892), Bakunin's former comrade and one of the leading militants of the Italian Federation, together with Errico Malatesta, was instrumental in convincing the Italian Federation to adopt an anarchist communist stance. The following excerpts from his 1880 speech to the Jura Federation, Anarchy and Communism, *have been translated by Nicolas Walter and are reprinted with the kind permission of Christine Walter.*

ANARCHY, TODAY, IS ATTACK; it is war against every authority, every power, every State. In the future society, Anarchy will be defence, the prevention of the re-establishment of any authority, any power, any State: Full and complete liberty of the individual who, freely and driven only by his needs, by his tastes and his sympathies, unites with other individuals in a group or association; free development of the association, which is federated with others in the commune or the district; free development of the communes which are federated in the region; and so on—the regions in the nation; the nations in humanity.

Communism, the question which particularly concerns us today, is the second term of our revolutionary ideal. *Communism*, at present, is still attack; it is not the destruction of authority, but it is the taking of possession, in the name of all humanity, of all the wealth existing in the world. In the future society, Communism will be the enjoyment of all existing wealth by all men and according to the principle: FROM EACH ACCORDING TO HIS FACULTIES TO EACH ACCORDING TO HIS NEEDS, that is to say: FROM EACH AND TO EACH ACCORDING TO HIS WILL.

It is, however, necessary to point out—and this above all in reply to our opponents, the authoritarian communists or Statists—that the taking of possession and the enjoyment of all the existing wealth must be, according to us, the deed of the people itself. Because the people, humanity, is not the same as the individuals who managed to seize the wealth and hold it in their hands, some have tried to conclude from this, it is true, that we should for this reason establish a whole class of rulers—of representatives and trustees of the common wealth. But we do not share this opinion. No intermediaries; no representatives who always end by representing only themselves; no mediators of equality, any more than mediators of liberty; no new government, no new State, whether it is called Popular or Democratic, Revolutionary or Provisional!

Since the common wealth is spread over the whole earth, and since all of it belongs by right to the whole of humanity, those who find this wealth within their reach and are in a position to use it will use it in common. The people of some country will use the land, the machines, the workshops, the houses, etc., of the country, and they will make use of it in common. Since they are part of humanity, they will exercise here, by deed and directly, their right to a share of the human wealth. But if an inhabitant of Peking came into this country, he would have the same rights as the others: he would enjoy, in common with the others, all the wealth of the country, in the same way that he had done in Peking…

But we are asked: Is Communism practicable? Shall we have enough products to allow each person the right to take from them at will, without demanding from individuals more work than they would like to give?

We reply: Yes, it will certainly be possible to apply this principle, *from each and to each according to his will*, because in the future society production will be so abundant that there will be no need to limit consumption or to demand from men more work than they would be able or willing to give.

This immense increase in production, of which we cannot give a true impression even today, may be predicted by examining the causes which will stimulate it. These causes may be reduced to three main ones:

1. The harmony of co-operation in various branches of human activity, replacing the present struggle which arises from competition;

2. The introduction on an immense scale of machines of all kinds;

3. The considerable economy in the power of labour, the instruments of labour and raw materials, arising from the suppression of dangerous or useless production.

Competition, struggle, is one of the basic principles of capitalist production, having for its motto: MORS TUA VITA MEA, *your death is my life*. The ruin of one makes the fortune of another. And this bitter struggle spreads from nation to nation, from region to region, from individual to individual, between workers as well as between capitalists. It is war to the knife, a fight at all levels—hand to hand, in squads, in platoons, in regiments, in divisions. One worker finds work where another loses it; one industry or several industries may prosper when another industry or industries may fail.

Well, imagine when, in the future society, this individualist principle of capitalist production, *each for himself and against all, and all against each*, will be replaced by the true principle of human sociability: EACH FOR ALL AND ALL FOR EACH—what an enormous change will be obtained in the results of production! Imagine what the increase of production will be when each man, far from having to struggle against all the others, will be helped by them; when he will have them not as enemies but as co-operators. If the collective labour of ten men achieves results absolutely impossible to an isolated man, how great will be the results obtained by the grand co-operation of all the men who today are working in opposition against one another!

And machines? The impact of these powerful auxiliaries of labour, however great it seems to us today, is only very minimal in comparison with what it will be in the society to come.

The machine today is opposed often by the ignorance of the capitalist, but even more often by his interest. How many machines remain unused solely because they do not return an immediate profit to the capitalist! Is a coal-mining company, for example, going to put itself to the expense of safeguarding the interests of the workers and building costly apparatus to carry the miners into the pits? Is the municipality going to introduce a machine to break stones, when this terrible work provides it with the means of giving cheap relief to the hungry? How many discoveries, how many applications of science remain a dead letter solely because they don't bring the capitalist enough!

The worker himself is opposed to machines today, and with reason, since they are for him the monster which comes to drive him from the factory, to starve him, degrade him, torture him, crush him. Yet what a great interest he will have, on the contrary, in increasing their number when he will no longer be at the service of the machines and when, on the contrary, the machines will themselves be at his service, helping him and working for his benefit!

So we must take account of the immense economy which will be made by the three elements of labour—strength, instruments and materials—which are horribly wasted today, since they are used for the production of things which are absolutely useless, when they are not actually harmful to humanity.

How many workers, how many materials and how many instruments of labour are used today for the armies of land and sea, to build ships, fortresses, cannons and all the arsenals of offensive and defensive weapons! How much strength is used to produce articles of luxury which serve only to satisfy the needs of vanity and corruption!

And when all this strength, all these materials, all these instruments of labour are used in industry for the production of articles which will themselves be used for production, what a prodigious increase of production we shall see emerge!

Yes, Communism is practicable: We shall indeed be able to let each take at will what he needs, since there will be enough for all; we shan't need to ask for more work than each wants to give, because there will be enough products for the morrow.

And it is thanks to this abundance that work will lose the ignoble character of enslavement and will have only the attraction of a moral and physical need, like that of study, of living with nature.

...[I]f after putting the instruments of labour and the raw materials in common, we retained the individual distribution of the products of labour, we would be forced to retain money, sharing out a greater or lesser accumulation of wealth according to the greater or lesser merit—or rather, skill—of individuals. Equality will thus have disappeared, since he who manages to acquire more wealth will already be raised by that very thing above the level of others...

The individual distribution of products would re-establish not only inequality between men, but also inequality between different kinds of work. We would see the immediate reappearance of *clean* and *dirty* work, of high and low work; the former would be for the rich, the second would be the lot of the poorer. Then it would not be vocation and personal taste which would decide a man to devote himself to one form of activity rather than another; it would be interest, the hope of winning more in some profession. Thus would be reborn idleness and industry, merit and demerit, good and evil, vice and virtue; and, in consequence, reward on one side and punishment on the other: law, judge, policeman, and jail.

...With collective labour imposed on us by the necessity of mass production and the application of machinery on a large scale, with this ever-increasing tendency of modern labour to make use of the labour of previous generations, how could we determine what is the share of the product of one and the share of the product of another? It is absolutely impossible, and our opponents recognize this so well themselves that they end by saying: "Well, we shall take as a basis for distribution the hours of labour." But at the same time they themselves admit that this would be unjust, since three hours of labour by Peter may be worth five hours of labour by Paul...

But one fine day we saw the rise again of a new shade of socialists...the apostles of the following thesis.

"There exist," they say, "values of use and values of production. Use values are those which we use to satisfy our own personal needs: that is, the house we live in, the food we consume, clothes, books, etc.; whereas production values are those we use for production: that is, the factory, the stores, the stable, shops, machines and instruments of labour of every kind, the soil, materials of labour, etc. The former values, which are used to satisfy the needs of the individual, should be distributed individually; whereas the latter, those which are used by everyone for production, should be distributed collectively."

...But I ask you, you who give the charming title of production values to the coal which is used to fuel the machine, the oil used to lubricate it, the oil which lights its operation—why deny it to the bread and meat which feed me, the oil which I dress my salad with, the gas which lights my labour, to everything which keeps alive and operating the most perfect of all machines, man, the father of all machines?

You class among production values the meadow and the stable which are used to keep cattle and horses, and you want to exclude from them houses and gardens which are used for the most noble of animals: man.

So where is your logic?

Besides, even you who make yourselves the apostles of this theory, you know perfectly well that this demarcation doesn't exist in reality and that, if it is difficult to trace today, it will completely disappear on the day when we shall all be producers at the same time as consumers.

...All are agreed that we are necessarily moving towards communism, but it is pointed out to us that at the start, since the products will not be abundant enough, we shall have to establish rationing, sharing, and that the best method of sharing the products of labour would be that based on the amount of labour which each will have done.

To this we reply that, in the future society, even when we may be obliged to have rationing, we should remain communist; that is to say, the rationing should be carried out not according to *merit* but according to *need*.

Let us take the family, that small-scale model of communism—a communism which is authoritarian rather than anarchist, to be sure, but this doesn't alter anything in our example.

In the family the father brings, let us suppose, a hundred sous a day, the eldest son three francs, a younger boy forty sous, and the child only twenty sous a day. All bring their pay to the mother who keeps the cash and gives them food to eat. They all bring unequally; but, at mealtime, each is served in his own way and according to his own appetite. There is no rationing. But let hard times come, and let poverty prevent the mother from continuing to allow for the appetite or taste of each in the distribution of the meal. There must be rationing; and, whether by the initiative of the mother or by the unspoken custom of all, the helpings are reduced. But look, this sharing is not done according to merit, for the younger boy and the child above all receive the largest share; and, as for the choice portion, it is kept for the old woman who brings in nothing at all. So even during famine, within the family this principle is applied of rationing according to need. Would it be otherwise in the great humanitarian family of the future?

33. Kropotkin: The Conquest of Bread (1892)

By the 1880's Kropotkin had become one of the leading exponents of anarchist communism, the basic principles of which he set forth in a series of pamphlets and articles. In 1892 he published his most eloquent and influential argument for anarchist communism, The Conquest of Bread *(Montreal: Black Rose Books, 1990; reprint of 1906 English edition). It was soon translated into several languages and had a considerable impact on the anarchist movement, not only in Europe but also throughout Latin America and Asia, particularly China. The following excerpts are taken from the chapter on the wage system, which has been widely translated and published in pamphlet form. The "collectivists" Kropotkin refers to were for the most part Marxist state socialists.*

WE HAVE SAID THAT CERTAIN collectivist writers desire that a distinction should be made between qualified or professional work and simple work. They pretend that an hour's work of an engineer, an architect, or a doctor, must be considered as two or three hours' work of a blacksmith, a mason, or a hospital nurse. And the same distinction must be made between all sorts of trades necessitating a more or less long apprenticeship and the simple toil of day labourers.

Well, to establish this distinction would be to maintain all the inequalities of present society. It would mean fixing a dividing line, from the beginning, between the workers and those who pretend to govern them. It would mean dividing society into two very distinct classes—the aristocracy of knowledge above the horny-handed lower orders—the one doomed to serve the other; the one working with its hands to feed and clothe those who, profiting by their leisure, study how to govern their fosterers…

We know that if engineers, scientists, or doctors are paid ten or a hundred times more than a labourer, and that a weaver earns three times more than an agricultural labourer, and ten times more than a girl in a match factory, it is...by reason of a monopoly of education, or a monopoly of industry. Engineers, scientists, and doctors merely exploit their capital—their diplomas—as middle-class employers exploit a factory, or as nobles used to exploit their titles of nobility

Let them, therefore, not...tell us that a student who has gaily spent his youth in a university has a *right* to a wage ten times greater than the son of a miner who has grown pale in a mine since the age of eleven; or that a weaver has a *right* to a wage three or four times greater than that of an agricultural labourer. The cost of teaching a weaver his work is not four times greater than the cost of teaching a peasant his. The weaver simply benefits by the advantages his industry reaps in Europe, in comparison with countries that have as yet no industries...

To make a distinction between simple and professional work in a new society would result in the Revolution sanctioning and recognizing as a principle a brutal fact we submit to nowadays, but that we nevertheless find unjust...

Services rendered to society, be they work in factory or field, or mental services, *cannot be* valued in money. There can be no exact measure of value (of what has been wrongly-termed exchange value), nor of use value, with regard to production. If two individuals work for the community five hours a day, year in year out, at different work which is equally agreeable to them, we may say that on the whole their labour is equivalent. But we cannot divide their work, and say that the result of any particular day, hour, or minute of work of the one is worth the result of a minute or hour of the other.

We may roughly say that the man who during his lifetime has deprived himself of leisure during ten hours a day has given far more to society than the one who has only deprived himself of leisure during five hours a day, or who has not deprived himself at all. But we cannot take what he has done during two hours and say that the yield is worth twice as much as the yield of another individual, working only one hour, and remunerate him in proportion. It would be disregarding all that is complex in industry, in agriculture, in the whole life of present society; it would be ignoring to what extent all individual work is the result of past and present labour of society as a whole. It would mean believing ourselves to be living in the Stone Age, whereas we are living in an age of steel.

If you enter a coal mine you will see a man in charge of a huge machine that raises and lowers a cage. In his hand he holds a lever that stops and reverses the course of the machine; he lowers it and the cage turns back in the twinkling of an eye; he raises it, he lowers it again with a giddy swiftness. All attention, he follows with his eyes fixed on the wall an indicator that shows him, on a small scale, at which point of the shaft the cage is at each second of its progress; as soon as the indicator has reached a certain level he suddenly stops the course of the cage, not a yard higher nor lower than the required spot. And no sooner have the colliers unloaded their coal-wagons, and pushed empty ones instead, than he reverses the lever and again sends the cage back into space.

During eight or ten consecutive hours he must pay the closest attention. Should his brain relax for a moment, the cage would inevitably strike against the gear, break its wheels, snap the rope, crush men, and obstruct work in the mine. Should he waste three seconds at each touch of the lever, in our modern perfected mines, the extraction would be reduced from twenty to fifty tons a day.

Is it he who is of greatest use in the mine? Or, is it perhaps the boy who signals to him from below to raise the cage? Is it the miner at the bottom of the shaft, who risks his life every instant, and who will some day be killed by fire-damp? Or is it the engineer, who would lose the layer of coal, and would cause the miners to dig on rock by a simple mistake in his calculations? And lastly, is it the mine owner who has put all his capital into the mine, and who has perhaps, contrary to expert advice asserted that excellent coal would be found there?

All the miners engaged in this mine contribute to the extraction of coal in proportion to their strength, their energy, their knowledge, their intelligence, and their skill. And we may say that all have the right to live, to satisfy their needs, and even their whims, when the necessaries of life have been secured for all. But how can we appraise their work?

And, moreover, is the coal they have extracted *their* work? Is it not also the work of men who have built the railway leading to the mine and the roads that radiate from all its stations? Is it not also the work of those that have tilled and sown the fields, extracted iron, cut wood in the forests, built the machines that burn coal, and so on?

No distinction can be drawn between the work of each man. Measuring the work by its results leads us to absurdity; dividing and measuring them by the hours spent on the work also leads us to absurdity. One thing remains: put the *needs* above the *works*, and first of all recognize the right to live, and later on, to the comforts of life, for all those who take their share in production.

34. Kropotkin: Fields, Factories and Workshops (1898)

Kropotkin was especially concerned with the division between intellectual, or brain, work, and manual labour. In Fields, Factories and Workshops *(London: Thomas Nelson & Sons, 1912; originally published 1898; abridged edition: Montreal: Black Rose Books, 1994, ed. George Woodcock), he set forth his ideas on how to combine the two by decentralizing industry and eliminating, as far as possible, the division of labour. These ideas were particularly influential in China and Japan.*

POLITICAL ECONOMY HAS HITHERTO insisted chiefly upon division. We proclaim integration; and we maintain that the ideal of society—that is, the state towards which society is already marching—is a society of integrated, combined labour. A society where each individual is a producer of both manual and intellectual work; where each able-bodied human being is a worker, and where each worker works both in the field and the industrial workshop; where every aggregation of individuals, large enough to dispose of a certain variety of natural resources—it may be a nation, or rather a region—produces and itself consumes most of its own agricultural and manufactured produce...

The scattering of industries over the country—so as to bring the factory amidst the fields, to make agriculture derive all those profits which it always finds in being combined with industry...and to produce a combination of industrial with agricultural work—is surely the next step to be made, as soon as a reorganization of our present conditions is possible...This step is imposed by the very necessity of producing for the producers themselves. It is imposed by the necessity for each healthy man and woman to spend a part of their lives in manual work in the free air; and it will be rendered the more necessary when the great social movements, which have now become unavoidable, come to disturb the present international trade, and compel each nation to revert to her own resources for her own maintenance. Humanity as a whole, as well as each separate individual, will be gainers by the change, and the change will take place...

We maintain that in the interests of both science and industry, as well as of society as a whole, every human being, without distinction of birth, ought to receive such an education as would enable him, or her, to combine a thorough knowledge of science with a thorough knowledge of handicraft. We fully recognize the necessity of specialization of knowledge, but we maintain that specialization must follow general education, and that general education must be given in science and handicraft alike. To the division of society into brain workers and manual workers we oppose the combination of both kinds of activities; and instead of "technical education," which means the maintenance of the present division between brain work and manual work, we advocate *education integrale*, or complete education, which means the disappearance of that pernicious distinction...

Have the factory and the workshop at the gates of your fields and gardens, and work in them. Not those large establishments, of course, in which huge masses of metals have to be dealt with and which are better placed at certain spots indicated by Nature, but the countless variety of workshops and factories which are required to satisfy the infinite diversity of tastes among civilized men. Not those factories in which children lose all the appearance of children in the atmosphere of an industrial hell, but those airy and hygienic, and consequently economical, factories in which human life is of more account than machinery and the making of extra profits, of which we already find a few samples here and there; factories and workshops into which men, women and children will not be driven by hunger, but will be attracted by the desire of finding an activity suited to their tastes, and where, aided by the motor and the machine, they will choose the branch of activity which best suits their inclinations...

For centuries science and so-called practical wisdom have said to man: "It is good to be rich, to be able to satisfy, at least, your material needs; but the only means to be rich is to so train your mind and capacities as to be able to compel other men—slaves, serfs or wage-earners—to make these riches for you. You have no choice. Either you must stand in the ranks of the peasants and the artisans who, whatsoever economists and moralists may promise them in the future, are now periodically doomed to starve after each bad crop or during their strikes and to be shot down by their own sons the moment they lose patience. Or you must train your faculties so as to be a military commander of the masses, or to be accepted as one of the wheels of the governing machinery of the State, or to become a manager of men in commerce or industry." For many centuries there was no other choice, and men followed that advice, without finding in it happiness, either for themselves and their own children, or for those whom they pretended to preserve from worse misfortunes.

But modern knowledge has another issue to offer to thinking men. It tells them that in order to be rich they need not take the bread from the mouths of others; but that the more rational outcome would be a society in which men, with the work of their own hands and intelligence, and by the aid of the machinery already invented and to be invented, should themselves create all imaginable riches. Technics and science will not be lagging behind if production takes such a direction. Guided by observation, analysis and experiment, they will answer all possible demands. They will reduce the time which is necessary for producing wealth to any desired amount, so as to leave to everyone as much leisure as he or she may ask for. They surely cannot guarantee happiness, because happiness depends as much, or even more, upon the individual himself as upon his surroundings. But they guarantee, at least, the happiness that can be found in the full and varied exercise of the different capacities of the human being, in work that need not be overwork, and in the consciousness that one is not endeavouring to base his own happiness upon the misery of others.

35. Luigi Galleani: The End of Anarchism (1907)

Luigi Galleani (1861-1931) was an intransigent Italian anarchist communist critical of all conventional organization, including trade unions and any attempts to create an "anarchist party." Although published in 1925, The End of Anarchism *actually dates from 1907. Malatesta, one of the "organizationalists" criticized by Galleani, nevertheless described it as "a clear, serene, eloquent exposition of communist anarchism," although he personally found it "too optimistic, too simplistic and too trusting in natural harmonies" (Malatesta,* The Anarchist Revolution, *London: Freedom Press, 1995, page 65, fn.). The following extracts are taken from the 1982 Cienfuegos Press edition, trans. M. Sartin and R. D'Attilio, and are reprinted with the kind permission of Stuart Christie.*

LIBERTARIAN COMMUNISM...should be inspired by the unsuppressible right of each organism to go all the way and under the best possible conditions in its ascent from the most elementary to superior and more complex forms; it should be the unsuppressible right of every person to grow, to develop his faculties in every way, to achieve his full and integral development.

Now, this ascent of the organism from a rudimentary to a fully developed state is marked by a series of ever-more, growing and varied needs claiming satisfaction, and its progressive development results from the more or less complete satisfaction of those numberless and infinitely diverse needs...

A farmer who lives in an Alpine valley, in the present conditions of his development, may have satisfied all his needs—eaten, drunk, and rested to his heart's content; while a worker who lives in London, in Paris, or in Berlin, may willingly give up a quarter of his salary and several hours of his rest, in order to satisfy a whole category of needs totally unknown to the farmer stranded among the gorges of the Alps or the peaks of the Apennine mountains—to spend an hour of intense and moving life at the theatre, at the museum or at the library, to buy a recently published book or the latest issue of a newspaper, to enjoy a performance of Wagner or a lecture at the Sorbonne.

Since these needs vary, not only according to time and place, but also according to the temperament, disposition and development of each individual, it is clear that only he or she who experiences and feels them is in a position to appreciate them and to measure adequately the satisfaction they may give.

Therefore, in drawing the measure of each person's share in the total social production from *need*, from the complex and infinite needs of each organism, rather than from the social use-value of each one's labour, anarchist-communism is inspired not only by a logical motive, but also by an eminently practical criterion of equality and justice...

As the ways and measure of the satisfaction of needs vary from person to person, according to their development and to the particular environment in which they live, *while the right to satisfy them in the manner which each person, the sole judge, deems convenient, remains equal for all,* equality and justice could not receive a more real and sincere sanction than that which is given by the libertarian communist conception of society. All have an equal right to live a full life—the strong and the weak, the intelligent and the dull, the capable and the inept; and, without regard to the contribution each one may have given to the total production of society, they all have the same right to satisfy their needs and to reach the superior forms of higher development...

At present, work has a servile character; it is not chosen freely according to one's aptitudes; it does not give any satisfaction whatever, material or moral; it offers only risks, deprivations, humiliations; it is uncertain, painful, excessive, paid in inverse proportion to its duration; it is sought reluctantly, executed with disgust; it is endured, in short, as a punishment, as a curse. The aversions it arouses at the present time are understandable, as is understandable the horror with which work, this inevitable condition of life, is looked at by the unfortunates who bear on their faces, on their eyes, on their tortured flesh, the stigma of all the aberrations and degenerations caused by centuries of slavery, of deprivations, of poverty, of grief, of brutality—all compressed into a state of arrested development, which makes them incapable of any fertile function or of any original action.

However, transplant that rickety progeny of sclerotics, drunkards, arthritics and prostitutes to a healthier social climate, to a world of equals where production is ruled by collective interest, not by whim and speculation; where it is limited to what is necessary and pleasant, excluding all that is stupid, useless, or harmful, from miser's safes to monstrous battleships; make room within the ranks of redeeming labour for all the energies that now lie stagnant, tricked by all kinds of lies and frauds, by all the evil doings of usury, inquisition and murder—in monasteries, barracks, jails, in the endless circles of bureaucracy; look at the progress of the last fifty years, and calculate the progress that is bound to take place during the next fifty years through the application of science to industry; open to everyone the theatres and the schools, the gymnasiums and the academies; let there be air and bread for everyone, sun and joy, life and love—and then tell us if work, short in hours, varied in kind, freely chosen by every worker according to his own preference, in whom security of intellectual and physical life will have accumulated and kept alive all kinds of energy; tell us then, if any one will refuse to participate in a work which has become a source of joy to the spirit, a physiological necessity and a universally acknowledged condition of life and of universal progress...

In order to believe in the possibility, in the realization of a society without private property and without government, it is not necessary that men be angels. It will be enough that this society be capable of satisfying the needs of all its members on the land which has become again the great mother of us all, made fertile by human labour, redeemed from all humiliations and yokes. The bourgeois, who are in a position to satisfy these needs in large measure are the best witnesses to the fact that if energy can be diverted, it cannot be constrained, so that our opponents' fears of inertia and vagrancy are plainly absurd: fencing, horsemanship, boating, motoring, mountain-climbing, oceanic cruising, politics, diplomacy, philanthropy, tropical and polar expeditions are nothing but the different aspects, physical or intellectual, frivolous or noble, of the energy and vital exuberance which burst forth from the full satisfaction of needs enjoyed by the ruling classes.

When everyone's physical, intellectual and moral needs are fully satisfied, we shall have in every human being the exuberance of energy that is at present the exclusive privilege of the ruling classes...

Modestly, but firmly, we are opposed to those anarchists who call themselves organizationalists, whether they wish to organize an anarchist party politically, or whether, in order to strengthen it, they aim to base it on labour organizations as they exist now, or on other ones they might organize that correspond more to their aims.

A political party, any political party, has its program: i.e., its constitutional charter; in assemblies of group representatives, it has its parliament; in its management, its boards and executive committees, it has its government. In short, it is a graduated superstructure of bodies, a true hierarchy, no matter how disguised, in which all stages are connected by a single bond, discipline, which punishes infractions with sanctions that go from censure to excommunication, to expulsion.

The anarchist party cannot help but be a party like the others. Worse! A government like any other government, enslaved, like all the others, by its constitution which, like all other constitutions, laws and codes, would be overtaken, on the day after its promulgation, by events and needs, by the pressing necessities of the struggle. A government, absurd and illegitimate like the others, based on delegation and representation, though it would be only too clear and obvious, especially from the experience of the anarchists, that every delegate and deputy could represent only his own ideas and feelings, not those of his constituents, which are infinitely variable on any subject. A government, intrusive and arbitrary, like any other government, because its preoccupation with directorial responsibility will, at every development, in every stage of its hierarchy, push it to adopt—always moved, of course, by the most noble and generous purpose—provisions, decisions, measures to which the card-carrying members will submit for the sake of discipline, even though they may be contrary to their opinion and their interest. A government, all absorbing like any other, because it wants and has an organ for every function, of little or no use, but through which everybody must pass, against which all initiatives will have to collide, and before which all original and unorthodox projects will appear suspicious, if not outright subversive…

Many who have been with an organization of any kind have had the bitter occasion to watch its indolence and its negligence. They end up doubting whether the organization is set up to defend the workers and support their aspirations, wondering whether it isn't at the critical moment, an obstacle or impediment, instead. They can tell you if we are exaggerating.

It would not help to object that here we deal with anarchists, selected people, who know what they want, who are able to choose their road, and who have the good legs and strength to climb it. Like the members of all the vanguard parties, anarchists are children of bourgeois society, carrying its stigma, and, understandably, the crowds that join them are not better and expect the maximum result from the least effort. We have been forced into too many compromise arrangements to be willing to seek more…wherever possible, we must avoid, we must shun, we must reject compromise and renunciation. We must be ourselves, according to the strict character outlined by our faith and our convictions. These certainly would not draw forth a good omen for the libertarian future if we could not proceed on our own, without the proxies and the tutors, which are inseparable from the notion of organization, be it either the political organization of the anarchist party or the organization of the craft and trade unions…

It has been firmly established that the labour organizations, those that are managed by somnolent conservatives, as well as the red ones led by the so-called revolutionary syndicalists, recognize and consent to the existing economic system in all its manifestations and relations. They limit their demands to immediate and partial improvements, high salaries, shorter hours, old-age pensions, unemployment benefits, social security, laws protecting women's and children's working conditions, factory inspections, etc., etc. They are the main purpose for which the organization was established, and it is clear that an anarchist cannot assume the responsibility for sponsoring aspirations of this kind...without denying all his anarchist and revolutionary convictions, without aligning himself with the reformist crowds whose spearhead he pretends to be.

Our place is in opposition, continually demonstrating with all possible vigilance and criticism the vanity of such aims, the futility of such efforts, the disappointing results; relentlessly pointing out, in contrast, the concrete and integral emancipation that could be achieved quickly and easily with different ways and other means.

The outcome of every agitation, of every union struggle would confirm the foresight and the fairness of our criticism. Even if it is not easy to hope that an organization might soon follow our suggestions, it is nevertheless believable that the more intelligent and bold among its members would be inclined to favour our point of view. They would form a nucleus ready to fight with passion in the struggles of the future, attracting their fellow workers to shake the authority of their union leaders.

...[W]e, ourselves, have to start the revolution from within ourselves, by discarding old superstitions, selfishness, self-imposed ignorance, foolish vanities and moral deficiencies.

We are children of the bourgeois regime, heirs to all its degradations, materially and actually incapable of shedding its bestial yoke at this time, except for a few, and *we are revolutionary only when and insofar as we know how to resist and react against the wickedness, corruption and violence of our environment*. And, when, through experience, we have become worthy of the cause, we will be able to arouse the same need of moral elevation and freedom that will spread in an ever-widening concentric movement, reaching those groups farthest from us, like the effect of a stone cast into a pond.

The revolution cannot be made by the anarchists alone, at a pre-established time and by pre-arranged movements; but if a movement should burst out tomorrow—no matter where—they could place themselves in the forefront, or near it, with the sole aim of pointing it towards decisive positions or solutions, and in so doing, counteracting the usual intriguers who take advantage of the good faith and sacrifices of the proletariat to foster their own interests and political fortune...

Anarchy does not claim to be the last word, but only a new, more enlightened, more advanced and more human step along the ascending path of the endless future...

For each herald that falls along the slopes of progress, hundreds arise, valiant and confident, raising the standard and carrying it high and undaunted from trench to trench, erecting it in triumph over the ruins of an old world condemned both by reason and by history, a symbol of resurrection and of liberation.

All that is needed in this immutable task is to persist: *to kindle in the minds of the proletariat the flame of the idea: to kindle in their hearts faith in liberty and injustice: to give to their anxiously stretched out arms a torch and an axe*.

The purest and noblest exaltation of our ideal in the hearts of the people is a constant and intrepid education; a cautious but vigorous preparation for the armed insurrection.

"A program?"

A purpose—perhaps only a condition. But with this condition: *Anarchy will be!*

Chapter 9
Anarchy And Anarchism

36. José Llunas Pujols: What is Anarchy (1882)

The anarchist movement in Spain developed out of the Spanish sections of the First International, which sided with the anti-authoritarian wing following the split in the International in 1872. The Spanish government attempted to suppress the International but by 1881 the Spanish sections were revived under a new name, the Workers' Federation of the Spanish Region. While some members of the Federation tried to avoid the anarchist label, speaking instead of "autonomy," others were more direct. In August 1882, in a passage translated by Paul Sharkey, several sections declared:

> Our Anarchy is not disorder nor is it chaos as our foes maliciously imagine. The word Anarchy signifies non-government, for which reason we anarchists support the abolition of the political and juridical States currently in existence and seek to replace them with a free federation of free associations of free producers. In our organization, we already practice the anarchist principle, the most graphic expression of Freedom and Autonomy. Every individual is free and autonomous within his Section. The latter is free and autonomous within the Local Federation and within its Union, and the Local Federations are free and autonomous within the Region; just as the Spanish Region is free and autonomous with regard to other regions where the federated workers are, as we are, sensible of the great need for our emancipation, the abolition of frontiers, and for the world, for humanity, to cease being divided into classes, all of which will melt back into that of the free producers.

José Llunas Pujols (1850-1905), a veteran of the International active in the revived Federation, advocated a collectivist form of anarchism, based on direct democracy. The following excerpts, translated by Paul Sharkey, are taken from two of Llunas' 1882 essays, "What is Anarchy" and "Collectivism."

WHAT, THEN, IS AN-ARCHY IN PRACTICE? The whole organization of society stripped of power, domination or the authority of some over others.

According to this definition, we shall have this: hierarchies not existing in a society *organized along anarchist lines*, the system being founded upon the free will of all its individuals...

[Administration is] the only thing required by and indispensable in any civilized society, or, to put it at its plainest, in any *collective body*.

And in order to carry out the *Administration* in a manner whereby no one abdicates his rights or his autonomy, commissions or delegations are elected as the collective deems useful.

...Since a collective as a whole cannot write a letter or forward a sum of money, or do an infinity of tasks which only individuals can perform, it follows that *delegating* these tasks to the most qualified person subject to *a code of conduct prescribed in advance*, is not only not an *abdication* of freedom but rather the *accomplishment* of the most sacred duty of anarchy, which is the *organization of Administration*.

Let us suppose that a workers' body is set up without a steering committee or any hierarchical office; that it meets in a general assembly once a week or more often, at which everything pertinent to its operations is decided; that it chooses receivers, a treasurer, a bookkeeper, an archivist, a secretary, etc. to collect dues, retain its funds, audit its accounts, handle its archives and correspondence, etc., or appoints a commission with *exclusively administrative* functions and with a defined code of conduct or *Imperative Mandate*: the organization of that society would be *perfectly anarchist*...

Then let us take a look at the municipality of the future, *organized along anarchist lines*...the unit of organization would still be the trades section in each locality.

...[I]n order to organize an anarchist municipality, each unit (trades section) would delegate one or more persons with purely administrative powers or with an imperative mandate so that they could form a municipal or local administrative commission. These persons, subject to replacement and recall at any time through the ongoing suffrage of those who have given them their mandates, could never set themselves up as dictators...

All commissions or delegations appointed in an anarchist society should at all times be liable to replacement and recall through ongoing balloting of the Section or Sections by which they have been elected, thereby making it impossible for anybody to stake a claim to even the slightest bit of authority.

...[A]narchy is the abolition of all of the existing powers that be, political and religious, and of what is miscalled economic authority; but it is more than just the *aboli-*

tion, being also the *replacement*, not of some authorities by some others...but of one social order by another, of one social organization...by another...founded upon the consent of all its associates. The political State and theology would thus be supplanted by Administration and Science.

...[A]s anarchists we want knowledge to be accessible to all, we want the most comprehensively rounded education for every individual, so that in creating a society of free men, we might also be making one of intelligent beings.

Thus by making education the cornerstone of the anarchist system, we have...the finest and most wholesome barrier against harmful passions; whereas authority uses punishment in order to repress, knowledge makes [us] moral through persuasion and by making this understood: that every human entitlement carries within itself an imprescriptible obligation to respect others.

In short, we have seen what anarchy is: *abolition* of all the existing powers that be and their *replacement* by the labour body in its various manifestations...

What we mean by *collectivism is a society organized on the basis of collective ownership, economic federation and the complete emancipation of the human being...*

[In the collectivist society] the individual will be required to work in order to meet his needs as is presently the case and will also be the case tomorrow. Combination is the only option if more and better is to be produced. From which it follows that, of their own volition, people will organize themselves into producer associations and federations that will oversee the exchange of products with one another at cost.

Thus the factory corporation will oversee the administration of the factories where all their members will be working; the shoemakers their workshops; the type-setters their presses; the farmworkers the land; the miners their mines, the seamen their vessels, etc., etc.

All citizens, assembled in a local congress, will look into and determine the educational establishments and organize the staffing of assistance and security, public works, hygiene, statistics, etc., which organizational set-up may at any time be revised by congresses, on the advice of groups or of commissions elected for that very purpose...

In each of the regions that will naturally be formed—in that many of the current political boundaries are arbitrary—the Trades Federations and Communal Federations will set up purely administrative federal commissions, and, as the body liaising between all the Unions, Federations and Communes, will look after all regional public services...as well as all roads, railways, telegraphs, canals, general statistics, etc. [The Commission] of one Region will oversee the maintenance of relations with the other regional commissions for the sake of solidarity and universal harmony, as well as for all matters of an international or cosmopolitan character.

...[M]an will be free in the productive society; every worker group will be free within the Local and Trades Federation; the localities will be free within their Counties or Regions, and the Regions free within the entire human family which will finally have achieved its complete redemption (reprinted in Max Nettlau, *La Première International en Espagne, 1868-1888*, Dordrecht: D. Reidel, 1969).

37. Charlotte Wilson: Anarchism (1886)

Charlotte Wilson (1854-1944) was active in the anarchist movement in England in the 1880's and 1890's, helping to found, with Kropotkin and others, the anarchist newspaper, Freedom, in 1886, the same year she wrote this essay on anarchism for the Fabian Society (reprinted in Anarchist Essays, London: Freedom Press, 2000, ed. N. Walter).

LIFE IN COMMON HAS DEVELOPED social instinct in two conflicting directions, and the history of our experience in thought and action is the record of this strife within each individual, and its reflection within each society. One tendency is towards domination; in other words, towards the assertion of the lesser, sensuous self as against the similar self in others, without seeing that, by this attitude, true individuality impoverishes, empties and reduces itself to nonentity. The other tendency is towards equal brotherhood, or to the self-affirmation and fulfillment of the greater and only true and human self, which includes all nature, and thus dissolves the illusion of mere atomic individualism.

Anarchism is the conscious recognition that the first of these tendencies is, and always has been, fatal to real social union, whether the coercion it implies be justified on the plea of superior strength or superior wisdom, of divine right or necessity, of utility or expedience; whether it takes the form of force or fraud, of exacted conformity to an arbitrary legal system or an arbitrary ethical standard, of open robbery or legal appropriation of the universal birthright of land and the fruits of social labour. To compromise with this tendency is to prefer the narrower to the wider expediency, and to delay the possibility of that moral development which alone can make the individual one in feeling with his fellows, and organic society, as we are beginning to conceive of it, a realizable ideal.

The leading manifestations of this obstructive tendency at the present moment are Property, or domination over things, the denial of the claim of others to their use; and Authority, the government of man by man, embodied in majority rule; that theory of representation which, whilst admitting the claim of the individual to self-guidance, renders him the slave of the simulacrum that now stands for society.

Therefore, the first aim of Anarchism is to assert and make good the dignity of the individual human being, by his deliverance from every description of arbitrary restraint—economic, political and social; and, by so doing, to make apparent in their true force the real social bonds which already knit men together, and, unrecognized, are the actual basis of such common life as we possess. The means of doing this rest with each man's conscience and his opportunities. Until it is done, any definite proposals for the reorganization of society are absurd. It is only possible to draw out a very general theory as to the probable course of social reconstruction from the observation of the growing tendencies.

Anarchists believe the existing organization of the State only necessary in the interests of monopoly, and they aim at the simultaneous overthrow of both monopoly and State. They hold the centralized "administration of productive processes" a mere reflection of the present middle-class government by representation upon the vague conception of the future. They look rather for voluntary productive and distributive associations utilizing a common capital, loosely federated trade and district communities practising eventually complete free communism in production and consumption. They believe that in an industrial community in which wealth is necessarily a social, not an industrial, product, the claims which any individual can fairly put forward to a share in such wealth are: firstly, that he needs it; secondly, that he has contributed towards it to the best of his ability; thirdly (as regards any special article), that he has thrown so much of his own personality into its creation that he can best utilize it.

When this conception of the relation between wealth and the individual has been allowed to supersede the idea now upheld by force, that the inherent advantage of possessing wealth is to prevent others from using it, each worker will be entirely free to do as nature prompts—i.e., to throw his whole soul into the labour he has chosen, and make it the spontaneous expression of his intensest purpose and desire. Under such conditions only, labour becomes pleasure, and its produce a work of art. But all coercive organization working with machine-like regularity is fatal to the realization of this idea. It has never proved possible to perfectly free human beings to co-operate spontaneously with the precision of machines. Spontaneity, or artificial order and symmetry must be sacrificed. And as spontaneity is life, and the order and symmetry of any given epoch only the forms in which life temporarily clothes itself, Anarchists have no fears that in discarding the Collectivist dream of the scientific regulation of industry, and inventing no formulas for social conditions as yet unrealized, they are neglecting the essential for the visionary.

The like reasoning is applicable to the moral aspect of social relations. Crime as we know it is a symptom of the strain upon human fellowship involved in the false and artificial social arrangements which are enforced by authority, and its main cause and sanction will disappear with the destruction of monopoly and the State. Crime resulting from defective mental and physical development can surely be dealt with both more scientifically and more humanely, by fraternal medical treatment and improved education, than by brute force, however elaborated and disguised.

As for the expression of the common life of the community, and the practical persuasion and assistance desirable to raise those who have lagged behind the average of moral development, it is enough to note the marvellous growth of public opinion since the emancipation of platform and press to become aware that no artificial machinery is needful to enforce social verdicts and social codes of conduct without the aid of written laws administered by organized violence. Indeed, when arbitrary restraints are removed, this form of the rule of universal mediocrity is, and always has been, a serious danger to individual freedom; but as it is a natural, not an artificial, result of life in common, it can only be counteracted by broader moral culture.

Anarchism is not a Utopia, but a faith based upon the scientific observation of social phenomena. In it the individualist revolt against authority...and the Socialist revolt against private ownership of the means of production, which is the foundation of Collectivism, find their common issue. It is a moral and intellectual protest against the unreality of a society which, as Emerson says, "is everywhere in conspiracy against the manhood of every one of its members." Its one purpose is by direct personal action to bring about a revolution in every department of human existence, social, political and economic. Every man owes it to himself and to his fellows to be free.

38. Élisée Reclus: Anarchy (1894)

In his time, Élisée Reclus (1830-1905) was as venerated as Kropotkin by the international anarchist movement. Reclus had been associated with Bakunin in the First International and fought for the Paris Commune. He was one of the first anarchists to advocate libertarian communism, and to adapt Darwinian ideas regarding evolution to anarchist notions of revolution, seeing the latter as the outcome of multifarious, gradual, sometimes imperceptible and unconscious changes in society (see Selection 74). The following text was originally presented as a talk in June 1894. It was published as "L'Anarchie" in Jean Grave's Les Temps nouveaux *(May 25–June 1, 1895). This translation is taken form John P. Clark and Camille Martin's selection of*

Reclus' writings, Anarchy, Geography, Modernity: The Radical Social Thought of Élisée Reclus *(Lanham: Lexington Books, 2004), which also contains an extensive interpretive essay by Clark regarding Reclus' social and political thought, and is reprinted here with his kind permission.*

IN ALL AGES THERE HAVE BEEN FREE MEN, those contemptuous of the law, men living without any master and in accordance with the primordial law of their own existence and their own thought. Even in the earliest ages we find everywhere tribes made up of men managing their own affairs as they wish, without any externally imposed law, having no rule of behaviour other than "their own volition and free will," as Rabelais expresses it [in Gargantua and Pantagruel, Book 1, Chapter 57].

But if anarchy is as old as humanity, those who represent it nevertheless bring something new to the world. They have a keen awareness of the goal to be attained, and from all corners of the earth they join together to pursue their ideal of the eradication of every form of government. The dream of worldwide freedom is no longer a purely philosophical or literary utopia...It has become a practical goal that is actively pursued by masses of people united in their resolute quest for the birth of a society in which there are no more masters, no more official custodians of public morals, no more jailers, torturers and executioners, no more rich or poor. Instead there will be only brothers who have their share of daily bread, who have equal rights, and who coexist in peace and heartfelt unity that comes not out of obedience to law, which is always accompanied by dreadful threats, but rather from mutual respect for the interest of all, and from the scientific study of natural laws.

...[T]he conquest of power has almost always been the great preoccupation of revolutionaries, including the best intentioned of them. The prevailing system of education does not allow them to imagine a free society operating without a conventional government, and as soon as they have overthrown their hated masters, they hasten to replace them with new ones who are destined, according to the ancient maxim, to "make the people happy." Generally, no one has dared to prepare for a change of princes or dynasties without having paid homage or pledged obedience to some future sovereign. "The king is dead! Long live the king!" cried the eternally loyal subjects—even as they revolted. For many centuries this has been the unvarying course of history. "How could one possibly live without masters!" said the slaves, the spouses, the children, and the workers of the cities and countryside, as they quite deliberately placed their shoulders under the yoke, like the ox that pulls the plow...

In contrast to this instinct, anarchy truly represents a new spirit. One can in no way reproach the libertarians for seeking to get rid of a government only to put themselves in its place. "Get out of the way to make room for me!" are words that they would be appalled to speak. They would condemn to shame and contempt, or at least to pity, anyone who, stung by the tarantula of power, aspires to an office under the pretext of "making his fellow citizens happy." Anarchists contend that the state and all that it implies are not any kind of pure essence, much less a philosophical abstraction, but rather a collection of individuals placed in a specific milieu and subjected to its influence. Those individuals are raised up above their fellow citizens in dignity, power, and preferential treatment, and are consequently compelled to think themselves superior to the common people. Yet in reality the multitude of temptations besetting them almost inevitably leads them to fall below the general level.

This is what we constantly repeat to our brothers—including our fraternal enemies, the state socialists—"Watch out for your leaders and representatives!" Like you they are surely motivated by the best of intentions. They fervently desire the abolition of private property and of the tyrannical state. But new relationships and conditions change them little by little. Their morality changes along with their self-interest, and, thinking themselves eternally loyal to the cause and to their constituents, they inevitably become disloyal. As repositories of power they will also make use of the instruments of power: the army, moralizers, judges, police, and informers. More than three thousand years ago the Hindu poet of the Mahabharata expressed the wisdom of the centuries on this subject: "He who rides in a chariot will never be the friend of the one who goes on foot!"

Thus the anarchists have the firmest principles in this area. In their view, the conquest of power can only serve to prolong the duration of the enslavement that accompanies it. So it is not without reason that even though the term "anarchist" ultimately has only a negative connotation, it remains the one by which we are universally known. One might label us "libertarians," as many among us willingly call themselves, or even "harmonists," since we see agreement based on free will as the constituting element of the future society. But these designations fail to distinguish us adequately from the socialists. It is in fact our struggle against all official power that distinguishes us most essentially. Each individuality seems to us to be the center of the universe and each has the same right to its integral development, without interference from any power that supervises, reprimands or castigates it...

We find everywhere, in all social relations, positions of superiority and subordination. In short...the guiding principle of the state itself and of all the particular states that make it up, is hierarchy, by which is meant "holy" archy or "sacred" authority, for that is the true meaning of the word. This sacrosanct system of domination encompasses a long succession of superimposed classes in which the highest have the right to command and the lowest have the duty to obey. The official morality consists in bowing humbly to one's superiors and in proudly holding up one's head before one's subordinates. Each person must have, like Janus, two faces, with two smiles: one flattering, solicitous, and even servile, and the other haughty and nobly condescending. The principle of authority (which is the proper name for this phenomenon) demands that the superior should never give the impression of being wrong, and that in every verbal exchange he should have the last word. But above all, his orders must be carried out. That simplifies everything: there is no more need for quibbling, explanations, hesitations, discussions, or misgivings. Things move along all by themselves, for better or worse. And if a master isn't around to command in person, one has ready-made formulas—orders, decrees, or laws handed down from absolute masters and legislators at various levels. These formulas substitute for direct orders and one can follow them without having to consider whether they are in accord with the inner voice of one's conscience.

Between equals, the task is more difficult, but also more exalted. We must search fiercely for the truth, discover our own personal duty, learn to know ourselves, engage continually in our own education, and act in ways that respect the rights and interests of our comrades. Only then can one become a truly moral being and awaken to a feeling of responsibility. Morality is not a command to which one submits, a word that one repeats, something purely external to the individual. It must become a part of one's being, the very product of one's life. This is the way that we anarchists understand morality. Are we not justified in comparing this conception favourably with the one bequeathed to us by our ancestors?

...[S]ome doubt may remain in your minds whether anarchy has ever been any more than a mere ideal, an intellectual exercise, or subject of dialectic. You may wonder whether it has ever been realized concretely, or whether any spontaneous organization has ever sprung forth, putting into practice the power of comrades working together freely, without the command of any master. But such doubts can easily be laid to rest. Yes, libertarian organizations have always existed. Yes, they constantly arise once again, each year in greater numbers, as a result of advances in individual initiative. To begin with, I could cite diverse tribal peoples called "savages," who even in our own day live in perfect social harmony, needing neither rulers nor laws, prisons nor police. But I will not stress such examples, despite their significance. I fear that some might object that these primitive societies lack complexity in comparison to the infinitely complicated organism of our modern world. Let us therefore set aside these primitive tribes and focus entirely on fully constituted nations that possess developed political and social systems.

...Since the point at which human society emerged from prehistory, awakened to the arts, sciences, and industry, and was able to hand down its experience to us through written records, the greatest periods in the lives of nations have always been those in which men, shaken by revolution, have suffered least under the long-lasting and heavy burden of a duly-constituted government. Judged by the progress in discovery, the flowering of thought, and the beauty of their art, the two greatest epochs for humanity were both tumultuous epochs, ages of "imperiled liberty." Order reigned over the immense empires of the Medes and the Persians, but nothing great came out of it. On the other hand, while republican Greece was in a constant state of unrest, shaken by continual upheavals, it gave birth to the founders of all that we think exalted and noble in modern civilization. It is impossible for us to engage in thought or to produce any work of art without recalling those free Hellenes who were our precursors and who remain our models. Two thousand years later, after an age of darkness and tyranny that seemed incapable of ever coming to an end, Italy, Flanders and the Europe of the Free Cities reawakened. Countless revolutions shook the world...In addition, the fire of free thought burst forth and humanity began once again to flourish. In the works of Raphaël, de Vinci and Michelangelo it felt the vigor of youth once more.

...Galileo, while locked away in the prisons of the Inquisition, could only murmur secretly, "Still, it moves!" But thanks to the revolutions and the fury of free thought, we can today cry from the housetops and in the public squares, "The world moves, and it will continue to move!"

In addition to this great movement that gradually transforms all of society in the direction of free thought, free morality and freedom of action, in short, toward the essentials of anarchy, there has also existed a history of direct social experimentation that has manifested itself in the founding of libertarian and communitarian colonies...These efforts to create model communities all have the major failing of being created outside the normal conditions of life, that is to say, far from the cities where people intermingle, where ideas spring up, and where intellects are reinvigorated...

But where anarchist practice really triumphs is in the course of everyday life among common people who would not be able to endure their dreadful struggle for existence if they did not engage in spontaneous mutual aid, putting aside differences and conflicts of interest. When one of them falls ill, other poor people take in his children, feeding them, sharing the meager sustenance of the week, seeking to make ends meet by doubling their hours of work. A sort of communism is instituted among neighbours through lending, in which there is a constant coming and going of household implements and provisions. Poverty unites the unfortunate in a fraternal league. Together they are hungry; together they are satisfied. Anarchist morality and practice are the rule even in bourgeois gatherings where they might seem to be entirely absent. Imagine a party in the countryside at which some participant, whether the host or one of the guests, would put on airs of superiority, order people around, or impose his whims rudely on everyone! Wouldn't this completely destroy all the pleasure and joy of the occasion? True geniality can only exist between those who are free and equal, between those who can enjoy themselves in whatever way suits them best, in separate groups if they wish, or drawing closer to one another and intermingling as they please, for the hours spent in this way are the most agreeable ones.

39. Jean Grave: Moribund Society and Anarchy (1893)

At the invitation of Élisée Reclus, Jean Grave (1854-1939) became the editor of Le Révolté *[*The Rebel*] in 1883, after Kropotkin, one of its founding editors, and several other anarchists were imprisoned in France for advocating anarchy. In 1887, Grave changed the name of the publication to* La Révolte *[*Revolt*], which he continued to publish until it was suppressed by the French government in 1894 and Grave was also imprisoned for publishing anarchist propaganda. He began a new paper in 1895,* Les Temps nouveaux *[*New Times*], which lasted until the First World War in 1914, publishing the works of leading anarchist theorists, including Kropotkin and Reclus, as well as contemporary art and literature by anarchist artists and sympathizers, such as the painter, Camille Pissarro (1830-1903), and the writer, Octave Mirbeau (1850-1917). The following excerpts are taken from Voltairine de Cleyre's 1899 translation of Grave's* Moribund Society and Anarchy *(San Francisco: A. Isaak, 1899), originally published in French in 1893 (P. V. Stock), with a preface by Octave Mirbeau.*

THE STRONGEST OBJECTION...persons have so far been able to bring against the Anarchists is to say to them, "Your theories are very fine, but they cannot be realized." This is not an argument. "Why can they not be realized?" we ask, and instead of answering us with reasons they bring forward their fears. They tell us that with man's evil nature it is to be feared that he would profit by his liberty to stop working altogether; that when no mediating power existed it might happen that the stronger would exploit the weaker, etc. The Anarchists have shown the lack of foundation for these fears by proving that this evil tendency in man, these shortcomings in his character, are stimulated and encouraged by the present social organization which sets one against the other, forcing them to tear from each other the pittance it apportions with such exceeding parsimony. They also show...that every social system based upon authority cannot but beget evil effects; since power is vested in persons subject to the same defects as other men, it is clear that if men do not know how to govern themselves, still less do they know how to govern others...

If we were a political party anxious to get into power, we might make a lot of promises to people in order to get ourselves carried to the top; but it is a different thing with Anarchy; we have nothing to promise, nothing to ask, nothing to give. And when after having pointed out the facts which demonstrate the tendency of humanity towards this ideal, our opponents object that our ideas are impossible, nothing remains to us but to come back to the proofs of the abuses proceeding from all our institutions, the falsity of the bases upon which these rest, the emptiness of these reforms by which charlatans would divert the people's attention, and to remind them of the alternative open to them—either to continue to submit to exploitation or to revolt—at the same time demonstrating to them that the success of this revolution will depend upon the energy with which they "will" the realization of what they know to be good. This is our task: the rest depends on others, not on us.

For our own part we are not exactly partisans of a propaganda accomplished by means of sonorous or sentimental phrases; their effect is to make people hope for an immediate triumph, which is impossible...

Our ideal is to fulfill a less brilliant and grandiose task, but a more lasting one. Instead of confining our efforts to capturing people through sentiment, we seek above all to win them through logic and reason. We certainly do not want to underrate those whose ability consists in winning people through an appeal to feeling. To each his task, according to his temperament and his conceptions. But for ourselves we prefer securing *conviction* rather than *belief*. All those who take part in the propaganda should know what difficulties await them, that they may be ready to meet them and not be discouraged by the first obstacle in the way...

Another very generally accepted prejudice among Anarchists is to consider the masses as plastic dough, which may be molded at will and about which there is no necessity of troubling oneself. This notion comes from the fact that, having made one step in advance of the rest, these people consider themselves in a way as prophets, and as much more intelligent than common mortals.

"We shall make the masses do so-and-so," "we shall lead them at our backs," etc. Verily a dictator would not talk differently. This way of regarding the masses is an inheritance from our authoritarian past. Not that we wish to deny the influence of minorities upon the crowd; it is because we are convinced of such influence that we are so concerned. But we think that, in the time of revolution, the only weight the Anarchists can have with the masses will be through action: putting our ideas in practice, preaching by example; by this means only can the crowd be led. Yet we should be thoroughly aware that, in spite of all, these acts will have no effect upon the masses unless their understanding has been thoroughly prepared by a clear and well-defined propaganda, unless they themselves stand on their own feet, prompted by ideas previously received. Now, if we shall succeed in disseminating our ideas, their influence will make itself felt; and it is only on condition that we know how to explain and render them comprehensible that we shall have any chance of sharing in the social transformation. Hence we need not be afraid of not obtaining followers, but rather to be on the watch for hindrance from those who consider themselves leaders.

In times of revolution its precursors are always outdone by the masses. Let us spread our ideas, explain them, elucidate them, remodel them if necessary. Let us not fear to look the truth in the face. And this propaganda, far from alienating the adherents of our cause, cannot but help to attract thereto all who thirst after justice and liberty.

40. Gustav Landauer: Anarchism in Germany (1895)

Anarchistic ideas first received expression in Germany during the 18th century among members of the Illuminati, *a secret society for free thought that spread throughout German speaking areas in Europe. One of the founders of the* Illuminati, *Adam Wieshaupt (1748-1830), presented an address to the society in which he spoke of national states disappearing "from the face of the earth without violence," with reason becoming "the only law for humanity" (as quoted in Max Nettlau,* A Short History of Anarchism, *London: Freedom Press, 1996; originally published 1932-34, pp. 22-23). During the 1840's, a variety of writers adopted an anarchist position of one sort or another, not only Max Stirner, but also some of the other Young Hegelians, such as Arnold Ruge and Edgar Bauer, Karl Grün and the journalist Wilhelm Marr. Marx, Engels and their supporters in Germany engaged in lengthy polemics against anarchist ideas and actions, misrepresenting and even vilifying them. By the 1890's the German socialist movement was dominated by the orthodox Marxist Social Democratic Party. It was within the Social Democratic Party that Gustav Landauer (1870-1919) first became active in the socialist movement in the early 1890's, quickly associating himself with a dissident group of young libertarian socialists, the Berliner Jungen. He later wrote a critique of the Social Democratic Party, one of his few publications translated into English,* Social Democracy in Germany *(London: Freedom Press,*

1896). He was murdered in 1919 by troops sent by the then Social Democratic government to suppress the revolution in Bavaria, in which Landauer had played a prominent role. The following excerpts from Landauer's 1895 essay, "Anarchism in Germany," are taken from a selection of Laundauer's essays, which also includes "Social Democracy in Germany," published by the Barbary Coast Collective in San Francisco.

ANARCHISM'S LONE OBJECTIVE IS to reach a point at which the belligerence of some humans against humanity, in whatever form, comes to a halt. And with this end point in mind, people must transcend themselves in the spirit of brother and sisterhood, so that each individual, drawing on natural ability, can develop freely...

Anarchism seeks just one thing: the forging of alliances among all those advocating a common interest when one needs to wrest concessions from nature by engaging in difficult, daily struggle. And when interests among people diverge, individuals will simply follow their own discretion; and it is again the union of various confederations that will protect the individual from the harmful actions of any individuals. It should be guarded against, however, that these confederations take on disproportionate power. It is in this sense that we call ourselves anarchists: we are for the benefit of the multitude because we detest all violence which deprives [them of] enjoyment and autonomy as a result of deeply seeded cultural factors.

We repudiate, above all, the colossal image that impresses the delusive stamp of authority, leaving only the imprint of docile adoration behind. We are talking in particular about the rigid institutions of long historical standing, into which people are born and to which they accommodate themselves, whether they regard them as reasonable and beneficial or not. Especially when it comes to the organs of coercive state power, the individual has ultimately but one choice: submission. The lone justification being that those who came before acquiesced in the same way as their descendants now do. The alternative is to radically depart from the *terra firma* of received life, for today there remains hardly a corner where the state hasn't laid its peremptory hands...Currently, humanity's real redemption lies not in compulsion and spiritual tutelage, were it even with the best intentions, but rather in freedom.

On the basis of state-imposed servitude, reinforced by the blind faith the masses devote to musty traditionalists and other remnants of a bygone era—above all to dynasties and patriarchies—the oppressive system of privileged private wealth rests. No world traditions, not even those with the weight of millennia behind them, can make justify before anarchists the custom that so few are able to lay real claim to ownership of land. Those who enjoy the fruits of its bounty play no actual role in harvesting it, yet they deny its yield to their toiling fellow man. No earthly power or widespread prejudice will deter anarchists from the conviction that the deprived and destitute must name what is theirs, that which is due the last and most wretched among them: land on which to stand, to stroll, to rest, and to work. He who complacently enjoys custody of inherited "rights" and privilege, (a custody secured only by enclosure behind high walls) reposing on moneybags, has once and for all alms to pay. These alms are paid to the oppressive regime, and its armed footsoldiers—deployed as they are against the "enemy within"—whose continued power is secured by the dull patience and dissolute will of the masses. All this while enormous masses of people—who have the same talents and needs as the oppressors themselves—must eke out a pittance for such necessities as the clothing on their backs.

Anarchists do not even claim, however, that the majority of oppressed people today even consider themselves victims. It may also be the case that among our own ranks, compassion and love are not necessarily the right words to describe our deepest motives. As for my animating force, it lies in the repugnance at the humanity that encircles us, a rage at the indolence of the rich who blithely build their happiness on the ruins of the joyless existence of the dehumanized multitude. My rage dissipates not one iota when I consider the extent of the squalor to which the oppressed are subjected. As they emerged from the mother's womb, the haves and the have-nots are as indistinguishable as one egg is from another. And then, at the end of their miserable lives, spent as it is among the outcasts of society: slogging, these skeletons—the shadow remaining from an exhausting struggle for life—have scarcely enough money to bury their kin with dignity...

We contend that no language can be loud and decisive enough for the uplifting of our compatriots, so that they may be incited out of their engrained daily drudgery. A renewed social form must be spurred on, through the transcendence of the present spiritual inertia, in pursuit of energetic action, designed to break barriers, and to prepare new ground for our seed. *That* is propaganda of the deed, as I understand it. Everything else is passion, despair, or a great misconception. It hasn't a thing to do with killing people; rather, it regards the rejuvenation of human spirit and will along with the productive energies unleashed by large communities.

Large-scale communities, I say. For, it is a great mistake...that anarchism means individualism and therefore stands, when so misunderstood, in opposition to socialism. Certainly, socialism for us means something quite different from the "abolition of the private ownership of the means of production." Our socialism doesn't speak even of collective property, since behind it hides nothing other than the domination of a bureaucratic cabal. No, we speak rather of, to use Benedikt Friedlander's [libertarian socialist (1866-1908)], delightful expression, the "ownerlessness of nature's bounty." This means, once people have recognized their real interests, they will develop strong alliances that will guarantee everyone a share of the Earth's plenty. And when individuals or groups claim the means of production for their own purposes, then those remaining shall receive equitable compensation...

I have no misgivings in saying that strong organizations will exist in anarchist society too, just as I am certain that some already existing organizations will "grow into" Anarchism... by that I mean, the organizations of real producers, namely, the workers...Of course, it absolutely doesn't occur to us to construct an artifice of historical development, by which—as a matter of material necessity—the working class, to one extent or another, is called by Providence to take for itself the role of the present day ruling class, to say nothing of the founding of the dictatorship of the proletariat. I have no hesitation in clarifying that class struggle fails to have this meaning for me. I am in no way of the opinion that once an individual has passed a certain threshold of wealth, that he then becomes an irredeemable reprobate, undeserving of any place in the coming society. It is, obviously, no more a scandal to have been born a bourgeois than a proletarian. More to the point, we anarchists are ready to regard anyone, regardless of their social class of origin, who considers our perspective correct and is willing to live a life that comports with the consequences of this belief, as a comrade.

However, the person who has recognized the truth in Anarchism, will certainly not spend all his time in clubs or conventions disputing which method the future society will employ for the washing of dishes or the efficacious cleaning of boots. Rather, this person, as far as personal courage and station in life allow, will without doubt demand the step-by-step improvement of his life's condition. Insight alone tells him that the improvement of his economic lot, as present circumstances dictate, remains intimately linked with the success of vigorous mass actions by workers. As long as the owners and the powerful have at their disposal all of the means they allow themselves to uphold the wretched conditions of today, so too will organized people fight back with all allowable methods for the comprehensive improvement of their lot. We don't preach class war but we acknowledge that it is often forced on the persons who desire an improvement in their condition. It isn't a matter of the destruction of modern culture, it's rather a matter of a vast army of those previously locked out, and who have by now acquired an appetite to also sit at the table and feast.

Those barely keeping their heads above water, to say nothing of the jobless and down-trodden, are not well served by talk of revolution and future paradise. That's why relentless class struggle remains self-evident for those whose only recourse for the betterment of their life station, in today's society, is the determination of solidarity and the energy of engagement. The lower orders of society will never—in light of recent and mounting evidence of injustice—be brought so low as to accept a ceasefire in striving for the formation of a society which does everyone justice and therefore deserves the title "just."

Anarchists do not comprise a political party, since our scorn for the state forecloses our treading on the same ground with it and especially since we despise bargaining and haggling. We Anarchists want to be preachers: a revolution of spirit is, for us, the first order. What end can come from the obstinacy of today's elite when they repress the aspirations and desires of the masses of our people? We shall not abdicate responsibility, rather, we will quietly take it on, safe in the knowledge that future generations will thank us for helping them respect themselves once again. The consciousness that we will not only not see the culmination of our victory, but rather will suffer fresh disappointments and setbacks—to say nothing of persecution—will not hold us back. In spite of this, we will devote ourselves to our life's work and to the expansion of enlightenment to all layers of society. We think, along with Schopenhauer: "Life is short and even though truth appears remote, the truth lives long: so tell the truth!" Of course, most anyone, after a bit of honest and courageous study, can name his own truth. Whoever believes it is in order to demand the imposition of "his Truth" along with the violent suppression of those with a divergent belief, may wish to wander down that road. The anarchists will walk down theirs.

41. Kropotkin: On Anarchism (1896)

Kropotkin wrote several articles and pamphlets on anarchism, one of his better known being his often reprinted essay, "Anarchism: Its Philosophy and Ideal," first published in 1896 (reprinted in Fugitive Writings, *Montreal: Black Rose Books, 1993, ed. George Woodcock), which sets forth Kropotkin's conception of anarchy as an efflorescence of free associations.*

IN PROPORTION AS THE HUMAN MIND frees itself from ideas inculcated by minorities of priests, military chiefs and judges, all striving to establish their domination, and of scientists paid to perpetuate it, a conception of society arises in which there is no longer room for those dominating minorities. A society entering into possession of the social capital accumulated by the labour of preceding generations, organizing itself so as to make use of this capital in the interests of all, and constituting itself without reconstituting the power of the ruling minorities. It comprises in its midst an infinite variety of capacities, temperaments and individual energies: it excludes none. It even calls for struggles and contentions; because we know that periods of contests, so long as they were freely fought out without the weight of constituted authority being thrown on one side of the balance, were periods when human genius took its mightiest flights and achieved the greatest aims. Acknowledging, as a fact, the equal rights of its members to the treasures accumulated in the past, it no longer recognizes a division between exploited and exploiters, governed and governors, dominated and dominators, and it seeks to establish a certain harmonious compatibility in its midst—not by subjecting all its members to an authority that is fictitiously supposed to represent society, not by crying to establish uniformity, but by urging all men to develop free initiative, free action, free association.

It seeks the most complete development of individuality combined with the highest development of voluntary association in all its aspects, in all possible degrees, for all imaginable aims; ever changing, ever modified associations which carry in themselves the elements of their durability and constantly assume new forms which answer best to the multiple aspirations of all.

A society to which pre-established forms, crystallized by law, are repugnant; which looks for harmony in an ever-changing and fugitive equilibrium between a multitude of varied forces and influences of every kind, following their own course,—these forces themselves promoting the energies which are favourable to their march towards progress, towards the liberty of developing in broad daylight and counterbalancing one another.

...[I]f man, since his origin, has always lived in societies, the State is but one of the forms of social life, quite recent as far as regards European societies. Men lived thousands of years before the first States were constituted; Greece and Rome existed for centuries before the Macedonian and Roman Empires were built up, and for us modern Europeans the centralized States date but from the sixteenth century. It was only then, after the defeat of the free medieval communes had been completed that the mutual insurance company between military, judicial, landlord, and capitalist authority, which we call the "State," could be fully established...

We know well the means by which this association of lord, priest, merchant, judge, soldier, and king founded its domination. It was by the annihilation of all free unions: of village communities, guilds, trades unions, fraternities, and medieval cities. It was by confiscating the land of the communes and the riches of the guilds. It was by the absolute and ferocious prohibition of all kinds of free agreement between men. It was by massacre, the wheel, the gibbet, the sword, and fire that church and State established their domination, and that they succeeded henceforth to reign over an incoherent agglomeration of "subjects" who had no more direct union among themselves.

It is only recently that we began to reconquer, by struggle, by revolt, the first steps of the right of association that was freely practiced by the artisans and the tillers of the soil through the whole of the middle ages.

And, already now, Europe is covered by thousands of voluntary associations for study and teaching, for industry, commerce, science, art, literature, exploitation, resistance to exploitation, amusement, serious work, gratification and self-denial, for all that makes up the life of an active and thinking being. We see these societies rising in all nooks and corners of all domains: political, economic, artistic, intellectual. Some are as short lived as roses, some hold their own for several decades, and all strive—while maintaining the independence of each group, circle, branch, or section—to federate, to unite, across frontiers as well as among each nation; to cover all the life of civilized men with a net, meshes of which are intersected and interwoven. Their numbers can already be reckoned by tens of thousands, they comprise millions of adherents—although less than fifty years have elapsed since church and State began to tolerate a few of them—very few, indeed.

These societies already begin to encroach everywhere on the functions of the State, and strive to substitute free action of volunteers for that of a centralized State. In England we see insurance companies arise against theft; societies for coast defence, volunteer societies for land defence, which the State endeavours to get under its thumb, thereby making them instruments of domination, although their original aim was to do without the State. Were it not for church and State, free societies would have already conquered the whole of the immense domain of education. And, in spite of all difficulties, they begin to invade this domain as well, and make their influence already felt.

And when we mark the progress already accomplished in that direction, in spite of and against the State, which tries by all means to maintain its supremacy of recent origin; when we see how voluntary societies invade everything and are only impeded in their development by the State, we are forced to recognize a powerful *tendency*, a latent force in modern society. And we ask ourselves this question: If five, ten, or twenty years hence—it matters little—the workers succeed by revolt in destroying the said mutual insurance societies of landlords, bankers, priests, judges, and soldiers; if the people become masters of their destiny for a few months, and lay hands on the riches they have created, and which belong to them by right—will they really begin to reconstitute that blood-sucker, the State? Or will they not rather try to organize from the simple to the complex according to mutual agreement and to the infinitely varied, ever-changing needs of each locality, in order to secure the possession of those riches for themselves, to mutually guarantee one another's life, and to produce what will be found necessary for life?

...It is often said that anarchists live in a world of dreams to come, and do not see the things which happen today. We see them only too well, and in their true colours, and that is what makes us carry the hatchet into the forest of prejudices that besets us.

Far from living in a world of visions and imagining men better than they are, we see them as they are; and that is why we affirm that the best of men is made essentially bad by the exercise of authority, and that the theory of the "balancing of powers" and "control of authorities" is a hypocritical formula, invented by those who have seized power, to make the "sovereign people," whom they despise, believe that the people themselves are governing. It is because we know men that we say to those who imagine that men would devour one another without those governors: "You reason like the king, who, being sent across the frontier, called out, 'What will become of my poor subjects without me?' "

Ah, if men were those superior beings that the utopians of authority like to speak to us of, if we could close our eyes to reality and live like them in a world of dreams and illusions as to the superiority of those who think themselves called to power, perhaps we also should do like them; perhaps we also should believe in the virtues of those who govern.

If the gentlemen in power were really so intelligent and so devoted to the public cause, as panegyrists of authority love to represent, what a pretty government and paternal utopia we should be able to construct! The employer would never be the tyrant of the worker; he would be the father! The factory would be a palace of delight, and never would masses of workers be doomed to physical deterioration. A judge would not have the ferocity to condemn the wife and children of the one whom he sends to prison to suffer years of hunger and misery and to die some day of anemia; never would a public prosecutor ask for the head of the accused for the unique pleasure of showing off his oratorical talent; and nowhere would we find a jailer or an executioner to do the bidding of judges who have not the courage to carry out their sentences themselves.

Oh, the beautiful utopia, the lovely Christmas dream we can make as soon as we admit that those who govern represent a superior caste, and have hardly any or no knowledge of simple mortals' weaknesses! It would then suffice to make them control one another in hierarchical fashion, to let them exchange fifty papers, at most, among different administrators, when the wind blows down a tree on the national road. Or, if need be, they would have only to be valued at their proper worth, during elections, by those same masses of mortals which are supposed to be endowed with all stupidity in their mutual relations but become wisdom itself when they have to elect their masters.

All the science of government, imagined by those who govern, is imbued with these utopias. But we know men too well to dream such dreams. We have not two measures for the virtues of the governed and those of the governors; we know that we ourselves are not without faults and that the best of us would soon be corrupted by the exercise of power. We take men for what they are worth—and that is why we hate the government of man by man, and why we work with all our might—perhaps not strong enough—to put an end to it.

But it is not enough to destroy. We must also know how to build, and it is owing to not having thought about it that the masses have always been led astray in all their revolutions. After having demolished they abandoned the care of reconstruction to the middle-class people who possessed a more or less precise conception of what they wished to realize, and who consequently reconstituted authority to their own advantage.

That is why anarchism, when it works to destroy authority in all its aspects, when it demands the abrogation of laws and the abolition of the mechanism that serves to impose them, when it refuses all hierarchical organization and preaches free agreement, at the same time strives to maintain and enlarge the precious kernel of social customs without which no human or animal society can exist. Only instead of demanding that those social customs should be maintained through the authority of a few, it demands it from the continued action of all.

42. E. Armand: Mini-Manual of the Anarchist Individualist (1911)

Individualist anarchism, by its very nature, could never aspire to become a revolutionary movement; it will always be a form of individual rebellion against authority. However, by the 1890's, thanks in large part to the influence of the German philosopher, Friedrich Nietzsche (1844-1900), and the rediscovery of Max Stirner, individualist anarchism began to attract a number of adherents, one of the most eloquent and prolific being E. Armand (1872-1962, pseudonym of Ernest Lucien Juin), who wrote the following "Mini-Manual of the Anarchist Individualist" in 1911. As with his older American counterpart, the individualist anarchist Benjamin Tucker (1854-1939), Armand's anarchism is a curious amalgam of Proudhonian economics and Stirnerian amoralism. The translation is by Paul Sharkey.

TO BE AN ANARCHIST IS TO DENY authority and reject its economic corollary: exploitation. And in every sphere of human activity at that. The anarchist seeks to live without gods or masters; without bosses or leaders; a-legally, bereft of laws as well as of prejudices; amorally, free of obligations as well as of collective morality. He wishes to live freely, to live out his own particular conception of life. In his heart of hearts he is always an a-social being, a refractory, an outsider, an onlooker, a watcher from the sidelines, a misfit. And though he may be obliged to live in a society the very make-up of which is offensive to his temperament, he moves through it like an alien. If, within it, he makes the necessary concessions—albeit with the after-thought that he can call them back—lest he risk or sacrifice his life foolishly or to no purpose, this is because he looks upon them as personal weapons in his defence of self in the struggle for existence. The anarchist aims to live his life as fully as possible, morally, intellectually and economically, without bothering about the rest of the world, be they exploiters or exploited: without any thought of lording it over or exploiting others, but ready to retaliate with all the means at his disposal against any who might meddle in his life or forbid him to express his thinking in writing or by word of mouth.

The anarchist's enemy is the State and all the institutions designed to maintain or perpetuate its hold upon the individual. There is no reconciliation possible between the anarchist and any form of society built upon authority, whether it be vested in an autocrat, an aristocracy or a democracy. No common ground between the anarchist and any setting governed by the decisions of a majority or the whims of an elite. The anarchist arms himself equally against State-supplied education and that dispensed by the Church. He is the adversary of Monopolies and privileges, whether they be intellectual, moral or economic. In short, he is the irreconcilable opponent of all rule, every social system and every state of affairs that implies the lordship of man or milieu over the individual and exploitation of the individual by fellow-man or milieu.

The anarchist's handiwork is above all a critical endeavour. The anarchist goes on his way sowing revolt against that which oppresses, hobbles or works against the unfettered development of the individual. For a start, we must rid our minds of preconceived notions, liberate temperaments fettered by fear and create minds released from fretting about other people's reactions and the conventions of society: at which point the anarchist will encourage those willing to be his fellow-travellers to mount a practical rebellion against the determinism of their social context, to assert their individuality, sculpt their self-image and achieve the greatest possible independence from their moral, intellectual and economic surroundings. He will urge the ignoramus to educate himself, the lackadaisical to shake a leg, the weak to become strong, the stooped to hold himself erect. He will urge the under-endowed and less apt to delve deep within themselves for every possible resource rather than to look to others…

He does not believe that the ills from which men suffer derive exclusively from capitalism, nor from private property. He considers that they are primarily due to the flawed mentality of men, taken as a block. The masters are only such because there are slaves, and gods only subsist because of the faithful on their knees. The individualist anarchist has no interest in violent revolution designed to switch the mode of product-distribution to collectivist or communist lines, which would bring scarcely any change in the general mind-set and would do nothing to hasten the emancipation of the individual. The latter would be as much of a subordinate under a communist system as he is today to the benevolence of the Milieu: he would be as poor and as wretched as he is now. Instead of being under the yoke of the present tiny capitalist minority, he would be overwhelmed by the economic machine. He would have nothing that he could call his own. He would be a producer, a consumer, a net contributor to or borrower from the common store, but autonomous? Never.

The individualist anarchist stands apart from the communist anarchist in this regard, that (besides ownership of the consumer goods representing an extension of his personality) he regards ownership of the means of production and free disposal of his produce as the quintessential guarantee of the autonomy of the individual. The understanding is that such ownership boils down to the chance to deploy (as individuals, couples, family groups, etc.) the requisite plot of soil or machinery of production to meet the requirements of the social unit, provided that the proprietor does not transfer it to someone else or rely upon the services of someone else in operating it.

The individualist anarchist draws the line at living at any price…He argues that he has an entitlement to defend himself against any social context (State, society, milieu, grouping, etc.) that will countenance, agree to, perpetuate, sanction or facilitate:

a) subordination of the individual to the milieu, the former being placed in a manifestly inferior position in that he cannot deal with the other on a man-to-man, equal-to-equal basis;

b) (in any context) mandatory mutual aid, solidarity and association;

c) denial of the individual's inalienable title to the means of production and to the full and unrestricted disposal of produce;

d) the exploitation of anyone by one of his neighbours who will set him to work in his employ and for his benefit;

e) greed, which is to say the opportunity for an individual, couple or family group to own more than strictly required for their normal upkeep;

f) the monopoly enjoyed by the State or any form of executive which might take its place, which is to say its meddling in a centralizing, administrative, directive or organizational capacity in relations between individuals, in any sphere whatever;

g) lending for interest, usury, speculation, monetary exchange rates, inheritance, etc.

...Relations between individualist anarchists are founded upon a basis of "reciprocity." "Comradeship" is essentially on an individual basis and is never imposed. A "comrade" is someone with whom they, as individuals, are pleased to associate, someone who makes an appreciable effort to feel alive, who participates in their propagation of educational criticism and selection of persons; who respects the individual's style of life and does not trespass against the development of his fellow-traveller and his nearest and dearest.

The individualist anarchist is never slave to some model formula or received text. He acknowledges only opinions. He has only theses to propose. And acknowledges no boundary. If he espouses a particular lifestyle, it is in order to derive greater freedom, greater happiness, greater well-being from it and not in order to sacrifice himself to it. And he tinkers with it and reshapes it when he realizes that remaining faithful to it would do injury to his autonomy. He has no desire to let himself be governed by *a priori* principles: he builds his behavioural code, *a posteriori*, upon his experiences and it is never final and is at all times subject to such amendments and changes as further experience and the need to equip himself with fresh weapons in his battle with his surroundings may recommend...

The individualist anarchist is only ever answerable to himself for his deeds and actions.

The individualist anarchist looks upon association merely as an expedient, a makeshift arrangement. So only in urgent circumstances is he willing to enter into association and then only of his own free will. And, as a general rule, he is willing to enter into short-term arrangements only, it being understood throughout that every contract can be voided the moment it injures one of the contracting parties.

The individualist anarchist lays down no specific sexual morality. It is up to every individual, of whichever sex, to determine his or her own sexual, emotional or sentimental life. The essential point is that in intimate relations between anarchists of different sexes, violence and constraint should play no part. He considers that economic independence and control of her fertility are the prerequisites for the emancipation of woman.

The individualist anarchist wants to live, wants to be able to enjoy life—life in all its manifestations—as an individual. While retaining mastery of his will and looking upon his knowledge, his faculties, his senses and his body's many organs of perception as so many servants at the disposal of his "ego." He does not run scared but refuses to be belittled. And knows very well that anyone who lets himself be carried away by his emotions or ruled by his inclinations is a slave. He seeks to hold on to his "mastery of self" in order to embark upon whatever adventures his individual questing and speculation may suggest…

The individualist anarchist will take a hand in associations formed by certain comrades with an eye to shrugging off the obsession of a Milieu that they find repugnant. Refusal to perform military service and to pay taxes can expect his whole-hearted sympathy; free unions, singular or multiple, by way of protests against the established morality; illegalism (with certain reservations) as a violent break with an economic compact imposed by force; abstinence from any act, any toil, any function that implies maintenance or consolidation of the imposed intellectual, ethical or economic system; trading of basic necessities between individualist anarchists owning the requisite machinery of production, dispensing with any capitalist intermediary, etc.—these are the acts of revolt essentially consonant with the individualist anarchist character.

Chapter 10
Propaganda By The Deed

43. Paul Brousse: Propaganda By the Deed (1877)

Propaganda by the deed is often wrongly equated with terrorism, when it really means nothing more than leading by example, on the basis that actions speak louder than words. While this concept was articulated by earlier revolutionaries, such as Carlo Pisacane (Selection 16) and Bakunin (Selection 28), it was made current by Paul Brousse (1844-1912), at the time one of the most militant members of the anti-authoritarian International, whose article on the subject was printed in the Bulletin of the Jura Federation *in August 1877, translated here by Paul Sharkey. The events referred to involved a demonstration in Berne, Switzerland, in which Brousse took part, where the workers showed the revolutionary red flag, and an abortive uprising in Benevento, Italy, in which Cafiero and Malatesta participated.*

OF WHAT DO THE MASSES CONSIST? Of peasants, workers, most of the time toiling eleven and twelve hours per day. They make their way home worn out from fatigue and have little inclination to read socialist pamphlets or newspapers: they sleep, they go for a stroll or devote their evenings to the family.

Well, what if there is a way of grabbing these people's attention, of showing them what they cannot read, of teaching them socialism by means of actions and making them see, feel, touch?...When one resorts to that line of reasoning one is on the trail that leads, beside theoretical propaganda, to propaganda by the deed.

Propaganda by the deed is a mighty means of rousing the popular consciousness. Let us take an example. Prior to the Paris Commune, who in France was conversant with the principle of communal autonomy? No one. Yet Proudhon had written magnificent books. Who read those books? A handful of literati. But once the idea was brought out into the open air, in the heart of the capital, onto the steps of the City Hall, when it took on flesh and life, it shook the peasant in his cottage, the worker at his fireside, and peasants and workers alike had to reflect on this huge question mark posted in the public square. Now that idea made inroads. In France, right around the world, for or against, everybody has picked his side...

Once attention has been aroused, it needs to be given sustenance. So the deed must contain at least one lesson.

Take for example the 18 March [1877] demonstration in Berne.

The Swiss bourgeoisie nurtures in the mind of the Swiss workingman a prejudice that he enjoys every possible freedom. We never weary of repeating to him: "No serious public freedom without economic equality. And what is it that underpins inequality? The State!" The people has little grasp of such abstractions; but offer it a tangible fact and it gets the point. Show it the article in the constitution allowing him to bring out the red flag, then bring out that flag: the State and the police will attack him; defend him: crowds will show up for the ensuing meeting; a few words of plain talk, and the people get the point. 18 March 1877 was a practical demonstration laid on for Swiss working folk in the public square, that they do not, as they thought they did, enjoy freedom.

Our friends from Benevento went one better. They did not bother to demonstrate just one self-evident fact to the people. They took over two small communes, and there, by burning the archives, they showed the people how much respect they should have for property. They handed tax monies back to the people and the weapons that had been confiscated from them; in so doing they showed the people the sort of contempt they should have for government. Is it not possible that the people said to itself: "We should be a lot happier if what these good young fellows want were some day to come to pass!" From that to helping them is but a step and a step easily taken.

We could go further.

Just once take over a commune, introduce collective ownership there, organize the trades bodies and production, district groups and consumption; let the instruments of production be placed in the hands of the workers, let the workers and their families move into salubrious accommodation and the idlers be tossed into the streets; if attacked, fight back, defend oneself, and if one loses, what matter? The idea will have been launched, not on paper, not in a newspaper, not on a chart; no longer will it be sculpted in marble, carved in stone nor cast in bronze: having sprung to life, it will march, in flesh and blood, at the head of the people.

And the people will salute it as it goes on its way.

44. Carlo Cafiero: Action (1880)

Despite the failure of the 1877 Benevento uprising, Carlo Cafiero continued to advocate revolutionary action, as he did in this 1880 article published in Le Révolté, *which has sometimes been wrongly attributed to Kropotkin. The translation is by Nicolas Walter, and is reprinted with the kind permission of Christine Walter.*

"IDEALS SPRING FROM DEEDS, and not the other way round," said Carlo Pisacane in his political testament, and he was right. It is the people who make progress as well as revolution: the constructive and destructive aspects of the same process. It is the people who are sacrificed every day to maintain universal production, and it is the people again who feed with their blood the torch which lights up human destiny...Just as the deed gave rise to the revolutionary idea, so it is the deed again which must put it into practice...

So it is action which is needed, action and action again. In taking action, we are working at the same time for theory and for practice, for it is action which gives rise to ideas, and which is also responsible for spreading them across the world.

But what kind of action shall we take? Should we go or send others on our behalf to Parliament, or even to municipal councils? No, a thousand times No! We have nothing to do with the intrigues of the bourgeoisie. We have no need to get involved with the games of our oppressors, unless we wish to take part in their oppression. "To go to Parliament is to parley; and to parley is to make peace," said a German ex-revolutionary, who did plenty of parleying after that.

Our action must be permanent rebellion, by word, by writing, by dagger, by gun, by dynamite, sometimes even by ballot when it is a case of voting for an ineligible candidate like Blanqui or Trinquet. We are consistent, and we shall use every weapon which can be used for rebellion. Everything is right for us which is not legal.

"But when should we begin to take our action, and open our attack?" friends sometimes ask us. "Shouldn't we wait until our strength is organized? To attack before you are ready is to expose yourself and risk failure."

Friends, if we go on waiting until we are strong enough before attacking—we shall never attack, and we shall be like the good man who vowed that he wouldn't go into the sea until he had learned to swim. It is precisely revolutionary action which develops our strength, just as exercise develops the strength of our muscles...

How shall we begin our action?

Just look for an opportunity, and it will soon appear. Everywhere that rebellion can be sensed and the sound of battle can be heard, that is where we must be. Don't wait to take part in a movement which appears with the label of official socialism on it. Every popular movement already carries with it the seeds of the revolutionary socialism: we must take part in it to ensure its growth. A clear and precise ideal of revolution is formulated only by an infinitesimal minority, and if we wait to take part in a struggle which appears exactly as we have imagined it in our minds—we shall wait forever. Don't imitate the dogmatists who ask for the formula before anything else: the people carry the living revolution in their hearts, and we must fight and die with them.

And when the supporters of legal or parliamentary action come and criticize us for not having anything to do with the people when they vote, we shall reply to them: "Certainly, we refuse to have anything to do with the people when they are down on their knees in front of their god, their king, or their master; but we shall always be with them when they are standing upright against their powerful enemies. *For us, abstention from politics is not abstention from revolution; our refusal to take part in any parliamentary, legal or reactionary action is the measure of our devotion to a violent and anarchist revolution, to the revolution of the rabble and the poor.*"

45. Kropotkin: Expropriation (1885)

Kropotkin's 1885 collection of articles, Words of a Rebel *(Montreal: Black Rose Books, 1992), contains some of his most revolutionary writings from* Le Révolté, *the anarchist paper Kropotkin helped found in 1879. In this passage from the chapter on revolutionary government, translated by Nicolas Walter, Kropotkin argues, much as Varlet had before him (Selection 5), that "revolutionary government" is a contradiction in terms:*

TO OVERTHROW A GOVERNMENT—this is everything for a bourgeois revolutionary. For us, it is only the beginning of the Social Revolution. Once the machine of the State is out of order, the hierarchy of officials fallen into disarray and no longer knowing which direction to move in, the soldiers losing confidence in their leaders—in a word, once the army of the defenders of Capital is put to flight—it is then that the great work of the destruction of the institutions which serve to perpetuate economic and political slavery arises before us. The possibility of acting freely is acquired—what are the revolutionaries going to do?

To this question it is only the anarchists who reply: "No government, anarchy!" All the others say: "A revolutionary government!" They differ only over the form to give this government. Some want it elected by universal suffrage, as a State or as a Commune; others declare for a revolutionary dictatorship. A "revolutionary government!" These two words sound very strangely to those who realize what the Social

Revolution should mean and what a government does mean. The two words contradict one another, destroy one another. We have of course seen despotic governments—it is the essence of all government to take the side of reaction against the revolution, and to have an inevitable tendency towards despotism—but we have never seen a revolutionary government, and for a good reason. It is that revolution—the synonym of "disorder," of the upsetting and overthrowing in a few days of time-honoured institutions, of the violent demolition of the established forms of property, the destruction of castes, the rapid transformation of received ideas about morality (or rather about the hypocrisy which takes its place), of individual liberty, and of spontaneous action—is precisely the opposite, the negation of government, this being the synonym of "established order," of conservatism, of the maintenance of existing institutions, the negation of initiative and individual action...

In order that the taking possession of the social wealth should become an accomplished fact, it is necessary that the people should have a free hand, that they should shake off the slavery to which they are too much accustomed, that they should act according to their own will, that they should move forward without waiting for orders from anyone...

The economic change which will result from the Social Revolution will be so immense and so profound, it must so change all the relations based today on property and exchange, that it is impossible for one or any individual to elaborate the different forms which must spring up in the society of the future. This elaboration of new social forms can be made only by the collective work of the masses. To satisfy the immense variety of conditions and needs which will spring up as soon as private property is abolished, it is necessary to have the flexibility of the collective spirit of the country. Any external authority will only be a hindrance, an obstacle to that organic work which should be done, and besides a source of discord and hatred...

For us who understand that the moment is near for giving a mortal blow to the bourgeoisie, that the time is not far off when the people will be able to lay hands on all social wealth and reduce the class of exploiters to impotence—for us, I say, there can be no hesitation in the matter. We shall throw ourselves body and soul into the social revolution, and since on this path a government, whatever colour it wears, is an obstacle, we shall reduce to impotence and sweep away all ambitious men who try to impose themselves upon us as rulers of our destinies. Enough of governments; make way for the people, for anarchy!

In the chapter on expropriation, translated by George Woodcock, Kropotkin sets forth in more detail how to make the social revolution:

If social wealth remains in the hands of the few who possess it today; if the factory, the warehouse and the workshop remain the property of the owner; if the railways and the other means of transport continue in the hands of the companies and individuals who have made them monopolies; if the mansions in the cities and the villas of landlords remain in the possession of their present owners instead of being placed, on the day of the revolution, at the free disposition of all the workers; if all the accumulated treasures, in the banks or in the houses of the rich, do not return immediately to the collectivity—because all of us have contributed to produce them; if the insurgent people does not take possession of all the goods and provisions accumulated in the great cities and does not organize affairs so that they are put at the disposal of those who need them; if the land, finally, remains the property of bankers and usurers—to whom it belongs today, in fact if not by right—and if the great properties are not taken away from the great proprietors to be placed in the hands of those who wish to cultivate the soil; if, finally, there emerges a new class of rulers who give orders to the ruled, the insurrection will not have been a revolution, and we shall have to start all over again...

Expropriation—that is the guiding word of the coming revolution, without which it will fail in its historic mission: the complete expropriation of all those who have the means of exploiting human beings; the return to the community...of everything that in the hands of anyone can be used to exploit others...

If on the morrow of the revolution the popular masses have only words at their disposal, if they do not recognize by facts whose evidence is as blinding as sunlight that the situation has been transformed to their advantage, and if the overturning of power ends up as merely a change of persons and formulas, nothing will have been achieved. There will remain only one more disillusionment. And we shall have to put ourselves once again to the ungrateful task of Sisyphus, rolling his eternal rock.

For the revolution to be anything more than a word, for the reaction not to lead us on the morrow to the same situation as on the eve, the conquest on the day itself must be worth the trouble of defending; the poor of yesterday must not find themselves even poorer today...

Only a general expropriation can satisfy the multitudes who suffer and are oppressed...But for expropriation to respond to the need, which is to put an end to private property and return all to all, it must be carried out on a vast scale. On a small scale, it will be seen only as a mere pillage; on a large scale it is the beginning of social reorganization...

Without the gardens and fields that give us produce indispensable for life, without the granaries, the warehouses, the shops that gather together the products of work, without the factories and workshops that provide textiles and metalwork, without the means of defence, without the railways and other ways of communication that allow us to exchange our products with the neighbouring free communes and combine our efforts for resistance and attack, we are condemned in advance to perish; we shall stifle like a fish out of water which can no longer breathe though bathed entirely in the vast ocean of air…

But destroy without delay everything that should be overthrown; the penal fortresses and the prisons, the forts directed against the towns and the unhealthy quarters where you have so long breathed an air heavy with poison. Install yourselves in the palaces and mansions, and make a bonfire of the piles of bricks and worm-eaten wood that were your hovels. The instinct to destroy, which is so natural and so just because it is also an urge to renew, will find much to satisfy it. So many outworn things to replace! For everything will have to be remade: houses, whole towns, agricultural and industrial plant, in fact every material aspect of society.

46. Jean Grave: Means and Ends (1893)

In these passages from Moribund Society and Anarchy, *Jean Grave emphasizes the need for anarchist methods to be consistent with anarchist ends.*

AT THE OUTSET ANARCHISTS MUST renounce the warfare of army against army, battles arrayed on fields, struggles laid out by strategists and tacticians maneuvering armed bodies as the chess-player maneuvers his figures upon the chess-board. The struggle should be directed chiefly towards the destruction of institutions. The burning up of deeds, registers of land-surveys, proceedings of notaries and solicitors, tax-collectors' books; the ignoring of the limits of holdings, destruction of the regulations of the civil staff, etc.; the expropriation of the capitalists, taking possession in the name of all, putting articles of consumption freely at the disposal of all—all this is the work of small and scattered groups, of skirmishes, not regular battles. And this is the warfare which the Anarchists must seek to encourage everywhere in order to harass government, compel them to scatter their forces; tire them out and decimate them piecemeal. No need of leaders for blows like these; as soon as someone realizes what should be done he preaches by example, acting so as to attract others to him, who follow him if they are partisans of the enterprise but do not, by the fact of their adherence, abdicate their own initiative in following him who seems most fit to direct the enterprise, especially since someone else may, in the course of the struggle, perceive the possibility of another maneuver, whereupon he will not go and ask authority from the first to make the attempt but will make it known to those who are struggling with him. These, in turn, will assist or reject the undertaking as seems most practicable.

In Anarchy those who know teach those who do not know; the first to conceive an idea puts it into practice, explaining it to those whom he wishes to interest in it. But there is no temporary abdication, no authority; there are only equals who mutually aid each other according to their respective faculties, abandoning none of their rights, no part of their autonomy. The surest means of making Anarchy triumph is to act like an Anarchist...

"The end justifies the means" is the motto of the Jesuits, which some Anarchists have thought fit to apply to Anarchy, but which is not in reality applicable save to him who seeks egoistic satisfaction for his purely personal needs, without troubling himself about those whom he wounds or crushes by the way. When satisfaction is sought in the exercise of justice and solidarity the means employed must always be adapted to the end, under pain of producing the exact contrary of one's expectations.

47. Leo Tolstoy: On Non-violent Resistance (1900)

Although Tolstoy (1828-1910) rejected the anarchist label, he also rejected all forms of coercive power and advocated non-violent resistance to authority. Tolstoy's main disagreement with the anarchists was over the question of violence. On other issues, he wrote, "The Anarchists are right...in the negation of the existing order, and in the assertion that, without Authority, there could not be worse violence than that of Authority under existing conditions. They are mistaken only in thinking that Anarchy can be instituted by a revolution" (from "On Anarchy," in Government is Violence: Essays on Anarchism and Pacifism, *London: Phoenix Press, 1990, page 68). The following excerpts are taken from his 1900 pamphlet,* The Slavery of Our Times.

APART FROM OUTBURSTS OF REVENGE or anger, violence is used only in order to compel some people, against their own will, to do the will of others. But the necessity to do what other people wish against your own will is slavery. And, therefore, as long as any violence, designed to compel some people to do the will of others, exists, there will be slavery.

All the attempts to abolish slavery by violence are like extinguishing fire with fire, stopping water with water, or filling up one hole by digging another. Therefore, the means of escape from slavery, if such means exist, must be found, not in setting up fresh violence, but in abolishing whatever renders governmental violence possible...

People must feel that their participation in the criminal activity of Governments, whether by giving part of their work in the form of money, or by direct participation in military service, is not, as is generally supposed, an indifferent action, but, besides being harmful to oneself and one's brothers, is a participation in the crimes unceasingly committed by all Governments and a preparation for new crimes which Governments, by maintaining disciplined armies, are always preparing.

The age of veneration for Governments, notwithstanding all the hypnotic influence they employ to maintain their position, is more and more passing away. And it is time for people to understand that not only are Governments not necessary, but are harmful and most highly immoral institutions, in which an honest, self-respecting man cannot and must not take part, and the advantages of which he cannot and should not enjoy.

And as soon as people clearly understand that, they will naturally cease to take part in such deeds—that is, cease to give the Governments soldiers and money. And as soon as a majority of people ceases to do this, the fraud which enslaves people will be abolished. Only in this way can people be freed from slavery.

...[I]f a man, whether slave or slave owner, really wishes to better not *his* position alone, but the position of people in general, he must not himself do those wrong things which enslave him and his brothers. In order not to do the evil which produces misery for himself and for his brothers, he should firstly *neither willingly nor under compulsion take any part in Government activity, and should therefore be neither a soldier, nor a Field Marshal, nor a Minister of State, nor a tax collector, nor a witness, nor an alderman, nor a juryman, nor a governor, nor a Member of Parliament, nor, in fact, hold any office connected with violence.* That is one thing.

Secondly, *such a man should not voluntarily pay taxes to Governments, either directly or indirectly; nor should he accept money collected by taxes, either as salary, or as pension, or as a reward; nor should he make use of Government institutions, supported by taxes collected by violence from the people.* That is the second thing.

Thirdly, such a man *should not appeal to Government violence for the protection of his own possessions in land or in other things, nor to defend him and his near ones; but should only possess land and all products of his own or other people's toil in so far as others do not claim them from him.* "But such an activity is impossible; to refuse all participation in Government affairs, means to refuse to live," is what people will say. "A man who refuses military service will be imprisoned; a man who does not pay taxes will be punished, and the tax will be collected from his property; a man who, having no other means of livelihood, refuses Government service, will perish of hunger with his family; the same will befall a man who rejects Government protection for his property and his person; not to make use of things that are taxed, or of Government institutions, is quite impossible, as the most necessary articles are often taxed; and just in the same way it is impossible to do without Government institutions, such as the post, the roads, etc."

It is quite true that it is difficult for a man of our times to stand aside from all participation in Government violence. But the fact that not everyone can so arrange his life as not to participate, in some degree, in Government violence, does not at all show that it is not possible to free oneself from it more and more. Not every man will have the strength to refuse conscription (though there are and will be such men), but each man can abstain from voluntarily entering the army, the police force, and the judicial or revenue service; and can give the preference to a worse paid private service rather than to a better paid public service.

Not every man will have the strength to renounce his landed estates (though there are people who do that), but every man can, understanding the wrongfulness of such property, diminish its extent. Not every man can renounce the possession of capital (there are some who do), or the use of articles defended by violence, but each man can, by diminishing his own requirements, be less and less in need of articles which provoke other people to envy. Not every official can renounce his Government salary (though there are men who prefer hunger to dishonest Government employment), but every one can prefer a smaller salary to a larger one for the sake of having duties less bound up with violence. Not every one can refuse to make use of government schools (although there are some who do), but every one can give the preference to private schools, and each can make less and less use of articles that are taxed, and of Government institutions.

Between the existing order, based on brute force, and the ideal of a society based on reasonable agreement confirmed by custom, there are an infinite number of steps, which mankind are ascending, and the approach to the ideal is only accomplished to the extent to which people free themselves from participation in violence, from taking advantage of it, and from being accustomed to it...

There is only one way to abolish Government violence: that people should abstain from participating in violence. Therefore, whether it be difficult or not to abstain from participating in governmental violence, and whether the good results of such abstinence will or will not be soon apparent, are superfluous questions; because to liberate people from slavery there is only that one way, and no other!

48. Errico Malatesta: Violence as a Social Factor (1895)

Errico Malatesta (1853-1932) was renowned in the international anarchist movement as an organizer, revolutionary, editor and writer. He began his career in the Italian Federation of the First International, associated with Bakunin. He was one of the first Internationalists to adopt an anarchist communist position. He was with Carlo Cafiero at Benevento, and was imprisoned many times for his revolutionary activities. He was active not only in Italy, but also in Latin America, the United States and England. The following article, "Violence as a Social Factor," was first published in the English anarchist paper, The Torch, *in April 1895, in response to some comments by a pacifist named T.H. Bell criticizing anarchists for having recourse to violence and terrorism.*

VIOLENCE, I.E., PHYSICAL FORCE used to another's hurt, which is the most brutal form the struggle between men can assume, is eminently corrupting. It tends, by its very nature, to suffocate the best sentiments of man, and to develop all the anti-social qualities: ferocity, hatred, revenge, the spirit of domination and tyranny, contempt of the weak, servility towards the strong.

And this harmful tendency arises also when violence is used for a good end. The love of justice which impelled one to the struggle, amid all the good original intentions, is not sufficient guarantee against the depraving influence exerted by violence on the mind and actions of him who uses it. In the whirl of battle one too often loses sight of the goal for which one fights, and one only thinks of returning, a hundred-fold if possible, the blows received; and when at last victory crowns the efforts of the party who fought for justice and humanity it is already corrupt and incapable of realizing the program by which it was inspired.

How many men who enter on a political struggle inspired with the love of humanity, of liberty, and of toleration, end by becoming cruel and inexorable proscribers.

How many sects have started with the idea of doing a work of justice in punishing some oppressor whom official "justice" could not or would not strike, have ended by becoming the instruments of private vengeance and base cupidity…

And the Anarchists who rebel against every sort of oppression and struggle for the integral liberty of each and who ought thus to shrink instinctively from all acts of violence which cease to be mere resistance to oppression and become oppressive in their turn…also are liable to fall into the abyss of brutal force.

…[F]acts have proved that the Anarchists are not free from the errors and faults of authoritarian parties, and that, in their case as in that of the rest of humanity, atavistic instincts and the influence of the environment are often stronger than the best theories and noblest intentions.

The excitement caused by some recent explosions and the admiration for the courage with which the bomb-throwers faced death, sufficed to cause many Anarchists to forget their program, and to enter on a path which is the most absolute negation of all anarchist ideas and sentiments.

Hatred and revenge seemed to have become the moral basis of Anarchism. "The bourgeoisie does as bad and worse." Such is the argument with which they tried to justify and exalt every brutal deed.

"The masses are brutalized; we must force our ideas on them by violence." "One has the right to kill those who preach false theories." "The masses allow us to be oppressed; let us revenge ourselves on the masses." "The more workers one kills the fewer slaves remain." Such are the ideas current in certain Anarchist circles...an Anarchist review, in a controversy on the different tendencies of the Anarchist movement, replied to a comrade with this unanswerable argument: "There will be bombs for you also."

It is true that these ultra-authoritarians, who so strangely persist in calling themselves Anarchists, are but a small fraction who acquired a momentary importance owing to exceptional circumstances. But we must remember that, generally speaking, they entered the movement inspired with those feelings of love and respect for the liberty of others which distinguish the true Anarchist, and only in consequence of a sort of moral intoxication produced by the violent struggle, they got to defend and extol acts and maxims worthy of the greatest tyrants. Nor must we forget that we have all, or nearly all, run the same danger, and that if most of us have stopped in time it is perhaps due to these mad exaggerations which have shown us beforehand into what an abyss we were in danger of falling.

Thus the danger of being corrupted by the use of violence, and of despising the people, and becoming cruel as well as fanatical persecutors, exists for all. And if in the coming revolution this moral degradation of the Anarchists were to prevail on a large scale, what would become of Anarchist ideas? And what would be the outcome of the Revolution?

...Let us not consider humanity as a metaphysical conception devoid of reality, and let us not transform the love of others into a continuous, absurd, and impossible self-sacrifice.

Humanity is the sum total of human units, and everyone who defends in himself those rights which he recognizes in others, defends them to the advantage of all.

Altruism cannot go beyond loving others as one loves oneself, otherwise it ceases to be a practical reality, and becomes a misty idea which may attract some minds inclined to mysticism, but can certainly not become a moral law to be lived up to.

The object of the ideally moral man is that all men may have as little suffering and as much joy as possible.

Supposing the predominant instinct of self-preservation be eliminated, the moral man, when obliged to fight, should act in such fashion that the total ill inflicted on the diverse combatants be as small as possible. Consequently he should not do another a great evil to avoid suffering a small one. For instance he should not kill a man to avoid being punched; but he would not hesitate to break his legs if he could not do otherwise to prevent his killing him. And when it is a question of like evils, such as killing so as not to be killed, even then it seems to me that it is an advantage to society that the aggressor should die rather than the aggressed.

But if self-defence is a right one may renounce, the defence of others at the risk of hurting the aggressor is a duty of solidarity...

Is it true...that the masses can emancipate themselves today without resorting to violent means?

Today, above the great majority of mankind who derive a scanty livelihood by their labour or who die through want of work, there exists a privileged class, who, having monopolized the means of existence and the management of social interests, shamefully exploit the former and deny the latter the means of work and life. This class, who are influenced solely by a thirst for power and profit, show no inclination (as facts prove) to voluntarily renounce their privileges, and to merge their private interests in the common good. On the contrary, it is ever arming itself with more powerful means of repression, and systematically uses violence not only to check every direct attack on their privileges, but also to crush in the bud every movement, every pacific organization, whose growth might endanger their power.

What means does Bell advise for getting out of this situation?

Propaganda, organization, moral resistance? Certainly these are the essential factors in social evolution, and it is from them that we must start, and without these revolutionary violence would be senseless, nay impossible...

Bell...admits the right of the workers to break in the doors of a factory in order to seize the machinery, but he does not recognize their right to injure the factory-owner. And in this he is right if the owner should allow the workers to proceed without opposing them with force. But unfortunately the policemen will come with their truncheons and revolvers. What should the workers do then? Should they allow themselves to be taken and sent to prison? That is a game one soon gets tired of.

Bell certainly admits that the workers have the right to organize for the defeat of the bourgeoisie by means of a general strike. But what if the government sends down soldiers to slaughter them? Or what if the bourgeoisie, which after all can afford to wait, holds out? It will be absolutely necessary for the strikers, if they do not wish to be starved out at the end of the second day, to seize on food wherever they can find it, and as it will not be given up to them without resistance, they will be obliged to take [it] by force. So they will either have to fight or consider themselves as conquered...

In reality Bell's error consists in this, that while discussing the methods of attaining an ideal he presupposes that the ideal is already attained.

If it were really possible to progress peacefully, if the partisans of a social system different to that which we desire did not force us to submit to it, then we might say that we were living under Anarchy.

For, what is Anarchy? We do not wish to impose on others any hard and fast system, nor do we pretend, at least I do not, to possess the secret of a perfect social system. We wish that each social group be able, within the limits imposed by the liberty of others, to experiment on the mode of life which it believes to be the best, and we believe in the efficacy of persuasion and example. If society did not deny us this right we should have no right to complain, and we would simply have to strive to make our system the most successful, so as to prove that it was the better. It is only because today one class has the monopoly of power and riches, and is therefore able to force the people, at the end of a bayonet, to work for it, that we have the right, and that it is our duty, to fight for attaining, with the aid of force, those conditions which render it possible to experiment on better forms of society.

In short it is our duty to call attention to the dangers attendant on the use of violence, to insist on the principle of the inviolability of human life, to combat the spirit of hatred and revenge, and to preach love and toleration. But to blind ourselves to the true conditions of the struggle, to renounce the use of force for the purpose of repelling and attacking force, relying on the fanciful efficacy of "passive resistance," and in the name of a mystical morality to deny the right of self-defence, or to restrain it to the point of rendering it illusionary, can only end in nothing, or in leaving a free field of action to the oppressors.

If we really wish to strive for the emancipation of the people, do not let us reject in principle the means without which the struggle can never be ended; and, remember, the most energetic measures are also the most efficient and the least wasteful. Only do not let us lose sight of the fact that ours is a struggle inspired by love and not by hatred, and that it is our duty to do all in our power to see that the necessary violence does not degenerate into mere ferocity, and that it be used only as a weapon in the struggle of right against wrong.

49. Gustav Landauer: Destroying the State by Creating Socialism (1910/15)

The first passage set forth below is taken from Gustav Landauer's article, "Weak Statesmen, Weaker People," first published in Landauer's paper, Der Sozialist *(*The Socialist*), in 1910. Landauer argues that the State is an ensemble of social relations, and that we destroy it by entering into new social relationships, not by one swift revolutionary blow. This particular passage from Landauer's writings was made famous by his friend and literary executor, the philosopher Martin Buber (1878-1965), who republished the entire article in his posthumous collection of Landauer's writings,* Beginnen: Aufsätze über Sozialismus *(Cologne: Verlag, 1924), and commented upon it in his chapter on Landauer in* Paths In Utopia *(Boston: Beacon Press, 1958). The second passage is from a later article, "Stand Up, Socialist," originally published in the inaugural issue of Ernst Joël's pacifist journal,* Der Aufbruch *(*The Awakening*, Vol. 1, No. 1, January 1915). The translations are by Robert Ludlow.*

Weak Statesmen, Weaker People (1910)

WE SOCIALISTS, WHO ARE AWARE OF HOW, after more than a hundred years, socialism—that is to say, the direct affinity of real interests—fights against politics—the rule of the privileged with the help of fictions—we who, to the best of our abilities, by awakening the spirit and building social realities, want to support this powerful trend of history, which is destined to lead our peoples to freedom and the great levelling; we have under no circumstances anything to do with politics [*Staatspolitik*]. But if we were to see that the power of the demonic [*Ungeist*] and the politics of brute force still had so much strength that great personalities, powerful politicians were arising, we would have some respect for such men in the other—the enemy—camp, and could at times even ask whether the power of the old still had a long life ahead of it.

More and more however we see—in other lands just as in Germany—that the power of the state no longer is based in the spirit and the natural force of its representatives, but rather more and more because the people, even the most unsatisfied, even the proletarian masses, know nothing at all of their task: to separate themselves from the state and to found the new [society] that is destined to replace it. Here on the one side state power and the impotence of the helpless masses, torn into separate pieces—here on the other side socialist organization, a society [*Gesellschaft*] of societies, an association [*Bund*] of associations, the people—that must be the conflict, the two sides that stand against each other as reality. Weaker and weaker will be the state power, the governing principle, the nature of those who represent the old ways—and the entire old system will be irretrievably lost, if only the people begin to constitute themselves outside the State. But the people have not yet grasped that the state has a function, and is an inevitable necessity, as long as that which is certain to replace it is not present: the socialist reality.

One can overturn a table and smash a windowpane; but they are puffed-up word-spewers [Wortemacher] and gullible word-adorers [Wortanbeter], who hold the state for such a thing—akin to a fetish—that one can smash in order to destroy. The state is a relationship between human beings, a way by which people relate to one another; and one destroys it by entering into other relationships, by behaving differently to one another. The absolute monarch can say: I am the state; we, who have found ourselves imprisoned within the absolute state, we must recognize the truth: we are the state—and are it as long as we are not otherwise, as long as we have not created the institutions that constitute a genuine community and society of human beings.

Stand Up, Socialist! (1915)

Socialism is a matter of the conduct and behaviour of people, but first of all the conduct and behaviour of socialists: from the living relationships of economy and community which they create among themselves. Evolving socialism lives only in people when it lives out of them. Nature and spirit do not let themselves be derided or put off for another day: what shall become, must grow; what shall grow, must begin in embryo; and what the beginners see as a matter for humanity, they must begin for the sake of their own humanity and as if it were for themselves alone. Is it not wondrous? Socialism is an image of the beholders, who see before them, clear and beckoning, the possibility of total transformation; it begins however as the deeds of the doers, who remove themselves from the whole as it is now to save their souls, in order to serve their God.

To be socialists appears to mean nothing other than our lucid insight that the world, the spirits, the souls could be wholly changed if the social bases were changed (and anarchism adds to this, that the new bases should be such that they, like every growing organism, unite within themselves stability and renewal, cosmic and chaotic powers, the principle of preservation and the principal of revolution). We are intent for a while—for a long while—on nothing other than heralding this great work to the people, and demanding it of them. In the end what comes to light is that in this realization of the intellect [Geist], what is essential is not its content, but rather the posture and orientation of the spirit [Geist] itself. The essential in socialism is its productivity, its will to reshape the world. Out of the recognition that the people of our time are products of their conditions, comes to true socialists the will and necessity not to let themselves be beaten down, but rather to productively create new conditions for their lives. Socialism unites within itself the ability to grasp, through experience, the nature of a social norm, with the will to overcome it; the recognition of being bound and controlled by a degrading state of affairs was already the first step towards liberation from this bondage.

For two decades there has been fear even of this truth, that socialism is the power of creativity and of sacrifice, that it requires religious intensity and heroism, that in the beginning it is the work of the few; the fear that every productive individual knows, fear of the daemonic that seizes the weak soul in the weak body, forces it out of its boundaries, and sends it on the path of accomplishment. This fear of the deed [Werkangst] on the part of those called to creation has warped the productive efforts of socialism into a theory of the laws of development, and the political party [the German Social Democratic Party] relying on it. And all that industrious nature [Wesen] was irrelevant [unwesentlich]; and all that talking and hustle and bustle about extraneous diversions was the timid excuse of those who, hearing themselves called by their God, cowered down like gnomes behind the hedge formed of their preoccupation with their fear [Angstbeschäftigung].

There is nothing left to do but get back on our feet and put the destination in our methods. The world, in which the spirit builds itself the body, has even in the machine age by no means become mechanistic. The miracle in which superstition believes, the miracle that materialism and mechanism assume—that the great thing comes without great effort and that fully-grown socialism grows not out of the childhood beginnings of socialism, but out of the colossal deformed body of capitalism—this miracle will not come, and soon people will no longer believe in it. Socialism begins with the act of the socialist, the act that will be all the harder, the smaller the number of those who dare and want to try. Who else shall do what he has recognized to be right, other than the recognizer himself? We are at all times dependent and at all times free. We are in no way damned to temporary idleness and waiting—merely making propaganda, and making demands. There is a great deal we can do, that a united band can set up and carry out, if it does not shrink back from efforts, problems, persecution, and ridicule. Finally give yourself up to your task, socialist! Given that a beginning will not come any other way, you need—for the masses, for the peoples, for humanity, for the turning around of history, for decency in economic relationships, community living, between the sexes [Geschlechter] and in upbringing—at first not the broad masses, but rather only companions. They are here today, as they are always here, if you are only here: the task is there, but you do not follow your calling, you let yourself wait. If you join yourselves together, and pace out the boundaries of the realm that is at this moment possible for your small growing band of companions, you will become aware: there is no end to what is possible.

50. Voltairine de Cleyre: Direct Action (1912)

Voltairine de Cleyre (1866-1912), described by Emma Goldman as "the greatest woman Anarchist of America," was an early anarchist feminist and a gifted writer. She wrote regularly for the anarchist press, including this article on "Direct Action," from 1912, originally published as a pamphlet by Emma Goldman's Mother Earth press. She died a few months later at the age of forty-five, partly due to the lingering effects of a shot from a deranged assassin nine and a half years earlier. True to her anarchist principles, she refused to press charges and pleaded for clemency on her attempted assassin's behalf.

DIRECT ACTION…THROUGH THE misapprehension, or else the deliberate misrepresentation, of certain journalists…suddenly acquired in the popular mind the interpretation, "Forcible Attacks on Life and Property." This was either very ignorant or very dishonest of the journalists; but it has had the effect of making a good many people curious to know all about Direct Action.

As a matter of fact, those who are so lustily and so inordinately condemning it will find on examination that they themselves have on many occasions practiced direct action, and will do so again.

Every person who ever thought he had a right to assert, and went boldly and asserted it, himself, or jointly with others that shared his convictions, was a direct actionist…

Every person who ever had a plan to do anything, and went and did it, or who laid his plan before others, and won their co-operation to do it with him, without going to external authorities to please do the thing for them, was a direct actionist. All co-operative experiments are essentially direct action.

Every person who ever in his life had a difference with anyone to settle, and went straight to the other persons involved to settle it, either by a peaceable plan or otherwise, was a direct actionist. Examples of such action are strikes and boycotts…

These actions are generally not due to any one's reasoning overmuch on the respective merits of directness or indirectness, but are the spontaneous retorts of those who feel oppressed by a situation. In other words, all people are, most of the time, believers in the principle of direct action, and practicers of it. However, most people are also indirect or political actionists. And they are both these things at the same time, without making much of an analysis of either. There are only a limited number of persons who eschew political action under any and all circumstances; but there is nobody, nobody at all, who has ever been so "impossible" as to eschew direct action altogether...

Those who, by the essence of their belief, are committed to Direct Action only are—just who? Why, the non-resistants; precisely those who do not believe in violence at all! Now do not make the mistake of inferring that I say direct action means non-resistance; not by any means. Direct action may be the extreme of violence, or it may be as peaceful as the waters of the Brook of Siloa that go softly. What I say is, that the real non-resistants can believe in direct action only, never in political action. For the basis of all political action is coercion; even when the State does good things, it finally rests on a club, a gun, or a prison, for its power to carry them through.

...It is by and because of the direct acts of the forerunners of social change, whether they be of peaceful or warlike nature, that the Human Conscience, the conscience of the mass, becomes aroused to the need for change. It would be very stupid to say that no good results are ever brought about by political action; sometimes good things do come about that way. But never until individual rebellion, followed by mass rebellion, has forced it. Direct action is always the clamorer, the initiator, through which the great sum of indifferentists become aware that oppression is getting intolerable.

We have now oppression in the land—and not only in this land, but throughout all those parts of the world which enjoy the very mixed blessings of Civilization. And just as in the question of chattel slavery, so this form of slavery has been begetting both direct action and political action. A certain percent of our population...is producing the material wealth upon which all the rest of us live; just as it was 4,000,000 chattel blacks who supported all the crowd of parasites above them. These are the *land workers* and the *industrial workers*.

Through the unprophesied and unprophesiable operation of institutions which no individual of us created, but found in existence when he came here, these workers, the most absolutely necessary part of the whole social structure, without whose services none can either eat, or clothe, or shelter himself, are just the ones who get the least to eat, to wear, and to be housed withal—to say nothing of their share of the other social benefits which the rest of us are supposed to furnish, such as education and artistic gratification.

These workers have, in one form or another, mutually joined their forces to see what betterment of their condition they could get; primarily by direct action, secondarily by political action...organized for the purpose of wringing from the masters in the economic field a little better price, a little better conditions, a little shorter hours; or on the other hand, to resist a reduction in price, worse conditions, or longer hours...They were not committed to any particular political policy when they were organized, but were associated for direct action of their own initiation, either positive or defensive.

The strike is their natural weapon, that which they themselves forged. It is the direct blow of the strike which nine times out of ten the boss is afraid of. (Of course there are occasions when he is glad of one, but that's unusual.) And the reason he dreads a strike is not so much because he thinks he cannot win out against it, but simply and solely because he does not want an interruption of his business. The ordinary boss isn't in much dread of a "class-conscious vote"; there are plenty of shops where you can talk Socialism or any other political program all day long; but if you begin to talk Unionism you may forthwith expect to be discharged or at best warned to shut up. Why? Not because the boss is so wise as to know that political action is a swamp in which the workingman gets mired, or because he understands that political Socialism is fast becoming a middle-class movement; not at all. He thinks Socialism is a very bad thing; but it's a good way off! But he knows that if his shop is unionized, he will have trouble right away. His hands will be rebellious, he will be put to expense to improve his factory conditions, he will have to keep workingmen that he doesn't like, and in case of strike he may expect injury to his machinery or his buildings...

Well, I have already stated that some good is occasionally accomplished by political action—not necessarily working-class party action either. But I am abundantly convinced that the occasional good accomplished is more than counterbalanced by the evil; just as I am convinced that though there are occasional evils resulting through direct action, they are more than counterbalanced by the good.

Nearly all the laws which were originally framed with the intention of benefiting the workers, have either turned into weapons in their enemies' hands, or become dead letters, unless the workers through their organizations have directly enforced their observance. So that in the end, it is direct action that has to be relied on anyway. As an example of getting the tarred end of a law, glance at the anti-trust law, which was supposed to benefit the people in general, and the working class in particular. About two weeks since, some 250 union leaders were cited to answer to the charge of being trust formers, as the answer of the Illinois Central to its strikers.

But the evil of pinning faith to indirect action is far greater than any such minor results. The main evil is that it destroys initiative, quenches the individual rebellious spirit, teaches people to rely on someone else to do for them what they should do for themselves; finally renders organic the anomalous idea that by massing supineness together until a majority is acquired, then through the peculiar magic of that majority, this supineness is to be transformed into energy. That is, people who have lost the habit of striking for themselves as individuals, who have submitted to every injustice while waiting for the majority to grow, are going to become metamorphosed into human high-explosives by a mere process of packing!

I quite agree that the sources of life, and all the natural wealth of the earth, and the tools necessary to co-operative production, must become freely accessible to all. It is a positive certainty to me that unionism must widen and deepen its purposes, or it will go under; and I feel sure that the logic of the situation will force them to see it gradually. They must learn that the workers' problem can never be solved by beating up scabs, so long as their own policy of limiting their membership by high initiation fees and other restrictions helps to make scabs. They must learn that the course of growth is not so much along the line of higher wages, but shorter hours, which will enable them to increase membership, to take in everybody who is willing to come into the union. They must learn that if they want to win battles, all allied workers must act together, act quickly (serving no notice on bosses), and retain their freedom so to do at all times. And finally they must learn that even then (when they have a complete organization), they can win nothing permanent unless they strike for everything—not for a wage, not for a minor improvement, but for the whole natural wealth of the earth. And proceed to the direct expropriation of it all!

They must learn that their power does not lie in their voting strength, that their power lies in their ability to stop production.

...[W]hat the working-class can do, when once they grow into a solidified organization, is to show the possessing class, through a sudden cessation of all work, that the whole social structure rests on them; that the possessions of the others are absolutely worthless to them without the workers' activity; that such protests, such strikes, are inherent in the system of property, and will continually recur until the whole thing is abolished—and having shown that, effectively, proceed to expropriate.

Chapter 11
Law And Morality

51. William Godwin: Of Law (1797)

In the following selection, taken from the Book VII of An Enquiry Concerning Political Justice *(see Selection 4), Godwin criticizes the very notion of the rule of law.*

IF IT BE DEEMED CRIMINAL IN ANY society to wear clothes of a particular texture, or buttons of a particular composition, it is unavoidable to exclaim that it is high time the jurisprudence of that society should inform its members what are the fantastic rules by which they mean to proceed. But, if a society be contented with the rules of justice, and do not assume to itself the right of distorting or adding to those rules, there law is evidently a less necessary institution. The rules of justice would be more clearly and effectually taught by an actual intercourse with human society, unrestrained by the fetters of prepossession, than they can be by catechisms and codes.

One result of the institution of law is that the institution, once begun, can never be brought to a close. Edict is heaped upon edict, and volume upon volume. This will be most the case where the government is most popular, and its proceedings have most in them of the nature of deliberation. Surely this is no slight indication that the principle is wrong, and that, of consequence, the further we proceed in the path it marks out to us, the more we shall be bewildered…

There is no maxim more clear than this, "Every case is a rule to itself." No action of any man was ever the same as any other action had ever the same degree of utility or injury. It should seem to be the business of justice to distinguish the qualities of men, and not, which has hitherto been the practice, to confound them. But what has been the result of an attempt to do this in relation to law? As new cases occur, the law is perpetually found deficient. How should it be otherwise? Lawgivers have not the faculty of unlimited prescience, and cannot define that which is boundless. The alternative that remains is either to wrest the law to include a case which was never in the contemplation of its authors, or to make a new law to provide for this particular case. Much has been done in the first of these modes. The quibbles of lawyers, and the arts by which they refine and distort the sense of the law, are proverbial. But, though much is done, everything cannot be thus done. The abuse will sometimes be too palpable. Not to say that the very education that enables the lawyer, when he is employed for the prosecutor, to find out offences the lawgiver never meant, enables him, when he is employed for the defendant, to discover subterfuges that reduce the law to nullity. It is therefore perpetually necessary to make new laws. These laws, in order to escape evasion, are frequently tedious, minute and circumlocutory. The volume in which justice records her prescriptions is forever increasing, and the world would not contain the books that might be written.

The consequence of the infinitude of law is its uncertainty. This strikes at the principle upon which law is founded. Laws were made to put an end to ambiguity, and that each man might know what he had to expect. How well have they answered this purpose? Let us instance in the article of property. Two men go to law for a certain estate. They would not go to law if they had not both of them an opinion of the success. But we may suppose them partial in their own case. They would not continue to go to law if they were not both promised success by their lawyers. Law was made that a plain man might know what he had to expect; and yet the most skillful practitioners differ about the event of my suit. It will sometimes happen that the most celebrated pleader in the kingdom, or the first counsel in the service of the crown, shall assure me of infallible success, five minutes before another law-officer, styled the keeper of the king's conscience, by some unexpected juggle decides it against me. Would the issue have been equally uncertain if I had had nothing to trust to but the plain unperverted sense of a jury of my neighbours, founded in the ideas they entertained of general justice? Lawyers have absurdly maintained that the expensiveness of law is necessary to prevent the unbounded multiplication of suits; but the true source of this multiplication is uncertainty. Men do not quarrel about that which is evident, but that which is obscure.

He that would study the laws of a country accustomed to legal security must begin with the volumes of the statutes. He must add a strict enquiry into the common or unwritten law; and he ought to digress into the civil, the ecclesiastical and canon law. To understand the intention of the authors of a law, he must be acquainted with their characters and views, and with the various circumstances to which it owed its rise, and by which it was modified while under deliberation. To understand the weight and interpretation that will be allowed to it in a court of justice, he must have studied the whole collection of records, decisions and precedents. Law was originally devised that ordinary men might know what they had to expect; and there is not, at this day, a lawyer existing in Great Britain vainglorious enough to pretend that he has mastered the code. Nor must it be forgotten that time and industry, even were they infinite, would not suffice. It is a labyrinth without end; it is a mass of contradictions that cannot be disentangled. Study will enable the lawyer to find in it plausible, perhaps unanswerable, arguments for any side of almost any question; but it would argue the utmost folly to suppose that the study of law can lead to knowledge and certainty.

A further consideration that will demonstrate the absurdity of law in its most general acceptation is that it is of the nature of prophecy. Its task is to describe what will be the actions of mankind, and to dictate decisions respecting them...Law tends, no less than creeds, catechisms and tests, to fix the human mind in a stagnant condition, and to substitute a principle of permanence in the room of that unceasing progress which is the only salubrious element of mind...

The fable of Procrustes presents us with a faint shadow of the perpetual effort of law. In defiance of the great principle of natural philosophy, that there are not so much as two atoms of matter of the same form through the whole universe, it endeavours to reduce the actions of men, which are composed of a thousand evanescent elements, to one standard...It was in the contemplation of this system of jurisprudence that the strange maxim was invented that "strict justice would often prove the highest injustice." There is no more real justice in endeavouring to reduce the actions of men into classes than there was in the scheme to which we have just alluded, of reducing all men to the same stature. If, on the contrary, justice be a result flowing from the contemplation of all the circumstances of each individual case, if only the criterion of justice be general utility, the inevitable consequence is that the more we have of justice, the more we shall have of truth, virtue and happiness.

From all these considerations we can scarcely hesitate to conclude universally that law is an institution of the most pernicious tendency...merely relative to the exercise of political force, and must perish when the necessity for that force ceases, if the influence of truth do not still sooner extirpate it from the practice of mankind.

52. Kropotkin: Law and Authority (1886)

In this essay, Kropotkin argues that law serves a dual purpose—firstly, it codifies and enforces accepted moral standards, and secondly, it furthers the particular interests of the ruling classes. According to Kropotkin, the former purpose is unnecessary, and the latter purpose is positively harmful. "Law and Authority" was published as a pamphlet by Freedom Press in 1886, and forms one of the chapters in Kropotkin's Words of a Rebel *(Montreal: Black Rose Books, 1992).*

"THE YEAR I OF LIBERTY" HAS NEVER lasted more than a day, for after proclaiming it men put themselves the very next morning under the yoke of law and authority. Indeed, for some thousands of years, those who govern us have done nothing but ring the changes upon "Respect for law, obedience to authority." This is the moral atmosphere in which parents bring up their children, and school only serves to confirm the impression. Cleverly assorted scraps of spurious science are inculcated upon the children to prove the necessity of law; obedience to the law is made a religion; moral goodness and the law of the masters are fused into one and the same divinity. The historical hero of the schoolroom is the man who obeys the law, and defends it against rebels.

Later when we enter upon public life, society and literature, impressing us day-by-day and hour-by-hour as the water-drop hollows the stone, continue to inculcate the same prejudice. Books of history, of political science, of social economy, are stuffed with this respect for law. Even the physical sciences have been pressed into the service by introducing artificial modes of expression, borrowed from theology and arbitrary power, into knowledge which is purely the result of observation. Thus our intelligence is successfully befogged, and always to maintain our respect for law. The same work is done by newspapers. They have not an article which does not preach respect for law, even where the third page proves every day the imbecility of that law, and shows how it is dragged through every variety of mud and filth by those charged with its administration. Servility before the law has become a virtue, and I doubt if there was ever even a revolutionist who did not begin in his youth as the defender of law against what are generally called "abuses," although these last are inevitable consequences of the law itself...

But times and tempers are changed. Rebels are everywhere to be found who no longer wish to obey the law without knowing whence it comes, what are its uses, and whither arises the obligation to submit to it, and the reverence with which it is encompassed. The rebels of our day are criticizing the very foundations of society which have hitherto been held sacred, and first and foremost amongst them that fetish, law.

The critics analyze the sources of law, and find there either a god, product of the terrors of the savage, and stupid, paltry, and malicious as the priests who vouch for its supernatural origin, or else, bloodshed, conquest by fire and sword. They study the characteristics of law, and instead of perpetual growth corresponding to that of the human race, they find its distinctive trait to be immobility, a tendency to crystallize what should be modified and developed day by day. They ask how law has been maintained, and in its service they see the atrocities of Byzantinism, the cruelties of the Inquisition, the tortures of the middle ages, living flesh torn by the lash of the executioner, chains, clubs, axes, the gloomy dungeons of prisons, agony, curses, and tears. In our own day they see, as before, the axe, the cord, the rifle, the prison; on the one hand, the brutalized prisoner, reduced to the condition of a caged beast by the debasement of his whole moral being, and on the other, the judge, stripped of every feeling which does honour to human nature living like a visionary in a world of legal fictions, reveling in the infliction of imprisonment and death, without even suspecting, in the cold malignity of his madness, the abyss of degradation into which he has himself fallen before the eyes of those whom he condemns...

Relatively speaking, law is a product of modern times. For ages and ages mankind lived without any written law...During that period, human relations were simply regulated by customs, habits, and usages, made sacred by constant repetition, and acquired by each person in childhood, exactly as he learned how to obtain his food by hunting, cattle-rearing, or agriculture...

Many travelers have depicted the manners of absolutely independent tribes, where laws and chiefs are unknown, but where the members of the tribe have given up stabbing one another in every dispute, because the habit of living in society has ended by developing certain feelings of fraternity and oneness of interest, and they prefer appealing to a third person to settle their differences. The hospitality of primitive peoples, respect for human life, the sense of reciprocal obligation, compassion for the weak, courage, extending even to the sacrifice of self for others which is first learnt for the sake of children and friends, and later for that of members of the same community—all these qualities are developed in man anterior to all law, independently of all religion, as in the case of the social animals. Such feelings and practices are the inevitable results of social life. Without being, as say priests and metaphysicans, inherent in man, such qualities are the consequence of life in common.

But side by side with these customs, necessary to the life of societies and the preservation of the race, other desires, other passions, and therefore other habits and customs evolve in human association. The desire to dominate others and impose one's own will upon them; the desire to seize upon the products of the labour of a neighbouring tribe; the desire to surround oneself with comforts without producing anything, while slaves provide their master with the means of procuring every sort of pleasure and luxury—these selfish, personal desires give rise to another current of habits and customs. The priest and the warrior, the charlatan who makes a profit out of superstition, and after freeing himself from the fear of the devil cultivates it in others; and the bully, who procures the invasion and pillage of his neighbours that he may return laden with booty and followed by slaves. These two, hand in hand, have succeeded in imposing upon primitive society customs advantageous to both of them, but tending to perpetuate their domination of the masses. Profiting by the indolence, the fears, the inertia of the crowd, and thanks to the continual repetition of the same acts, they have permanently established customs which have become a solid basis for their own domination.

...[A]s society became more and more divided into two hostile classes, one seeking to establish its domination, the other struggling to escape, the strife began. Now the conqueror was in a hurry to secure the results of his actions in a permanent form, he tried to place them beyond question, to make them holy and venerable by every means in his power. Law made its appearance under the sanction of the priest, and the warrior's club was placed at its service. Its office was to render immutable such customs as were to the advantage of the dominant minority. Military authority undertook to ensure obedience. This new function was a fresh guarantee to the power of the warrior; now he had not only mere brute force at his service; he was the defender of law.

If law, however, presented nothing but a collection of prescriptions serviceable to rulers, it would find some difficulty in insuring acceptance and obedience. Well, the legislators confounded in one code the two currents of custom of which we have just been speaking, the maxims which represent principles of morality and social union wrought out as a result of life in common, and the mandates which are meant to ensure eternal existence to inequality. Customs, absolutely essential to the very being of society, are, in the code, cleverly intermingled with usages imposed by the ruling caste, and both claim equal respect from the crowd. "Do not kill," says the code, and hastens to add, "And pay tithes to the priest." "Do not steal," says the code, and immediately after, "He who refuses to pay taxes, shall have his hand struck off."

Such was law; and it has maintained its two-fold character to this day. Its origin is the desire of the ruling class to give permanence to customs imposed by themselves for their own advantage. Its character is the skillful commingling of customs useful to society, customs which have no need of law to insure respect, with other customs useful only to rulers, injurious to the mass of the people, and maintained only by the fear of punishment.

Like individual capital, which was born of fraud and violence, and developed under the auspices of authority, law has no title to the respect of men. Born of violence and superstition, and established in the interests of conqueror, priest, and rich exploiter, it must be utterly destroyed on the day when the people desire to break their chains...

The millions of laws which exist for the regulation of humanity appear upon investigation to be divided into three principal categories: protection of property, protection of persons, protection of government. And by analyzing each of these three categories, we arrive at the same logical and necessary conclusion: *the uselessness and hurtfulness of law*.

Socialists know what is meant by protection of property. Laws on property are not made to guarantee either to the individual or to society the enjoyment of the produce of their own labour. On the contrary, they are made to rob the producer of a part of what he has created, and to secure to certain other people that portion of the produce which they have stolen either from the producer or from society as a whole. When, for example, the law establishes Mr. So-and-So's right to a house, it is not establishing his right to a cottage he has built for himself, or to a house he has erected with the help of some of his friends. In that case no one would have disputed his right. On the contrary, the law is establishing his right to a house which is *not* the product of his labour; first of all because he has had it built for him by others to whom he has not paid the full value of their work, and next because that house represents a social value which he could not have produced for himself. The law is establishing his right to what belongs to everybody in general and to nobody in particular. The same house built in the midst of Siberia would not have the value it possesses in a large town, and, as we know, that value arises from the labour of something like fifty generations of men who have built the town, beautified it, supplied it with water and gas, fine promenades, colleges, theatres, shops, railways, and roads leading in all directions. Thus, by recognizing the right of Mr. So-and-So to a particular house in Paris, London, or Rouen, the law is unjustly appropriating to him a certain portion of the produce of the labour of mankind in general. And it is precisely because this appropriation and all other forms of property bearing the same character are a crying injustice, that a whole arsenal of laws and a whole army of soldiers, policemen, and judges are needed to maintain it against the good sense and just feeling inherent in humanity...

As all the laws about property which make up thick volumes of codes and are the delight of our lawyers have no other object than to protect the unjust appropriation of human labour by certain monopolists, there is no reason for their existence, and, on the day of the revolution, social revolutionists are thoroughly determined to put an end to them. Indeed, a bonfire might be made with perfect justice of all laws bearing upon the so-called "rights of property," all title-deeds, all registers, in a word, of all that which is in any way connected with an institution which will soon be looked upon as a blot in the history of humanity, as humiliating as the slavery and serfdom of past ages.

The remarks just made upon laws concerning property are quite as applicable to the second category of laws: those for the maintenance of government, i.e., constitutional law.

It again is a complete arsenal of laws, decrees, ordinances, orders in council, and what not, all serving to protect the diverse forms of representative government, delegated or usurped, beneath which humanity is writhing. We know very well—anarchists have often enough pointed it out in their perpetual criticism of the various forms of government—that the mission of all governments, monarchical, constitutional, or republican, is to protect and maintain by force the privileges of the classes in possession, the aristocracy, priesthood and bourgeoisie. A good third of our laws—and each country possesses some tens of thousands of them—the fundamental laws on taxes, excise duties, the organization of ministerial departments and their offices, of the army, the police, the church, etc., have no other end than to maintain, patch up, and develop the administrative machine. And this machine in its turn serves almost entirely to protect the privileges of the possessing classes. Analyze all these laws, observe them in action day by day, and you will discover that not one is worth preserving.

About such laws there can be no two opinions. Not only anarchists, but more or less revolutionary radicals also, are agreed that the only use to be made of laws concerning the organization of government is to fling them into the fire.

The third category of law still remains to be considered; that relating to the protection of the person and the detection and prevention of "crime." This is the most important because most prejudices attach to it; because, if law enjoys a certain amount of consideration, it is in consequence of the belief that this species of law is absolutely indispensable to the maintenance of security in our societies. These are laws developed from the nucleus of customs useful to human communities, which have been turned to account by rulers to sanctify their own domination. The authority of the chiefs of tribes, of rich families in towns, and of the king, depended upon their judicial functions, and even down to the present day, whenever the necessity of government is spoken of, its function as supreme judge is the thing implied. "Without a government men would tear one another to pieces," argues the village orator.

"The ultimate end of all government is to secure twelve honest jurymen to every accused person," said Burke.

Well, in spite of all the prejudices existing on this subject, it is quite time that anarchists should boldly declare this category of laws as useless and injurious as the preceding ones.

First of all, as to so-called "crimes"—assaults upon persons—it is well known that two-thirds, and often as many as three-fourths, of such "crimes" are instigated by the desire to obtain possession of someone's wealth. This immense class of so-called "crimes and misdemeanors" will disappear on the day on which private property ceases to exist. "But," it will be said, "there will always be brutes who will attempt the lives of their fellow citizens, who will lay their hands to a knife in every quarrel, and avenge the slightest offence by murder, if there are no laws to restrain and punishments to withhold them." This refrain is repeated every time the right of society *to punish* is called in question.

Yet there is one fact concerning this head which at the present time is thoroughly established; the severity of punishment does not diminish the amount of crime. Hang, and, if you like, quarter murderers, and the number of murders will not decrease by one. On the other hand, abolish the penalty of death, and there will not be one murder more; there will be fewer. Statistics prove it...

Moreover, it is also a well known fact that the fear of punishment has never stopped a single murderer. He who kills his neighbour from revenge or misery does not reason much about consequences; and there have been few murderers who were not firmly convinced that they should escape prosecution.

Without speaking of a society in which a man will receive a better education, in which the development of all his faculties, and the possibility of exercising them, will procure him so many enjoyments that he will not seek to poison them by remorse—even in our society, even with those sad products of misery whom we see today in the public houses of great cities—on the day when no punishment is inflicted upon murderers, the number of murders will not be augmented by a single case. And it is extremely probable that it will be, on the contrary, diminished by all those cases which are due at present to habitual criminals, who have been brutalized in prisons.

We are continually being told of the benefits conferred by law, and the beneficial effect of penalties, but have the speakers ever attempted to strike a balance between the benefits attributed to laws and penalties, and the degrading effect of these penalties upon humanity? Only calculate all the evil passions awakened in mankind by the atrocious punishments formerly inflicted in our streets! Man is the cruelest animal upon earth. And who has pampered and developed the cruel instincts unknown, even among monkeys, if it is not the king, the judge, and the priests, armed with law, who caused flesh to be torn off in strips, boiling pitch to be poured into wounds, limbs to be dislocated, bones to be crushed, men to be sawn asunder to maintain their authority? Only estimate the torrent of depravity let loose in human society by the "informing" which is countenanced by judges, and paid in hard cash by governments, under pretext of assisting in the discovery of "crime." Only go into the jails and study what man becomes when he is deprived of freedom and shut up with other depraved beings, steeped in the vice and corruption which oozes from the very walls of our existing prisons. Only remember that the more these prisons are reformed, the more detestable they become. Our model modern penitentiaries are a hundred-fold more abominable than the dungeons of the middle ages. Finally, consider what corruption, what depravity of mind is kept up among men by the idea of obedience, the very essence of law; of chastisement; of authority having the right to punish, to judge irrespective of our conscience and the esteem of our friends; of the necessity for executioners, jailers, and informers—in a word, by all the attributes of law and authority. Consider all this, and you will assuredly agree with us in saying that a law inflicting penalties is an abomination which should cease to exist.

People without political organization, and therefore less depraved than ourselves, have perfectly understood that the man who is called "criminal" is simply unfortunate; that the remedy is not to flog him, to chain him up, or to kill him on the scaffold or in prison, but to help him by the most brotherly care, by treatment based on equality, by the usages of life among honest men. In the next revolution we hope that this cry will go forth:

> Burn the guillotines; demolish the prisons; drive away the judges, policemen and informers—the impurest race upon the face of the earth; treat as a brother the man who has been led by passion to do ill to his fellow; above all, take from the ignoble products of middle-class idleness the possibility of displaying their vices in attractive colours; and be sure that but few crimes will mar our society.

The main supports of crime are idleness, law and authority; laws about property, laws about government, laws about penalties and misdemeanors; and authority, which takes upon itself to manufacture these laws and to apply them.

No more laws! No more judges! Liberty, equality, and practical human sympathy are the only effectual barriers we can oppose to the anti-social instincts of certain among us.

53. Errico Malatesta: The Duties of the Present Hour (1894)

In the 1890's various governments passed repressive laws as part of a campaign against anarchists and other revolutionaries, allegedly in response to anarchist terrorism. In this article from the August 1894 edition of Liberty, *an anarchist communist paper published in England by James Tochatti (1852-1928), Malatesta, while rejecting terrorism, advocates principled resistance to these repressive laws.*

REACTION IS LET LOOSE UPON US from all sides. The bourgeoisie, infuriated by the fear of losing their privileges, will use all means of repression to suppress not only the Anarchist and Socialist, but every progressive movement.

It is quite certain that they will not be able to prevent those outrages which served as the pretext of this present reaction; on the contrary, the measures which bar all other outlets to the active temper of some seem expressly calculated to provoke and multiply them.

But, unfortunately, it is not quite certain that they may not succeed in hampering our propaganda by rendering the circulation of our press very difficult, by imprisoning a great number of our comrades, and by leaving no other means of revolutionary activity open to us than secret meetings, which may be very useful for the actual execution of actions determined on, but which cannot make an idea enter into the mass of the proletariat.

We would be wrong to console ourselves with the old illusion that persecutions are *always* useful to the development of the ideas which are persecuted. This is wrong, as almost all generalizations are. Persecutions may help or hinder the triumph of a cause, according to the relation existing between the power of persecution and the power of resistance of the persecuted; and past history contains examples of persecutions which stopped and destroyed a movement as well as of others which brought about a revolution.

Hence we must face, without weakness or illusion, the situation into which the *bourgeoisie* has placed us today and study the means to resist the storm and to derive from it the greatest possible profit for our cause.

There are comrades who expect the triumph of our ideas from the multiplication of acts of individual violence. Well, we may differ in our opinions on the moral value and the practical effect of individual acts in general and of each act in particular, and there are in fact on this subject among Anarchists various divergent and even directly opposed currents of opinion; but one thing is certain, namely, that with a number of bombs and a number of blows of the knife, a society like bourgeois society cannot be overthrown, being based, as it is, on an enormous mass of private interests and prejudices, and sustained, more than it is by the force of arms, by the inertia of the masses and their habits of submission.

Other things are necessary to bring about a revolution, and specially the Anarchist revolution. It is necessary that the people be conscious of their rights and their strength; it is necessary that they be ready to fight and ready to take the conduct of their affairs into their own hands. It must be the constant preoccupation of the revolutionists, the point towards which all their activity must aim, to bring about this state of mind among the masses. The brilliant acts of a few individuals may help in this work, but cannot replace it, and in reality, they are only useful if they are the result of a collective movement of spirit of the masses...being accomplished under such circumstances that the masses understand them, sympathize with, and profit by them...

Who expects the emancipation of mankind to come, not from the persistent and harmonious co-operation of all men of progress, but from the accidental or providential happening of some acts of heroism, is not better advised than one who expects it from the intervention of an ingenious legislator or of a victorious general...

What have we to do in the present situation?

Before all, in my opinion, we must as much as possible resist the laws; I might almost say we must ignore them.

The degree of freedom, as well as the degree of exploitation under which we live, is not at all, or only in a small measure, dependent upon the letter of the law: it depends before all upon the resistance offered to the laws. One can be relatively free, notwithstanding the existence of draconian laws, provided custom is opposed to the government making use of them; while, on the other side, in spite of all guarantees granted by laws, one may be at the mercy of all the violence of the police, if they feel that they can, without being punished, make short work of the liberty of the citizens...

The results of the new laws which are being forged against us will depend to a large degree, upon our own attitude. If we offer energetic resistance, they will at once appear to public opinion as a shameless violation of all human right and will be condemned to speedy extinction or to remain a dead letter. If, on the contrary, we accommodate ourselves to them, they will rank with contemporary political customs, which will, later on, have the disastrous result of giving fresh importance to the struggle for political liberties (of speaking, writing, meeting, combining, associating) and be the cause more or less of losing sight of the social question.

We are to be prevented from expressing our ideas: let us do so none the less and that more than ever. They want to proscribe the very name of Anarchist: let us shout aloud that we are Anarchists. The right of association is to be denied us: let us associate as we can, and proclaim that we are associated, and mean to be. This kind of action, I am quite aware, is not without difficulty in the state things are in at present, and can only be pursued within the limits and in the way which commonsense will dictate to everybody according to the different circumstances they live under. But let us always remember that the oppression of governments has no other limits than the resistance offered to it.

Those Socialists who imagine to escape the reaction by severing their cause from that of the Anarchists, not only give proof of a narrowness of view which is incompatible with aims of radical reorganization of the social system, but they betray stupidly their proper interest. If we should be crushed, their turn would come very soon.

But before all we must go among the people: this is the way of salvation for our cause.

While our ideas oblige us to put all our hopes in the masses, because we do not believe in the possibility of imposing the good by force and we do not want to be commanded, we have despised and neglected all manifestations of popular life; we contented ourselves with simply preaching abstract theories or with acts of individual revolt, and we have become isolated. Hence the want of success of what I will call, the first period of the Anarchist movement. After more than twenty years of propaganda and struggle, after so much devotion and so many martyrs, we are today nearly strangers to the great popular commotions which agitate Europe and America, and we find ourselves in a situation which permits the governments to foster, without plainly appearing absurd, hopes to suppress us by some police measures.

Let us reconsider our position.

Today, that which always ought to have been our duty, which was the logical outcome of our ideas, the condition which our conception of the revolution and reorganization of society imposes on us, namely, to live among the people and to win them over to our ideas by actively taking part in their struggles and sufferings, today this has become an absolute necessity imposed upon us by the situation which we have to live under.

54. Kropotkin: Mutual Aid (1902) and Anarchist Morality (1890)

Despite opposition from religious elements, it did not take long for Charles Darwin's theory of natural selection to be used as an ideological justification for capitalist exploitation, under the rubric of "the struggle for existence" and "survival of the fittest." Kropotkin, as a scientist and an anarchist, was a determined critic of "Social Darwinism," which he regarded as unsci-

entific and immoral. In Mutual Aid: A Factor of Evolution *(Montreal: Black Rose Books, 1989; originally published 1902), which began as a series of articles published in the* Nineteenth Century *from 1890 through 1896, Kropotkin presents a wealth of evidence to show that cooperation, or mutual aid, is a positive factor in evolution, more conducive to the survival of the species than individual competition within the species. Kropotkin's theory of mutual aid is meant to provide an evolutionary explanation for moral behaviour, not to justify a particular moral view, but to establish the natural basis of all morality. It was in "Anarchist Morality," and other writings, that Kropotkin set forth his positive ideas regarding an anarchist approach to morality. "Anarchist Morality" was first published in* La Révolte *in 1890; it was published in English by Freedom Press in 1892, and has been republished many times since. It is included in Kropotkin's* Fugitive Writings *(Montreal: Black Rose Books, 1993, ed. George Woodcock).*

Mutual Aid (1902)

IT IS NOT LOVE TO MY NEIGHBOUR—whom I often do not know at all—which induces me to seize a pail of water and to rush towards his house when I see it on fire; it is a far wider, even though more vague feeling or instinct of human solidarity and sociability which moves me. So it is also with animals. It is not love, and not even sympathy (understood in its proper sense) which induces a herd of ruminants or of horses to form a ring in order to resist an attack of wolves; not love which induces wolves to form a pack for hunting; not love which induces kittens or lambs to play, or a dozen of species of young birds to spend their days together in the autumn; and it is neither love nor personal sympathy which induces many thousand fallow-deer scattered over a territory as large as France to form into a score of separate herds, all marching towards a given spot, in order to cross there a river. It is a feeling infinitely wider than love or personal sympathy—an instinct that has been slowly developed among animals and men in the course of an extremely long evolution, and which has taught animals and men alike the force they can borrow from the practice of mutual aid and support, and the joys they can find in social life.

The importance of this distinction will be easily appreciated by the student of animal psychology, and the more so by the student of human ethics. Love, sympathy and self-sacrifice certainly play an immense part in the progressive development of our moral feelings. But it is not love and not even sympathy upon which Society is based in mankind. It is the conscience—be it only at the stage of an instinct—of human solidarity. It is the unconscious recognition of the force that is borrowed by each man from the practice of mutual aid; of the close dependency of every one's happiness upon the happiness of all; and of the sense of justice, or equity, which brings the individual to consider the rights of every other individual as equal to his own. Upon this broad and necessary foundation the still higher moral feelings are developed...

We have heard so much lately of the "harsh, pitiless struggle for life," which was said to be carried on by every animal against all other animals, every "savage" against all other "savages," and every civilized man against all his co-citizens—and these assertions have so much become an article of faith—that it was necessary, first of all, to oppose to them a wide series of facts showing animal and human life under a quite different aspect. It was necessary to indicate the overwhelming importance which sociable habits play in Nature and in the progressive evolution of both the animal species and human beings: to prove that they secure to animals a better protection from their enemies, very often facilities for getting food and (winter provisions, migrations, etc.), longevity, therefore a greater facility for the development of intellectual faculties; and that they have given to men, in addition to the same advantages, the possibility of working out those institutions which have enabled mankind to survive in its hard struggle against Nature, and to progress, notwithstanding all the vicissitudes of its history.

But whatever the opinions as to the first origin of the mutual-aid feeling or instinct may be—whether a biological or a supernatural cause is ascribed to it—we must trace its existence as far back as to the lowest stages of the animal world; and from these stages we can follow its uninterrupted evolution, in opposition to a number of contrary agencies, through all degrees of human development, up to the present times. Even the new religions which were born from time to time—always at epochs when the mutual-aid principle was falling into decay in the theocracies and despotic States of the East, or at the decline of the Roman Empire—even the new religions have only reaffirmed that same principle. They found their first supporters among the humble, in the lowest, downtrodden layers of society, where the mutual-aid principle is the necessary foundation of every-day life; and the new forms of union which were introduced in the earliest Buddhist and Christian communities, in the Moravian brotherhoods and so on, took the character of a return to the best aspects of mutual aid in early tribal life.

Each time, however, that an attempt to return to this old principle was made, its fundamental idea itself was widened. From the clan it was extended to the stem, to the federation of stems, to the nation, and finally—in ideal, at least—to the whole of mankind. It was also refined at the same time. In primitive Buddhism, in primitive Christianity, in the writings of some of the Mussulman teachers, in the early movements of the Reform, and especially in the ethical and philosophical movements of the last century and of our own times, the total abandonment of the idea of revenge, or of "due reward"—of good for good and evil for evil—is affirmed more and more vigorously. The higher conception of "no revenge for wrongs," and of freely giving more than one expects to receive from his neighbours, is proclaimed as being the real principle of morality—a principle superior to mere equivalence, equity, or justice, and more conducive to happiness. And man is appealed to to be guided in his acts, not merely by love, which is always personal, or at the best tribal, but by the perception of his oneness with each human being. In the practice of mutual aid, which we can retrace to the earliest beginnings of evolution, we thus find the positive and undoubted origin of our ethical conceptions; and we can affirm that in the ethical progress of man, mutual support—not mutual struggle—has had the leading part. In its wide extension, even at the present time, we also see the best guarantee of a still loftier evolution of our race.

Anarchist Morality (1890)

We do not wish to be ruled. And by this very fact, do we not declare that we ourselves wish to rule nobody? We do not wish to be deceived, we wish always to be told nothing but the truth. And by this very fact, do we not declare that we ourselves do not wish to deceive anybody, that we promise to always tell the truth, nothing but the truth, the whole truth? We do not wish to have the fruits of our labour stolen from us. And by that very fact, do we not declare that we respect the fruits of others' labour?

...By what right indeed can we demand that we should be treated in one fashion, reserving it to ourselves to treat others in a fashion entirely different? Our sense of equality revolts at such an idea...

By proclaiming ourselves anarchists, we proclaim beforehand that we disavow any way of treating others in which we should not like them to treat us; that we will no longer tolerate the inequality that has allowed some among us to use their strength, their cunning or their ability after a fashion in which it would annoy us to have such qualities used against ourselves. Equality in all things, the synonym of equity, this is anarchism in very deed. It is not only against the abstract trinity of law, religion, and authority that we declare war. By becoming anarchists we declare war against all this wave of deceit, cunning, exploitation, depravity, vice—in a word, inequality—which they have poured into all our hearts. We declare war against their way of acting, against their way of thinking. The governed, the deceived, the exploited, the prostitute, wound above all else our sense of equality. It is in the name of equality that we are determined to have no more prostituted, exploited, deceived and governed men and women...

We have revolted and invited others to revolt against those who assume the right to treat their fellows otherwise than they would be treated themselves; against those who, not themselves wishing to be deceived, exploited, prostituted or ill-used, yet behave thus to others. Lying and brutality are repulsive, we have said, not because they are disapproved by codes of morality, but because such conduct revolts the sense of equality in everyone to whom equality is not an empty word. And above all does it revolt him who is a true anarchist in his way of thinking and acting.

If nothing but this simple, natural, obvious principle were generally applied in life, a very lofty morality would be the result; a morality comprising all that moralists have taught.

The principle of equality sums up the teachings of moralists. But it also contains something more. This something more is respect for the individual. By proclaiming our morality of equality, or anarchism, we refuse to assume a right which moralists have always taken upon themselves to claim, that of mutilating the individual in the name of some ideal. We do not recognize this right at all, for ourselves or anyone else.

We recognize the full and complete liberty of the individual; we desire for him plentitude of existence, the free development of all his faculties. We wish to impose nothing upon him; thus returning to the principle which Fourier placed in opposition to religious morality when he said: "Leave men absolutely free. Do not mutilate them as religions have done enough and to spare. Do not fear even their passions. In a *free* society these are not dangerous."

Provided that you yourself do not abdicate your freedom, provided that you yourself do not allow others to enslave you, and provided that to the violent and anti-social passions of this or that person you oppose your equally vigorous social passions, you have nothing to fear from liberty.

We renounce the idea of mutilating the individual in the name of any ideal whatsoever. All we reserve to ourselves is the frank expression of our sympathies and antipathies towards what seems to us good or bad...

And yet if societies knew only this principle of equality, if each man practiced merely the equity of a trader, taking care all day long not to give others anything more than he was receiving from them, society would die of it. The very principle of equality itself would disappear from our relations. For, if it is to be maintained, something grander, more lovely, more vigorous than mere equity must perpetually find a place in life.

And this thing greater than justice is here.

Until now humanity has never been without large natures overflowing with tenderness, with intelligence, with goodwill, and using their feeling, their intellect, their active force in the service of the human race without asking anything in return.

This fertility of mind, of feeling or of goodwill takes all possible forms. It is in the passionate seeker after truth, who renounces all other pleasures to throw his energy into the search for what he believes true and right contrary to the affirmations of the ignoramuses around him. It is in the inventor who lives from day to day forgetting even his food, scarcely touching the bread with which perhaps some woman devoted to him feeds him like a child, while he follows out the invention he thinks destined to change the face of the world. It is in the ardent revolutionist to whom the joys of art, of science, even of family life, seem bitter, so long as they cannot be shared by all, and who works despite misery and persecution for the regeneration of the world. It is in the youth who, hearing of the atrocities of invasion, and taking literally the heroic legends of patriotism, inscribes himself in a volunteer corps and marches bravely through snow and hunger until he falls beneath the bullets. It was in the Paris street arab, with his quick intelligence and bright choice of aversions and sympathies, who ran to the ramparts with his little brother, stood steady amid the rain of shells, and died murmuring: "Long live the Commune!" It is in the man who is revolted at the sight of a wrong without waiting to ask what will be its result to himself, and when all backs are bent stands up to unmask the iniquity and brand the exploiter, the petty despot of a factory or great tyrant of an empire. Finally it is in all those numberless acts of devotion less striking and therefore unknown and almost always misprized, which may be continually observed, especially among women, if we will take the trouble to open our eyes and notice what lies at the very foundation of human life, and enables it to enfold itself one way or another in spite of the exploitation and oppression it undergoes…

Such men and women as these make true morality, the only morality worthy the name. All the rest is merely equality in relations. Without their courage, their devotion, humanity would remain besotted in the mire of petty calculations. It is such men and women as these who prepare the morality of the future, that which will come when our children have ceased to *reckon*, and have grown up to the idea that the best use for all energy, courage and love is to expend it where the need of such a force is most strongly felt.

Chapter 12
Anarcho-Syndicalism

55. The Pittsburgh Proclamation (1883)

Anarcho-syndicalism represents an amalgam of anarchism and revolutionary trade unionism ("syndicalisme" in French). The anarcho-syndicalists took to heart the admonition from the founding Statutes of the First International that "the emancipation of the workers must be the workers' own doing" (Selection 19). The roots of anarcho-syndicalism can be traced back to Proudhon (see Selections 12 and 18), Bakunin (Selection 25) and the anti-authoritarian sections of the First International (Selections 26 and 27). The revolutionary principles of the anti-authoritarian sections of the First International continued to have adherents in various parts of Europe and Latin America. The Workers' Federation of the Spanish Region, which adopted an anarchist stance (Selection 36), can be considered one of the first anarcho-syndicalist organizations. An early variant of anarcho-syndicalism was introduced into North America by a group of revolutionary socialists who in 1883 helped found an affiliate of the anti-authoritarian International, the International Working People's Association, also known as the "Black International," at a congress in Pittsburgh. The congress was attended by delegates from across the United States, with proxies from British Columbia and Mexico. Anarchists from Chicago and the midwestern United States, including Albert Parsons (1848-1887) and August Spies (1855- 1887), persuaded a majority of delegates to endorse what became known as the "Chicago idea," the organization of the workers into federated, autonomous trade unions that would spearhead the social revolution and serve as the basis for a new society, fighting for immediate improvements, such as the eight-hour day, but always with the ultimate goal of social revolution in mind. Parsons and Spies helped draft the Congress' statement of principles, which became known as the Pittsburgh Proclamation. In 1887 they were executed, together with Adolph Fischer and George Engel, ostensibly for their role in the Chicago Haymarket bombing, for which there was no real evidence, but in reality for their revolutionary activities and anarchist views, making them the "Haymarket Martyrs." The main author of the Proclamation was Johann Most (1846-1906), at the time a collectivist anarchist and fervent ad-

vocate of armed insurrection. Most had been a radical Social Democratic member of the German parliament, forced into exile when Bismarck suppressed the socialist movement in Germany. The concluding passages of the Proclamation include even then clearly recognizable quotations from Marx and Engel's Communist Manifesto. *Most had previously published a popular summary of Marx's* Capital. *Hundreds of thousands of copies of the Proclamation were published in English and German, and it was translated into several other languages including French, Spanish, Yiddish and Czech.*

OUR PRESENT SOCIETY IS FOUNDED upon the exploitation of the propertyless class by the propertied. This exploitation is such that the propertied (capitalists) buy the working force body and soul of the propertyless, for the price of the mere cost of existence (wages) and take for themselves, i.e. steal, the amount of new values (products) which exceeds the price, whereby wages are made to represent the necessities instead of the earnings of the wage-labourer.

As the non-possessing classes are forced by their poverty to offer for sale to the propertied their working forces, and as our present production on a grand scale enforces technical development with immense rapidity, so that by the application of an always decreasing number of [the] human working force, an always increasing amount of products is created; so does the supply of working force increase constantly, while the demand therefor decreases. This is the reason why the workers compete more and more intensely in selling themselves, causing their wages to sink, or at least on the average, never raising them above the margin necessary for keeping intact their working ability.

While by this process the propertyless are entirely debarred from entering the ranks of the propertied, even by the most strenuous exertions, the propertied, by means of the ever-increasing plundering of the working class, are becoming richer day by day, without in any way being themselves productive.

If now and then one of the propertyless class become rich it is not by their own labour but from opportunities which they have to speculate upon, and absorb, the labour-product of others.

With the accumulation of individual wealth, the greed and power of the propertied grows. They use all the means for competing among themselves for the robbery of the people. In this struggle generally the less-propertied (middle-class) are overcome, while the great capitalists, par excellence, swell their wealth enormously, concentrate entire branches of production as well as trade and intercommunication into their hands and develop into monopolists. The increase of products, accompanied by simultaneous decrease of the average income of the working mass of the people, leads to so-called "business" and "commercial" crises, when the misery of the wage-workers is forced to the extreme...

The increasing eradication of working forces from the productive process annually increases the percentage of the propertyless population, which becomes pauperized and is driven to "crime," vagabondage, prostitution, suicide, starvation and general depravity. This system is unjust, insane and murderous. It is therefore necessary to totally destroy it with and by all means, and with the greatest energy on the part of every one who suffers by it, and who does not want to be made culpable for its continued existence by his inactivity.

Agitation for the purpose of organization; organization for the purpose of rebellion. In these few words the ways are marked which the workers must take if they want to be rid of their chains; as the economic condition is the same in all countries of so-called "civilization"; as the governments of all Monarchies and Republics work hand in hand for the purpose of opposing all movements of the thinking part of the workers; as finally the victory in the decisive combat of the proletarians against their oppressors can only be gained by the simultaneous struggle along the whole line of the bourgeois (capitalistic) society, so therefore the international fraternity of people as expressed in the International Working People's Association presents itself as a self-evident necessity.

True order should take its place. This can only be achieved when all implements of labour, the soil and other premises of production, in short, capital produced by labour, is changed into societary property. Only by this presupposition is destroyed every possibility of the future spoilation of man by man. Only by common, undivided capital can all be enabled to enjoy in their fullness the fruits of the common toil. Only by the impossibility of accumulating individual (private) capital can everyone be compelled to work who makes a demand to live.

This order of things allows production to regulate itself according to the demand of the whole people, so that nobody need work more than a few hours a day, and that all nevertheless can satisfy their needs. Hereby time and opportunity are given for opening to the people the way to the highest possible civilization; the privileges of higher intelligence fall with the privileges of wealth and birth. To the achievement of such a system the political organizations of the capitalistic classes —be they Monarchies or Republics—form the barriers. These political structures (States), which are completely in the hands of the propertied, have no other purpose than the upholding of the present disorder of exploitation.

All laws are directed against the working people. In so far as the opposite appears to be the case, they serve on one hand to blind the worker, while on the other hand they are simply evaded. Even the school serves only the purpose of furnishing the offspring of the wealthy with those qualities necessary to uphold their class domination. The children of the poor get scarcely a formal elementary training, and this, too, is mainly directed to such branches as tend to produce prejudices, arrogance and servility; in short, want of sense. The Church finally seeks to make complete idiots out of the mass and to make them forego the paradise on earth by promising a fictitious heaven. The capitalistic press, on the other hand, takes care of the confusion of spirits in public life. All these institutions, far from aiding in the education of the masses, have for their object the keeping in ignorance of the people. They are all in the pay and under the direct control of the capitalistic classes. The workers can therefore expect no help from any capitalistic party in their struggle against the existing system. They must achieve their liberation by their own efforts. As in former times a privileged class never surrendered its tyranny, neither can it be expected that the capitalists of this age will give up their rulership without being forced to do it…

The political institutions of our time are the agencies of the propertied class; their mission is the upholding of the privileges of their masters; any reform in your own behalf would curtail these privileges. To this they will not and cannot consent, for it would be suicidal to themselves.

That they will not resign their privileges voluntarily we know; that they will not make any concessions to us we likewise know. Since we must then rely upon the kindness of our masters for whatever redress we have, and knowing that from them no good may be expected, there remains but one recourse—FORCE! Our forefathers have not only told us that against despots force is justifiable, because it is the only means, but they themselves have set the immemorial example.

By force our ancestors liberated themselves from political oppression, by force their children will have to liberate themselves from economic bondage. "It is, therefore, your right, it is your duty," says Jefferson—"to arm!"

What we would achieve is, therefore, plainly and simply:

First:—Destruction of the existing class rule, by all means, i.e., by energetic, relentless, revolutionary and international action.

Second:—Establishment of a free society based upon co-operative organization of production.

Third:—Free exchange of equivalent products by and between the productive organizations without commerce and profit-mongery.

Fourth:—Organization of education on a secular, scientific and equal basis for both sexes.

Fifth:—Equal rights for all without distinction of sex or race.

Sixth:—Regulation of all public affairs by free contracts between the autonomous (independent) communes and associations, resting on a federalistic basis.

Whoever agrees with this ideal let him grasp our outstretched brother hands!

Proletarians of all countries, unite!

Fellow-workmen, all we need for the achievement of this great end is ORGANIZATION and UNITY!

There exists now no great obstacle to that unity. The work of peaceful education and revolutionary conspiracy well can and ought to run in parallel lines.

The day has come for solidarity. Join our ranks! Let the drum beat defiantly the roll of battle: "Workmen of all countries unite! You have nothing to lose but your chains; you have a world to win!"

Tremble, oppressors of the world! Not far beyond your purblind sight there dawns the scarlet and sable lights of the JUDGMENT DAY!

56. Fernand Pelloutier: Anarchism and the Workers' Unions (1895)

Anarchists had been active in the trade union movement since at least the time of the First International. However, by the 1890's some anarchists had come to regard trade unions as essentially reformist organizations. Fernand Pelloutier (1867-1901) was a French anarchist who argued against such views, sensing a renewed militancy among the workers as they became disillusioned with the political machinations of the various socialist parties. He urged his anarchist comrades to get involved in the trade unions, as he had done, becoming secretary of the Federation of Bourses du Travail in 1895, helping to lay the basis for the revolutionary syndicalist organization, the Confédération Générale du Travail (CGT). This article originally appeared in Jean Grave's Les Temps nouveaux *in 1895. The translation is by Paul Sharkey. It is reprinted from his translation of Daniel Guerin's anthology of anarchist writings,* No Gods, No Masters *(San Francisco: AK Press, 1998), with the kind permission of the publisher.*

THE NEW WATCHWORD "NO MORE POLITICKING!" had spread through the workshops. A number of union members deserted the churches devoted to the cult of electioneering. So the trade union terrain seemed to some anarchists ripe to receive and nurture their doctrine, and came to the aid of those who, freed at last of parliamentary tutelage, now strove to focus their attention and that of their comrades upon the study of economic laws.

This entry into the trade union of some libertarians made a considerable impact. For one thing, it taught the masses the true meaning of anarchism, a doctrine which, in order to make headway can very readily, let us say it again, manage without the individual dynamiter; and, through a natural linkage of ideas, it showed union members what this trades organization of which they had previously had only the narrowest conception is and may yet become.

Nobody believes or expects that the coming revolution, however formidable it should be, will realize unadulterated anarchist communism. By virtue of the fact that it will erupt, no doubt, before the work of anarchist education has been completed, men will not be quite mature enough to organize themselves absolutely without assistance, and for a long time yet the demands of caprice will stifle the voice of reason in them. As a result (and this seems a good time to spell it out), while we do preach perfect communism, it is not in the certainty or expectation of communism's being the social form of the future: it is in order to further men's education, and round it off as completely as possible, so that, by the time that the day of conflagration comes, they will have attained maximum emancipation. But must the transitional state to be endured necessarily or inevitably be the collectivist [state socialist] jail? Might it not consist of libertarian organization confined to the needs of production and consumption alone, with all political institutions having been done away with? Such is the problem with which many minds have—rightly—been grappling for many a long year.

Now, what is the trade union? An association which one is free to join or quit, one without a president, with no officials other than a secretary and a treasurer subject to instant revocation, of men who study and debate kindred professional concerns. And who are these men? Producers, the very same who create all public wealth. Do they await the approval of the law before they come together, reach agreement and act? No: as far as they are concerned, lawful constitution is merely an amusing means of making revolutionary propaganda under government guarantee, and anyway, how many of them do not and will not ever figure in the unions' formal annual returns?

Do they use the parliamentary mechanism in order to arrive at their resolutions? Not any more: they hold discussions and the most widely-held view has the force of law, but it is a law without sanction, observed precisely because it is subject to the endorsement of the individual, except, of course, when it comes to resisting the employers. Finally, while they appoint a chairman, a delegated supervisor, for every session, this is not now the result of habit, for, once appointed, that chairman is utterly overlooked and himself frequently forgets the powers vested in him by his comrades. As a laboratory of economic struggles, detached from election contests, favouring the general strike with all that that implies, governing itself along anarchic lines, the trade union is thus the simultaneously revolutionary and libertarian organization that alone will be able to counter and successfully reduce the noxious influence of the collectivist politicians. Suppose now that, on the day the revolution breaks out, virtually every single producer is organized into the unions: will these not represent, ready to step into the shoes of the present organization, a quasi-libertarian organization, in fact suppressing all political power, an organization whose every part, being master of the instruments of production, would settle all of its affairs for itself, in sovereign fashion and through the freely given consent of its members? And would this not amount to the "free association of free producers?"

To be sure, there are many objections: the federal agencies may turn into authorities: wily persons may come to govern the trade unions just the way the parliamentary socialists govern the political groupings: but such objections are only partly valid. In keeping with the spirit of the trade unions, the federal councils are merely half-way houses generated by the need to spread and make economic struggles more and more formidable, but which the success of the revolution would make redundant, and which, also, the groups from which they emanate monitor with too jealous an eye for them ever to successfully win a directorial authority. On the other hand, the permanent revocability of officials reduces their function and their profile to very little, and often indeed having done their duty is not enough for them to retain their comrades' confidence. Then again, trades organization is still only in the embryonic stages. Once rid of politicians' tyranny, it can stride out freely and, like the child learning to take his first steps, toddle along the road of independence. But who can say where a softly-softly approach and, rather more, the fruits of freedom will have carried them in ten years' time? It is up to libertarian socialists to commit all of their efforts to getting them there. "The Federal Committee of the Bourses du Travail" —say the official minutes carried by the Bulletin de la Bourse de Narbonne—"has as its task the instruction of the people regarding the pointlessness of a revolution that would make do with the substitution of one State for another, even should this be a socialist State." That committee, states another minute..."should strive to prepare an organization which, in the event of a transformation of society, may see to the operation of the economy through the free grouping and render any political institution superfluous. Its goal being the abolition of authority in any of its forms, its task is to accustom the workers to shrug off tutelage."

Thus, on the one hand, the "unionized" are today in a position to understand, study and receive libertarian teachings: on the other, anarchists need not fear that, in taking part in the corporative movement, they will be required to forswear their independence. The former are ready to accept and the latter can strengthen an organization whose resolutions are the products of free agreement: which, to borrow Grave's words (*La Societe future,* p. 202) "has neither laws, nor statutes, nor regulations to which each individual may be obliged to submit on pain of some pre-determined penalty;" which individuals are at liberty to quit as they see fit, except, let me repeat, when battle has been joined with the enemy; which, when all is said and done, may be a practical schooling in anarchism.

Let free men then enter the trade union, and let the propagation of their ideas prepare the workers, the artisans of wealth there to understand that they should regulate their affairs for themselves, and then, when the time comes, smash not only existing political forms, but any attempt to reconstitute a new power. That will show the authorities how well-founded was their fear, posing as disdain, of "syndicalism," and how ephemeral was their teaching, evaporated before it was even able to put down roots!

57. Antonio Pellicer Paraire: The Organization of Labour (1900)

Antonio Pellicer Paraire (1851-1916) was a typesetter active in the Workers' Federation of the Spanish Region (Selection 36) in the 1880's, who argued against sectarianism among the various tendencies within the anarchist movement in favour of a principled but realistic approach. He travelled to Cuba, Mexico and the United States before settling in Argentina in 1891. In a series of articles published in the Buenos Aires anarchist newspaper, La Protesta Humana, *in 1900, he argued in favour of labour organization while warning of the dangers of authoritarianism, centralization and bureaucratization. These articles helped lay the groundwork for the creation of the Workers' Federation of Argentina in 1901. The translation is by Paul Sharkey.*

ONE WING OF THE WORKERS' MOVEMENT which we may call the revolutionary wing is made up of all who whole-heartedly believe and labour righteously for the success of the ideal; and the other wing, which we may call the economic wing, is made up of the toiling masses who fight to better their circumstances by countering the abuses of the employers, not yet persuaded that if the efforts they deployed in securing such partial improvements were to be committed to pursuit of complete emancipation, the latter would be achieved at less cost and in less time.

But it has to be admitted that things are as they are and so parallel or dual organization has to be accepted; revolutionary organization, rooted in ideals, is more straightforward and easier, because it involves those best versed in the goal pursued. Groups for individual tasks and understanding between these groups in more transcendental matters: there we have revolutionary organization. Economic organization is rather more complicated and tricky because of the great masses involved and the multiplicity of its intentions. Which is why that system of organization has proved slow work, to which the finest intellects have made their contributions, because such organization too is the real lever of revolutionary might and may yet represent the new society within the old.

So such organization, which we describe as economic in order to distinguish it from the revolutionary, in order to avoid misunderstandings, rather than out of any intention to say that they are not both at once economic *and* revolutionary, is the one that is truly still in need of further examination.

Each individual should cling to his freedom and his rights, equal with the rights and freedom of his co-associates, and should not allow his freedom and his rights to be infringed by anything or anyone in his handiwork, in his centres, in the bosom of society, in what is being created for the good of all. Trade union association being a product of wills coalescing around specific purposes, those wills need to be active; which is to say that each and every person works on behalf of the proposed aim and does not allow some people to shoulder all the burden while others remain indifferent to every effort, because that leads to a victimhood of laziness or bossiness.

We must ensure that the associate finds society not merely a support in his struggle against capital as he presses home his demands, but also the source of the greatest possible number of gratifications and relief from all his most pressing needs. In short: let the collective be complementary to the individual in whatever the latter cannot achieve by his own unaided efforts, in a setting of the most perfect comradeship, without bullying or tyranny…

The first task for a trades society to tackle should be federation with other societies from the same trade existing in the region, and, should there be none, to set about forming some and federating with them.

…[O]ccasionally, the use of the word federation and even the federative principle has been shunned because of the use made of those terms in authoritarian bodies and in State constitutions. Such wariness is well founded, because a federal or federative regime based on authoritarian units is not destructive of authoritarian unity, but is, all things considered, just as despotic as a unitary system.

It should not be forgotten that every ideal carries within itself an implicit logical procedure. One cannot, if one aspires to good and to freedom, adopt a barrack-like or monastery-like approach, because that will never lead to anything but despotism. One takes possession of freedom by exercising it. And those who preach emancipation to the workers and subject them to authoritarian regulation and deliver them up like sheep to an administrative junta-turned-Executive Authority are deceiving, lying to, suborning, duping and betraying the workers.

Essentially it is up to the trades federation to ensure success in the workers' struggle against capital; the local federation, in addition to this labour solidarity, also boasts a more direct social aspect, intervention in public affairs, albeit in defence of workers' interests; there we have the commune in action, the people acting out its duty and its rights; in this respect, its importance may be great and should be greater with every passing day...

Issues without number come within their direct purview, not to mention all social issues...all of them matters that may and should occupy the workers, mobilizing public opinion, and channelling all exertions and efforts towards the whittling down to nothing of the activity of the public authorities, this being the war of freedom against tyranny, for the more authoritarianism dwindles, the more firmly ensconced freedom becomes and, with it, the safer the welfare of society.

...[T]he local federation [should] be set up along the lines of the revolutionary commune, ongoing, pro-active action by the working people in every matter that impacts upon their freedom and their lives.

Instead of a local council, it seems to us that these functions would be better performed by a local assembly; it would be a vigilant representative of the people, since the latter cannot be permanently on hand, given that under normal circumstances it does not have the material time to do so, and knows that even though its day to day work occupies all its time, there are good comrades available to keep it briefed on developments so that, should the need arise, it can rally round and directly exercise a right of which it may not be divested even for a single minute, not having given such power away to anyone.

Thus the local councils are prevented from turning into parodies of the municipal corporations or councils, insofar as the local assembly represents the people in action...

The local federation, starting from the notion of labour and operating as a social organism, lays the groundwork for the society of the future.

To what did the International aspire? Intelligent action of the proletariat the world over, without regard to race, creed or nationality...

So, what do we require for a worldwide federation of free communes, that being the natural tendency of the local federations?

Simply this: that the principle of association gain ground, that associations federate pretty much along the lines we have set out, as mutually homogeneous units, without chauvinistic or racial frictions, with all of the groups retaining their autonomy and independence, free of meddling by other groups and with no one having methods, systems, theories, schools of thought, beliefs, or any faith shoved down his throat, the individual being free, right from his very first attachment to his fellow-citizens, his brethren from the workshop, who speak the same language and are comprehensively like-minded, through to a worldwide understanding, and need not feel aggrieved in his feelings, dislikes or prejudices, should he have any. (Reprinted in Diego Abad de Santillan, *La FORA: Ideologia y Trayectoria*, Buenos Aires: Editorial Proyeccion, 1971.)

58. The Workers' Federation of the Uruguayan Region (FORU): Declarations from the 3rd Congress (1911)

Anarchists played an important role in the revolutionary labour movements in Latin America. Around the turn of the century, they were particularly active in Mexico, Brazil, Argentina and Uruguay. While the revolutionary syndicalist CGT in France adopted an "apolitical" stance in its famous Charter of Amiens in 1906, the Latin American anarcho-syndicalist federations, such as the Workers' Federation of the Argentine Region (FORA)—the successor to the Workers' Federation of Argentina—and the Workers' Federation of the Uruguyan Region (FORU), adopted an explicitly anarchist program. The "Pact of Solidarity" adopted at the founding Congress of the FORA in 1904 declared:

> We must not forget that a union is merely an economic by-product of the capitalist system, born from the needs of this epoch. To preserve it after the revolution would imply preserving the capitalist system that gave rise to it. We, as anarchists, accept the unions as weapons in the struggle and we try to ensure that they should approximate as closely [as possible] to our revolutionary ideals. We recommend the widest possible study of the economic-philosophical principles of anarchist communism. This education, going on from concentrating on achieving the eight-hour day, will emancipate us from mental slavery and consequently lead to the hoped for social revolution. (As quoted by P. Yerrill and L. Rosser, Revolutionary Unionism in Latin America: The FORA in Argentina, London: ASP, 1987, pp. 19-20)

The following declarations from the 3rd Congress of the FORU in 1911 detail the type of organizational structure adopted by the anarcho-syndicalists which they felt was consonant with their anarchist ideals. The translation is by Paul Sharkey.

CONSIDERING: THAT THE GROWTH of science tends more and more to reduce men's exertions in the production of what is required in order to meet their needs; that the very same prolific output has led to workers' being dismissed from workshop, mine, factory and field, leaving them stranded, making life harder and harder for them, because of this very expansion in the numbers of unproductive wage-slaves; that for his upkeep every man has need of a number of utterly indispensable items and thus must dedicate a given amount of time to production thereof, as the most elementary justice proclaims; that this society carries within itself the seeds of its destruction in the perennial imbalance between the needs created by progress per se and the wherewithal for the meeting of those needs, an imbalance that triggers the ongoing rebellions that we are witnessing in the form of strikes; that the discovery of a new instrument for the creation of wealth and the honing of that instrument has plunged thousands of households into poverty, when logic tells us that increased ease of production should be matched by a general betterment of people's lives; that this paradox is symptomatic of our present flawed social constitution; that this flawed constitution lies at the root of internecine wars, outrages and degeneracy, making a mockery of the comprehensive notion of humanity we have received from the most modern thinkers, operating on the basis of observation and inductive scientific reasoning with regard to social phenomena; that this economic change should also be mirrored in every institution; that history is evolving towards freedom of the individual; that this is crucial if social freedom is to be realized; that such freedom is not lost through combining forces with other producers, but is, rather, magnified by the intensity and scale it lends to the potential of the individual; that man is sociable and thus that the freedom of one is not bounded by the freedom of his neighbour, as the bourgeois would have it, but, rather, finds its complement in the freedom of his neighbour; that codified, tax laws are no match for the scientific laws actually experienced by peoples and managed and framed by the people itself in its ongoing striving for improvement; come the economic transformation which will do away with the class antagonisms that currently make man a predator upon his fellow-man, and establish a population of free producers; finally, the serf and the seigneur, the aristocrat and the plebeian, the bourgeois and the proletarian, the master and the slave, whose differences have stained history with blood, may at last embrace under the single designation of brothers.

The Third Congress of the Workers' Federation of the Uruguayan Region (FORU) declares: That all its efforts should be geared towards bringing about the complete emancipation of the proletariat, by establishing *sociedades de resistencia*, federations of kindred trades, local federations and consolidating the national federation so that, moving on from the simple to the complex, and broadening the narrow horizons within which producers have lived up to now, and by affording them more bread, more sustenance, more intelligence, more life, we may join with the exploited in the whole great confederation of all of the earth's producers and, on the basis of such fellowship, stride on, steadfast and determined, to the conquest of economic and social emancipation:

1. Organizing the Republic's working class into trades associations.

2. Establishing trades and allied trades Federations on the footing of these workers' associations.

3. Localities are to form Local Federations; the departments, Departmental Federations; nations, Regional Federations; and the entire world, one International Federation, complete with a Liaison Centre or Bureau for the larger Federations among these groupings.

4. As is also the case with the Central Bureau appointed to handle liaison and campaigning, members serving on bodies representing the Trades Federations or Allied Trades Federations, while enjoying complete autonomy in their internal lives and liaisons, are to wield no authority and may at any time be replaced through a vote of the majority of the federated associations assembled in Congress, or by the determination of the federated associations as expressed through their respective local trades Federations.

5. In every locality where...affiliated federations have been set up, these may declare that they have contracted into a free local agreement.

...8. All of the member associations of this Federation undertake to practice the fullest moral and material solidarity towards one another, making every effort and sacrifice that circumstances may demand of them, so that the workers may always emerge victorious from struggles provoked by the bourgeoisie and in pressing the demands of the proletariat.

9. For effective solidarity in all struggles undertaken by the federated associations, wherever possible, they should consult with their respective Federations in order to discover precisely what means or resources are accessible to the member associations.

10. Associations are free and autonomous within the Local Federation; free and autonomous within the Trades and Allied Trades Federation; free and autono-

mous within the Area Federation, as well as free and autonomous within the Regional Federation.

11. Associations, Local Federations, Trades or Allied Trades Federations and Area Federations, by virtue of being autonomous, will administer themselves howsoever they may deem fit and they are to take up and implement all of the accords they deem necessary for achieving the purpose they set themselves.

12. As every association enjoys freedom of initiative within its respective Federation, each and every member has a moral duty to advance whatever suggestions they see fit, and, once accepted by their respective Federation, this should be conveyed to the Federal Council so that the latter in turn may communicate it to all affiliated associations and Federations, for implementation by all which find it acceptable.

...16. The accords of this Congress, unless rescinded by a majority of associations party to the compact, are to be binding upon all associations currently affiliated and any which may join hereafter.

...18. This solidarity compact can at any time be revised by Congresses or through a majority vote of the Federated Associations; but the Federation entered into is not open for discussion as long as there are two associations left upholding this compact.

...Our wholly economic organization is different from and in opposition to all political parties, since, just as the latter organize with a view to conquering State power, we organize for the destruction of all bourgeois and political institutions until we can establish a Free Federation of free producers in their place. (Reprinted in C. M. Rama and A. J. Cappelletti, *El Anarquismo en America Latina*, Caracas: Biblioteca Ayachucho, 1990)

59. Emma Goldman: On Syndicalism (1913)

Emma Goldman (1869-1940) first became active in the anarchist movement in the United States following the arrests and trial of the Haymarket Martyrs in Chicago (Selection 55). After their execution, she worked with Johann Most in New York, living with a group of young anarchists, including her lifelong comrade, Alexander Berkman. She became a noted public speaker, writer and agitator. She led a garment workers strike in 1889 and remained associated with anarchists in the labour movement throughout her career. The following excerpts are taken from her article, "Syndicalism: Its Theory and Practice," originally published in her paper, Mother Earth, *and as a pamphlet, in 1913.*

SYNDICALISM IS, IN ESSENCE, the economic expression of Anarchism. That circumstance accounts for the presence of so many Anarchists in the Syndicalist movement. Like Anarchism, Syndicalism prepares the workers along direct economic lines, as conscious factors in the great struggles of today, as well as conscious factors in the task of reconstructing society along autonomous industrial lines, as against the paralyzing spirit of centralization with its bureaucratic machinery of corruption, inherent in all political parties.

Realizing that the diametrically opposed interests of capital and labour can never be reconciled, Syndicalism must needs repudiate the old, rusticated, worn-out methods of trade unionism, and declare for an open war against the capitalist regime, as well as against every institution which today supports and protects capitalism.

As a logical sequence Syndicalism, in its daily warfare against capitalism, rejects the contract system, because it does not consider labour and capital equals, hence cannot consent to an agreement which the one has the power to break, while the other must submit to without redress.

For similar reasons Syndicalism rejects negotiations in labour disputes, because such a procedure serves only to give the enemy time to prepare his end of the fight, thus defeating the very object the workers set out to accomplish. Also, Syndicalism stands for spontaneity, both as a preserver of the fighting strength of labour and also because it takes the enemy unawares, hence compels him to a speedy settlement or causes him great loss.

Syndicalism objects to a large union treasury, because money is as corrupting an element in the ranks of labour as it is in those of capitalism...However, the main reason for the opposition of Syndicalism to large treasuries consists in the fact that they create class distinctions and jealousies within the ranks of labour, so detrimental to the spirit of solidarity. The worker whose organization has a large purse considers himself superior to his poorer brother, just as he regards himself better than the man who earns fifty cents less per day...

Syndicalism has grown out of the disappointment of the workers with politics and parliamentary methods. In the course of its development Syndicalism has learned to see in the State—with its mouthpiece, the representative system—one of the strongest supporters of capitalism; just as it has learned that the army and the church are the chief pillars of the State. It is therefore that Syndicalism has turned its back upon parliamentarism and political machines, and has set its face toward the economic arena wherein alone gladiator Labour can meet his foe successfully...

Time and again has the army been used to shoot down strikers and to indicate the sickening idea of patriotism, for the purpose of dividing the workers against themselves and helping the masters to the spoils. The inroads that Syndicalist agitation has made into the superstition of patriotism are evident from the dread of the ruling class for the loyalty of the army, and the rigid persecution of the anti-militarists. Naturally, for the ruling class realizes much better than the workers that when the soldiers will refuse to obey their superiors, the whole system of capitalism will be doomed.

Indeed, why should the workers sacrifice their children that the latter may be used to shoot their own parents? Therefore Syndicalism is not merely logical in its anti-military agitation; it is most practical and far-reaching, inasmuch as it robs the enemy of his strongest weapon against labour.

Now, as to the methods employed by Syndicalism—Direct Action, Sabotage, and the General Strike.

Direct Action: Conscious individual or collective effort to protest against, or remedy, social conditions through the systematic assertion of the economic power of the workers...

Sabotage is mainly concerned with obstructing, by every possible method, the regular process of production, thereby demonstrating the determination of the workers to give according to what they receive, and no more...In other words, sabotage is merely a weapon of defence in the industrial warfare, which is the more effective, because it touches capitalism in its most vital spot, the pocket.

By the General Strike, Syndicalism means a stoppage of work, the cessation of labour. Nor need such a strike be postponed until all the workers of a particular place or country are ready for it... the General Strike may be started by one industry and exert a tremendous force. It is as if one man suddenly raised the cry "Stop the thief!" Immediately others will take up the cry, till the air rings with it. The General Strike, initiated by one determined organization, by one industry or by a small, conscious minority among the workers, is the industrial cry of "Stop the thief," which is soon taken up by many other industries, spreading like wildfire in a very short time.

One of the objections of politicians to the General Strike is that the workers also would suffer for the necessaries of life. In the first place, the workers are past masters in going hungry; secondly, it is certain that a General Strike is surer of prompt settlement than an ordinary strike...Besides, Syndicalism recognizes the right of the producers to the things which they have created; namely, the right of the workers to help themselves if the strike does not meet with speedy settlement.

When [Georges] Sorel [French intellectual (1847-1922)] maintains that the General Strike is an inspiration necessary for the people to give their life meaning, he is expressing a thought which the Anarchists have never tired of emphasizing. Yet I do not hold with Sorel that the General Strike is a "social myth" that may never be realized. I think that the General Strike will become a fact the moment labour understands its full value—its destructive as well as constructive value, as indeed many workers all over the world are beginning to realize.

These ideas and methods of Syndicalism some may consider entirely negative, though they are far from it in their effect upon society today. But Syndicalism has also a directly positive aspect. In fact, much more time and effort is being devoted to that phase than to the others. Various forms of Syndicalist activity are designed to prepare the workers, even within present social and industrial conditions, for the life of a new and better society. To that end the masses are trained in the spirit of mutual aid and brotherhood, their initiative and self-reliance developed, and an *esprit de corps* maintained whose very soul is solidarity of purpose and the community of interests of the international proletariat.

Chief among these activities are the *mutualitées*, or mutual aid societies, established by the French Syndicalists. Their object is, foremost, to secure work for unemployed members, and to further that spirit of mutual assistance which rests upon the consciousness of labour's identity of interests throughout the world...

Besides the *mutualitées*, the French Syndicalists have established other activities tending to weld labour in closer bonds of solidarity and mutual aid. Among these are the efforts to assist workingmen journeying from place to place. The practical as well as ethical value of such assistance is inestimable. It serves to instill the spirit of fellowship and gives a sense of security in the feeling of oneness with the large family of labour...

No less in importance than the mutual aid activities of the Syndicalists is the cooperation established by them between the city and the country, the factory worker and the peasant or farmer, the latter providing the workers with food supplies during the strikes, or taking care of the strikers' children...

And all these Syndicalist activities are permeated with the spirit of educational work, carried on systematically by evening classes on all vital subjects treated from an unbiased, libertarian standpoint—not the adulterated "knowledge" with which the minds are stuffed in our public schools. The scope of the education is truly phenomenal, including sex hygiene, the care of women during pregnancy and confinement, the care of home and children, sanitation and general hygiene; in fact, every branch of human knowledge—science, history, art—receives thorough attention, together with the practical application in the established workingmen's libraries, dispensaries, concerts and festivals, in which the greatest artists and litterateurs of Paris consider it an honour to participate.

One of the most vital efforts of Syndicalism is to prepare the workers, *now*, for their role in a free society. Thus the Syndicalist organizations supply its members with textbooks on every trade and industry, of a character that is calculated to make the worker an adept in his chosen line, a master of his craft, for the purpose of familiarizing him with all the branches of his industry, so that when labour finally takes over production and distribution, the people will be fully prepared to manage successfully their own affairs...

This method of applied education not only trains the worker in his daily struggle, but serves also to equip him for the battle royal and the future, when he is to assume his place in society as an intelligent, conscious being and useful producer, once capitalism is abolished.

Nearly all leading Syndicalists agree with the Anarchists that a free society can exist only through voluntary association, and that its ultimate success will depend upon the intellectual and moral development of the workers who will supplant the wage system with a new social arrangement, based on solidarity and economic well-being for all. That is Syndicalism, in theory and practice.

60. Pierre Monatte and Errico Malatesta: Syndicalism—For and Against (1907)

In 1907 an international anarchist congress was held in Amsterdam. Among the topics debated was the relationship between syndicalism and anarchism. Pierre Monatte (1881-1960) spoke in support of the French Confédération Générale du Travail, defending its apolitical stance and urging anarchists to join the syndicalist movement. Errico Malatesta criticized the syndicalists on a number of grounds, offering a broader conception of anarchism that was not exclusively working class. The following excerpts are taken from George Woodcock's The Anarchist Reader *(London: Fontana, 1977), and are reprinted with the kind permission of the Writers' Trust of Canada on behalf of the Woodcock estate.*

Pierre Monatte

ONE WOULD HAVE TO BE BLIND not to see what there is in common between anarchism and syndicalism. Both seek to root out capitalism and the wage system by means of the social revolution. Syndicalism exists as the proof of a reawakening of the working-class movement, and it revives in anarchism a consciousness of its origins among the workers; on the other hand, the anarchists have contributed not a little towards bringing the working-class movement into the revolutionary path and towards popularizing the idea of direct action. In such ways syndicalism and anarchism have influenced each other to their mutual benefit.

It is in France, among the militants of the Confédération Générale du Travail, that the ideas of revolutionary syndicalism emerged and were developed. The Confederation occupies an entirely unique place in the international working-class movement. It is the only organization that, in declaring itself entirely revolutionary, has no attachments to any of the political parties, not even the most advanced of them. In most countries other than France, social democracy plays the leading role. In France, the CGT leaves far behind it, both in terms of numerical strength and of the influence it exercises, the Socialist party; claiming to represent *only* the working class, it has firmly repulsed all the advances that have been made to it over the past years. Autonomy has been its strength and it intends to remain autonomous.

This stand of the CGT, its refusal to have dealings with the political parties, has earned it the title of "anarchist" in the mouths of its exasperated adversaries. Yet nothing could be more false. The CGT, a vast grouping of syndicates and labour unions, has no official doctrine. All doctrines are represented within it and enjoy equal tolerance. A number of anarchists serve on the confederal committee; there they meet and work with socialists, the majority of whom—it should be noted in passing—are no less hostile than the anarchists to any idea of an alliance between the syndicates and the Socialist party.

...[N]either the realization of working-class unity, nor the coalition of revolutionaries would have been able on its own to lead the CGT to its present level of prosperity and influence, if we had not remained faithful, in our syndicalist practice, to the fundamental principle which in fact excludes syndicates based on opinions: *only one syndicate for each profession and town*. The consequence of this principle is the political neutralization of the syndicate, which neither can nor should be either anarchist, or Guesdist, or Allemanist, or Blanquist, but simply working-class. In the syndicate divergences of opinion, which are often so subtle and artificial, take second place, and in this way agreement is possible. In practical life, interests come before ideas; in spite of all the quarrels between the schools and the sects, the interests of the workers, by the very fact that they are all subject to the law of wages, are identical. And that is the secret of the accord that was established between them, the accord that made the strength of syndicalism and allowed it last year, at the Congress of Amiens, proudly to affirm its self-sufficiency...

It is important that the proletarians of all countries should profit from the syndicalist experience of the French proletariat. And it is the task of the anarchists to make sure that the experience is repeated everywhere that there is a working class working towards its emancipation. To that partisan unionism which has produced, in

Russia for example, anarchist unions, and in Belgium and Germany Christian and social democratic unions, the anarchists should oppose a syndicalism in the French style, a syndicalism that is neutral or, more exactly, independent. In the same way as there is one working class, there should be, in each industry and each town, no more than one working class organization, a single syndicate. Only on that condition can the class struggle—ceasing to be hindered at every moment by the squabbles of rival schools and sects—develop in all its breadth and achieve its maximum effect.

Syndicalism, as the Congress of Amiens proclaimed in 1906, is sufficient unto itself. That statement, I know, has never been fully understood, even by the anarchists. It means that the working class, having at last attained majority, means to be self-sufficient and to rely on no one else for its emancipation. What fault can an anarchist find with a will to action so finely expressed?

Syndicalism does not waste time promising to the workers an earthly paradise. It calls on them to conquer it, assuring them that their actions will never be entirely in vain. It is a school of will, of energy, and of fertile thinking. It opens to anarchism, which has been too long closed in upon itself, new perspectives and new hopes. Let all anarchists then come to syndicalism; their work will be all the more fertile for it, their blows against the social regime all the more decisive.

Errico Malatesta

The conclusion Monatte has reached is that syndicalism is a necessary and sufficient means of social revolution. In other words, Monatte has proclaimed *that syndicalism is sufficient unto itself.* And that, in my view, is a radically false doctrine…

Today, as in the past, I would like to see the anarchists entering the working-class movement. Today, as yesterday, I am a syndicalist in the sense that I am an upholder of the syndicates. I do not ask for anarchist syndicates, which would immediately give legitimacy to social democratic, republican, royalist and all other kinds of syndicates, and which would divide the working class more than ever against itself. I do not even want to see *red* syndicates, because I do not want to see *yellow* syndicates [employer controlled unions]. I would like far more to see syndicates wide open to all workers without regard for opinions, syndicates that are absolutely *neutral*.

Therefore I favour the most active participation in the working-class movement. But I do so above all in the interests of our propaganda whose scope in this way will be greatly widened. But in no way should that participation be considered as tantamount to a renunciation of our most cherished ideas. Within the syndicate we must remain anarchists, in all the strength and breadth of that definition. The working-class movement, in my eyes, is no more than a means—though doubtless it is the best of all the means that are available to us. But I refuse to take that means as an end, and in the same way I would not want us to lose sight of the totality of anarchist conceptions, or, to put it more simply, our other means of propaganda and agitation.

The syndicalists, on the other hand, are inclined to turn the means into an end, to regard the part as the whole...

Yet, even if it fortifies itself with the somewhat useless epithet of revolutionary, syndicalism is no more—and will never be more—than a legalitarian and even conservative movement, with no other accessible end but the amelioration of the conditions of work. I need not look for any further proof than that which is offered to us by the great North American unions. Having shown themselves, when they were still weak, as imbued with the most radical revolutionism, these unions have become, in so far as they have gained power and wealth, completely conservative organizations, entirely concerned with making their members into the aristocrats of the factory, the workshop or the mine, and far less hostile to paternalistic capitalism than they are to non-organized workers, to that proletariat in rags so condemned by the social democrat! But that ever-growing unemployed proletariat, which is of no account to syndicalism, or which—rather—is merely an obstacle to it, we—the other anarchists—cannot forget, and it is our duty to defend it because its members have most to suffer.

Let me repeat: the anarchists must enter the working-class unions, first of all to carry on anarchist propaganda there, and then because it is the only way in which—on the day we all hope for—we may have at our disposition groups who are capable of taking over the direction of production; we must enter the unions, finally, to struggle energetically against that detestable state of mind that makes the syndicates disinclined to defend anything but special interests.

In my view, the basic error of Monatte and of all the revolutionary syndicalists arises from a much too simplistic conception of the class struggle. It is the conception according to which the economic interests of all the workers—of the working-class—are identical, the conception according to which it is enough for workers to take in hand the defence of their own interests, and the interests of the whole proletariat will be at the same time defended against capitalism.

I suggest that the reality is quite different. Like the bourgeoisie, like everyone else, the workers are subject to that law of universal competition which derives from the existence of government and private property and which will only disappear when they are extinguished. Thus, in the true sense of the word, there are no classes because there are no class interests. In the heart of the working "class," as in the heart of the bourgeoisie, competition and struggle continue. The economic interests of one category of workers will be irrevocably opposed to those of another category. And everywhere one sees workers who both economically and morally are far nearer to the bourgeoisie than they are to the proletariat...I don't need to remind you how often in strikes the workers employ violence—against the police and the managers? Not in the least, but against the *blacklegs* who nevertheless are workers just as exploited as themselves and even more humiliated, while the true enemies of the workers, the real obstacles to social equality, are still the police and the employers.

Nevertheless, moral solidarity is possible among the workers even in the absence of economic solidarity. The workers who isolate themselves in the defence of their corporate interests may not be aware of it, but it will emerge on the day when a common will towards social transformation turns them into new men. In present-day society, solidarity can only result from a communion that develops under the aegis of a shared ideal. It is the role of the anarchists to awaken the syndicates to that ideal, to orient them gradually towards the social revolution—at the risk of harm to those "immediate advantages" to which at present they seem so partial.

One cannot deny that syndicalist action involves us in certain perils. The greatest of these perils undoubtedly lies in the acceptance by the militant of office in the syndicates, particularly when it is paid office. Let us take it as a general rule: the anarchist who becomes a permanent and paid official in a syndicate is lost to propaganda, lost to anarchism! Henceforward he is under obligation to those who pay him and, since these are not all anarchists, the salaried official—placed between his conscience and his interest—must either follow his conscience and lose his position, or follow his interest—and then, goodbye to anarchism!

The presence of the official in the working-class movement is a danger comparable only to that of parliamentarism: both of them lead to corruption, and from corruption to death is not a very long step.

And now, let us consider the general strike. Personally, I accept the principle and for years I have been propagating it to the best of my powers. The general strike has always seemed to me an excellent means for starting the social revolution. Yet we must be on our guard against falling into the disastrous illusion that the general strike makes armed insurrection unnecessary.

We are told that by means of halting production abruptly the workers will succeed in a few days in starving out the bourgeoisie who, dying with hunger, will be obliged to surrender. I can think of no more grandiose absurdity. The first to die of hunger during a general strike would not be the bourgeois, who dispose of all the stores, but the workers who have only their toil on which to live.

The general strike as it is foretold to us is a pure utopia. Either the worker, dying with hunger after three days of striking, will go back with bowed head to the workshop, and we can chalk up yet another defeat. Or he will seek to take over production by main force. Who will he find waiting to stop him? Soldiers, policemen, apart from the bourgeois themselves, and then the matter cannot help resolving into shooting and bombs. It will be insurrection, and victory will be to the strongest.

Let us therefore prepare for that inevitable insurrection instead of limiting ourselves to looking forward to the general strike as a panacea for all ills...

But even if we consider it in realistic terms, the general strike is still one of the weapons with two edges which it is necessary to employ with great caution. The provision of subsistence cannot be suspended indefinitely. Sooner or later it will be necessary to seize the means of feeding people, and for that we cannot wait until the strike has developed into an insurrection.

It is not so much to cease work that we should call on the workers, but rather to continue it for their own benefit. Without that, the general strike will soon be transformed into a general famine, even though one might have been energetic enough to seize hold immediately of all the produce accumulated in the shops. Basically, the idea of the general strike emerges from a totally erroneous belief: the belief that by taking over the products accumulated by the bourgeoisie, humanity can continue consuming, without producing, for no one knows how many months and years...

In the past I deplored that the comrades isolated themselves from the working-class movement. Today I deplore that many of us, falling into the contrary extreme, let themselves be swallowed up in the same movement. Once again, working-class organization, the strike, the general strike, direct action, boycott, sabotage and armed insurrection itself, are only *means*. Anarchy is the *end*. The anarchist revolution which we desire far exceeds the interests of a single class: it proposes the complete liberation of enslaved humanity, from the triple viewpoint, economic, political and moral. And let us therefore be on our guard against any unilateral and simplistic plan of action. Syndicalism is an excellent means of action by reason of the working-class forces which it puts at our disposition, but it cannot be our sole means. Even less must we lose sight of the one end that is worth our effort: Anarchy!

Chapter 13
Art And Anarchy

61. Oscar Wilde: The Soul of Man Under Socialism (1891)

The role of art and the artist in society is something anarchists have commented on since Proudhon, whose Du Principe de l'art et de sa destination sociale *(Paris: Garnier), was published posthumously in 1865. Proudhon advocated a realistic approach, which should not be confused with Marxist "socialist realism," something which came much later and had nothing to do with Proudhon or anarchism. Proudhon rejected the idealization through art of existing social realities, including the situation of the working class, which was far from ideal, and proposed, as Godwin had before him, that we should stop hiding from reality and see "things as they really are" (Proudhon,* Selected Writings, *New York: Doubleday, 1969, ed. S. Edwards, page 215). He commended his friend, the painter Gustave Courbet (1819-1877), for having "the courage to depict us not as nature intended us to be, but as our passions and vices have made us," adding that it was not Courbet's fault "if people recoil at the sight of their own image" (*Selected Writings, *pp. 216-217).*

In God and the State, *Bakunin described art, in contrast to science, as "the return of abstraction to life" (Selection 24). Kropotkin argued that artists in capitalist society were condemned to decorating "the parlours of shopkeepers," unless they put their talents "at the service of the revolution" (*Words of a Rebel, *Montreal: Black Rose, 1992, pages 54 and 58). After the revolution, artists will become "an integral part of a living whole that would not be complete without them, any more than they would be complete without it," and art will become a part of everyday life, blended with industry, surrounding "man, in the street, in the interior and exterior of public monuments," with everyone enjoying the "comfort and leisure" to enable them to engage in whatever artistic activities they may choose (*The Conquest of Bread, *Montreal: Black Rose, 1990, pages 141-142).*

Before socialism took up too many of his evenings, Oscar Wilde (1854-1900), the poet, playwright and novelist, briefly identified himself as an anarchist and wrote a pamphlet entitled,

The Soul of Man Under Socialism *(Chicago: Charles H. Kerr, 1984; originally published in the February 1891* Fortnightly Review*), in which he emphasized the importance of the utopian imagination and the unavoidable conflict between art and authority, advocating a kind of anarchist individualism.*

A MAP OF THE WORLD THAT DOES NOT include Utopia is not worth even glancing at, for it leaves out the one country at which Humanity is always landing. And when Humanity lands there, it looks out, and, seeing a better country, sets sail. Progress is the realization of Utopias...

An individual who has to make things for the use of others, and with reference to their wants and their wishes, does not work with interest, and consequently cannot put into his work what is best in him. Upon the other hand, whenever a community or a powerful section of a community, or a government of any kind, attempts to dictate to the artist what he is to do, Art either entirely vanishes, or becomes stereotyped, or degenerates into a low and ignoble form of craft. *A work of art is the unique result of a unique temperament. Its beauty comes from the fact that the author is what he is. It has nothing to do with the fact that other people want what they want*. Indeed, the moment that an artist takes notice of what other people want, and tries to supply the demand, he ceases to be an artist, and becomes a dull or an amusing craftsman, an honest or a dishonest tradesman. He has no further claim to be considered as an artist. *Art is the most intense mode of individualism that the world has known...*

And it is to be noted that it is the fact that Art is this intense form of individualism that makes the public try to exercise over it an authority that is as immoral as it is ridiculous, and as corrupting as it is contemptible...They are continually asking Art to be popular, to please their want of taste, to flatter their absurd vanity, to tell them what they have been told before, to show them what they ought to be tired of seeing, to amuse them when they feel heavy after eating too much, and to distract their thoughts when they are wearied of their own stupidity. *Now Art should never try to be popular. The public should try to make itself artistic*. There is a very wide difference. If a man of science were told that the results of his experiments, and the conclusions that he arrived at, should be of such a character that they would not upset the received popular notions on the subject, or disturb popular prejudice, or hurt the sensibilities of people who knew nothing about science; if a philosopher were told that he had a perfect right to speculate in the highest spheres of thought, provided that he arrived at the same conclusions as were held by those who had never thought in any sphere at all—well, nowadays the man of science and the philosopher would be considerably amused. Yet it is really a very few years since both philosophy and science were subjected to brutal popular control, to authority in fact—the authority of either the general ignorance of the community, or the terror and greed for power of an ecclesiastical or governmental class. Of course, we have to a very great extent got rid of any attempt on the part of the community or the Church, or the Government, to interfere with the individualism of speculative thought, but the attempt to interfere with the individualism of imaginative art still lingers. In fact, it does more than linger: it is aggressive, offensive, and brutalizing...

The one thing that the public dislike is novelty. Any attempt to extend the subject matter of art is extremely distasteful to the public; and yet the vitality and progress of art depend in a large measure on the continual extension of subject-matter. The public dislike novelty because they are afraid of it. It represents to them a mode of Individualism, an assertion on the part of the artist that he selects his own subject, and treats it as he chooses. The public are quite right in their attitude. Art is Individualism, and Individualism is a disturbing and disintegrating force. Therein lies its immense value. For what it seeks to disturb is monotony of type, slavery of custom, tyranny of habit, and the reduction of man to the level of a machine. In Art, the public accept what has been, because they cannot alter it, not because they appreciate it...

The fact is, the public make use of the classics of a country as a means of checking the progress of Art. They degrade the classics into authorities. They use them as bludgeons for preventing the free expression of Beauty in new forms. They are always asking a writer why he does not write like somebody else, or a painter why he does not paint like somebody else, quite oblivious of the fact that if either of them did anything of the kind he would cease to be an artist. A fresh mode of Beauty is absolutely distasteful to them, and whenever it appears they get so angry and bewildered that they always use two stupid expressions—one is that the work of art is grossly unintelligible; the other, that the work of art is grossly immoral. What they mean by these words seems to me to be this. When they say a work is grossly unintelligible, they mean that the artist has said or made a beautiful thing that is new; when they describe a work as grossly immoral, they mean that the artist has said or made a beautiful thing that is true. The former expression has reference to style; the latter to subject-matter...

People sometimes inquire what form of government is most suitable for an artist to live under. To this question there is only one answer. *The form of government that is most suitable to the artist is no government at all.* Authority over him and his art is ridiculous.

...It is to be noted also that Individualism does not come to man with any sickly cant about duty, which merely means doing what other people want because they want it; or any hideous cant about self-sacrifice, which is merely a survival of savage mutilation. *In fact, it does not come to man with any claims upon him at all. It comes naturally and inevitably out of man*. It is the point to which all development tends. It is the differentiation to which all organisms grow. It is the perfection that is inherent in every mode of life, and towards which every mode of life quickens. And so Individualism exercises no compulsion over man. On the contrary, it says to man that he should suffer no compulsion to be exercised over him. It does not try to force people to be good. It knows that people are good when they are let alone. Man will develop Individualism out of himself.

62. Bernard Lazare: Anarchy and Literature (1894)

During the 1890's in France a wide variety of artists became associated with anarchism, including painters such as Camille Pissarro, Paul Signac, Charles Maurin and Maximilien Luce, and writers and poets such as Paul Adam, Adolphe Retté, and Octave Mirbeau. Bernard Lazare (1865-1903), who later played an important role in the Dreyfus Affair, was a French writer and journalist who edited, with Paul Adam, the avant-garde literary journal, Les Entretiens Politiques et Littéraires. *Lazare identified himself as an anarchist at this time and testified as a character witness on behalf of Jean Grave at his February 1894 trial. The following excerpts, translated by Paul Sharkey, are taken from his contemporaneous article, "Anarchy and Literature," published in* La Révolte's Literary Supplement, *shortly before the French government forced its closure in March 1894. Lazare refers to Auguste Vaillant (1861-1894) who was executed in February 1894 for bombing the French Chamber of Deputies (causing only minor injuries), Ravachol (François Koeningstein, 1859-1892), who was executed in 1892 for a series of crimes, including bombings to avenge the police killings of peaceful demonstrators, and Louis Jules Léauthier (1872-1894), who stabbed a Serbian diplomat because he was a "bourgeois" and was later executed along with several other anarchist prisoners following a failed uprising at the notorious French penal colony, Devil's Island.*

WE HAD THE AUDACITY TO BELIEVE THAT not everything was for the best in the best of all possible worlds, and we stated and state still that modern society is despicable, founded upon theft, dishonesty, hypocrisy and turpitude. One of us attacked the voracious ogre of militarism, one that other bloody idol that goes under the name of fatherland, another committed the abomination of rejecting war, butchery, ceaseless looting, hatred of peoples and races and issued a call to universal brotherhood, and somebody else again spoke ill of the oppressive State, the heartless rule of law, the narrowness and wrong-headed basis of justice, vanity and property, villainy and conventional morality.

And so their beefs with us are plain: we are anarchists—nothing wrong with that—but anarchist dilettantes…If I have things right, the meaning is that our ideas, our theories or our doctrines are pantomime doctrines, theories and ideas that we embrace for effect, that they are our equivalent of the romantics' red waistcoat, in short, that we espouse them so as to shock the bourgeois and, in the last analysis, are play-actors bereft of all conviction.

This notion is a great credit to the brains that hatched it and I do not find it unpleasant. Anything else coming from its authors would have come as a surprise to me. It is self-evident that only after one has judged oneself does one pass judgment on others. Now, most of our accusers who are coming to the end of a glittering career or who are entering the lists in the hope of following in the footsteps of their elders, have always earned a living from their opinions, or indeed have formed opinions in order to make a living from them. They have marketed and priced them, and, having only ever had ideas that were commodities, they have a hard time understanding the notion that a man might be disinterested or a true believer. While there may be a few sincere souls among those taking exception to our writings, they then woke up to the excellence of the privileges in which they share, and cannot comprehend how they could be assailed other than as a pastime or out of jealousy, or indeed, to conjure up new personal stipends. The world being founded upon falsehood, the only virtue grudgingly acknowledged is sincerity, especially as those who aspire to this ideological loyalism can only prove it through what they write and this is the very thing that is being called into question. We have no evidence to present, besides that contained in our writings, other than the insincerity of our adversaries, whose abjurations are legendary, and we must wonder whether in fighting us they are not indirectly pleading their own cause, for it would be acknowledging a shameful vileness, would it not, to concede that there are some persons capable of letting themselves be prompted by motives other than monetary?

However, this dilettantism of ours is not, they say, solely characterized by lack of bona fides and by affectation. Our speech, our writing and our failure to act bear witness to our dilettante status. Which really is an abominable feature of ours, and if Vaillant is an odious criminal for throwing that bomb, we, on the other hand, are odious sycophants because we first of all were beaten to it and then because we primed him just as we did Ravachol and Léauthier, and will go on to prime others, unless somebody stops us first.

These two arguments are contradictory, and the contradiction derives from the construction placed upon the word "act" and action itself. Act does not just mean physical action: the picking up of rifle, dagger or dynamite; there is intellectual action and we know that only too well because we stand accused of targeting those around us for it. So the charge of inactivity is unfounded and at best it might be argued that we understand action more as Diderot, Rousseau or the Encyclopaedists did, than in the manner of an Orsini, Fieschi or Saint-Réjaut (to borrow examples from right across the spectrum). There is no denying that, and by my reckoning in so doing we fulfill our role as intellectuals—I am deliberately using that word which the brainless gentlemen of the press throw in our faces by way of insult. Yes, as they would have us confess, we are the cause, or one of the causes, driving men to revolt, so there is no denying that we are activists. We could not be dilettantes unless we were to shrug off responsibility for our words and our writings. Now, who ever told you that we refused to accept that responsibility? For my own part, I accept it fully and blatantly, minimal though it may be, in that it makes only an infinitesimal addition to the responsibility accepted by poets, philosophers, novelists, dramatists, thinkers and all independent authors in every age, down through the ages. Since you condemn us, condemn our elders too: condemn Rabelais, condemn Montaigne, condemn La Bruyère, condemn Voltaire, condemn Heine, Hugo, Byron, Shelley, all the rebels, all the libertarians. We will certainly find ourselves in a company every bit as good as yours and, between them and you, we long ago made our choice.

It may well be that simpletons, primitives, reckless types already soured by poverty and by despair have drunk from some page of ours the craving for something better and, in their naiveté, thought that they might hasten the arrival of that something better by lashing out. But did we create these embittered, desperate wretches, or was that you?

Are we the source of the distress and destitution that still beset millions? Is it thanks to us and to our libertarianism, to our protestations that poor wretches perishing from hunger and cold are picked up off the streets, boulevards and squares? Was it not you who made them ready to give us a hearing, you, the stalwarts and pillars of society and of order? You prattle about responsibilities: so claim your own share, just as we claim ours!

Make something of a confession, therefore, and appoint one of your representatives to take on this task some day and we will be reconciled with some splendid, rabid mentors, honourable champions of forcefulness. What can you say? You will say: "We believed in one thing only—money: we have spent our lives championing it and in its pursuit, we have idolized the mighty and the rich, we have run after the thieving financiers and shady politicians and scooped up the coins spilling from their pockets, we have thrown our support behind all rapine, every abomination, and if we have ever shown any sign of pity, that pity was lucrative and we knew how to turn a profit from it. We sold ourselves to all who made us an offer, everybody who could pay our price." Deep down, good fellows, if you do not come over to the Revolution, it is no doubt because you think that it has no immediate profit to offer you.

So what can we tell you and what matter to us are your carping, your insults and your nonsense? We believe in everything that you deny, love everything that you detest, we hate everything that you hold dear; we have faith in our ideas and you have no ideas, only appetites; we are minds and you bellies, and every fibre of our being opposes you and we despise you every bit as much as you abominate us.

Which of us is right? Time will tell. Perhaps you reckon that tomorrow will be yours, that the hue and cry you have started is not going to end and that, worn out by your yapping, tied down by the ropes you are trying to throw over us, we will fall silent. Stop deluding yourselves. No law can halt free thought, no penalty can stop us from uttering truth and justice according to our lights, and the Idea, gagged, bound and beaten, will emerge all the more lively, splendid and mighty.

63. Jean Grave: The Artist as Equal, Not Master (1899)

In his 1899 publication, L'Anarchie, son but, ses moyens *(Paris: P. V. Stock), Jean Grave argues against artistic elitism, on the basis that true freedom for the artist can only be achieved through the freedom of the masses. This translation is taken from Alvin F. Sanborn's* Paris and the Social Revolution *(Boston: Small, Maynard & Co., 1905), with some minor modifications.*

IT IS NOT ONLY TO THOSE WHO ARE dying of want that anarchy addresses itself. To satisfy one's hunger is a primordial right that takes precedence over all other rights and stands at the head of the claims of a human being. But anarchy embraces all the aspirations and neglects no need. The list of its demands includes all the demands of humanity.

Mirbeau, in his *Mauvais Bergers*, makes one of the characters proclaim to workmen on strike their right to beauty. And, indeed, every being has a right not only to what sustains life, but also to whatever renders it easy, enlivens it, and embellishes it. They are rare, alas! in our social state, who can live their lives fully.

Some there are whose physical needs are satisfied, but who are inhibited in their evolution by a social organization which is conditioned by the narrowness of conception of the average intellect,—artists, litterateurs, savants, all who think, suffer morally, if not physically, from the present order of things.

Daily they are wounded by the pettiness of current existence, and disheartened by the mediocrity of the public to whom they address themselves, and whom they must consider if they wish to sell their works—a situation which leads those who would not die of hunger to compromise, to vulgar and mediocre art.

Their education has led many of them to believe that they are of an essence superior to the peasant, to the manual worker, from whom, for that matter, they are for the most part descended. They have been persuaded that it is necessary, if their "talent" is to develop and their imagination is to have full swing, that the "vile multitude" take upon its shoulders the heavy tasks, devote itself to serving them, and wear itself out in making, by its labour, life easy for them; that they must have, if their genius is to attain its complete fruition, the same atmosphere of luxury and of idleness as the aristocratic classes.

A healthy conception of things teaches that a human being, to be complete, must exercise his limbs as well as his brain, that labour is degrading only because it has been made a sign of servitude, and that a man truly worthy of the name does not need to impose the cares of his existence on others...

The artist and the litterateur belong to the masses. They cannot isolate themselves, and inevitably feel the effects of the surrounding mediocrity. It is vain for them to entrench themselves behind the privileges of the ruling classes, to attempt to withdraw into their "ivory tower": if there is debasement for him who is reduced to performing the vilest tasks to satisfy his hunger, the morality of those who condemn him to it is not superior to his own; if obedience degrades, command, far from exalting character, degrades it also.

To live their dream, realize their aspirations, they, too, must work—for the moral and intellectual elevation of the masses. They, too, must understand that their own development is made up of the intellectuality of all; that, whatever the heights they believe they have attained, they belong to the multitude. If they strain to rise above the multitude, a thousand bonds hold them to it, fetter their action and their thought, preventing them forever from reaching the summits they have glimpsed. A society normally constituted does not admit slaves, but a mutual exchange of services between equals.

Chapter 14
Anarchy And Education

64. Bakunin: Integral Education (1869)

From the time of Godwin, anarchists have recognized the importance of education as a means of social liberation, on the one hand, and as an authoritarian means of social control, on the other. While Proudhon had advocated general vocational training as a means of lessening the negative effects of the division of labour (Selection 12), it was Bakunin who developed the concept of "integral education," which was meant to help overcome the division between intellectual and manual labour, an idea Kropotkin expanded upon in Fields, Factories and Workshops *(Selection 34). The following extracts are taken from Bakunin's essay, "L'Instruction intégrale," originally published as a series of articles in the Swiss Internationalist paper,* L'Egalité, *in 1869. The translation is taken from Robert Cutler's* The Basic Bakunin *(New York: Prometheus, 1992), and is reprinted with his kind permission. For consistency, I have changed the references to "all-round education" back to "integral education," as that is how the concept is referred to in the other selections.*

THE FIRST QUESTION WE MUST NOW consider is whether the working masses can be fully emancipated so long as the education that they receive is inferior to that given to the members of the bourgeoisie, or, in general, so long as any class of any size enjoys, because of its birth, the privileges of a better upbringing and a fuller education. Doesn't this question answer itself? Isn't it obvious that of two persons endowed with nearly equal natural intelligence, the one who knows more, who is broader-minded thanks to scientific learning, who grasps more easily and fully the nature of his surroundings because he better understands those facts which are called the laws of nature and society and which interconnect natural and social events—that that person will feel freer in nature and society, and that he will also in fact be the cleverer and stronger of the two? The one who knows more will naturally rule over the one who knows less; and if between two classes just this one difference in education and upbringing existed, it would be enough to produce all the others in short order, and the human world would find itself in its present state, divided anew into a large number of slaves and a small number of rulers, the former working for the latter, as is the case now.

Now you understand why bourgeois socialists call for only *some* education for the people, a little more than they have now, and why we socialist-democrats call for *integral education* for them, *total* education as full as the intellectual development of the times allows, so that in the future no *class* can rule over the working masses, exploiting them, superior to them because it knows more...

But, they will say...it is impossible for all humanity to devote itself to scientific learning; it would die of hunger. While some study, accordingly, the others must work to produce the vital necessities, first of all for themselves and then also for those persons who have consecrated themselves exclusively to labours of the intellect. For these latter work not just for themselves: don't their scientific discoveries, through application to industry and agriculture as well as to political and social life generally, both broaden human understanding and improve the situation of every human being without exception? Don't artistic creations ennoble everyone's life?

No, not at all. And our greatest criticism of science and the arts is precisely that they spread their good deeds and exercise their beneficial influence only over a very small portion of society, to the exclusion of the vast majority and hence also to their detriment.

...Someone will ask: If everybody is educated, who will want to work? Our answer is simple: *Everyone shall work and everyone shall be educated*. A frequent objection to this reply is that such a combination of industrial and intellectual labour can only hurt both, that workers will be poor scholars and scholars will be poor workers. Yes, [this is true] in present-day society, where both manual and mental labour are distorted by the wholly artificial separation to which they have both been condemned. But we are convinced that well-rounded living persons must develop muscular and mental activities equally and that these activities, far from harming each other, not only will not impede each other but instead will support, broaden, and reinforce each other; the scholar's science will become more fertile, more useful, and broader in scope when the scholar ceases being a stranger to manual labour, and the educated worker will work more intelligently and therefore more productively than the unlearned worker.

From this it follows, in the interest of both labour and science, that there should no longer be either workers or scholars but only human beings...

But once equality has triumphed and is well established, will various individuals' abilities and their levels of energy cease to differ? Some will exist, perhaps not so many as now, but certainly some will always exist. It is proverbial that the same tree never bears two identical leaves, and this will probably always be true. And it is even truer with regard to human beings, who are much more complex than leaves. But this diversity is hardly an evil. On the contrary, as the German philosopher Feuerbach rightly observed, it is a resource of the human race. Thanks to this diversity, humanity is a collective whole in which the one individual complements all the others and needs them. As a result, this infinite diversity of human individuals is the fundamental cause and the very basis of their solidarity. It is an all-powerful argument for equality.

Even in modern society, if we disregard the differences artificially created by a thousand social causes, such as upbringing, education, and economic and political standing—which differ not only among social strata but nearly from family to family—we will see that from the standpoint of intellectual abilities and moral strength, excluding geniuses and idiots, the vast majority of individuals either are quite similar or at least balance each other out (since one who is weaker in a given respect nearly always makes up the difference by being equivalently stronger in another respect), with the result that it becomes impossible to say whether one individual from this mass rises much above or sinks much below another. The vast majority of human individuals are not identical, but they are equivalent and hence equal…

Education ought to be equal for everyone in all respects. It must therefore be integral education, that is, it should prepare every child of each sex for the life of thought as well as for the life of labour. This way, all children are equally able to become full human beings…

Since, on the one hand, no mind however powerful can encompass every specialty of every science, and since, on the other hand, a general knowledge of all sciences is absolutely necessary for the mind to be fully developed, instruction will naturally be divided into two parts: the general part, which will furnish both the basic elements of every science without exception and a very real, not superficial knowledge of the whole that they form together; and the special part, which will be divided of necessity into several groups or faculties, each of which will cover in full the particular aspects of a given number of sciences that are intrinsically very complementary…

Undoubtedly some adolescents, influenced by either their own or someone else's secondary interest, will be mistaken in the choice of their scientific specialty, initially choosing a faculty and career not quite best suited to their aptitudes. But since we are sincere, unhypocritical partisans of *individual freedom*; since we detest with all our heart, in the name of this freedom, the principle of authority and every possible manifestation of that divine, anti-human principle; since we detest and condemn, from the full depth of our love for freedom, the authority both of the father and of the schoolmaster; since we find them equally demoralizing and disastrous (for daily experience shows us that the head of the family and the schoolmaster, in spite of and even as a result of their acknowledged and proverbial wisdom, are worse [judges] of their children's abilities than are the children themselves, because they follow an indisputable, irrevocable, and entirely human law that leads every domineering person astray, leading every schoolmaster and family head to give much greater weight to their own tastes than to the natural aptitudes of the child in their arbitrary determination of their children's future); finally, since the mistakes of despotism are always more disastrous and less rectifiable than those of freedom: [for all these reasons] we support fully and completely, against every official, semi-official, paternal, and pedantic tutor in the world, the freedom of children to choose and decide their own career.

If they err, the error itself will be an effective lesson for the future, and the general education which they will have received will help them guide themselves back onto the path indicated to them by their own nature. Like mature persons, children become wise only through experiences of their own, and never through those of others.

Along with *scientific* or *theoretical* instruction, in integral education there must inevitably be *industrial or practical instruction*. This is the only way to train the full human being, the worker who understands what he is doing…

Alongside scientific and industrial instruction there will have to be practical instruction as well, or rather, a series of experiments in morality, not divine morality but human morality. Divine morality is based on two immoral principles: respect for authority and contempt for humanity. Human morality, on the contrary, is founded on contempt for authority and respect for the freedom of humanity…

For individuals to be moralized and become fully human, three things are necessary: a hygienic birth; rational, integral education, accompanied by an upbringing based on respect for labour, reason, equality, and freedom; and a social environment wherein each human individual will enjoy full freedom and really be, *de jure* and *de facto*, the equal of every other.

Does this environment exist? No. Therefore it must be established. If, in the existing social environment, we cannot even successfully establish schools which would give their students an education and upbringing as perfect as we might imagine, could we successfully create just, free, moral persons? No, because on leaving school they would enter a society governed by totally opposite principles, and, because society is always stronger than individuals, it would soon prevail over them, that is, demoralize them. What is more, the very foundation of such schools is impossible in the present social environment. For social life embraces everything, pervading the schools as well as the life of families and individuals who are a part of it.

Instructors, professors, and parents are all members of this society, all more or less stultified or demoralized by it. How would they give students what they themselves lack? One can preach morality successfully only by example; and since a socialist morality is entirely the opposite of current morality, the schoolmasters, who are inevitably more or less dominated by the latter morality, will act in front of their pupils in a manner wholly contrary to what they preach. As a result, a socialist upbringing is impossible not only in modern families but in the schools as well.

But integral education is equally impossible under present conditions: the members of the bourgeoisie will hear nothing of their children becoming workers, and workers are deprived of every resource for giving their children a scientific education...

Yes, certainly, the workers do everything possible to obtain all the education they can in the material circumstances in which they currently find themselves. But without being led astray by the Sirens' song of the bourgeois socialists and the members of the bourgeoisie, they will above all concentrate their efforts on the great question of their economic emancipation, which is the mother of all their other emancipations.

65. Francisco Ferrer: The Modern School (1908)

Francisco Ferrer y Guardia (1859-1909) was a libertarian educator executed by the Spanish government in 1909 for allegedly fomenting an insurrection in Barcelona known as the "Tragic Week." In reality, his crime was to advocate secular, humanist and rationalist education in a country whose educational system was dominated by a reactionary Catholic Church. In 1901, Ferrer founded the Escuela Moderna, or Modern School, in Barcelona, modeled after libertarian schools in France, such as Paul Robin's (1837-1912) free school in Cempuis, that provided male and female students with the "integral education" of which Bakunin spoke. Ferrer was also active in the Spanish anarcho-syndicalist movement, publishing a journal, La Huelga General *(*The General Strike*) in 1901-1903, until it was suppressed by the authorities. The Spanish government shut down Ferrer's Modern School in 1906, but he continued to promote the principles of libertarian education, publishing* L'Ecole Renovée *in 1908, the journal of the International League for the Rational Education of Children, to which several prominent libertarians belonged, including Sébastien Faure, who had founded another free school in France, La Ruche, in 1904 (Selection 66). The following article sets forth Ferrer's ed-*

ucational program from the inaugural issue of L'Ecole Renovée, *which was widely reprinted, particularly after Ferrer's execution on October 13, 1909. In the wake of Ferrer's death, which sparked widespread outrage, Modern Schools were founded throughout Europe and in Latin America, the United States, China and Japan. The following translation was first published in the November 1909 issue of Emma Goldman's* Mother Earth *newspaper, and has recently been reprinted in* Anarchy! An Anthology of Emma Goldman's Mother Earth *(Washington: Counterpoint, 2001), ed. P. Glassgold.*

TO THOSE WHO WISH TO RENOVATE the education of children two methods are open: to work for the transformation of the school by studying the child, so as to prove scientifically that the present organization of education is defective and to bring about progressive modification; or, to found new schools in which shall be directly applied those principles corresponding directly to the ideal of society and of its units, as held by those who eschew the conventionalities, prejudices, cruelties, trickeries, and falsehoods upon which modern society is based.

The first method certainly offers great advantages. It corresponds to that evolutionary conception which all men of science defend and which alone, according to them, can succeed.

In theory they are right, and we are quite ready to recognize it. It is evident that experiments in psychology and physiology must lead to important changes in matters of education: that teachers, being better able to understand the child, will know better how to adapt their instruction to natural laws. I even grant that such evolution will be in the direction of liberty, for I am convinced that constraint arises only from ignorance and that the educator who is really worthy of the name will obtain his results through the spontaneous response of the child, whose desires he will learn to know and whose development he will try to further by giving it every possible gratification.

But in reality, I do not believe that those who struggle for human emancipation can expect much from this method. Governments have ever been careful to hold a high hand over the education of the people. They know, better than anyone else, that their power is based almost entirely on the school. Hence, they monopolize it more and more. The time is past when they opposed the diffusion of instruction and when they sought to restrain the education of the masses. These tactics were formerly possible, because the economic life of the nations allowed the prevalence of popular ignorance, that ignorance which renders mastery easy. But circumstances have changed. The progress of science, discoveries of all kinds, have revolutionized the conditions of labour and production. It is no longer possible for a people to remain ignorant: it must be educated in order that the economic situation of one country may hold its own and make headway against the universal competition. In consequence, governments want education; they want a more and more complete organization of the school, not because they hope for the renovation of society through education, but because they need individuals, workmen, perfected instruments of labour, to make their industrial enterprises and the capital employed in them profitable. And we have seen the most reactionary governments follow this movement; they have realized perfectly that their former tactics were becoming dangerous to the economic life of the nations and that it is necessary to adapt popular education to new necessities.

But it would be a great mistake to suppose that the directors have not foreseen the dangers which the intelligent development of the people might create for them and that it was necessary for them to change their methods of keeping the mastery. These methods have likewise been adapted to the new conditions of life, and they have laboured to keep a hold over the evolution of ideas. At the same time that they seek to preserve the beliefs upon which social discipline was formerly based, they have sought to give to conceptions born of scientific effort a signification which could do no harm to established institutions. And to that end they took possession of the school. They who formerly left the priests in charge of the education of the people, because the priests were perfectly suited to the task, their instruction being at the service of authority, now took up everywhere the direction of scholarly education.

The danger, for them, lay in the awakening of human intelligence to the new outlook on life; the awakening, in the depths of men's consciousness, of a will towards emancipation. It would have been foolish to combat the evolving forces; they had to be driven into channels. That is the reason why, far from adhering to the old procedures of government, they adopted new ones, and evidently efficacious ones. It did not require great genius to find this solution; the simple pressure of facts led the men in power to understand what they must oppose to the apparent perils.

They founded schools, laboured to spread education on all sides, and if there were those among them who at first resisted this impulse—for its diverse tendencies favoured certain antagonistic political parties—all soon understood that it was better to yield to it, and that the best tactics were to assure the defence of their interests and their principles by new means. Forthwith began terrible struggles for the conquest of the School; in every country these struggles are still continuing with intensity; here, bourgeois republican society triumphs; there, clericalism. All sides know the importance of the game and recoil at no sacrifice to secure a victory. Everyone's cry is: "For and by the School." And the good people ought to be touched by so much solicitude! Everybody thirsts for their elevation by education, and by consequence—their happiness! Formerly some could say: "These others want to keep you in ignorance that they may the better exploit you: we want to see you educated and free." Now that is no longer possible; they have built schools on every corner, for every sort of instruction.

It is in this unanimous change of ideas among the ruling classes in respect to the school that I find reason to be suspicious of their goodwill and the explanation of the facts which actuate my doubts as to the efficacy of the methods of renovation which certain reformers want to put in operation. These reformers are, moreover, very indifferent, generally speaking, to the social significance of education; they are men very ardent in the search of scientific truth, but who avoid all questions foreign to the object of their studies. They study patiently to know the child and will some day tell us—their science is young yet—what methods of education are most suitable for its integral development.

Now this, in some sort, professional indifference is very prejudicial, I think, to the cause they intend to serve.

I do not mean to say that they are unconscious of the realities of the social environment, and I know that they expect the best results for the general welfare from their task. They say: In trying to discover the secrets of the life of the human being, in seeking the processes of its normal physical and psychic development, we give education a form which cannot but be favourable to the liberation of energies. We do not wish to devote our attention directly to the liberation of the school: as savants moreover we cannot, for we are not yet able exactly to define what is to be done. We shall proceed by slow degrees, convinced that the school will be transformed just in proportion to our discoveries by the force of events themselves...

This reasoning is apparently logical, and no one would dare to contradict it. And yet it is mixed considerably with illusion. Yes, if the governing powers had, as men, the same ideas as benevolent reformers, if they were really concerned for the continuous reorganization of society in the sense of the progressive disappearance of slavery, we might admit that scientific effort alone would improve the destiny of nations. But we should reckon without our host. We know too well that those who dispute for power have in view nothing but the defence of their own interests; that they busy themselves only with conquering what they want for themselves, for the satisfaction of their appetites. Long ago we ceased to believe in the words with which they mask their ambitions. Certain naïve persons still refuse to believe that there is not among them, all the same, some little sincerity and imagine that they, too, sometimes desire the happiness of their fellows. But these become fewer and fewer, and the Positivism of the century has become far too cruel for us to deceive ourselves any longer as to the intentions of those who govern us.

Just as they knew how to get out of the difficulty, when the necessity for education became evident, in such a way as to prevent that education from becoming a danger, just so they will know how to organize the school in accordance with the new discoveries of science that nothing may endanger their supremacy. These are ideas which are certainly not received without difficulty; but when one has seen, from close by, what takes place and how things are in reality arranged, one can no longer be caught by the whistling of words.

Oh, what have people not expected, what do they not expect still, from education! The majority of progressive men expect everything from it, and it is only in these later days that some begin to understand that it offers nothing but illusions. We perceive the utter uselessness of this learning acquired in the schools by the systems of education at present in practice; we see that we expected and hoped in vain. It is because the organization of the school, far from spreading the ideal which we imagined, has made education the most powerful means of enslavement in the hands of the governing powers today. Their teachers are only the conscious or unconscious instruments of these powers, modeled moreover according to their principles; they have from their youth up, and more than anyone else, been subjected to the discipline of their authority; few indeed are those who have escaped the influence of this domination; and these remain powerless, because the school organization constrains them so strongly that they cannot but obey it. It is not my purpose here to examine the nature of this organization. It is sufficiently well known for me to characterize it in one word: constraint. The school imprisons children physically, intellectually, and morally, in order to direct the development of their faculties in the paths desired. It deprives them of contact with nature in order to model them after its own pattern. And this is the explanation of all which I have here set forth: The care which governments have taken to direct the education of the people and the bankruptcy of the hopes of believers in liberty. The education of today is nothing more than drill. I refuse to believe that the systems employed have been combined with any exact design for bringing about the results desired. That would suppose genius. But things take place precisely as if this education responded to some vast entire conception in a manner really remarkable. It could not have been better done. What accomplished it was simply that the leading inspiration was the principle of discipline and of authority which guides social organizers at all times. They have but one clearly defined idea, one will, namely: Children must be accustomed to obey, to believe, to think according to the social dogmas which govern us. Hence, education cannot be other than such as it is today. It is not a matter of seconding the spontaneous development of the faculties of the child, of leaving it free to satisfy its physical, intellectual, and moral needs; it is a matter of imposing ready-made ideas upon it; a matter even of preventing it from ever thinking otherwise than is willed for the maintenance of the institutions of this society; it is a matter of making it an individual strictly adapted to the social mechanism.

No one should be astonished that such an education has this evil influence upon human emancipation. I repeat, it is but a means of domination in the hands of the governing powers. They have never wanted the uplift of the individual, but his enslavement; and it is perfectly useless to hope anything from the school of today.

Now, what has been resulting up until today will continue to result in the future. There is no reason for governments to change their system. They have succeeded in making education serve for their advantage; they will likewise know how to make use of any improvements that may be proposed to their advantage.

It is sufficient that they maintain the spirit of the school, the authoritarian discipline which reigns therein, for all innovations to be turned to their profit. And they will watch [for] their opportunity; be sure of that.

I would like to call the attention of my readers to this idea: All the value of education rests in respect for the physical, intellectual, and moral will of the child. Just as in science no demonstration is possible save by facts, just so there is no real education save that which is exempt from all dogmatism, which leaves to the child itself the direction of its effort and confines itself to the seconding of that effort. Now there is nothing easier than to alter this purpose, and nothing harder than to respect it. Education is always imposing, violating, constraining; the real educator is he who can best protect the child against his (the teacher's) own ideas, his peculiar whims; he who can best appeal to the child's own energies.

One may judge by this with what ease education receives the stamp they wish to put upon it and how easy is the task of those who wish to enslave the individual. The best of methods become in their hands only the more powerful and perfect instruments of domination. Our own ideal is certainly that of science, and we demand that we be given the power to educate the child by favouring its development through the satisfaction of all its needs in proportion as these arise and grow.

We are convinced that the education of the future will be of an entirely spontaneous nature; certainly we cannot as yet realize it, but the evolution of methods in the direction of a wider comprehension of the phenomena of life, and the fact that all advances toward perfection mean the overcoming of some constraint, all this indicates that we are in the right when we hope for the deliverance of the child through science.

Is this the ideal of those who control the present school organization? Is this what they, too, want to realize? and they, too, do they aspire to overcome restraint? Not at all. They will employ the newest and most effective means to the same end as now, that is to say, the formation of beings who will accept all the conventions, all the prejudices, all the lies upon which society is founded.

Let us not fear to say that we want men capable of evolving without stopping, capable of destroying and renewing their environments without cessation, of renewing themselves also; men whose intellectual independence will be their greatest force, who will attach themselves to nothing, always ready to accept what is best, happy in the triumph of new ideas, aspiring to live multiple lives in one life. Society fears such men; we must not then hope it will ever want an education able to give them to us.

What, then, is our own mission? What method are we going to choose to contribute to the renovation of the school?

We shall follow the labours of the scientists who study the child with the greatest attention, and we shall eagerly seek for means of applying their experience to the education we wish to build up, in the direction of an ever fuller liberation of the individual. But how can we attain our end? Shall it not be by putting ourselves directly to the work favouring the foundation of new schools, which shall be ruled as much as possible by this spirit of liberty, which we forefeel will dominate the entire work of education in the future?

A trial has been made which, for the present, has already given excellent results. We can destroy all which in the present school answers to the organization of constraint, the artificial surroundings by which the children are separated from nature and life, the intellectual and moral discipline made use of to impose ready-made ideas upon them, beliefs which deprave and annihilate natural bent. Without fear of deceiving ourselves, we can restore the child to the environment which entices it, the environment of nature in which he will be in contact with all that he loves and in which impressions of life will replace fastidious book learning. If we did no more than that, we should already have prepared in great part the deliverance of the child.

In such conditions we might already freely apply the data of science and labour most fruitfully.

I know very well that we could not thus realize all our hopes, that we should often be forced, for lack of knowledge, to employ undesirable methods; but a certitude would sustain us in our effort, namely, that even without reaching our aim completely we should do more and better in our still imperfect work than the present school accomplishes. I like the free spontaneity of a child who knows nothing, better than the word knowledge and intellectual deformity of a child who has been subjected to our present education.

What we have attempted at Barcelona others have attempted elsewhere, and we have all seen that the work is possible. And I think it should be begun without delay. We should not wait until the study of the child has been completed before undertaking the renovation of the school; if we must wait for that, we shall never do anything. We will apply what we do know and, progressively, all that we shall learn. Already, a complete plan of rational education is possible, and, in such schools as we conceive, children may develop, happy and free, according to their natural tendencies. We shall labour to perfect and extend it. (Further reading: Paul Avrich, *The Modern School Movement*, Princeton: Princeton University Press, 1980)

66. Sébastien Faure: Libertarian Education (1910)

Sébastien Faure (1858-1942) first became active in the anarchist movement in Paris in the late 1880's. He was a talented public speaker, going on numerous tours throughout France to spread the anarchist idea. In 1894 he was put on trial, along with Jean Grave (already imprisoned for his anarchist propaganda) and several other prominent anarchists, such as Emile Pouget (1860-1931) and the art critic, Felix Fénéon (1861-1944), in what became known as the "Trial of the Thirty." Despite the public being excluded from Faure's cross-examination out of fear of his oratorical skills, he was acquitted along with most of the defendants. In 1895, with Louise Michel, he launched the anarchist paper, Le Libertaire, *popularizing the use of the word "libertarian" as a synonym for "anarchist." In 1904 he founded a free school called "La Ruche" (the Beehive), which lasted until 1917, when, amid war, it was forced to close. The following excerpts from Faure's 1910 pamphlet,* "La Ruche"—Propos d'Educateur, *have been translated by Paul Sharkey.*

WHEN IT COMES INTO THE WORLD, when its existence is like a blank sheet upon which nothing has yet be written, the child is neither good nor bad. He is both. The heir to all preceding generations, he carries within himself, in germ, all the qualities and all the shortcomings of his ancestors; all their virtues and all their vices, all their strengths and all their weaknesses, all their ignorance and all their learning, all their savagery and all their indulgence, all their defeats and all their victories, all their greatness and all their pettiness, all their courage and all their cowardice, all their rebelliousness and all their subservience, all their advances and all their set-backs, all their sublimity and all their wretchedness.

He is as capable of the most sensitive actions as of the most irrational acts; he is fitted for the noblest acts as well as for the vilest; he can climb the heights or plumb the depths.

Education and social surroundings will turn this little amorphous, inconsistent, frail and eminently impressionable creature into what he will become thereafter.

...[S]trictness makes for deceivers, faint-hearts and cowards. It is deadly to openness, confidence and real courage. It erects dangerous barriers of mutual mistrust between Educator and child: it sours the hearts of the little ones and alienates them from the affections of their elders; it introduces a Master-Slave relationship rather than a Friend-Friend relationship between Educator and child...

The result of a regimen of constraint is regulation of the child's every move; consequently, it leads to classification of all of the latter under the headings mandatory and forbidden, the rewarded and the punished; for there would be no constraint if the child was not required to conform to prescriptions and prohibitions, and if abiding by the former and breaching the latter did not bring consequences in the form of reward or punishment as the case may be.

"If you do such a thing you will be rewarded."

"If you do something else, you will be punished."

That is the whole story.

...[T]he constraint system exercises none of the child's nobler faculties; it makes no appeal to his reasoning, does not speak to his heart, has nothing to say to his dignity and nothing to his conscience.

It does not prompt any high-minded feelings in him; moves him to no purposeful effort; arouses no noble aspiration; prompts no unselfish impulse; and no productive exercise.

It does not focus the considered attention of the child on immediate or longer-term, direct or indirect consequences for himself and others, beyond this implication: reward in one instance and punishment in the other.

It leaves no room for initiative. Seeing two avenues of action open to him, avenues at the entrance to which two signposts have been carefully placed, one reading, in curt and trenchant terms "What must be done; the avenue of reward," while the other displays this inscription "What must not be done; the avenue of punishment," he struggles to decide whether the action asked of him is to be classified among the musts or the must-nots, without bothering to wonder why he should act thus without the course upon which he embarks bringing him any other satisfaction than some reward to be collected or punishment to be avoided.

Undetectably, this constraint system produces grey, drab, colourless, insipid beings bereft of all determination, passion or personality; a slavish, cowardly, sheepish breed, incapable of manly or sublime deeds, the execution of which presupposes and requires a dose of liveliness, fire, independence and enthusiasm, but instead one perfectly capable of cruelty and abjection, especially in circumstances where personal accountability is eclipsed by mob activity.

The system of freedom leads to quite different outcomes.

It is characterized by risk throughout the entire learning period. So, at the outset, when the child is pretty much ignorant of all the consequences implicit in his actions, the educator bombards him with warnings, advice, explanations and the thousand ingenious ways in which his support can be fed in and his watchful eye exercised, because, while he is under an obligation to respect the child's freedom, he also has an obligation to shield him from all of the various dangers that surround him. Gradually and as the child, better informed with each passing day, becomes more alive to the precise implications of his actions, such guardianship should be relaxed so that the child acquires the habit of clearing away the dangers he meets along the way...

If he is always kept under guard, if he is not allowed to budge without securing leave to do so, out of fear of stumbling, dangers, obstacles—which is to say out of fear of the mistakes he may make, the influences to which he will be exposed and the consequences his conduct might have for himself and for others—he remains forever trapped in the bear-hug of constraint, like the infant in his mother's arms, and will never learn to navigate life's shoals; even as an adult he will still be the little personality-less and limp creature he was as a child.

And on the day that he comes of age and is left to his own devices due to the death or departure of those who had taken on the task of thinking for him and deciding for him, he will have to think, decide and act for himself and will find that he has no inner reason to guide him, no heart to drive him, no will to move him, no conscience to reassure him...

The greatest moralizing force is example. Evil is contagious; so is Good. Example exercises a well-nigh omnipotent influence over the child by reason of his malleability...

If you do not want your children to lie to you, never deceive them; if you don't want them to fight with one another, never strike them; if you don't want them to use coarse language, never curse at them.

If you want them to trust you, prove that you trust them. If you want them to listen to you, speak to them as if they were capable of understanding you; if you want them to love you, do not be stingy with your affection for them; if you want them to cuddle and be open with you, do not be sparing in your kissing and cuddling of them.

Example is all-powerful…

All who are not blinkered by partisanship are gradually coming around to the idea that there is a lot less danger in having boys and girls live and grow side by side than in systematically keeping them separated from each other. Simple observation shows that unwholesome curiosity and dangerous precociousness grow out of the systematic separation of these children at an age when they are beginning to sense the earliest stirrings of sexual life.

Can we so delude ourselves as to believe that, for boys and girls to be kept apart, we need only forbid the former to speak to the latter and the latter to play with the former?

Experience shows that the result of such bans is the very opposite of what was expected.

As long as children are young enough not to be troubled by the approach of the opposite sex, it cannot be other than dangerous and immoral to forewarn them of misdemeanours they are not even tempted to commit.

And once boys and girls reach an age where they feel vaguely moved by an exchanged glance, a fleeting contact, a furtive touch, a held hand, a word, then even if one throws up the highest barriers between them, one will only succeed in fuelling the emotion, and fanning the desire to repeat the encounter…

The practice of co-education poses the delicate matter of sex education.

Delicate? Why should it be any more delicate than any other? Why should apprising the child which has reached the age and degree of awareness where this matter comes into play, of the conditions in which the perpetuation of the human race takes place, be any more delicate than informing it about the reproductive practices of other species?

The unease which a conversation or a course on this matter causes the educator derives almost entirely from the mystery with which the master senses the matter is shrouded as far as the child is concerned; and that mystery itself derives from the circumlocutions, reservations, oratorical euphemisms and innuendo with which the topic is customarily treated in the presence of children. If it were dealt with candidly, tackled head-on and studied just like any other element of the natural sciences, all of the awkwardness and embarrassment would evaporate.

The hypocritical fathers of the official morality who preach virtue and who generally practice vice as long as nobody gets to know about it, ask that children be kept in ignorance of certain subjects.

Ignorance is always an evil, a danger.

How many of the misdemeanours and foolish acts committed by children can be ascribed entirely to lack of experience, to ignorance! A far-sighted mother and father should always enlighten their children. The child will find out eventually: so why hide things from him? Could it be to spare his blushes? Keeping secrets encourages him to concoct, with regard to things about which he frets, false notions about which he will consult with his friends or neighbours. Nor will there be any shortage of people to misdirect him later, by which time there will be no time left to step in and brief him in all candour. So why conceal from him something that he will inevitably discover at some point? This is an unforgivable lack of foresight.

...True morality consists of shedding the requisite light upon such matters, a light that the child will some day be able to find for himself. Better that those who love him should provide it than those who do not know him.

Chapter 15
Women, Love And Marriage

67. Bakunin: Against Patriarchal Authority (1873)

Bakunin, in contrast to Proudhon, was very much opposed to patriarchal authority. In his essay on integral education (Selection 64), he denounced the authority of the father over his children. In his revolutionary programs and manifestos, he consistently advocated equal rights for women. In his Revolutionary Catechism *from 1866 he wrote: "Woman, differing from man but not inferior to him, intelligent, industrious and free like him, is declared his equal both in rights and in all political and social functions and duties" (*Selected Writings, *New York: Grove Press, 1974, ed. A. Lehning, page 83). Consequently, he called for:*

> Abolition not of the natural family but of the legal family founded on law and property. Religious and civil marriage to be replaced by free marriage. Adult men and women have the right to unite and separate as they please, nor has society the right to hinder their union or to force them to maintain it. With the abolition of the right of inheritance and the education of children assured by society, all the legal reasons for the irrevocability of marriage will disappear. The union of a man and a woman must be free, for a free choice is the indispensable condition for moral sincerity. In marriage, man and woman must enjoy absolute liberty. Neither violence nor passion nor rights surrendered in the past can justify an invasion by one of the liberty of another, and every such invasion shall be considered a crime. (Bakunin on Anarchism, Montreal: Black Rose Books, 1980, pp. 93-94)

Within the First International, the anti-authoritarian federalists associated with Bakunin, such as Eugene Varlin, adopted a similar position, which was opposed by Proudhon's followers, the French mutualists. But it was not just the Proudhonians in the First International who derided Bakunin's ideas regarding the equality of the sexes. In his note opposite Bakunin's statement in the Program of the International Socialist Alliance *(1868) that the Alliance stood above all for "the political, economic and social equalization of individuals of either sex" (Bakunin,* Selected Writings, *page 174), Marx called Bakunin a hermaphrodite, and ridiculed his wife for having added her signature to the program. Bakunin's relationship with his wife Antonia was the subject of considerable scorn because, consistent with his anarchist principles, he never sought to restrain her relationships with other men yet acted as a loving father to her children.*

In the following extracts from Statism and Anarchy *(1873), reprinted in* Bakunin on Anarchism, *Bakunin returns to the theme of patriarchal domination. Unlike other Russian socialists of his era, Bakunin had no illusions regarding the authoritarian and patriarchal social structure of the Russian peasant commune, the Mir, which others saw as the basis for a peasant socialism.*

THE IDEAL OF THE RUSSIAN PEOPLE IS overshadowed by three…traits which we must combat with all our energy…1) paternalism, 2) the absorption of the individual by the Mir, 3) confidence in the Tsar…The last two, absorption of the individual by the Mir and the cult of the Tsar, are the natural and inevitable effects of the first, i.e., the paternalism ruling the people. This is a great historic evil, the worst of all…

This evil deforms all Russian life, and indeed paralyzes it, with its crass family sluggishness, the chronic lying, the avid hypocrisy, and finally, the servility which renders life insupportable. The despotism of the husband, of the father, of the eldest brother over the family (already an immoral institution by virtue of its juridical-economic inequalities), turn it into a school of violence and triumphant bestiality, of cowardice and the daily perversions of the family home. The expression "whitewashed graveyard" is a good description of the Russian family.

…[The family patriarch] is simultaneously a slave and a despot: a despot exerting his tyranny over all those under his roof and dependent on his will. The only masters he recognizes are the *Mir* and the Tsar. If he is the head of the family, he will behave like an absolute despot, but he will be the servant of the *Mir* and the slave of the Tsar. The rural community is his universe; there is only his family and on a higher level the clan. This explains why the patriarchal principle dominates the *Mir*, an odious tyranny, a cowardly submission, and the absolute negation of all individual and family rights…

One of the greatest misfortunes in Russia is that each community constitutes a closed circle. No community finds it necessary to have the least organic connection with other communities. They are linked by the intermediary of the Tsar, the "little father," and only by the supreme patriarchal power vested in him. It is clear that disunion paralyzes the people, condemns its almost always local revolts to certain defeat and at the same time consolidates the victory of despotism…

The struggle against the patriarchal regime is at present raging in almost every village and in every family. In the rural community, the *Mir* has degenerated to the point where it has become an instrument of the State. The power and the arbitrary bureaucratic will of the State is hated by the people and the revolt against this power and this arbitrary will is at the same time a revolt against the despotism of the rural community and of the *Mir*.

68. Louise Michel: Women's Rights (1886)

Following the Paris Commune (Selection 30), Louise Michel was imprisoned and then exiled in 1873 to a French penal colony in New Caledonia. On the way there she became an avowed anarchist. Reflecting on the defeat of the Commune, she later wrote: "Dishonest men, in power, are harmful; honest men, in power, are ineffective. Liberty and power cannot possibly go together" (as quoted in Edith Thomas, Louise Michel, *Montreal: Black Rose Books, 1980, page 341). After a general pardon was granted to the Communards in 1880, she returned to France to advocate anarchy and social revolution. She was arrested and imprisoned several more times, the most severe sentence of 6 years being imposed in 1883 for leading a demonstration through Paris carrying the black flag of anarchy. Although she spent most of the 1890's in voluntary exile in England, she frequently returned to France for speaking tours, with the theme of women's rights being a common topic. The following excerpts are taken from the chapter on "Women's Rights" in* The Red Virgin: Memoirs of Louise Michel *(Tuscaloosa: University of Alabama Press, 1981; originally published 1886), ed. and trans. B. Lowry and E. E. Gunter, and are reprinted with the kind permission of the publisher.*

ALL THE WOMEN READING THESE MEMOIRS must remember that we women are not judged the same way men are. When men accuse some other man of a crime, they do not accuse him of such a stupid one that an observer wonders if they are serious. But that is how they deal with a woman; she is accused of things so stupid they defy belief. If she is not duped by the claims of popular sovereignty put forth to delude people, or if she is not fooled by the hypocritical concessions which hoodwink most women, she will be indicted. Then, if a woman is courageous, or if she grasps some bit of knowledge easily, men claim she is only a "pathological" case.

At this moment man is master, and women are intermediate beings, standing between man and beast. It is painful for me to admit that we are a separate caste, made one across the ages.

For many years the human race has been lying in its cocoon with its wings folded; now it is time for humanity to unfold its wings. The human race that is emerging from its cocoon will not understand why we lay supine so long.

The first thing that must change is the relationship between the sexes. Humanity has two parts, men and women, and we ought to be walking hand in hand; instead there is antagonism, and it will last as long as the "stronger" half controls, or thinks it controls, the "weaker" half.

How marvelous it would be if only the equality of the sexes were recognized, but while we wait, women are still, as Molière said, "the soup of man." The strong sex condescends to soothe us by defining us as the beautiful sex. Nonsense! It's been a damned long time since we women have had any justice from the "strong" sex.

We women are not bad revolutionaries. Without begging anyone, we are taking our place in the struggle; otherwise, we could go ahead and pass motions until the world ends and gain nothing. For my part, comrades, I have refused to be any man's "soup," and I've gone through life with the masses without giving any slaves to the Caesars.

Let me tell men a few truths. They claim man's strength is derived from woman's cowardice, but his strength is less than it appears to be. Men rule with a lot of uproar, while it is women who govern without noise.

But governing from the shadows is valueless. If women's mysterious power were transformed into equality, all the pitiful vanities and contemptible deceptions would disappear. Never again would there be either a master's brutality or a slave's perfidy.

...In New Caledonia I saw warriors loading their women as if they were mules. Whenever someone might see them, they posed haughtily, carrying only their warrior's spear. But if the gorges and mountains closed up and hid them from view, or if the path were deserted, then the warrior, moved by pity, would unload some of the burden from his human mule and carry it himself. Thus lightened, the woman breathed deeply; now she had no more than one child hanging on her back and one or two others hanging on her legs. But if a shadow appeared on the horizon—even if only a cow or a horse—quickly the load went back on the woman's back, and the warrior made a great pretense of adjusting it. Oh dear, if someone had seen him—a warrior who thinks women are worth something! But most women after a lifetime of being treated like this no longer wanted anything more.

Is it not the same everywhere? Human stupidity throws old prejudices over us like a winding-sheet over a corpse. Are there not stupid arguments about the inferiority of women? Maternity or other circumstances are supposed to keep women from being good fighters. That argument assumes people are always going to be stupid enough to butcher each other. Anyway, when a thing is worth the pain, women are not the last to join the struggle. The yeast of rebellion which lies at the bottom of every woman's heart rises quickly when combat stirs it up, particularly when combat promises to lessen squalor and stinks less than a charnel house.

Calm down, men. We are not stupid enough to want to run things. Our taking power would only make some kind of authority last longer; you men keep the power instead, so that authority may wither away more quickly. I must add that even "more quickly" will still be too long.

We women are disgusted, and further villainies only inspire us to act. We jeer a little also. We jeer at the incredible sight of big shots, cheap punks, hoods, old men, young men, scoundrels—all turned into idiots by accepting as truth a whole heap of nonsensical ideas which have dominated the thinking of the human race. We jeer at the sight of those male creatures judging women's intellects by weighing the brains of women in their dirty paws.

Do men sense the rising tide of us women, famished for learning? We ask only this of the old world: the little knowledge that it has. All those men who wish to do nothing are jealous of us. They are jealous of us because we want to take from the world what is sweetest: knowledge and learning.

I have never understood why there was a sex whose intelligence people tried to cripple as if there were already too much intelligence in the world. Little girls are brought up in foolishness and are expressly disarmed so that men can deceive them more easily. That is what men want. It is precisely as if someone threw you into the water after having forbidden you to learn to swim or even after having tied your arms and legs. It is all done under the pretext of preserving the innocence of little girls.

Men are happy to let a girl dream. And most of those dreams would not disturb her as they do now if she knew them as simple questions of science. She would be in fact more truly innocent then, for she could move calmly through visions which now trouble her. Nothing that comes from science or nature would bother her. Does a corpse disturb people who are used to the dissecting room? When nature, living or dead, appears to an educated woman, she does not blush. There is no mystery, for mystery is destroyed when the cadaver is dissected. Nature and science are clean; the veils that men throw over them are not.

…"Civilized" men prepare young girls to be deceived, and then make it a crime for them to fall, but also make it almost an honour for the seducer. What an uproar when men find an unruly animal in the flock! I wonder what would happen if the lamb no longer wanted to be slaughtered. Most likely, men would slaughter them just the same, whether or not they stretched their necks out for the knife. What difference does it make? The difference is that it is better not to stretch your neck out to your murderer.

There is a roadside market where men sell the daughters of the people. The daughter of the rich is sold for her dowry and is given to whomever her family wishes. The daughter of the poor is taken by whoever wants her. Neither girl is ever asked her own wishes.

In our world, the proletarian is a slave; the wife of a proletarian is even more a slave. Women's wages are simply a snare because they are so meager that they are illusory. Why do so many women not work? There are two reasons. Some women cannot find work, and others would rather die of hunger, living in a cave, than do a job which gives them back less than enough to live on and which enriches the entrepreneur at the same time.

Prostitution is the same. We practice Caledonian morality, and men don't count women for much here either. There are some women who hold tight to life. But then, forced on by hunger, cold, and misery, they are lured into shame by the pimps and whores who live from that kind of work. In every rotten thing, there are maggots. Those unfortunate women let themselves be formed into battalions in the mournful army that marches from the hospital to the charnel house.

When I hear of one of these miserable creatures taking from a man's pocket more than he would have given her, I think, "So much the better." Why should we close our eyes? If there were not so many buyers, that sordid market would not exist. And when some honest woman, insulted and pursued, kills the scoundrel who is chasing her, I think, "Bravo, she has rid others of the danger and avenged her sisters." But too few women do it.

If women, these accursed—even the socialist Proudhon said they can only be housewives and courtesans, and indeed they cannot be anything else in the present world—if, as I say, these women are often dangerous, to whom does the blame belong? Who has, for his pleasure, developed their coquetry and all the other vices agreeable to men? Men have selected these vices through the ages.

We women have weapons now, the weapons of slaves, silent and terrible. No one has to put them into our hands. It is done.

I admit that a man, too, suffers in this accursed society, but no sadness can compare to a woman's. In the street, she is merchandise. In the convents, where she hides as if in a tomb, ignorance binds her, and rules take her up in their machinelike gears and pulverize her heart and brain. In the world, she bends under mortification. In her home, her burdens crush her. And men want to keep her that way. They do not want her to encroach upon either their functions or their titles.

Be reassured, "gentlemen." We do not need any of your titles to take over your functions when it pleases us to do so. Your titles. Bah! We do not want rubbish. Do what you want to with them. They are too flawed and limited for women. The time is not far off when you will come and offer them to us in order to try to dress them up a little by dividing them with us.

Keep those rags and tatters. We want none of them. What we do want is knowledge and education and liberty. We know what our rights are, and we demand them. Are we not standing next to you fighting the supreme fight? Are you not strong enough, men, to make part of that supreme fight a struggle for the rights of women? And then men and women together will gain the rights of all humanity.

Beyond our tormented epoch will come the time when men and women will move through life together as good companions, and they will no more argue about which sex is superior than races will argue about which race is foremost in the world.

69. Carmen Lareva: Free Love (1896)

In place of the legal family, under the name of "free love," anarchists advocated individual freedom and voluntary unions. The concept of free love was controversial, frequently misrepresented and misunderstood. In this article, "Free Love: Why Do We Want It," originally published in 1896 in the Argentine feminist anarchist-communist journal, La Voz de la Mujer *(*Woman's Voice*), Carmen Lareva clarifies the idea and dispels some of the misconceptions associated with it.* La Voz de la Mujer *was probably one of the first explicitly feminist anarchist papers. It has been recently reprinted in book form:* La Voz de la Mujer: periódico comunista-anárquico, 1896-1897 *(Buenos Aires: Universidad Nacional de Quilmes, 1997). The translation is by Paul Sharkey.*

THE IGNORANT BELIEVE AND THE MALICIOUS say that the Anarchist idea flies in the face of everything fine and beautiful, of art, the sciences and, above all, home life.

In fact, time after time we have had occasion to hear this from the lips of some working women: "Oh, some splendid idea, this Anarchist idea of yours is! You want all us women—wives, daughters, mothers and sisters—turned into concubines, sordid playthings for man's unrestrained passions!"

It is to those who talk this way and think this way that we address ourselves. Let us see.

We hold that in society as it exists there is no one and nothing more disgraced than hapless woman. Scarcely have we attained puberty than we become targets for lubricious, cynically sexual leering by the stronger sex. Of the exploiter and exploited classes alike. Later, on reaching "womanhood," we are most often tricked into the quagmires of impurity, or held to the scorn and ridicule of a society which looks upon our downfall as anything but idealistic and loving, and sees it quite simply as a "lapse."

If we achieve what some women believe will bring them happiness, namely marriage, then we are even worse off, a thousand times worse off. Our status being what it is, our "spouse's" loss of work, his meagre earnings, illness, etc., turn what might otherwise have been the last word in bliss into a grave and terrifying burden upon our "husbands." Indeed, there is nothing so lovely, poetic, tender, pleasing and winsome as a child, a son—the last word in wedded bliss!—but woe betide the poor man! Woe betide the household upon which poverty settles and which holds a little one in need of our care, caresses and attention. Woe betide that household! It will not be long before a thousand squabbles and countless woes beset it. Do you know why? Because the new-born makes a thousand demands that prevent the young mother from helping her partner to bear the costs of running the home, which, indeed, grow even as their incomes shrink, whereupon what should be the dearest wish and greatest happiness of the household comes to be regarded as a burden, a hindrance and a source of upset and impoverishment that the greatest care must be taken to avert, through *coitus interruptus* and fraudulent and aberrant intercourse with its whole sequel of nauseating diseases. Hence the thousands upon thousands of nauseating and repulsive practices whereby the nuptial bed is turned into a sink of disgusting obscenities and hence the degradation, the boredom, the diseases and the much trumpeted "trespass" against "honour." Adultery!

Do away with the cause and the effect disappears, and with poverty abolished, the vileness too will be gone, and the home, far from being what it is today, would be a paradise of pleasures and delights.

How often have we heard confidences from our female friends who have been the scapegoats for such acts!—So what? came our partner's response when we cast such deeds up to him: Don't you know how expensive a business it is to raise a child? Midwife, doctor, medical bills, dietary costs, care and then there is the wet nurse: how could I cope when, with two of us working now, we can barely scrape a living? How could I manage on my own with expenses increasing and income shrinking? Never mind children! To the devil with them!

How do you like that? Dear female comrades, is that love, home life, tenderness? It is painful to think that a woman must go through this: yet, go through it she must!

Now, in proclaiming free love, a free union of the sexes, it is our staunch belief that it can banish all of these distasteful experiences. Freely united and with nothing to fear, in that we would have made provision for the upkeep of those beings, the fruits of love, which might spring from the union of those who, soaring on the wings of love, melted into a single being, of course both would be happy and free; as partners in their respective actions, they would have no cause to fear anything from each other.

We have been told that if love, if union, etc., were free, as we wish them to be, the man would be continually switching from one woman to the next and that, with nothing to fear from society or the law, there would be no more fidelity, whereas today, because the law punishes the adulteress or adulterer, out of a fear of social stigma, spouses put up with each other's failings and waywardness.

Nothing, dear female comrades, could be further from the truth. What both of the sexes are looking for is not the gratification of a more or less carnal appetite. No, what they are after is happiness, bliss, tranquility and decency and every semi-educated creature looks to procreate and achieve his dream, his yearning; today's society is so materially and cynically selfish because, capital being what one needs in order to buy or procure one's pleasures and needs, everybody makes a greater or lesser effort to acquire it.

Moreover, we, the "dregs" of society as we are called, living as we do from an early age subject to work as it is currently practiced, not merely degrading and mortifying, but also brutalizing, naturally do not have the education over which the bourgeois also wield a monopoly, in their eagerness to wield a monopoly upon everything, and so we are not conversant with the thousand delights which it affords those of higher status: things such as painting, music, poetry, sculpture, etc., etc., and this being the case, there is no question but that in everything we do during our wretched lives, we are a lot more materialistic than we ought to be and than we would be if we were to be educated, not just the way the bourgeoisie is today, but even better. Art elevates one's feelings and, without even the slightest glimmer of these, plainly we cannot attain such heights.

Education not being free and we not having enough time to acquire it, how are we to be educated? Who does not know that from our most tender years we are swallowed up and tormented by the workshop? We will get no education there. Very much the opposite. We will find everything there, everything except that! And time after time, wretched female workers have been targets of bourgeois lust, quickly dispatched to uneasy graves and cast, defenceless, into the increasingly hungry, insatiable chasm of vice under a mantle of mud and tears, while little more than children, gladly embracing perdition as a means of escape from the derision and sneers of their tormentors!

In this society, this is all quite natural, given the extent of the ignorance in which we wallow. Take some famished soul and offer him a crust of bread, no matter how blackened, and at the same time offer him a rebec [stringed musical instrument], a painting or a poem, even should these be an immortal creation by Shakespeare or Lord Byron, and which would he go for first? The bread! Rather than the book or the rebec; plainly, before it can manifest its presence, the spirit has needs that must be met and material needs take precedence over and are more pressing than the spiritual.

So there is no disputing that in a society whose members or component parts have been educated pretty much to perfection, couples can come together freely and without fear that their happiness will be in any way diminished by the absence of a blessing from a third party.

In their eagerness to be all-governing, the law and society compel us to do blind homage to them in this ritual. We women do not believe in such blessings or ritual, which, to us, is like taking two dogs frolicking in the street and telling them, as we join them together: "You have my leave to be happy." In which case they would carry on just as if we had done the opposite.

When the time comes, the dying bourgeois have to pass on the spoils of their thievery to their children, and they must be parcelled out here or there: because, unless they do so, the law would not recognize their inheritance. It is a business arrangement and in their eyes business takes priority over all.

But in a society where there will be no place for such "deals," there will be no need for such nonsense. Marriage, as the current dictum has it, or rather the blessing ceremony, merely symbolizes society's assent to the act, so, should another society embrace the practice of free union of the sexes, plainly it would be giving its endorsement to that practice and that would be that. But for their fear of the criticism of others, many women and men would be content with free unions and this is the only thing stopping them; so let us allow them to get on with it and let us do as we please and whatever we may please to do without detriment to any.

As for fear of punishment being a preservative against marital infidelity, it is not our belief that this sophism is worth even the effort required to refute it. Anyone will grant that it is a "lapse" which, ninety times out of every hundred, can occur without the authorities and the law knowing, etc., and we believe too that a person who, for fear of punishment, stays "faithful" to a commitment into which she may well have been tricked or otherwise inveigled, might as well be "unfaithful," except that it would be better if she were...to walk out because, if she loves another male or female, this is plainly because she does not love the person with whom society requires her to share her bread and her roof and, while this may not quite amount to prostitution, it comes close, very close to that, because in so doing, she is required to feign love of someone she simply detests, to deceive and be a hypocrite, in short, to give herself to a man or woman whom she despises. In which case it is only natural that it will not be long before their household is beset by squabbling, friction and a thousand other things and happenings to embitter the lives of both partners.

If they were free in their actions, this would not happen and they might enjoy whatever culture our society of the future will have to offer. (Further reading: Jose Moya, "Italians in Buenos Aires' Anarchist Movement: Gender, Ideology and Women's Participation, 1890-1910," in *Women, Gender and Transnational Lives: Italian Workers of the World*, Toronto: University of Toronto, 2002, ed. D. Gabaccia and F. Iacovetta)

70. Emma Goldman: Marriage (1897), Prostitution and Love (1910)

Free love had been preached by various sexual radicals in the United States for some time, despite repressive obscenity laws that were used to prosecute and imprison its various advocates. In 1876, the anarchist Ezra Heywood (1829-1893) published Cupid's Yokes *(Princeton: Cooperative Publishing), in which he denounced the institution of marriage as contrary to women's freedom. In 1877 he was arrested for distributing obscene material, and was sentenced to two years in prison. He continued to fight for free speech and died in 1893 shortly after completing another two year sentence for publishing articles on oral sex, sex education and birth control. One of the articles had originally been published in* Lucifer, The Light Bearer, *by another anarchist, Moses Harman (1830-1910), who was also imprisoned. Emma Goldman was a great admirer of them both, meeting Harman in 1893, describing him as a "courageous champion of free motherhood and woman's economic and sexual emancipation" (*Living My Life, *Vol.1, New York: Dover, 1970, page 219). She often wrote and spoke about marriage and free love in the years to follow. The following essay, "Marriage," was originally published in July 1897 in the* Firebrand, *an anarchist paper published by the Isaak family (who later published Voltairine de Cleyre's translation of Jean Grave's* Moribund Society and Anarchy*). It has recently been reprinted in* Emma Goldman: a documentary history of the American years, *ed. C. Falk, B. Pateman, J. M. Moran (Berkeley: University of California Press, 2003). The* Firebrand *was suppressed soon after the publication of Emma Goldman's article, ostensibly for publishing a Walt Whitman poem.*

AT ALL TIMES, AND IN ALL AGES, HAVE THE suppressed striven to break the chains of mental and physical slavery. After thousands of noble lives have been sacrificed at the stake and on the gallows, and others have perished in prisons, or at the merciless hands of inquisitions, have the ideas of those brave heroes been accomplished. Thus have religious dogmas, feudalism and black slavery been abolished, and new ideas, more progressive, broader and dearer, have come to the front, and again we see poor downtrodden humanity fighting for its rights and independence. But the crudest, most tyrannical of all institutions—marriage, stands firm as ever, and woe unto those who dare to even doubt its sacredness. Its mere discussion is enough to infuriate not only Christians and conservatives alone, but even Liberals, Freethinkers, and Radicals. What is it that causes all these people to uphold marriage? What makes them cling to this prejudice? (for it is nothing else but prejudice). It is because marriage relations are the foundation of private property, ergo, the foundation of our cruel and inhuman system. With wealth and superfluity on one side, and idleness, exploitation, poverty, starvation, and crime on the other; hence to abolish marriage, means to abolish everything above mentioned. Some progressive people are trying to reform and better our marriage laws. They no longer permit the church to interfere in their matrimonial relations, others even go further, they marry free, that is without the consent of the law; but, nevertheless, this form of marriage is just as binding, just as "sacred," as the old form, because it is not the form or the kind of marriage relation we have, but…the thing itself that is objectionable, hurtful and degrading. It always gives the man the right and power over his wife, not only over her body, but also over her actions, her wishes; in fact, over her whole life. And how can it be otherwise?

Behind the relations of any individual man and woman to each other, stands the historical age evolved relations between the two sexes in general, which have led up to the difference in the position and privileges of the two sexes today…

Among the rich class it has long been out of fashion to fall in love. Men of society marry after a life of debauchery and lust, to build up their ruined constitution. Others again have lost their capital, in gambling sports or business speculation, and decide that an heiress would be just the thing they need, knowing well, that the marriage tie will in no way hinder them from squandering the income of their wealthy bride. The rich girl having been brought up to be practical and sensible, and having been accustomed to live, breathe, eat, smile, walk and dress only according to fashion, holds out her millions to some title, or to a man with a good social standing. She has one consolation, and that is, that society allows more freedom of action to a married woman and should she be disappointed in marriage she will be in a position to gratify her wishes otherwise. We know, the walls of boudoirs and salons are deaf and dumb, and a little pleasure within these walls is no crime.

With the men and women among the working-class, marriage is quite a different thing. Love is not so rare as among the upper class, and very often helps both to endure disappointments and sorrows in life, but even here the majority of marriages last only for a short while, to be swallowed up in the monotony of the every day life and the struggle for existence. Here also, the workingman marries because he grows tired of a boardinghouse life, and out of a desire to build a home of his own, where he will find his comfort. His main object, therefore, is to find a girl that will make a good cook and housekeeper; one that will look out only for his happiness, for his pleasures; one that will look up to him as her lord, her master, her defender, her supporter; the only ideal worth while living for. Another man hopes that the girl he'll marry will be able to work and help to put away a few cents for rainy days, but after a few months of so-called happiness he awakens to the bitter reality that his wife is soon to become a mother, that she cannot work, that the expenses grow bigger, and that while he before managed to get along with the small earning allowed him by his "kind" master, this earning is not sufficient to support a family.

The girl who has spent her childhood, and part of her womanhood, in the factory feels her strength leaving her and pictures to herself the dreadful condition of ever having to remain a shopgirl; never certain of her work, she is, therefore, compelled to look out for a man, a good husband, which means one who can support her, and give her a good home. Both, the man and the girl, marry for the same purpose, with the only exception that the man is not expected to give up his individuality, his name, his independence, whereas, the girl has to sell herself body and soul, for the pleasure of being someone's wife; hence they do not stand on equal terms, and where there is no equality there can be no harmony. The consequence is that shortly after the first few months, or to make all allowance possible, after the first year, both come to the conclusion that marriage is a failure.

As their conditions grow worse and worse, and with the increase of children the woman grows despondent, miserable, dissatisfied and weak. Her beauty soon leaves her, and from hard work, sleepless nights, worry about the little ones and disagreement and quarrels with her husband, she soon becomes a physical wreck and curses the moment that made her a poor man's wife. Such a dreary, miserable life is certainly not inclined to maintain love or respect for each other. The man can at least forget his misery in the company of a few friends; he can absorb himself in politics, or he can drown his misfortune in a glass of beer. The woman is chained to the house by a thousand duties; she cannot, like her husband, enjoy some recreation because she either has no means for it, or she is refused the same rights as her husband, by public opinion. She has to carry the cross with her until death, because our marriage laws know of no mercy, unless she wishes to lay bare her married life before the critical eye of Mrs. Grundy, and even then she can only break the chains which tie her to the man she hates if she takes all the blame on her own shoulders, and if she has energy enough to stand before the world disgraced for the rest of her life. How many have the courage to do that?

...The poor woman has to consider her little ones; she is less fortunate than her rich sister, and yet the woman who remains in bondage is called respectable: never mind if her whole life is a long chain of lies, deceit and treachery, she yet dares to look down with disgust upon her sisters who have been forced by society to sell their charms and affections on the street. No matter how poor, how miserable a married woman may be, she will yet think herself above the other, whom she calls a prostitute, who is an outcast, hated and despised by everyone, even those who do not hesitate to buy her embrace, look upon the poor wretch as a necessary evil...The sole difference between her and the married woman is, that the one has sold herself into chattel slavery during life, for a home or a title, and the other one sells herself for the length of time she desires; she has the right to choose the man she bestows her affections upon, whereas the married woman has no right whatsoever; she must submit to the embrace of her lord, no matter how loathsome this embrace may be to her, she must obey his commands; she has to bear him children, even at the cost of her own strength and health; in a word, she prostitutes herself every hour, every day of her life. I can find no other name for the horrid, humiliating and degrading condition of my married sisters than prostitution of the worst kind, with the only exception that the one is legal, the other illegal.

...But whether legal or illegal, prostitution in any form is unnatural, hurtful and despicable, and I know only too well that the conditions cannot be changed until this infernal system is abolished, but I also know that it is not only the economic dependence of women which has caused her enslavement, but also her ignorance and prejudice, and I also know that many of my sisters could be made free even now, were it not for our marriage institutions which keep them in ignorance, stupidity and prejudice. I therefore consider it my greatest duty to denounce marriage, not only the old form, but the so-called modern marriage, the idea of taking a wife and housekeeper, the idea of private possession of one sex by the other. I demand the independence of woman; her right to support herself; to live for herself; to love whomever she pleases, or as many as she pleases. I demand freedom for both sexes, freedom of action, freedom in love and freedom in motherhood.

Do not tell me that all this can only be accomplished under Anarchy; this is entirely wrong. If we want to accomplish Anarchy, we must first have free women at least, those women who are economically just as independent as their brothers are, and unless we have free women, we cannot have free mothers, and if mothers are not free, we cannot expect the young generation to assist us in the accomplishment of our aim, that is the establishment of an Anarchist society.

In "The Traffic in Women," from her 1910 Mother Earth publication, Anarchism and Other Essays, *Emma Goldman addressed the problem of prostitution directly:*

IT WOULD BE ONE-SIDED AND EXTREMELY superficial to maintain that the economic factor is the only cause of prostitution. There are others no less important and vital. That, too, our reformers know, but dare discuss even less than the institution that saps the very life out of both men and women. I refer to the sex question, the very mention of which causes most people moral spasms.

It is a conceded fact that woman is being reared as a sex commodity, and yet she is kept in absolute ignorance of the meaning and importance of sex. Everything dealing with that subject is suppressed, and persons who attempt to bring light into this terrible darkness are persecuted and thrown into prison. Yet it is nevertheless true that so long as a girl is not to know how to take care of herself, not to know the function of the most important part of her life, we need not be surprised if she becomes an easy prey to prostitution, or to any other form of a relationship which degrades her to the position of an object for mere sex gratification.

It is due to this ignorance that the entire life and nature of the girl is thwarted and crippled. We have long ago taken it as a self-evident fact that the boy may follow the call of the wild; that is to say, that the boy may, as soon as his sex nature asserts itself, satisfy that nature; but our moralists are scandalized at the very thought that the nature of a girl should assert itself...

Society considers the sex experiences of a man as attributes of his general development, while similar experiences in the life of a woman are looked upon as a terrible calamity, a loss of honour and of all that is good and noble in a human being. This double standard of morality has played no little part in the creation and perpetuation of prostitution. It involves the keeping of the young in absolute ignorance on sex matters, which alleged "innocence," together with an overwrought and stifled sex nature, helps to bring about a state of affairs that our Puritans are so anxious to avoid or prevent...

The meanest, most depraved and decrepit man still considers himself too good to take as his wife the woman whose grace he was quite willing to buy, even though he might thereby save her from a life of horror...Fully fifty per cent of married men are patrons of brothels. It is through this virtuous element that the married women—nay, even the children—are infected with venereal diseases. Yet society has not a word of condemnation for the man, while no law is too monstrous to be set in motion against the helpless victim. She is not only preyed upon by those who use her, but she is also absolutely at the mercy of every policeman and miserable detective on the beat, the officials at the station house, the authorities in every prison...

We must rise above our foolish notions of "better than thou," and learn to recognize in the prostitute a product of social conditions. Such a realization will sweep away the attitude of hypocrisy, and insure a greater understanding and more humane treatment. As to a thorough eradication of prostitution, nothing can accomplish that save a complete transvaluation of all accepted values—especially the moral ones—coupled with the abolition of industrial slavery.

In "Marriage and Love," also included in Anarchism and Other Essays *(New York: Mother Earth, 1910), Emma Goldman added these comments on "free love":*

FREE LOVE? AS IF LOVE IS ANYTHING BUT FREE! Man has bought brains, but all the millions in the world have failed to buy love. Man has subdued bodies, but all the power on earth has been unable to subdue love. Man has conquered whole nations, but all his armies could not conquer love. Man has chained and fettered the spirit, but he has been utterly helpless before love. High on a throne, with all the splendor and pomp his gold can command, man is yet poor and desolate, if love passes him by. And if it stays, the poorest hovel is radiant with warmth, with life and colour. Thus love has the magic power to make of a beggar a king. Yes, love is free; it can dwell in no other atmosphere. In freedom it gives itself unreservedly, abundantly, completely. All the laws on the statutes, all the courts in the universe, cannot tear it from the soil, once love has taken root. If, however, the soil is sterile, how can marriage make it bear fruit? It is like the last desperate struggle of fleeting life against death.

Love needs no protection; it is its own protection. So long as love begets life no child is deserted, or hungry, or famished for the want of affection...

The defenders of authority dread the advent of a free motherhood, lest it will rob them of their prey. Who would fight wars? Who would create wealth? Who would make the policeman, the jailer, if woman were to refuse the indiscriminate breeding of children? The race, the race! shouts the king, the president, the capitalist, the priest. The race must be preserved, though woman be degraded to a mere machine—and the marriage institution is our only safety valve against the pernicious sex-awakening of woman. But in vain these frantic efforts to maintain a state of bondage. In vain, too, the edicts of the Church, the mad attacks of rulers, in vain even the arm of the law. Woman no longer wants to be a party to the production of a race of sickly, feeble, decrepit, wretched human beings, who have neither the strength nor moral courage to throw off the yoke of poverty and slavery. Instead she desires fewer and better children, begotten and reared in love and through free choice; not by compulsion, as marriage imposes. Our pseudo-moralists have yet to learn the deep sense of responsibility toward the child, that love in freedom has awakened in the breast of woman. Rather would she forego forever the glory of motherhood than bring forth life in an atmosphere that breathes only destruction and death. And if she does become a mother, it is to give to the child the deepest and best her being can yield. To grow with the child is her motto; she knows that in that manner alone can she help build true manhood and womanhood...

In our present pygmy state love is indeed a stranger to most people. Misunderstood and shunned, it rarely takes root; or if it does, it soon withers and dies. Its delicate fiber cannot endure the stress and strain of the daily grind. Its soul is too complex to adjust itself to the slimy woof of our social fabric. It weeps and moans and suffers with those who have need of it, yet lack the capacity to rise to love's summit.

Some day, some day men and women will rise, they will reach the mountain peak, they will meet big and strong and free, ready to receive, to partake, and to bask in the golden rays of love. What fancy, what imagination, what poetic genius can foresee even approximately the potentialities of such a force in the life of men and women. If the world is ever to give birth to true companionship and oneness, not marriage, but love will be the parent.

Chapter 16
The Mexican Revolution

71. Voltairine de Cleyre: The Mexican Revolution (1911)

Anarchist ideas were first introduced into Mexico during the 1860's. From 1868 to 1869, the anarchist Julio Chavez Lopez led a peasant uprising in Chalco province, which spread to neighbouring provinces before Chavez Lopez was captured and shot by firing squad. The insurgents would seize whatever arms and funds they could find, burn the municipal land titles, and redistribute the land among the peasants. In his 1869 manifesto, Chavez Lopez called for the abolition of government and exploitation, declaring that: "We want: the land in order to plant it in peace and harvest it in tranquility; to leave the system of exploitation and give liberty to all in order that they might farm in the place that best accommodates them without having to pay tribute; to give the people the liberty to reunite in whatever manner they consider most convenient...without the need of outsiders who give orders and castigate...Long live socialism! Long live liberty!" (as quoted by John M. Hart, Anarchism and the Mexican Working Class, 1860-1931, *Austin: University of Texas, 1987, page 39).*

Anarchists also played a prominent role in the National Congress of Mexican Workers. Founded in 1876, it affiliated with the anti-authoritarian International in 1881, but was dissolved by the Díaz dictatorship shortly thereafter.

There was a resurgence of anarchist activity in the years leading up to the 1910 Mexican Revolution, the first great revolution of the twentieth century. Ricardo Flores Magón and the Partido Liberal Mexicano (PLM) attempted armed insurrections in 1906 and 1908, but the U.S. authorities conducted a series of preemptive arrests of many of the would-be participants before they could marshal their forces on the U.S. side of the border. Several PLM members were arrested and imprisoned in the aftermath, including Ricardo Flores Magón, with most of them remaining in various U.S. jails until the very eve of the Mexican Revolution.

Emma Goldman met with the PLM leadership in 1905, throwing her support behind the Mexican revolutionary cause. In 1908, when many of the PLM leaders were in jail and their paper suppressed, she published their "Manifesto to the American People" in Mother Earth.

The following selections are taken from a series of articles by Voltairine de Cleyre that appeared in Mother Earth *beginning with the December 1911 issue (Vol. 6, No. 10), under the title of "The Mexican Revolution." This essay is included in her posthumous* Selected Works *(New York: Mother Earth, 1914), ed. Alexander Berkman.*

WHAT IS A REVOLUTION? AND WHAT is this revolution?

A revolution means some great and subversive change in the social institutions of a people, whether sexual, religious, political, or economic. The movement of the Reformation was a great religious revolution; a profound alteration in human thought—a refashioning of the human mind. The general movement towards political change in Europe and America about the close of the eighteenth century was a revolution. The American and the French revolutions were only prominent individual incidents in it, culminations of the teachings of the *Rights of Man*.

The present unrest of the world in its economic relations, as manifested from day to day in the opposing combinations of men and money, in strikes and bread-riots, in literature and movements of all kinds demanding a readjustment of the whole or of parts of our wealth-owning and wealth-distributing system—this unrest is the revolution of our time, the *economic revolution*, which is seeking social change and will go on until it is accomplished...

The Mexican Revolution is one of the prominent manifestations of this world-wide economic revolt...It began in the bitter and outraged hearts of the peasants, who for generations have suffered under a ready-made system of exploitation, imported and foisted upon them, by which they have been dispossessed of their homes, compelled to become slave-tenants of those who robbed them; and under Díaz, in case of rebellion to be deported to a distant province, a killing climate, and hellish labour. It will end only when that bitterness is assuaged by very great alteration in the landholding system or until the people have been absolutely crushed into subjection by a strong military power, whether that power be a native or a foreign one.

Now the political overthrow [of Díaz] of last May [1911], which was followed by the substitution of one political manager for another, did not at all touch the economic situation. It promised, of course; politicians always promise. It promised to consider measures for altering conditions; in the meantime, proprietors are assured that the new government intends to respect the rights of landlords and capitalists, and exhorts the workers to be patient and—*frugal!*...The idea that such a condition can be dealt with by the immemorial remedy offered by tyrants to slaves is like the idea of sweeping out the sea with a broom...

The Indian population—especially the Yaquis and the Moquis—have always disputed the usurpations of the invaders' government, from the days of the early conquest until now, and will undoubtedly continue to dispute them as long as there is an Indian left, or until their right to use the soil out of which they sprang *without paying tribute in any shape* is freely recognized.

The communistic customs of these people are very interesting, and very instructive, too; they have gone on practicing them all these hundreds of years, in spite of the foreign civilization that was being grafted upon Mexico (grafted in all senses of the word); and it was not until forty years ago (indeed the worst of it not till twenty-five years ago) that the increasing power of the government made it possible to destroy this ancient life of the people.

By them, the woods, the waters, and the lands were held in common. Anyone might cut wood from the forest to build his cabin, make use of the rivers to irrigate his field or garden patch (and this is a right whose acknowledgment none but those who know the aridity of the southwest can fully appreciate the imperative necessity for). Tillable lands were allotted by mutual agreement before sowing, and reverted to the tribe after harvesting, for reallotment. Pasturage, the right to collect fuel, were for all. The habits of mutual aid which always arise among sparsely settled communities are instinctive with them. Neighbour assisted neighbour to build his cabin, to plough his ground, to gather and store his crop.

No legal machinery existed—no tax-gatherer, no justice, no jailer. All that they had to do with the hated foreign civilization was to pay the periodical rent-collector and to get out of the way of the recruiting officer when he came around. Those two personages they regarded with spite and dread; but as the major portion of their lives was not in immediate contact with them, they could still keep on in their old way of life in the main.

With the development of the Díaz regime, which came into power in 1876 …this Indian life has been broken up, violated with as ruthless a hand as ever tore up a people by the roots and cast them out as weeds to wither in the sun…

When the revolution burst out, the Yaquis and other Indian people said to the revolutionists: "Promise us our lands back, and we will fight with you." And they are keeping their word magnificently. All during the summer they have kept up the warfare. Early in September, the Chihuahua papers reported a band of 1,000 Yaquis in Sonora about to attack El Anil; a week later 500 Yaquis had seized the former quarters of the federal troops at Pitahaya. This week it is reported that federal troops are dispatched to Ponoitlan, a town in Jalisco, to quell the Indians who have risen in revolt again because their delusion that the Maderist government was to restore their land has been dispelled. Like reports from Sinaloa. In the terrible state of Yucatan, the Mayas are in active rebellion; the reports say that "The authorities and leading citizens of various towns" have been seized by the malcontents and put in prison. What is more interesting is that the peons have seized not only "the leading citizens," but still more to the purpose have seized the plantations, parceled them, and are already gathering the crops for themselves.

...[T]he main thing, the mighty thing, the regenerative revolution is the REAPPROPRIATION OF THE LAND BY THE PEASANTS. Thousands upon thousands of them are doing it.

Ignorant peasants: peasants who know nothing about the jargon of land reformers or of Socialists. Yes: that's just the glory of it! Just the fact that it *is* done by ignorant people; that is, people ignorant of book theories; but *not* ignorant, not so ignorant by half, of life on the land, as the theory spinners of the cities. Their minds are simple and direct; they act accordingly. For them, there is *one way* to "get back to the land": i.e., to ignore the machinery of paper landholding (in many instances they have burned the records of the title deeds) and proceed to plough the ground, to sow and plant and gather, and *keep the product themselves*.

72. Praxedis Guerrero: To Die On Your Feet (1910)

Praxedis Guerrero (1882-1910) joined the PLM in 1906. He was from a wealthy Mexican family, but renounced his inheritance, went to the United States, and became a worker. He was one of the few PLM leaders to evade arrest and was thus able to return to Mexico in December 1910 as part of an armed group of revolutionaries determined to bring about the social revolution. He was killed on December 29, 1910 during a battle with Mexican troops. Guerrero's anarchism is based on a theory of environmental determinism common among 19th century and early 20th century thinkers. The focus of revolutionary activity must therefore be on transforming the environment, rather than attacking individuals. The following selections from his writings, originally published in the PLM paper, Regeneración, *have been translated by Ward S. Albro and are taken from his book,* To Die On Your Feet: The Life, Times, and Writings of Praxedis Guerrero *(Fort Worth: Texas Christian University Press, 1996). They are reprinted here with the kind permission of the publisher.*

Puntos Rojos (Socialist Aphorisms)

SOW A LITTLE SEED OF REBELLION AND you will determine a harvest of freedoms.

Passivism and mildness do not imply kindness, any more than rebelliousness implies savagery.

"We are hungry and thirsty for justice," can be heard everywhere; but how many of those hungry dare to take the bread, and how many of those thirsty risk to drink the water that is on the way to the revolution?

If it seems to you that by walking, you won't reach freedom, then run.

To live in order to be free, or to die in order to stop being slaves.

For some sensitive spirits it is more painful and barbarian to see a thousand men die in the revolution than to see millions of men, women, and children live and die in the jails and in exploitation.

The features of the tyrant represent a description of the people who obey him.

Who is more responsible: the tyrant who oppresses the people, or the people who created him?

If you feel the urge to bow down before a despot, go ahead, but pick up a rock to finish the salutation with dignity.

A cause does not succeed because of its kindness and its justice: it succeeds because of the efforts of its supporters.

There are many thieves in Mexico. There are people so degenerate that steal the insignificance of a piece of bread, when they could afford the luxury of starving to death.

The Purpose Of The Revolution

"Why, if you want freedom, do you not kill the tyrant and thus avoid the horrors of a major fratricidal war? Why do you not murder the despot who oppresses people and who has put a price on your head?"—I have been asked many times. Because I am not an enemy of the tyrant, I have replied; because if I were to kill the man, tyranny would still be left standing, and it is the latter I combat; because if I were to blindly hurl myself against him, I would be doing what a dog does, when it bites a rock, hurting itself, but not knowing nor understanding where the pain comes from.

Tyranny is the logical result of a social disease, whose present remedy is the Revolution, since the pacific resistance of the doctrine of Tolstoy would only produce in these times the annihilation of the few who might ever have understood or practiced its simplicity.

Inviolable laws of nature rule over all things and beings; cause is the creator of effect; the environment determines in an absolute manner the appearance and the qualities of the product…However bloodthirsty and ferocious they may be, tyrannies and despotisms cannot break that law, because it has no loopholes. They exist, therefore, in a special environmental state that prevails around them and from which they are the result. If they offend, if they cause harm, if they obstruct, we must seek their annulment in the transformation of that morbid environment, and not in the simple murder of the tyrant. The isolated death of one man, be he tsar, sultan, dictator or president, is ineffective if one wishes to destroy tyranny. It would be like trying to dry up a swamp by, from time to time, killing the reptiles that are born in it.

If things were otherwise, nothing would be more practical or simple than to go to the individual and to destroy him…

For most people, revolution and war have the same meaning: a mistake which, in the light of misplaced judgments, makes the last resort of the oppressed look like barbarity. War has the invariable characteristics of hatred and national or personal ambitions; it creates a relative benefit for an individual or a group, paid for with the blood and the sacrifice of the masses. Revolution is the abrupt upheaval of the human tendency toward improvement, when a fairly numerous part of humanity is subjected by violence to a state incompatible to its needs and aspirations. Wars can be fought against a man, but never a revolution; the first destroys, perpetuating injustices; the latter mixes, shakes, confuses, disrupts, and casts the purifying fire of new ideas—the old elements poisoned by prejudices and eaten away by moths—to produce, from the scalding pot of the catastrophe, a more benign environment for the development and expansion of all beings. Revolution is the flood that spills over the dryness of the dead countryside, spreading the mud of life that transforms the uncultivated land of forced peace, where only reptiles live, into fertile fields suitable for the splendid blooming of higher species.

Tyrants do not just appear in nations through a phenomenon of self-generation. The universal law of determinism lifts them on the backs of the people. The same law, manifested in the powerful revolutionary transformation, will make them fall forever, asphyxiated, like a fish deprived of its liquid environment. (*Regeneración*, September 17, 1910)

The Means And The End

Could there exist a tyrant over a people who did not provide him with the elements to sustain himself? A common wrongdoer can commit his misdeeds without the complicity of his victims; a despot cannot live or tyrannize without the cooperation of his, or a numerous part of them. Tyranny is the crime of the unconscious collectivities against themselves and must be attacked as a social disease by means of the Revolution, considering the death of the tyrants as an unavoidable incident of the struggle, an incident, and nothing more, but not an act of justice.

…Science, by denying the free will of the enemy, destroys the basis of the present barbaric penal institutions; revolutionaries do not establish different criteria for the acts of a bigger or a smaller wrongdoer, nor do we have to seek evasive answers, to glaze over the violence that unavoidably and necessarily has to accompany the liberation movement. We deplore it and we find it disgusting, but in the alternative of continuing indefinitely enslaved, or appealing to the use of force, we choose the passing horrors of the armed struggle, without hatred toward the irresponsible tyrant, whose head will not roll to the ground just because justice demands it, but because the consequences of the long-lived despotism suffered by the people and the necessities of the moment will impose it, and when the time comes, in which the broken fences of passivism give way sincerely to the desires of freedom, exasperated by the confinement they have suffered, by the difficulties that have always had to be manifested.

We are going to the violent struggle without making it into an ideal of ours, without dreaming about the execution of the tyrants as the ultimate victory of justice.

Our violence is not justice, it is simply a necessity fulfilled in spite of emotions and idealisms, which alone are insufficient to guarantee a conquest of progress in the lives of people. Our violence would have no purpose without the violence of the despotism; nor could it be explained if the majority of the victims of the tyrant were neither conscious nor unconscious accomplices of the unjust present system; if the evolutionary power of human aspirations could find an unrestricted stage to extend itself in the social environment, the production of violence and its practice would be nonsensical; but this is now the practical environment to break old molds which the evolution of passivism would take centuries to gnaw. (*Regeneración*, November 5, 1910)

73. Ricardo Flores Magón: Land and Liberty (1911-1918)

When Ricardo Flores Magón (1874-1922) helped found the PLM in 1905, it did not have a clear ideological orientation. Its fundamental purpose was to overthrow the Díaz dictatorship. Concerned that he would alienate some of the PLM's supporters, he did not openly advocate anarchism until 1911. PLM forces, joined by members of the Industrial Workers of the World (the "Wobblies," a revolutionary syndicalist organization based primarily in the United States), enjoyed some success in Baja California at the beginning of 1911 but were defeated by Madero's forces. In 1912, Flores Magón was sentenced to two years in prison for violating U.S. "neutrality" laws. He recommenced publication of Regeneración *upon his release in 1914, denouncing the new Carranza government in Mexico. In 1916 he was imprisoned again, this time for distributing* Regeneración *by mail, on the ground that it was an "indecent" publication containing articles denouncing Carranza, U.S. business interests in Mexico and the murder of Mexicans by Texas Rangers. In 1918 he was sentenced to twenty years in jail for publishing an anarchist manifesto, reproduced here as the final selection. By then the U.S. had entered the First World War in Europe, and the Russian Revolution had begun. He died, allegedly of a heart attack, in Leavenworth Penitentiary in November 1922. The following extracts are taken from Ricardo Flores Magón,* Land and Liberty: Anarchist Influences in the Mexican Revolution *(Montreal: Black Rose, 1977), ed. D. Poole.*

TO ARMS! TO ARMS FOR LAND AND LIBERTY!

The Earth is the property of all. When, millions and millions of years ago, the Earth had not yet separated itself from the chaotic cluster, which, as time passed on, was to dower the firmament with new suns; and when, as the result of gradual cooling, planets became more or less fitted for organic life, this planet had no owner. Neither did the Earth have any owner when humanity was converting every old tree trunk and every mountain cavern into a dwelling place and a refuge from the inclemency of the weather and from wild beasts. Neither did the Earth have any owner when humanity, having advanced still farther along the thorny path of progress, had reached the pastoral period, in which there were pastures whereon the tribe, with herds in common, settled. The first owner appeared with the first man who had slaves to work his fields, and who, that he might make himself master of those slaves and of those fields, found it necessary to take up arms and levy war against a hostile tribe. Violence, then, was the origin of private property in the land, and by violence it has been upheld to our own days.

Invasions, wars of conquest, political revolutions, wars for the control of markets, and acts of spoilation carried through by governors or those under their protection—these constitute the titles to private property in land; titles sealed with the blood of enslavement of humanity. Yet this monstrous origin of a right which is absurd, since it is based on crime, does not hinder the law from calling that right "sacred" inasmuch as those who have withheld the land are the very ones who have written the law.

Private property in land is based on crime and, by that very fact, is an immoral institution. That institution is the front of all the ills that afflict the human being. Vice, crime, prostitution, despotism, are born of it. For its protection there have become necessary the army, the judiciary, parliament, police, the prison, the scaffold, the church, the government and a swarm of employers and drones, supported by the very ones who have not so much as a clod of earth on which to rest their heads, since they have come into life after the Earth has been divided up among a few bandits who appropriated it by force, or among the descendants of those bandits, who have come into possession through the so-called right of inheritance.

The Earth is the element from which everything necessary for life is extracted or produced. From it we get the useful metals, coal, rock, sand, lime, salts. By its cultivation we produce every kind of fruit, for nourishment and pleasure. Its prairies yield food for the cattle; its forests offer us their woods, its fountains are the generative waters of life and beauty. And all this belongs to a few; makes happy a few; gives power to a few; though nature made it for all.

Of this tremendous injustice are born all the ills that afflict the human species and produce his misery. Misery makes man vile; misery prostitutes him; misery pushes him to crime; misery bestializes the face, the body and the intelligence.

Degraded and—which is worse—unconscious of their shame, generations succeed one another, living in the midst of wealth and abundance without tasting that happiness a few have monopolized. With the Earth belonging to a few, those who possess none of it must hire themselves to those who do possess it, if they are to keep their hides and skeletons on foot. The humiliation of hire or hunger—this is the dilemma with which private property in land faces each as he enters life! an iron dilemma which forces humanity itself to put on itself the chains of slavery, if it would avoid perishing by starvation or giving itself up to crime or prostitution.

Ask yourselves today why governments oppress, why men rob and murder, why women prostitute themselves! Behind the iron bars of those charnel houses of body and soul which men call prisons, thousands of unfortunates are paying, in torture of body and agony of soul, for that crime, which the law has lifted into the category of a sacred right—private property in land. In the defiling atmosphere of the house of public prostitution thousands of young women are prostituting their bodies and crippling their self-respect, as the result of private property in land. In the asylum, in the hospitals, in the foundling institutions, in all those gloomy abodes wherein misery, abandonment and human misery take refuge, men and women, the aged and the child, are suffering from the consequences of private property in land. And convicts and beggars, the prostitute, the orphan and the infirm are lifting their eyes to heaven; in the hope of finding there, beyond the stars which they can see, that happiness of which the owners of this Earth are robbing them.

Meanwhile the human herd, unconscious of its right to life, turns and bends its back to develop by its toil for others this Earth which Nature has placed at its own service, thus perpetuating [by] its own submissiveness the empire of injustice. But, from the slavish and bemired mass rebels arise; from the sea of backs there emerge the heads of the first revolutionaries. The herd trembles for it foresees chastisement. Tyranny trembles, for it foresees attack. And breaking the silence, a shout, like the roar of thunder, rolls over the backs and reaches even to the thrones: "The Land!"

...Silent slaves of the clod; resigned peons of the field; throw down the plough! The clarions of Acayucan and Jiminez, of Palomas and Las Vacas, of Viesca and Valladolid are calling you to war; that you may take possession of this Earth to which you give your sweat, though it denies you its fruits because you have consented, in your submissiveness, that idle hands shall become masters of what belongs to you, of what belongs to all humanity, of what cannot belong to a few but to all men and women who, by the very fact that they are living, have a right to share in common, by reason of their toil, all that wealth which the Earth is capable of producing.

Slaves! Take the Winchester in hand! Work the Land; but only after you have taken it into your own possession! To work it now is to rivet your chains, for you are producing more wealth for the masters, and wealth is power, wealth is strength, physical and moral, and the strong will hold you always in subjection. Be strong yourselves! Be strong and rich, all of you, by making yourselves masters of the Land! But for this you need the gun. Buy it or borrow it, in the last resort! Throw yourselves into the struggle, shouting with all your strength "Land and Liberty!" (*Regeneración*, October 1910)

Manifesto Issued By The Junta Of The Mexican Liberal Party, September 23, 1911

MEXICANS: The Organizing Junta of the Mexican Liberal Party views with sympathy your efforts to put in practice the lofty ideals of political, economic and social emancipation, the triumph of which on earth will bring to an end the already sufficiently extensive quarrel between man and man, which has its origin in that inequality of fortune which springs from the principle of private property. To abolish that principle means to annihilate all the political, economic, social, religious and moral institutions that form the environment within which are asphyxiated the free initiative and the free association of human beings who, that they may not perish, find themselves obliged to carry on among themselves a frenzied competition from which there issue triumphant not the best, not the most self-sacrificing, not those most richly endowed, physically, morally or intellectually, but the most crafty, the most egotistic, the least scrupulous, the hardest-hearted, those who place their own well-being above all considerations of human solidarity and human justice.

But for the principle of private property there would be no reason for government, which is needed solely to keep the disinherited from going to extremes in their complaints or rebellions against those who have got into their possession the social wealth. Nor would there be any reason for the church, whose exclusive object is to strangle in the human being the innate spirit of revolt against oppression and exploitation, by the preaching of patience, of resignation and of humility; silencing the cries of the most powerful and fruitful instincts by the practice of immoral penances, cruel and injurious to personal health and—that the poor may not aspire to the enjoyment of this earth and become a danger to the privileges of the rich—by promising the humblest, the most resigned, the most patient a heaven located in the infinite, beyond the farthest stars the eye can reach.

Capital, Authority, the Church—there you have the sombre trinity that makes of this beauteous earth a paradise for those who, by cunning, violence and crime, have been successful in gathering into their clutches the product of the toiler's sweat, of the blood, of the tears and sacrifices of thousands of generations of workers; but a hell for those who, with muscle and intelligence, till the soil, set the machinery in motion, build the houses and transport the products.

Thus humanity remains divided into two classes whose interests are diametrically opposed—the capitalist class and the working class; the class that has possession of the land, the machinery of production and the means of transporting wealth, and the class that must rely on its muscle and intelligence to support itself.

Between these two social classes there cannot exist any bond of friendship or fraternity, for the possessing class always seeks to perpetuate the existing economic, political and social system which guarantees it tranquil enjoyment of the fruits of its robberies, while the working class exerts itself to destroy the iniquitous system and institute one in which the land, the houses, the machinery of production and the means of transportation shall be for the common use…

In these moments of confusion so propitious for the attack on oppression and exploitation; in these moments in which Authority, weakened, unbalanced, vacillating, attacked on every side by unchained passions, by tempests of appetites that have sprung into life, and hope immediately to glut themselves; in these moments of anxiety, agony and terror on the part of the privileged, compact masses of the disinherited are invading the lands, burning the title deeds, laying their creative hands on the soil and threatening with their fists all that was respectable yesterday—Authority, Capital, the Clergy. They are turning the furrow, scattering the seed and await, with emotion, the first fruit of free labour. These, Mexicans, are the first practical results of the propaganda and of the action of soldiers of the proletariat, of the generous upholders of our equalitarian principles, of our brothers who are bidding defiance to all imposition and all exploitation with the cry—a cry of death for all those above, but of life and hope for all those below—"Long Live Land and Liberty."

Expropriation must be pursued to the end, at all costs, while this grand movement lasts. This is what has been done and is being done by our brothers of Morelos, of Southern Puebla, of Michoacan, of Guerrero, Veracruz, of the Northern portion of the State of Tamaulipas, of Durango, Sonora, Sinaloa, Jalisco, Chihuahua, Oaxaca, Yucatan, Quintana Roo, and parts of other States, as even the Mexican bourgeois press itself has had to confess. There the proletariat has taken possession of the land without waiting for a paternal government to deign to make it happy, for it knows that nothing good is to be expected of governments and that the emancipation of the workers must be the task of the workers themselves.

These first acts of expropriation have been crowned with most pleasing success; but they must not be limited to taking possession of the land and the implements of agriculture alone. There must be a resolute taking possession, of all the industries by those working in them, who should bring it about similarly that the lands, the mines, the factories, the workshops, the foundries, the railroads, the shipping, the stores of all kinds and the houses shall be in the power of each and every one of the inhabitants, without distinction of sex.

The inhabitants of each region in which such an act of supreme justice has been effected will only have to agree that all that is found in the stores, warehouses, granaries, etc., shall be brought to a place of access by all, where men and women of reliability can make an exact inventory of what has been collected and can calculate the time it will last—the necessities and the number of inhabitants that will have to use it being taken into account—from the moment of expropriation, until the first crops shall have been raised and the other industries shall have turned out their first products.

When such an inventory has been made the workers in the different industries will understand, fraternally and among themselves, how to so regulate production that none shall want while this movement is going on, and that only those who are not willing to work shall die of hunger—the aged, the incapacitated, and the children, who have a right to enjoy all, being excepted.

Everything produced will be sent to the community's general store, from which all will have the right to take what their necessities require, on the exhibition [of] proof that they are working at such and such an industry.

The human being aspires to satisfy wants with the least possible expenditure of effort, and the best way to obtain that result is to work the land and other industries in common. If the land is divided up and each family takes a piece there will be grave danger of falling anew into the capitalist system, since there will not be wanting men of cunning or grasping habits who may get more than others and in the long run exploit their fellows. Apart from that danger is the fact that if each family works its little patch of land it will have to toil as much or more than it does today under the system of individual property to obtain the miserable result now achieved; but, if there is joint ownership of the land and the peasants work it in common, they will toil less and produce more. Of course there will be enough for each to have his own house and a ground-plot for his own pleasure. What has been said as to working the land in common applies to working the factories, working shops, etc., in common. Let each, according to his temperament, tastes, and inclinations choose the kind of work that suits him best, provided he produces sufficient to cover his necessary wants and does not become a charge on the community.

Operating in the manner pointed out, that is to say, expropriation being followed immediately by the organization of production, free of masters and based on the necessities of the inhabitants of each region, nobody will suffer want, in spite of the armed movement going on, until the time when, that movement having terminated with the disappearance of the last bourgeois and the last agent of authority, and the law which upholds privilege having been shattered, everything having been placed in the hands of the toilers, we shall meet in fraternal embrace and celebrate with cries of joy in [the] inauguration of a system that will guarantee to every human being Bread and Liberty...

It is the duty of us poor people to work and struggle to break the chains that make us slaves. To leave the solution of our problems to the educated and rich is to put ourselves voluntarily in their clutches. We, the plebians; we, the tatterdemalions; we, the starvelings; we who have no place wherein to lay our heads and live tortured by uncertainty as to whence will come tomorrow's bread for our women and little ones; we, who when we have reached old age, are ignominiously discharged because we can no longer work; it is for us to make powerful efforts and a thousand sacrifices to destroy to its lowest foundations the edifice of the old society which has been a fond mother to the rich and vicious and a hard-hearted stepmother to the workers and the virtuous...

Rise, all of you, as one man! In the hands of all are tranquility, well-being, liberty, the satisfaction of all healthy appetites. But we must not leave ourselves to the guidance of directors. Let each be master of himself. Let all be arranged by the mutual consent of free individualities. Death to slavery! Death to hunger! Long life to "Land and Liberty!"

...As long as there are rich and poor, governors and governed, there will be no peace, nor is it to be desired that there should be; for such a peace would be founded on the political, economic and social inequality of millions of human beings who suffer hunger, outrages, the prison and death, while a small minority enjoys pleasures and liberties of all kinds for doing nothing.

On with the struggle! On with expropriation, for the benefit of all and not of the few! This is no war of bandits, but of men and women who desire that all may be brothers and enjoy, as such, the good things to which nature invites us and which the brawn and intelligence of man have created, the one condition being that each should devote himself to truly useful work. Liberty and well-being are within our grasp. The same effort and the same sacrifices that are required to raise to power a governor—that is to say, a tyrant—will achieve the expropriation of the fortunes the rich keep from you. It is for you, then, to choose. Either a new governor—that is to say, a new yoke—or life-redeeming expropriation and the abolition of all imposition, be that imposition religious, political or of any other kind. (*Regeneración*, January 1912)

Manifesto of The Organising Junta of The Mexican Liberal Party to The Members of The Party, The Anarchists of The World And The Workers in General

COMRADES: The clock of history is nearing the time, when, with its inexorable hand, it will indicate the instant in which this already dying society will finally die.

The death of the old society is near. It will happen very soon, and only those interested in its continuing existence, those who profit from injustice and those who see with horror the Social Revolution where they will have to work side by side with their former slaves will deny this.

Everything indicates, with force of evidence, that the death of bourgeois society will not be long in coming. The citizen looks grimly at the policeman whom he considered yesterday as his protector and support. The assiduous reader of the bourgeois press sweeps men aside and drops with dismay the prostituted sheet in which appears the declarations of the chiefs of states. The workers strike without caring if national interests are damaged or not, already aware that the fatherland does not belong to them but to the rich. You can see faces in the street that clearly show their interior discontent while their arms are agitating to build barricades. You hear murmurs in the bars, in the theatres, in the trains and in each home, especially in ours, the homes of the poor. You cry when a son leaves for the war, or you can die of a broken heart when you think that tomorrow, or even today, that young man who was the happiness of the home, who, with his freshness and kindness turned the sad existence of his old parents into one of happiness, will be armed and facing a young man like himself, a young man he cannot hate because he does not know.

The flames of discontent are encouraged and fanned by a tyranny, which in all countries is becoming increasingly cruel and arrogant. Everywhere fists become clenched, minds become exalted, hearts beat with violence, and those who do not murmur, shout, longing for the moment when their hardened hands will drop the work tools and take up the rifle that is waiting for the hero's caress.

Comrades: The moment is solemn. It is the moment before the greatest political and social catastrophe that history has recorded: the insurrection of all the people against their present conditions.

It will certainly be the blind impulse of the suffering masses. It will be, without doubt, the chaotic explosion of anger, unrestrained by the guard's revolver or the hangman's gallows. It will be the overflowing of all indignation, of all bitterness, and in the chaos that will follow new tyrants will be born, because in such cases with regularity charlatans become leaders.

Therefore, it rests with you, the conscientious, to prepare the people's minds for this moment, but not for the insurrection, as that will be born of tyranny.

Prepare the people, not only to await this great event with serenity, but also prepare them for those who would drag them along the paths of flowers and in the end subject them to the same enslavement that they suffer today.

For the rebellion to succeed without unconsciously forging with its own hands new chains that will again enslave the people, it is necessary that we, who do not believe in Government, that we, who are convinced that Government in all its forms and whoever is at its head is a tyranny because it is not an institution created to protect the weak, but to protect the strong, must use every circumstance to spread, without fear, our sacred anarchist ideal, the only human, the only just and the only true.

Failing to do this is to betray the aspirations of the people for a liberty whose only limits are natural ones, a liberty that will not endanger the conservation of the species.

Failing to do this is to leave the poor in the hands of those who will sacrifice them to their own interests. Failing to do this will affirm the conviction of our enemies who claim "that the day is far off when we will be able to implant new ideas."

Activity, activity and more activity is what we must have at this moment.

Let each man and each woman that loves the anarchist ideal spread it with tenacity, without thinking of danger or taking notice of ridicule or considering the consequence.

To work comrades, and the future will be our ideal. (*Regeneración*, March 1918) (Further reading: Ward S. Albro, *Always a Rebel: Ricardo Flores Magón and the Mexican Revolution*, Fort Worth: Texas Christian University Press, 1992 and Colin M. MacLachlan, *Anarchism and the Mexican Revolution: The Political Trials of Ricardo Flores Magón in the United States*, Berkeley: University of California Press, 1991.)

Chapter 17
War And Revolution In Europe

74. Élisée Reclus: Evolution and Revolution (1891)

Evolution and Revolution *(London: W. Reeves, 1891) was one of Élisée Reclus' most popular and widely translated pamphlets, later expanded into his book,* Evolution, Revolution and the Anarchic Ideal *(Paris: Stock, 1898, in French). The idea that revolution was an aspect of progressive evolution became a common tenet among anarchists the world over.*

THESE TWO WORDS, EVOLUTION AND REVOLUTION, closely resemble one another, and yet they are constantly used in their social and political sense as though their meaning were absolutely antagonistic. The word Evolution, synonymous with gradual and continuous development in morals and ideas, is brought forward in certain circles as though it were the antithesis of that fearful word, Revolution, which implies changes more or less sudden in their action, and entailing some sort of catastrophe. And yet is it possible that a transformation can take place in ideas without bringing about some abrupt displacements in the equilibrium of life? Must not revolution necessarily follow evolution, as action follows the desire to act? They are fundamentally one and the same thing, differing only according to the time of their appearance…

To begin with, we must clearly establish the fact, that if the word evolution is willingly accepted by the very persons who look upon revolutionists with horror, it is because they do not fully realize what the term implies, for they would not have the thing at any price. They speak well of progress in general, but they resent progress in any particular direction. They consider that existing society, bad as it is, and as they themselves acknowledge it to be, is worth preserving; it is enough for them that it realizes their own ideal of wealth, power or comfort…

But if the word evolution serves but to conceal a lie in the mouths of those who most willingly pronounce it, it is a reality for revolutionists; it is they who are the true evolutionists.

Escaping from all formulas, which to them have lost their meaning, they seek for truth outside the teaching of the schools; they criticize all that rulers call order, all that teachers call morality; they grow, they develop, they live, and seek to communicate their life. What they have learned they proclaim; what they know they desire to practice. The existing state of things seems to them iniquitous, and they wish to modify it in accordance with a new ideal of justice. It does not suffice them to have freed their own minds, they wish to emancipate those of others also, to liberate society from all servitude. Logical in their evolution, they desire what their mind has conceived, and act upon their desire.

...[I]t is certain that the actual world is divided into two camps, those who desire to maintain poverty, i.e., hunger for others, and those who demand comforts for all. The forces in these two camps seem at first sight very unequal. The supporters of existing society have boundless estates, incomes counted by hundreds of thousands, all the powers of the State, with its armies of officials, soldiers, policemen, magistrates, and a whole arsenal of laws and ordinances. And what can the Socialists, the artificers of the new society, oppose to all this organized force? Does it seem that they can do nothing? Without money or troops they would indeed succumb if they did not represent the evolution of ideas and of morality. They are nothing, but they have the progress of human thought on their side. They are borne along on the stream of the times...

The external form of society must alter in correspondence with the impelling force within; there is no better established historical fact. The sap makes the tree and gives it leaves and flowers; the blood makes the man; the ideas make the society. And yet there is not a conservative who does not lament that ideas and morality, and all that goes to make up the deeper life of man, have been modified since "the good old times." Is it not a necessary result of the inner working of men's minds that social forms must change and a proportionate revolution take place?

...[F]reedom of the human will is now asserting itself in every direction; it is preparing no small and partial revolutions, but one universal Revolution. It is throughout society as a whole, and every branch of its activity, that changes are making ready. Conservatives are not in the least mistaken when they speak in general terms of Revolutionists as enemies of religion, the family and property. Yes: Socialists do reject the authority of dogma and the intervention of the supernatural in nature, and, in this sense however earnest their striving for the realization of their ideal, they are the enemies of religion. Yes: they do desire the suppression of the marriage market; they desire that unions should be free, depending only on mutual affection and respect for self and for the dignity of others, and, in this sense, however loving and devoted to those whose lives are associated with theirs, they are certainly the enemies of the legal family. Yes: they do desire to put an end to the monopoly of land and capital, and to restore them to all, and, in this sense, however glad they may be to secure to every one the enjoyment of the fruits of the earth, they are the enemies of property…

The right of the strongest is now evoked against social claims. Darwin's theory, which has lately made its appearance in the scientific world, is believed to tell against us. And it is, in fact, the right of the strongest which triumphs when fortune is monopolized. He who is materially the fittest, the most wily, the most favoured by birth, education, and friends; he who is best armed and confronted by the feeblest foe, has the greatest chance of success; he is able better than the rest to erect a citadel, from the summit of which he may look down on his unfortunate brethren. Thus is determined the rude struggle of conflicting egoisms. Formerly this blood-and-fire theory was not openly avowed; it would have appeared too violent, and honeyed words were preferable. But the discoveries of science relative to the struggle between species for existence and the survival of the fittest have permitted the advocates of force to withdraw from their mode of expression all that seemed too insolent. "See," they say, "it is an inevitable law! Thus decrees the fate of mankind!"

We ought to congratulate ourselves that the question is thus simplified, for it is so much the nearer to its solution. Force reigns, say the advocates of social inequality! Yes, it is force which reigns! proclaims modern industry louder and louder in its brutal perfection. But may not the speech of economists and traders be taken up by revolutionists? The law of the strongest will not always and necessarily operate for the benefit of commerce. "Might surpasses right," said Bismark, quoting from many others; but it is possible to make ready for the day when might will be at the service of right. If it is true that ideas of solidarity are spreading; if it is true that the conquests of science end by penetrating the lowest strata; if it is true that truth is becoming common property; if evolution towards justice *is* taking place, will not the workers, who have at once the right and the might, make use of both to bring about a revolution for the benefit of all? What can isolated individuals, however strong in money, intelligence, and cunning, do against associated masses?

In no modern revolution have the privileged classes been known to fight their own battles. They always depend on armies of the poor, whom they have taught what is called loyalty to the flag, and trained to what is called "the maintenance of order." Five millions of men, without counting the superior and inferior police, are employed in Europe in this work. But these armies may become disorganized, they may call to mind the nearness of their own past and future relations with the mass of the people, and the hand which guides them may grow unsteady. Being in great part drawn from the proletariat, they may become to *bourgeois* society what the barbarians in the pay of the Empire became to that of Rome—an element of dissolution. History abounds in examples of the frenzy which seizes upon those in power. When the miserable and disinherited of the earth shall unite in their own interest, trade with trade, nation with nation, race with race; when they shall fully awake to their sufferings and their purpose, doubt not that an occasion will assuredly present itself for the employment of their might in the service of right; and powerful as may be the Master of those days, he will be weak before the starving masses leagued against him. To the great evolution now taking place will succeed the long expected, the great revolution.

75. Tolstoy: Compulsory Military Service (1893)

As a consistent pacifist, Tolstoy was opposed to compulsory military service, regarding armed force as the very basis of state power. The following excerpts are taken from The Kingdom of God is Within You *(New York: Cassell Publishing, 1894; originally published in Russian, 1893), translated by Constance Garnett.*

ARMIES…ARE NEEDED BY GOVERNMENTS and by the ruling classes above all to support the present order, which, far from being the result of the people's needs, is often in direct antagonism to them, and is only beneficial to the government and ruling classes.

To keep their subjects in oppression and to be able to enjoy the fruits of their labour the government must have armed forces.

But there is not only one government. There are other governments, exploiting their subjects by violence in the same way, and always ready to pounce down on any other government and carry off the fruits of the toil of its enslaved subjects. And so every government needs an army also to protect its booty from its neighbour brigands. Every government is thus involuntarily reduced to the necessity of emulating one another in the increase of their armies…

Every increase in the army of one state, with the aim of self-defence against its subjects, becomes a source of danger for neighbouring states and calls for a similar increase in their armies.

The armed forces have reached their present number of millions not only through the menace of danger from neighbouring states, but principally through the necessity of subduing every effort at revolt on the part of the subjects.

Both causes, mutually dependent, contribute to the same result at once; troops are required against internal forces and also to keep up a position with other states. One is the result of the other. The despotism of a government always increases with the strength of the army and its external successes, and the aggressiveness of a government increases with its internal despotism.

The rivalry of the European states in constantly increasing their forces has reduced them to the necessity of having recourse to universal military service, since by that means the greatest possible number of soldiers is obtained at the least possible expense. Germany first hit on this device. And directly one state adopted it the others were obliged to do the same. And by this means all citizens are under arms to support the iniquities practiced upon them; all citizens have become their own oppressors.

Universal military service was an inevitable logical necessity, to which we were bound to come. But it is also the last expression of the inconsistency inherent in the social conception of life, when violence is needed to maintain it. This inconsistency has become obvious in universal military service. In fact, the whole significance of the social conception of life consists in man's recognition of the barbarity of strife between individuals, and the transitoriness of personal life itself, and the transference of the aim of life to groups of persons. But with universal military service it comes to pass that men, after making every sacrifice to get rid of the cruelty of strife and the insecurity of existence, are called upon to face all the perils they had meant to avoid. And in addition to this the state, for whose sake individuals renounced their personal advantages, is exposed again to the same risks of insecurity and lack of permanence as the individual himself was in previous times.

Governments were to give men freedom from the cruelty of personal strife and security in the permanence of the state order of existence. But instead of doing that they expose the individuals to the same necessity of strife, substituting strife with individuals of other states for strife with neighbours. And the danger of destruction for the individual, and the state too, they leave just as it was.

Universal military service may be compared to the efforts of a man to prop up his falling house who so surrounds it and fills it with props and buttresses and planks and scaffolding that he manages to keep the house standing only by making it impossible to live in it.

In the same way universal military service destroys all the benefits of the social order of life which it is employed to maintain.

The advantages of social organization are security of property and labour and associated action for the improvement of existence—universal military service destroys all this.

The taxes raised from the people for war preparations absorb the greater part of the produce of labour which the army ought to defend.

The withdrawing of all men from the ordinary course of life destroys the possibility of labour itself. The danger of war, ever ready to break out, renders all reforms of social life vain and fruitless.

In former days if a man were told that if he did not acknowledge the authority of the state, he would be exposed to attack from enemies domestic and foreign, that he would have to resist them alone, and would be liable to be killed, and that therefore it would be to his advantage to put up with some hardships to secure himself from these calamities, he might well believe it, seeing that the sacrifices he made to the state were only partial and gave him the hope of a tranquil existence in a permanent state. But now, when the sacrifices have been increased tenfold and the promised advantages are disappearing, it would be a natural reflection that submission to authority is absolutely useless.

But the fatal significance of universal military service, as the manifestation of the contradiction inherent in the social conception of life, is not only apparent in that. The greatest manifestation of this contradiction consists in the fact that every citizen in being made a soldier becomes a prop of the government organization, and shares the responsibility of everything the government does, even though he may not admit its legitimacy.

Governments assert that armies are needed above all for external defence, but that is not true. They are needed principally against their subjects, and every man, under universal military service, becomes an accomplice in all the acts of violence of the government against the citizens without any choice of his own.

To convince oneself of this one need only remember what things are done in every state, in the name of order and the public welfare, of which the execution always falls to the army. All civil outbreaks for dynastic or other party reasons, all the executions that follow on such disturbances, all repression of insurrections, and military intervention to break up meetings and to suppress strikes, all forced extortion of taxes, all the iniquitous distributions of land, all the restrictions on labour—are either carried out directly by the military or by the police with the army at their back. Anyone who serves his time in the army shares the responsibility of all these things, about which he is, in some cases, dubious, while very often they are directly opposed to his conscience. People are unwilling to be turned out of the land they have cultivated for generations, or they are unwilling to disperse when the government authority orders them, or they are unwilling to pay the taxes required of them, or to recognize laws as binding on them when they have had no hand in making them, or to be deprived of their nationality—and I, in the fulfillment of my military duty, must go and shoot them for it. How can I help asking myself when I take part in such punishments, whether they are just, and whether I ought to assist in carrying them out?

Universal service is the extreme limit of violence necessary for the support of the whole state organization, and it is the extreme limit to which submission on the part of the subjects can go. It is the keystone of the whole edifice, and its fall will bring it all down.

76. Jean Grave: Against Militarism and Colonialism (1893)

In the following extracts from Voltairine de Cleyre's translation of Jean Grave's Moribund Society and Anarchy *(San Francisco: A. Isaak, 1899), Grave draws the connection between militarism and colonialism, denouncing both. Anti-militarism was a consistent theme in anarchist literature and within the anarchist movement. It was mainly as a result of publishing these passages that Grave was imprisoned by the French authorities in 1894.*

WHAT, IN REALITY, DOES THE WORD "country" represent, beyond the natural affection one has for his family and his neighbours, and the attachment engendered by the habit of living upon one's native soil? Nothing, less than nothing, to the major portion of those who go off to get their heads broken in wars of whose causes they are ignorant and whose cost they alone pay, as workers and combatants! Successful or disastrous, these wars cannot alter their situation in the least. Conquerors or conquered they are the ever-to-be-exploited, submissive cattle, subject to impress, which the capitalist class is anxious to keep under its thumb.

If we agree to the interpretation given it by those who talk the most about it, "the country" is the soil, the territory belonging to the State of which one is a subject. But States have only arbitrary limits; such limitation most frequently depends upon the issue of battles. Political groups were not always constituted in the same manner as they exist today, and tomorrow, if it pleases those who exploit us to make war, the issue of another battle may cause a portion of the country to pass under the yoke of another nationality. Has it not always been the same throughout the ages? As, in consequence of the wars they have made upon each other, nations have appropriated, then lost again or retaken the provinces which separated their frontiers, it follows that the patriotism of these provinces, tossed first to this side then to that, consisted in fighting sometimes under one flag, sometimes under another, in killing their allies of the day before, in struggling side by side with their enemies of the day after—first proof of the absurdity of patriotism!

And, moreover, what can be more arbitrary than frontiers? For what reason do men located on this side of a fictitious line belong to a nation more than those on the other side? The arbitrariness of these distinctions is so evident that nowadays the racial spirit is claimed as the justification for parceling peoples into distinct nations. But here again the distinction is of no value and rests upon no serious foundation, for every nation is itself but an amalgamation of races quite different from each other, not to speak of the interminglings and crossings which the relations operating among nations, more and more developed, more and more intimate, bring about every day… the human race is moving too rapidly towards unification and the absorption of the variations which divide it, to leave any distinctions remaining save those of climate and environment which will have been too profound to be completely modified.

But wherein the inconsistency is still greater, on the part of the major portion of those who go to get themselves killed without having any motive for hatred against those designated to them as their enemies, is that this soil which they thus go forth to defend or to conquer does not and will not belong to them. This soil belongs to a minority of property-owners, who, sheltered from all danger, bask tranquilly in their chimney-corners, while the workers foolishly go out to slay each other, stupidly permitting themselves to take up arms for the purpose of wresting from others the soil which will serve—their masters, as a means to exploit themselves—the workers—still further. We have seen in fact that property does not belong to those who possess it: robbery, pillage, assassination, disguised under the pompous names of conquest, colonization, civilization, patriotism, have been its not least important factors…if the workers were logical, instead of defending "the country" by fighting—*other workers*, they would begin by getting rid of those who command and exploit them; they would invite all the workers, of whatever nationality, to do the same, and would all unite in production and consumption at their ease. The earth is vast enough to support everybody. It is not lack of room nor the scarcity of provisions that has brought about these bloody wars in which thousands of men have cut each other's throats for the greater glory and profit of a few; on the contrary, it is these iniquitous wars to which the desires of rulers, the rivalries of the ambitious, the commercial competition of the great capitalists have given birth, which have fenced off the peoples as distinct nations, and which, in the middle ages, brought about those plagues and famines that mowed down those whom the wars had spared…

The history of the proletariat proves to us that national governments are not afraid to shoot down their "subjects" when the latter demand a few liberties. What more, then, could foreign exploiters do? Our enemy is *the master*, no matter to what nationality he belongs! Whatever the excuse with which a declaration of war be decorated or disguised, there can be nothing in it at bottom but a question of *bourgeois* interest: whether it be disputes on the subject of political precedence, commercial treaties, or the annexation of colonial countries, it is the advantage of the privileged alone—of rulers, merchants, or manufacturers—which is at stake. The republicans of today humbug us nicely when they congratulate us upon the fact that their wars are no longer made in the interest of dynasties, the republic having replaced kings. Caste interest has replaced dynastic interest,—that is all; what difference does it make to the worker? Conquerors, or conquered, we shall continue to pay the tax, to die of hunger when out of work; the almshouse or the hospital will continue to be our refuge at old age. And the capitalistic class would like us to interest ourselves in their quarrels! What have we to gain by it?

As to fearing a worse condition, the stoppage of progress in case a nation should disappear, this is failing to take into account what international relations are nowadays, and the general diffusion of ideas. A nation, today, might be divided, parceled out, dismembered, its name taken away; yet you could not succeed, short of utter extermination, in changing its proper foundation, which is diversity of character and temperament, the very nature of the races composing it. And if war were declared, all these liberties, real or pretended, which are claimed as our especial lot, would be speedily suspended, the Socialist propaganda muzzled, authority reinstated in the hands of the military power; and we should no longer have anything for the most thorough absolutism to envy.

War, consequently, can bring no good to the workers; we have no interests engaged in it, nothing to defend but our skins; it is our lookout to defend them still better by not exposing ourselves to get holes put through them, for the greater profit of those who exploit and govern us. The *bourgeoisie*, on the other hand, have an interest in war; it enables them to preserve the armies which keep the people respectful, and defend their institutions; through it they can succeed in forcing the products of "their industry" on others, opening up new markets with cannon shots. They alone subscribe to the loans which war necessitates, the interest upon which we, the workers, alone pay. Let the capitalists fight themselves, then, if they want to; once more: it is no concern of ours. And, moreover, let us revolt once for all; let us endanger the privileges of the *bourgeoisie*, and it will not be long till we see those who preach patriotism to *us*, appealing to the armies of their conquerors, be they German, Russian, or of no matter what country…they have frontiers between their slaves, but for themselves they mock at such when their interests are at stake.

There is no "country" for the man truly worthy of the name; or at least there is but one—that in which he struggles for true right, in which he lives and has his affections; but it may extend over the whole earth! Humanity is not to be chucked into little pigeon-holes, wherein each is to shut himself up in his corner, regarding the rest as enemies. To the genuine individual all men are brothers and have equal rights to live and to evolve according to their own wills, upon this earth which is large enough and fruitful enough to nourish all. As to your countries by convention, the workers have no interest in them, and nothing in them to defend; consequently, on whichever side of the frontier they may chance to have been born, they should not, on that account, have any motive for mutual hatred. Instead of going on cutting each other's throats, as they have done up to the present, they ought to stretch out their hands across the frontiers and unite all their efforts in making war upon their real, their only, enemies: authority and capital...

Colonization is extending too widely, in the present epoch, for us to neglect to treat separately of this hybrid product of patriotism and mercantilism combined—brigandage and highway robbery for the benefit of the ruling classes! A private individual goes into his neighbour's house, breaks everything he lays his hands on, seizes everything he finds convenient for his own use: he is a criminal; society condemns him. But if a government find itself driven to a standstill by an internal situation which necessitates some external "diversion;" if it be encumbered at home by unemployed hands of which it knows not how to rid itself; of products which it cannot get distributed; let this government declare war against remote peoples which it knows to be too feeble to resist it, let it take possession of their country, subject them to an entire system of exploitation, force its products upon them, massacre them if they attempt to escape this exploitation with which it weighs them down—oh, then, this is moral! From the moment you operate on a grand scale it merits the approbation of honest men. It is no longer called robbery or assassination; there is an honourable word for covering up the dishonourable deeds that government commits: this is called "civilizing" undeveloped peoples...

It is nothing astonishing that these high feats of arms obtain the approval and applause of the *bourgeois* world. The *bourgeoisie* is interested in these strokes of brigandage; they serve as a pretext for maintaining permanent armies; they occupy the pretorians who, during these slaughters, set their hands to more serious "labour;" these armies themselves serve to unload a whole pack of idiots and worthless persons by whom the *bourgeoisie* would be much embarrassed, and who, by virtue of a few yards of gilt stripes, are made their most furious defenders. These conquests facilitate an entire series of financial schemes by means of which they may skim off the savings of speculators in search of doubtful enterprises. They will monopolize the stolen or conquered lands. These wars cause massacres of workers whose excessive numbers embarrass them; the conquered countries being in "need" of an administration there is a new market for a whole army of office-seekers and ambitious persons whom they thus harness to their chariot, whereas had these latter remained unemployed its route might have been hampered thereby. Still better, there are peoples to exploit, to be yoked in their service, upon whom their products may be forced, whom they may decimate without being held accountable to any one. In view of these advantages the *bourgeoisie* need not hesitate; and the French *bourgeoisie* have so well understood this that they have launched headlong into colonial enterprises. But what astonishes and disheartens us is that there are workers who approve of these infamies; who feel no remorse in lending a hand to these rascalities, and do not understand the flagrant injustice of massacring people in their own homes, in order to mould them to a way of living not natural to them...

Messieurs the bourgeois being embarrassed with products which they cannot dispose of, find nothing better to do than to go and declare war against poor devils powerless to defend themselves, in order to impose these products upon them. To be sure it would be easy enough to come to an understanding with them; one might traffic with them by means of barter, not being overscrupulous, even, about the value of the objects exchanged..."Yes, it is possible...but the devil of it is that to operate in such a way takes time and patience; it is impossible to go in on a grand scale; one must figure on competition; 'commerce must be protected'."—We know what that means: two or three fast battleships, in double-quick order, half-a-dozen gunboats, a body of troops to be landed—salute! Civilization is going to perform its work! We have taken a people, strong, robust, and healthy; in forty or fifty years from now we shall have them turned into a horde of anemics, brutalized, miserable, decimated, corrupted, who will shortly disappear from the surface of the globe. Then the civilizing job will be finished!

77. Élisée Reclus: The Modern State (1905)

The following excerpts are taken from Reclus' 1905 essay, "The Modern State," originally published in Volume 6 of L'Homme et la Terre *(Paris: Librairie Universelle, 1905-8), in which Reclus discusses the connection between the patriarchal family and political authority, and the nature of modern bureaucracy. The translation is from Clark and Martin's selection of Reclus' writings,* Anarchy, Geography, Modernity *(Lanham: Lexington Books, 2004), and is reprinted with their kind permission.*

IT HAS OFTEN BEEN REPEATED THAT the family unit is the primordial cell of humanity. This is only relatively true, for two men who meet and strike up a friendship, a band (even among animals) that forms to hunt or fish, a concert of voices or instruments that join in unison, an association to realize ideas through common action—all constitute original groupings in the great global society. Nevertheless, it is certain that familial associations, whether manifested in polygyny, polyandry, monogamy, or free unions, exercise a direct influence on the form of the state through the effects of their ethics. What one sees on a large scale parallels what one sees on the small scale. The authority that prevails in government corresponds to that which holds sway in families, though ordinarily in lesser proportions, for the government is incapable of pressuring widely dispersed individuals in the way that one spouse can pressure the other who lives under the same roof.

Just as familial practices naturally harden into "principles" for all those involved, so government takes on the form of distinct political bodies encompassing various segments of the human race that are separated from one another. The causes of this separation vary and intermingle. In one place, a difference in language has demarcated two groups. In another, economic conditions arising from a specific soil, from particular products, or from historical paths going in different directions have created the boundaries that divide them. Then, on top of all the primary causes, whether arising from nature or from stages of social evolution, is added a layer of conflicts that every authoritarian society always produces. Thus through the ceaseless interplay of interests, ambitions, and forces of attraction and repulsion, states become demarcated. Despite their constant vicissitudes, these entities claim to have a sort of collective personality, and demand from those under their jurisdiction that peculiar feeling of love, devotion, and sacrifice called "patriotism." But should a conqueror pass through and erase the existing borders, the subjects must, by order of that authority, modify their feelings and reorient themselves in relation to the new sun around which they now revolve.

Just as property is the right of use and abuse, authority is the right to command rightly or wrongly. This is grasped quite well by the masters, and also by the governed, whether they slavishly obey, or feel the spirit of rebellion awakening in them…

The state and the various elements that constitute it have the great disadvantage of acting according to a mechanism so regular and so ponderous that it is impossible for them to modify their movements and adapt to new realities. Not only does bureaucracy not assist in the economic workings of society, but it is doubly harmful to it. First, it impedes individual initiative in every way, and even prevents its emergence; and second, it delays, halts, and immobilizes the works that are entrusted to it. The cogs of the administrative machine work precisely in the opposite direction from those functioning in an industrial establishment. The latter strives to reduce the number of useless articles, and to produce the greatest possible results with the simplest mechanism. By contrast, the administrative hierarchy does its utmost to multiply the number of employees and subordinates, directors, auditors, and inspectors. Work becomes so complicated as to be impossible. As soon as business arises that is outside of the normal routine, the administration is as disturbed as a company of frogs would be if a stone were thrown into their swamp. Everything becomes a pretext for a delay or a reprimand...

In certain respects, minor officials exercise their power more absolutely than persons of high rank, who are by their very importance constrained by a certain propriety...Often they even risk being removed from office through the intervention of deliberative bodies and of bringing their superiors down with them. But the petty official need not have the slightest fear of being held responsible in this way, so long as he is shielded by a powerful boss. In this case, all upper-level administration, including ministers and even the king, will vouch for his irreproachable conduct. The uncouth can give free rein to crass behavior, the violent can lash out as they please, and the cruel can enjoy torturing at their leisure. What a hellish life it is to endure the hatred of a drill sergeant, a jailer, or the warden of a chain gang! Sanctioned by law, rules, tradition, and the indulgence of his superiors, the tyrant becomes judge, jury, and executioner. Of course, while giving vent to his anger, he is always supposed to have dispensed infallible justice in all its splendor. And when cruel fate has made him the satrap of some distant colony, who will be able to oppose his caprice? He joins the ranks of kings and gods...

Whereas the soldier obeys orders out of fear, the official's motivation stems not only from forced obedience but also from conviction. Being himself a part of the government, he expresses its spirit in his whole manner of thinking and in his ambitions. He represents the state in his own person. Moreover, the vast army of bureaucrats in office has a reserve force of a still greater army of all the candidates for offices, supplicants and beggars of favours, friends, and relations. Just as the rich depend on the broad masses of the poor and starving, who are similar to them in their appetites and their love of lucre, so do the masses, who are oppressed, persecuted, and abused by state employees of all sorts, support the state indirectly, since they are composed of individuals who are each preoccupied with soliciting jobs.

Naturally, this unlimited expansion of power, this minute allocation of positions, honours, and meager rewards, to the point of ridiculous salaries and the mere possibility of future remuneration, has two consequences with opposing implications. On the one hand, the ambition to govern becomes widespread, even universal, so that the natural tendency of the ordinary citizen is to participate in the management of public affairs. Millions of men feel a solidarity in the maintenance of the state, which is their property, their affair...On the other hand, this state, divided into innumerable fragments, showering privileges on one or another individual whom all know and have no particular reason to admire or fear, but whom they may even despise—this banal government, being all too well understood, no longer dominates the multitudes through the impression of terrifying majesty that once belonged to masters who were all but invisible, and who only appeared before the public surrounded by judges, attendants, and executioners. Not only does the state no longer inspire mysterious and sacred fear, it even provokes laughter and contempt.

78. Otto Gross: Overcoming Cultural Crisis (1913)

Otto Gross (1877-1920) was a radical psychoanalyst close to Carl Jung (1875-1961) and respected by Sigmund Freud (1856-1939). He was the first person to relate the emerging theory of psychoanalysis to anarchism. He was part of the early counter-cultural community in Ascona, Switzerland, and later associated with members of the Berlin Dada movement and Franz Kafka, with whom he planned to publish a journal, "Against the Will to Power." He was involuntarily institutionalized in psychiatric facilities on more than one occasion, as a dangerous anarchist and for drug addiction. He died on the streets of Berlin in February 1920.

The following passages are from Gross' article, "On Overcoming the Cultural Crisis," originally published in the anti-authoritarian, avant-garde German paper, Die Aktion, *in April 1913, in reply to an article by Gustav Landauer attacking psychoanalysis. The translation is by Dr. John Turner of the University of Wales Swansea, courtesy of Gottfried Heuer and the International Otto Gross Society (www.ottogross.org).*

THE PSYCHOLOGY OF THE UNCONSCIOUS is the philosophy of revolution: i.e., this is what it is appointed to become because it ferments insurrection within the psyche, and liberates individuality from the bonds of its own unconscious. It is appointed to make us inwardly capable of freedom, appointed because it is the preparatory work for the revolution.

The incomparable revaluation of all values, with which the imminent future will be filled, begins in this present time with Nietzsche's thinking about the depths of the soul and with Freud's discovery of the so-called psychoanalytic technique. This latter is the practical method which for the first time makes it possible to liberate the unconscious for empirical knowledge: i.e., for us it has now become possible to know ourselves. With this a new ethic is born, which will rest upon the moral imperative to seek real knowledge about oneself and one's fellow men.

What is so overpowering in this new obligation to apprehend the truth is that until today we have known nothing of the question that matters incomparably above all others—the question of what is intrinsic, essential in our own being, our inner life, our self and that of our fellow human beings; we have never even been in a position to inquire about these things. What we are learning to know is that, as we are today, each one of us possesses and recognizes as his own only a fraction of the totality embraced by his psychic personality.

In every psyche without exception the unity of the functioning whole, the unity of consciousness, is torn in two, an unconscious has split itself off and maintains its existence by keeping itself apart from the guidance and control of consciousness, apart from any kind of self-observation, especially that directed at itself.

I must assume that knowledge of the Freudian method and its important results is already widespread. Since Freud we understand all that is inappropriate and inadequate in our mental life to be the results of inner experiences whose emotional content excited intense conflict in us. At the time of those experiences—especially in early childhood—the conflict seemed insoluble, and they were excluded from the continuity of the inner life as it is known to the conscious ego. Since then they have continued to motivate us from the unconscious in an uncontrollably destructive and oppositional way. I believe that what is really decisive for the occurrence of repressions is to be found in the inner conflict...rather than in relation to the sexual impulse. Sexuality is the universal motive for an infinite number of internal conflicts, though not in itself but as the object of a sexual morality which stands in insoluble conflict with everything that is of value and belongs to willing and reality.

It appears that at the deepest level the real nature of these conflicts may always be traced back to *one* comprehensive principle, to the conflict between that which belongs to oneself and that which belongs to the other, between that which is innately individual and that which has been suggested to us, i.e. that which is educated or otherwise forced into us.

This conflict of individuality with *an authority that has penetrated into our own innermost self* belongs more to the period of childhood than to any other time.

The tragedy is correspondingly greater as a person's individuality is more richly endowed, is stronger in its own particular nature. The earlier and the more intensely that the capacity to withstand suggestion and interference begins its protective function, the earlier and the more intensely will the self-divisive conflict be deepened and exacerbated. The only natures to be spared are those in whom the predisposition towards individuality is so weakly developed and is so little capable of resistance that, under the pressure of suggestion from social surroundings, and the influence of education, it succumbs, in a manner of speaking, to atrophy and disappears altogether—natures whose guiding motives are at last composed entirely of alien, handed-down standards of evaluation and habits of reaction. In such second-rate characters a certain apparent health can sustain itself, i.e., a peaceful and harmonious functioning of the whole of the soul or, more accurately, of what remains of the soul. On the other hand, each individual who stands in any way higher than this normal contemporary state of things is not, in existing conditions, in a position to escape pathogenic conflict and to attain his *individual health*, i.e., the full harmonious development of the highest possibilities of his innate individual character.

It is understood from all this that such characters hitherto, no matter in what outward form they manifest themselves—whether they are opposed to laws and morality, or lead us positively beyond the average, or collapse internally and become ill—have been perceived with either disgust, veneration or pity as disturbing exceptions whom people try to eliminate. It will come to be understood that, already today, there exists the demand to approve these people as the healthy, the warriors, the progressives, and to learn from and through them.

Not one of the revolutions in recorded history has succeeded in establishing freedom for individuality. They have petered out ineffectively, each time as precursors of a new bourgeoisie, they have ended with the precipitate desire of people to reinstall themselves in conditions generally agreed to be normal. They have collapsed because the revolutionary of yesterday carried authority within himself. Only now can it be recognized that *the root of all authority lies in the family*, that the combination of sexuality and authority, as it shows itself in the patriarchal family still prevailing today, claps every individuality in chains.

The times of crisis in advanced cultures have so far always been attended by complaints about the loosening of the ties of marriage and family life...but people could never hear in this "immoral tendency" the life-affirming ethical crying out of humanity for redemption. Everything went to wrack and ruin, and the problem of emancipation from original sin, from the enslavement of women for the sake of their children, remained unsolved.

The revolutionary of today, who with the help of the psychology of the unconscious sees the relations between the sexes in a free and propitious future, fights against rape in its most primordial form, against the father and against patriarchy.

The coming revolution is the revolution for matriarchy [mother right]. It does not matter under what outward form and by what means it comes about.

79. Gustav Landauer: For Socialism (1911)

In his 1911 publication, For Socialism, *Gustav Landauer rejects the essentially Marxist notion that capitalist production processes and modern technology are progressive forces that are preparing the way for the triumph of socialism. The following selections are taken from the David J. Parent translation published by Telos Press (St. Louis: 1978), reprinted with the kind permission of the publisher.*

THE DECREASE OF WORKING HOURS creates longer free time for the workers. However much one may rejoice at this fact, one must not ignore what results such achievements have often had: greater exploitation of the workers' strength, increased intensity of work. Often the highly capitalized entrepreneur, e.g., a large stock company, has every reason to rejoice over the workers' victory. All entrepreneurs of a certain sector have, for instance, been forced to shorten working hours, but the large enterprises are often able to compensate for these losses by introducing new machines which chain the worker even more constantly in the service of the high-speed machinery…

The industrialist will, moreover, in order to regain what the shortening of the working time takes from him, not even have to modify the mechanical apparatus of his enterprise. In the factory there is an additional mechanism not constructed of iron and steel: the work system. A few new regulations, a few new supervisory and foreman positions often speed up an enterprise more than new machines…

The accelerated work system has only temporary effect, but the machine is relentless. It has its definite number of rounds, its given output, and the worker no longer depends on a more or less human person, but on a metal devil created by men to exploit human energies. The psychological consideration of man's joy in his work plays a subordinate role here; every worker knows and feels with particular bitterness that machines, tools and animals are better treated than working men…The workers have often been called slaves in a tone of the utmost indignation. However, one should know what one says, and use even a word like "slave" in its sober, literal sense. A slave was a *protégé*, who had to be guided psychologically, for his death cost money: a new slave had to be bought. The terrible thing about the relationship of the modern worker to his master is precisely that he is no such slave, that in most cases the entrepreneur can be completely indifferent as to whether the worker lives or dies. He lives for the capitalist; but he dies for himself. He can be replaced. Machines and horses have to be bought, which involves both procurement costs and secondly, operating costs. So it was with the slave, who first had to be bought and trained even as a child and then provided with subsistence. The modern entrepreneur gets the modern worker free of charge; whether he pays a subsistence wage to one or to the other is indifferent.

Here again in this depersonalization and dehumanization of the relationship between the entrepreneur and the worker, the capitalist system, modern technology and state centralism go hand in hand. The capitalist system itself reduces the worker to a number. Technology, allied with capitalism, makes him a cog in the wheels of the machine. Finally the state sees to it that the capitalist not only has no reason to mourn the worker's death, but even in cases of death or accident has no need to become personally involved with him in any way. The state's insurance institutions can certainly be regarded from many aspects, but this one should not be overlooked. They too replace living humanity by a blindly functioning mechanism.

The limits of technology, as it has been incorporated into capitalism, have gone beyond the bounds of humanity. There is not much concern for the workers' life or health (here one must not think only of the machines; one should also recall the dangerous metal wastes in the polluted air of work-shops and factories, the poisoning of the air over entire cities), and certainly there is no concern for the worker's joy of life or comfort during work.

The Marxists and the masses of workers who are influenced by them are completely unaware of how fundamentally the technology of the socialists differs from capitalist technology in this regard. Technology will, in a cultured people, have to be directed according to the psychology of free people who want to use it. When the workers themselves determine under what conditions they want to work, they will make a compromise between the amount of time they want to spend outside of production and the intensity of work they are willing to accept within production. There will be considerable individual differences; some will work very fast and energetically, so that afterwards they can spend a very long time in rest and recreation, while others will prefer not to degrade any hours of the day to a mere means, and they will want their work itself to be pleasurable and proceed at a comfortable pace. Their slogan will be "Haste makes waste" and their technology will be adapted to their nature...

The capitalist production process is a key point for the emancipation of work only in a negative respect. It does not lead to socialism by its own further development and immanent laws; not through the workers' struggle in their role as producers can it be transformed decisively in favour of labour, but only if the workers stop playing their role as capitalist producers. Whatever any man, even the worker, does within the structure of capitalism, everything draws him only deeper and deeper into capitalist entanglement. In this role the workers too are participants in capitalism, though their interests are not self-selected but are indoctrinated into them by the capitalists and though in every essential they reap not the advantages but the disadvantages of the injustice into which they are placed. Liberation is possible only for those who can step out of capitalism mentally and physically, who cease playing a role in it and begin to be men.

80. Malatesta: Anarchists Have Forgotten Their Principles (1914)

At the International Anarchist Congress in Amsterdam in August 1907, where Malatesta debated Monatte on revolutionary syndicalism (Selection 60), the delegates passed the following motion:

> Anarchists, seeking the comprehensive deliverance of humanity and the complete freedom of the individual, are naturally, essentially, the declared enemies of all armed force vested in the hands of the State—be it army, gendarmerie, police or magistracy.
>
> They urge their comrades—and in general all who aspire to freedom, to struggle in accordance with their circumstances and temperament, and by all means, by individual revolt, isolated or collective refusal to serve, passive and active disobedience and military strike—to destroy root and branch the instruments of domination.
>
> They express the hope that all the peoples concerned will respond to any declaration of war by insurrection.
>
> They declare their view that the anarchists must set the example. (*Anarchisme & Syndicalisme: Le Congres Anarchiste International d'Amsterdam,* 1907, Rennes: Nautilus, 1997, translated by Paul Sharkey)

After the First World War began in August 1914 and the hoped for insurrection did not materialize, the majority of anarchists remained committed anti-militarists opposed to the war. A few very prominent anarchists adopted a pro-war stance in support of the countries allied against Germany and the Austro-Hungarian Empire (with even fewer, such as the anarchist historian, Max Nettlau, supporting Austria and Germany). Kropotkin and Jean Grave were among the pro-war, anti-German group, as was the "revolutionary syndicalist" CGT in France, including Pierre Monatte. Malatesta published the following article, "Anarchists Have Forgotten Their Principles," in the November 1914 issue of Freedom, *the English anarchist paper, in response to this betrayal (reprinted in Malatesta,* Life and Ideas, *London: Freedom Press, 1965, ed. V. Richards).*

I AM NOT A "PACIFIST." I FIGHT, AS WE ALL do, for the triumph of peace and of fraternity among all human beings; but I know that a desire not to fight can only be fulfilled when neither side wants to, and that so long as men will be found who want to violate the liberties of others, it is incumbent on these others to defend themselves if they do not wish to be eternally beaten; and I also know that to attack is often the best, or the only, effective means of defending oneself. Besides, I think that the oppressed are always in a state of legitimate self-defence, and have always the right to attack the oppressors. I admit, therefore, that there are wars that are necessary, holy wars: and these are wars of liberation, such as are generally "civil wars"—i.e., revolutions.

But what has the present war in common with human emancipation, which is our cause?

Today we hear Socialists speak, just like any bourgeois, of "France," or "Germany," and of other political and national agglomerations—results of historical struggles—as of homogeneous ethnographic units, each having its proper interests, aspirations, and mission, in opposition to the interests, aspirations, and mission of rival units. This may be true relatively, so long as the oppressed, and chiefly the workers, have no self-consciousness, fail to recognize the injustice of their inferior position, and make themselves the docile tools of the oppressors. There is, then, the dominating class only that counts; and this class, owing to its desire to conserve and to enlarge its power, even its prejudices and its own ideas, may find it convenient to excite racial ambitions and hatred, and send its nation, its flock, against "foreign" countries, with a view to releasing them from their present oppressors, and submitting them to its own political and economical domination.

But the mission of those who, like us, wish the end of all oppression and of all exploitation of man by man, is to awaken a consciousness of the antagonism of interests between dominators and dominated, between exploiters and workers, and to develop the class struggle inside each country, and the solidarity among all workers across the frontiers, as against any prejudice and any passion of either race or nationality.

And this we have always done. We have always preached that the workers of all countries are brothers, and that the enemy—the "foreigner"—is the exploiter, whether born near us or in a far-off country, whether speaking the same language or any other. We have always chosen our friends, our companions-in-arms, as well as our enemies, because of the ideas they profess and of the position they occupy in the social struggle, and never for reasons of race or nationality. We have always fought against patriotism, which is a survival of the past, and serves well the interests of the oppressors; and we were proud of being internationalists, not only in words, but by the deep feelings of our souls.

And now that the most atrocious consequences of capitalist and State domination should indicate, even to the blind, that we were in the right, most of the Socialists and many Anarchists in the belligerent countries associate themselves with the Governments and the bourgeoisie of their respective countries, forgetting Socialism, the class struggle, international fraternity, and the rest.

What a downfall!

It is possible that present events may have shown that national feelings are more alive, while feelings of international brotherhood are less rooted, than we thought; but this should be one more reason for intensifying, not abandoning, our anti-patriotic propaganda. These events also show that in France, for example, religious sentiment is stronger, and the priests have a greater influence than we imagined. Is this a reason for our conversion to Roman Catholicism?

I understand that circumstances may arise owing to which the help of all is necessary for the general well-being: such as an epidemic, an earthquake, an invasion of barbarians, who kill and destroy all that comes under their hands. In such a case the class struggle, the differences of social standing must be forgotten, and common cause must be made against the common danger; but on the condition that these differences are forgotten on both sides. If any one is in prison during an earthquake, and there is a danger of his being crushed to death, it is our duty to save everybody, even the jailers—on condition that the jailers begin by opening the prison doors. But if the jailers take all precautions for the safe custody of the prisoners during and after the catastrophe, it is then the duty of the prisoners towards themselves as well as towards their comrades in captivity to leave the jailers to their troubles, and profit by the occasion to save themselves.

If, when foreign soldiers invade the *sacred soil of the Fatherland*, the privileged class were to renounce their privileges, and would act so that the "Fatherland" really became the common property of all the inhabitants, it would then be right that all should fight against the invaders. But if kings wish to remain kings, and the landlords wish to take care of *their* lands and of *their* houses, and the merchants wish to take care of *their* goods, and even sell them at a higher price, then the workers, the Socialists and Anarchists, should leave them to their own devices, while being themselves on the look-out for an opportunity to get rid of the oppressors inside the country, as well as of those coming from outside.

In all circumstances, it is the duty of the Socialists, and especially of the Anarchists, to do everything that can weaken the State and the capitalist class, and to take as the only guide to their conduct the interests of Socialism; or, if they are materially powerless to act efficaciously for their own cause, at least to refuse any voluntary help to the cause of the enemy, and stand aside to save at least their principles—which means to save the future.

81. International Anarchist Manifesto Against War (1915)

In early 1915, an international group of anarchists, including Malatesta, Alexander Berkman and Emma Goldman, published a manifesto against war, from which the following excerpts have been taken. It was widely translated and republished in the international anarchist press, such as Goldman's Mother Earth, *and the English anarchist paper,* Freedom *(March 1915; reprinted in* Freedom Centenary Edition, *London: Freedom Press, 1986).*

ARMED CONFLICT, RESTRICTED OR WIDESPREAD, colonial or European, is the natural consequence and the inevitable and fatal outcome of a society that is founded on the exploitation of the workers, rests on the savage struggle of the classes, and compels Labour to submit to the domination of a minority of parasites who hold both political and economic power.

The war was inevitable. Wherever it originated, it had to come. It is not in vain that for half a century there has been a feverish preparation of the most formidable armaments, and a ceaseless increase in the budgets of death. It is not by constantly improving the weapons of war, and by concentrating the mind and the will of all upon the better organization of the military machine that people work for peace.

Therefore, it is foolish and childish, after having multiplied the causes and occasions of conflict, to seek to fix the responsibility on this or that Government...Each does its very best to produce the most indisputable and the most decisive documents in order to establish its good faith and to present itself as the immaculate defender of right and liberty, and the champion of civilization.

Civilization? Who, then, represents it just now? Is it the German State, with its formidable militarism, and so powerful that it has stifled every disposition to revolt? Is it the Russian State, to whom the knout, the gibbet, and Siberia are the sole means of persuasion? Is it the French State, with its *Biribi*, its bloody conquests in Tonkin, Madagascar, Morocco, and its compulsory enlistment of black troops? France, that detains in its prisons, for years, comrades guilty only of having written and spoken against war? Is it the English State, which exploits, divides, and oppresses the populations of its immense colonial Empire?

No; none of the belligerents is entitled to invoke the name of civilization, or to declare itself in a state of legitimate defence.

The truth is, that the cause of wars, of that which at present stains with blood the plains of Europe, as of all wars that have preceded it, rests solely in the existence of the State, which is the political form of privilege.

The State has arisen out of military force, it has developed through the use of military force, and it is still on military force that it must logically rest in order to maintain its omnipotence. Whatever the form it may assume, the State is nothing but organized oppression for the advantage of a privileged minority. The present conflict illustrates this in the most striking manner. All forms of the State are engaged in the present war: absolutism with Russia, absolutism softened by Parliamentary institutions with Germany, the State ruling over peoples of quite different races with Austria, a democratic Constitutional regime with England, and a democratic Republican regime with France.

The misfortune of the peoples, who were deeply attached to peace, is that, in order to avoid war, they placed their confidence in the State with its intriguing diplomatists, in democracy, and in political parties (not excluding those in opposition, like Parliamentary Socialism). This confidence has been deliberately betrayed, and continues to be so, when Governments, with the aid of the whole of their press, persuade their respective peoples that this war is a war of liberation.

We are resolutely against all wars between peoples, and in neutral countries, like Italy, where the Governments seek to throw fresh peoples into the fiery furnace of war, our comrades have been, are, and ever will be most energetically opposed to war.

The role of the Anarchists in the present tragedy, whatever may be the place or the situation in which they find themselves, is to continue to proclaim that there is but one war of liberation: that which in all countries is waged by the oppressed against the oppressors, by the exploited against the exploiters. Our part is to summon the slaves to revolt against their masters.

Anarchist action and propaganda should assiduously and perseveringly aim at weakening and dissolving the various States, at cultivating the spirit of revolt, and arousing discontent in peoples and armies.

To all the soldiers of all countries, who believe they are fighting for justice and liberty, we have to declare that their heroism and their valour will but serve to perpetuate hatred, tyranny, and misery.

To the workers in factory and mine it is necessary to recall that the rifles they now have in their hands have been used against them in the days of strike and of revolt, and that later on they will be again used against them in order to compel them to undergo and endure capitalist exploitation.

To the workers on farm and field it is necessary to show that after the war they will be obliged once more to bend beneath the yoke and to continue to cultivate the lands of their lords and to feed the rich.

To all the outcasts, that they should not part with their arms until they have settled accounts with their oppressors, until they have taken land and factory and workshop for themselves.

To mothers, wives, and daughters, the victims of increased misery and privation, let us show who are the ones really responsible for their sorrows and for the massacre of their fathers, sons, and husbands.

We must take advantage of all the movements of revolt, of all the discontent, in order to foment insurrection, and to organize the revolution to which we look to put an end to all social wrongs.

No despondency, even before a calamity like the present war. It is in periods thus troubled, in which many thousands of men heroically give their lives for an idea, that we must show these men the generosity, greatness, and beauty of the Anarchist ideal: Social justice realized through the free organization of producers; war and militarism done away with forever; and complete freedom won, by the abolition of the State and its organs of destruction.

82. Emma Goldman: The Road to Universal Slaughter (1915)

When the United States did not immediately enter the war, there was a concerted propaganda campaign in favour of U.S. involvement under the rubric of "Preparedness," resulting in a massive increase in U.S. military forces. In response, Emma Goldman published this essay, "Prepardedness: The Road to Universal Slaughter," in Mother Earth, *Vol. X, No. 10, December 1915, and also as a pamphlet.*

In February 1917, revolution broke out in Russia. In April 1917, the United States entered the war and, as Emma Goldman had predicted, began an aggressive attack on radicals at home. Goldman and Berkman, actively campaigning against conscription, were arrested in June 1917, sentenced to two years in prison and deported to Russia upon their release, while distribution of Mother Earth *and Berkman's paper,* The Blast, *was effectively prohibited.*

EVER SINCE THE BEGINNING OF THE EUROPEAN conflagration, the whole human race almost has fallen into the deathly grip of the war anesthesis, overcome by the mad teaming fumes of a blood soaked chloroform, which has obscured its vision and paralyzed its heart. Indeed, with the exception of some savage tribes, who know nothing of Christian religion or of brotherly love, and who also know nothing of dreadnaughts, submarines, munition manufacture and war loans, the rest of the race is under this terrible narcosis. The human mind seems to be conscious of but one thing, murderous speculation. Our whole civilization, our entire culture is concentrated in the mad demand for the most perfected weapons of slaughter.

Ammunition! Ammunition! O, Lord, thou who rulest heaven and earth, thou God of love, of mercy and of justice, provide us with enough ammunition to destroy our enemy. Such is the prayer which is ascending daily to the Christian heaven. Just like cattle, panic-stricken in the face of fire, throw themselves into the very flames, so all of the European people have fallen over each other into the devouring flames of the furies of war, and America, pushed to the very brink by unscrupulous politicians, by ranting demagogues, and by military sharks, is preparing for the same terrible feat.

In the face of this approaching disaster, it behooves men and women not yet overcome by the war madness to raise their voice of protest, to call the attention of the people to the crime and outrage which are about to be perpetrated upon them.

America is essentially the melting pot. No national unit composing it is in a position to boast of superior race purity, particular historic mission, or higher culture. Yet the jingoes and war speculators are filling the air with the sentimental slogan of hypocritical nationalism, "America for Americans," "America first, last, and all the time." This cry has caught the popular fancy from one end of the country to another. In order to maintain America, military preparedness must be engaged in at once. A billion dollars of the people's sweat and blood is to be expended for dreadnaughts and submarines for the army and the navy, all to protect this precious America.

The pathos of it all is that the America which is to be protected by a huge military force is not the America of the people, but that of the privileged class; the class which robs and exploits the masses, and controls their lives from the cradle to the grave. No less pathetic is it that so few people realize that preparedness never leads to peace, but that it is indeed the road to universal slaughter...

Since the war began, miles of paper and oceans of ink have been used to prove the barbarity, the cruelty, the oppression of Prussian militarism. Conservatives and radicals alike are giving their support to the Allies for no other reason than to help crush that militarism, in the presence of which, they say, there can be no peace or progress in Europe. But though America grows fat on the manufacture of munitions and war loans to the Allies to help crush Prussians the same cry is now being raised in America which, if carried into national action, would build up an American militarism far more terrible than German or Prussian militarism could ever be, and that because nowhere in the world has capitalism become so brazen in its greed and nowhere is the state so ready to kneel at the feet of capital....

Preparedness is not directed only against the external enemy; it aims much more at the internal enemy. It concerns that element of labour which has learned not to hope for anything from our institutions, that awakened part of the working people which has realized that the war of classes underlies all wars among nations, and that if war is justified at all it is the war against economic dependence and political slavery, the two dominant issues involved in the struggle of the classes...

Just as it is with all the other institutions in our confused life, which were supposedly created for the good of the people and have accomplished the very reverse, so it will be with preparedness. Supposedly, America is to prepare for peace; but in reality it will be the cause of war. It always has been thus—all through bloodstained history, and it will continue until nation will refuse to fight against nation, and until the people of the world will stop preparing for slaughter. Preparedness is like the seed of a poisonous plant; placed in the soil, it will bear poisonous fruit. The European mass destruction is the fruit of that poisonous seed. It is imperative that the American workers realize this before they are driven by the jingoes into the madness that is forever haunted by the spectre of danger and invasion; they must know that to prepare for peace means to invite war, means to unloose the furies of death over land and seas.

That which has driven the masses of Europe into the trenches and to the battlefields is not their inner longing for war; it must be traced to the cut-throat competition for military equipment, for more efficient armies, for larger warships, for more powerful cannon. You cannot build up a standing army and then throw it back into a box like tin soldiers. Armies equipped to the teeth with weapons, with highly developed instruments of murder and backed by their military interests, have their own dynamic functions. We have but to examine into the nature of militarism to realize the truism of this contention.

Militarism consumes the strongest and most productive elements of each nation. Militarism swallows the largest part of the national revenue. Almost nothing is spent on education, art, literature and science compared with the amount devoted to militarism in times of peace, while in times of war everything else is set at naught; all life stagnates, all effort is curtailed; the very sweat and blood of the masses are used to feed this insatiable monster—militarism. Under such circumstances, it must become more arrogant, more aggressive, more bloated with its own importance. If for no other reason, it is out of surplus energy that militarism must act to remain alive;

therefore it will seek an enemy or create one artificially. In this civilized purpose and method, militarism is sustained by the state, protected by the laws of the land, is fostered by the home and the school, and glorified by public opinion. In other words, the function of militarism is to kill. It cannot live except through murder.

But the most dominant factor of military preparedness and the one which inevitably leads to war, is the creation of group interests, which consciously and deliberately work for the increase of armament whose purposes are furthered by creating the war hysteria. This group interest embraces all those engaged in the manufacture and sale of munitions and in military equipment for personal gain and profit…

It is not enough to claim being neutral; a neutrality which sheds crocodile tears with one eye and keeps the other riveted upon the profits from war supplies and war loans, is not neutrality. It is a hypocritical cloak to cover the country's crimes. Nor is it enough to join the bourgeois pacifists, who proclaim peace among the nations, while helping to perpetuate the war among the classes, a war which, in reality, is at the bottom of all other wars.

It is this war of the classes that we must concentrate upon, and in that connection the war against false values, against evil institutions, against all social atrocities. Those who appreciate the urgent need of co-operating in great struggles must oppose military preparedness imposed by the state and capitalism for the destruction of the masses. They must organize the preparedness of the masses for the overthrow of both capitalism and the state. Industrial and economic preparedness is what the workers need. That alone leads to revolution at the bottom as against mass destruction from on top. That alone leads to true internationalism of labour against Kaiserdom, Kingdom, diplomacies, military cliques and bureaucracy. That alone will give the people the means to take their children out of the slums, out of the sweat shops and the cotton mills. That alone will enable them to inculcate in the coming generation a new ideal of brotherhood, to rear them in play and song and beauty; to bring up men and women, not automatons. That alone will enable woman to become the real mother of the race, who will give to the world creative men, and not soldiers who destroy. That alone leads to economic and social freedom, and does away with all wars, all crimes, and all injustice.

Chapter 18
The Russian Revolution

83. Gregory Maksimov: The Soviets (1917)

The Soviets were popular democratic institutions that first emerged in St. Petersburg during the 1905 Russian Revolution. The original Soviets were assemblies of factory workers, soldiers and peasants. Inevitably, various political factions sought to control them. When the Soviets were reconstituted following the February 1917 Russian Revolution, most of the delegates were affiliated with one or another of the political parties. The Soviets became a popular counter-power to the Provisional Government led by the moderate Social Revolutionary, Alexander Kerensky (1881-1970). Gregory Maksimov (or G. P. Maximoff, 1893-1950) was an anarcho-syndicalist active in St. Petersburg, organizing the first conference of Petrograd Factory Committees in June 1917. In November 1917 (October on the old Russian calendar, hence the "October Revolution"), the Bolsheviks seized power in a coup d'etat, proclaiming a revolutionary Soviet government. Many anarchists took part in the October Revolution, regarding the Bolsheviks as genuine revolutionaries at the time. The Bolsheviks immediately began to consolidate their power. As a result, by December 1917, Maksimov was denouncing the Soviets as tools of reaction, and defending the revolutionary role of the factory committees. The following selection is taken from his December 1917 article, "The Soviets of Workers', Soldiers' and Peasants' Deputies," translated by Paul Avrich in his (out of print) collection of Russian anarchist writings, The Anarchists in the Russian Revolution *(London: Thames & Hudson, 1973), reprinted here with the kind permission of the publisher.*

I. BEFORE THE "SECOND OCTOBER REVOLUTION" the soviets were political, anarchistic, class organizations mixed with a classless intelligentsia element.

II. They served as centres in which the will of the proletariat was crystallized, without compulsion or force but by discussion, by the will of the majority without coercing the will of the minority.

III. The acts of the soviets before 24 October 1917 had a revolutionary character, for the soviets had been brought into being by the proletariat spontaneously, by revolutionary means, and with that element of improvisation which springs from the needs of each locality and which entails (a) the revolutionizing of the masses, (b) the development of their activity and self-reliance, and (c) the strengthening of their faith in their own creative powers.

IV. At that time the soviets were the best form of political organization that had ever existed, because they afforded the opportunity at any time to recall, re-elect and replace "deputies" by others who better expressed the will of their constituents, that is, because they permitted the electors to control their elected representatives.

V. The soviets were a temporary transitional form between a representative parliamentary system and full popular rule.

Thus the soviets were a revolutionary force, alive, creative, active, alert—in a word, progressive. And the forces defending them were also revolutionary and progressive. Those forces (organizations, institutions, parties, groups, individuals) which stood to the right of the soviets were defenders of the earlier forms of government and of old institutions. They were hostile to the soviets, that is, counter-revolutionary, reactionary. Therefore, when a life-and-death struggle was being waged with these hostile forces we joined ranks temporarily with the soviets as the most revolutionary forces; joined ranks because a defeat for the revolutionary segment of democracy would have meant the defeat of the revolution itself; joined ranks in the provinces because, even though the slogan "all power to the soviets" did not satisfy us, it was nevertheless more progressive than the demands of right-wing democracy and at least partly fulfilled our demands for the decentralization, dispersal and final elimination of authority and its replacement by autonomous and independent organizational units.

As a result of the above, during the struggle between the two sides, we have stood on the side of the revolutionary forces against the forces of reaction. We have been guided by the slogan "march apart, strike together." But this must be our guiding slogan only until such time as those with whom we are striking together become a "real" force, an actual authority, that is, an element of stagnation, of compulsion—in a word, of reaction. With the forces of revolution this happens immediately after their victory, when their enemies are defeated and annihilated. It happens because the throne on which the vanquished has sat, and on which the victors will now sit, cannot be put at the top of the stairway of social progress but only one step higher than under the former regime. In accordance with the inexorable laws of progress, the moment the revolutionary force becomes a ruling power it loses its revolutionary character, grows stagnant and calls into being a new force that is more revolutionary and progressive. Once the revolutionary force aspires to domination, it becomes stagnant and repressive because it strives to hold on to its power, allowing nothing and no one to limit it. As a result (and here a simple law of physics comes into play: that every action has an equal and opposite reaction) there arises a new dissatisfaction, from which emerges a new force of opposition, more alive, progressive and revolutionary in that it aims to expand the victory where the victors aim only to consolidate it then quiet things down.

This is why the Bolsheviks, before their victory over Menshevism [a rival socialist party], defencism and opportunism, were a revolutionary force. But they have now become, in keeping with the laws of progress, a force of stagnation, a force seeking to restrain the revolutionary pressures of life, a force striving to squeeze life into the artificial framework of their program, with the result that they have given rise to a new force, progressive and revolutionary, that will seek to destroy this framework and to widen the sphere of revolutionary activity. Such a force, at the present moment, is anarchism.

Our aid to the Bolsheviks must end at the point where their victory begins. We must open a new front, for we have fulfilled the demands of progress. We will leave the present field of battle. We will go with the Bolsheviks no longer, for their "constructive" work has begun, directed towards what we have always fought and what is a brake on progress—the strengthening of the state. It is not our cause to strengthen what we have resolved to destroy. We must go to the lower classes to organize the work of the third—and perhaps the last—revolution. And just as we earlier took part in the soviets, we must now, with the transfer of power to their hands, struggle against them as law-making and statist organs. Therefore:

1. The Soviets are now organs of power, a legal apparatus on county, district and provincial level.

2. Russia, having recognized a new form of social life, a Republic of (completely autonomous) soviets, has not yet jettisoned as unnecessary baggage the principle of statehood. The state remains, for the soviets are organizations of power, a new type of (class) parliament, each a miniature half-free state at the county, district and provincial levels.

3. The soviets are legal, state organs, organs of a modernized representative system, and we know, as Kropotkin has said [in *Words of a Rebel*], "representative government, whether it is called a Parliament, a Convention or Council of the Commune, or whether it gives itself any other more or less absurd title, and

> whether it is nominated by the prefects of a Bonaparte or arch-liberally elected by an insurgent city, will always seek to extend its legislation, to increase its power by meddling with everything, all the time killing the initiative of the individual and the group to supplant them by law."

This tendency of representative bodies, I should add, in no way depends on their make-up. Whatever the composition of the soviets, they will surely follow the above path; to turn the soviets from this path is inconceivable. Thus to take part in the soviets with the aim of achieving a majority and guiding their activities in the direction we desire would be to accept parliamentary tactics and to renounce the revolution. It would mean becoming statist anarchists who believe in the power of laws and decrees, having lost their faith in the independence and creativity of the masses. It would mean, finally, that we believe in the liberating force of the state.

No, we must fight, and fight relentlessly, against this existing form of the soviets, because:

> 1. The soviets have become organs of power in which the misguided proletariat has accepted the forms of law. As a result, the soviets have been transformed from revolutionary organizations into organizations of stagnation, of the domination of the majority over the minority, and obstacles on the road towards the further development of progress and freedom.
>
> 2. Their acts are now acts of law which kill the spirit of the revolution and of the revolutionary creativity of the masses, encouraging sluggishness, inertia, complacency and apathy, and fostering a belief not in their own creative powers but in the might of their elected officials...
>
> 3. They are not organs linking together autonomous local organizations of workers.
>
> 4. They are now organs of political struggle and intrigue among the so-called workers' and socialist parties, and adversely affect the cause of the liberation of the workers.

Thus we must now wage a struggle against the soviets not as forms in general, not as soviets *per se*, but as they are presently constituted. We must work for their conversion from centres of authority and decrees into non-authoritarian centres, regulating and keeping things in order but not suppressing the freedom and independence of local workers' organizations. They must become the centres which link together these autonomous organizations. The struggle for such soviets must be conducted, for the most part, outside the confines of the soviets and among the broad masses.

But bearing in mind that not all soviets have the same clearly defined (that is, twisted and authoritarian) character, it is by no means forbidden, at least in some cases, to carry on this struggle inside the soviets. However, the main struggle for the creation of non-authoritarian soviets must be conducted outside the soviets, and it is to this struggle that first priority must be given.

84. All-Russian Conference of Anarcho-Syndicalists: Resolution on Trade Unions and Factory Committees (1918)

Maksimov and the Russian anarcho-syndicalists took a critical view of trade unions, which were dominated by the political parties and then co-opted by the Bolsheviks after the October Revolution. They continued to support the revolutionary factory committees as a genuine alternative to the Soviets and the trade unions. The following resolution was adopted by the delegates to the First All-Russian Conference of Anarcho-Syndicalists held in Moscow in 1918 (reprinted from The Anarchists in the Russian Revolution, *London: Thames & Hudson, 1973, with the kind permission of the publisher).*

I. The desperate economic situation of the country, brought about by the rapacity and warfare of the imperialist bourgeoisie, requires an immediate and fundamental revolution in the area of economic relations. It requires the immediate abolition of the state capitalist system and its replacement by a socialist system on anarchist-communist lines.

II. The workers' organizations must take a most active part in this cause, each in its own defined sphere of life, refusing to allow the slightest interference from the state or any statist organizations whatever.

III. As the unfolding revolution has shown, the trade unions cannot serve as the axis of the labour movement, for they correspond neither in form nor in essence to the changing political and economic situation. What is now needed is a new form of workers' organization, one that fully corresponds in structure as well as in essence to the new revolutionary forms of political and economic life. This—the cherished offspring of the great workers' revolution—is the factory committee. From now on the entire focus of the workers' aspirations must be transferred to these organizational forms.

IV. The trade unions, as they are commonly understood, are dead organizations. Henceforth they must become a branch of the factory committees, carrying on completely autonomous work in the following areas: a) cultural and educational (at least wherever proletarian cultural and educational organizations have not yet taken firm root); b) mutual aid; c) the organization of charity. But the unions must in no way interfere with the work of the factory committees, labour exchanges, or workers' consumer cooperatives.

V. The factory committee is a fighting organizational form of the entire workers' movement, more perfect than the soviet of workers', soldiers' and peasants' deputies in that it is a basic self-governing producers' organization under the continuous and alert control of the workers. On its shoulders the revolution has placed the task of reconstructing economic life along communist lines. In those areas of production where it is not possible to establish factory committees, the trade unions will carry out their functions.

VI. The factory committee is our young, fresh, future organization in full flower and strength. The trade union is our bygone, decrepit, outmoded, defunct organization. The factory committee is one of the most perfect forms of labour organization within the framework of the present crumbling state capitalist order, and the primary social organism in the future anarchist-communist society. All other forms of labour organization must yield before it and become its component parts. With the aid of the factory committees and their industry-wide federations, the working class will destroy both the existing economic slavery and its new form of state capitalism which is falsely labelled "socialism."

85. Manifestos of the Makhnovist Movement (1920)

After the October Revolution, Russia was soon plunged into civil war. The Bolsheviks negotiated a truce with the Germans, allowing for the German occupation of Ukraine. An insurrectionary peasant army under the leadership of Nestor Makhno (1889-1934) fought to expel the Germans and to overthrow the local overlords ("hetmen"). After the Germans withdrew at the end of the First World War, various White (Czarist) and Red (Bolshevik) armies invaded Ukraine to re-establish their dominance. Makhno, a committed anarchist, fought against them both at various times, while at others allying with the Red Army against the counter-revolutionary White forces. The following Makhnovist manifestos are reprinted from Peter Arshinov's History of the Makhnovist Movement (1918-1921)*, London: Freedom Press, 1987; originally published 1923.*

Declaration of the Revolutionary Insurgent Army of the Ukraine (Makhnovist)

FELLOW WORKERS! THE REVOLUTIONARY Insurgent Army of the Ukraine (Makhnovist) was called into existence as a protest against the oppression of the workers and peasants by the bourgeois-landlord authority on the one hand and the Bolshevik-Communist dictatorship on the other.

Setting for itself one goal—the battle for total liberation of the working people of the Ukraine from the oppression of various authorities and the creation of a TRUE SOVIET SOCIALIST ORDER, the insurgent Makhnovist army fought stubbornly on several fronts for the achievement of these goals and at the present time is bringing to a victorious conclusion the struggle against the Denikinist [White] army, liberating region after region, in which every coercive power and every coercive organization is in the process of being removed.

Many peasants and workers are asking: What will happen now? What is to be done? How shall we treat the decrees of the exiled authorities, etc.

All of these questions will be answered finally and in detail at the All-Ukrainian worker-peasant Congress, which must convene immediately, as soon as there is an opportunity for the workers and peasants to come together. This congress will map out and decide all the urgent questions of peasant-worker life.

In view of the fact that the congress will be convened at an indefinite time, the insurgent Makhnovist army finds it necessary to put up the following announcement concerning worker-peasant life:

1. All decrees of the Denikin (volunteer) authority are abolished. Those decrees of the Communist authority which conflict with the interests of the peasants and workers are also repealed. Note: Which decrees of the Communist authority are harmful to the working people must be decided by the working people themselves—the peasants in assemblies, the workers in their factories and workshops.

2. The lands of the service gentry, of the monasteries, of the princes and other enemies of the toiling masses, with all their livestock and goods, are passed on to the use of those peasants who support themselves solely through their own labour. This transfer will be carried out in an orderly fashion determined in common at peasant assemblies, which must remember in this matter not only each of their own personal interests, but also bear in mind the common interest of all the oppressed, working peasantry.

3. Factories, workshops, mines and other tools and means of production become the property of the working class as a whole, which will run all enterprises themselves, through their trade unions, getting production under way and striving to tie together all industry in the country in a single, unitary organization.

4. It is being proposed that all peasant and worker organizations start the construction of free worker-peasant soviets. Only labourers who are contributing

work necessary to the social economy should participate in the soviets. Representatives of political organizations have no place in worker-peasant soviets, since their participation in a workers' soviet will transform the latter into deputies of the party and can lead to the downfall of the soviet system.

5. The existence of the Cheka [the Bolshevik secret police], of party committees and similar compulsory authoritative and disciplinary institutions is intolerable in the midst of free peasants and workers.

6. Freedom of speech, press, assembly, unions and the like are inalienable rights of every worker and any restriction on them is a counter-revolutionary act.

7. State militia, policemen and armies are abolished. Instead of them the people will organize their own self-defence. Self-defence can be organized only by workers and peasants.

8. The worker-peasant soviets, the self-defence groups of workers and peasants and also every peasant and worker must not permit any counter-revolutionary manifestation whatsoever by the bourgeoisie and officers. Nor should they tolerate the appearance of banditry. Everyone convicted of counter-revolution or banditry will be shot on the spot.

9. Soviet and Ukrainian money must be accepted equally with other monies. Those guilty of violation of this are subject to revolutionary punishment.

10. The exchange of work products and goods will remain free; for the time being this activity will not be taken over by the worker-peasant organizations. But at the same time, it is proposed that the exchange of work products take place chiefly BETWEEN WORKING PEOPLE.

11. All individuals deliberately obstructing the distribution of this declaration will be considered counter-revolutionary. (January 7, 1920)

Who Are the Makhnovists and What Are They Fighting For?

I. The Makhnovists are peasants and workers who rose as early as 1918 against the coercion of the German-Magyar, Austrian and Hetman bourgeois authority in the Ukraine. The Makhnovists are those working people who raised the battle standard against the Denikinists and any kind of oppression, violence and lies, wherever they originated. The Makhnovists are the very workers by whose labour the bourgeoisie in general and now the Soviet bourgeoisie in particular rules and grows rich and fat.

II. WHY DO WE CALL OURSELVES MAKHNOVISTS? Because, first, in the terrible days of reaction in the Ukraine, we saw in our ranks an unfailing friend and leader,

MAKHNO, whose voice of protest against any kind of coercion of the working people rang out in all the Ukraine, calling for a battle against all oppressors, pillagers and political charlatans who betray us; and who is now marching together with us in our common ranks unwaveringly toward the final goal: liberation of the working people from any kind of oppression.

...IV. HOW DO THE MAKHNOVISTS UNDERSTAND THE SOVIET SYSTEM? The working people themselves must freely choose their own soviets, which will carry out the will and desires of the working people themselves, that is to say, ADMINISTRATIVE, not ruling, soviets.

The land, the factories, the workshops, the mines, the railroads and the other wealth of the people must belong to the working people themselves, to those who work in them, that is to say, they must be socialized.

V. WHAT ROAD LEADS TO THE ACHIEVEMENT OF THE MAKHNOVIST GOALS? An implacable revolution and consistent struggle against all lies, arbitrariness and coercion, wherever they come from, a struggle to the death, a struggle for free speech, for the righteous cause, a struggle with weapons in hand. Only through the abolition of all rulers, through the destruction of the whole foundation of their lies, in state affairs as well as in political and economic affairs. And only through the destruction of the state by means of a social revolution can the genuine Worker-Peasant soviet system be realized and can we arrive at SOCIALISM. (April 27, 1920)

Pause! Read! Consider!

Comrade in the Red Army! You were sent by your commissars and commanders to capture the insurgent Makhnovists. Following orders from your chiefs, you will destroy peaceful villages, search, arrest and kill people you don't know but whom they have pointed out to you as enemies of the people. They tell you that the Makhnovists are bandits and counter-revolutionaries.

They tell you; they order you; they do not ask you; they send you; and, like obedient slaves of your leaders, you go to capture and kill. Whom? For what? Why?

Think about it, comrade Red Army Man! Think about it you toiling peasant and worker, taken by force into the cabal of the new masters, who claim the stirring title of worker-peasant authority.

We, the revolutionary insurgent Makhnovists, are also peasants and workers like our brothers in the Red Army. We rose against oppression; we are fighting for a better and brighter life. Our frank ideal is the achievement of a non-authoritarian labourers' society without parasites and without commissar-bureaucrats. Our immediate goal is the establishment of the free soviet order, without the authority of the

Bolsheviks, without pressure from any party whatsoever. For this the government of the Bolshevik-Communists sends punitive expeditions upon us. They hurry to make peace with Denikin, with the Polish landlords, and other white guard scum, in order to crush more easily the popular movement of revolutionary insurgents, who are rising for the oppressed against the yoke of any authority.

The threats of the white-red high command do not scare us.

WE WILL ANSWER VIOLENCE WITH VIOLENCE.

When necessary, we, a small handful, will put to flight the legions of the bureaucratic Red Army. For we are freedom-loving revolutionary insurgents and the cause we defend is a just cause. Comrade! Think about it, who are you with and who are you against?

Don't be a slave—be a man. (June 1920)

86. Peter Arshinov: The Makhnovshchina and Anarchism (1921)

Peter Arshinov (1887-1937) was a revolutionary socialist and briefly, during the 1905 Russian Revolution, a member of the Bolshevik Party. In 1906 he became an anarchist. Returning to his native Ukraine, he was involved in the bombing of a police station and assassinated a railroad boss responsible for the persecution and deaths of many workers. He was imprisoned, and facing a death sentence, escaped in 1907. He travelled through Europe for a couple of years, returning to Russia in 1909 to resume his revolutionary activities. In 1910, he was again arrested and sentenced to twenty years in prison. He was sent to the Butyrki prison in Moscow, where he met Nestor Makhno, who was serving a life sentence for his involvement in the assassination of a police chief by his local anarchist group. In March 1917, as a result of the February Revolution, both Arshinov and Makhno were freed from prison. Makhno returned immediately to Ukraine, while Arshinov stayed for a time in Moscow, working with the Moscow Federation of Anarchist Groups. They met again in Moscow in 1918, but it was only after Makhno began a mass insurgency in 1919 that Arshinov went back to Ukraine to join the Makhnovist movement (the Makhnovshchina), where he remained until its defeat in 1921. The following excerpts are taken from Arshinov's 1923 publication, History of the Makhnovist Movement (1918-1921), *translated by Lorraine and Fredy Perlman.*

THE ANARCHIST IDEAL IS LARGE AND RICH in its diversity. Nevertheless, the role of anarchists in the social struggle of the masses is extremely modest. Their task is to help the masses take the right road in the struggle and in the construction of the new society. If the mass movement has not entered the stage of decisive collision, their duty is to help the masses clarify the significance, the tasks and the goals, of the struggle ahead; their duty is to help the masses make the necessary military preparations and organize their forces. If the movement has already entered the stage of decisive collision, anarchists should join the movement without losing an instant; they should help the masses free themselves from erroneous deviations, support their first creative efforts, assist them intellectually, always striving to help the movement remain on the path which leads toward the essential goals of the workers. This is the basic and, in fact, the only task of anarchists in the first phase of the revolution. The working class, once it has mastered the struggle and begins its social construction, will no longer surrender to anyone the initiative in creative work. The working class will then direct itself by its own thought; it will create its society according to its own plans. Whether or not this will be an anarchist plan, the plan as well as the society based on it will emerge from the depths of emancipated labour, shaped and framed by its thought and its will.

When we examine the Makhnovshchina, we are immediately aware of two basic aspects of this movement: 1) its truly proletarian origins as a popular movement of the lowest strata of society: the movement sprang up from below, and from beginning to end it was the popular masses themselves who supported, developed, and directed it; 2) it deliberately leaned on certain incontestably anarchist principles from the very beginning: (a) the right of workers to full initiative, (b) the right of workers to economic and social self-management, (c) the principle of statelessness in social construction...

In the Makhnovshchina we have an anarchist movement of the working masses—not completely realized, not entirely crystallized, but striving toward the anarchist ideal and moving along the anarchist path.

But precisely because this movement grew out of the depths of the masses, it did not have the necessary theoretical forces, the powers of generalization indispensable to any widespread social movement. This shortcoming manifested itself in the fact that the movement, in the face of the general situation, did not succeed in developing its ideas and its slogans, or in elaborating its concrete and practical forms. This is why the movement developed slowly and painfully, especially in view of the numerous enemy forces which attacked it from all sides...

The basic shortcoming of the movement resides in the fact that during its last two years it concentrated mainly on military activities. This was not an organic flaw of the movement itself, but rather its misfortune—it was imposed on the movement by the situation in the Ukraine.

Three years of uninterrupted civil wars made the southern Ukraine a permanent battlefield. Numerous armies of various parties traversed it in every direction, wreaking material, social and moral destruction on the peasants. This exhausted the peasants. It destroyed their first experiments in the field of workers' self-management. Their spirit of social creativity was crushed. These conditions tore the Makhnovshchina away from its healthy foundation, away from socially creative work among the masses, and forced it to concentrate on war—revolutionary war, it is true, but war nevertheless...

The Makhnovshchina understands the social revolution in its true sense. It understands that the victory and consolidation of the revolution, the development of the well being which can flow from it, cannot be realized without a close alliance between the working classes of the cities and those of the countryside. The peasants understand that without urban workers and powerful industrial enterprises they will be deprived of most of the benefits which the social revolution makes possible. Furthermore, they consider the urban workers to be their brothers, members of the same family of workers.

There can be no doubt that, at the moment of the victory of the social revolution, the peasants will give their entire support to the workers. This will be voluntary and truly revolutionary support given directly to the urban proletariat. In the present-day situation, the bread taken by force from the peasants nourishes mainly the enormous governmental machine. The peasants see and understand perfectly that this expensive bureaucratic machine is not in any way needed by them or by the workers, and that in relation to the workers it plays the same role as that of a prison administration toward the inmates. This is why the peasants do not have the slightest desire to give their bread voluntarily to the State. This is why they are so hostile in their relations with the contemporary tax collectors—the commissars and the various supply organs of the State.

But the peasants always try to enter into direct relations with the urban workers. This question was raised more than once at peasant congresses, and the peasants always resolved it in a revolutionary and positive manner. At the time of the social revolution, when the masses of urban proletarians become truly independent and relate directly to the peasants through their own organizations, the peasants will furnish the indispensable foodstuffs and raw materials, knowing that in the near future the workers will place the entire gigantic power of industry at the service of the needs of the workers of the city and the countryside...

Statists lie when they claim that the masses are capable only of destroying the old, that they are great and heroic only when they engage in destruction, and that in creative work they are inert and vulgar. In the realm of creative activity, in the realm of daily work, the masses are capable of great deeds and of heroism. But they must feel a solid foundation under their feet; they must feel truly free; they must know that the work they do is their own; they must see in every social measure which is adopted the manifestation of their will, their hopes and their aspirations. In short, the masses must direct themselves in the largest meaning of those words…

Proletarians of the world, look into the depths of your own beings, seek out the truth and realize it yourselves: you will find it nowhere else.

Such is the watchword of the Russian revolution.

87. Voline: The Unknown Revolution (1947)

Voline (V. M. Eichenbaum, 1882-1945) joined with the Makhnovshchina in 1919 when the Bolsheviks began a concerted attempt to crush the anarchist movement within areas under Bolshevik control. He had been involved in the founding of the first workers' Soviet in St. Petersburg in 1905. In 1907 he was sent into internal exile but escaped to France, where he met various anarchists, including Sébastien Faure, with whom he later collaborated on the latter's Encyclopédie anarchiste *(Paris: Librairie internationale), 1926-1934. He actively opposed the First World War, and had to leave France for the United States in 1915 to avoid internment. He joined the editorial board of the anarcho-syndicalist paper,* Golos Truda, *which was then being published from out of New York. When news of the February Revolution reached them, the entire group returned to Russia to publish* Golos Truda *in Petrograd (St. Petersburg). In 1918 he helped found the anarchist Nabat Confederation in Ukraine, but had to flee to areas under Makhnovist control when the Bolsheviks began their clampdown on the anarchist movement. He was ultimately captured by Bolshevik forces and narrowly escaped execution. He and several other anarchists, including Gregory Maksimov, went on a hunger strike during the Red Trade Union International Congress in Moscow in 1921, eventually winning their release from prison but being forced into exile. He died in France in 1945. His analysis of the Russian Revolution, from which the following passages are taken, was published posthumously in 1947 as* The Unknown Revolution *(Montreal: Black Rose Books, 1993).*

THE BOLSHEVIK IDEA WAS TO BUILD, on the ruins of the bourgeois state, a new "Workers' State" to constitute a "workers' and peasants' government," and to establish a "dictatorship of the proletariat."

The Anarchist idea [was and] is to transform the economic and social bases of society *without having recourse to a political state*, to a government, or to a dictatorship of any sort. That is, to achieve the Revolution and resolve its problems not by *political or statist* means, but by means of natural and free activity, *economic and social, of the associations of the workers themselves*, after having overthrown the last capitalist government.

To co-ordinate action, the first conception envisaged a certain political power, organizing the life of the State with the help of the government and its agents and according to formal directives from the "centre."

The other conception conjectured the complete abandonment of political and statist organization; and the utilization of a *direct and federative* alliance and collaboration of the economic, social, technical, or other agencies (unions, co-operatives, various associations, etc.) locally, regionally, nationally, internationally; therefore a centralization, *not political nor statist*, going from the central government to the periphery *commanded* by it, but *economic and technical*, following needs and real interests, going from the periphery to the centres, and established in a logical and natural way, according to concrete necessity, without domination or command.

It should be noted how absurd—or biased—is the reproach aimed at the Anarchists that they know only how "to destroy," and that they have no "positive" constructive ideas, especially when this charge is hurled by those of the "left." Discussions between the political parties of the extreme left and the Anarchists have always been about the positive and constructive tasks which are to be accomplished after the destruction of the bourgeois State (on which subject everybody is in agreement). What would be the way of building the new society then: statist, centralist, and political, or federalist, a-political, and simply social? Such was always the theme of the controversies between them; an irrefutable proof that the essential preoccupation of the Anarchists was always future construction.

To the thesis of the parties, a political and centralized "transitional" State, the Anarchists opposed theirs: progressive but *immediate* passage to the economic and federative community. The political parties based their arguments on the social structure left by the centuries and past regimes, and they pretended that this model was compatible with constructive ideas. The Anarchists believed that new construction required, *from the beginning*, new methods, *and they recommended those methods*. Whether their thesis was true or false, it proved in any case that they knew clearly what they wanted, and that they had strictly constructive ideas.

As a general rule, an erroneous interpretation—or, more often, one that was deliberately inaccurate—pretended that the libertarian conception implied the absence of all organization. Nothing is farther from the truth. It is a question, not of "organization or non-organization," but of two different principles of organization. All revolutions necessarily begin in a more or less spontaneous manner, therefore in a confused, chaotic way. It goes without saying—and the libertarians understood this as well as the others—that if a revolution remains in that primitive stage, it will fail.

Immediately after the spontaneous impetus, the principle of organization has to intervene in a revolution as in all other human activity. And it is then that the grave question arises: What should be the manner and basis of this organization?

One school maintains that a central directing group—an "elite" group—ought to be formed to take in hand the whole work, lead it according to its conception, impose the latter on the whole collectivity, establish a government and organize a State, dictate its will to the populace, impose its "laws" by force and violence, combat, suppress, and even eliminate, those who are not in agreement with it.

Their opponents [the Anarchists] consider that such a conception is absurd, contrary to the fundamental principles of human evolution, and, in the last analysis, more than sterile—and harmful to the work undertaken. Naturally, the Anarchists say, it is necessary that society be organized. But this new organization should be done freely, socially, and, certainly, from the bottom. The principle of organization should arise, not from a centre created in advance to monopolize the whole and impose itself on it, but—what is exactly the opposite—from all quarters, to lead to points of co-ordination, natural centers designed to serve all these quarters...

The basic idea of Anarchism is simple: no party, political or ideological group, placed above or outside the labouring masses to "govern" or "guide" them ever succeeds in emancipating them, even if it sincerely desires to do so. Effective emancipation can be achieved only by the *direct, widespread, and independent action of those concerned, of the workers themselves*, grouped, not under the banner of a political party or of an ideological formation, but in their own class organizations (productive workers' unions, factory committees, co-operatives, etc.) on the basis of concrete action and self-government, *helped, but not governed*, by revolutionaries working in the very midst of, and not above the mass, in the professional, technical, defence, and other branches.

All political or ideological groupings which seek to "guide" the masses toward their emancipation by the political or governmental route, are taking a false trail, leading to failure and ending inevitably by installing a new system of economic and social privileges, thus giving rise, under another aspect, to a regime of oppression and exploitation for the workers—therefore another variety of capitalism—instead of helping the Revolution to direct them to their emancipation.

This thesis necessarily leads to another: The Anarchist idea and the true emancipating revolution cannot be achieved by *the Anarchists as such*, but only by the vast masses concerned—the Anarchists, or rather, the revolutionaries in general, being called in only to enlighten and aid them under certain circumstances. If the Anarchists pretended to be able to achieve the Social Revolution by "guiding" the masses, such a pretension would be an illusion, as was that of the Bolsheviki, and for the same reason.

That is not all. In view of the immensity—one might say the universality—and the nature of the task, the working class alone cannot lead the true Revolution to a satisfactory conclusion. If it has the pretentiousness of acting alone and imposing itself upon the other elements of the population by dictatorship, and forcibly making them follow it, it will meet with the same failure. One must understand nothing about social phenomena nor of the nature of men and things to believe the contrary...

Three conditions are indispensable—in the following order of importance—for a revolution to succeed conclusively.

> 1. It is necessary that great masses—millions of persons in several countries—driven by imperative necessity, participate in it of their own free will.
>
> 2. That, by reason of this fact, the more advanced elements, the revolutionists, part of the working class, *et al.*, do not have recourse to coercive measures of a political nature.
>
> 3. That for these two reasons, the huge "neutral" mass, carried without compulsion by the far-sweeping current, by the free enthusiasm of millions of humans, and by the first positive results of this gigantic movement, accept of their own free will the *fait accompli* and come over more and more to the side of the true revolution.

Thus the achievement of the true emancipating revolution requires the active participation, the strict collaboration, conscious and without reservations, of millions of men of all social conditions, declassed, unemployed, levelled, and thrown into the Revolution by the force of events.

But, in order that these millions of men be driven into a place from which there is no escape, it is necessary above everything else that this force dislodge them from the beaten track of their daily existence. And for this to happen, it is necessary that this existence, the existing society itself, become impossible; *that it be ruined from top to bottom—its economy, its social regime, its politics, its manners, customs, and prejudices.*

Such is the course history takes when the times are ripe for the *true* revolution, for *true* emancipation.

It is here that we touch upon the heart of the problem.

I think that in Russia this destruction had not gone far enough. Thus the political idea had not been destroyed, which permitted the Bolsheviks to take power, impose their dictatorship, and consolidate themselves. Other false principles and prejudices likewise remained.

The destruction which had preceded the revolution of 1917 was sufficient to stop the war and modify the forms of power and capitalism. But it was not sizeable enough to destroy them *in their very essence*, to impel millions of men to abandon the false modern social principles (State, politics, power, government, etc.) and act themselves on completely new bases, and have done forever with capitalism and power, *in all their previous forms*.

This insufficiency of destruction was, in my opinion, the fundamental cause which arrested the Russian Revolution and led to its deformation by the Bolsheviki.

...[T]he Bolsheviki did not "push the Revolution as far as possible." Retaining power, with all its forces and advantages, they, on the contrary, *kept it down*. And, subsequently, having taken over the capitalist property, they succeeded, after a fierce struggle against popular total revolution, in turning it to their own advantage, restoring under another form the capitalist exploitation of the masses...

The historical evolution of humanity has reached a stage where continuity of progress requires *free* labour, exempt from all submission, from all constraint, from all exploitation of man by man. Economically, technically, socially, and even morally, *such labour is, from now on, not only possible but historically indispensable*. The "lever" of this vast social transformation (of which, through several decades, we have been experiencing the tragic convulsions) is the Revolution. To be truly progressive and "justified" that revolution must necessarily lead to a system in which human labour will be effectively and totally emancipated.

In order that the labouring masses may pass from slave labour to free labour, they must, from the beginning of the Revolution, carry it out themselves, in full freedom, in complete independence. Only on this condition can they, concretely and immediately, take in hand the task which is now imposed upon them by history—the building of a society based on emancipated labour.

All modern revolutions which are not carried out by the masses themselves will not lead to the historically indicated result. So they will be neither progressive nor "justified" but perverted, turned from their true course, and finally lost. Led by new masters and guardians, again kept from all initiative and from all essentially free responsible activity, and compelled as in the past to follow docilely this "'chief" or that "guide" who has imposed himself on them, the labouring masses will revert to their time-honoured habit of "following" and will remain an "amorphous herd," submissive and shorn. And the *true* revolution simply will not be accomplished.

88. Alexander Berkman: The Bolshevik Myth (1925)

After Alexander Berkman (1870-1936) and Emma Goldman were released from prison in 1919, they and another 247 undesirables were deported to Russia on the S. S. Buford, victims of the first large-scale "Red Scare" campaign in the United States (of which Ricardo Flores Magón and Sacco and Vanzetti were also victims). Arriving in Russia in January 1920, unaware of the growing repression, they were initially sympathetic to the Bolsheviks. But as they became better acquainted with the situation in Russia, and came into contact with various Russian anarchists who had managed to escape imprisonment or death, their views of the Bolsheviks began to change. Berkman travelled to Ukraine to find out the truth about the Makhnovshchina, which was subject to a vicious Bolshevik propaganda campaign of lies and vilification. Despite Bolshevik claims to the contrary, it became clear that anarchists of all persuasions, even the "anarchists of ideas," as well as "bandits" like Makhno, were regarded by the Bolsheviks as enemies to be ruthlessly crushed. Berkman later encouraged Maksimov to write a detailed account of Bolshevik repression, which was published by the Berkman Memorial Fund in 1940 as The Guillotine at Work: Twenty Years of Terror in Russia *(volume one was republished by Cienfuegos Press in 1979 under the name of G. P. Maximoff, entitled,* The Guillotine at Work, Vol. 1: The Leninist Counter-Revolution*). For Berkman, the final straw came in March 1921, when the Bolsheviks massacred the Kronstadt sailors, who had rebelled against Bolshevik authority, calling for such "counter-revolutionary" measures as elections by secret ballot, freedom of the press, freedom of assembly and the liberation of political prisoners. The following extracts are taken from the afterword to Berkman's* The Bolshevik Myth *(New York: Boni and Liveright, 1925), published separately by Berkman when the publisher rejected it as an "anti-climax," which Berkman then used as the name of his pamphlet. It is included in the 1989 Pluto Press edition of* The Bolshevik Myth.

TERRORISM HAS ALWAYS BEEN THE ultima ratio of government alarmed for its existence. Terrorism is tempting with its tremendous possibilities. It offers a mechanical solution, as it were, in hopeless situations. Psychologically it is explained as a matter of self-defence, as the necessity of throwing off responsibility the better to strike the enemy.

But the principles of terrorism unavoidably rebound to the fatal injury of liberty and revolution. Absolute power corrupts and defeats its partisans no less than its opponents. A people that knows not liberty becomes accustomed to dictatorship. Fighting despotism and counter-revolution, terrorism itself becomes their efficient school.

Once on the road of terrorism, the State necessarily becomes estranged from the people. It must reduce to the possible minimum the circle of persons vested with extraordinary powers, in the name of the safety of the State. And then is born what may be called the panic of authority. The dictator, the despot is always cowardly. He suspects treason everywhere. And the more terrified he becomes, the wilder rages his frightened imagination, incapable of distinguishing real danger from fancied. He sows broadcast discontent, antagonism, hatred. Having chosen this course, the State is doomed to follow it to the very end.

The Russian people remained silent, and in their name—in the guise of mortal combat with counter-revolution—the government initiated the most merciless warfare against all opponents of the Communist Party. Every vestige of liberty was torn out by the roots. Freedom of thought, of the press, of public assembly, self-determination of the worker and of his unions, the freedom of labour—all were declared old rubbish, doctrinaire nonsense, "bourgeois prejudices," or intrigues of reviving counter-revolution.

That was the Bolshevik reply to the revolutionary enthusiasm and deep faith which inspired the masses in the beginning of their great struggle for liberty and justice—a reply that expressed itself in the policy of compromise abroad and terrorism at home.

Thrust back from direct participation in the constructive work of the Revolution, harassed at every step, the victim of constant supervision and control by the Party, the proletariat became accustomed to consider the Revolution and its further fortunes as the personal affair of the Communists. In vain did the Bolsheviki point to the world war as the cause of Russia's economic breakdown; in vain did they ascribe it to the blockade and the attacks of armed counter-revolution. Not in them is the real source of the collapse and débacle.

No blockade, no wars with foreign reaction could dismay or conquer the revolutionary people whose unexampled heroism, self-sacrifice and perseverance defeated all its external enemies. On the contrary, civil war really helped the Bolsheviki. It served to keep alive popular enthusiasm and nurtured the hope that, with the end of war, the ruling Party will make effective the new revolutionary principles and secure the people in the enjoyment of the fruits of the Revolution. The masses looked forward to the yearned-for opportunity for social and economic liberty. Paradoxical as it may sound, the Communist dictatorship had no better ally, in the sense of strengthening and prolonging its life, than the reactionary forces which fought against it.

It was only the termination of the wars which permitted a full view of the economic and psychologic demoralization to which the blindly despotic policy of the dictatorship brought Russia. Then it became evident that the most formidable danger to the Revolution was not outside, but *within* the country: a danger resulting from the very nature of the social and economic arrangements which characterize the system of Bolshevism.

Its distinctive features—inherent social antagonisms—are abolished only formally in the Soviet Republic. In reality those antagonisms exist and are very deep-seated The exploitation of labour, the enslavement of the worker and peasant, the cancellation of the citizen as a human being, as a personality, and his transformation into a microscopic part of the universal economic mechanism owned by the government; the creation of privileged groups favored by the State; the system of compulsory labour service and its punitive organs—these are the characteristics of Bolshevism.

Bolshevism, with its Party dictatorship and State Communism, is not and can never become the threshold of a free, non-authoritarian Communist society, because the very essence and nature of governmental, compulsory Communism excludes such an evolution. Its economic and political centralization, its governmentalization and bureaucratization of every sphere of activity and effort, its inevitable militarization and degradation of the human spirit mechanically destroy every germ of new life and extinguish the stimuli of creative, constructive work.

The historic struggle of the labouring masses for liberty necessarily and unavoidably proceeds outside the sphere of governmental influence. The struggle against oppression—political, economic and social—against the exploitation of man by man, or of the individual by the government, is always simultaneously also a struggle against government as such. The political State, whatever its form, and constructive revolutionary effort are irreconcilable. They are mutually exclusive. Every revolution in the course of its development faces this alternative: to build freely, independently and despite of the government, or to choose government with all the limitation and stagnation it involves. The path of the Social Revolution, of the constructive self-reliance of the organized, conscious masses, is in the direction of non-government; that is, of Anarchy. Not the State, not government, but systematic and coordinated social reconstruction by the toilers is necessary for the upbuilding of the new society. Not the State and its police methods, but the solidaric cooperation of all working elements—the proletariat, the peasantry, the revolutionary intelligentsia—mutually helping each other in their voluntary associations, will emancipate us from the State superstition and bridge the passage between the abolished old civilization and Free Communism. Not by order of some central authority, but organically, from life itself, must grow up the closely-knit federation of the united industrial, agrarian, and other associations; by the workers themselves must they be organized and managed, and then—and only then—will the great aspiration of labour for social regeneration have a sound, firm foundation. Only such an organization of the commonwealth will make room for the really free, creative, new humanity, and will be the actual threshold of non-governmental, Anarchist Communism.

We live on the eve of tremendous social changes. The old forms of life are breaking and falling apart. New elements are coming into being, seeking adequate expression. The pillars of present-day civilization are being shattered. The principles of private ownership, the conception of human personality, of social life and liberty are being transvalued. Bolshevism came to the world as the revolutionary symbol, the promise of the better day. To millions of the disinherited and enslaved it became the new religion, the beacon of social salvation. But Bolshevism has failed, utterly and absolutely. As Christianity, once the hope of the submerged, has driven Christ and his spirit from the Church, so has Bolshevism crucified the Russian Revolution, betrayed the people, and is now seeking to dupe other millions with its Judas kiss.

It is imperative to unmask the great delusion, which otherwise might lead the Western workers to the same abyss as their brothers in Russia. It is incumbent upon those who have seen through the myth to expose its true nature, to unveil the social menace that hides behind it—the red Jesuitism that would throw the world back to the dark ages and the Inquisition.

Bolshevism is of the past. The future belongs to man and his liberty.

89. Emma Goldman: The Transvaluation of Values (1924)

Emma Goldman and Alexander Berkman left Russia together in December 1921. In September 1921, their anarchist comrades, Fanya Baron and the poet Lev Chernyi, had been summarily executed by the Bolshevik secret police, the Cheka, as "bandits." Berkman had met with Fanya Baron just the day before. She was planning the escape of her husband, Aaron Baron, who had been arrested with Voline and other members of the Nabat Confederation in November 1920 (he went on to endure 18 years of imprisonment and internal exile, only to be "liquidated" when released from custody in 1938). The following extracts are taken from Goldman's My Disillusionment in Russia *(London: C. W. Daniel, 1925; originally published 1924), in which she argues that the fundamental task of the social revolution is the "transvaluation of values," a concept that has its roots in the philosophy of Nietzsche.*

THE DOMINANT, ALMOST GENERAL, idea of revolution—particularly the Socialist idea—is that revolution is a violent change of social conditions through which one social class, the working class, becomes dominant over another class, the capitalist class. It is the conception of a purely physical change, and as such it involves only political scene shifting and institutional rearrangements. Bourgeois dictatorship is replaced by the "dictatorship of the proletariat"—or by that of its "advance guard," the Communist Party; Lenin takes the seat of the Romanovs, the Imperial Cabinet is rechristened Soviet of People's Commissars, Trotsky is appointed Minister of War, and a labourer becomes the Military Governor General of Moscow. That is, in essence, the Bolshevik conception of revolution, as translated into actual practice. And with a few minor alterations it is also the idea of revolution held by all other Socialist parties.

This conception is inherently and fatally false. Revolution is indeed a violent process. But if it is to result only in a change of dictatorship, in a shifting of names and political personalities, then it is hardly worthwhile. It is surely not worth all the struggle and sacrifice, the stupendous loss in human life and cultural values that result from every revolution. If such a revolution were even to bring greater social well being (which has not been the case in Russia) then it would also not be worth the terrific price paid: mere improvement can be brought about without bloody revolution. It is not palliatives or reforms that are the real aim and purpose of revolution, as I conceive it.

In my opinion—a thousandfold strengthened by the Russian experience—the great mission of revolution, of the SOCIAL REVOLUTION, is a *fundamental transvaluation of values*. A transvaluation not only of social, but also of human values. The latter are even preëminent, for they are the basis of all social values. Our institutions and conditions rest upon deep-seated ideas. To change those conditions and at the same time leave the underlying ideas and values intact means only a superficial transformation, one that cannot be permanent or bring real betterment. It is a change of form only, not of substance, as so tragically proven by Russia.

It is at once the great failure and the great tragedy of the Russian Revolution that it attempted (in the leadership of the ruling political party) to change only institutions and conditions while ignoring entirely the human and social values involved in the Revolution. Worse yet, in its mad passion for power, the Communist State even sought to strengthen and deepen the very ideas and conceptions which the Revolution had come to destroy. It supported and encouraged all the worst anti-social qualities and systematically destroyed the already awakened conception of the new revolutionary values. The sense of justice and equality, the love of liberty and of human brotherhood—these fundamentals of the real regeneration of society—the Communist State suppressed to the point of extermination. Man's instinctive sense of equity was branded as weak sentimentality; human dignity and liberty became a bourgeois superstition; the sanctity of life, which is the very essence of social reconstruction, was condemned as un-revolutionary, almost counter-revolutionary. This fearful perversion of fundamental values bore within itself the seed of destruction. With the conception that the Revolution was only a means of securing political power, it was inevitable that all revolutionary values should be subordinated to the needs of the Socialist State; indeed, exploited to further the security of the newly acquired governmental power. "Reasons of State," masked as the "interests of the Revolution and of the People," became the sole criterion of action, even of feeling. Violence, the tragic inevitability of revolutionary upheavals, became an established custom, a habit, and was presently enthroned as the most powerful and "ideal" institution…

This perversion of the ethical values soon crystallized into the all-dominating slogan of the Communist Party: THE END JUSTIFIES ALL MEANS…In the wake of this slogan followed lying, deceit, hypocrisy and treachery, murder, open and secret…

There is no greater fallacy than the belief that aims and purposes are one thing, while methods and tactics are another. This conception is a potent menace to social regeneration. All human experience teaches that methods and means cannot be separated from the ultimate aim. The means employed become, through individual habit and social practice, part and parcel of the final purpose; they influence it, modify it, and presently the aims and means become identical. From the day of my arrival in Russia I felt it, at first vaguely, then ever more consciously and clearly. The great and inspiring aims of the Revolution became so clouded with and obscured by the methods used by the ruling political power that it was hard to distinguish what was temporary means and what final purpose. Psychologically and socially the means necessarily influence and alter the aims. The whole history of man is continuous proof of the maxim that to divest one's methods of ethical concepts means to sink into the depths of utter demoralization. In that lies the real tragedy of the Bolshevik philosophy as applied to the Russian Revolution. May this lesson not be in vain.

No revolution can ever succeed as a factor of liberation unless the MEANS used to further it be identical in spirit and tendency with the PURPOSES to be achieved. Revolution is the negation of the existing, a violent protest against man's inhumanity to man with all the thousand and one slaveries it involves. It is the destroyer of dominant values upon which a complex system of injustice, oppression, and wrong has been built up by ignorance and brutality. It is the herald of NEW VALUES, ushering in a transformation of the basic relations of man to man, and of man to society. It is not a mere reformer, patching up some social evils; not a mere changer of forms and institutions; not only a re-distributor of social well-being. It is all that, yet more, much more. It is, first and foremost, the TRANSVALUATOR, the bearer of new values. It is the great TEACHER of the NEW ETHICS, inspiring man with a new concept of life and its manifestations in social relationships. It is the mental and spiritual regenerator.

Its first ethical precept is the identity of means used and aims sought. The ultimate end of all revolutionary social change is to establish the sanctity of human life, the dignity of man, the right of every human being to liberty and well-being. Unless this be the essential aim of revolution, violent social changes would have no justification. For *external* social alterations can be, and have been, accomplished by the normal processes of evolution. Revolution, on the contrary, signifies not mere *external* change, but *internal*, basic, fundamental change. That internal change of concepts and ideas, permeating ever-larger social strata, finally culminates in the violent upheaval known as revolution. Shall that climax reverse the process of transvaluation, turn against it, betray it? That is what happened in Russia. On the contrary, the revolution itself must quicken and further the process of which it is the cumulative expression; its main mission is to inspire it, to carry it to greater heights, give it fullest scope for expression. Only thus is revolution true to itself. Applied in practice it means that the period of the actual revolution, the so-called transitory stage, must be the introduction, the prelude to the new social conditions. It is the threshold to the NEW LIFE, the new HOUSE OF MAN AND HUMANITY. As such it must be of the spirit of the new life, harmonious with the construction of the new edifice.

Today is the parent of tomorrow. The present casts its shadow far into the future. That is the law of life, individual and social. Revolution that divests itself of ethical values thereby lays the foundation of injustice, deceit, and oppression for the future society. The *means* used to *prepare* the future become its *cornerstone*. Witness the tragic condition of Russia. The methods of State centralization have paralyzed individual initiative and effort; the tyranny of the dictatorship has cowed the people into slavish submission and all but extinguished the fires of liberty; organized terrorism has depraved and brutalized the masses and stifled every idealistic aspiration; institutionalized murder has cheapened human life, and all sense of the dignity of man and the value of life has been eliminated; coercion at every step has made effort bitter, labour a punishment, has turned the whole of existence into a scheme of mutual deceit, and has revived the lowest and most brutal instincts of man. A sorry heritage to begin a new life of freedom and brotherhood.

It cannot be sufficiently emphasized that revolution is in vain unless inspired by its ultimate ideal. Revolutionary methods must be in tune with revolutionary aims. The means used to further the revolution must harmonize with its purposes. In short, the ethical values which the revolution is to establish in the new society must be *initiated* with the revolutionary activities of the so-called transitional period. The latter can serve as a real and dependable bridge to the better life only if built of the same material as the life to be achieved. Revolution is the mirror of the coming day; it is the child that is to be the Man of Tomorrow.

Chapter 19
Anarchism In Latin America

90. Comrades of the Chaco: Anarchist Manifesto (1892)

Anarchist ideas were introduced into Latin America by European immigrants during the 1860's. The anti-authoritarian International generated significant support in several Latin American countries, and anarchists helped organize some of the first trade unions. The two largest Latin American anarchist movements were in Argentina and Brazil, but anarchists were active throughout Latin America. The following manifesto was published in 1892 by a Paraguayan anarchist communist group calling itself "The Comrades of the Chaco" (reprinted in El Anarquismo en America Latina, *Caracas: Biblioteca Ayacucho, 1990, ed. A. J. Cappelletti and C. M. Rama). Paraguay was a particularly impoverished country plagued by seemingly interminable political conflict among its ruling classes and with neighbouring states. The translation is by Paul Sharkey.*

WE ARE ANARCHIST-COMMUNISTS and, being such, mean to spread complete emancipation of the proletariat while fighting to abolish the iniquitous exploitation of man by his neighbour, and we pledge all our moral and material resources to the eradication of all tyranny and the establishment of genuine liberty, equality and fraternity in the family of man.

The essential reason for publication of this manifesto is to express our malaise. For which the current (so mistakenly described as civilized) social system is to blame; as well as to say what we are and what we want, with revolutionary selflessness and the conviction that our cries of indignation will rouse capital's new slaves from the languor of their slumbers. We are in an age of enlightenment when we can see very clearly that everything in nature, such as land, water, air, sunshine, moonlight and the other elements that go to make up the Universe, belong to every being on this planet of ours, since those elements created us and sustain our existence.

It is high time that it was acknowledged that everything artificial in our earthly home, like cities, vast tracts of uncultivated land, canals, ports, sea lanes and land routes, instruments of labour and all the advances of science, are the handiwork of many generations and of thousands upon thousands of workers and thus are equally the property of all and not the sole preserve of a privileged class, phoney politicians, swindlers, clericals, murderers of humanity who protect the big thieves and the murderers and butchers of innocents and exploiters of the working man; in short, everything around us that exists belongs to all workers since we helped create it with our sweat and our blood; we did, and not the band of leeches who, with their constitutions, codes, imaginary gods and holy madonnas have made themselves gods and governors so that they might live off the backs of the producer and steal the gold that we ourselves have extracted from the bowels of the earth...

It is we workers, bricklayers, who erect magnificent, grand, airy palaces and it is a crime if we allow others who command and kill us in the name of fatherland and law to live there while we live in a filthy hovel and, in most instances, do not even have a roof over our heads.

It is we who produce the food and it is a crime for us to allow our children to perish of hunger just so that those who do not lift a finger, other than to turn our wives and children into prostitutes, can stuff themselves until they die.

It is we that weave the rich tapestries and cashmere, make elegant garments and go about in rags as a result of letting ourselves be robbed without putting up any resistance, whereupon these thieves treat us as filthy scoundrels on account of our cravenness and we find ourselves in the ranks of the degraded.

We are the ones who make picture books for our education and then vegetate in the crassest ignorance because we let them be read by those who think themselves superior to us, and who reward our slavishness by calling us ignoramuses and brutes; rightly so, because any man who does not bridle at a tyranny that diminishes his human dignity, is a lesser animal than the rest, since they, who have no capacity for reason, rebel against those who would enslave them.

In short, we workers are the producers of all the wealth of society and in repayment for so very many sacrifices, we find ourselves enslaved, humiliated, oppressed and exploited; in short, we are the victims of this struggle and warfare in the workers' ranks, a struggle and a war stoked by politicians who are driven to provoke butchery in the family of man because of their ambition to rule and rob.

91. Manuel González Prada: Our Indians (1904)

Manuel González Prada (1848-1919) was a Peruvian poet, writer and intellectual who moved toward an anarchist position around 1902. He was familiar with the major anarchist writers, and shared with Kropotkin an admiration for the French moral philosopher, Jean Marie

Guyau (1854-1888), and opposition to Social Darwinism (Selection 54). He was one of the first Latin American writers to discuss the issue of indigenous peoples. The following excerpts are taken from his 1904 essay, "Our Indians," translated here by Paul Sharkey. A collection of González Prada's writings, translated by F. H. Fornoff, including a good selection from his anarchist period, has recently been published as Free Pages and Other Essays: Anarchist Musings *(Oxford: Oxford University Press, 2003).*

WHAT A HANDY INVENTION ETHNOLOGY is in the hands of some! Once one has accepted that Mankind is divided into superior races and inferior races and acknowledged the white man's superiority and thus his right to sole governance of the Planet, there cannot be anything more natural than suppression of the black man in Africa, the redskin in the United States, the Tagalog in the Philippines and the Indian in Peru.

Just as the supreme law of existence works itself out by selecting or eliminating the weak on the basis of their failure to adapt, so the violent eliminators or suppressors are merely accelerating Nature's slow and sluggish trend, abandoning the tortoise's slow gait for the gallop of the horse. Many do not spell it out but let it be read between the lines, like Pearson when he speaks of the fellowship between civilized men of European stock in the face of Nature and human barbarism. For human barbarism read un-white men.

But not only is the suppression of the black and yellow peoples decreed: within the white race itself peoples are sorted into those destined for greatness and survival and peoples doomed to degeneration and extinction...Some pessimists, thinking themselves the Deucalions of the coming flood and even Nietzschean supermen, weigh up the disappearance of their race as if they were talking about pre-historic creatures or events on the Moon. It has not yet been formulated but the maxim stands: the crimes and vices of the English or Americans are inherent in the human race and not symptomatic of the decadence of a people; on the other hand, the crimes and vices of Frenchmen or Italians are freakish and symptomatic of racial degeneracy...

Is the suffering of the Indian less under the Republic than under Spanish rule? The *corregidores* and *encomiendas* may have gone, but the forced labour and impressment endure. The suffering we put him through is enough to bring the execration of humane persons down upon our heads. We keep him in ignorance and servitude, debase him in the barracks, brutalize him with alcohol and dispatch him to self-destruction in civil wars and, from time to time, orchestrate man-hunts and slaughters...

Unwritten it may be, but the axiom according to which the Indian has no rights, only obligations, is honoured. Where he is concerned, the complaint of an individual is regarded as insubordination, collective claims as conspiracy to revolt. The Spanish royalists used to butcher the Indian when he tried to shrug off the yoke of the conquerors, but we nationalist republicans exterminate him when he takes exception to onerous taxation, or wearies of silently enduring the iniquities of some satrap.

Our form of government boils down to a big lie, because a state where two or three million individuals live outside the law does not deserve to be called a democratic republic. Whereas along the coast there is an inkling of guarantees under a sham republic, in the interior the violation of every right under a blatant feudal regime is palpable. The writ of Codes does not run there, nor do courts of justice carry any weight, because hacienda owners and lordliness settle every quarrel by claiming the roles of judge and bailiff for themselves. Far from supporting the weak and the poor, the political authorities nearly always abet the rich and strong. There are regions where justices of the peace and governors are counted as part of the hacienda's slave force. What governor, what sub-prefect, let alone prefect, would dare face down a hacienda owner?

A hacienda comes about through the amassing of tiny plots wrested from their lawful owners and the lord wields the authority of a Norman baron over his peons. Not only has he a say in the appointment of governors, mayors and justices of the peace, but he conducts weddings, appoints heirs, disposes of inheritances and has the sons submit to a slavery that normally lasts their life-time just to clear the debts of the father. He enforces fearful punishments like the foot-stocks, flogging, the pillory and death; or as droll as head-shaving or cold water enemas. It would be a miracle if someone with no regard for life or property were to have any regard for female honour; every Indian woman, single or married, may find herself the target of the master's brutish lusts. Abduction, violation and rape do not mean much when the belief is that Indian women are there to be taken by force. And for all that, the Indian never addresses his master without kneeling before him and kissing his hand. Let it not be said that the lords of the land act that way out of ignorance or for want of education; the children of some hacienda owners are shipped off to Europe in their childhood, educated in France or England and return to Peru with all of the appearances of civilized folk; but once they are back on their haciendas, the European veneer comes off and they act even more inhumanely and violently than their fathers; haciendas are tantamount to kingships in the heart of the Republic and the hacienda owners act like autocrats in the bosom of democracy...

In order to excuse the dereliction of Government and the inhumanity of the exploiters, some...pessimists place the mark of shame upon the Indian's forehead: they charge that he shies away from civilization. Anyone would think that splendid schools teeming with very well-paid erudite teachers had been thrown up in all our townships only to find their classrooms empty because the children, under instructions from their parents, refuse to attend for education. One would also think that the Indians are refusing to follow the morally edifying example set by the ruling classes or have no scruples about nailing to a cross all who peddle high-minded and unselfish notions. The Indian gets what he is given: fanaticism and fire-water.

So, what do we mean by civilization? Morality illumines industry and art, learning and science like a beacon at the top of a great pyramid. Not theological morality, which looks for some posthumous sanction, but rather human morality which looks for no sanction and would look no further than the Earth. The greatest accomplishment of morality, for individuals and societies alike, consists of its having turned man's strife with his neighbour into a mutual agreement to live. Where there is no justice, mercy nor goodwill, civilization is nowhere to be found; where the "struggle for existence" is enunciated as the rule of society, barbarism rules. What is the point of amassing the learning of an Aristotle when one is a tiger at heart? What matter the artistic gifts of a Michelangelo when one has the heart of a swine? Rather than going around the world spreading the light of art or science, better to go around dispensing the milk of human kindness. Societies where doing good has graduated from being an obligation to being a habit and where the act of kindness has turned into an instinctive impulse deserve the description highly civilized. Have Peru's rulers attained that degree of morality? Are they entitled to look upon the Indian as a creature incapable of civilization?

...As long as the Indian attends lessons in school or is educated through simply rubbing shoulders with civilized folk, he acquires the same level of morality and culture as the descendant of the Spaniard. We are forever rubbing shoulders with yellow-skinned folk who dress, eat, live and think just like soft-spoken gentlemen from Lima. We see Indians in parliaments, town councils, on the bench, in the universities and athenaeums, where they seem to be no more venal and no more ignorant than folk from other races. In the hurly-burly of national politics there is no way of sorting out the blame and being able to state what damage was done by the mestizos, the mulatos and the whites. There is such a mish-mash of blood and colouring, every individual represents so many licit or illicit dalliances, that when faced by many a Peruvian we would be baffled as to the contribution of the black man or yellow man to their make-up: none deserves the description of pure-bred white man, even if he has blue eyes and blond hair...

Some educationists (competing with the snake-oil salesmen) imagine that if a man can name the tributaries of the Amazon and the average temperature in Berlin, half the job of resolving all society's ills is done and dusted. If, through some superhuman effort, the illiterate of this nation were to wake up tomorrow morning not just knowing how to read and write but holding university degrees, the Indian problem would still not have been resolved: a proletariat of ignoramuses would give way to one of B.A.s and PhDs. The most civilized nations are awash with doctors without patients, lawyers without clients, engineers without projects, writers without public, artists without patrons and teachers without students and they make up a countless army of enlightened brains and empty stomachs. But where haciendas along the coast occupy four or five thousand acres and where ranches in the sierras measure thirty or even fifty leagues, a nation must be split into lords and serfs…

There are two ways in which the Indian's circumstances might be improved; either the hearts of his oppressors soften to the extent that they concede the rights of the oppressed; or enough manliness is injected into the minds of the oppressed to chasten the oppressors. If the Indian were to spend on rifles and cartridges all of the money that he fritters away on drink and fiestas, if he were to hide a weapon in some corner of his hovel or some hollow in the rocks, his circumstances would alter and he would command respect for his property and his life. He would answer violence with violence, teaching a lesson to the master that rustles his sheep, the trooper that press-gangs him in the Government's name, the bully who carries off his livestock and draught animals.

Preach not humility and resignation to the Indian: rather pride and rebelliousness. What has he gained from three or four hundred years of forbearance and patience? The fewer the authorities he tolerates, the greater the number of harms he avoids. There is one telling fact: greater well-being is to be found in the districts furthest removed from the great haciendas, and there is more order and tranquility in the towns that are least visited by the authorities.

In short: the Indian will be redeemed through his own exertions, not through the humanization of his oppressors. Every white man, pretty much, is a Pizarro, a Valverde or an Areche.

92. Rafael Barrett: Striving for Anarchism (1909/10)

Rafael Barrett (1876-1910) was born in Spain and studied in Paris before emigrating to Latin America in 1904. He eventually settled in Paraguay, where he fought in the revolt against the Colorado Party. He briefly served as a secretary for the railway but resigned rather than exploit the workers. He became a popular journalist who supported the anarchist cause. Jailed and then deported from Paraguay, he spent his last few years in Uruguay before succumbing to ill health. The first piece to follow is from his article, "My Anarchism," originally published in the March 1909 edition of the Paraguayan anarchist paper, Rebelión. *The second piece is an excerpt from his book,* Moralidades actuales *(Montevideo: Bertani, 1910), entitled "Striving." A good selection of his writings is included in* El Anarquismo en America Latina, *(Caracas: Biblioteca Ayacucho, 1990). The translations are by Paul Sharkey.*

My Anarchism

THE IGNORANT CONSIDER THAT ANARCHY is disorder, and that in the absence of government society will always revert to chaos. They cannot conceive of order other than as something imposed from without by force of arms.

Anarchism, as I understand it, boils down to political free enquiry.

We need to rid ourselves of respect for the law. The law is not accountable. It is an obstacle to all real progress. It is a notion that we have to abolish.

The laws and constitutions that govern peoples by force are a sham. They are not the products of men's research and common advancement. They are the creatures of a barbarous minority that resorts to brute force in order to indulge its avarice and cruelty....

Nine tenths of the world's population, thanks to written laws, know the degradation of poverty. It does not require much knowledge of sociology, when one thinks of the wonderful talent for assimilation and creativity displayed by the children of the "lower" orders, to appreciate the monstrous lunacy of that extravagant waste of human energy. The law rides roughshod over the mother's womb!

We fit the law the way a Chinese woman's foot fits its binding, or the way the baobab tree fits the Japanese vase. Voluntarily stunted!

Are we afraid of the "chaos" that might follow should we remove the restraints, if we should shatter the vase and plant ourselves on solid ground and face into the vastness? What does it matter what forms the future will take? Reality will unveil them. We are sure that they are going to be fine and noble like the tree sprouting freely.

Let our ideal be as lofty as may be. Let us not be "practical." Let's not try to "improve" the law and substitute one set of restraints for another. The more unattainable the ideal appears, the better. The sailor plots his course by the stars. So let our focus be on the longer term. In that way we can identify the shorter term. And speed our success.

Striving

Life is a weapon. Where should it strike, against which obstacle should our muscle-power be deployed, how shall we crown our desires? Is it the better choice to burn ourselves out all in one go and die the ardent death of a bullet shattering against the wall, or grow old on the never-ending road and outlive hope? The powers that fate has momentarily let fall into our hands are stormy forces indeed. For him who has a weather eye open and his ear cocked, who has risen once above the flesh, reality is anguish. Groans of agony and cries of victory call out to us in the night. Our passions, like a pack of straining hounds, scent danger and glory. We sense that we are masters of the impossible and our greedy spirit is torn asunder.

To step on to the virgin beach, to rouse the slumbering wonder, to feel the breath of the unknown, the quivering of a new form: these I crave. Better to distort than to repeat. Better to destroy than to imitate. Let the monsters come, just as long as they be young. Evil is what we are leaving behind in our wake. Beauty is the mystery being given birth. And this sublime fact, the advent of that which never was before, must strike to the very depths of our being. Gods for a minute, what matter to us are the sufferings of the fray, what matter the dark outcome as long as we can throw back at Nature: You did not create me in vain!

Man needs to take a look at himself and say: I am an instrument. Let us banish from our souls the familiar feeling of silent labour and give our admiration to the beauty of the world. We are but a means, but the end is great. We are the stray sparks from a prodigious conflagration. The majesty of the Universe shines above us and makes our humble exertions sacred. Little though we may be, we shall be all, provided we give ourselves completely. We have stepped out of the shadows in order to warm ourselves at the fire; we were born to spread our substance around and ennoble things. Our mission is to broadcast our body parts and our intellect; to open up our insides until our genius and our blood spill on to the earth. We exist only insofar as we give; for us to deny ourselves is to fade away in ignominy. We are a promise; the vehicle of unfathomable intentions. We live for our fruits; the only crime is sterility.

Our exertions link up with the countless exertions of space and time and blend with the efforts of the universe. Our cry echoes through the infinite vastness. When we move, we make the stars tremble. Not an atom, not a single idea is lost in eternity. We are the siblings of the stones in our huts, of the sensitive trees and the speeding insects. We are siblings even of the imbeciles and criminals, failed experiments, the bankrupted children of our common mother. We are the siblings even of the fatalism that kills us. By fighting and winning we do our bit for the grand endeavour, and we do our bit when we are defeated too. Pain and annihilation have their uses too. From behind the endless, savage warfare comes the song of a vast harmony. Slowly our nerves strain, binding us to the unknown. Slowly our reason spreads its laws into unknown territory. Slowly science marshals phenomena into a higher unity, the inkling of which is essentially religious, because it is not religion that science destroys but religions. Queer notions cross our minds. A muddled and grandiose dream settles over humanity. The horizon is dense with shadows and in our hearts dawn smiles.

We do not yet understand. We are merely afforded the right to love. Driven on by supreme determinations welling up within us, we tumble into the bottomless enigma. We heed the wordless voice rising in our consciousness and tentatively we toil and fight. Our heroism consists of our ignorance. We are on the move, we know not where and we will not be stopped. The tragic encouragement of the irreparable caresses our sweating breasts.

93. Teodoro Antilli: Class Struggle and Social Struggle (1924)

Teodoro Antilli was active in the Argentine anarchist movement during a period of severe repression. In late 1909 a state of siege was imposed, many anarchists were imprisoned and their presses, offices and cultural centres were ransacked and closed. Antilli was involved in the publication of the anarchist paper, La Battala, *but was arrested in May 1910 along with hundreds of others amid renewed attacks on the anarcho-syndicalist FORA (Selection 58). In 1913, Antilli was imprisoned for publishing an article accusing an assistant prison governor of raping an anarchist prisoner. He was involved in the general strike of January 1919, which was ruthlessly suppressed. Over 700 workers were killed, thousands more wounded, and over 50,000 imprisoned in what came to be known as the "Tragic Week." All anarchist papers, including Antilli's, were banned. In 1921, another 1,100 workers were massacred during the anarchist rebellion in Patagonia. Antilli and his next paper,* La Antorcha, *supported the actions of Severino Di Giovanni, a militant Italian anarchist refugee from fascism who began a campaign of illegal actions, including bank robberies and assassinations, in face of this brutal reaction. The following extracts, translated by Paul Sharkey, are taken from Antilli's* Salud a la Anarquia! *[*Here's to Anarchy!*] (Buenos Aires: La Antorcha, 1924, reprinted in* El Anarquismo en America Latina, *Caracas: Biblioteca Ayacucho, 1990).*

WE SHOULD, IT OCCURS TO US, OFFER a full explanation of our notion of "social struggle" as opposed to "class struggle." As we see it, they are as different as narrow is from wide and the eternal from the ephemeral. Suggesting actions of differing scopes. In fact, someone locked into the class struggle is ill equipped to understand comprehensive social struggle. ...If I accept that there is only class struggle, success for me will be enough. My quarrel is with the propertied and the capitalists. If I join forces with other workers like myself and set up, say, a cooperative, the class struggle will be over as far as we are concerned; we shall have won, as indeed the cooperators and socialists contend. Yet the state of society will not have been changed and the class struggle will be over as far as we are concerned because we have made ourselves capitalists, the inner circle of a business that visits its exploitation on outsiders, making every one of us, in equal measure, an exploiter, instead of our being split into exploiters and exploited...If I extend this to thinking about the entire social system as a "class struggle," then all that is required is that my class should dictate to the other class, in which case I too shall have emerged the victor.

"Social struggle," as we understand it, is not just setting a course for revolution and extinguishing the existence of the bourgeoisie; it is also, since we hold that the social also means the sociable, the elimination of all imposition, especially political imposition, by one man upon another; we see humanity as having fought for countless centuries past to achieve a genuinely free society; we plunge into these raging waters and, let there be no mistake about this, we accept all the consequences and, chiefly, the Revolution. Social struggle, therefore, is something humane and all-embracing; the aim is not merely to change society, but that society should be hospitable for men, and every source of oppression or tyranny banished, which is to say, a genuinely free society...

The term "social struggle," as we employ it, is that all-encompassing. And we want this borne in mind lest it be confused with class struggle carried through to Revolution. We bring into the Revolution a social struggle as well...Class struggle carried through to Revolution has as its aim a "proletarian dictatorship." Social struggle carried through to Revolution has as its object the freedom of Humanity and the ennobling of all of its members.

94. López Arango and Abad de Santillán: Anarchism in the Labour Movement (1925)

Emilio López Arango (1894-1929) was one of the editors of the leading Argentine anarchist paper, La Protesta, *and a member of the anarcho-syndicalist bakers' union, which Malatesta had helped found in 1887. He was originally from Spain, as was Diego Abad de Santillán (1897-1983). Abad de Santillán joined López Arango and others first in publishing the anarchist papers,* La Campana, *and then* La Protesta. *Abad de Santillán later contributed articles from Europe where he became involved with the revived anti-authoritarian International Workers Association (IWA), an international federation of anarcho-syndicalist organizations (Selection 114), in 1922. In 1925, López Arango and Abad de Santillán wrote* El Anarquismo en el movimiento obrero [Anarchism in the Labour Movement] *(Barcelona: Cosmos, 1925), in which they emphasized the anarchist component of anarcho-syndicalism, being equally critical of pure syndicalism and Marxist-Leninism. As with Antilli, despite their strong disagreements over the question of violence, they reject a narrowly working class conception of anarchism, as Malatesta had done before them (Selection 60). The translation is by Paul Sharkey.*

WE DO NOT WHIMSICALLY CONFOUND the workers' movement with syndicalism; syndicalism, as we see it, is a revolutionary theory, one of the many that pop up along the path of the revolution in order to misdirect its aims or clip the wings of the combative idealism of the masses. And plainly, given a choice between this theory and anarchism, we cannot hesitate for a single moment, in that we contend that one comes to freedom only through freedom and that the revolution will be anarchic, which is to say, libertarian, or it will not be at all…

The a-political reformists stand on the road to dictatorship: they counter the communist formula of proletarian dictatorship and the workers' State with the class-based call for "all power to the unions." But in point of fact, setting aside the communists' political persuasions and their confessed dictatorial aims, neutral syndicalism actually embraces all of the Marxist contingencies: it takes capitalism's economic dominion as the basis for the accomplishment of economic aims that defy all political and ideological characterization.

We ought not to forget that the Syndicate is, as an economic by-product of capitalist organization, a social phenomenon spawned by the needs of its day. Clinging to its structures after the revolution would be tantamount to clinging to the cause that spawned it: capitalism.

The notion of class strikes us as a contradiction of the principles championed by anarchism. We consider it the last refuge of authoritarianism, and while fighting to liberate the workers' movement from the political parties, we are, if we assert the notion of class, preparing the ground for a new dominion.

The fact that revolutionaries emerge almost exclusively from the ranks of the oppressed and exploited does not mean that the revolution is a class affair: for those oppressed and exploited who do their bit for the task of transforming society have arrived at an egalitarian outlook on life that rules out the narrow interests of the revolutionaries themselves, taken as a particular group.

The proletariat as a class is an abstract invention…In actuality, the proletariat is a motley collection which in part passively endures the blights of society, in part enters into tactical or express alliances with the bourgeoisie and the reaction, and in part also bands together to fight for Freedom and Justice…

In our view, anarchism is not some laboratory discovery nor the fruit of inspired thinkers, but rather a spontaneous movement of the oppressed and exploited who have grasped the human predicament, the harmfulness of privilege and the uselessness of the State, and who are eager to fight for a social order that will afford man some scope for free development…

We anarchists have no magical powers: we do not imagine ourselves the creators of universal happiness, direct creators at any rate, and we acknowledge and declare as much. In this we also stand apart from those revolutionaries who in actual fact simply yearn to impose their wishes upon more or less well-meaning peoples…

The anarchist revolution will redeem men from the mortal sin of abdication of personality, but the anarchist revolution is not made in accordance with such and such a more or less libertarian program, but is made by means of destruction of the State and all authority. It is a matter of very little consequence to us whether the revolution of the future will be founded upon the family, the social group, branches of industry, the commune or the individual. What concerns us is that the building of a free social order is a collective endeavour in which men do not mortgage their freedom, be it voluntarily or under coercion. The anarchist revolution is, today, the natural revolution, which will not let itself be led astray nor hijacked by authority-wielding groups, parties or classes.

95. The American Continental Workers' Association (1929)

López Arango and Abad de Santillán were also involved in the Congress of the American Continental Workers' Association (ACAT) in 1929, at which the various Latin American anarcho-syndicalist trade union organizations created a continental federation affiliated with the revamped IWA. López Arango was murdered shortly thereafter, allegedly by Severino Di Giovanni and his gang, against whose violent tactics López Arango had waged a long campaign in La Protesta. *In 1930, with the repressive dictatorship of General Uriburu in Argentina forcing the anarchist movement underground, Abad de Santillán returned to Spain where he was to play an important role in the CNT-FAI. Anarcho-syndicalist movements in other parts of Latin America were also suppressed, making the resolutions from the 1929 ACAT Congress one of the last programmatic statements of Latin American anarcho-syndicalism prior to the Second World War. The following material from the Congress has been reprinted in* El Anarquismo en America Latina *(Caracas: Biblioteca Ayacucho, 1990). The translation is by Paul Sharkey.*

SOCIAL ORGANIZATION:—THERE ARE TWO courses offered by proletarian and socialist movements as a way of overcoming the present situation: conquest of the State in order to effect a political transformation of society by means of decrees, and the organizing of economic life on the basis of the labour of one and all. The first resolution means to build the new social organization from the top down; the second means to effect it from the ground upwards; the keynote of the one is authority, of the other, freedom.

The American Continental Workers' Association (ACAT) which learns from the experiences of the past half century of struggles and takes due account of the lessons of reality and life, repudiates conquest of the political State as a means to proletarian emancipation and stakes all its hopes on organizing labour on the solid foundations of freedom, usefulness and solidarity.

As a result, it aspires to a social system in which labour will be the foundation and guarantee of freedom and justice for all.

ABOLISHING THE STATE:—A social system rooted in the concerted labour of free associations of free producers makes nonsense of the State which has always been the tool of the domination of one parasitical caste or class, to the detriment of the producer masses, and which loses its *raison d'être* once economic equalization, the expropriation of the expropriators, has ensured that all human beings are equal, where life, the instruments of labour and access to products are concerned.

The American Continental Workers' Association, as spokesman for the interests of those who produce rather than of those who exploit labour and profit from others' labours, seeks a society of free and equal beings and thus an anarchist society.

ABOLISHING MONOPOLIES:—Capitalism, which is the most unjust form of economics conceivable, and not always the most productive and advantageous in terms of production *per se*, has its deepest roots in the recognition and championing of monopolistic, exclusive, inherited property.

The ACAT rejects any notion of monopoly over the use of society's resources and asserts the full entitlement of humanity at present and in the future to equal access, according to need, to the benefits of nature and human labour. While acknowledging no particular form of organizing future economic relations, it recommends communism as the system holding out the promise of a broader guarantee of social well-being and freedom of the individual.

MAN FREE IN A FREE SOCIETY:—As far as capitalism and the State in the ascendant are concerned, the ideal consists of increasing enslavement and oppression of the broad masses for the benefit of privileged, monopolistic minorities. The ultimate ideal of the ACAT is man free in a free society and it urges realization of this through simultaneous revolutionary suppression of the machinery of the State and capitalist economic organization, in the conviction that the abolition of one and retention of the other will inevitably lead, as experience has shown, to restoration of the very order one sought to destroy.

Libertarian socialism is achievable only through social revolution. As a result, revolutionary workers must prepare themselves intellectually and practically to assume possession of the means of production, distribution and transport for automatic use on the morrow of the revolution, as well as devising forms of liaison between the various productive groups or locations, without the latter constituting the only form of economic coexistence and provided that the fundamental principles set out in our aims are observed.

Fighting Methods...

2. ...the fighting methods of the ACAT and its affiliated organizations are strikes, partial and general, sabotage and, in instances where it may be necessary to practice solidarity across national borders, the boycott.

3. Official arbitration and governmental interference in the settlement of quarrels between capital and labour are rejected. Consequently, the policy of collaboration between classes is to be resisted, and indeed the labour organizations signatory to this solidarity pact undertake to combat draft legislation in their respective countries that is designed to make State intervention in strikes and other social disputes mandatory.

4. The libertarian workers' organizations are founded on federalism. Individuals are free to join the union, the unions make up federations and these together make up the national body. Unity of the proletariat is built from the ground up, with both the individual and the group retaining their autonomy within the workers' International...Federalism is the idea of an organizational convergence that persists as long as there are interests at the practical, factory level common to a factory, a village, a region, bearing in mind that man's first duty is to the surroundings in which he lives as a social being and then to his calling as a producer.

5. The American Continental Workers' Association proclaims its opposition to all politics and rejects all compromise or alliance with parties which accept class collaboration and with trade union groupings that operate under the auspices of the State, be it parliamentary or a dictatorship.

6. The ACAT expresses its sympathy with any proletarian revolutionary venture designed to secure comprehensive political, economic and social emancipation by means of armed insurrection.

7. As an aspiration for the future, the ACAT commends anarchist communism, on the understanding that spreading the philosophical ideas of anarchism ought to be the ongoing concern of all revolutionaries aspiring to abolish the State's political and legal tyranny along with the economic tyranny of capital.

Short-Term Aims

Without abjuring its general aims, and indeed as an effective means of accelerating the realization of them, the ACAT pursues the following short-term goals:

1. The securing of better pay rates, which is to say, a greater share for workers in the benefits of production.

2. Reduction in working hours.

3. Defence of social, economic and moral gains by all of the means of revolutionary direct action not at odds with the lofty aims we pursue.

4. Relentless struggle against militarism and war, through propaganda on behalf of a boycott of the arms industry, individual and collective refusal to serve in the army, bringing the officer class into moral disrepute, and, in the event of war, a revolutionary general strike and sabotage.

5. Ignoring the artificial barriers raised by statist nationhood and proclamation of the worldwide homeland of labour and the common interests of workers the world over.

6. Popularization and affirmation of a profoundly libertarian mentality and of thoughtful production as the pre-requisite for a promising social transformation.

7. Constant practice of solidarity on behalf of victims of the revolutionary struggle against capitalism and the State.

8. Encouragement and support for all social and cultural trends and movements which, while not agreeing with us entirely *vis-a-vis* ultimate goals, contribute through their actions and propaganda towards the undermining of the mainstays of political authoritarianism and economic privilege, without ever abandoning our own internal cohesion or losing sight of the goals peculiar to the labour liberation movement…

Against the Worldwide Reaction

…We regard the fight against the reversion of minds and of social and political institutions to medievalism as one of the prime revolutionary duties of the hour.

In this fight we must combat militarism, war and reaction—three different manifestations of the same principle and the same aspiration—with equal intensity.

In the particular struggle against militarism, we recommend:

a) Individual refusal to serve in the military; and collective refusal, to the same end.

b) Propagation of the ideas of responsibility which bring the function of the serviceman into disrepute and make it a duty upon the proletariat to decline to work for the army, in peace time or in war time.

c) The preparation and propagation of the idea of a complete boycott of supplies, munitions, transport services, etc., for the army and its stalwarts.

d) The sponsoring of children's literature that counters the militaristic poison issuing from State schools.

The aforementioned are recognized as effective measures against war, in addition to the revolutionary general strike or popular uprising with a resultant escalation in the struggle and propaganda.

The fight against reaction, which is a complement to the fight against militarism and war, should be waged primarily through the affirmation of the solidarity of moral and material interests of the oppressed and exploited in every land, through a deliberate and ongoing boycott of statism, through the exposure of the reaction implicit in labour and social legislation, through a campaign against the insatiable demands of the machinery of domination and oppression, through the pressure for freedom and equality for all human beings and, lastly, through the honing and escalation of the ongoing material and psychological conspiracy against the iniquitousness of privilege and despotism.

The Immigration Issue

...Emigration should be ascribed not just to over-population of the old world, but also and primarily to capitalist economic policy. The capitalist governments of the European nations have an interest in getting rid of the discontented segments of the unemployed proletariat, so as to douse a source of malaise.

For their part, the capitalist governments of the recipient countries are eager to welcome as much man-power as possible so as to meet the demands of the labour market and reduce wages...

Before embarking upon emigration, emigrant workers should contact the workers' organizations of the intended destination countries, if possible through the good offices of their own organizations, for a pre-departure briefing on working conditions, wage levels, market conditions, etc. In so doing they are looking out for their own interests, for they need not, through ignorance of the situation, agree to work in dire conditions nor find themselves in the painful position of having to undercut the wages of their fellow workers or endangering the gains secured by the workers' organizations.

Congress issues an urgent appeal to emigrant workers to organize themselves into revolutionary trade unions for the defence of their class interests. The worldwide organization of capitalism must be confronted by the worldwide working class, organized along international, revolutionary and libertarian lines. Only through the abolition of economic exploitation and political domination, only after all artificial borders and the class distinctions upheld by violence have been done away with can relations between the workers of every country and intercourse between peoples be harmonious...

Against Exploitation in All Its Guises

The continental conference of revolutionary workers, while looking with utter belief and confidence to a complete transformation of the political order and bourgeois economic order in times to come, recognizes the urgent necessity of the struggle for bread and day-to-day improvements as expressive of the proletariat's determination to carry out that transformation.

Also, it notes the multiplicity of the forms of man's exploitation of his neighbour—in industry, where man appears as producer; in business, where he appears as consumer; in financial speculation, in the realm of agrarian and latifundian capitalism, etc.—and is of the view that the definitive revolutionary work, as with everyday defence, should be carried out on every possible front.

Chapter 20
Chinese Anarchism

96. He Zhen: Women's Liberation (1907)

Anarchist ideas in China can be traced back to the early Daoist philosophers (Selection 1). Around the beginning of the 20th century, anarchist ideas again began to circulate in China and among Chinese intellectuals and students abroad. He Zhen was an early Chinese anarchist feminist living in Tokyo who, with her husband, Liu Shipei (1884-1919), founded the Society for the Study of Socialism in 1907. Together they published one of the first Chinese anarchist journals, Natural Justice. *The position of women in Chinese society was to become an important issue for the Chinese anarchists. At the time, footbinding and concubinage were still common practices. The following excerpts are from her article, "Problems of Women's Liberation," originally published in* Natural Justice *in September and October 1907. The translation is by Hsiao-Pei Yen of the University of Oregon (History Department).*

THE WORLD IN THE LAST FEW THOUSAND years has been...a world constructed by class hierarchy and dominated by men. To make the world better, we need to eliminate the system of male domination and practice equality so men and women will share the world together. All these changes begin with women's liberation.

For thousand of years, China's social structure forced women to be submissive slaves. In ancient times, women were treated as men's property. To prevent licentiousness, men established moral teachings that emphasized the difference between the sexes. Over time, the difference between males and females was seen as natural law. Women were confined to their private quarters, seldom could they travel...women's responsibility has been limited to raising children and managing the household.

Chinese religion believes that descendents contain the ancestors' spirits, so people think propagation is a way to achieve immortality. The Chinese political system treats offspring as property, so people consider procreation as a means to obtain wealth. Therefore, with both religion and the political system supporting men's sexual indulgence, men treat women as a tool for human breeding. Moreover, Chinese men are seldom willing to deal with trivial household chores; instead, they have women do all the physical labour as well as care for the children. There are other causes that make raising children and managing the household women's lifelong career. Firstly, men treat women as their private property. Secondly, the low living standard in pre-modern times made men's labour alone enough to feed the family, so women of well-off families seldom had work other than raising children and managing the household. So all vices of slavery and idleness gather around women…Only in poor families do women often rely on themselves for living. They work in the fields; they are hired as maids; at worst, they become prostitutes. For those women, although they are physically less confined, they never achieve spiritual liberation. Indeed, those who obtain physical liberation are actually the most exploited, the most humiliated, and the most degraded…

Men want to avoid women's liberation because they are afraid that liberation will lead to women's promiscuous behavior. The more restrictions men impose on women, the stronger women's desire for transgression becomes. Women will seize any available opportunity to unbridle themselves. Similarly, even though stealing is forbidden, once the thief understands the value of the object, the desire to steal it will only be strengthened. Thus, it is confinement, not liberation, that leads to women's adultery. How can Chinese people say that liberation makes women promiscuous? They do not understand the real cause. The more they forbid women's liberation, the more degenerate female virtues become. This is why Chinese women do not advance…

True liberation means complete freedom from all confinement. The contemporary Western marriage system is confined by conditions of power, wealth, morality, and law. Although the marriage is said to be voluntary, do all men and women in the West only marry for love? Men often seduce women with their wealth; women of wealthy families are also able to attract more suitors. Sometimes, rich men even force poor women to marry them. This is the confinement of marriage by wealth. In some cases, men marry women of prestigious backgrounds as a means for their advancement; in other cases, men of prestige and women of low social status are not able to marry because of their class difference. This is the confinement of marriage by power. There is simply no marriage of freedom!…Although women receive the same education as men do in modern societies ruled by law, they seldom have the chance to study politics and law, not to mention to be enrolled in army and police academies. Although women are said to have equal opportunity with men in the modern state governed by bureaucracy, they hold no public office. Gender equality exists only in name.

The liberation of women should bring women the enjoyment of true equality and freedom. The Western system today only brings women freedom and equality in name. The freedom they claim to have is not true freedom, but false freedom! The equality is false equality! Without true freedom, women lack full advancement; without true equality, human rights are not enjoyed by everybody. Asian women, in awe of the development of Western civilization, believe that Western women are liberated and share full freedom and equality with men. They want to follow the footsteps of Western women. Alas! As we are in the era of women's revolution, I do not want women to have only false freedom and false equality; I strongly hope women will obtain true freedom and true equality!

In recent years, people began searching for women's liberation in Chinese society. Women's liberation can be achieved either actively or passively. What does achieving liberation actively mean? It is when women strive for and advocate their own liberation. What does achieving liberation passively mean? It is when liberation is granted to women by men. Chinese women's liberation today has been mainly promoted through the passive way. When most of the advocates of the women's liberation movement are men, women do not gain as much as men. Why have men, who in the past wholeheartedly promoted female confinement and female constraint, turned to support women's liberation and gender equality in recent years? There are three explanations. Firstly, Chinese men worship naked power. They believe that China should follow the system of the major civilizing forces of the world, such as Europe, America, and Japan. If Chinese men forbid the practice of footbinding among their wives and daughters, put them in school, and have them educated, then China would be considered civilized. Chinese men would enjoy the fame of civilization, and so would their families. When those "civilized" men appear in public with their "civilized" wives and daughters, they will be applauded for their accomplishment. Do those men promote women's liberation for the sake of women? They only use women to achieve their own fame. Their selfish concern proves that they treat women as their private property. If women's advancement did not affect their reputation, they would not be so interested in women's liberation. Chinese men's privatization of women was first manifested in their effort to confine women in the old society of tradition; it is now demonstrated by their plea for female liberation on the Western model.

Secondly, Chinese men's promotion of women's liberation has to do with China's economic stagnation. Middle-class families have difficulty supporting their female members. Men realize that they do not gain from the confinement of women;

instead it devastates their economy. So they advocate women's independence and see women's economic dependence on men as their worst enemy. Chinese men encourage their daughters to enter girls' schools. Women from less affluent families study handicrafts, such as embroidery, knitting, sewing and cooking. The fortunate ones enter teachers' schools. The more advanced women receive professional training, such as medicine and science, outside the regular curriculum. Men promote female education not for the betterment of women but for their own advantage. Upon their graduation, women can afford to live on their own by becoming teachers or skilled workers. They are also forced to support their families. With their daughters now sharing the family burden, or even becoming the major breadwinner, men can enjoy more of their leisure time or use their money on their mistresses and prostitutes. While men indulge in pleasure without restraint, their daughters suffer from the solitude of hardship. Men advocate women's independence for men's own profit. That is the second reason why Chinese men promote women's liberation.

Thirdly, Chinese men value family and have great expectations for their offspring. However, they are not competent to deal with the task of managing the household and raising the children all by themselves. They want women to take the responsibility. Therefore, home economics becomes the most popular subject in girls' schools in China. Even China's newly established party (the Revolutionary Alliance) has claimed that domestic education is the foundation of all education. It is implied that a civilized woman can manage her household better than a backward woman; a civilized woman can educate her children better than a backward woman. In fact, the family belongs to the man, so taking care of the family is like serving the man; the children also belong to the man because they adopt their father's surname instead of their mother's. That is why men want to use women for their own purpose. In conclusion, the above three reasons demonstrate that men selfishly take advantage of women's liberation. They claim to help women obtain independence and become civilized; however, they promise women hope of liberation but actually thrust women into hardship. In traditional society, men had superior status to women but women enjoyed more physical freedom and leisure time; in today's society, men are still superior to women, although women share men's work and men share women's pleasure. Why should women feel happy about being used by men? Foolish women praise men for initiating women's liberation. They do not realize that they are doing exactly the same as those who highly praise the Manchu constitutionalists. The Manchu have drafted a constitution, but they are not willing to grant political power to the people. Similarly, men's promotion of women's liberation does not mean women will gain real power from men.

I am not saying that men should do all the work, nor am I suggesting that women's rights should not be expanded and women should perform their duties willingly. What I am arguing is: the women's rights movement should be fought for by women, not be granted by men. If women take orders from men, they have already lost their own freedom; if women receive rights from men, they have already become men's dependents. When women's liberation is in the power of men, men take advantage of women and ultimately subordinate women to them. This is why I advocate that women should seek their own liberation without relying on men to give it to them. Today Chinese women all look to men as the answer to their liberation. They are willing to take a passive role because they lack self-consciousness. Without self-consciousness, women are manipulated by men and yet they honour men. Aren't these women the most shameless?

I have talked about the drawbacks of women's passive liberation. Undoubtedly, there are some Chinese women who have longed for freedom and equality and do not want to be restrained by traditions. Their promotion of liberation seems to be conducted by their own will. However, we need to explore their true motivation. What they really want is to indulge themselves in unfettered sexual desires in the name of freedom and equality. They narrowly interpret liberation as the way to set free sexual desires. They do not understand that true liberation can only be achieved if women advance themselves to gain the power of transforming society. When women are only interested in love and sex, their spirit of saving mankind will be replaced by excessive desires and therefore their mission will not be accomplished. It is justifiable if women's obsession comes from their pursuit of free love. But very few Chinese women fit into this category. Some simply cannot resist temptation and will go with any man; some are seduced and become decadent. Some trade their bodies for wealth: they either make money through prostitution or by coquettishly flirting with rich men. To disgrace oneself in pursuit of wealth is the most degrading behavior. Can we call such conduct an act of freedom? Moreover, since the term "liberation" originally meant to be free from slavery, how can we make a connection between prostitutes and liberated women? Those women mistake liberation for sexual indulgence, so it is difficult for them to realize that they have already become the most debased prostitutes.

Today Caucasian women understand the drawbacks of gender inequality and identify the uneven distribution of power as the origin of gender inequality. They form organizations to strive for women's suffrage…

The majority of women are already oppressed by both the government and by men. The electoral system simply increases their oppression by introducing a third ruling group: elite women. Even if the oppression remains the same, the majority of women are still taken advantage of by the minority of women…

When a few women in power dominate the majority of powerless women, unequal class differentiation is brought into existence among women. If the majority of women do not want to be controlled by men, why do they want to be controlled by women? Therefore, instead of competing with men for power, women should strive for overthrowing men's rule. Once men are stripped of their privilege, they will become the equal of women. There will be no submissive women nor submissive men. This is the liberation of women. This is radical reform. Why should we be content with the existing parliamentary system and the suffrage movement as the ultimate goal? Only if interested women could transform their movement from that of entering the government to exterminating the government! (*Natural Justice*, Vol.7-10, September-October 1907)

97. Chu Minyi: Universal Revolution (1907)

Around the same time that He Zhen and Liu Shipei began publishing anarchist material from out of Tokyo, another group of Chinese anarchists in Paris started publishing the New Era, *a journal containing their own original work as well as extensive translations of the writings of European anarchists such as Kropotkin, Reclus, Malatesta and Bakunin. Chu Minyi (1884-1946) was a regular contributor to* New Era. *The following excerpts are taken from his article, "Universal Revolution," originally published in* New Era *in the fall of 1907. The translation is by Guannan Li of the University of Oregon (History Department). Chu Minyi's view of revolution as part of a broader process of social evolution can also be found in Reclus and Kropotkin's writings.*

NO REVOLUTION, NO SOCIAL PROGRESS. When justice flourishes, revolution approaches justice as well as peace. In the past, bloody destruction was called revolution. Nowadays, ideas in speeches and books can result in revolution. Everybody knows justice. Everyone will resist that which does not accord with justice. Therefore, might cannot arbitrarily repress the masses; the rich cannot enslave people. Government cannot abuse its power; money cannot buy ease. If nobody wants to be a soldier, armies cannot form, and war ends automatically. If nobody wants to accept the law, reward and punishment will be ineffective, and people will automatically break away from regulation. When might is overthrown, everybody can fulfill his position and get what he needs. They can work and study freely and enjoy freedom…

Revolution relies on justice. Might does not accord with justice. So revolution is against might. Government is the most powerful location of might. So to oppose might is to overthrow government. However, opposition to government must be approved by the majority. Now is still not the time. The majority are still restricted by morality, indulging their interests and reputation, and afraid of misfortune. In most cases, people who assist might will damage others' interests and benefit themselves. This causes the society of inequality. Therefore, revolutions in this century are still not peaceful. Relying on weaponry, government protects its regime with guns. How could revolutionaries fight government in the battlefield? Illegally smuggling weaponry is strictly forbidden; drilling the army underground is prohibited. This is still not the time to use the revolutionary army to overthrow government. If everyone agrees with popularizing revolution, might will fall down automatically.

When justice is apparent, people will know the necessity of revolution and understand that revolution is evolution. The more people endorse it, the easier to realize it, and the quicker progress is made. If revolution is endorsed just by one person or a few people, it will be more dangerous and progress very slowly, because the majority will still not understand its necessity and will oppose it. Revolution kills people like flies and disasters always happen…If revolution is endorsed by most people, it will be less dangerous and progress very quickly, because few people will oppose it. So revolution succeeds by the majority's agreement. If revolution is endorsed by everybody, it is peaceful and also progresses very quickly because there is no more opposition. Everything which accords with justice will be carried out accordingly; everything which violates justice will be discarded accordingly. This is what is called social revolution.

Government relies on weaponry to protect might. It can abuse its power. Since civilians have no arms, they have to tolerate what the government does to them…In pre-modern times, if government did not follow the way, people could protest and overthrow it. Nowadays there is a popular adage, "Guns fire and revolutionary armies die out." Might uses weaponry to consolidate itself. So if we are going to overthrow government, we must first destroy its base. The only way is to oppose weaponry, and let those who are oppressed by might be aware of the fact that weaponry only victimizes their property and lives to ensure might's personal property and interests. Moreover, killing somebody for no reason is the most inhuman conduct. People who understand this will not be willing to do it. If everyone has the same idea, weaponry will be automatically discarded and government will lose its foundation. Even though there is no revolutionary army, government will be destroyed by itself. Otherwise, if we also advocate the weaponry that might relies on, although it is not used for conquering the land to serve our own interests and we just want to use it once to kill the enemy of humanity, we can only hope that it will work forever. The enemy of humanity uses weaponry to protect its might, oppress and exploit people, and oppose revolution. How could we still advocate and encourage weaponry? For me the only way to eliminate the enemy of humanity is to popularize revolution, vindicate justice, and educate soldiers in the common ways. Otherwise, how could we persuade soldiers to turn their back when they march for battle? If we could do this in the common ways, it would not be necessary for us at the same time to advocate the expansion of weaponry. We should protest it and make sure that might has no basis to consolidate itself. If we advocate and expand it, and neglect popularizing revolution and vindicating justice, people will be deceived easily by the wrong, indulge in selfish interests forced on them by the situation, and finally be used by might. It is like killing a person and then placing the weapon in his hands. How dangerous it is!

...Those who with ambition advocate and expand military power with the goal of revenge go against justice. Alas! I don't know how to distinguish these people from those who work for their own interests in the name of the people. It also recalls to me the words, "violence begets violence."

So opposition to weaponry not only destroys governments' power base, it also avoids the killing caused by war. This is really the right way to maintain humanity...

Government relies on weaponry to secure itself, and at the same time oppresses brave opponents. Relying on law, it also manages to restrict opponents...

The human being is human because of freedom. Restricted by others (thus unfree), you are even inferior to the animal...The law restricts humankind and violates freedom. So the law does not accord with justice. We should oppose it. Then might has no disguise to deceive and fool the common people, and we break away from its restrictions to achieve freedom. It is because the law violates freedom and does not accord with justice that we should eliminate it. Then might has nothing to rely on to restrict the people. And we get complete freedom...

The mighty want to enjoy supreme glory forever. Unless they encourage the commoners to sacrifice their lives and property for them, they must submit to insult or rule by other powerful countries. Humiliation will decrease their glory; submission will end it. Therefore, the idea that people will be enslaved and live in pain if the country submits is in the interests of the mighty. If there were no government that cared about its glory and beat the drum of nationalism and militarism, how could people belonging to two sides have different feelings? Although there are ordinarily no wars between the two sides, why must there be war despite the people? Benefiting themselves and imperiling others—xenophobia and discrimination always originate from this. Alas! Government actually ruins people's minds and disturbs the peace...

No government, no boundaries; no boundaries, universal harmony comes. People will not enslave others, and vice versa; people will not depend on others, and vice versa; people will not harm others, and vice versa. This is what is called freedom, equality, and humanitarianism...

When people are born into the world, they deserve to have clothing, food, and housing. How could people born into the world have no clothing to resist cold, no food to resist hunger, and no housing to resist sunlight, dew, wind, frost, rain, and snow? If one starves or freezes to death, this is society's fault. Because of hunger and cold, more than tens of millions of people die each year. Although clothes for the rich pile up like a hill, food rises like a sea, they never think about the poor people. The granary is full; the national treasury is substantial. But the starving and frozen are everywhere. This is the result of the private ownership of property. Workers who work hard all their lives still cannot afford a life; sons of the rich who inherit property from their ancestors lead parasitical lives. One is a life of toil, the other of ease; one is a life of pain, the other of happiness. How unequal it is!...It is this private ownership that makes people struggle with each other...Renting a piece of land, a single peasant cannot feed himself. How can a family which has many members? Workers who enter a factory to get a job must rely on capitalists. They work very hard everyday to ensure food. Once they get sick or laid off, their families are thrown into a terrible situation. Alas! If property is not eliminated, the gap between the poor and the rich will become bigger. How can we tolerate the fact that a few capitalists are satisfied with their ease, but a great number of commoners end up with miserable lives? So to oppose property is to eliminate capitalists' ferocity and save commoners from hardship. When private property is eliminated and property is collectively owned, there will be no difference between the poor and rich. Worries about hunger and coldness will end. People will work and enjoy life together, work and rest together. Isn't this the phenomenon of communist society?

...Religion restricts the mind, hinders progress, and makes people submissive. Superstition emerges out of it. Slavishness takes root from obedience. So-called high priests and saints...frightened people by exploiting their weakness and their mortal fear of death; they animated them by visions of immortal spirits. They terrified people by promising harm for their dissolute lives...They made people willing to abandon life here and now in exchange for happiness in heaven...They rendered life an elusive dream, and the afterlife the real thing. Thus people came to undervalue this life...

Religion has been turned into the tool of government. It advances with politics. Politics hinders the evolution of humanity visibly, religion does this invisibly...We should replace religion with education, dispel superstition by science. How wrong it is for people to still regard religion as the way to redemption!

...Religion is also the opposite of revolution. Revolution aims at progress, religion adores conservation; revolution emphasizes action, religion adores inaction. If we aim at progress, society will reform daily. If we admire conservation, the world becomes more and more corrupt. If we emphasize action, new enterprise and a new society emerge daily. If we admire inaction, the abhorrent and disgusting become more and more prevalent. So religion hinders the universalization of revolution. To popularize revolution, we must oppose religion. Religion will also delay the development of science. To develop science, we must oppose religion. Therefore, opposition to religion must popularize revolution and develop science...

Revolutionaries are not viewed in a favourable light by most people who cannot understand their ideas and methods of overthrowing government. However, revolutionaries cannot allow might to tyrannize people and hinder evolution. They have to practice assassination to kill one or two enemies of humanity. They hope their action will make people more aware of their plight, and also terrify the mighty...Assassination will help arouse revolutionary agitation and quicken social evolution. Once agitation begins, the revolutionary engine will get started. Phony revolutionaries use revolution as a pretext, and only care about their own interests and fame. They easily retreat, or turn against revolution. Real revolutionaries believe in truth and justice. They march forward bravely. When might uses cruel killing and fierce torture to intimidate people, its cruelty is instead manifested, which awakens those who trust in the existing order and oppose revolutionaries. They start to understand why anarchists kill the enemies of humanity and destroy violent governments. Most truthful people do not dare to attack might but submit to the existing order, and rebuke revolution. The assassins not only arouse revolutionary agitation and jumpstart the engine of revolution, they create revolutionary movements.

...Assassination is for the elimination of evil, not for one's own interests; for justice, not for fame; for the elimination of might, not for revenge. If assassination is for personal interest, it is not assassination but murder; if it is for fame, it is not assassination, but gratuitous violence; if it is for revenge, it is not assassination, but frantic killing. Only killing that has proper goals may be called assassination. Only people who have courage and purpose may attempt it. Assassination originates from extreme justice and sincerity. If people just rely on courage and temporary anger to do it, they will never understand the principle, and assassination will be used only for personal interests. Or they just do it for revenge...Alas! How can this be assassination! Government slaughters the masses, and then relies on the law to justify it as legal killing. If assassination does not accord with justice, there would be no difference from government. Assassins have to be benevolent and righteous people.

Why are the rich always happy and the poor prisoners of toil? Because the rich rely on property to enslave the poor; they do not work but enjoy ease and happiness. The poor work with neither ease nor happiness. This is the greatest inequality. If we submit to it in order to maintain humanity, the rich will get richer, the poor will get poorer. What is the way to resist? Strikes, which serve to prevent the rich from using their wealth to avoid hardship and impugn the poor...

Strikes help workers break away from enslavement, but not for rest and more money. Once they have eliminated enslavement, workers will not be restricted by others; they will seek social reform, pursue public welfare, work according to their ability, get what they need, bear the same hardships, and enjoy the same ease and happiness. This is called natural life.

Free work and natural life need the exercise not only of strength but also of the mind. Workers can choose work according to their temperament, and exercise both body and mind. The mind seeks knowledge; the body pursues physical force. Use of the mind alone will result in weak physical strength; use of the body alone will result in underdeveloped mind. Neither is healthy. The mind should secure strength; the body should secure the mind. Interdependence of the two is the healthiest way...

Those who get used to parochialism, and are consumed with self-interest, cannot develop intellectually. When the intellect does develop, people extend former love of king and family to love of country, former love of one's own body and parents to love of the race, and former love of country and race to love of humankind and the world. Philanthropy is natural. People always change their preference according to parochialism and interests. However, once they overcome this, philanthropy can be realized.

Parochialism is because of family. Family is because of marriage. If we want to eliminate custom, we must start with the family. To eliminate family, we must eliminate marriage. When marriage is eliminated, family cannot come into being. Then people will rise above their own interests. If there is no parochialism, then people will help each other. Then people from all over the world will belong to one family. The world can thus achieve great harmony. Then there is no difference between king and minister, father and son, husband and wife, and brothers. There is only friends' love. So love can be universal.

Interests are people's key concerns. They struggle for subsistence. The superior win and the inferior lose. Their struggle is over clothing, food, and housing. Therefore, private property is highly valued. Because individuals are weak, they gather together. When the group is big and powerful, they always win; when the group is small and weak, they always lose...They have to set up government to maintain their advantages. Thus national boundaries are set up. Therefore, to eliminate interest, we must start with national boundaries. To eliminate national boundaries, we must start with private property. When private property has been eliminated, there will be no way to determine national and racial boundaries. Then people will abandon ideas of interest. Humankind will achieve equality and enjoy great harmony. There will be no national and racial boundaries, but only philanthropy. Love will thus be universal. (*New Era*, Nos. 15, 17, 18, 20 & 23, September-November 1907)

98. Wu Zhihui: Education as Revolution (1908)

Wu Zhihui (1869-1953) was an influential member of the Paris group that published the New Era. *He regarded education as a particularly important part of the anarchist social revolution and later helped to found the Labour University in China, where some of his ideas were put into practice, but only for a brief period while it served the purposes of the Guomindang government prior to its suppression of the anarchist movement. The following excerpts are from his article, "On Anarchist Advocacy of Education as Revolution," originally published in the* New Era *in September 1908. The translation is by Guannan Li of the University of Oregon (History Department).*

THE GOAL OF POLITICAL REVOLUTION is the struggle for rights. It equates public morality with national sovereignty. Therefore, when political revolution occurs, it easily turns into mob action by the revolutionary party. At first, they grab power from the monarchs. Then they fight against and indiscriminately slaughter and coerce each other. The only thing they dare not openly transgress is the motherland and national sovereignty.

...Those who advocate political revolution use rights as a catalyst to arouse emotions. In this case, rights are opposed to public morality. Here, revolution and education are viewed as two separate things. So bad effects are inevitable.

The call for constitutionalism in political revolution is especially contemptible... even if they captured political power, the coercive imperial house would remain in existence...

Anarchist revolution is totally different. Anarchists aim at arousing public morality, are concerned with the mutual interaction between the individual and the society, and are willing to abnegate all personal rights in order to pursue collective happiness. This actually emphasizes education, not revolution. When education is popularized, everyone abandons old habits and starts a new life. Revolution, thus, is just a certain effect of this transformation. In terms of these effects, there is nothing wrong with a revolutionary advocacy that seeks before the revolution to institute a revolutionary education that paves the way for revolution.

So the anarchists' revolution is not political revolution; it is education...education is revolution. Daily education is daily revolution. The smaller effects of education are small changes in social customs. This is called the small revolution...When the effect of education is to suddenly transform old customs in the entire society, this is called the grand revolution...[T]here is actually no completion to the true revolution. Truth and justice progress everyday. So long as education does not stop, neither does revolution...

Anarchist education consists of the morality included in truth and public morality, such as philanthropy, liberty and freedom, etc., and the knowledge included in truth and public morality, such as the experimental sciences. Besides these, there is no education.

Some injudicious people think education and revolution are separate. Their revolution aims at arousing emotions for rebellion. The education they have in mind is the one carried out by the pedagogues in schools where inferior methods and slave education prevail. To cultivate public morality, they advocate the reform of consciousness. However, the more they cultivate, the more they stray away. Thus, the cultivation of public morality finally fails, and the ephemeral revolution ends up with unthinking rebellion. This is because they never recognize that education is revolution, and revolution the revelation of public morality. Only progressive anarchist-educationalists have a full view of public morality as revolution. (*New Era*, No. 65, September 19, 1908)

99. Shifu: Goals and Methods of the Anarchist-Communist Party (1914)

During his short life, Shifu (Liu Sifu, 1884-1915) came to epitomize the dedicated anarchist revolutionary in China. First he abandoned his studies and joined the Revolutionary Alliance, the republican movement led by Sun Yat-sen. He was involved in an assassination attempt in 1907 and jailed for two years. He became acquainted with anarchist ideas while in jail, reading both Natural Justice *and the* New Era. *After his release, he joined the China Assassination Corps. Following the Revolution of 1911, he adopted an explicitly anarchist position, forming the Conscience Society and then the Cock-crow Society in Guangzhou, publishing what was to become the leading anarchist paper in China,* The People's Voice. *In 1913 he renamed himself Shifu and began organizing workers (the Chinese anarchists were among the first to organize Chinese workers into trade unions). In 1914 he started the Society of Anarchist-Communist Comrades. The group's manifesto, "Goals and Methods of the Anarchist-Communist Party," was published in* The People's Voice *in July 1914, on the eve of the First World War. It illustrates the influence of Kropotkin among the Chinese anarchists, not only in respect to anarchist communism, but also in relation to his concept of "mutual aid"(Selection 54). Shifu died of tuberculosis in 1915, but* The People's Voice *continued publishing until 1922, and many of Shifu's comrades went on to play a prominent role in the Chinese anarchist movement. This translation is by Edward S. Krebs, author of the definitive biography of Shifu:* Shifu, Soul of Chinese Anarchism *(Lanham: Rowman & Littlefield, 1998).*

WHAT IS THE ANARCHIST-COMMUNIST PARTY? What are the goals of the Anarchist-Communist Party? Here they are in simple and direct language:

1. All the important items of production—land, mines, factories, farming tools, machinery, and the like—will be taken back and returned to the common ownership of society; the right of private property will be eradicated, and money will be abolished.

2. All the important items of production are things common to society, and those involved in production may use them freely. (For example, those who farm may freely use land and the tools of cultivation, and will not need to rent from a landlord as at present, or be used by a landlord; those in industry may freely use the machinery in factories to produce goods and will not be employed by factory owners as at present.)

3. There will be no classes of capitalist and labourer; everyone should engage in labour. (Such careers as agriculture, construction, communications, education, medicine, child care, and all other kinds of effort in which humankind is involved for livelihood, all these are labour.) Each person recognizing what he or she is suited for and able to do, will work freely without oppression or limitation.

4. The products of labour—food, clothing, housing, and everything else that is useful—all are the common possessions of society. Everyone may use them freely, and everyone will enjoy all wealth in common.

5. There will not be any kind of government. Whether central or local, all government organizations will be abolished.

6. There will be no armies, police, or jails.

7. There will be no laws or rules.

8. All kinds of public associations will be organized freely in order to reform all kinds of work and manage all aspects of production so that we may provide for the masses of people. (For example, those adept at farming can unite with their comrades and organize an agricultural society, and those adept at mining can organize a mining society.) These public organizations will range from the simple to the complex. These will be organized by the workers in each kind of work, and there will be no leaders or managers. Those who take these responsibilities will also be seen as workers, and they will not have the authority to manage others. In these associations there will also be no statutes or regulations to restrict people's freedom.

9. The marriage system will be abolished; men and women will unite freely. The offspring will be cared for together in public hospitals. The sons and daughters born will receive care in public nurseries.

10. All the youth will go to school and receive an education, from the age of six to the age of twenty or twenty-five. Both males and females should attain to the highest level of learning according to their abilities.

11. Both men and women will devote themselves to labour after completing their education until the age of forty-five or fifty. After this they will retire to a public old people's home. All who are sick or have other health problems will be examined and treated in a public hospital.

12. All religions and creeds will be abolished. As to morality, people will be free, with no duties or restrictions; this will allow the natural morality of "mutual aid" to develop freely to its fulfillment.

13. Each person will work two to four hours at most every day. In the remaining time each day, people will be free to study science in order to help with the progress of society. For recreation they may pursue the fine arts and the practical arts in order to develop their individual physical and mental powers.

14. In schools and education we will select a suitable international language so that the different languages and literatures of each nation will gradually be eliminated, and the far and the near, the east and west, will have no boundaries at all.

The above also are some of the methods that our party uses to achieve our goals. If we wish to achieve such goals, we need to use the following methods:

1. Use newspapers, books, lectures, schools, and other methods to spread our ideas among the common people so that a majority of them will understand the

promise and fullness of our principles and the beauty of social organization in the future, and know that labour is man's natural duty and mutual aid his inherent virtue.

2. During the period of propaganda, all should consider the circumstances of time and place to make use of two sorts of methods: first, resistance, such as refusal to pay taxes or to participate in military service, strikes, boycotts, and similar actions; second, disturbances, including assassination, violence, and the like. These two methods for opposing authority and extending our principles in order to hasten the tide of revolution, spreading it far and near—are ways to speed and strengthen propaganda.

3. The great people's revolution is the fulfillment of propaganda; the masses will set off an incident, overthrowing government and the capitalists, and rebuilding a proper society.

4. The great people's revolution is a great world revolution. Our party will unite in all countries, not just one country at a time. The present is the period of propaganda: all our comrades should pursue these methods as appropriate to the places where they are and to the strength at their disposal. Then when the opportunity is ripe, the great world revolution will commence, probably starting in Europe—perhaps in France, Germany, England, Spain, Italy, Russia or one of the other nations where propaganda has already become extremely widespread. One day the triggering incident will occur, perhaps with several countries rising together, or perhaps in just one country; then other countries will hear of it and all respond. Labour unions will strike, and armies will lay down their arms. The governments of Europe will be toppled one after another. In North and South America and in Asia, our party will join in and rise up. The speed of our success will be unimaginable. In China today, nothing is more important than to catch up, devoting our utmost effort to propaganda in order to prevent the possibility that a day would come when that incident would occur in Europe, but propaganda in the East would not be ripe; that would hold back the world's progress.

The above are the methods for achieving our goals.

If people have doubts about our principles, it can only be because "they are difficult to put into effect." Or they are concerned that the morality of this generation is inadequate; if the day came when there were no government, surely there would be all sorts of problems and workers might steal the goods needed by society, or they think that with so many people throughout the land, it would be difficult to reach the masses with our propaganda, and it would be impossible for a minority of people in our party to oppose the power of government in the many countries. These two areas of doubt are what many people today are concerned with on these two kinds of questions; here I wish to explain how these questions can be dealt with:

1. We say that in order to realize the society of anarchist communism, we must first propagate our principles and seek the agreement of the majority of ordinary people. If the majority of people understand the beauty of these principles, then it should be easy enough to handle the lack of understanding of the minority. So why should we worry about any problems? Furthermore, under anarchism people do not need to have serious problems implementing morality: this is nothing other than "labour" and "mutual aid." These two qualities are part of the capacity of humanity and do not come from some external inspiration. In order to improve society and have the conditions of our life advance day by day to where it should be, this natural morality must be able to develop freely. In earlier times, work and even the most pleasant things were distresses and not as conditions today. Now, with science and invention, and without the restraints of money, we can use machinery for everything; no matter what kind of task, we can have efficiency and time-saving, and maintain good hygiene in our work. Thus with a few hours each day, which will be like a daily exercise routine, we can get all the work done, so how could anyone wish to avoid it? With the speed of machinery and the numbers of workers, the wealth of production will be inconceivable. There can only be a surplus of the goods that we need; there will be no worry about them being inadequate. And why would anyone want to steal these goods? But if there are still recalcitrants who would want others to serve them, and themselves sit happily after a full meal, our people would oppose them with the principle of anti-authoritarianism and reject them from society. How could such a small group of people cause problems?

2. Anything that does not accord with universal principles is difficult to propagate, and anything that does is easy to propagate. The universal principles of anarchist communism are shared in the consciences of all people, so how could it be difficult to propagate them? Surely our strength is up to this task! Consider that anarchism appeared in Europe only sixty years ago, and it has only been forty years since party people commenced propaganda work, but today in every country of Europe things are developing especially well, advancing a thousand miles a day! Anarchist groups are spreading far and wide, and books and news-

> papers are everywhere. What we Chinese are receiving with such great enthusiasm is already old hat in Europe. At the international congress of anarchism in London this year, they made plans to launch an international organization of anarchists. It is not long until the worldwide revolution! It is even more satisfying to realize that, except for the capitalists, in European society there are only workers. Today the great principles of socialism and anarchism are already deeply implanted in the minds of the workers' parties, and in the activities of workers' parties in recent years we already see the incipient emergence of anarchism. Governments look to their armies to take care of things, but in the militia organizations of every country you have those who in ordinary times are the workers! Thus over the past several years when governments sought to put down strikes, the troops would not obey the commands to disperse them, or they would put down their arms and join the workers: they would not attack their brothers and friends on behalf of the government. And so when the great revolution begins one day soon, the soldiers also will rise up against the government—of this we can be sure. What do we have to fear from flesh-eating governments and capitalists?! As to the current situation in China, although the propagation of our principles really is not as broad as in Europe, if we and our comrades in East Asia can bring together all our planning and all our strength and sacrifice for about twenty years, giving all our effort to propaganda, I will dare to say that our ideas will be spread throughout the East Asian continent. At that time our progress in Europe will be even more difficult to imagine. The time of realization is surely something we ourselves will see; do not think it is an ideal that cannot be realized.

Alas, war clouds fill every part of Europe, and millions of workers are about to be sacrificed for the wealthy and the nobility. The evils of government have come to this and now are totally revealed! The day when hostilities cease will be the day when the death sentence for government and the capitalists is proclaimed. The tide of anarchism will then burst forth and rise. We vow that the common people of East Asia will awake from their dreams and rouse themselves with urgency, and we trust that they will not linger on in backwardness. (*People's Voice,* No. 17, July 1914)

100. Huang Lingshuang: Writings on Evolution, Freedom and Marxism (1917-29)

Huang Lingshuang (1898-1982) was a member of the anarchist communist group started by Shifu's brother, Liu Shixin, in Guangzhou. He later helped found the first anarchist group in Beijing. He was one of the earliest Chinese anarchist critics of Marxism following the Russian Revolution. The first selection is from Huang Lingshuang's "Declaration" to the inaugural issue of the anarchist paper, Evolution, *originally published in January 1917. The second selection is from the forward to* Records of Freedom, *the publication of the anarchist Truth Society in Beijing, originally published in July 1917. The third selection is from Huang Lingshuang's "Critique of Marxism," originally published in* New Youth *in May 1919. These writings illustrate the continuing influence of Kropotkin among Chinese anarchists. The final selection is from Huang Lingshuang's* Social Evolution *(Shanghai: World Books, 1929), in which he distinguishes cultural evolution from biological and social evolution (a distinction which was never clearly made by Kropotkin), and criticizes concepts of universal stages of historical development, consistent with his earlier critique of Marxism. The translations are by Shuping Wan, associate professor of history at Montgomery College (Department of History and Political Science).*

Declaration to Evolution (1917)

SOCIETY IS THE TOTALITY OF ORGANISMS. With every organism, from each according to his capacity, to each according to his needs, seeking help from his group, the human being should be able to spend less time to bring more happiness. Thus we can understand that the way of the development of human society is through the development of morals. This is the aim: to bring happiness to all human beings in the world. Therefore, in discussions of social evolution the question is what kind of system best suits society, and how can we increase the amount of human happiness and improve its quality…Modern anarchism means to demonstrate this truth. Now that the truth is clarified, it is time for us to start a revolution and realize the aim of this truth. What does revolution mean? The (Chinese) term "geming" is called "revolution" in the Western language. "Re" means "geng" (more), and "evolution" means "jinhua." If we combine "re" and "evolution," we get the term "revolution," which simply means "more-evolution." However, the kind of revolution we advocate is quite different from those superficial revolutions. For example, when the Entente triumphed over Germany and Austria-Hungary, many people took it as the triumph of justice over power. The kind of authoritarian power in our minds refers to more than the militarism of Germany and Austria-Hungary and Nietzsche's "superman." In our society everything that prevents the whole of humankind from realizing freedom and happiness, such as politics, religion, law, capitalism, is an authoritarian power. We should make further progress and totally abolish them. The world revolution by the common people leads to their life of "mutual aid" (form each according to his capacity, to each according to his needs). This is the truth of evolution (no government and no private property), and this is the final victory of truth over power! This is what our journal stands for. (*Evolution*, Vol.1, No.1, January 10, 1917)

Forward to *Records of Freedom* (1917)

The evolution of the world is so slow. After thousands of years of turmoil the republic has just arrived. It seems that the common people enjoy a little more happiness than before. However, when the powerful people discover that the common people are seeking happiness for themselves, they use every cruel means to block the newly emerging trend. The ideal society is still far away. Touched by inequality in contemporary society and the helplessness of numerous people, we have become aware of the need to transform society. It is our goal to realize anarchism as political organization and communism as economic ideal. Now that the goal is set, we are determined to overcome all difficulties to realize it. It is nothing for us to endure hardships and sufferings. We appreciate the beauty of anarchism and the goodness of communism, and understand that our ideal cannot be achieved overnight. Our priority is to instill anarchist communism into the common people and raise their self-consciousness. There are two ways to approach this. The violent approach is to use bombs and handguns...the peaceful approach is to use education and persuasion to improve the morals and knowledge of the majority, and to work with one heart. It seems that the two approaches are quite different, but they are by no means contradictory to each other. Personally, I believe the peaceful approach is more effective.

Alas, don't you see how evil the contemporary social system is? Are you going to turn a blind eye to it? We have to do all we can to catch up and work with the progressive people all over the world to transform the system. In the *Classics of Poetry* there is a line: "The rain and wind bring in darkness and gloominess, but the cock never stops its crow." Despite the limitation of our ability we will do our part to facilitate the work and make a wave. It is our great hope that the enlightened peopled in society will share our concern. (*Records of Freedom*, July 1, 1917)

Critique of Marxism (1919)

Marx's idea of politics can be found in "The Communist Manifesto," coauthored with Engels (there was confrontation in the International Working Men's Association between Marx and Bakunin, an anarchist. Actually, Marx's idea of communism is the contemporary idea of collectivism, while Bakunin's idea of collectivism is the contemporary idea of communism). In the Manifesto there are ten measures, which can be seen as the policies of social democracy. What are these policies all about?

1. abolition of property;

2. management of transportation by the state;

3. concentration of factories and instruments of production in the hands of the state;

4. establishment of industrial armies, especially for agriculture.

The most severe criticism of these policies came from anarchists, whose communism is quite different from Marx's collectivism. Anarchists believe that in a historical perspective the state is organized solely for the protection of the privileges and property of the few. By now all the power of education, state religion and national defence has been concentrated in the hands of the state. If we endow the state with more power, such as control of the land, mines, railways, banks, insurance, will the tyranny of the state be even harsher (these are Kropotkin's words in the *Encyclopedia Britannica*)? Can we guarantee that our leaders will not become a Napoleon or a Yuan Shikai [Chinese strongman]? Moreover, socialism should not be the suppression of individual freedom. The government of the social democratic party wants to establish industrial armies and agricultural armies. Isn't this a suppression of the individual? There are also some problems in their principle of distribution. Society is different from an individual. In the light of socialism, the possessions of society should belong to the public rather than to the individual. According to Marx's idea of collectivism, things, such as houses and clothes, may be privately owned. I believe that private ownership of property is contradictory to the principle of socialism. Is it problematic if in the same house the cattle-shed is public property while the bedrooms are privately owned? Moreover, the Marxists advocate to each according to his capacity. If so, men of strong ability would enjoy rewards while men of poor ability would lose their means of living. Poor ability is caused by one's physiological condition. This does not result from his laziness. Such a method of distribution has nothing to do with human happiness. Anarchist communists want to subvert the organization of the state and allow the common people to establish a variety of associations to run enterprises, such as educational associations and agricultural associations. Step by step these associations will become complex enough to deal with all business in society so as to abolish all kinds of authoritarian power and bring equality and happiness to every individual. Their principle of labour is "from each according to his capacity," and their principle of distribution is "to each according to his needs." This is the focus of the difference between anarchists and Marxists. (*New Youth*, Vol.6, No.5, May 1919)

Social Evolution (1929)

The degree of human social life is evaluated by the degree of cultural development. Culture is a unique characteristic of human society, and coexists with human life...Social evolution started before the appearance of humankind, and cultural evolution started at the very beginning of human life. The development of culture and human life started simultaneously. Social evolution originated from organic evolution, and cultural evolution originated from social evolution.

What is the place of social evolution and cultural evolution in the progress of world evolution? We know that world evolution is a natural sequence. At the very beginning there were merely physical and chemical phenomena in the world; after a long period of development life and society came into being. The final and the highest product of progressive evolution is culture...

If we want to understand the fact of social evolution, we must realize that the methods and concepts used to study organic evolution are unable to provide sufficient assistance in our study of social evolution.

First, the subject of organic science (plants or animals) is relevant to inheritance, but culture is not inherited...and has no relevance to race. Culture is superorganic and beyond the sphere of biology; secondly, human physiology has not changed much since the end of the glacial epoch. The Neanderthal, who has been considered to be the earliest ancestor of human beings, had a very large skull; the Cro-Magnon, who was more advanced and similar to the modern man, had obviously large brain capacity. According to anthropology, their physical strength and brain capacity were little different from those of modern man, but there is an enormous difference between their stone-age culture and modern culture.

In sum it is safe to say that social evolution depends on the development of culture, and cultural evolution determines the direction of social evolution...

In the nineteenth century geologists, paleontologists, and biologists proposed many theories of developmental stages. They held that without exception all organic life went through [these stages] from the earliest geological epoch to the modern epoch. This led to the idea of the developmental stages of society. [Herbert] Spencer held that the political and social systems of society experienced many changes, which proceeded in a certain sequence, from simple systems to complex systems. [Lewis] Morgan's *Ancient Society* can be seen as the "comprehensive" model of this kind of conception of evolution...

The anthropologists of our time do not accept such an argument. Instead of making a sweeping generalization, they have paid much attention to the study of the cultural traits of particular groups, which has led them to reject the proposition that without exception all nations have to go though the same social or cultural stages...

We also reject the proposition that there are necessary stages of economic progress. First, there is hardly any standard way to measure the unit of, for example, technology or economy, organization or type of commerce, or means of exchange, none of which can be seen as the basis for the economic stage of a nation. The stage of economic life includes a great number of interrelated factors. Among them we cannot find a single factor that bears particular importance. The economy is very intricate, and a cultural complex includes not only economic but also psychological and social factors. More often than not these factors can change the nature and function of economic factors in society. The same economic and technological conditions do not necessarily result in the same culture. It is true that economic life exercises its influence on culture, but economic life is not the factor that can change all social factors; secondly, economic change, like historical change, has a strong system of continuity, it is not so easy to create a division, and the change in different aspects of the economy does not occur at the same rate. Very few groups in the world have gone through all the assigned stages without transcendence. The theory of economic stages, therefore, is as implausible as Morgan's theory of cultural stages.

102. Li Pei Kan: On Theory and Practice (1921-1927)

Li Pei Kan (or Li Feigan) (1904-), writing under the name of Ba Jin (or Pa Chin), was one of China's best known writers of the twentieth century. His novel, Family *(Garden City: Anchor Books, 1972; originally published 1931), is a classic of modern Chinese literature. His pseudonym was a contraction of the Chinese names for Bakunin and Kropotkin, but he was particularly influenced by Emma Goldman, whom he described as his "spiritual mother." He corresponded with her for many years and translated several of her and Alexander Berkman's writings into Chinese. He played an active role in the Chinese anarchist movement and refused to join either the Guomindang (Nationalist Party) or the Communist Party, unlike other prominent figures in the Chinese anarchist movement, such as Wu Zhihui (Selection 98), who collaborated with the Guomindang. The following excerpts are from articles Li Pei Kan published in the anarchist press during the 1920's. At the beginning of that decade, the anarchists were the most influential revolutionary group in China; by the end of that decade, they had been eclipsed by the Communists and suppressed by the Guomindang. The translations are by Shuping Wan of Montgomery College.*

How to Build a Society of Genuine Freedom and Equality (1921)

THESE DAYS "FREEDOM" AND "EQUALITY" have become the pet phrases of some people. If you ask them what freedom means, they will answer: "Freedom refers to freedom of speech, press, organization, and correspondence." If you ask them what equality means, they will answer: "Every citizen is equal before the law without discrimination." However, this is not genuine freedom and equality...

The obstacle to people's freedom is government. Since the establishment of government, the people have completely lost their freedom and are controlled by the government. We want to have mutual love among our brothers and sisters all over the world, but governments always force us to be patriotic, to be soldiers, and to kill our compatriots of the world. Even in China the situation is terrible, and the Chinese kill the Chinese. These years in the provinces of Hunan, Shanxi, and Sichuan the blood runs like a river and the dead bodies are heaped up like a mountain. Such terrible misery is exactly the benefit that government has brought us.

Capitalists monopolize the common property that belongs to the whole world, and the poor people lose their means of living. Instead of punishing those capitalists, the government protects them by means of law. The people do not have any possessions, and in order to survive they have to resort to robbery. They are actually forced to do so by the capitalists, but the government calls them robbers, and executes them by shooting. This is not to justify robbery. We just want to take back some of our confiscated possessions. Why do we deserve to be executed by shooting while those capitalists who rob the common possessions of the world deserve a comfortable life? If the poor people do not resort to robbery, the only option is to become beggars. Sometimes the government and capitalists show their benevolence, grant to the poor a tiny share of the money they have robbed, and call it by the fine-sounding name of philanthropy. They falsely accuse us of enjoying begging rather than working. Readers! Don't we want to work? The truth is that they don't give us a job opportunity and just pour abuse upon us. Therefore, the so-called freedom and equality mentioned above seem to have nothing to do with the people! Is this genuine freedom and equality? I don't think so. What is genuine freedom and equality? I believe that only anarchism means genuine freedom and communism means genuine equality. The only way to build a society of genuine freedom and equality is social revolution.

What is anarchism? Anarchism advocates that the government and all the organizations attached to it should be abolished and that all the instruments of production and products should belong to the whole people. From each according to his capacity, to each according to his needs. Each one performs the duty that fits his capacity best. Some can be doctors and some can be mine workers. Less hours for hard jobs, and longer hours for easy jobs. Food, clothes, and houses are all provided by certain institutions. Everyone enjoys equal education with no distinction...

Without political laws there is genuine freedom; without capitalists there is genuine equality.

My labouring friends! Please imagine the freedom and equality in a society without authoritarian powers! Do you want to have such a society? If yes, you should wage a social revolution and overthrow the evil politics. The society of freedom and equality will then be realized. Unite all your friends immediately! If you continue to tolerate your sufferings, you will simply allow yourselves to be meat on the chopping block of the capitalists! Believe me! (*Semi-Monthly*, No. 17, April 1, 1921)

Patriotism and the Road to Happiness for the Chinese (1921)

Day by day China has become an apathetic society without any happiness. Now some youth of consciousness advocate that the only way to save China from this miserable situation is to promote "patriotism," and take "patriotism" as the only way to happiness for the Chinese. As a result the sound of "patriotism" can be heard all over the country. This is a terrible phenomenon. I believe that "patriotism" is an obstacle to human evolution. As a member of humankind my conscience drives me to refute such a fallacy and to offer my suggestion of "the way to happiness for the Chinese." The following words come out of my conscience. I believe that in such a big country like China there should be at least some people of conscience who may support my ideas.

...Except for some cruel warlords and politicians, human beings are all opposed to and condemn wars, and the origins of wars actually come from "patriotism." If human beings love each other and work together peacefully, how could there be wars? "Patriotism" started to rise in the "era of animal desire," when the state came into being. The state is characterized by hypocrisy and selfishness. In order to satisfy its animal desire, the state pushes its people to invade other countries and to die. The victory of war brings pleasures to warlords and politicians, and the loss of the war takes the flesh and blood of the people as military expenses. Is war of any benefit to the common people? Unfortunately, the common people are totally unaware that so-called patriotism is a weapon used to kill their dearest ones. "Patriotism" is a monster that kills people. For example, in the late nineteenth century the German government promoted patriotic sentiment and implemented conscription. All adults, including intellectuals and priests, would have to go to perform military service, and to kill people under the instruction of the militarists and politicians. They were ordered to kill workers on strike, and even their parents and brothers. Alas! What else can be more savage and cruel than this?

...I believe that the promotion of patriotism can never bring more happiness to the Chinese; instead it can only bring them more misery. The only way for the Chinese to seek happiness is to abolish the following institutions:

I. GOVERNMENT: Government is an institution of authoritarian power. It protects laws, kills us, deprives us of our means of living, insults us, and helps the capitalists kill the poor. We human beings were born to be free by nature, but the government has created so many laws to bind us up; we love peace, but the government pushes us to the war; we are supposed to practice mutual aid with our compatriots all over the world, but the government tells us to compete with each other. Everything that the government does is contradictory to the will of the vast majority of the people. Above all government is the basis for patriotism. If we want to seek happiness, our priority is to overthrow the government.

II. PRIVATE PROPERTY: Private property is the result of plunder. Property originally belonged to all human beings, but a small number of people, by means of their power and knowledge, took public property as their own. This led the weak people to be homeless, and the powerful people to buy others' labour. They enjoy what the labourers produce while the labourers have nothing left for themselves. Private property is the number one inequality in the world. Also, private property has led to rivalry, theft, robbery, and moral degeneration. It is private property that has maintained the existence of government for such a long time. Therefore, the abolition of private property will make it easier to abolish the government.

III. RELIGION: Religion shackles human thought and hinders human evolution. While we want to seek truth, it teaches us superstition; while we want to be progressive, it asks us to be conservative. Some priests say: "God is omnipotent. God is truth, justice, kindness, beauty, power, and vitality, and man is falsity, injustice, evil, ugliness, impotence, and death; God is the master, and man is the slave. Man alone is not capable of achieving justice, truth, and ever-lasting life, and must follow God's revelations. God created the world, and monarchs and officials represent God and deserve to be served by the people."...This is the essence of Christianity, and similarities can be found in other less powerful religions. Bakunin's comment is great: "If God really did exist, it would be necessary to abolish him." Let's do this.

The institutions discussed above are all our enemies. Before we can embark on the way to happiness we must abolish them. Afterwards we will redistribute property, initiate free associations, practice the principles of mutual aid, from each according to his capacity, to each according to his needs, one for all, and all for one. Is this not a happy life? However, we have to pay a price before we can obtain happiness. What is the price? It is the warm blood of many people. Bakunin said: "Nothing in the world is more exciting and more enjoyable than the revolutionary endeavor! Would you rather let your life linger by bowing down to despotic power or bravely risk your life fighting against the tyrant to the end?" How exciting and courageous! I hope our friends will join us and contribute our warm blood to the most exciting and the most enjoyable revolutionary endeavor. Let us march together to the road of happiness! (*Awakening the People*, No. 1, September 1, 1921)

Anarchism and the Question of Practice (1927)

Anarchism is a product of the mass movement, and can never divorce itself from practice. In fact, anarchism is not an idle dream that transcends time. It could not have emerged before the Industrial Revolution, and could not have developed before the French revolution. Many Chinese hold that Lao Tzu and Chuang Tzu were China's [first] anarchists. This is very misleading. Taoism shares nothing with modern anarchism. The time of Lao Tzu and Chuang Tzu could not have produced the ideas of modern anarchism.

I think that many people have some misunderstanding of the doctrine of anarchism. It is true that anarchists are opposed to war, but the kind of war that anarchists are opposed to is the war resulting from the power struggle among warlords and politicians. We do support the struggle of the oppressed against the oppressors, and the struggle of the proletariat against the bourgeoisie, because it is a war for self-defence and liberty, which Malatesta considered to be "necessary and sacred." We also support the war of colonies against their metropolitan states and the war of the weaker nations against imperialist powers, although the goal of such wars is a little different from our ideal. Some people are opposed to class struggle, which, they argue, is contradictory to the happiness of all humanity. There was an article in the *People's Voice* (No. 33), which also reflected such a point of view. Anarchists are by no means opposed to class struggle, and actually advocate class struggle. Anarchism is the ideal and ideology of the exploited class...in the class struggle. It can be misleading simply to advocate seeking happiness for all humanity, as humanity is not a whole, and it was divided into two antagonistic classes long ago. "Anarchism has never been the ideal of the ruling class" (Kropotkin). "The real creator of anarchism is the revolutionary working class" (Aliz).

No practical problem can be more important than the problem of the Chinese revolution. It is the problem of the initiation of social revolution that occurs in our minds all the time. We are materialists...We understand that the arrival of social revolution cannot be determined by our good wishes. It results from social evolution and is determined by the needs of history. Within the limits permitted by material conditions the effort of the individual may facilitate social evolution, but it is not the only factor in social evolution...

There is no contradiction between revolution and evolution. Reclus said: "Evolution and revolution are the same phenomenon of a sequence of actions: evolution comes before revolution and develops into revolution." Anarchism cannot be realized in a very short period. Its success requires an accumulation of uninterrupted revolution and construction. Aliz made a good comment: "The realization of anarchism does not come all of a sudden. We have no way to fully realize the ideal of anarchism at one full stroke, and have to realize it step by step." It is impossible for us to fully realize the ideal of anarchism under China's current conditions. Our ideal, the ideal of future society, is a correct one. It is not an illusion, but its realization is limited by material conditions. In other words, the ideal society will not suddenly appear like a miracle; it comes gradually. Every effort we make may speed up its arrival, but there are still limitations. This may not be as ideal as we wish, but this is a fact. If there is social revolution in China, we want to fully realize the ideal society of anarchism; but is it possible to practice the principle of from each according to his capacity and to each according to his needs when China's economy is underdeveloped, and daily necessities and even food still depend on imports from foreign countries? Under such conditions we have to make compromises. This does not mean that we have to accept failure. We do need to make some preparations before the revolution comes, and allow the workers to develop industry by means of cooperation. Even after the revolution starts, it will still be impossible for us to reach the ideal society of anarchism in a single bound. We have to move towards our ideal step by step...

This is only a hypothesis about China's situation after the social revolution takes place, but we really don't know if it may happen in the near future. First, China's material conditions are not mature; second, the gap between Chinese anarchists and the masses is still very wide. Some anarchists are only interested in the propaganda of some principles among the people, but they never ask themselves if their propaganda is accessible to the people and what the people really want. How can we engage ourselves in the movement of workers without knowledge of their immediate concerns? It is hardly possible to ask them to wage a revolution with an empty stomach. It is true that social revolution may not occur in China immediately, but we should start our preparations and facilitate its inauguration...

China has entered the era of revolution. Many of the revolutionary movements in China are not the movements of the Nationalist Party [Guomindang] but the movements of the people. Tens of thousands of workers are on strike, and numerous young people fight in the battlefields. Under the white terror many people are devoting themselves to the revolution. They have not the slightest fear of jail or death. Some people say that those revolutionaries are misled by a small number of people, that their dream is wealth and power, that they are running dogs of new warlords, that they are loyal followers of the Three People's Principles [of the Nationalist Party], and that they want to set up a bourgeois government. This is absolutely not true. It is true that there is a difference between the northern expedition of the Nationalist Army and China's revolutionary movement, the independent war of a semi-colonial country and the aim of anarchists, but we anarchists are not opposed to it and simply want to go even farther. Before we can abolish capitalism, we are by no means opposed to any kind of anti-imperialist movement. I hate Soviet Russia, but I hate imperialist powers even more; I hate the Nationalist Party, but I hate warlords even more. The reason is simple. Soviet Russia is not as evil as the imperialist powers, and the Nationalist Party and warlords are not jackals from the same lair. Certainly it would be wonderful if we could offer the people something better. It does not bother a bourgeois scholar to look on unconcerned and make empty talk in opposition, but to a revolutionary it is a crime. "Perfection or nothing" is the idea of an individualist, not the idea of a revolutionary who fights for the interests of the people, because such an idea does not reflect the needs of the people. If you have no means to bring "perfect" happiness to the people, how can you deny their opportunity to enjoy a slight portion of happiness? We should understand that this revolutionary movement is not monopolized by a particular political party. Without the participation and support of the people, how can those warlords be defeated? We anarchists did not play an influential role in the movement. This was our mistake. If we simply look on and denigrate this movement merely as a power struggle or war among warlords, and describe the Nationalist Party and Zhang Zoling [Manchurian warlord] as jackals from the same lair, then those right-wing conservatives would certainly be very happy and say thanks to us!

...The propositions of the Nationalist Party are contradictory to ours, and in principle this party is our enemy. It is well known that the Nationalist Party wants to construct a good government, and we want to overthrow all kinds of government.

Nevertheless, we have no objection to some causes such as the overthrow of warlords, and the overthrow of imperialism, but we want to move forward even further and reject the government of the Nationalist Party and its construction. (Several years ago when I put the slogan "self-reliance of the weaker nations to overthrow all imperialism" on the cover of the first issue of the *People*, some comrades in Wuchang and Hunan wrote letters against this slogan. They said that the slogan was superficial. Before the abolition of capitalism, they argued, to call for the overthrow of imperialism was to attend to trifles to the neglect of essentials. They also said that anarchists should not accept the idea that there were weaker nations in humanity. I don't agree with them. We do not deny the existence of weaker nations as a fact, but should weaker nations remain slaves of imperialist powers until the realization of anarchist society? Can colonies and semi-colonies never get independence before the abolition of capitalism?) Most of the common people agree with the Nationalist Party merely on some slogans, but disagree with it on many issues. At present the Nationalist Party is the leader of the people...If we go to the people, throw ourselves into the revolutionary torrent, and lead the people to move towards a greater aim, then the people will naturally distance themselves from the Nationalist Party and follow us, which can bring more anarchist influence to the revolutionary movement, and make a deep impression of anarchism in the mind of the people. If we work in this way, although anarchist society may not be fully realized immediately, the people will move in this direction (at least better than the current situation). If we make an effort, we sow a seed; if we attempt to build a dike to contain the revolutionary trend, we are doomed to be submerged...

At present the revolution in China has gone beyond the aims of the Nationalist Party. For example, the peasants rise to overthrow local tyrants and evil gentry, peasants' associations everywhere make resistance against landlords, and workers organize labour unions to make resistance against capitalists. This is wonderful news...I believe that if we make ourselves a part of the revolutionary torrent, we will be able to create some new slogans such as "peasants' autonomy," "peasants' management of land," "abolition of foremanship." In time of turmoil and war we can burn down some county executive offices, or go to help the peasants organize communes to enable them to run their own affairs without the government's involvement. We should join the labour movement as workers, think about the concerns of our fellow workers and create new slogans, such as the reduction of working hours, protection of workers' means of living, and workers' education. Among the important issues in contemporary China, the priority should be advocating workers' rights to directly supervise all equipment in the factory, to abolish foremanship, and to negotiate with factory owners through the labour union. In regard to the slogan of taking over the factories by the workers, I think for the time being this is not feasible, although we can advocate it at an appropriate time. In practice our slogans must be relevant to the immediate concerns of the people...

We can criticize the principles of the Nationalist Party and the Communist Party, but we should not denigrate them...But, some people hold that we should join the Nationalist Party, to which I am strongly opposed.

In sum, if we throw ourselves into China's revolutionary torrent, although we are unable to fully realize anarchist society overnight, we may bring the Chinese people closer to the ideal of anarchism, and bring more anarchist influence to the movement. This would certainly be a much better attitude than looking on unconcerned and making indiscreet criticisms. (*People's Bell,* 1927)

(Further reading: Arif Dirlik, *Anarchism in the Chinese Revolution*, Berkeley: University of California, 1991; Peter Zarrow, *Anarchism and Chinese Political Culture*, New York: Columbia University, 1990.)

Chapter 21
Anarchism In Japan And Korea

102. Kôtoku Shûsui: Letter from Prison (1910)

Kôtoku [Denjiro] Shûsui (1871-1911) was one of the first Japanese socialists and, later, one of the founders of the Japanese anarchist movement. He began as an orthodox Marxist Social Democrat but moved away from parliamentary socialism, declaring himself an anarchist in 1905 upon his release from jail for publishing subversive literature. He went to the United States and established contacts there with various anarchists and members of the Industrial Workers of the World. Upon his return to Japan he became a prominent advocate of direct action. He was involved in the publication of several anarchist papers and translated the writings of European anarchists into Japanese, including Kropotkin's The Conquest of Bread *(Selection 33). He was subjected to constant harassment by the Japanese authorities and was charged with high treason in 1910, along with many other Japanese anarchists, including his companion, Kanno Sugako. Kôtoku, Kanno and 9 other anarchists were executed in January 1911. Several others were sentenced to death but had their sentences commuted to life in prison. The following excerpts are from his "Letter from Prison," written to his attorneys in December 1910. The translation by Yoshiharu Hashimoto, originally published in* A Short History of the Anarchist Movement in Japan *(Tokyo: Idea Publishing, 1979), has been modified by the editor for stylistic reasons.*

WHENEVER THE ANARCHIST MOVEMENT is mentioned, there are many people who understand it as assassination of a sovereign by pistol or bomb, which shows their ignorance of anarchism. You, the attorneys, know already that anarchism is a kind of philosophy similar to that of Lao Tzu and Chuang Tzu, which taught us we must progress in accordance with the general tendency to fulfill our freedom and happiness, because that tendency is natural in human society, to be realized with mutual aid and communal life, united by morality and charity, without government compulsion as it is now.

Therefore, it is needless to say that the anarchist hates oppression, disdains bondage as well as violence, and no one else loves freedom and justice like him...

In truth, assassins did emerge from among the anarchists, but that does not mean all anarchists without fail are assassins. Furthermore, many assassins came not only from the anarchists, but also from the state socialists, the republicans, the Minkenka, patriots and loyalists...the number of assassinations by anarchists is few in comparison to the other parties...If an idea is declared terrorist due to the appearance of an assassin, there is no more violent idea than the loyal or patriotic one...violence is usually initiated by government officials, the rich and the aristocrats, while the militant and the worker are provoked, so exploited that they are compelled to revolt with violence as a last resort...

The problem is how to make an anarchist revolution when you do not attack the sovereign with a bomb...[our] REVOLUTION...means a fundamental transformation of political and social institutions, not a change of rulers...the revolution occurs spontaneously, neither individual nor party can induce it...Therefore, we cannot plan in advance how to initiate a revolution and how to proceed with it...Based on the presupposition...that the institutions and hierarchy of today will not keep up with the advance and development of society and humanity...their overthrow and the creation of new institutions will become inevitable...

Considering this evolutionary process, we believe that after the decay of individual competition and the institution of private property, a communistic society will follow, with anarchistic libertarian institutions driving away modern state despotism; thus, we want to have such a revolution...

Although we cannot predict under what conditions a revolution shall be realized and how it will be achieved, in any case the participants in the revolution for freedom and peace for the masses must try to limit the use of violence...such [violent] collisions have in fact been provoked usually by the obstinate conservative elements fighting against the general tendency [of evolutionary progress]...

The revolutionary anarchist movement, properly so-called, does not seek to induce a revolution immediately, nor is it a mutinous assault. Far from it, it includes all efforts such as the cultivation of one's understanding and knowledge, and the discipline to contribute one's service to the coming revolution. Publishing newspapers and journals, writing and distributing books and leaflets, speeches and meetings, all of these means are used to explain the reasons for and the vicissitudes of the tendency of social evolution, thereby cultivating the knowledge related to them.

In addition, organizing trade unions with various cooperatives is an advantageous vocation for us to develop the capacity of living in a commune either at the time of or in the aftermath of a revolution...

Some may say that a movement is useless if the revolution can only come spontaneously, but that is not true. Whenever an old regime and the old institutions have reached their apogee, society has begun to decline on its own accord. Where there is no idea and knowledge of the general tendency [of social evolution], of the new institutions and organization that will replace the old, and no ability to participate, society withers away along with the old regime, without sprouting the new bud of revolution. In contrast, if we are prepared with knowledge and ability, a new bud will spring forth even though the original stock shall have died...

There are no institutions or organizations that do not ceaselessly fluctuate and evolve, for the human being is dynamic as well as society. It is necessary to advance and to renew in accordance with the times. A small period of such advancement and renewal is called a reformation or an innovation; a big one, a revolution. In order to prevent the decay and downfall of society, I believe it is necessary to propagate new ideas and new thinking; in other words, a revolutionary movement is indispensable...

I was surprised to hear that direct action was understood as synonymous with violent revolution and bomb throwing...What it means is that the workers, in order to promote their own advantage, as a group, for the sake of the trade union, must act for themselves without relying on slow moving parliaments; not indirect action through the intermediary of the parliamentarian, but direct action by the workers themselves, without representatives...Instead of asking parliament to make factory laws to improve or regulate the work place, the workers negotiate directly with the owners; if the latter refuse to negotiate, the former push on to the general strike...Another example: a protester advocating the expropriation of food from the rich when the hungry workers lie on the street...Then expropriation is another method of direct action...

Just because someone is in favour of direct action does not mean that he supports everything not subjected to parliamentary procedure; nor should direct action be confused with riot, murder, robbery or even fraud because they do not go through parliament either...

I believe it does not serve as a revolution to raise a disturbance without any cause in a peaceful country, causing vain sacrifice with destruction of property and human lives. But when the tyranny of the rich and the government reaches its zenith, and the people are driven to the verge of ruin, it is worthwhile for a future revolution to help them.

103. Ôsugi Sakae: Social Idealism (1920)

After the execution of Kôtoku Shûsui in 1911, Ôsugi Sakae (1885-1923) became one of the leading anarchists in Japan. He had escaped arrest in the high treason trial that sent Kôtoku, Kanno and the others to their deaths because he was already in prison for his anarchist activities. He advocated and practiced free love, and was an early Japanese proponent of anarcho-syndicalism. Initially sympathetic to the Russian Revolution, he became a critic of Bolshevism and translated essays by Emma Goldman and Alexander Berkman exposing the Bolshevik dictatorship. In 1923, Ôsugi, his lover, the anarchist feminist Itô Noe, and Ôsugi's six year old nephew were brutally murdered by the Japanese military police. The following excerpts are from Yoshiharu Hashimoto's translation of Ôsugi's declaration from 1920, "A Socialized Idealism," in A Short History of the Anarchist Movement in Japan *(Tokyo: Idea Publishing, 1979). The translation has been modified by the editor for stylistic reasons.*

KROPOTKIN OFTEN SAID THAT A WORKER ought to have an idea of the society of the future that he intends to construct. Unless he grasps this notion, the worker will be an instrument of revolution, never a master of it.

In truth, up till now, the worker has been used in every revolution as an instrument to destroy the old regime, and has had no share in the construction of the new society. Indeed, the workers have destroyed most of the old, but left the rest in others' hands, so that the so-called new society belongs to others, like the former society…

Suppose, however, that the worker had no notion of a new social organization: if he could participate in the destruction of the old society as well as in the construction of the new one, he would be master of the revolution.

Suppose that the worker had an idea, but it was the product of someone else's knowledge: he could not be a true master of the revolution…Therefore, when the worker wants to be a true master of the revolution, in other words, to construct a new society for himself, he should cultivate his autonomy; above all, the emancipation of the worker is the task of the worker himself…

You may complain that "we do not understand what idea or ideals we should hold whatever notion or ideal of a new social organization you may suggest." There are many examples put before the worker: anarchism, social democracy, syndicalism and guild socialism. However, the worker does not know which is the better choice at the present time. Each of them has a plausible rationale. Thus, the worker does not understand, in truth, which is best. Moreover, he must think about advancing his own life before examining an idea or ideal by comparing these different examples. While he is engaged in his own urgent business, he gradually conceives of his position in relation to that between capitalist and worker, then between the government and the capitalist. Even he realizes the fundamental defect in the present social order. Further, he awakens his free spirit, which is even stronger than the conception of his position that he develops during his efforts to change working conditions. It is a fact that I have seen among the workers, that the worker tries to link his free spirit to the social knowledge that he has obtained before accepting the social idea or ideal as it is presented to him. The worker has been preparing his conclusions under the influence of the various examples presented to him instead of acquiring his own....

An idea or ideal is a great power or light as it is. But such power or light will decrease when it is separated from the reality where it is cultivated...

It is the same with an idea or ideal of the future society that the worker undertakes to construct. The anarchist, social democratic and syndicalist ideas or ideals of a future society may imply a power or light constructed by Western or American workers. It is better for them to advance under their own power or light. Yet there is a considerable distance between their reality and that of a Japanese worker...

There is no other means than to promote the reality conforming to their temperament and surroundings, while we seek our own idea or ideal.

Then we can make it our motto: to act like a believer, to think like a sceptic.

104. Itô Noe: The Facts of Anarchy (1921)

Itô Noe (1895-1923) was a Japanese anarchist feminist and later the companion of Ôsugi Sakae, with whom she was murdered by the Japanese military police in 1923. She was a leading figure in the Japanese feminist Bluestocking Society, and translated Emma Goldman into Japanese. The following excerpts are taken from her article, "The Facts of Anarchy," originally published in 1921 in Rodo Undo *(the* Labour Movement*). Itô Noe argues that the Japanese peasant village was a functioning anarchist society based on mutual agreement and mutual aid. The translation by Yoshiharu Hashimoto, originally published in* A Short History of the Anarchist Movement in Japan *(Tokyo: Idea Publishing, 1979), has been modified by the editor for stylistic reasons.*

WE HAVE OFTEN HEARD THE ABUSE that the ideal of anarchist communism is an unrealizable fancy. Everyone clings to the superstitious belief that autonomy cannot be achieved without the support of a central government. In particular, some socialists... sneer at the "dream" of anarchism. Yet I have found that it is not a dream, but something aspects of which have been realized in the autonomy of the villages inherited from our ancestors. In some remote districts where there is no so-called "culture," I have discovered a simple mutual aid...and a social life based on mutual agreement. It is completely different from "administration" under central government, being a mutual aid organization generated by necessity and continued in parallel with the official administration since before the time when there was an "administrative organ."

Now I want to depict the facts that I have seen personally at my native village...

There are sixty to seventy houses divided into six small associations, and these six associations federate with each other as the occasion demands...There are no chains of command or officials. The spirit of the associations, inherited from their ancestors, is "to assist each other in times of trouble."

...[At village meetings] everyone frankly speaks his own thoughts...There is no fearful atmosphere to make one too timid to express his own opinion...In fact, there is no discrimination, whether he is a village master or a daily labourer...There is neither haughtiness nor humility....

How are decisions made? They do it together. Generally, if it is practical or based on clear facts, even more if everyone has offered his knowledge and opinions, the decision will be reached spontaneously...

When a sick person must take to his bed, the news will be reported to the association. The members will rush to the house. Some will get a doctor, others will report it to his relatives; they go on these errands or nurse him kindly...

In cases of childbirth, the women of the association come together. They take care of everything until the mother rises again. Everything else, whenever help is needed, the association will provide it without complaint. Of course there will be two or three families out of favour with the members. With respect to helping such families, although the members may speak ill of them or even complain, they will never refuse to help, for they distinguish between their work for the association and their personal antipathies.

Administrative tasks are shared by the members. If a particular task is long lasting, shifts are arranged so that there is no inconvenience. The responsibility of each member to the association is not coerced or unwilling. He performs his role...so as to follow his conscience...No command or supervision is needed...

After the satisfactory resolution of a particular task, an association formed for that purpose is dissolved. The unit of federation [in each village] is not the association, but each home...

The police seem useless to the association. Quarrels...are mainly settled by the association...A couple from a certain family stole something. The victim had proof and previous knowledge. The victimized family summoned the couple [before the association] and scolded them. Both the victims and the thieves agreed as a settlement of the matter to the announcement that the couple would be expelled from the assembly if they committed the crime again...

Expulsion is the last resort...When one receives this punishment, no one dares to associate with him...So they think of the seriousness of this punishment and do not impose it on someone unless his deed is intolerable. As far as I know, I have not heard of this great punishment being imposed on a family...

Egoistic urban life is intolerable to those accustomed to village life. Where there is no hope of success besides poverty, it is far more comfortable and warm to support each other under the protection of the association.

105. Shin Chaeho: Declaration of the Korean Revolution (1923)

Shin Chaeho (1880-1936) was a Korean revolutionary active in the Korean national liberation movement following Japan's annexation of Korea in 1910. He wrote the following "Declaration of the Korean Revolution" for a Korean national liberation group, the Righteous Group (Uiyoldan), based in China. Despite its nationalist and anti-Japanese tone, the Declaration illustrates Shin Chaeho's shift towards anarchism in its advocacy of a "direct revolution" of the masses that would destroy exploitation and social inequality. In 1927, Shin Chaeho joined the Eastern Anarchist Federation, which had members from Korea, China, Vietnam, Taiwan and Japan. He was arrested by Japanese authorities in Taiwan in 1928 for raising funds for the Korean anarchist movement in China and sentenced to ten years in prison, where he died in 1936. The translation is by Dongyoun Hwang of Soka University of America (Asian Studies Department).

TO SUSTAIN THE KOREAN PEOPLE'S survival, we need to wipe out Robber Japan. The expulsion of Robber Japan can only be accomplished by a revolution...

But where do we begin to engage in a revolution?

After the revolutions of the old days, people used to become the slaves of the state, and, above them, there used to be lords and masters, a privileged group dominating them. Consequently, the so-called revolution was nothing but an altered name for the privileged group. In other words, a revolution used to just replace one privileged group with another. Therefore, people determined their orientation toward revolution according to their understanding of which group of the new/old lords and masters was more generous, more ruthless, more virtuous, or more vicious. Evidently, as a result, people had no direct relations with revolution. Accordingly, a slogan such as "behead the king, console the people" became the sole goal of the revolution...However, today's revolution is one that the masses make for themselves, and, for that reason, we call it a "revolution of the masses" and a "direct revolution." Since it shall be a direct revolution of the masses, the fermentation and expansion of their enthusiasm for it transcends any numerical comparison in the revolution between the weak and the strong. The result of the revolution, whether a success or a failure, always goes beyond the ordinary meaning of warfare: the masses without money and arms defeat a monarch with millions of soldiers and hundreds of thousands of wealth, and expel foreign invaders. The first step toward our revolution, therefore, is to demand the awakening of the masses.

How can the masses be awakened?

The masses will awaken neither by having a divine person, a sage, or a gallant hero, who makes the masses "awaken," nor by hearing vehement statements such as "masses, let's awaken" and "the masses, be awakened."

Destruction by the masses and for the masses of all obstacles, such as inequality, unnaturalness, and absurdity, that stand in the way of improving the masses' livelihood, is the only way to "awaken the masses." In other words, the masses who have awakened in advance should become the revolutionary forerunners for the whole masses...

Because of starvation, cold, plight, pain, wives' shouting, children's crying, pressures to pay taxes, pressures to pay back private loans, no freedom of action, and other various pressures, the general masses can neither live nor die. In this situation, the robber has instituted the politics of robbery that are the main causes of the pressures. If the robber is knocked down, all the facilities of the robber are destroyed and good news [about this] reaches the four seas; all the masses, then, would shed sympathetic tears. Consequently, all of them would realize that, besides death from starvation, there is rather a road called revolution. If the brave out of righteous indignation and the weak out of pain could come along the road and relentlessly advance to influence the masses universally, so that they could make a great revolution under nation-wide unity, that would definitely make a day when the crafty, cunning and cruel Robber Japan would be expelled. Therefore, if we want to awaken the masses, overthrow the rule of the Robber, and thus open up a new life for our nation, raising one hundred thousand soldiers and launching a rebellion should be considered, for they are incomparable to throwing a bomb or to the thousands of billions of sheets of newspaper and magazine writings.

If a violent revolution of the masses does not occur, so be it. However, when it does, like a stone rolling down from a cliff, it won't stop until it reaches its destination...

The road to revolution shall be opened through destruction. However, we destroy in order not just to destroy but to construct. If we do not know how to construct, that means we do not know how to destroy, and, if we do not know how to destroy, that means we do not know how to construct. Construction is distinguishable from destruction only in its form, but, in spirit, destruction means construction. The reasons why we are to destroy the Japanese forces are:

1. To destroy the rule of a foreign race. Why? Since at the top of "Korea" resides a foreign race, "Japan," a despotic country, Korea under the despotism of a foreign race is not an authentic Korea. To discover the authentic Korea, we destroy the rule of a foreign race.

2. To destroy a privileged class. Why? Since at the top of the Korean "masses" sits the Governor General or others who are the members of a privileged class composed of a gang of robbers who oppress the masses, the Korean masses under the oppression of the privileged class are not the free masses of Korea. To discover the free masses of Korea, we overthrow the privileged class.

3. To destroy the system of economic exploitation. Why? Since the economy under the exploitive system is not an economy organized by the masses themselves for the sake of their livelihood but an economy organized to feed the robber, we are to destroy the system of economic exploitation and to develop the livelihood of the masses.

4. To destroy social inequality. Why? Since the strong exists above the weak and the high above the low, a society full of any inequalities will become one in which people exploit, usurp, hate and detest each other. In society, at first for the happiness of the minority, damage is inflicted upon the masses, the majority, and, at last, the minority inflict damage upon each other...To promote the happiness of all the masses, therefore, we destroy social inequality.

5. To destroy servile cultural thoughts. Why? Are these not something produced by the strong to support the strong in the form of religion, ethics, literature, fine arts, customs, and public morals? Haven't they served the strong as various tools for its pleasure? Aren't they narcotics that enslave the masses? While the minority class becomes the strong, the majority masses end up being the weak. That the weak could not resist an unjust oppression is entirely due to the fact that they are fettered by servile cultural thoughts. If we do not cut off the chains of these restraints and put forward a culture of the masses, the general masses, weak in thinking of their rights and lacking their interest in advancing freedom, would just circulate through fate as slaves. Therefore, to advocate the culture of the masses, we must destroy servile cultural thoughts.

In other words, in order to construct a Korea made of the "authentic Korea," the free Korean masses, the economy of the masses, the society of the masses, and the culture of the masses, we attempt to break through such phenomena as the rule of a foreign race, the exploitive system, social inequality, and servile cultural thoughts... We understand by now: that destruction and construction are inseparable, not two but one; that prior to the destruction by the masses exists the construction by the masses; that the Korean masses now will destroy the forces of Robber Japan only through the masses' violence, as those forces are the obstacles standing in the way of constructing a new Korea; and that the Korean masses encounter Robber Japan on "a single bridge" where the two realize that one of them shall be ruined by the other. So, we, the twenty-million masses, will be united and march toward the road to violence and destruction.

The masses are the supreme headquarters of our revolution.

Violence is our only weapon for our revolution.

We go to the masses and go hand in hand with the masses.

With ceaseless violence-assassination, destruction, and rebellion, we will overthrow the rule of Robber Japan,

Transform all the absurd systems in our life, and construct an ideal Korea in which one human being will not be able to oppress other human beings and one society will not be able to exploit other societies. (*Collected Writings of Shin Chaeho*, ed. Danjae Shin Chaeho, Vol. 3, Seoul: Hyeongseol chulpansa, 1975; second edition, 1987)

106. Hatta Shûzô: On Syndicalism (1927)

In Japan, as elsewhere, anarchists were active in the labour movement. In 1926, the All-Japan Libertarian Federation of Labour Unions (Zenkoku Jiren) was founded. It included both anarcho-syndicalist and anarchist communist elements. In its statement of principles the Federation declared:

> We base our movement for the emancipation of the workers and tenant farmers on the class struggle.
>
> We reject participation in politics and insist on economic action.
>
> We advocate free federation organized by industry and forsake centralism.
>
> We oppose imperialist invasion and advocate the international solidarity of the workers.

Hatta Shûzô (1886-1934) was an advocate of "pure anarchism," a Japanese variant of anarchist communism, and an uncompromising critic of anarcho-syndicalism. He drew a distinc-

tion between class struggle and revolutionary transformation, writing that "it is a major mistake to declare, as the syndicalists do, that the revolution will be brought about by the class struggle. Even if a change in society came about by means of the class struggle, it would not mean that a genuine revolution had occurred." This is because "in a society which is based on the division of labour, those engaged in vital production (since it forms the basis of production) would have more power over the machinery of coordination than those engaged in other lines of production. There would therefore be a real danger of the [re]appearance of classes" (as quoted by John Crump, The Anarchist Movement in Japan, *London: Pirate Press, 1996). In the following excerpts from an article originally published in 1927, Hatta Shûzô sets forth his critique of anarcho-syndicalism and briefly describes the "pure anarchist" alternative. The translation by Yoshiharu Hashimoto, originally published in* A Short History of the Anarchist Movement in Japan *(Tokyo: Idea Publishing, 1979), has been modified by the editor for stylistic reasons.*

THERE ARE THREE TYPES OF TRADE UNIONISM. One has as its object maintaining the livelihood of the worker. Another is organized as the agent of the Bolsheviks. The third is the syndicalist union that fights against capitalism face to face. The syndicalists have themselves gradually divided into two: one group seeks to advance the position of the workers; the other seeks to achieve communism. What we must determine is whether this is a corruption of syndicalism or an inherent defect in syndicalism itself...

What is there to syndicalism? I am convinced both anarchism and Marxism...By examining this point, we understand it is based on the conception of class struggle as declared in the Charter of Amiens...As you know, the class struggle arose from modern capitalism. The industrial working class is pitted against the capitalist class in relation to the contradiction of profit. The rising working class becomes class conscious and begins the class struggle, expecting the complete emancipation of the working class through a final battle with the capitalists. This is the Marxist theory behind syndicalism...

Secondly, syndicalism has adopted the notion of the "creative violence" of the minority. According to the revolutionary syndicalists, the true emancipation of the working class is achieved through a creative dynamic wherein a few convinced militants inspire the majority.

Thirdly, syndicalism has adopted the industrial factors that have historically arisen within capitalism and seeks to control the new social organization by means of a division of labour. Of course, syndicalism emphasizes knowledge of local demand, but it adopts the division of labour as a form of economic organization upon which to construct a society of producers. In this sense it contains Marx's economic theory and that of socialism in general.

Thus, the theory of syndicalism adopts most of the Marxist theory and then adds from anarchism the notion of the creative violence of the minority...

Despite the enthusiasm of syndicalism and its abundance of activists, it gradually falls into reformism and cannot maintain concurrence with anarchism because syndicalism...has two contradictory theories at its base (i.e., Marxism and anarchism). The class struggle requires a majority that does not agree with the violence of the minority; with enforced cohesion, the enthusiasm of the minority will decline and it will fall into reformism too...

Syndicalism advocates the division of labour as the productive organization in the future society. It is without doubt that all production is carried out by division in society...Its typical characteristics are, in the first place, the mechanization of labour; secondly, someone engaging in one kind of production has no responsibility for, understanding of or interest in other industries; thirdly, it needs a special coordinating body to preside over the divided work...carried out by persons who do not engage in that work. Power will emerge from that group without fail. In contrast, in Kropotkin's communal organization, coordinated production is performed autonomously on a human scale, so that people are able to take responsibility, to understand and to have an interest directly in other industries, even as they are engaged in one system of production. Because they can coordinate the work process themselves there is no superior body and there is no place of power. Where production is based on the division of labour with the people who work in the important industries acquiring power over the coordinating body, in contrast to those who work in less important industries, then there is the possibility of class division again emerging. Moreover, the division of labour does not imply that "man produces for himself with his own hands," so production and consumption do not cohere at all. We cannot hope for true freedom where there is no freedom of production and consumption...An anarchist society cannot be achieved unless it is a commune as proposed by Kropotkin, with inner coordination [of production] that does not depend on a division of labour...I hope the present labour unions will advance with the method and in the spirit of anarchism, not mere syndicalism, Bolshevism or reformism.

Hatta argued that in an anarchist communist society, production would be based on consumption, instead of consumption being determined by the demands of production, as in a capitalist or even a syndicalist economy, which is a denial of the individual freedom to satisfy one's desires:

> In a locally decentralized communist system, production springs from consumption. In place of consumption arising out of production, as in a system based on centralized power, consumption becomes the causal source of production in a system of decentralized production. (As quoted in John Crump, Hatta Shûzô and Pure Anarchism in Interwar Japan, New York: St. Martin's, 1993)

107. Kubo Yuzuru: On Class Struggle and the Daily Struggle (1928)

Kubo Yuzuru (1903-1961) was a Japanese anarcho-syndicalist. In this article, "Of the Class Struggle and the Daily Struggle," originally published in Kokushoku Undo *in 1928, he responds to some of the criticisms of anarcho-syndicalism made by the "pure anarchists." Ironically, the Zenkoku Jiren labour federation adopted a "pure anarchist" position in 1928, and the anarcho-syndicalists broke away to form a separate anarcho-syndicalist organization. By 1931, the Zenkoku Jiren had over 16,000 members, while the anarcho-syndicalist federation, the Libertarian Federal Council of Labour Unions of Japan (Nihon Rôdô Kumiai Jiyû Rengô Kyôgikai, referred to as the Jikyô), had a membership of around 3,000. As Hatta Shûzô argued in the selection above, the "pure anarchists" did not oppose trade unions as such; rather, they argued that the unions should be animated by an anarchist spirit, with the goal of a decentralized, classless, anarchist communist society always in mind. The translation of Kubo's article by Yoshiharu Hashimoto, originally published in* A Short History of the Anarchist Movement in Japan *(Tokyo: Idea Publishing, 1979), has been modified by the editor for stylistic reasons.*

IT IS NO WONDER THAT THE ANARCHIST promotes class struggle and the daily struggle, for there is no reason to prevent such propaganda by the deed. There may be a few intolerant ideologues among Japanese anarchists who accuse class struggle of being an amalgam of Marxism. But the tactic of class struggle is not the monopoly of the Marxists...

Capitalism divides society into two classes, such as the oppressor and the oppressed, the exploiter and the exploited. There we come face to face with the confrontation of classes and the strife between them. The existence of classes engenders class struggle. Where class struggle is a fact, there our movement will be. Really, the problem is one of goals and the method of struggle. Then we can see two main tendencies of class struggle, one based on authoritarian Marxism, the other on free federation. According to the Marxist conception of class struggle, the proletariat will take over the position of the capitalist class by usurping political power through political struggle. Its object being political power...it means the monopoly of a party...

That is, Marxist class struggle does not bring an end to the strife or the contradiction of classes, but reverses the positions of the opposed classes. Nominally it is the dictatorship of the proletariat, although in fact the Marxists do not concern themselves with their fellow workers' intentions of emancipation, despite their possession of numerical strength. There [in Marxism] the ideas of free federation and spontaneity, essential factors for building the new society, are killed. Therefore, we are vehemently opposed to them.

Our class struggle is based on the principles of communal property and anti-authoritarianism, to put an end to class confrontation, in short, to create a new society where there is neither exploiter nor exploited, neither master nor slave, revived with spontaneity and mutual free agreement as an integral whole. After all, our class struggle is to achieve the radical transformation of economic and political institutions by means of the workers' organizations based on the ideal of free federation. Their [the Marxists'] goal is to replace one ruling class with another, but ours is to put an end to class antagonism. Because of the aggravation of the class struggle, you may condemn us as Marxists; then the free federations of labour unions that in the past...had a revolutionary platform based on class struggle ought to be condemned as Marxist too. There are some who dismiss the class struggle but deny it by referring to the elimination of class contradictions. This is...a pretext for avoiding the terminology of class struggle. It also seems to proclaim the ceasing of struggle against the master and capitalist...There are a number of tactics in Marxist strategy borrowed from the syndicalists and anarchists...you narrow-minded people remind me of the fable of a dog having a fish in its mouth who barked at its own reflection and lost the fish, as you indiscriminately accuse us of merely using the same phraseology as the Bolsheviks...

It is possible to argue that the anarchist movement is divided into economic and political phases. The movement related to the economic field deals with the struggle to obtain daily bread for the worker. The desire to obtain better bread, to conquer bread, has been, in fact, the source of modern socialism. If the workers were without the desire for the good of tomorrow, there never would have been a liberation movement. Anarchism originated from the fact of the struggle of the workers. Without that, there would be no anarchism...[Anarchism] has far greater meaning than to denigrate the workers' economic struggles as mere reformism. We do not neglect the fact that there is a distance between raising wages, reforming conditions and the ideal society. Nevertheless, it is our role to move step by step against the foundations of capitalism. I need not point out that raising wages and improving working conditions are not our goals *per se*. On the contrary, they are nothing more than a means or rationale, yet by such means we ought to rouse direct action and cultivate a bud of anarchism through daily struggle, which I believe will be the preparation for revolution...

Besides the economic struggle, there is also the political struggle. Besides economic oppression by the capitalist, there is also political tyranny...We ought to lead a direct struggle of revolutionary movements of the people against all political institutions and oppressive measures, such as the heavy tax burden for the benefit of the capitalists. Then we create awareness of anti-authoritarianism. We should seize every opportunity in economic and political struggles so that anarchist thought may prevail...We urge grabbing every chance and utilizing any moment...to shake the foundations of society...That is to say, the daily struggle is a ceaseless struggle.

108. The Talhwan: What We Advocate (1928)

The Talhwan *was the publication of the Korean Anarchist Federation in China. "Talhwan" is the Korean translation of "conquest"; the title of the paper is believed to have been inspired by Kropotkin's* The Conquest of Bread *(Selection 33). The following excerpts are taken from the inaugural issue of the* Talhwan *published in June 1928. The translation is by Dongyoun Hwang of Soka University of America (Asian Studies Department).*

ALL PRODUCTS OF CONTEMPORARY SOCIETY were produced by the joint effort of the workers, and modern civilization was created by the blood and sweat of the masses in the past. Neither an individual nor a government, therefore, can have rights to monopolize the products and own civilization exclusively, no matter what. Since the past, however, capitalism, advancing together with government, has monopolized everything and created the property of a privileged class.

In order for us to live, we cannot help retaking (*talhwan*) the possessions that initially belonged to all human beings. In other words, we advocate that we should accomplish public ownership of property.

Although the struggle between labour and capital may differ in every place according to the status of capitalism and its institutions, the proletariat in every place must be united by taking the same stand for the principles of the struggle. Their present, sole goal is to retake the civilization of a capitalist class and, then, return it to the whole masses. By doing so, the capitalist society will be replaced with a new society founded upon the principles of freedom and equality that guarantee the autonomy of the producers.

We do not allow the existence of a government, no matter what kind of form it may take. Let's look at the human past! In the age of feudalism, monarchial governments supported a system of serfdom serving the interests of the imperial family and the aristocratic class. In the age of capitalism, democratic governments, for the protection of the interests of the bourgeoisie, use a representative system in politics that creates a privileged class, and the wage slave system for its economic system that makes great but subtle machines by utilizing numerous workers' bones, blood and sweat, thus finally enslaving human beings to machines. And, now let's look at the crumbling so-called [Soviet] government of peasants and workers! The regime of the petit bourgeoisie, called the Communist (?) Party, to maintain its despotic and dictatorial politics, carries out state capitalism, which is an extended form of individual capitalism that concentrates capital in the hands of the government. While the [Soviet] government, mounting a cunning scheme called the New Economic Policy, acknowledges the ownership and free business activities of individual capital in the name of regulated capital…it turns out that in truth the ordinary people of Russia are subject to the dual oppressions of individual capitalism and state capitalism…[N]o matter what kind of form it takes, government is a tool for the minority with power to oppress the masses, and an obstacle that stands in the way of realizing mutual human fraternity. Therefore, we do not allow for its existence…

Capitalism of the past worked with feudalism of the past, and modern capitalism works with the bourgeois government. Consequently, government could not survive without capitalism and vice versa… capital itself is a gift snatched by the strong and powerful. In theory or in practice, capital has already lost all its values. It has forced human beings to do harm to other human beings, denying them the basic necessities of life. Therefore, capital is called the source of all crimes and evils. Accordingly, we admit that, whether they are individual capitalists or state capitalists, all of those who steal the possessions of the masses are robbers.

We are absolutely against something called power, no matter what rules and forms it has. We do not allow others to gain power; we ourselves, at the same time, do not demand power. In fact, a thing called power is a protector of private property and a mechanism that makes human beings oppressed.

While we are going to wipe out the present bourgeoisie and capitalist society, it is not…that we want to get rid of all social organizations. Rather, we only demand a society in which progress and civilization are comparatively well integrated with each other. Our primary principle is that each individual in society consumes according to one's own demand and produces according to one's own ability.

We believe that a society, no matter what kind of society it is, after abolishing private property, cannot help tending and advancing toward the state of common property (*gongsan*) with the idea of non-government (*mujeongbu*). We think that the common property system can be fulfilled only with non-government and non-government can be carried out only with the common property system. The common property system we argue for here does not imply a compulsory communism, a government-patronized communism, which in keeping with Marx's collectivism concentrates capital in government. Rather, it implies a free communism under the autonomy of producers' organizations, namely anarcho-communism (*mujeongbu gongsan ju'eui*) under which there is no government.

With these principles, we are going to give back to the oppressed class of the Korean masses a colony, called Korea...after retaking it from the hands of the Japanese capitalist government. We are going to refuse forever to come to terms with the capitalist class of our native country under the situation that fighting Japan has become...[an] excuse for establishing the national united front. Although the capitalist class is a special class in a colony, viewed from the standpoint of its own interests, it will eventually compromise with the conquering capitalist class...

It is in order to retake the masses and their possessions now under the control of a compulsory power, to restore the true life of human beings, and to provoke a spontaneous surge of the masses that we publish *The Conquest*.

109. Takamure Itsue: A Vision of Anarchist Love (1930)

Takamure Itsue (1894-1964) was a prominent anarchist feminist in Japan during the inter-war years and one of the founders of the anarchist feminist group, the Fujin Sensen (the Women's Front). The following excerpts are from her article, "A Vision of Anarchist Love," originally published in 1930. The translation is by Yasuko Sato of the University of Nevada (History Department).

WHAT I MEAN HERE BY ANARCHIST LOVE is unfettered love. However, those who have hitherto been too subjected to the fetters of social convention hastily interpret such love as a pathological setback, hence as "wanton" and "promiscuous."

Similarly, many people think of anarchism as a principle that upholds an unsettling degree of disorder. Denouncing it as undermining the legitimacy of the police or the state, those who are pitifully parochial believe that the maintenance of peace in this world is possible only by means of police and state. But this idea is a consequence of being deceived by the ruling authorities. Anyone who studies history can easily envision peaceful and communitarian orders of society free from police and state. Everybody is innately capable of mutual aid and love. Only when mutual aid and love are fully realized will our society be peaceful, and we will be able to accomplish great endeavors…

In the course of time, we gradually become indifferent to political administration. With the assumption that those above will manage skillfully, we consider everything to be tiresome and allow them to handle it. In the process, we degenerate into the totally spiritless, uncritical "ignorant masses." The "system of control" is thus one that "nourishes the ignorant masses." Having thoroughly been degraded into the ignorant masses, we become even unable to ruminate on such matters as "autonomy" and "self-government."

Insofar as we maintain such a complacent attitude, we will never be redeemed. We must continue living a life that is endlessly unrewarded and full of pain and distress.

Now, it is time for us to rise up. We must rise up and wipe out all evils completely. To achieve this end, we must not be seduced by other reformist ideas such as Marxism, which is so inconsistent and deceptive as to call for gradual reforms through a better system of control.

Our political consciousness consists not in participating in politics, but in denying it. This means being absolutely opposed to politics, controls, and oppressive power—all these things.

Analogously, every sphere [of human activity] should be like this. All phenomena in the world are interconnected and organic. Even in the matter of love, we need to strive strenuously for free love by abolishing traditional views of love as a "shackle." Free love signifies none other than anarchist love…

Men have an irresponsible attitude toward the problem of love. They are in a carefree position, able to regard sexual intercourse only as an excretion. Such is not the case with women. For them, love is immensely real, leading immediately to pregnancy and childbearing. These are the differences that separate male and female views on the issue of love.

…[O]ne of the reasons why male-dominated society belittles the issue of love as a private affair has to do with the male "sex," although, of course, this does not account for everything. By making use of the male "sex," the ruling class has cunningly accelerated this tendency. This is because the ruling class is concerned only with the object of direct exploitation, that is, with the production of commodities. They are insatiably intent on turning all of the exploited into a single efficient industrial machine. This being the case, the problem of sexuality is rather vexatious, and those in power conceive of such "human" demands, daily life and all as mere extravagance for everyone except themselves. (They certainly favour the birth of babies as eggs for their industrial machines, but invariably, this birth has to occur under restricted conditions. In other words, babies are allowed to be born only to be chained up within the confinement of the marriage system.) Under these circumstances, it is only natural that romance between humans should be wholly despised, rejected, and denounced...

We may safely assume that, in the case of men, except for those who have an unusual degree of objectivity and a warm humanity, very few arrive at social consciousness through sexual liaisons. The same is not true of women. They take on the burdens of pregnancy and childbirth through sexual encounters.

However young they may be, women cannot afford to remain unconcerned in present-day society by perceiving love merely as a "romance" or "poem." When in love, they cannot avoid devoting some thought to the "realistic, all too realistic" problem of pregnancy. They confront the "social, all too social" problem of childbearing.

Thus for women, love is an extraordinary event. The fact that love is an inevitability for young people makes the problem all the more serious. Women today cannot detachedly say, "why not love?" when pregnancy and childbirth, the consequences of love, are dismissed as private affairs, all the responsibilities of which are relentlessly imposed upon frail women. In addition, the more humane love is, the more brutally it is suppressed, and of course the damage is inflicted solely on women.

In a society like ours, sexual acts are utterly impossible except within the confines of [family] chains or in the form of perverse lascivious acts women do not desire. It would not be possible to painfully experience such misery, anxiety, and discontent without rapidly turning them into social consciousness. For women, sexual intercourse is directly linked to pregnancy and childbirth. Hence, women's sexual conduct is not merely romantic or poetic, but manifests in full measure a society itself.

...[I]n an attempt to carry out rapacious exploitation by making people believe that what is done "for the nation" and "for God" is the only thing that matters, [the ruling class] thinks about how to get rid of all troublesome human desires and uniformly regiments people by leading them away from those unproductive activities as much as possible. That is, each individual is paired with another individual of the opposite sex and made to privately own him or her under fixed conditions. With this, it is supposed that the lives of children born of such arrangements can be fitted into the couple's own responsibilities. It has been thought that the origins of marriage institutions have been construed only in terms of the inheritance of private property, but this is not quite right. We also need to know that they originated from a ruling-class view of sexual desire as private and contemptuous (in the sense that the sexual desire of the ruled is deemed to be bothersome, and that various duties arising from it are ignored).

Since the feudal age, marriages for the inheritance of family names and property (marriages for childbearing) have been falling into decay. Obviously, marriage in the capitalist age is distinctive in that it is "childless," centered on contraception...

Thus envisaged, if its origins are simply "for the sake of property inheritance," the institution of marriage should have already disintegrated in the capitalist era. Nonetheless, Ben Lindsey and others are vigorously calling for the legalization of capitalist marriage, and it is entirely legalized in Soviet Russia. This suggests that the marriage system is still necessary for certain reasons. That is, for reasons that are beneficial for the ruling class: the reduction of [labour power] to uniformity through the concept of marriage as a private affair and the attribution of various kinds of responsibilities to [the private sphere].

...It is only on the level of ineffectual law or morality that husbands are connected to their wives, and after all, it is only mothers—inseparably bound up with their babies—who are compelled to take care of them. Furthermore, in places like America and Russia where uninhibited love prevails, men are neither affectionate toward their regular children nor certain whether they are truly their own, so they seek to evade [paternal responsibility] as much as possible. It is argued, therefore, that the most difficult and numerous cases that dominate most of the courts in contemporary Russia are about sex. As long as they dream of their liberation only on the level of politics and law, women will never be liberated. This is because politics and law are no more than bureaucratic lawsuits and scraps of paper...

According to Ms. Ellis in England: "Women have cyclic sexual impulses. Nevertheless, as a result of the marriage system, a woman's sexual organs are seen as her husband's possessions, and she is constantly exposed to his sexual drive regardless of whether or not she has sexual impulses..."

It should now be obvious that healthy sexual conduct is natural sexual intercourse between a man and a woman via the spontaneity of their mutual love. In effect, since the emergence of oppressive society, such sexual activities have been heavily repressed and vulgarized. Because they have been ruthlessly institutionalized for the convenience and maintenance of oppressive power, the sexual life we now see before our eyes presents an almost hellish picture.

...We are told that in capitalist society people no longer desire to have children, since sex life exists only for pleasure.

While this tendency has promoted contraception, the headway made by contraception has accelerated this tendency. Although their individual motivations may be different, the bourgeoisie, the proletariat, farmers, women—no one among them—disavows contraception. The world is moving into an astonishing era of birth control...

Why did capitalist marriage—marriage centered on contraception—come into existence? One of the primary reasons is that the proletariat faces economic difficulties, while capitalist production, concurrent with advances in machinery, has lowered the rates of necessary human labour. Another reason is the turbulent incongruities and contradictions generated by the marriage system since the dawn of history.

Notably, in recent times women's self-consciousness has formulated this phenomenon not as mere lustfulness, but as a kind of rebellious action. Admittedly, women have "resisted childbearing" since the dawn of the history of oppressive power. (Society confined women to dungeons and denied them genuinely free childbirth by imposing painfully involuntary births, as if in prison cells. Since then, women's rebellious spirit has completely nullified the meaning of their social contribution through childbirth, because childbirth in dire confinement is simply a humiliation for women.) Ultimately, women's desire takes the form of promoting birth control, and they have come to play a leading role in the drama of rebellion...

One contemporary form of anarchist love may show an American face; it is free love through the full utilization of contraception. If women themselves have become abnormal, this is not applicable; but as long as they have not, as long as their position is to seek genuine anarchist love, they will never be satisfied with recreational sex. Therefore, even in conjunction with free love featuring birth control, anarchist love will be pursued in a faithful manner. The spirit of a sexual life based on respect and love—even if momentary—will never be lost. A rendezvous will begin with respect and earnest longing, and parting will also take place with respect and serene kindness. We may experience ardent love for a short while without knowing when and where, and there is no reason to deny the freedom of realizing that love.

Nevertheless, we may have an eternal love that is both passionate and quiet, full of respect. It will evoke a sense of "peaceful union." In such cases, as an inevitable consequence of that love, we will never involve ourselves in another love, because that is impossible...

Anarchist love can never be phrased in terms of fulfilling one's selfish interests, because it is not mere selfish love between lovers themselves but an outgrowth of respect and love for all people.

At times, it may thus be necessary for us to bury in silence the ardent love that our hearts incidentally start embracing by virtue of our strong reason or to illuminate it from a broader perspective. In such cases, then our love could be tragic, but that is inescapable. Since we must respect and love the positions of all people without exception, it would not do for our conduct to ever be easy.

110. Japanese Libertarian Federation: What To Do About War (1931)

The following article, "What To Do About War?", was published in the Japanese Libertarian Federation paper, Jiyu Rengo Shinbun, *No. 64, in November 1931, when Japan was in the process of occupying Manchuria. The invasion of Manchuria also marked renewed suppression of the Japanese anarchist movement, which was effectively destroyed by 1937. The article was originally published in* Esperanto *to make it accessible to an international audience. The translation is by John Crump, reprinted in* Anarchist Opposition to War *(Seattle: Charlatan Stew, 1995).*

THE JAPANESE MILITARISTS HAVE MOBILIZED their army to China on the pretext "For the peace of the Orient" or "To defend the Japanese people in China." They always use, whenever a state crisis occurs, such beautiful expressions as "For Our fatherland" or "For justice" and try to stir up the people's patriotism. But what is the fatherland? For whom does it exist? Never forget that all states exist only for the wealthy. It is the same with war. War brings injury or death to the young men of the poor, and hunger and cold to their aged parents and young brothers and sisters. But to the wealthy it brings enormous riches and honour.

The true cause of the mobilization to China is none other than the ambition of the Japanese capitalist class and military to conquer Manchuria. Japan has its own Monroe doctrine. Japanese capitalism cannot develop, or even survive, without Manchuria. That is why its government is inclined to risk anything so as not to lose its many privileges in China. Therefore it has approved the enormous expense of the mobilization, despite the fact that it is experiencing a deficit in the current year's income of the state treasury. American capital has flowed into China in larger and larger amounts. This represents an enormous menace to the Japanese capitalist class. In other words, now Japan is forced to oppose American capital in China. In fact, this is the direct cause of the mobilization.

From another point of view, we can see that this incident is a drama written by the Japanese military as a militaristic demonstration to all pacifists, cosmopolitans and socialists within Japan, and to other countries in general, and China in particular. Even we Japanese have been surprised at the rapid mobilization. How were they able to make preparations so rapidly? It is clear that the mobilization was totally prepared for long ago. That is the drama. Did we say drama? In this way the military have engineered the opportunity to demonstrate and establish their strength, which has been weakened of late by disarmament and pacifist public opinion. Of course, a secret agreement had been reached between the military and the capitalists, because they both belong to the ruling class.

In this situation, what must we do? The Communists say "Defend and come to the aid of the Chinese revolution!" But who will benefit in China when Japanese power is totally eliminated from that country? It will be none other than the newly rising Chinese bourgeoisie and the capitalists of other countries. We must keenly observe and criticize all that takes place. In the face of war, we must not make the mistake which our comrade Kropotkin and others made during the World War. Of course, we opposed the mobilization. But we found that merely one-sided opposition is a very feeble response. The sole method to eradicate war from our world is for us, acting as the popular masses, to reject it in all countries simultaneously. We must cease military production, refuse military service and disobey the officers. Complete international unity of the anarchists would signal our victory, not only economically but in the war against war.

ANARCHIST GROUPS OF ALL COUNTRIES, UNITE!

ABOLISH IMPERIALIST WAR!

Chapter 22
The Interwar Years

111. Gustav Landauer: Revolution of the Spirit (1919)

Throughout the First World War, Gustav Landauer had taken a consistently anti-war stand. In early 1918, mass strikes against the war began in Germany. Landauer's writings quickly rose in popularity, especially his 1911 publication, For Socialism *(Selection 79). In late October 1918, naval mutinies broke out in Kiel, and in November workers' and soldiers' councils were formed. The majority Social Democrats proclaimed a republic, pre-empting the radical socialists, led by Karl Liebknecht and Rosa Luxembourg. Landauer went to Bavaria, where the independent socialist, Kurt Eisner, had already proclaimed a social republic. Landauer joined with the anarchist Erich Mühsam (1868-1934) in supporting a Revolutionary Workers' Council that advocated a direct democracy of broadly based workers' councils in opposition to parliamentary democracy. Unlike the radical Marxists involved in the council movement, who called for the "dictatorship of the proletariat," Landauer argued that the councils should include all members of the community and called for "the 'abolition of the proletariat' as a distinct class" (Eugene Lunn,* Prophet of Community: The Romantic Socialism of Gustav Landauer, *Berkeley: University of California, 1973, page 301). In January 1919, the "Spartacist" uprising was crushed in Berlin, and Liebknecht and Luxemburg were murdered by military forces. The revolutionary council movement continued in Bavaria, with Landauer taking an active role. Eisner was assassinated in February 1919. The Social Democrats tried to set up a new government in March 1919 and supported the violent suppression of street protests. When three demonstrators were killed by security forces with the approval of the Social Democrats, Landauer commented, "In the whole of natural history I know of no more revolting creature than the Social Democratic Party" (as quoted in Lunn, page 321). The Social Democratic government retreated to Nuremburg and a Council Republic was declared in Munich in April 1919. Landauer participated in the Council Republic, but it lasted for only one week; then the Communists seized power after an attempted coup by troops loyal to the Social Democratic government. Landauer at first offered his support to the Communists, which they rejected, but when it became clear that they intended to adopt the authoritarian methods of the Bolsheviks, Landauer withdrew his offer. Two weeks later he was brutally beaten and shot to death by reactionary troops sent by the central Social Democratic government in Berlin to crush the Bavarian revolution. Hundreds of others were also slaughtered. The Social Democratic minister of national defence, Gustav Noske, congratulated the commander of the troops for the "discreet and wholly successful way in which you have conducted your operations in Munich" (as quoted in Lunn, page 340).*

The following excerpts are from the forward to the second edition of For Socialism, *which Landauer wrote in Munich in early January 1919 while there was still hope for genuine revolutionary transformation along communitarian anarchist lines. The translation by David J. Parent is from the Telos Press edition (St. Louis, 1978), and is reprinted with the kind permission of the publisher.*

THE GOVERNMENT HAS COLLAPSED; socialism is the only salvation. It certainly did not result as a blossom of capitalism; it is the heir and repudiated son waiting at the door behind which the corpse of his unnatural father rots. Nor can socialism be added to the beautiful body of society as an apex of national wealth and a sumptuous economy; it must be created almost out of nothing amid chaos. In despair I called for socialism; but out of that despair I drew great hope and joyous resolution, and the despair which I and the likes of me bore in our hearts has not become a permanent condition. May those who must now begin the work of construction not lack hope, a desire to work, knowledge, and an enduring creativity.

Everything said here about the collapse applies fully only to Germany at present and to the nations which, voluntarily or not, have shared its fate. As was said, not capitalism as such has collapsed by virtue of its immanent impossibility, but the capitalism of one group of nations, acting in conjunction with autocracy and militarism, has been ruined by the liberally administered capitalism of another, militarily weaker, capitalistically stronger area, in final conjunction with the volcanic eruption of popular rage of its own people. I will not predict when and in what form the collapse of the other, more clever representative of capitalism and imperialism will occur. The social causes necessary for any revolution to take place are present everywhere. However, the need for political liberation, the only reason for a revolution to move toward a goal and become more than a revolt, is of varying strength in those countries which have experienced democratic political revolutions. The following seems to be evident: the more free political mobility exists in a country, and the greater the adaptability of government institutions to democracy, the more terrible and unproductive, however, the struggle will be when social hardship, injustice and degradation finally generate the phantom of a revolution and, consequently an all-too-real civil war, if steps are not taken to establish socialism immediately...

For the revolution can only be a political one. It would not gain the support of the enslaved masses, if they did not also desire to break free of social oppression and economic hardship. However, the transformation of social institutions, of property relations, of the type of economy cannot come by way of revolution. In these matters, action from below can only shake off, destroy and abandon something; action from above, even by a revolutionary government, can only abolish and command, whereas socialism must be built, erected, organized out of a new spirit. This new spirit prevails mightily and ardently in the revolution. Robots become men. Cold, unimaginative men are fired with enthusiasm. The entire *status quo*, including opinions, positive and negative, is cast into doubt. Reason, which formerly focused only on selfish interest, becomes rational thinking and thousands of men sit or pace restlessly in their rooms, for the first time in their lives forging plans for the common welfare. Everything becomes accessible to the good. The incredible miracle is brought into the realm of possibility. The reality which is otherwise hidden in our souls, in the structures and rhythms of art, in the faith-structures of religion, in dream and love, in dancing limbs and gleaming glances, now presses for fulfillment. However, the tremendous danger remains that the old humdrum way and empty imitation will take hold of the revolutionaries and make them shallow, uncultured radicals, with the ringing rhetoric and violent gestures, who neither know, nor want to know, that the transformation of society can come only in love, work, and silence.

They also ignore another point, despite the experiences of past revolutions. All these revolutions were a great renewal, a bubbling refreshment, a high point of nations; but their permanent results were slight. Ultimately they brought a change only in the forms of political disenfranchisement. Political freedom, maturity, honest pride, self-determination and an organic, corporative coherence of the masses out of one unifying spirit, voluntary associations in public life—this can only be achieved by a great adjustment, by economic and social justice, by socialism. How could there be a commonwealth of true communities in our era, in which Christianity affirms the equality of all the children of men, in origin, rights and destiny; how could there be a free public life, pervaded by the all-fulfilling, dynamic spirit of enthusiastically progressive men and deep, strong women, if slavery, disinheritance and ostracism persist in any form and guise?

The political revolution which brings the spirit to power and makes it the strong imperative and decisive implementation, can clear the way for socialism, for a change of conditions by a renewed spirit. But decrees can, at most, incorporate men as government slaves into a new military-like economy; the new spirit of justice must create its own forms of economy. The idea must embrace the needs of the moment within its long-range view and shape them energetically. What was previously only an ideal, is realized by the work of renewal born out of the revolution.

The need for socialism is there. Capitalism is collapsing. It no longer works. The fiction that capital works has burst like a bubble; the only thing that attracted the capitalist to his sort of work, to the risk of his fortune and the leadership and administration of enterprise, namely profit, no longer attracts him. The age of the profitability of capital, of interest and usury, is over; the mad war-profits were a dance of death. If we are not to perish in our Germany, to perish really and literally, the only salvation is work, real work done, performed and organized by an unselfish, fraternal spirit. New forms of work must be developed, freed from a tribute payable to capital, ceaselessly creating new values and new realities, harvesting and transforming the products of nature for human needs. The age of the productivity of labour is beginning; otherwise we have reached the end of the line. Technology has placed both long known and newly discovered natural forces at man's service. The more people cultivate the earth and transform its products, the richer the harvest. Mankind can live in dignity and without care. No one need be another's slave, no one need be excluded and disinherited. Work, the means of life, need not become an arduous torment. All can live in openness to spirit, soul, play, and God. Revolutions and their painfully long, oppressive pre-history teach us that only the most extreme distress, only the feeling of sheer desperation brings the masses of men to reason, to the reason which, for wise men and children, always comes naturally; what horrors, ruins, hardships, scourges, plagues, conflagrations and wild cruelties are we to expect, if even at this fateful hour, reason, socialism, spiritual leadership and conformity to the spirit do not enter into men's minds?

...Our revolution can and should distribute lands on a grand scale. It can and should create a new and revitalized farm population, but it certainly cannot give the capitalist class joy in work and enterprise. For capitalists, the revolution is only the end of the war: collapse and ruin. The capitalists, their industrial managers and their dealers lose not only their income but also will lose their raw materials and world market. Moreover, the negative component of socialism is there and no power can remove it from the earth: the complete, hourly increasing disinclination of the workers, indeed their psychic inability to continue to hire themselves out under capitalist conditions.

Socialism, then, must be built; it must be set into operation amid the collapse, in conditions of distress, crisis, improvisations. I will now shout from the rooftops how out of the greatest need the greatest virtue must be established, and the new labour corporations out of the fall of capitalism and the pressing needs of the living masses. I will not fail to rebuke the proletarians of industry, who consider themselves the only workers, for their narrow-mindedness, the wild obstinacy, intransigence and crudeness of their intellectual and emotional life, their irresponsibility and incapacity for a positive economic organization and leadership of enterprises. By absolving men of guilt and declaring them creatures of social conditions, one does not make these products of society different than they are, while the new world will be built not with men's causes but with the men themselves.

...[S]ocialism is possible and necessary in every form of economy and technology. It has no use for the industrial and mercantile technology of capitalism nor for the mentality that produced this monstrosity. Because socialism must commence and because the realization of spirit and virtue is never mass-like and normal but rather results only from the self-sacrifice of the few and the new venture of pioneers, socialism must free itself from ruin out of poverty and joy in work. For its sake we must return to rural living and to a unification of industry, craftsmanship and agriculture, to save ourselves and learn justice and community. What Peter Kropotkin taught us about the methods of intensive soil cultivation and unification of intellectual and manual labour in his important and now famous book *Fields, Factories and Workshops* [Selection 34] as well as the new form of credit and monetary cooperative must all be tested now in our most drastic need and with creative pleasure. Necessity demands, voluntarily but under threat of famine, a new start and construction, without which we are lost.

Let me add one last word, the most serious one. If we convert the greatest hardship into the greatest virtue and transform the emergency labour made necessary by the crisis into the provisional beginning of socialism, our humiliation will be credited to our honour. Let us disregard the question as to how our socialist republic, arising out of defeat and ruin, will stand among the victorious nations and the mighty countries presently devoted to capitalism. Let us not beg, let us fear nothing, let us not flinch. Let us act among the nations, like Job activated by his suffering, abandoned by God and the world in order to serve God and the world. Let us construct our economy and the institutions of our society so that we can rejoice in hard work and a worthy life. One thing is certain: when things go well with us in poverty, when our souls are glad, poor and honourable men in all other nations, in all of them will follow our example. Nothing, nothing in the world has such irresistible power of conquest as goodness does. We were politically retarded, were the most arrogant and provoking lackeys; the harm that resulted for us with the inevitability of destiny has incensed us against our masters, moved us to revolution. So at one stroke, namely the blow that struck us, we assumed leadership. We are to lead the way to socialism; how else could we lead than through our example? Chaos is here. New activities and turmoil are on the horizon. Minds are awakening, souls rising to responsibility, hands taking action. May the revolution bring rebirth. May, since we need nothing so much as new, uncorrupted men rising up out of the unknown darkness and depths, may these renewers, purifiers, saviours not be lacking to our nation. Long live the revolution, and may it grow and rise to new levels in hard, wonderful years. May the nations be imbued with the new, creative spirit out of their task, out of the new conditions, out of the primeval, eternal and unconditional depths, the new spirit that really does create new conditions. May the revolution produce religion, a religion of action, life, love, that makes men happy, redeems them and overcomes impossible situations. What does life matter? We will die soon, we all die, we do not live at all. Nothing lives but what we make of ourselves, what we do with ourselves. Creation lives; not the creature, only the creator. Nothing lives but the action of honest hands and the governance of a pure, genuine spirit.

112. Errico Malatesta: An Anarchist Program (1920)

Malatesta returned to Italy in late 1919, where he campaigned ceaselessly for an anarchist social revolution amid the post-war turmoil that engulfed Italy as with the rest of Europe. He edited the daily anarchist paper, Umanità Nova, *which had a circulation of about 50,000, and drafted the following program which was adopted by the Unione Anarchica Italiana at its Congress in Bologna in July 1920. It sets forth a concise statement of Malatesta's mature anarchist position, which remained communist and insurrectionary. The translation by Vernon Richards is taken from* Errico Malatesta: His Life and Ideas *(London: Freedom Press, 1965).*

I. Aims And Objectives

WE BELIEVE THAT MOST OF THE ILLS THAT afflict mankind stem from a bad social organization; and that man could destroy them if he wished and knew how.

Present society is the result of age-long struggles of man against man. Not understanding the advantages that could accrue for all by cooperation and solidarity; seeing in every other man (with the possible exception of those closest to them by blood ties) a competitor and an enemy, each one of them sought to secure for himself, the greatest number of advantages possible without giving a thought to the interests of others.

In such a struggle, obviously the strongest or more fortunate were bound to win, and in one way or another subject and oppress the losers.

So long as man was unable to produce more than was strictly needed to keep alive, the conquerors could do no more than put to flight or massacre their victims, and seize the food they had gathered.

Then when with the discovery of grazing and agriculture a man could produce more than what he needed to live, the conquerors found it more profitable to reduce the conquered to a state of slavery, and put them to work for their advantage.

Later, the conquerors realized that it was more convenient, more profitable and certain to exploit the labour of others by other means: to retain for themselves the exclusive right to the land and working implements, and set free the disinherited who, finding themselves without the means of life, were obliged to have recourse to the landowners and work for them, on their terms.

Thus, step by step through a most complicated series of struggles of every description, of invasions, wars, rebellions, repressions, concessions won by struggle, associations of the oppressed united for defence, and of the conquerors for attack, we have arrived at the present state of society, in which some have inherited the land and all social wealth, while the mass of the people, disinherited in all respects, is exploited and oppressed by a small possessing class.

From all this stems the misery in which most workers live today, and which in turn creates the evils such as ignorance, crime, prostitution, diseases due to malnutrition, mental depression and premature death. From all this arises a special class (government) which, provided with the necessary means of repression, exists to legalize and protect the owning class from the demands of the workers; and then it uses the powers at its disposal to create privileges for itself and to subject, if it can, the owning class itself as well. From this the creation of another privileged class (the clergy), which by a series of fables about the will of God, and about an after-life etc., seeks to persuade the oppressed to accept oppression meekly, and (just as the government does), as well as serving the interest of the owning class, serves its own. From this the creation of an official science which, in all those matters serving the interests of the ruling class, is the negation of true science. From this the patriotic spirit, race hatred, wars and armed peace, sometimes more disastrous than wars themselves. From this the transformation of love into torment or sordid commerce.

From this hatred, more or less disguised, rivalry, suspicion among all men, insecurity and universal fear.

We want to change radically such a state of affairs. And since all these ills have their origin in the struggle between men, in the seeking after well-being through one's own efforts and for oneself and against everybody, we want to make amends, replacing hatred by love, competition by solidarity, the individual search for personal well-being by the fraternal cooperation for the well-being of all, oppression and imposition by liberty, the religious and pseudo-scientific lie by truth.

Therefore:

1. Abolition of private property in land, in raw materials and the instruments of labour, so that no one shall have the means of living by the exploitation of the labour of others, and that everybody, being assured of the means to produce and to live, shall be truly independent and in a position to unite freely among themselves for a common objective and according to their personal sympathies.

2. Abolition of government and of every power which makes the law and imposes it on others: therefore abolition of monarchies, republics, parliaments, armies, police forces, magistratures and any institution whatsoever endowed with coercive powers.

3. Organization of social life by means of free association and federations of producers and consumers, created and modified according to the wishes of their members, guided by science and experience, and free from any kind of imposition which does not spring from natural needs, to which everyone, convinced by a feeling of overriding necessity, voluntarily submits.

4. The means of life, for development and well-being, will be guaranteed to children and all who are prevented from providing for themselves.

5. War on religions and all lies, even if they shelter under the cloak of science. Scientific instruction for all to advanced level.

6. War on rivalries and patriotic prejudices. Abolition of frontiers; brotherhood among all peoples.

7. Reconstruction of the family, as will emerge from the practice of love, freed from every legal tie, from every economic and physical oppression, from every religious prejudice.

This is our ideal.

II. Ways And Means

We have outlined under a number of headings our objectives and the ideal for which we struggle.

But it is not enough to desire something; if one really wants it adequate means must be used to secure it, and these means are not arbitrary, but instead cannot but be conditioned by the ends we aspire to and by the circumstances in which the struggle takes place, for if we ignore the choice of means we would achieve other ends, possibly diametrically opposed to those we aspire to. And this would be the obvious and inevitable consequence of our choice of means. Whoever sets out on the highroad and takes a wrong turn does not go where he intends to go but where the road leads him.

It is therefore necessary to state what are the means which in our opinion lead to our desired ends, and which we propose to adopt.

Our ideal is not one which depends for its success on the individual considered in isolation. The question is of changing the way of life of society as a whole; of establishing among men relationships based on love and solidarity; of achieving the full material, moral and intellectual development not for isolated individuals or members of one class or of a particular political party, but for all mankind—and this is not something that can be imposed by force, but must emerge through the enlightened consciences of each one of us and be achieved with the free consent of all.

Our first task therefore must be to persuade people. We must make people aware of the misfortunes they suffer and of their chances to destroy them. We must awaken sympathy in everybody for the misfortunes of others and a warm desire for the good of all people.

To those who are cold and hungry we will demonstrate how possible and easy it could be to assure to everybody their material needs. To those who are oppressed and despised we shall show how it is possible to live happily in a world of people who are free and equal; to those who are tormented by hatred and bitterness we will point to the road that leads to peace and human warmth that comes through learning to love one's fellow beings.

And when we will have succeeded in arousing the sentiment of rebellion in the minds of men against the avoidable and unjust evils from which we suffer in society today, and in getting them to understand how they are caused and how it depends on human will to rid ourselves of them; and when we will have created a lively and strong desire in men to transform society for the good of all, then those who are convinced, will by their own efforts as well as by the example of those already convinced, unite and want to as well as be able to act for their common ideals.

As we have already pointed out, it would be ridiculous and contrary to our objectives to seek to impose freedom, love among men and the radical development of human faculties, by means of force. One must therefore rely on the free will of others, and all we can do is to provoke the development and the expression of the will of the people. But it would be equally absurd and contrary to our aims to admit that those who do not share our views should prevent us from expressing our will, so long as it does not deny them the same freedom.

Freedom for all, therefore, to propagate and to experiment with their ideas, with no other limitation than that which arises naturally from the equal liberty of everybody.

But to this are opposed—and with brute force—those who benefit from existing privileges and who today dominate and control all social life.

In their hands they have all the means of production; and thus they suppress not only the possibility of free experimentation in new ways of communal living, and the right of workers to live freely by their own efforts, but also the right to life itself; and they oblige whoever is not a boss to have to allow himself to be exploited and oppressed if he does not wish to die of hunger.

They have police forces, a judiciary, and armies created for the express purpose of defending their privileges; and they persecute, imprison and massacre those who would want to abolish those privileges and who claim the means of life and liberty for everyone.

Jealous of their present and immediate interests, corrupted by the spirit of domination, fearful of the future, they, the privileged class, are, generally speaking incapable of a generous gesture; are equally incapable of a wider concept of their interests. And it would be foolish to hope that they should freely give up property and power and adapt themselves to living as equals and with those who today they keep in subjection.

Leaving aside the lessons of history (which demonstrates that never has a privileged class divested itself of all or some of its privileges, and never has a government abandoned its power unless obliged to do so by force or the fear of force), there is enough contemporary evidence to convince anyone that the bourgeoisie and governments intend to use armed force to defend themselves, not only against complete expropriation, but equally against the smallest popular demands, and are always ready to engage in the most atrocious persecutions and the bloodiest massacres.

For those people who want to emancipate themselves, only one course is open: that of opposing force with force.

It follows from what we have said that we have to work to awaken in the oppressed the conscious desire for a radical social transformation, and to persuade them that by uniting they have the strength to win; we must propagate our ideal and prepare the required material and moral forces to overcome those of the enemy, and to organize the new society; and when we will have the strength needed we must, by taking advantage of favourable circumstances as they arise, or which we can ourselves create, make the social revolution, using force to destroy the government and to expropriate the owners of wealth, and by putting in common the means of life and production, and by preventing the setting up of new governments which would impose their will and hamper the reorganization of society by the people themselves.

All this is however less simple than it might appear at first sight. We have to deal with people as they are in society today, in the most miserable moral and material condition; and we would be deluding ourselves in thinking that propaganda is enough to raise them to that level of intellectual development which is needed to put our ideas into effect.

Between man and his social environment there is a reciprocal action. Men make society what it is and society makes men what they are, and the result is therefore a kind of vicious circle. To transform society men must be changed, and to transform men, society must be changed.

Poverty brutalizes man, and to abolish poverty men must have a social conscience and determination. Slavery teaches men to be slaves, and to free oneself from slavery there is a need for men who aspire to liberty. Ignorance has the effect of making men unaware of the causes of their misfortunes as well as the means of overcoming them, and to do away with ignorance people must have the time and the means to educate themselves.

Governments accustom people to submit to the Law and to believe that Law is essential to society; and to abolish government men must be convinced of the uselessness and the harmfulness of government.

How does one escape from this vicious circle?

Fortunately existing society has not been created by the inspired will of a dominating class, which has succeeded in reducing all its subjects to passive and unconscious instruments of its interests. It is the result of a thousand internecine struggles, of a thousand human and natural factors acting indifferently, without directive criteria; and thus there are no clear-cut divisions either between individuals or between classes.

Innumerable are the variations in material conditions; innumerable are the degrees of moral and intellectual development; and not always—we would almost say very rarely, does the place of any individual in society correspond with his abilities and his aspirations. Very often individuals accustomed to conditions of comfort fall on hard times and others, through exceptionally favourable circumstances, succeed in raising themselves above the conditions into which they were born. A large proportion of the working class has already succeeded either in emerging from a state of abject poverty, or was never in such a situation; no worker to speak of finds himself in a state of complete social unawareness, of complete acquiescence to the conditions imposed on him by the bosses. And the same institutions, such as have been produced by history, contain organic contradictions and are like the germs of death, which as they develop result in the dissolution of institutions and the need for transformation.

From this the possibility of progress—but not the possibility of bringing all men to the necessary level to want, and to achieve, anarchy, by means of propaganda, without a previous gradual transformation of the environment.

Progress must advance contemporaneously and along parallel lines between men and their environment. We must take advantage of all the means, all the possibilities and the opportunities that the present environment allows us to act on our fellow men and to develop their consciences and their demands; we must use all advance in human consciences to induce them to claim and to impose those major social transformations which are possible and which effectively serve to open the way to further advances later.

We must not wait to achieve anarchy, in the meantime limiting ourselves to simple propaganda. Were we to do so we would soon exhaust our field of action; that is, we would have converted all those who in the existing environment are susceptible to understand and accept our ideas, and our subsequent propaganda would fall on sterile ground; or if environmental transformations brought out new popular groupings capable of receiving new ideas, this would happen without our participation, and thus would prejudice our ideas.

We must seek to get all the people, or different sections of the people, to make demands, and impose itself and take for itself all the improvements and freedoms that it desires as and when it reaches the state of wanting them, and the power to demand them; and in always propagating all aspects of our program, and always struggling for its complete realization, we must push the people to want always more and to increase its pressures, until it has achieved complete emancipation.

III. The Economic Struggle

The oppression which today impinges most directly on the workers and which is the main cause of the moral and material frustrations under which they labour, is economic oppression, that is the exploitation to which bosses and business men subject them, thanks to their monopoly of all the most important means of production and distribution.

To destroy radically this oppression without any danger of it re-emerging, all people must be convinced of their right to the means of production, and be prepared to exercise this basic right by expropriating the land owners, the industrialists and financiers, and putting all social wealth at the disposal of the people.

But can this expropriation be put into effect today? Can we today pass directly, without intermediate steps, from the hell in which the workers now find themselves to the paradise of common property?

Facts demonstrate what the workers are capable of today.

Our task is the moral and material preparation of the people for this essential expropriation; and to attempt it again and again, every time a revolutionary upheaval offers us the chance to, until the final triumph. But in what way can we prepare the people? In what way must one prepare the conditions which make possible not only the material fact of expropriation, but the utilization to everybody's advantage of the common wealth?

We have already said that spoken and written propaganda alone cannot win over to our ideas the mass of the people. A practical education is needed, which must be alternately cause and effect in a gradual transformation of the environment. Parallel with the workers developing a sense of rebellion against the injustices and useless sufferings of which they are the victims, and the desire to better their conditions, they must be united and mutually dependent in the struggle to achieve their demands.

And we as anarchists and workers, must incite and encourage them to struggle, and join them in their struggle.

But are these improvements possible in a capitalist regime? Are they useful from the point of view of a future complete emancipation of the workers?

Whatever may be the practical results of the struggle for immediate gains, the greatest value lies in the struggle itself. For thereby workers learn that the bosses interests are opposed to theirs and that they cannot improve their conditions, and much less emancipate themselves, except by uniting and becoming stronger than the bosses. If they succeed in getting what they demand, they will be better off: they will earn more, work fewer hours and will have more time and energy to reflect on the things that matter to them, and will immediately make greater demands and have greater needs. If they do not succeed they will be led to study the causes of their failure and recognize the need for closer unity and greater activity and they will in the end understand that to make their victory secure and definitive, it is necessary to destroy capitalism. The revolutionary cause, the cause of the moral elevation and emancipation of the workers must benefit by the fact that workers unite and struggle for their interests.

But, once again, can the workers succeed in really improving their conditions in the present state of society?

This depends on the confluence of a great number of circumstances.

In spite of what some say, there exists no natural law (law of wages) which determines what part of a worker's labour should go to him; or if one wants to formulate a law, it could not be but this: wages cannot normally be less than what is needed to maintain life, nor can they normally rise such that no profit margin is left to the boss.

It is clear that in the first case workers would die, and therefore would stop drawing any wages, and in the second the bosses would stop employing labour and so would pay no more wages. But between these two impossible extremes there is an infinite scale of degrees ranging from the miserable conditions of many land workers to the almost respectable conditions of skilled workers in the large cities.

Wages, hours and other conditions of employment are the result of the struggle between bosses and workers. The former try to give the workers as little as possible and get them to work themselves to the bone; the latter try, or should try to work as little, and earn as much, as possible. Where workers accept any conditions, or even being discontented, do not know how to put up effective resistance to the bosses demands, they are soon reduced to bestial conditions of life. Where, instead, they have ideas as to how human beings should live and know how to join forces, and through refusal to work or the latent and open threat of rebellion, to win the bosses respect, in such cases, they are treated in a relatively decent way. One can therefore say that within certain limits, the wages he gets are what the worker (not as an individual, of course, but as a class) demands.

Through struggle, by resistance against the bosses, therefore, workers can up to a certain point, prevent a worsening of their conditions as well as obtaining real improvement. And the history of the workers' movement has already demonstrated this truth.

One must not however exaggerate the importance of this struggle between workers and bosses conducted exclusively in the economic field. Bosses can give in, and often they do in face of forcefully expressed demands so long as the demands are not too great; but if workers were to make demands (and it is imperative that they should) which would absorb all the bosses profits and be in effect an indirect form of expropriation, it is certain that the bosses would appeal to the government and would seek to use force to oblige the workers to remain in their state of wage slavery.

And even before, long before workers can expect to receive the full product of their labour, the economic struggle becomes impotent as a means of producing the improvements in living standards.

Workers produce everything and without them life would be impossible; therefore it would seem that by refusing to work they could demand whatever they wanted. But the union of all workers, even in one particular trade, and in one country is difficult to achieve, and opposing the union of workers are the bosses organizations. Workers live from day to day, and if they do not work they soon find themselves without food; whereas the bosses, because they have money, have access to all the goods in stock and can therefore sit back and wait until hunger reduces their employees to a more amenable frame of mind. The invention or the introduction of new machinery makes workers redundant and adds to the large army of unemployed, who are driven by hunger to sell their labour at any price. Immigration immediately creates problems in the countries where better working conditions exist, for the hordes of hungry workers, willy nilly, offer the bosses an opportunity to depress wages all round. And all these facts, which necessarily derive from the capitalist system, conspire in counteracting and often destroying advances made in working class consciousness and solidarity. And in every case the overriding fact remains that production under capitalism is organized by each capitalist for his personal profit and not, as would be natural, to satisfy the needs of the workers in the best possible way. Hence the chaos, the waste of human effort, the organized scarcity of goods, useless and harmful occupations, unemployment, abandoned land, under-use of plant and so on, all evils which cannot be avoided except by depriving the capitalists of the means of production and, it follows, the organization of production.

Soon then, those workers who want to free themselves, or even only to effectively improve their conditions, will be faced with the need to defend themselves from the government, with the need to attack the government, which by legalizing the right to property and protecting it with brute force, constitutes a barrier to human progress, which must be beaten down with force if one does not wish to remain indefinitely under present conditions or even worse.

From the economic struggle one must pass to the political struggle, that is to the struggle against government; and instead of opposing the capitalist millions with the workers' few pennies scraped together with difficulty, one must oppose the rifles and guns which defend property with the more effective means that the people will be able to find to defeat force by force.

IV. The Political Struggle

By the political struggle we mean the struggle against government. Government is the *ensemble* of all those individuals who hold the reins of power, however acquired, to make the law and to impose it on the governed, that is the public.

Government is the consequence of the spirit of domination and violence with which some men have imposed themselves on others, and is at the same time the creature as well as the creator of privilege and its natural defender.

It is wrongly said that today government performs the function of defender of capitalism but that once capitalism is abolished it would become the representative and administrator of the general interest. In the first place capitalism will not be destroyed until the workers, having rid themselves of government, take possession of all social wealth and themselves organize production and consumption in the interests of everybody without waiting for the initiative to come from government which, however willing to comply, would be incapable of doing so.

But there is a further question: if capitalism were to be destroyed and a government were to be left in office, the government, through the concession of all kinds of privileges, would create capitalism anew for, being unable to please everybody, it would need an economically powerful class to support it in return for the legal and material protection it would receive.

Consequently privilege cannot be abolished and freedom and equality established firmly and definitely without abolishing government—not this or that government but the very institution of government.

As in all questions of general interest, and especially this one, the consent of the people as a whole is needed, and therefore we must strain every nerve to persuade the people that government is useless as well as harmful, and that we can live better lives without government.

But, as we have repeated more than once, propaganda alone is impotent to convince everybody—and if we were to want to limit ourselves to preaching against government, and in the meantime waiting supinely for the day when the public will be convinced of the possibility and value of radically destroying every kind of government, then that day would never come.

While preaching against every kind of government, and demanding complete freedom, we must support all struggles for partial freedom, because we are convinced that one learns through struggle, and that once one begins to enjoy a little freedom one ends by wanting it all. We must always be with the people, and when we do not succeed in getting them to demand a lot we must still seek to get them to want something; and we must make every effort to get them to understand that however much or little they may demand should be obtained by their own efforts and that they should despise and detest whoever is part of, or aspires to, government.

Since government today has the power, through the legal system, to regulate daily life and to broaden or restrict the liberty of the citizen, and because we are still unable to tear this power from its grasp, we must seek to reduce its power and oblige governments to use it in the least harmful ways possible. But this we must do always remaining outside, and against, government, putting pressure on it through agitation in the streets, by threatening to take by force what we demand. Never must we accept any kind of legislative position, be it national or local, for in so doing we will neutralize the effectiveness of our activity as well as betraying the future of our cause.

The struggle against government, in the last analysis, is physical, material.

Governments make the law. They must therefore dispose of the material forces (police and army) to impose the law, for otherwise only those who wanted to would obey it, and it would no longer be the law, but a simple series of suggestions which all would be free to accept or reject. Governments have this power, however, and use it through the law, to strengthen their power, as well as to serve the interests of the ruling classes, by oppressing and exploiting the workers.

The only limit to the oppression of government is the power with which the people show themselves capable of opposing it. Conflict may be open or latent; but it always exists since the government does not pay attention to discontent and popular resistance except when it is faced with the danger of insurrection.

When the people meekly submit to the law, or their protests are feeble and confined to words, the government studies its own interests and ignores the needs of the people; when the protests are lively, insistent, threatening, the government, depending on whether it is more or less understanding, gives way or resorts to repression. But one always comes back to insurrection, for if the government does not give way, the people will end by rebelling; and if the government does give way, then the people gain confidence in themselves and make ever increasing demands, until such time as the incompatibility between freedom and authority becomes clear and the violent struggle is engaged.

It is therefore necessary to be prepared, morally and materially, so that when this does happen the people will emerge victorious.

A successful insurrection is the most potent factor in the emancipation of the people, for once the yoke has been shaken off, the people are free to provide themselves with those institutions which they think best, and the time lag between passing the law and the degree of civilization which the mass of the population has attained, is breached in one leap. The insurrection determines the revolution, that is, the speedy emergence of the latent forces built up during the "evolutionary" period.

Everything depends on what the people are capable of wanting.

In past insurrections, unaware of the real reasons for their misfortunes, they have always wanted very little, and have obtained very little.

What will they want in the next insurrection?

The answer, in part, depends on our propaganda and what efforts we put into it.

We shall have to push the people to expropriate the bosses and put all goods in common and organize their daily lives themselves, through freely constituted associations, without waiting for orders from outside and refusing to nominate or recognize any government or constituted body in whatever guise (constituent, dictatorship, etc.) even in a provisional capacity, which ascribes to itself the right to lay down the law and impose with force its will on others.

And if the mass of the population will not respond to our appeal we must—in the name of the right we have to be free even if others wish to remain slaves and because of the force of example—put into effect as many of our ideas as we can, refuse to recognize the new government and keep alive resistance and seek that those localities where our ideas are received with sympathy should constitute themselves into anarchist communities, rejecting all governmental interference and establishing free agreements with other communities which want to live their own lives.

We shall have to, above all, oppose with every means the re-establishment of the police and the armed forces, and use any opportunity to incite workers in non-anarchist localities to take advantage of the absence of repressive forces to implement the most far reaching demands that we can induce them to make.

And however things may go, to continue the struggle against the possessing class and the rulers without respite, having always in mind the complete economic, political and moral emancipation of all mankind.

V. Conclusion

What we want, therefore, is the complete destruction of the domination and exploitation of man by man; we want men united as brothers by a conscious and desired solidarity, all cooperating voluntarily for the well-being of all; we want society to be constituted for the purpose of supplying everybody with the means for achieving the maximum well-being, the maximum possible moral and spiritual development; we want bread, freedom, love, and science for everybody.

And in order to achieve these all important ends, it is necessary in our opinion that the means of production should be at the disposal of everybody and that no man, or groups of men, should be in a position to oblige others to submit to their will or to exercise their influence other than through the power of reason and by example.

Therefore: expropriation of landowners and capitalists for the benefit of all; and abolition of government.

And while waiting for the day when this can be achieved: the propagation of our ideas; unceasing struggle, violent or non-violent depending on the circumstances, against government and against the boss class to conquer as much freedom and well-being as we can for the benefit of everybody.

113. Luigi Fabbri: Fascism: The Preventive Counter-Revolution (1921)

The anarchists and revolutionary syndicalists in Italy tried to spur the Italian workers on to revolution, taking a leading role in the factory occupations that spread across Italy in 1920, which they hoped would mark the beginning of a general expropriation and the social revolution. The more moderate socialist parties effected a compromise, and then Mussolini and the Fascists began their counter-revolution in earnest, with the support of the bourgeoisie and the government. Malatesta, the anarcho-syndicalist, Amando Borghi (1882-1968), and many other anarchists were arrested in October 1920, within weeks of the ending of the factory occupations. Luigi Fabbri (1877-1935) was a friend of Malatesta, co-editor of Umanità Nova, *and a notable anarchist propagandist. He was one of the first to provide an anarchist analysis of fascism in his 1921 publication,* Fascism: The Preventive Counter-Revolution *(reprint: Pistoia: Licinio Capelli, 1975). The following excerpts have been translated by Paul Sharkey.*

THE FASCIST PHENOMENON IS NOT peculiar to Italy. It has surfaced in even more serious form in Spain and has raised its head in Germany, Hungary, the Americas and elsewhere. Nor were persecution and unlawful reaction mounted by private citizens unknown prior to the World War. In certain respects, they had precedents in the pogroms in Russia and the lynchings in the United States. What is more, the United States has always had a sort of private police in the service of the capitalists, acting in cahoots with the official police, but independently of government, in troubled times and during strikes...

Fascism, guerrilla warfare between fascists and socialists—or, to be more accurate, between the bourgeoisie and the proletariat—is nothing but the natural unleashing and material consequence of the class hostilities honed during the [first world] war and aggravated by a number of secondary circumstances and factors which only appear—and then only briefly—to have distorted its character, which triumphs and comes to the fore when least expected...

With the war, there emerged the greatest proletarian unanimity against the ruling class and this led to an extraordinary deepening of the gulf between the classes, with the one regarding the other as its declared enemy. And in particular, the ruling class, seeing its power threatened, lost its head. What disturbed it most, perhaps, was the feeling that it could not defend itself except through recourse to violence and civil war, which, in theory and through its laws, it had always condemned: it was undermining the very foundations and principles upon which the bourgeoisie had been constructing its institutions for close to a century.

The proletarian menace welded the ruling class, of which fascism today constitutes a sort of militia and rallying point, into a bloc. And the ruling class is not comprised solely of the bourgeoisie proper: it comprises and is made up also of the most backward-looking strata, all of the castes that eke out a parasitic existence under the aegis of the state or who man its ramparts; those who supply the government and the protected industries, the police (grown to mammoth proportions these days), the upper bureaucracy and judiciary are—all of them—more or less fascistic in outlook. Add to these the landowning bourgeoisie, which is backward-looking by nature and tradition, and always has its back to the wall of peasant demands, which in the long run it could not withstand except by renouncing all profit, which is to say the very privilege that property confers...

The fascists proper, the ones with the badges on their lapels, are relatively few in number but derive their strength from the closed ranks, direct and indirect aid and poorly concealed complicity of all of the various conservative forces in society...

It is primarily as the organization and agent of the violent armed defence of the ruling class against the proletariat, which, to their mind, has become unduly demanding, united and intrusive, that fascism represents a continuation of the war.

It would be too simplistic to say that the world war was a sort of international war on the proletariat and against revolution. There were other equally important factors and motives behind the war; but it is a fact that one of the things that triggered the conflict in Europe, one of the factors why no ruling class in any country—not in France, not in Germany, not in Russia, not in Austria, not in England, not in Italy—did what could have been...done to avert war—was precisely the hope that each of them had of being spared revolution, decapitating a working class that had become overly strong, defusing popular resistance through blood-letting on a vast scale, consolidating crowned heads and especially the rule of the banking and industrial plutocracy.

Many have, as the saying goes, paid the price for this: once the floodgates were opened, the surging currents swept away many of the crowned heads of Germany, Russia, Austria, etc., but everybody played his hand in the hope of emerging as the winner; which is to say, by defeating not just the enemy on the other side of the border, but also the enemy within, the organized proletariat, socialism and revolution…

The solid strength of fascism is the sort of strength that corresponds to a broad coalescence of interests—all the interests, ambitions and powers under threat from revolution, socialism and the proletariat. In a sense it was just what the conservatives needed precisely because…the classic forms of reaction were inadequate or damaging. On the one hand, the state had to be allowed to keep up the appearances of legality and liberalism, but at the same time, it had to be paralyzed: so that, outside the state, there would be a free hand to attack the proletariat on every front, even the most lawful and moderate, by any means necessary, including the most violent, heedless of democratic, legal or sentimental concerns or prejudices. In terms of conservatism, fascism—further abetted (and this has perhaps been its greatest stroke of luck), not merely by circumstances but by the very mistakes of the workers' and socialistic parties and organizations—has provided an outstanding answer to this need on the part of the bourgeoisie…

The much preached and yearned for revolution had failed to arrive, in spite of all the favourable openings: and in a sense it could be argued that it was not wanted. But the fact that it had hovered like a threat for nearly two years was enough to trigger counter-revolution. Thus there was a counter-revolution without there ever having been a revolution, a real preventive counter-revolution proper, of which fascism has been the most active and impressive factor…

The bourgeoisie which had not managed to weaken the proletariat through the indirect weapon of war—and had instead achieved the opposite effect, due to peculiarities of the Italian situation—renewed its pledge to succeed this time through the three-pronged concerted activity of illegal fascist violence, lawful government repression and economic pressures deriving from unemployment, partly inevitable but also in part deliberately contrived as a means of tightening the noose on the workers…

Had [the proletariat] resisted the first fascist attacks promptly with the requisite vigour and violence and the necessary commitment, fascism would have been still born. Instead, once the proletarian opted instead to appeal passively to the law, even that weak trench was demolished by the enemy from many sides, since—given that the socialists proved to be the weaker—the police and security forces no longer had any scruples about showing themselves allied with the fascists in the light of day; and the concerted onslaught by illegal and lawful forces, to which the judiciary would shortly be added, began.

...Initially reluctant, capitalism and the government—those in government, by which is meant, if not this or that minister personally then definitely the higher civil service, the prefects, the chiefs of police, etc.—realized that fascism was a useful weapon and soon ensured that it was given every assistance in terms of funding and arms, turning a blind eye to its breaches of the law and, where necessary, covering its back through intervention by armed forces which, on the pretext of restoring order, would rush to the aid of the fascists wherever the latter were beginning to take a beating instead of doling one out.

...[I]t would be naïvety itself for revolutionaries to ask capitalism and the state to target fascism with repressive measures that might otherwise produce further harmful effects. Moreover, any repression that goes beyond legitimate self-defence, any government backlash based upon jails and handcuffs, always has a criminal impact of its own. And revolutionaries cannot and should not be calling for arrests and convictions, handcuffs and jail terms.

In reality, revolutionaries, socialists and workers will see an end to government and capitalist connivance with fascism only when they summon up their own capacity for resistance, not sporadically and fitfully, not more or less as individuals or groups or in any unduly localized way, but across the board. When it comes to demanding a right, there is only one thing that the workers could ask for: that they be given equal treatment, and be left free to defend themselves every time that they are attacked; and defend themselves using the same resources as the fascists, to wit, their own organizations, their own meetings, their own flags, their own beliefs, their own lives. They would be entitled to ask that the police and the courts not reduce them to the condition of somebody whose arms are tied while others give him a savage beating. Or let the capitalist state cast aside all hypocrisy and stop playing two parts in the farce and take direct responsibility for the repression of the workers.

But these are pointless demands, unless backed by real force, both moral and material; and can only be pressed by way of a token demonstration of one's rights and for propaganda purposes. In point of fact, Italian jails are filled with workers and the heaviest sentences rain down on workers who during clashes made the mistake of using violence to defend themselves from the fascists...

Given the war, given that the only real preventive remedy against it—revolution—was not forthcoming, fascism or something of the sort was inevitable. The fascists, and those of their leaders who honestly believe that they are in charge of the movement, are in fact merely agents of a phenomenon that is stronger than them and by which they are dragged along.

...[T]here is no movement less idealistic and more preoccupied with material success than fascism; it is obsessed by its own material interests and the material interests of the ruling class. Fascism has the entire working class in its sights with its most spectacular acts of violence and vandalism, no matter who may argue the opposite; and the working class is being targeted precisely because it poses a threat to capitalist profits and trespasses against the interests of shopkeepers and employers in that, to date, it has represented an erosion or infringement of proprietary rights. Fascism is rather unmoved by anything else...From the word go, what was under attack was not Bolshevism but the proletariat as a whole...

Activist fascism served, but also, exploited the bourgeoisie's fear of Bolshevism, but it was also primarily the instrument and creature of capitalism's salvation from the proletariat...In fact, in every locality, in every region, the fascists' greatest violence was not reserved for their assault upon a certain political faction, the very one that they were arguing was a menace to the country, to the fatherland, etc.,...according to the fascists, Italy and the proletariat faced a different enemy in every district: the very party or organization that enjoyed the widest support and largest membership among the proletariat in that particular location...

Their destructive frenzy made no distinction between these various bodies: leagues or camere del lavoro, placement bureaux or federations, libraries or newspapers, consumer cooperatives or production cooperatives, workers' mutual societies or leisure circles, cafes, inns or private homes. Just as long as they belonged to the workers.

In all of these conflicts and countless attacks countless proletarians have lost their lives; and those wrapped in funeral shrouds and laid to rest in the mute earth have also been drawn from every persuasion and outlook, Catholics as well as anarchists, republicans as well as socialists, communists as well as reformists, or non-partisan workers. The only reason why they were targeted by murderous revolvers was because they were workers, toilers. What more telling evidence could there be that the fascists' guerrilla war is not waged against this or that specific party but against the working class as a class? The aim is to dismantle its strongholds everywhere, the focus of the proletariat's resistance to capitalism; and the intention is to cut down anyone who successfully defends the workers and earns their trust, no matter what colours they may fly....

Anybody making any serious efforts to defend himself and use violence in legitimate self-defence soon found that the security forces would wade in on the side of the fascists and against the victims. That which, in the fascists' case, has been endorsed, abetted, tolerated or benevolently contained, is violently, savagely repressed in the case of subversives...

In weighing up the violence of the two sides involved in this guerrilla warfare, the greatest mistake would be to consider only the bloody encounters that have claimed the odd victim. Although the latter may be many, they represent exceptions to the rule. The worst violence, the type that leaves the worst legacy of resentment behind it, is the day to day sort that kills, not one or two or three people, but rather threatens an entire class, the use of the cudgel offending the human dignity which many cherish more than life itself, destroying through its destruction of a workers' body or cooperative the economic standing or well-being of an entire group, trampling the most basic elements of everybody's freedom, banishing all security and striking terror, not in a few more or less responsible figures, but in whole populations, in members of the working class or people who refuse to join the Fascio, even should these people be politically inactive, indifferent or naïve. And this sort of violence, with its less lethal, less bloody aftermath, surfaces daily just about everywhere and is almost exclusively the handiwork of the fascists. In certain districts it has become so run-of-the-mill that it is no longer the subject of complaint or comment and is not even mentioned by the subversive press.

If we add such violence to the other sort, to the more murderous violence upon which the press is more inclined to concentrate, then any comparison between fascist violence and worker violence becomes impossible...

In its program fascism sets out its aspiration to govern Italy, to install *a strong sovereign state* to revive and protect the social function of *private ownership*. So it is a program of struggle not just against revolution but also against socialism and against the proletariat which strives for equality and freedom, liberation from wage slavery and an end to the exploitation of its labour, by any route...

Whether or not this program brings success to this party which owes its origins and name to fascism, out and out fascism as we know it today—which consists of systematically destroying and smashing the proletariat's political and economic organizations by one means or another, especially by violent, bullying means—the fascism which is peculiarly dear to the ruling classes, which feeds upon their aid and protection, the fascism upon which the industrialists and landowners depend to put pressure on the workers and peasants to accept lower wages and additional work, the fascism that is pretty much an umbrella for the parasitical and militaristic classes with their dreams of states of siege and military dictatorships, in short, the fascism of cudgel, revolver and arson, the one that hopes to surmount the crisis generated by the war through a preventive counter-revolution, that fascism is not going to walk away from violence and will carry on being what it is, unless it is defeated by a greater force. It has become an organism and, as such, cannot countenance suicide, no matter the relative logicality of its situation and the pointlessness of its actions in overall political and social terms…

Democracy has been chasing its shadow for over a hundred years and devised all sorts of shapes for it; but, no matter what the form, the state has remained the champion of the interests of one class against another, the supporter and ally of the ruling class against the oppressed classes. Fascism in Italy has been an obvious instance of this, laying the democratic view of the state to rest once and for all…

When a faction breaches the state's laws, embraces violence as a method and employs it according to its whims, over and above and in defiance of the law, it is in a state of rebellion. The state has the wherewithal to steer it back to normality; the violent, armed and contemptuous violence that it merits, that drowns it in blood, if need be. But in order to do that it needs to have an interest in so doing and such a terrible undertaking must hold out the promise of a reward that outweighs the expenditure. Now, insofar as fascism usurps the state and relegates it to a secondary position, the state might be induced to get rid of it; but other, stronger interests and dark dangers will deter it from taking on a force which, while it may well be a competitor and disrespectful, is yet not its enemy, not an opponent of its institutions but rather seeks to reinforce them (albeit by means that run the risk of compromising them) and, above all, champions the same social interests, the same class privileges over which the state itself mounts guard. Fascism is an ally of the state, an irksome, demanding, inconvenient, embarrassing and insubordinate ally—all of these things—but an ally nonetheless. How could the state give serious thought to destroying it?

…It may be that fascism, albeit moderating certain of its most irksome features which are offensive to humane feelings, may survive and consolidate as an instrument for violent compulsion, some sword of Damocles to dangle constantly over the heads of the working classes, so that the latter can never be fully at ease anywhere, even within the parameters of the law, and forever fearful of its rights being violated by some unforeseen and arbitrary violence.

In which case, for the working class and for all those who have embraced its cause, for all who see the proletariat's liberation from wage slavery as a pre-requisite to greater justice, greater well-being and greater freedom for all, the only option is to kill off fascism, to make its eradication a target, without retreating into some Moslem-like patience, without trusting fatalistically to fate, to natural evolution, the process of decomposition, the laws of economics and other kindred expressions through which men disguise their laziness and their reluctance to make the requisite effort of will.

Killing off fascism, of course, is not an excuse for slaughtering fascist personnel. Often the violence deployed against the latter merely feeds it rather than killing it off. That those attacked by the fascists at specific times and in specific places should defend themselves however they can and may is only natural and unavoidable...However, embarking upon a material struggle against fascism as an organism in itself, seeing no other enemy but this, would be a dismal affair: it would be like stripping the branches from a poisonous tree while leaving the trunk intact; like striking off some tentacles instead of striking at the octopus's head. It may be possible to inflict a few partial defeats on fascism this way and to claim fascist lives; but it will only serve to make the fight all the more bitter and might well bolster fascism and help to make it an even sturdier organism.

The fight against fascism can only be waged effectively if it is struck through the political and economic institutions of which it is an outgrowth and from which it draws sustenance. Moreover, revolutionaries aiming to bring down capitalism and the state, if they were to allow themselves to be drawn out by fascism like a lightning bolt diverted by the lightning rod, and to devote all of their efforts and exhaust themselves in the fight against fascism alone, would be playing into the hands of the very institutions that they would like to see demolished. Using the fascists as a bogeyman, the capitalistic state would not only succeed in protecting itself and living a easier life, but would also succeed in persuading a segment of the proletariat to work in co-operation with it and to take its side. Even today, while on the one hand capitalism uses fascism to blackmail the state, the state itself uses fascism to blackmail the proletariat, sending out the message: "Give up on your dreams of political and economic expropriation and order your leaders to cooperate with me in strengthening the institutions of state, or I will stand by as you are beaten and killed by the fascists and, if they are not up to the task, I will lend them a helping hand myself!"

As long as the proletariat is accustomed to viewing fascism as its special enemy, against whom it has a special fight, the government's blackmail ploy can always succeed;

and for as long as that blackmail does its job, the government has an interest in the continued survival of fascism (which is more or less disposed to follow its instructions)...

The bourgeoisie has learnt how to put this weapon to use; and if the proletariat fails to destroy its will to do so, by means of a practical demonstration that it knows how to dash it from bourgeois hands, the latter may—even if they set it aside for the moment—pick it up again at the first opportunity.

114. The IWA: Declaration of the Principles of Revolutionary Syndicalism (1922)

After the First World War, various anarcho-syndicalist and revolutionary syndicalist organizations regrouped, forming a new incarnation of the International Workers' Association (IWA) at a congress in Berlin in 1922, with delegations representing two million workers from 15 countries in Europe and Latin America. Distancing themselves from the Marxist-Leninists who were then in the process of creating a Moscow dominated Communist International, the Congress openly declared itself in favour of libertarian communism and opposed to all forms of state power, including the so-called "Dictatorship of the Proletariat" in Russia.

I. REVOLUTIONARY SYNDICALISM, BASING itself on the class struggle, aims for the union of all manual and intellectual workers in combative economic organizations, to prepare for and achieve their liberation from the double yoke of capital and the state. Its goal is the reorganization of all social life on the basis of libertarian communism via the collective revolutionary action of the working classes themselves. Since only the economic organizations of the proletariat are capable of achieving this objective, revolutionary syndicalism addresses itself to workers in their capacity as producers and creators of social wealth, in opposition to the modern labour parties, which it declares are incapable of the economic reorganization of society.

II. Revolutionary syndicalism is the staunch enemy of all social and economic monopoly, and aims at its abolition by the establishment of economic communes and administrative organs run by the workers in the fields and factories, forming a system of free councils without subordination to any authority or political party. As an alternative to the politics of states and parties, it posits the economic reorganization of production, replacing the rule of man over man with the simple administration of things. Consequently, its goal is not the conquest of political power, but the abolition of all state functions in the life of society. It considers that along with the disappearance of a property owning caste, must come the disappearance of a central ruling caste; and that no form of statism, even the so-called "Dictatorship of the Proletariat," can ever be an instrument for human liberation, but that on the contrary, it will always be the creator of new monopolies and new privileges.

III. Revolutionary syndicalism has a two-fold function: to carry on the day-to-day revolutionary struggle for the economic, social and intellectual advancement of the working class within the limits of present-day society, and to educate the masses so that they will be ready to independently manage the processes of production and distribution when the time comes to take possession of all the elements of social life. It does not accept the idea that the organization of a social system based exclusively on the producing class can be ordered by simple governmental decrees and maintains that it can only be obtained through the common action of all manual and intellectual workers, in every branch of industry, by the assumption of the administration of every individual operation by the producers themselves, such that every group, factory or branch of industry is an autonomous member of the universal economic organism that systematically shapes the entire production and general distribution processes on the basis of mutual accords and in the interests of the general community.

IV. Revolutionary syndicalism is opposed to all centralist endeavours and organizations, borrowed from the state and the church, which systematically stifle the spirit of initiative and independent thought. Centralism is an artificial organization, from the top down, that leaves in the hands of the few the affairs of the whole community. Through this process, the individual becomes a puppet guided and controlled from above. The good of society is subordinated to the interests of the few, variety is replaced by uniformity, personal responsibility is replaced by rigid discipline, and education is replaced by training. Consequently, revolutionary syndicalism is founded upon a federalist union, that is, upon an organization structured from the bottom up, a voluntary federation of all forces based on mutual interests and shared convictions.

V. Revolutionary syndicalism rejects all parliamentary activity and all collaboration with legislative bodies. Not even the freest voting system can bring about the disappearance of the clear contradictions at the core of present-day society; the whole parliamentary system has as its only goal to lend an air of legality to the reign of falsehood and social injustice, and to induce the slaves to put the imprimatur of the law upon their own slavery.

VI. Revolutionary syndicalism rejects all arbitrarily created political and national frontiers, and regards nationalism as merely the religion of the modern state, behind which is concealed the material interests of the propertied classes. It recognizes only natural regional differences, and demands the right of every minority to regulate its own affairs by mutual agreement with all the other economic, regional or national associations.

VII. For the identical reason, revolutionary syndicalism fights against militarism in all of its forms and considers anti-militarist propaganda one of its most important tasks in the struggle against the existing system. In furtherance of that goal, above all, are the refusal to participate in state military service, and the organized refusal of the workers to produce military equipment.

VIII. Revolutionary syndicalism stands on the footing of direct action and supports all struggles of the people that are not in contradiction to its goal of abolishing economic monopolies and state despotism. It endorses strikes, boycotts, sabotage, and so on, as its weapons. Direct action reaches its highest expression in the social general strike, which syndicalists at the same time envisage as the prelude to the social revolution.

IX. While syndicalists are opposed to all organized violence in the hands of any revolutionary government, they do not fail to realize that the decisive struggles between the capitalism of today and the free communism of tomorrow will not be without conflict. Consequently, they recognize violence as a means of defence against the violent methods of the ruling classes during the struggle for the possession of the factories and the fields by the revolutionary people. Just as the expropriation of the factories and the fields in practice can only be carried out and channelled along the path of social reorganization by the workers' revolutionary economic organizations, so must also the defence of the revolution be the task of the masses themselves and their economic organizations, and not of a particular military body, or any other organization, outside of the economic associations.

X. Only in the revolutionary economic organizations of the working class is found the means of its liberation, and the creative energy for the reconstruction of society on the path of libertarian communism. (Further reading: Wayne Thorpe, *"The Workers Themselves": Revolutionary Syndicalism and International Labour, 1913-1923*, Dordrecht: Kluwer, 1989).

115. The Platform and its Critics (1926-27)

The Organizational Platform of the Libertarian Communists *was a document published in 1926 by a group of exiled Russian anarchists, including Nestor Makhno (Selection 85), Peter Arshinov (Selection 86), and Ida Mett, author of* The Kronstadt Uprising *(Montreal: Black Rose, 1971; originally published 1938). The stated purpose of the Platform was to draw the lessons from the failure of anarchism in the Russian Revolution, and to provide an organi-*

zational basis for unity in the anarchist movement. The sections of the Platform reproduced below dealing with military defence and organization generated the most controversy. The text is taken from G. P. Maximoff [Maksimov], Constructive Anarchism *(Sydney: Monty Miller Press, 1988). A broader selection of responses, including replies from Arshinov and Makhno, can be found at the Nestor Makhno Archive: www.nestormakhno.info.*

IN THE SOCIAL REVOLUTION THE MOST critical moment is not during the suppression of authority, but following, that is, when the forces of the defeated regime launch a general offensive against the labourers, and when it is a question of safeguarding the conquests under attack. The very character of this offensive, just as the technique and development of the civil war, will oblige the labourers to create determined revolutionary military contingents. The essence and fundamental principles of these formations must be decided in advance. Denying the statist and authoritarian methods of government, we also deny the statist method of organizing the military forces of the labourers, in other words the principles of a statist army based on obligatory military service. Consistent with the fundamental positions of libertarian communism, the principle of voluntary service must be the basis of the military formations of labourers...

However, "voluntary service" and the action of partisans should not be understood in the narrow sense of the word, that is as a struggle of worker and peasant detachments against the local enemy, uncoordinated by a general plan of operation and each acting on its own responsibility, at its own risk. The action and tactics of the partisans in the period of their complete development should be guided by a common revolutionary strategy.

As in all wars, the civil war cannot be waged by the labourers with success unless they apply the two fundamental principles of all military action: unity in the plan of operations and unity of common command. The most critical moment of the revolution will come when the bourgeoisie march against the revolution in organized force. This critical moment obliges the labourers to adopt these principles of military strategy.

Thus, in view of the necessities imposed by military strategy and also the strategy of the counter-revolution the armed forces of the revolution should inevitably be based on a general revolutionary army with a common command and plan of operations. The following principles form the basis of this army:

a. the class character of the army;

b. voluntary service (all coercion will be completely excluded from the work of defending the revolution);

c. free revolutionary discipline (self-discipline) (voluntary service and revolutionary self-discipline are perfectly compatible, and give the revolutionary army greater morale than any army of the State);

d. the total submission of the revolutionary army to the masses of the workers and peasants as represented by the worker and peasant organizations common throughout the country, established by the masses in the controlling sectors of economic and social life.

In other words, the organ of the defence of the revolution, responsible for combating the counter-revolution on major military fronts as well as on an internal front (bourgeois plots, preparation for counter-revolutionary action) will be entirely under the jurisdiction of the productive organizations of workers and peasants to which it will submit, and by which it will receive its political direction…

The fundamental principles of organization of a General Union of anarchists should be as follows:

1. Theoretical Unity: Theory represents the force which directs the activity of persons and organizations along a defined path towards a determined goal. Naturally it should be common to all the persons and organizations adhering to the General Union. All activity by the General Union, both overall and in its details, should be in perfect concord with the theoretical principles professed by the union.

2. Tactical Unity or the Collective Method of Action: In the same way the tactical methods employed by separate members and groups within the Union should be unitary, that is, be in rigorous concord both with each other and with the general theory and tactic of the Union.

A common tactical line in the movement is of decisive importance for the existence of the organization and the whole movement: it removes the disastrous effect of several tactics in opposition to one another, it concentrates all the forces of the movement, gives them a common direction leading to a fixed objective.

3. Collective Responsibility: The practice of acting on one's personal responsibility should be decisively condemned and rejected in the ranks of the anarchist movement. The areas of revolutionary life, social and political, are above all profoundly collective by nature. Social revolutionary activity in these areas cannot be based on the personal responsibility of individual militants.

> The executive organ of the general anarchist movement, the Anarchist Union, taking a firm line against the tactic of irresponsible individualism, introduces in its ranks the principle of collective responsibility: the entire Union will be responsible for the political and revolutionary activity of each member; in the same way, each member will be responsible for the political and revolutionary activity of the Union as a whole.
>
> 4. Federalism: Anarchism has always denied centralized organization, both in the area of the social life of the masses and in its political action. The centralized system relies on the diminution of the critical spirit, initiative and independence of each individual and on the blind submission of the masses to the "centre." The natural and inevitable consequences of this system are the enslavement and mechanization of social life and the life of the organization.

Against centralism, anarchism has always professed and defended the principle of federalism, which reconciles the independence and initiative of individuals and the organization with service to the common cause.

In reconciling the idea of the independence and high degree of rights of each individual with the service of social needs and necessities, federalism opens the doors to every healthy manifestation of the faculties of every individual.

But quite often, the federalist principle has been deformed in anarchist ranks: it has too often been understood as the right, above all, to manifest one's "ego," without obligation to account for duties as regards the organization.

This false interpretation disorganized our movement in the past. It is time to put an end to it in a firm and irreversible manner.

Federation signifies the free agreement of individuals and organizations to work collectively towards common objectives.

However, such an agreement and the federal union based on it, will only become reality, rather than fiction or illusion, on the conditions *sine qua non* that all the participants in the agreement and the Union fulfill most completely the duties undertaken, and conform to communal decisions. In a social project, however vast the federalist basis on which it is built, there can be no decisions without their execution. It is even less admissible in an anarchist organization, which exclusively takes on obligations with regard to the workers and their social revolution. Consequently, the federalist type of anarchist organization, while recognizing each member's rights to independence, free opinion, individual liberty and initiative, requires each member to undertake fixed organization duties, and demands execution of communal decisions.

On this condition alone will the federalist principle find life, and the anarchist organization function correctly, and steer itself towards the defined objective.

The idea of the General Union of Anarchists poses the problem of the co-ordination and concurrence of the activities of all the forces of the anarchist movement.

Every organization adhering to the Union represents a vital cell of the common organism. Every cell should have its secretariat, executing and guiding theoretically the political and technical work of the organization.

With a view to the co-ordination of the activity of all the Union's adherent organizations, a special organ will be created: the executive committee of the Union. The committee will be in charge of the following functions: the execution of decisions taken by the Union with which it is entrusted; the theoretical and organizational orientation of the activity of isolated organizations consistent with the theoretical positions and the general tactical line of the Union; the monitoring of the general state of the movement; the maintenance of working and organizational links between all the organizations in the Union; and with other organizations.

The rights, responsibilities and practical tasks of the executive committee are fixed by the congress of the Union.

The General Union of Anarchists has a concrete and determined goal. In the name of the success of the social revolution it must above all attract and absorb the most revolutionary and strongly critical elements among the workers and peasants.

Extolling the social revolution, and further, being an anti-authoritarian organization which aspires to the abolition of class society, the General Union of Anarchists depends equally on the two fundamental classes of society: the workers and the peasants. It lays equal stress on the work of emancipating these two classes.

As regards the workers' trade unions and revolutionary organizations in the towns, the General Union of Anarchists will have to devote all its efforts to becoming their pioneer and their theoretical guide.

It adopts the same tasks with regard to the exploited peasant masses. As bases playing the same role as the revolutionary workers' trade unions, the Union strives to realize a network of revolutionary peasant economic organizations, furthermore, a specific peasants' union, founded on anti-authoritarian principles.

Born out of the mass of the labouring people, the General Union must take part in all the manifestations of their life, bringing to them on every occasion the spirit of organization, perseverance and offensive. Only in this way can it fulfill its task, its theoretical and historical mission in the social revolution of labour, and become the organized vanguard of their emancipating process.

In 1927, Voline (Selection 87) and several other Russian anarchists in exile, including Mollie Steimer (1897-1980) and Senya Fleshin (1894-1981), published a response to the Platform. The following excerpts are taken from Fighters for Anarchism: Mollie Steimer and Senya Fleshin *(Libertarian Publications Group, 1983), ed. and trans. Abe Bluestein.*

WE DO NOT AGREE WITH THE POSITION of the Platform "that the most important reason for the weakness of the anarchist movement is the absence of organizational principles." We believe that this issue is very important because the Platform seeks to establish a centralized organization (a party) that would create "a political and tactical line for the anarchist movement." This overemphasizes the importance and role of organization.

We are not against an anarchist organization; we understand the harmful consequences of a lack of organization in the anarchist movement; we consider the creation of an anarchist organization to be one of the most urgent tasks...But we do not believe that organization, as such, can be a cure-all. We do not exaggerate its importance, and we see no benefit or need to sacrifice anarchist principles and ideas for the sake of organization.

We see the following reasons for the weakness of the anarchist movement:

1. The confusion in our ideas about a series of fundamental issues, such as the conception of the social revolution, of violence, of the period of transition, of organization.

2. The difficulty of getting a large part of the population to accept our ideas. We must take into account existing prejudices, customs, education, the fact that the great mass of people will look for accommodation rather than radical change.

3. Repression...

The thesis of the Platform...can be summarized as follows: the masses must be directed. The contrary viewpoint was the prevailing one in our movement until now: individuals and conscious minorities, including their ideological organizations, cannot "direct the masses." We must learn from the masses constantly if we do not want to lead them down a blind alley...

This is how the problem should be seen. Their solution is very superficial and false because the central problem is not resolved: the revolutionary masses and the conscious minority or their ideological organization.

We do not believe that the anarchists should lead the masses; we believe that our role is to assist the masses only when they need such assistance. This is how we see our position: the anarchists are part of the membership in the economic and social mass organizations. They act and build as part of the whole. An immense field of action is opened to them for ideological, social and creative activity without assuming a position of superiority over the masses. Above all they must fulfill their ideological and ethical influence in a free and natural manner.

The anarchists and specific organizations (groups, federations, confederations) can only offer ideological assistance, but not in the role of leaders. The slightest suggestion of direction, of superiority, of leadership of the masses and developments inevitably implies that the masses must accept direction, must submit to it; this, in turn, gives the leaders a sense of being privileged like dictators, of becoming separated from the masses.

In other words, the principles of power come into play. This is a contradiction not only with the central ideas of anarchism, but also our conception of social revolution. The revolution must be the free creation of the masses, not controlled by ideological or political groups…

The authors of the Platform write: "The organization of production will be carried out by organizations created by the workers—soviets, factory committees—which will direct and organize production in the cities, the regions and the nations. They will be linked closely with the masses who elect and control them, and have the power of recall at anytime."

The Platform accepts a centralized, mechanical system, giving it the simple corrective of election…

As a matter of principle we are not against committees (factory committees, workshop committees), nor against the need for a relationship and coordination between them. But these organizations can have a negative aspect: immobility, bureaucracy, a tendency to authoritarianism that will not be changed automatically by the principle of voting. It seems to us that there will be a better guarantee in the creation of a series of other, more mobile, even provisional organs which arise and multiply according to needs that arise in the course of daily living and activities. Thus, in addition to organizations for distribution, for consumers, for housing, etc. All of these together offer a richer, more faithful reflection of the complexity of social life…

The position of the Platform on the role of the army as a "political defender," and "arm against reaction," surprises us. We believe that such an apparatus can have only a negative role for the social revolution. Only the people in arms, with their enthusiasm, their positive solutions to the essential problems of the revolution (particularly in production) can offer sufficient defence against the plots of the bourgeoisie…a leading organization (the Union) that orients the mass organizations (workers and peasants) in their political direction and is supported as needed by a centralized army is nothing more than a new political power...

The authors of the Platform forget they are following an old road in seeking to create an organization based on a single ideological and tactical conception. They are creating an organization that will have more or less hostile relations with other organizations that do not have exactly the same conceptions. They do not understand that this old road will lead inevitably to the same old results: the existence not of a single organization but of many organizations. They will not be in a cooperative, harmonious relationship, but rather in conflict with each other even though they are all anarchist: each organization will claim the sole, the profound truth. These organizations will be concerned with polemics against each other rather than developing propaganda and activities to help the anarchist movement in general...

The role and aim of an organization are fundamental. There cannot be a serious organization without a clear definition of this question. The aims of an organization are determined in a large part by its form. The authors of the Platform attribute the role of leading the masses, the unions and all other organizations, as well as all activities and developments to the anarchist organization...We reject any idea that the anarchists should lead the masses. We hope that their role will only be that of ideological collaboration, as participants and helpers fulfilling our social role in a modest manner. We have pointed out the nature of our work: the written and spoken word, revolutionary propaganda, cultural work, concrete living example, etc.

Despite being kept under house arrest by the Fascist regime in Italy, Malatesta managed to obtain a copy of the Platform and to publish the following response in the October 1927 issue of the Italian anarchist paper, Il Risveglio, *in Geneva. It has most recently been reprinted in Malatesta,* The Anarchist Revolution: Polemical Articles 1924-1931 *(London: Freedom Press, 1995).*

I BELIEVE IT IS NECESSARY ABOVE ALL and urgent for anarchists to come to terms with one another and organize as much and as well as possible in order to be able to influence the direction the mass of the people take in their struggle for change and emancipation...

But it is obvious that in order to achieve their ends, anarchist organizations must, in their constitution and operation, remain in harmony with the principles of anarchism; that is, they must know how to blend the free action of individuals with the necessity and the joy of cooperation which serve to develop the awareness and initiative of their members and as a means of education for the environment in which they operate and a moral and material preparation for the future we desire.

Does the project under discussion satisfy these demands?

It seems to me that it does not. Instead of arousing in anarchists a greater desire for organization, it seems deliberately designed to reinforce the prejudice of those comrades who believe that to organize means to submit to leaders and belong to an authoritarian, centralizing body that suffocates any attempt at free initiative. And in fact it contains precisely those proposals that some, in the face of evident truths and despite our protests, insist on attributing to all anarchists who are described as organizers. Let us examine the Platform.

First of all, it seems to me a mistake—and in any case impossible to realize—to believe that all anarchists can be grouped together in one "General Union"—that is, in the words of the Platform, in a *single*, active revolutionary body.

We anarchists can all say that we are of the same party, if by the word "party" we mean all who are *on the same side*, that is, who share the same general aspirations and who, in one way or another, struggle for the same ends against common adversaries and enemies. But this does not mean it is possible—or even desirable—for all of us to be gathered into one specific association. There are too many differences of environment and conditions of struggle; too many possible ways of action to choose among, and also too many differences of temperament and personal incompatibilities for a *General Union*, if taken seriously, not to become, instead of a means for coordinating and reviewing the efforts of all, an obstacle to individual activity and perhaps also a cause of more bitter internal strife...

Besides, even the authors of the Platform declare as "inept" any idea of creating an organization which gathers together the representatives of the different tendencies in anarchism. Such an organization, they say, "incorporating heterogeneous elements, both on a theoretical and practical level, would be no more than a mechanical collection (*assemblage*) of individuals who conceive all questions concerning the anarchist movement from a different point of view and would inevitably break up as soon as they were put to the test of events and real life."

That's fine. But then, if they recognize the existence of different tendencies they will surely have to leave them the right to organize in their own fashion and work for anarchy in the way that seems best to them. Or will they claim the right to expel, to *excommunicate* from anarchism all those who do not accept their program? Certainly they say they "want to assemble in a single organization" all the *sound elements* of the libertarian movement; and naturally they will tend to judge as *sound* only those who think as they do. But what will they do with the elements that are *not sound*?

Of course, among those who describe themselves as anarchists there are, as in any human groupings, elements of varying worth; and what is worse, there are some who spread ideas in the name of anarchism which have very little to do with anarchism. But how to avoid the problem? *Anarchist truth* cannot and must not become the monopoly of one individual or committee; nor can it depend on the decisions of real or fictitious majorities. All that is necessary—and sufficient—is for everyone to have and to exercise the widest freedom of criticism and for each one of us to maintain their own ideas and choose for themselves their own comrades. In the last resort the facts will decide who was right.

Let us therefore put aside the idea of bringing together *all* anarchists into a single organization and look at this *General Union* which the Russians propose to us for what it really is—namely the Union of a particular fraction of anarchists; and let us see whether the organizational method proposed conforms with anarchist methods and principles and if it could thereby help to bring about the triumph of anarchism.

Once again, it seems to me that it cannot.

I am not doubting the sincerity of the anarchist proposals of those Russian comrades. They want to bring about anarchist communism and are seeking the means of doing so as quickly as possible. But it is not enough to want something; one also has to adopt suitable means; to get to a certain place one must take the right path or end up somewhere else. Their organization, being typically authoritarian, far from helping to bring about the victory of anarchist communism, to which they aspire, could only falsify the anarchist spirit and lead to consequences that go against their intentions.

In fact, their *General Union* appears to consist of so many partial organizations with *secretariats* which *ideologically* direct the political and technical work; and to coordinate the activities of all the member organizations there is a *Union Executive Committee* whose task is to carry out the decisions of the Union and to oversee the "ideological and organizational conduct of the organizations in conformity with the ideology and general strategy of the Union."

Is this anarchist? This, in my view, is a government and a church. True, there are no police or bayonets, no faithful flock to accept the dictated *ideology*; but this only means that their government would be an impotent and impossible government and their church a nursery for heresies and schisms. The spirit, the tendency remains authoritarian and the educational effect would remain anti-anarchist.

...[I]f the Union is responsible for what each member does, how can it leave to its individual members and to the various groups the freedom to apply the common program in the way they think best? How can one be responsible for an action if he does not have the means to prevent it? Therefore, the Union and in its name the Executive Committee, would need to monitor the action of the individual members and order them what to do and what not to do; and since disapproval after the event cannot put right a previously accepted responsibility, no one would be able to do anything at all before having obtained the go-ahead, the permission of the committee. And on the other hand, can an individual accept responsibility for the actions of a collectivity before knowing what it will do and if he cannot prevent it doing what he disapproves of?

Moreover, the authors of the Platform say that it is the "Union" which proposes and disposes. But when they refer to the wishes of the Union do they perhaps also refer to the wishes of all the members? If so, for the Union to function it would need everyone always to have the same opinion on all questions. So if it is normal that everyone should be in agreement on the general and fundamental principles, because otherwise they would not be and remain united, it cannot be assumed that thinking beings will all and always be of the same opinion on what needs to be done in the different circumstances and on the choice of persons to whom to entrust executive and directional responsibilities.

In reality—as it emerges from the text of the Platform itself—the will of the Union can only mean the will of the majority, expressed through congresses which nominate and control the *Executive Committee* and decide on all the important questions. Naturally, the congresses would consist of representatives elected by the majority of member groups, and these representatives would decide on what to do, as ever by a majority of votes. So, in the best of cases, the decisions would be taken by the majority of a majority, and this could easily, especially when the opposing opinions are more than two, represent only a minority.

Furthermore it should be pointed out that, given the conditions in which anarchists live and struggle, their congresses are even less truly representative than the bourgeois parliaments. And their control over the executive bodies, if these have authoritarian powers, is rarely opportune and effective. In practice anarchist congresses are attended by whoever wishes and can, whoever has enough money and who has not been prevented by police measures. There are as many present who represent only themselves or a small number of friends as there are those truly representing the opinions and desires of a large collective. And unless precautions are taken against possible traitors and spies—indeed, because of the need for those very precautions—it is impossible to make a serious check on the representatives and the value of their mandate.

In any case this all comes down to a pure majority system, to pure parliamentarianism.

It is well known that anarchists do not accept majority government (*democracy*), any more than they accept government by the few (*aristocracy*, *oligarchy*, or dictatorship by one class or party) nor that of one individual (*autocracy*, *monarchy* or personal dictatorship).

Thousands of times anarchists have criticized so-called majority government, which anyway in practice always leads to domination by a small minority.

Do we need to repeat all this yet again for our Russian comrades?

Certainly anarchists recognize that where life is lived in common it is often necessary for the minority to come to accept the opinion of the majority. When there is an obvious need or usefulness in doing something and to do it requires the agreement of all, the few should feel the need to adapt to the wishes of the many. And usually, in the interests of living peacefully together and under conditions of equality, it is necessary for everyone to be motivated by a spirit of concord, tolerance and compromise. But such adaptation on the one hand by one group must on the other be reciprocal, voluntary and must stem from an awareness of need and of goodwill to prevent the running of social affairs from being paralyzed by obstinacy. It cannot be imposed as a principle and statutory norm. This is an ideal which, perhaps, in daily life in general, is difficult to attain in entirety, but it is a fact that in every human grouping anarchy is that much nearer where agreement between majority and minority is free and spontaneous and exempt from any imposition that does not derive from the natural order of things.

So if anarchists deny the right of the majority to govern human society in general—in which individuals are nonetheless constrained to accept certain restrictions, since they cannot isolate themselves without renouncing the conditions of human life—and if they want everything to be done by the free agreement of all, how is it possible for them to adopt the idea of government by majority in their essentially free and voluntary associations and begin to declare that anarchists should submit to the decisions of the majority before they have even heard what those might be?

It is understandable that non-anarchists would find Anarchy, defined as a free organization without the rule of the majority over the minority, or vice versa, an unrealizable utopia, or one realizable only in a distant future; but it is inconceivable that anyone who professes to anarchist ideas and wants to make Anarchy, or at least seriously approach its realization—today rather than tomorrow—should disown the basic principles of anarchism in the very act of proposing to fight for its victory.

In my view, an anarchist organization must be founded on a very different basis from the one proposed by those Russian comrades.

Full autonomy, full independence and therefore full responsibility of individuals and groups; free accord between those who believe it useful to unite in cooperating for a common aim; moral duty to see through commitments undertaken and to do nothing that would contradict the accepted program. It is on these bases that the practical structures, and the right tools to give life to the organization should be built and designed…But all this must be done freely, in such a way that the thought and initiative of individuals is not obstructed, and with the sole view of giving greater effect to efforts which, in isolation, would be either impossible or ineffective. Thus congresses of an anarchist organization, though suffering as representative bodies from all the above-mentioned imperfections, are free from any kind of authoritarianism, because they do not lay down the law; they do not impose their own resolutions on others. They serve to maintain and increase personal relationships among the most active comrades, to coordinate and encourage programmatic studies on the ways and means of taking action, to acquaint all on the situation in the various regions and the action most urgently needed in each; to formulate the various opinions current among the anarchists and draw up some kind of statistics from them—and their decisions are not obligatory rules but suggestions, recommendations, proposals to be submitted to all involved, and do not become binding and enforceable except on those who accept them, and for as long as they accept them.

The administrative bodies which they nominate—Correspondence Commission, etc.—have no executive powers, have no directive powers, unless on behalf of those who ask for and approve such initiatives, and have no authority to impose their own views—which they can certainly maintain and propagate as groups of comrades, but cannot present as the official opinion of the organization. They publish the resolutions of the congresses and the opinions and proposals which groups and individuals communicate to them; and they serve—for those who require such a service—to facilitate relations between the groups and cooperation between those who agree on the various initiatives. Whoever wants to is free to correspond with whomsoever he wishes, or to use the services of other committees nominated by special groups.

In an anarchist organization the individual members can express any opinion and use any tactic which is not in contradiction with accepted principles and which does not harm the activities of others. In any case a given organization lasts for as long as the reasons for union remain greater than the reasons for dissent. When they are no longer so, then the organization is dissolved and makes way for other, more homogeneous groups.

Clearly, the duration, the permanence of an organization depends on how successful it has been in the long struggle we must wage, and it is natural that any institution instinctively seeks to last indefinitely. But the duration of a libertarian organization must be the consequence of the spiritual affinity of its members and of the adaptability of its constitution to the continual changes of circumstances. When it is no longer able to accomplish a useful task it is better that it should die.

Those Russian comrades will perhaps find that an organization like the one I propose and similar to the ones that have existed, more or less satisfactorily at various times, is not very efficient.

I understand. Those comrades are obsessed with the success of the Bolsheviks in their country and, like the Bolsheviks, would like to gather the anarchists together in a sort of disciplined army which, under the ideological and practical direction of a few leaders, would march solidly to the attack of the existing regimes, and after having won a material victory would direct the constitution of a new society. And perhaps it is true that under such a system, were it possible that anarchists would involve themselves in it, and if the leaders were men of imagination, our material effectiveness would be greater. But with what results? Would what happened to socialism and communism in Russia not happen to anarchism?

Those comrades are anxious for success as we are too. But to live and to succeed we don't have to repudiate the reasons for living and alter the character of the victory to come.

We want to fight and win, but as anarchists—for Anarchy.

116. Voline: Anarchist Synthesis

In 1924, Sébastien Faure invited Voline to Paris, where he assisted him in the publication of the Encyclopédie anarchiste. *Both Faure and Voline were advocates of "anarchist synthesis," which sought to synthesize all that was best in the various strands of anarchist thought and to unify the anarchist movement, while trying to avoid what Voline regarded as the sectarian party spirit of the Platformists. The following excerpts are from Voline's entry under "Anarchist Synthesis" in the* Encyclopédie anarchiste *(Paris: Librairie internationale), 1926-1934. The translation is by Paul Sharkey.*

"ANARCHIST SYNTHESIS" IS THE NAME GIVEN to a trend presently emerging from within the libertarian movement and aiming to reconcile and thereafter to "synthesize" the various schools of thought which divide that movement into several more or less mutually hostile factions. Essentially, the aim is to some extent to achieve unity on theory, as well as to unite the anarchist movement into one harmonious, ordered, rounded whole. I say to some extent because of course the anarchist outlook could not and should not ever become rigid, immutable or stagnant. It must remain supple, lively, rich in terms of ideas and its various strands. But suppleness should not mean confusion. And, then again, there is a happy medium between immobility and flux. It is precisely that happy medium that the "Anarchist Synthesis" aims to identify, pin down and arrive at…

The three key ideas which…should be embraced by all serious anarchists in order to unite the movement, are as follows:

> 1. Definitive acceptance of the *syndicalist* principle, which points the way to the real *methodology of social revolution*.
>
> 2. Definitive acceptance of the (libertarian) *communist* principle, which lays the *organizational basis for the new society in the making*.
>
> 3. Definitive acceptance of the *individualist* principle, the utter emancipation and happiness of the individual being the *real goal of the social revolution and the new society*…

Is the existence of several inimical anarchist currents, squabbling with one another, a *positive* thing or a *negative* one? Does the disintegration of the libertarian idea and movement into several mutually hostile tendencies *further* or *frustrate* the success of the anarchist belief? If it be thought to further it, there is no point in further discussion. If, on the other hand, it is regarded as damaging, then we must draw all the requisite conclusions from that acknowledgment.

To that first question, our answer is this:

At the outset, the anarchist idea was still under-developed and confused and it was only natural and useful that every aspect of it should be analyzed, taken apart, scrutinized thoroughly, its components examined and measured alongside one another, etc. Which is what was done. Anarchism was broken down into several elements (or currents). Thus the overly general and vague whole was dissected and this helped us delve deeper and make a more thoroughgoing study of that whole as well as of its component parts. So at the time this dismemberment of the anarchist idea was a positive thing. Various persons probed the various strands of anarchism and the details and the whole gained in depth and precision as a result. But then, once this initial task had been accomplished, after the components of anarchist thinking (communism, individualism, syndicalism) had been turned over and over from every angle, minds ought to have turned to *rebuilding*, with these same well-honed components, the *organic whole* from which they had sprung. Following a thoroughgoing *analysis*, we had to return (shrewdly) to the restorative of *synthesis*.

Bizarrely, minds were no longer focused on this need. Persons interested in this or that given component of anarchism wound up *substituting it for the finished article*. Naturally, it was not long before they found themselves at loggerheads and ultimately in conflict with those who accorded *similar treatment* to different bits of the whole truth. So, instead of grappling with the idea of amalgamating the scattered shards (which, taken separately, were no longer of much use) into one organic whole, anarchists wrestled over many a long year with the pointless task of *hatefully* pitting their "currents" one against another. Everyone looked upon "his" current, "his" morsel as the *sole truth* and steadfastly opposed supporters of the others. And so began that marching on the spot within libertarian ranks, characterized by blinkered vision and mutual resentment, which has lingered even into our own day and which should be deemed *harmful* to the normal development of the anarchist outlook.

Our conclusion is plain. *Dismemberment of the anarchist idea into several strands has served its purpose. And outlived its usefulness. And has no further justification. It is now dragging the movement into a blind alley, doing it tremendous damage and has nothing —cannot have anything—positive left to offer*. The first phase—when anarchism was searching for its bearings, being defined and inevitably foundering in the process—is over. It belongs to the past. And it is high time that we took things a step further.

If the dissipation of anarchism today is a negative thing, a harmful thing, we should be looking for ways of bringing it to an end. We must rally the whole and put the scattered components back together and rediscover and consciously rebuild the synthesis on which we had turned our backs.

Whereupon a further question arises: Is such a synthesis feasible at present? Might it not be utopian? Could we furnish it with a certain theoretical grounding?

To which we answer: Yes. A synthesis of anarchism (or, if you prefer, a "synthetic" anarchism) is perfectly feasible. And not at all utopian. There are some quite powerful theoretical grounds working on its behalf. Let us briefly review a few of these, the most important ones, in logical succession:

1. If anarchism aspires to life, if it looks to success in the future, if it wishes to become an organic and permanent feature of life, one of its fertilizing, creative driving forces, then it must try to cling as close to life, its essence and its ultimate truth as possible. Its ideological underpinnings must match the elementary features of existence as closely as they can. In fact, it is plain that if anarchism's basic ideas were at odds with the real elements of life and evolution, anarchism could scarcely be lively. Now, what is life? Can we somehow define and encapsulate its essence and grasp and pin down its characteristic

features? Yes, we can. True, it is certainly not a matter of a scientific formula for life—no such formula exists—but rather of a pretty clear-cut, fair definition of its visible, palpable, conceivable essence. According to this line of reasoning, life is primarily a *great synthesis:* a vast, complicated whole, an organic, original whole made up of countless motley variations.

2. Life is a synthesis. So what are the essence and originality of that synthesis? The essence of life is the widest *variety* of its parts—which are in a state of perpetual *motion* at that—simultaneously and equally perpetually displaying a certain *unity*, or, rather, a certain *equilibrium*. The essence of life, the essence of the sublime synthesis is a constant striving for equilibrium, indeed the ongoing achievement of a certain equilibrium amid the greatest diversity and perpetual motion…

3. *Life is a synthesis*. Life (the universe, nature) is *equilibrium* (a sort of oneness) *in diversity and in motion* (or, if one prefers, diversity and motion in equilibrium). As a result, if anarchism wishes to march in step with life, if it wants to be one of its organic elements, if it wishes to be reconciled with it and to arrive at a real result, instead of finding itself at odds with it, only to be rejected in the end, it too must—without renouncing diversity or motion—also and always achieve equilibrium, synthesis and unity.

But it is not enough just to argue that anarchism *can* be synthetic; it *must* be so. Not only is a synthesis of anarchism feasible or desirable: it is *vital.* While retaining the lively diversity of its component parts, and avoiding stagnation and embracing movement—the essential features of its vitality—anarchism should at the same time seek equilibrium through that very diversity and movement.

Diversity and movement in the absence of equilibrium spell chaos. Equilibrium without diversity and movement spell stagnation and death. *Diversity plus movement in equilibrium: that is the synthesis of life*. Anarchism should be varied and mobile and at the same time balanced, synthetic and one. Otherwise it will not be life-like.

4. Note, finally, that the true basis of diversity and movement in life (with synthesis as the jumping-off point) is *creation*, to wit, the constant production of the new, new combinations, new movements, a new equilibrium. Life is a *creative* diversity. Life is equilibrium set *in uninterrupted creation*. As a result, no anarchist could argue that "his" current is the sole and constant truth and that all the other strands within anarchism are nonsense. On the contrary: it is non-

> sense for an anarchist to let himself be led up a blind alley by one single little truth, "*his own*" and for him thereby to forget life's real great truth: the perpetual calling forth of new forms, fresh combinations and a constantly renewed synthesis.

Life's synthesis is not stationary; it creates and is constantly modifying its elements and their mutual relations.

Anarchism means to partake, wheresoever it may, in life's creative activity. As a result, it should—insofar as its outlook allows—be broad-minded, tolerant and synthetic, while engaged in creative activity.

The anarchist should scrupulously and perspicaciously monitor all of the serious elements of libertarian thought and movement. Far from retreating into some singular element, he should be searching for some way to arrive at an equilibrium and synthesis of all given elements. Furthermore, he should analyze and constantly monitor his synthesis, comparing it against the elements of life itself, so that it may always be in perfect harmony with the latter. Indeed, life does not stand still; it changes. And as a result the role and mutual relations between the several elements of the anarchist synthesis will not always be the same: in different instances, it is going to be sometimes this or sometimes that element that is in need of underpinning, support and implementation...

We must discover and frame within the various strands of anarchism on the one hand, everything that ought to be regarded as phony, at odds with life's reality and in need of rejection: and, on the other, everything that ought to be registered as just, wholesome, acceptable. Next, all of these just and valid elements should be combined and a synthetic whole created from them. (It is primarily in this initial groundwork that a rapprochement between anarchists of differing persuasions and their tolerance towards one another might achieve the great status of a crucial first step.) And, finally, this assemblage would have to earn the acceptance of all of anarchism's serious, active militants as furnishing the basis for the formation of a united libertarian body, the members of which would thus be agreed upon a range of fundamentals acceptable to them all.

117. Alexander Berkman: The ABC of Communist Anarchism (1929)

After leaving Russia in late 1921, Alexander Berkman spent some time in Berlin, where he wrote his critique of the Bolsheviks (Selection 88). He then moved to France, where he spent the last years of his life. At the invitation of the Jewish Anarchist Federation of New York he wrote an anarchist primer to explain anarchist ideas to the general public. It was originally published as Now and After: The ABC of Communist Anarchism *(New York: Vanguard Press, 1929; AK Press reprint, 2004), from which the following excerpts have been taken.*

THE EXCHANGE OF COMMODITIES BY means of prices leads to profit making, to taking advantage and exploitation; in short, to some form of capitalism. If you do away with profits, you cannot have any price system, nor any system of wages or payment. That means that exchange must be according to value. But as value is uncertain or not ascertainable, exchange must consequently be free, without "equal" value, since such does not exist. In other words, labour and its products must be exchanged without price, without profit, freely, according to necessity. This logically leads to ownership in common and to joint use. Which is a sensible, just, and equitable system, and is known as Communism.

"But is it just that all should share alike?" you demand. "The man of brains and the dullard, the efficient and the inefficient, all the same? Should there be no distinction, no special recognition for those of ability?"

Let me in turn ask you, my friend, shall we punish the man whom nature has not endowed as generously as his stronger or more talented neighbour? Shall we add injustice to the handicap nature has put upon him? All we can reasonably expect from any man is that he do his best—can any one do more? And if John's best is not as good as his brother Jim's, it is his misfortune, but in no case a fault to be punished.

There is nothing more dangerous than discrimination. The moment you begin discriminating against the less capable, you establish conditions that breed dissatisfaction and resentment: you invite envy, discord, and strife. You would think it brutal to withhold from the less capable the air or water they need. Should not the same principle apply to the other wants of man? After all, the matter of food, clothing, and shelter is the smallest item in the world's economy.

The surest way to get one to do his best is not by discriminating against him, but by treating him on an equal footing with others. That is the most effective encouragement and stimulus. It is just and human.

"But what will you do with the lazy man, the man who does not want to work?" inquires your friend.

That is an interesting question, and you will probably be very much surprised when I say that there is really no such thing as laziness. What we call a lazy man is generally a square man in a round hole. That is, the right man in the wrong place. And you will always find that when a fellow is in the wrong place, he will be inefficient or shiftless. For so-called laziness and a good deal of inefficiency are merely unfitness, misplacement. If you are compelled to do the thing you are unfitted for by your inclinations or temperament, you will be inefficient at it; if you are forced to do work you are not interested in, you will be lazy at it...

Under present conditions there is little choice given the average man to devote himself to the tasks that appeal to his leanings and preferences. The accident of your birth and social station generally predetermines your trade or profession. The son of the financier does not, as a rule, become a woodchopper, though he may be more fit to handle logs than bank accounts. The middle classes send their children to colleges which turn them into doctors, lawyers, or engineers. But if your parents were workers who could not afford to let you study, the chances are that you will take any job which is offered you, or enter some trade that happens to afford you an apprenticeship. Your particular situation will decide your work or profession, not your natural preferences, inclinations, or abilities. Is it any wonder, then, that most people, the overwhelming majority, in fact, are misplaced? Ask the first hundred men you meet whether they would have selected the work they are doing, or whether they would continue in it, if they were free to choose, and ninety-nine of them will admit that they would prefer some other occupation. Necessity and material advantages, or the hope of them, keep most people in the wrong place.

It stands to reason that a person can give the best of himself only when his interest is in his work, when he feels a natural attraction to it, when he likes it. Then he will be industrious and efficient...The need of activity is one of the most fundamental urges of man. Watch the child and see how strong is his instinct for action, for movement, for doing something. Strong and continuous. It is the same with the healthy man. His energy and vitality demand expression. Permit him to do the work of his choice, the thing he loves, and his application will know neither weariness nor shirking...

Under Anarchism each will have the opportunity of following whatever occupation will appeal to his natural inclinations and aptitude. Work will become a pleasure instead of the deadening drudgery it is today. Laziness will be unknown, and the things created by interest and love will be objects of beauty and joy.

It is said that no two blades of grass are alike. Much less so are human beings. In the whole wide world no two persons are exactly similar even in physical appearance;

still more dissimilar are they in their physiological, mental, and psychical make-up. Yet in spite of this diversity and of a thousand and one differentiations of character we compel people to be alike today. Our life and habits, our behaviour and manners, even our thoughts and feelings are pressed into a uniform mold and fashioned into sameness. The spirit of authority, law, written and unwritten, tradition and custom force us into a common groove and make of man a will-less automaton without independence or individuality. This moral and intellectual bondage is more compelling than any physical coercion, more devastating to our manhood and development. All of us are its victims, and only the exceptionally strong succeed in breaking its chains, and that only partly…

But the general view that conformity is a natural trait is entirely false. On the contrary, given the least chance, unimpeded by the mental habits instilled from the very cradle, man evidences uniqueness and originality. Observe children, for instance, and you will see most varied differentiation in manner and attitude, in mental and psychic expression. You will discover an instinctive tendency to individuality and independence, to non-conformity, manifested in open and secret defiance of the will imposed from the outside, in rebellion against the authority of parent and teacher. The whole training and "education" of the child is a continuous process of stifling and crushing this tendency, the eradication of his distinctive characteristics, of his unlikeness to others, of his personality and originality. Yet even in spite of year-long repression, suppression, and molding, some originality persists in the child when it reaches maturity, which shows how deep are the springs of individuality…

Life in freedom, in Anarchy, will do more than liberate man merely from his present political and economic bondage. That will be only the first step, the preliminary to a truly human existence. Far greater and more significant will be the *results* of such liberty, its effects upon man's mind, upon his personality. The abolition of the coercive external will, and with it of the fear of authority, will loosen the bonds of moral compulsion no less than of economic and physical. Man's spirit will breathe freely, and that mental emancipation will be the birth of a new culture, of a new humanity. Imperatives and taboos will disappear, and man will begin to be himself, to develop and express his individual tendencies and uniqueness. Instead of "thou shalt not," the public conscience will say "thou mayest, taking full responsibility." That will be a training in human dignity and self-reliance, beginning at home and in school, which will produce a new race with a new attitude to life.

The man of the coming day will see and feel existence on an entirely different plane. Living to him will be an art and a joy. He will cease to consider it as a race where every one must try to become as good a runner as the fastest. He will regard leisure as more important than work, and work will fall into its proper, subordinate place as the means to leisure, to the enjoyment of life.

Life will mean the striving for finer cultural values, the penetration of nature's mysteries, the attainment of higher truth. Free to exercise the limitless possibilities of his mind, to pursue his love of knowledge, to apply his inventive genius, to create, and to soar on the wings of imagination, man will reach his full stature and become man indeed. He will grow and develop according to his nature. He will scorn uniformity, and human diversity will give him increased interest in, and a more satisfying sense of, the richness of being. Life to him will not consist in functioning but in living, and he will attain the greatest kind of freedom man is capable of, freedom in joy...

If your object is to secure liberty, you must learn to do without authority and compulsion. If you intend to live in peace and harmony with your fellow-men, you and they should cultivate brotherhood and respect for each other. If you want to work together with them for your mutual benefit, you must practice cooperation. The social revolution means much more than the reorganization of conditions only: it means the establishment of new human values and social relationships, a changed attitude of man to man, as of one free and independent to his equal; it means a different spirit in individual and collective life, and that spirit cannot be born overnight. It is a spirit to be cultivated, to be nurtured and reared, as the most delicate flower is, for indeed it is the flower of a new and beautiful existence...

New situations and changed conditions make us feel, think, and act in a different manner. But the new conditions themselves come about only as a result of new feelings and ideas. The social revolution is such a new condition. We must learn to think differently before the revolution can come. That alone can bring the revolution.

We must learn to think differently about government and authority, for as long as we think and act as we do today, there will be intolerance, persecution, and oppression, even when organized government is abolished. We must learn to respect the humanity of our fellow-man, not to invade him or coerce him, to consider his liberty as sacred as our own; to respect his freedom and his personality, to foreswear compulsion in any form: to understand that the cure for the evils of liberty is more liberty, that liberty is the mother of order.

And furthermore we must learn that equality means equal opportunity, that monopoly is the denial of it, and that only brotherhood secures equality. We can learn this only by freeing ourselves from the false ideas of capitalism and of property, of mine and thine, of the narrow conception of ownership.

By learning this we shall grow into the spirit of true liberty and solidarity, and know that free association is the soul of every achievement. We shall then realize that the social revolution is the work of cooperation, of solidaric purpose, of mutual effort...

What we call progress has been a painful but continuous march in the direction of limiting authority and the power of government and increasing the rights and liberties of the individual, of the masses. It has been a struggle that has taken thousands of years. The reason that it took such a long time—and is not ended yet—is because people did not know what the real trouble was: they fought against this and for that, they changed kings and formed new governments, they put out one ruler only to set up another, they drove away a "foreign" oppressor only to suffer the yoke of a native one, they abolished one form of tyranny, such as the Tsars, and submitted to that of a party dictatorship, and always and ever they shed their blood and heroically sacrificed their lives in the hope of securing liberty and welfare.

But they secured only new masters, because however desperately and nobly they fought, they never touched the *real source* of trouble, the *principle of authority* and *government*. They did not know that *that* was the fountainhead of enslavement and oppression, and therefore they never succeeded in gaining liberty.

But now we understand that true liberty is not a matter of changing kings or rulers. We know that the whole system of master and slave must go, that the entire social scheme is wrong, that government and compulsion must be abolished, that the very foundations of authority and monopoly must be uprooted...

The main purpose of the social revolution must be the *immediate* betterment of conditions for the masses. The success of the revolution fundamentally depends on it. This can be achieved only by organizing consumption and production so as to be of real benefit to the populace. In that lies the greatest—in fact, the only—security of the social revolution...

The object of revolution is to secure greater freedom, to increase the material welfare of the people. The aim of the social revolution, in particular, is to enable the masses *by their own efforts* to bring about conditions of material and social well-being, to rise to higher moral and spiritual levels...

Every revolution is accompanied by a great outburst of popular enthusiasm full of hope and aspiration. It is the spring-board of revolution. This high tide, spontaneous and powerful, opens up the human sources of initiative and activity. The sense of equality liberates the best there is in man and makes him consciously creative. These are the great motors of the social revolution, its moving forces. Their free and unhindered expression signifies the development and deepening of the revolution. Their suppression means decay and death. The revolution is safe, it grows and becomes strong, as long as the masses feel that they are direct participants in it, that they are fashioning their own lives, that *they* are making the revolution, that they *are* the revolution. But the moment their activities are usurped by a political party or are centered in some special organization, revolutionary effort becomes limited to a comparatively small circle from which the large masses are practically excluded. The natural result is that popular enthusiasm is dampened, interest gradually weakens, initiative languishes, creativeness wanes, and the revolution becomes the monopoly of a clique which presently turns dictator.

This is fatal to the revolution. The sole prevention of such a catastrophe lies in the continued active interest of the workers through their every-day participation in all matters pertaining to the revolution...

It cannot be emphasized too strongly how essential spiritual values are to the social revolution. These and the consciousness of the masses that the revolution also means material betterment are dynamic influences in the life and growth of the new society. Of the two factors the spiritual values are foremost. The history of previous revolutions proves that the masses were ever willing to suffer and to sacrifice material well-being for the sake of greater liberty and justice. Thus in Russia neither cold nor starvation could induce the peasants and workers to aid counter-revolution. All privation and misery notwithstanding they served heroically the interests of the great cause. It was only when they saw the Revolution monopolized by a political party, the newly won liberties curtailed, a dictatorship established, and injustice and inequality dominant again that they became indifferent to the Revolution, declined to participate in the sham, refused to cooperate, and even turned against it.

To forget ethical values, to introduce practices and methods inconsistent with or opposed to the high moral purposes of the revolution means to invite counter-revolution and disaster...

Understand well that the only really effective defence of the revolution lies in the attitude of the people. Popular discontent is the worst enemy of the revolution and its greatest danger. We must always bear in mind that the strength of the social revolution is organic, not mechanistic: not in mechanical, military measures lies its might, but in its industry, in its ability to reconstruct life, to establish liberty and justice. Let the people feel that it is indeed their own cause which is at stake, and the last man of them will fight like a lion in its behalf...Where the masses are conscious that the revolution and all its activities are in their own hands, that they themselves are managing things and are free to change their methods when they consider it necessary, counter-revolution can find no support and is harmless.

"But would you let counter-revolutionists incite the people if they tried to?"

By all means. Let them talk all they like. To restrain them would serve only to create a persecuted class and thereby enlist popular sympathy for them and their cause. To suppress speech and press is not only a theoretic offence against liberty: it is a direct blow at the very foundations of the revolution. It would, first of all, raise problems where none had existed before. It would introduce methods which must lead to discontent and opposition, to bitterness and strife, to prison, Cheka, and civil war. It would generate fear and distrust, would hatch conspiracies, and culminate in a reign of terror which has always killed revolutions in the past.

The social revolution must from the very start be based on entirely different principles, on a new conception and attitude. Full freedom is the very breath of its existence; and be it never forgotten that the cure for evil and disorder is *more* liberty, not suppression. Suppression leads only to violence and destruction…

No revolution has yet tried the true way of liberty. None has had sufficient faith in it. Force and suppression, persecution, revenge, and terror have characterized all revolutions in the past and have thereby defeated their original aims. The time has come to try new methods, new ways. The social revolution is to achieve the emancipation of man through liberty, but if we have no faith in the latter, revolution becomes a denial and betrayal of itself. Let us then have the courage of freedom: let it replace suppression and terror. Let liberty become our faith and our *deed* and we shall grow strong therein.

Only liberty can make the social revolution effective and wholesome. It alone can pave the way to greater heights and prepare a society where well-being and joy shall be the heritage of all. The day will dawn when man shall for the first time have full opportunity to grow and expand in the free and generous sunshine of Anarchy.

118. Marcus Graham: Against the Machine (1934)

Marcus Graham (1893-1985) was a Rumanian immigrant who became active in the anarchist movement in the United States during the First World War. He contributed to several anarchist publications before becoming editor of MAN!, *which began publication in January 1933, and continued publishing, despite police harassment, until it was suppressed by the U.S. government in 1940. The following article, "What Ought to be the Anarchist Attitude Towards the Machine," was originally published in the March 1934 issue of* MAN!, *and has been reprinted in* MAN! An Anthology of Anarchist Ideas, Essays, Poetry and Commentaries *(London: Cienfuegos Press, 1974), ed. Marcus Graham. It was written in response to those anarchists who saw machinery as liberating, labour-saving devices.*

MAN WILL NEVER BE ABLE TO MASTER the machine without the sacrifice of endangering human life. Why? Because man will always remain a human being whose very vibration of life is motivated by innumerable emotions, habits, intuitions, and impressions. It is perfectly all right for inventors to conceive safety devices of all sorts, and for aspiring socialist and communist politicians to promise the dawn of a day when the entire world will become such an accident-proof straitjacket that man will be enabled to control every sort of machine through the mere pressing of this or that button. But for an Anarchist—who aspires to unloosen wide and afar man's ingenuity, initiative and independence—to think likewise is, to put it mildly, quite a contradiction…

The "best" ruler over any people sooner or later becomes despotic by the very fact of having power in his hands. As Anarchists we are unequivocally opposed to any sort of rulership or exploitation of man over man. Why then turn around and give the same sort of power to any man over the use of the machine which at all times endangers the lives of others and often that of the wielder himself?

Hundreds of thousands of workers own some sort of automobile. And how many fatal accidents transpire every moment of their use? Certainly no one can vouchsafe the assertion that machine drivers intentionally get into accidents that sometimes cost their own lives….

All such facts should be of very grave concern to each and all of us Anarchists. For human life is to us the most sacred thing; we wish not only to achieve liberty for those that live, *but also to safeguard the right of every living soul not to be sacrificed upon the false altar of a false god—to wit, the machine.*

As an Anarchist I am in favour of the destruction of every power on earth that tends to hinder the liberation of mankind from all forms of oppression and rulership. But I am just as emphatically opposed to the endangering or destruction of a single human life in the name of a new devouring monster now preying upon mankind—the machine. Anarchy, to me, means an ethical conception of life. Liberty without encroachment upon anyone else's freedom, least of all, upon anyone else's life. *To forget that Anarchy is an ethical approach towards life in all the domains which tend to create happiness for each and all alike, is to forget the fundamental and basic principles of Anarchy…*

The assertion…that primitive man got tired of his sort of life and chose the machine as a substitute is far from correct. In examining any of the historical facts dealing with the manner in which the machine is adopted in any of the still primitive countries, it will be found that commercialism, signifying, of course, exploitation and rulership, is at the helm in fostering the machine in all such instances…

The machine, as a saviour of man, is also associated with the hatred toward toil now prevailing everywhere. But this is another error wrongly placed. Toil for one's own needs gives one self-expression and joy. It is the exploitation of toil that is the only curse that mankind suffers from.

The machine to me is an attempt to mechanize life. As an Anarchist I oppose such an unnatural anti-Anarchist approach towards the solution of our present enslavement. I am struggling and hoping for the dawn of that day when man shall at last come into his own: a natural, self-reliant, intuitive, colourful, handicraft creator of all those needs and things that will give us joy—the joy of the free life in a liberated society. (Vol. 2, No. 3, March 1934)

119. Wilhelm Reich and the Mass Psychology of Fascism (1935)

The following excerpts are taken from "The Crisis of International Socialism. New Trends in Marxism" by H.R., originally published in the Spanish anarchist publication, La Revista Blanca, *November 15, 1935 (Parts IV-V). "H.R." was probably Helmut Rudiger (1903-1966), a German anarcho-syndicalist then living in Spain. The part of his article reproduced here deals with Wilhelm Reich's groundbreaking work,* The Mass Psychology of Fascism *(New York: Farrar, Straus & Giroux, 1970; originally published 1933). The translation by Richard M. Cleminson of the University of Leeds is published here with his kind permission.*

PSYCHOANALYSIS, REICH SAYS, REVEALS to us the mechanism of sexual repression which acts in human psychology and he describes the negative consequences that this can have for an individual. Sex-economic analysis asks: What is the sociological motivation behind the repression of sexuality and why does the individual carry out that repression? The Church tells us this is necessary for the health of the soul for a better world. Freud himself believes that sexual repression is necessary in order to guarantee human society and the tasks of civilization. For Reich, however, the problem lies elsewhere. According to him, sexual repression is not a question of civilization but is explained by the needs of the social regime, that is, by the political interest that the ruling classes harbour. By studying the history of sexual repression we see that this does not begin in the first stages of civilization as such and that this repression is not an inevitable condition of human progress, but that instead it appears much later in the period of the formation of the private property of the means of production and at the same time of the division of society into classes. Sexual ideology is placed at the service of the material interests of the ruling class and the interests of exploitation to serve a social minority which has in its power the land and the instruments of labour. This state of things has its organic expression in monogamous marriage and in the patriarchal family. With this repression and oppression of sexual freedom, human feelings are altered, religion which is adverse to sexuality is born and the ruling class begins to construct a whole sexual political organization. This includes especially the churches in all their forms, and their ultimate aim is the suppression of sexuality and what little happiness there is in human existence. All this contains a sociological significance in respect of the increasing exploitation of the work of the disinherited classes.

Reich illustrates how the ruling classes give the proletariat, today more then ever before, substitutes in place of a sexuality restricted by the official morality of capitalist society. Such abnormal methods of satisfaction include militarism with its constant excitation in favour of sadism and with its fetishism of the uniform, nationalist fanaticism, etc. The major source of sexual oppression, however, today and in the earlier times of the creation of private property, continues to be the family and marriage. It is here that the authority of the male is born, of the father over the mother and children and which in the minds of women and children becomes the all powerful state. In place of confidence in themselves, the youth, women and the exploited classes hold authority in fear, are submissive to it and go through a process of "self-identification" of the suppressed individual with the authority that they are suppressed by. Here we have the model of the ideal subject. The person of this mentality and psychological structure will serve the state, the capitalist exploiter and the leaders of political parties faithfully.

Given the huge importance of the ideological foundations of capitalist exploitation, Reich defends the need for a conscious cultural program in class struggle, a process of intellectual preparation of the proletariat for its task of liberation. This process should have its basis in effective propaganda against official sexual morality. The author of this book states: "The more developed capitalism is, the greater the bourgeois infection of the proletariat. In turn, the revolutionary duties on the cultural front become more important, a task whose essential component is politico-social activity." Further, "Propaganda against hunger...was a too narrow base, even though it was the most important argument against capitalism. The young worker, for example, has a thousand sexual and cultural questions which remain after satisfying his hunger. The struggle against hunger is of the first order but it should not be wrought in isolation..."

Reich thus finds himself before the eternal question of the relations between man and society...There is a mutual interconnection here that is difficult to resolve either through simplistic deterministic statements or through voluntaristic extremism. But with respect to historical materialism, it is necessary to say quite frankly that its deterministic conception of history has caused huge damage to the anti-capitalist movement because it has weakened considerably the revolutionary energies of the working class, which believed that it could trust some pre-established historical laws that were to lead more or less automatically towards a better future for humanity. In this process of social development the proletariat would merely have to unite around its political party in order to wait for the hour of revolution and to transform society at a given moment by means of a *political* movement, while the economic transformation was already taking place organically in the heart of capitalism itself, which was, according to Marx, its own grave digger. Anarchism, by contrast, has always emphasized the supreme value of revolutionary will, of the task of education of the working class and the preparation of the individual revolutionary for the concrete tasks of social reconstruction. Anarcho-syndicalism calls for direct action in the daily struggle and the abolition of all authoritarian tendencies in union organization, in order to assist in the mission of creating a proletariat conscious of its own strength and capable of employing it practically, free from the guidance of so-called leaders. Let us now see what the psychological neo-Marxism of Reich says on this question of revolutionary will, and we shall see yet another confirmation of our old criticism of historical materialism:

"Men, certainly, make up society but they succumb to the laws that dominate them, independently of them. History teaches us that if we try to change only the spiritual structure of men, society resists. If we try to change only society, men resist. This shows that neither of the two elements can be substituted for the other since… *the subjective structure of man and the objective structure of society do not only correspond to one another—they are identical*."

In my opinion, the special value of Reich's work is this aspect of his research…

With respect to the psychoanalytic thesis of the author in the narrow sense of the term…one can naturally be rather skeptical…A completely healthy and well-balanced individual in terms of his sexual life may be a long way off from being a perfect socialist and a convinced revolutionary fighter. It could be said that no one could be a true revolutionary if they had not yet freed themselves from antiquated bourgeois sexual concepts and from authoritarian prejudices which are rooted in reactionary sexual morality. On the other hand, an individual completely free of bourgeois sexual prejudice may lack all sense of human solidarity. We recognize that Freud errs a great deal in not taking into account the political significance of sexual repression in the conservation of exploitative regimes. We must also recognize the importance of the repression of certain sexual tendencies for the benefit of human solidarity and civilization, something which Freud emphasizes throughout his work.

Furthermore, human psychology is a complex matter. Other psychological schools of thought have dedicated their research not only to sexuality as the principal wellspring of human beings but other aspects of the human soul. We have to take into account the results of all these psychological schools for the development of the educational process of revolutionary libertarian socialism. We will then be able to obtain sufficient tools to create a revolutionary ideology securely entrenched in the hearts and minds of the exploited masses...

The final conclusions by Reich...tell us nothing of the change in *revolutionary praxis* that must take place after the failure of authoritarian socialism in Germany. For Reich, it seems that his psychological studies are only valuable in terms of improving the arguments of speakers at meetings and for individual propaganda in the struggle for the support of the election of members of parliament or for the faithful party member. In addition, it is not sufficient to raise the question of the Russian legislation on sexuality and the family, as does Reich, however advanced it may be in comparison with that of other countries. The solution of the huge problems brought up by the book does not lie here.

If there is a radical conclusion truly to be made after reading Reich's [book]...it is that it is necessary to create a *libertarian* socialist movement in the broadest sense of the word and that *authority* is the greatest evil of the old workers' movement.

The struggle against capitalism and the construction of a society without classes can only be done by the constructive labour of freely associated individuals who are aware of their creative mission. What we need in Germany and everywhere else is not the single party in place of all those that currently exist, the many "workers'" parties that battle it out among themselves. What will take us to the social revolution cannot be the use of more psychologically refined methods in order to attract the masses to their revolutionary party leaders but instead *the liquidation of the party, of authoritarian organization as such*, and its substitution by federalist organization "open to all initiatives," *replacing all political beliefs by the tactic of direct action of the exploited*. Socialism is nothing more or less than the creation of new direct relations between men, between the producers and consumers who are one and same in the organization of the economic and cultural needs of people on an independent basis without the intervention of capitalists who will only exploit and political leaders who will always be, unavoidably, against individual freedom and dignity. These are the two requirements of humanity and it is they that make up the single indispensable basis of civilization worthy of the name. In this time of white and red dictatorships, of authoritarian madness, the desperate faith of the masses in the "totalitarian state" has been deceived a thousand times. The state appeared to them to be the only way out of the present chaos which seemed to be nothing else but the end of civilization itself. At this time, therefore, we need to construct the idea of the *total man* who in all senses liberates himself from the yoke of authority by beginning to build society from below, by means of new forms of work and distribution of the wealth created, without relying for one moment once and for all on those who promise happiness in exchange for political power being handed over to any boss or party, whatever they are called. As long as this lesson is not learned from the failure of Marxism in Germany, the painful events of central Europe will serve for nothing and the German people will continue its martyrdom under the emblem of the swastika or that of any other dictatorial organization or totalitarian and anti-human state that may follow the present regime. (Translation © Richard M. Cleminson)

120. Bart de Ligt: The Conquest of Violence (1937)

Bart de Ligt (1883-1938) was a revolutionary pacifist and libertarian socialist active in the international anti-militarist and peace movements. De Ligt was imprisoned in his native Holland during the First World War as a result of his anti-militarist and pacifist activities. He became a well-known advocate of nonviolent direct action. The July 1934 conference of the War Resisters International adopted his "Plan of Campaign against All War and All Preparation for War," which set forth a detailed plan for nonviolent resistance to militarism, war and war preparations. The following excerpts are taken from his book, The Conquest of Violence: An Essay on War and Revolution *(London: Pluto Press, 1989; originally published 1937, with an introduction by Aldous Huxley).*

TO THE ESSENTIALLY PARASITIC BOURGEOISIE, the use of...violence comes naturally, as we have said. On the other hand, the Bolsheviks, Socialists, Syndicalists and Anarchists, who wish to do away with every kind of parasitism, exploitation, and oppression, are battling for a world from which every form of brutal violence will be banished. That is why, when once the old means of violence are used by them there appears a flagrant contradiction between such means and the goal in sight.

For it is a fixed law that all means have their own abiding end, proceeding from the function for which they came into being, which can only be subordinated to other, loftier ends as far as the latter are attuned to the essential and, as it were, innate end. Besides, every end suggests its own means. To transgress this law inevitably brings about a tyranny of the means. For if these lead away from their intended goal, then the more people use them, the farther they get from the objective and the more their actions are determined by them. For example, it is impossible to educate people in liberty by force, just as it is impossible to breathe by coal gas. Life must have fresh air. And freedom must be awakened and stimulated by freedom and in freedom. It can never be born of violence. At the most, we may seek liberty as an antidote to our bondage, just as we cry out for fresh air when we are threatened with asphyxiation.

And so, when those who struggle for the abolition of class and race exploitation automatically employ in their revolution—the greatest and noblest in history—those very means of horizontal and vertical warfare that the capitalist class once employed against the feudal powers, aggravating them further by mediaeval cruelties such as inquisitions and tortures, abhorred by the bourgeoisie itself for a long time past, the result is a tragic contradiction...

Modern capitalism, no longer able to justify itself from either a practical or a moral point of view, inevitably finished up by adopting the methods of Fascism. Even in the most democratic countries, the middle classes, in order to impose their will, found themselves often unwillingly obliged to resort to all kinds of feudal expedients which once were repugnant to them. In our time, freedom of thought, of speech, of the Press, of organization and association, is being more and more curtailed, even in the classic lands of liberty like England, France and the Netherlands. There is not a single act today at which the capitalists will stop short in order to safeguard their "authority" and maintain the "right," that is to say, the privileges of the bourgeoisie. Those beauteous devices with which the bourgeoisie had so proudly adorned itself in its rise, have fallen away; and, stripped of those deceitful garments, it is seen for what it is and always has been.

Fascism, that is, a politico-economic state where the ruling class of each country behaves towards its own people as for several centuries it has behaved to the colonial peoples under its heel; Fascism, which takes from its victims one after the other, the few political and social rights which they enjoyed; Fascism which is always lowering wages and reducing human beings, men and women, to a state of slavery; Fascism is the last despairing stand which imperialist capitalism must inevitably make, unless the working-class opposes it with all its might. It is, we have reason to hope, the last effort of the upper middle-classes to check that social evolution which threatens to sweep away the selfish regime they have instituted. From the point of view of social psychology, we are up against the policy of despair and a system which takes advantage of the people's increasing misery to seduce them by a new Messianism: belief in the Strong Man, the Duce, the Führer. This condition of hopeless misery explains the brutality and cruelty of Fascism: on both sides, the upper classes and the down-trodden masses alike, people are no longer themselves, i.e. no longer human.

It may therefore be said that Fascism in a country is nothing but imperialism the wrong way up, turned against its own people, and that imperialism is only Fascism the wrong way up, turned against foreign peoples. In both cases, the essence of the thing is violence.

While capitalism has come by its very nature to Fascist methods, Socialism on the other hand must never fall back on them; to do so would attack its very roots. The violence and warfare which are characteristic conditions of the imperialist world do not go with the liberation of the individual and of society, which is the historic mission of the exploited classes. The greater the violence, the weaker the revolution, even where violence has deliberately been put at the service of revolution. The greater the revolution, that is to say, the social construction, the less there will be to deplore of violence and destruction.

...[T]he English cobbler James Harragan...had a way of ending his public utterances in favour of social revolution with the words, "Stay in, don't come out." Which means, that the workers must not strike by going home or into the streets, thus separating themselves from the means of production and giving themselves over to dire poverty but that, on the contrary, they must stay on the spot and control these means of production.

In the social revolution, therefore, it is a question of creating an entirely new collective order in every branch of production and distribution. The masses, workers and intellectuals alike, will only achieve this in as far as they have succeeded in establishing a due relation between the methods of co-operation and those of non-co-operation: they must refuse to undertake any work which is unworthy of men and harmful to mankind; they must refuse to bow to any employer or master whomsoever, even the so-called revolutionary State, and join solidly in the one and only system of free production. It may be that in their effort to achieve this, the masses fall back more or less into violence. But this can never be anything more than an accidental phenomenon, and, as we have said, a sign of weakness and not of strength. The readier the revolutionary masses are to accomplish their historical task, the less they will use violence. The important thing for them is in any case deliberately from now on to steer their whole revolutionary tactic towards non-violence.

For this reason we appeal to all who wish to free the world from capitalism, imperialism and militarism, to free themselves first and foremost from those bourgeois, feudal and barbarous prejudices concerning violence, which are completely obsolete, and to which the majority of men still cling. Just as it is the inevitable fate of all political or social power, even though it may be exercised in the name of the Revolution, not to be able any longer to rid itself of horizontal and vertical violence, so it is the task of the social revolution to go beyond this violence and to emancipate itself from it. If the masses of the people really raise themselves, they will substitute for the violence of the State the freedom which comes from self-government.

The traditional belief in horizontal and vertical violence is nothing but a kind of moral enslavement to the nobility, clergy and bourgeoisie. It is nothing but a kind of blind, savage Messianism. It is the intrusion of the past into the present, to the peril of the future. He who cannot break loose from this fatal heritage is doomed to confuse it more and more with the revolution, which in turn is corrupted by it. For if the Revolution does offer a real value, it is just this, that it has shaken off barbarism and based itself on its essential principles: universal solidarity and co-operation.

121. Rudolf Rocker: Nationalism and Culture (1937)

Rudolf Rocker (1873-1958) was a German anarcho-syndicalist and a moving force behind the refounding of the International Workers' Association in 1922 (Selection 114). He wrote extensively on a wide variety of topics, from anarchism and anarcho-syndicalism to Marxism and dictatorship. His book, Anarcho-Syndicalism *(London: Secker & Warburg, 1938; Pluto Press reprint, 1989, with a preface by Noam Chomsky), is one of the best introductions to the subject. The following extracts are taken from his more philosophically ambitious work,* Nationalism and Culture *(Los Angeles: Rocker Publications Committee, 1937; most recently reprinted by Black Rose Books), in which he analyzes the connection between power politics, capitalism and racism.*

THE MORBID DESIRE TO MAKE MILLIONS of men submissive to a definite will and to force whole empires into courses which are useful to the secret purposes of small minorities, is frequently more evident in the typical representatives of modern capitalism than are purely economic considerations or the prospect of greater material profit. The desire to heap up ever increasing profits today no longer satisfies the demands of the great capitalistic oligarchies. Every one of its members knows what enormous power the possession of great wealth places in the hands of the individual and the caste to which he belongs. This knowledge gives a tempting incentive and creates that typical consciousness of mastery whose consequences are frequently more destructive than the facts of monopoly itself. It is this mental attitude of the modern Grand Seigneur of industry and high finance which condemns all opposition and will tolerate no equality...

Because of his social position there are left no limits to the power lust of the modern capitalist. He can interfere with inconsiderate egoism in the lives of his fellowmen and play the part of Providence for others. Only when we take into consideration this passionate urge for political power over their own people as well as over foreign nations are we able really to understand the character of the typical representatives of modern capitalism. It is just this trait which makes them so dangerous to the social structure of the future.

Not without reason does modern monopolistic capitalism support the National Socialist and fascist reaction. This reaction is to help beat down any resistance of the working masses, in order to set up a realm of industrial serfdom in which productive man is to be regarded merely as an economic automaton without any influence whatsoever on the course and character of economic and social conditions…

Every power is animated by the wish to be the only power, because in the nature of its being it deems itself absolute and consequently opposes any bar which reminds it of the limits of its influence. Power is active consciousness of authority. Like God, it cannot endure any other God beside it. This is the reason why a struggle for hegemony immediately breaks out as soon as different power groups appear together or have to keep inside of territories adjacent to one another. Once a state has attained the strength which permits it to make decisive use of its power it will not rest satisfied until it has achieved dominance over all neighbouring states and has subjected them to its will. While not yet strong enough for this it is willing to compromise, but as soon as it feels itself powerful it will not hesitate to use any means to extend its rule, for the will to power follows its own laws, which it may mask but can never deny.

The desire to bring everything under one rule, to unite mechanically and to subject to its will every social activity, is fundamental in every power. It does not matter whether we are dealing with the person of the absolute monarch of former times, the national unity of a constitutionally elected representative government, or the centralistic aims of a party which has made the conquest of power its slogan. The fundamental principle of basing every social activity upon a definite norm which is not subject to change is the indispensable preliminary assumption of every will to power. Hence the urge for outward symbols presenting the illusion of a palpable unity in the expression of power in whose mystical greatness the silent reverence of the faithful subject can take root…

Political power always strives for uniformity. In its stupid desire to order and control all social events according to a definite principle, it is always eager to reduce all human activity to a single pattern. Thereby it comes into irreconcilable opposition with the creative forces of all higher culture, which is ever on the lookout for new forms and new organizations and consequently as definitely dependent on variety and universality in human undertakings as is political power on fixed forms and patterns. Between the struggles for political and economic power of the privileged minorities in society and the cultural activities of the people there always exists an inner conflict. They are efforts in opposite directions which will never voluntarily unite and can only be given a deceptive appearance of harmony by external compulsion and spiritual oppression...

The very fact that every system of rulership is founded on the will of a privileged minority which has subjugated the common people by cunning or brute force, while each particular phase of culture expresses merely the anonymous force of the community, is indicative of the inner antagonism between them. Power always reverts to individuals or small groups of individuals; culture has its roots in the community. Power is always the sterile element in society, denied all creative force. Culture embodies procreative will, creative urge, formative impulse, all yearning for expression. Power is comparable to hunger, the satisfaction of which keeps the individual alive up to a certain age limit. Culture, in the highest sense, is like the procreative urge, which keeps the species alive. The individual dies, but never society. States perish; cultures only change their scene of action and forms of expression...

But although power and culture are opposite poles in history, they nevertheless have a common field of activity in the social collaboration of men, and must necessarily find a *modus vivendi*. The more completely man's cultural activity comes under the control of power, the more clearly we recognize the fixation of its forms, the crippling of its creative imaginative vigour and the gradual atrophy of its productive will. On the other hand, the more vigorously social culture breaks through the limitations set by political power, the less is it hindered in its natural development by religious and political pressure. In this event it grows into an immediate danger to the permanence of power in general...

Compulsion does not unite, compulsion only separates men; for it lacks the inner drive of all social unions—the understanding which recognizes the facts and the sympathy which comprehends the feeling of the fellow man because it feels itself related to him. By subjecting men to a common compulsion one does not bring them closer to one another; rather one creates estrangements between them and breeds impulses of selfishness and separation. Social ties have permanence and completely fulfill their purpose only when they are based on good will and spring from the needs of men. Only under such conditions is a relationship possible where social union and the freedom of the individual are so closely intergrown that they can no longer be recognized as separate entities.

Just as in every revealed religion the individual has to win the promised heavenly kingdom for himself and does not concern himself too greatly about the salvation of others, being sufficiently occupied with achieving his own, so also within the state man tries to find ways and means of adjusting himself without cudgeling his brain too much about whether others succeed in doing so or not. It is the state which on principle undermines man's social feeling by assuming the part of adjuster in all affairs and trying to reduce them to the same formula, which is for its supporters the measure of all things. The more easily the state disposes of the personal needs of the citizens, the deeper and more ruthlessly it dips into their individual lives and disregards their private rights, the more successfully it stifles in them the feeling of social union, the easier it is for it to dissolve society into its separate parts and incorporate them as lifeless accessories into the gears of the political machine.

Modern technology is about to construct the "mechanical man" and has already achieved some very pretty results in this field. We already have automatons in human form which move to and fro with their iron limbs and perform certain services—give correct change, and other things of that sort. There is something uncanny about this invention which gives the illusion of calculated human action; yet it is only a concealed clockwork that without opposition obeys its master's will. But it would seem that the mechanical man is something more than a bizarre notion of modern technology. If the people of the European American cultural realm do not within reasonable time revert to their best traditions there is real danger that we shall rush on to the era of the mechanical man with giant strides.

The modern "mass man," this uprooted fellow traveller of modern technology in the age of capitalism, who is almost completely controlled by external influences and whirled up and down by every mood of the moment—because his soul is atrophied and he has lost that inner balance which can maintain itself only in a true communion—already comes dangerously close to the mechanical man. Capitalistic giant industry, division of labour, now achieving its greatest triumph in the Taylor system and the so-called rationalization of industry, a dreary barracks system drilled into the drafted citizens, the connected modern educational drill and all that is related to it—these are phenomena whose importance must not be underestimated while we are inquiring about the inner connections among existing conditions...

The unexpected development of capitalist industrialism has furthered the possibility of national mass suggestion in a measure undreamed of before. In the modern great cities and centres of industrial activity live, closely crowded, millions of men who by the pressure of the radio, cinema, education, party, and a hundred other means are constantly drilled spiritually and mentally into a definite, prescribed attitude and robbed of their personal, independent lives. In the processes of capitalistic giant industry labour has become soulless and has lost for the individual the quality of creative joy. By becoming a dreary end in itself it has degraded man into an eternal galley slave and robbed him of that which is most precious, the inner joy of accomplished work, the creative urge of the personality. The individual feels himself to be only an insignificant element of a gigantic mechanism in whose dull monotone every personal note dies out…

The machine, which was to have made work easier for men, has made it harder and has gradually changed its inventor himself into a machine who must adjust himself to every motion of the steel gears and levers. And just as they calculate the capacity of the marvellous mechanism to the tiniest fraction, they also calculate the muscle and nerve force of the living producers by definite scientific methods and will not realize that thereby they rob him of his soul and most deeply defile his humanity. We have come more and more under the dominance of mechanics and sacrificed living humanity to the dead rhythm of the machine without most of us even being conscious of the monstrosity of the procedure. Hence we frequently deal with such matters with indifference and in cold blood as if we handled dead things and not the destinies of men.

To maintain this state of things we make all our achievements in science and technology serve organized mass murder; we educate our youth into uniformed killers, deliver the people to the soulless tyranny of a bureaucracy, put men from the cradle to the grave under police supervision, erect everywhere jails and penitentiaries, and fill every land with whole armies of informers and spies. Should not such "order," from whose infected womb are born eternally brutal power, injustice, lies, crime and moral rottenness—like poisonous germs of destructive plagues—gradually convince even conservative minds that it is order too dearly bought?

The growth of technology at the expense of human personality, and especially the fatalistic submission with which the great majority surrender to this condition, is the reason why the desire for freedom is less alive among men today and has with many of them given place completely to a desire for economic security. This phenomenon need not appear so strange, for our whole evolution has reached a stage where nearly every man is either ruler or ruled; sometimes he is both. By this the attitude of dependence has been greatly strengthened, for a truly free man does not like to play the part of either the ruler or the ruled. He is, above all, concerned with making his inner values and personal powers effective in a way as to permit him to use his own judgment in all affairs and to be independent in action. Constant tutelage of our acting and thinking has made us weak and irresponsible; hence, the continued cry for the strong man who is to put an end to our distress. This call for a dictator is not a sign of strength, but a proof of inner lack of assurance and of weakness, even though those who utter it earnestly try to give themselves the appearance of resolution. What man most lacks he most desires. When one feels himself weak he seeks salvation from another's strength; when one is cowardly or too timid to move one's own hands for the forging of one's fate, one entrusts it to another...

Every class that has thus far attained to power has felt the need of stamping their rulership with the mark of the unalterable and predestined, till at last this becomes an inner certainty for the ruling castes themselves.

They regard themselves as the chosen ones and think that they recognize in themselves externally the marks of men of privilege. Thus arose in Spain the belief in the *sangre azul*, the "blue blood" of the nobility, which is first mentioned in the medieval chronicles of Castile. Today they appeal to the blood of the "noble race" which allegedly has been called to rule over all the peoples of the world. It is the old idea of power, this time disguised as race. Thus one of the best known defenders of the modern race idea declares with noble self-assurance: "All Nordic culture is power culture; all Nordic talent is talent for matters of power, for matters of enterprise and worldmaking, whether in the material or in the spiritual realm, in the state, in art, in research."

All advocates of the race doctrine have been and are the associates and defenders of every political and social reaction, advocates of the power principle in its most brutal form...In this respect the representatives of the modern race theory differ in not the slightest degree from their predecessors except that they are more soulless, outspoken and brutal, and therefore more dangerous at a time when the spiritual in people is crippled and their emotions have grown callous and dull because of the war and its horrible after effects. People of the brand of Ammon, Gunther, Hauser and Rosenberg, are in all their undertakings ruthless and hidebound reactionaries. What that leads to, the Third Reich of Hitler, Goering and Goebbels shows us realistically. When Gunther, in his *Rassenkunde des deutschen Volkes* speaks of a "gradation in rank of the Germans according to their blood" his concept is thoroughly that of a slave people who are arranged in a definite order of ranks that reminds us of the castes of the Indians and the Egyptians. One comprehends how this doctrine found such ready acceptance in the ranks of the great industrialists. The *Deutsche Arbeitgeberzeitung* wrote thus about Gunther's book: "What becomes of the dream of human equality after one takes even a single glance at this work? Not only do we regard the study of such a work as this as a source of the highest interest and instruction; we believe, too, that no politician can form a correct judgment without investigation of the problems here dealt with."

Of course! No better moral justification could be produced for the industrial bondage which our holders of industrial power keep before them as a picture of the future...

He who thinks that he sees in all political and social antagonisms merely blood determined manifestations of race, denies all conciliatory influence of ideas, all community of ethical feeling, and must at every crisis take refuge in brute force. In fact, the race theory is only the cult of power. Race becomes destiny, against which it is useless to struggle; therefore any appeal to the basic principles of humanity is just idle talk which cannot restrain the operation of the laws of nature. This delusion is not only a permanent danger to the peaceful relations of peoples with one another, it kills all sympathy within a people and flows logically into a state of the most brutal barbarism. Whither this leads is shown in Ernst Mann's *Moral der Kraft,* where we read: "Who because of his bravery in battle for the general welfare has acquired a serious wound or disease, even he has no right to become a burden to his fellow men as cripple or invalid. If he was brave enough to risk his life in battle, he should possess also the final courage to end his life himself. Suicide is the one heroic deed available to invalids and weaklings."

...Such lines of thought lead to total depravity and inflict on all human feeling deeper wounds than one suspects. The race theory is the leitmotif of a new barbarism which endangers all the intellectual and spiritual values in culture, threatening to smother the voice of the spirit with its "voice of the blood." And so belief in race becomes the most brutal violence to the personality of man, a base denial of all social justice. Like every other fatalism, so also race fatalism is a rejection of the spirit, a degrading of man to a mere blood vessel for the race. The doctrine of race when applied to the concept of the nation proves that this is not a community of descent, as has been so often asserted; and as it dissects the nation into its separate components it destroys the foundations of its existence. When in spite of this its adherents today so noisily proclaim themselves the representatives of the national interests, one can but recall the saying of Grillparzer: "The course of the new education runs from humanity through nationality to bestiality."

Chapter 23
The Spanish Revolution

122. Félix Martí Ibáñez: The Sexual Revolution (1934)

Félix Martí Ibáñez (1913-1972) was a doctor active in the Spanish anarcho-syndicalist trade union federation, the Confederación Nacional del Trabajo (the CNT). The following excerpts are from his article, "Eugenics and Sexual Morality. The Sexual Revolution," originally published in Estudios, *135, November 1934. The translation is by Richard M. Cleminson of the University of Leeds, author of* Anarchism, Science and Sex: Eugenics in Eastern Spain, 1900-1937 *(Bern: Peter Lang, 2000). It is published here with his kind permission.*

WE RECOGNIZE THAT THE REVOLUTIONARY subversion of contemporary social life will be the basis of a new state of things.

But beneath the revolutionary slogans, under the new order, many of the disgraceful social disorders which afflict us today will persist. And the sexual aspect may be included here.

I imagine that some will find this statement ill-advised. But let us pause and think. Sexual freedom and the liberal criteria as far as sexuality is concerned are things which affect the deepest and most hidden spiritual side of the personality. Things so intimate and so personal that a simple change in social reality may do little when confronted by our deepest biological tendencies…

It is precisely the sexual prejudices that are the most difficult to banish. This is because sex and life itself are mixed up in the final analysis—just as sex and death are united in our amorous tribulations.

The ideological orientation of social, political, economic or scientific matters is easily changed. An eloquent example is given by politicians and scientists, by those who abandon what seemed to be firmly held ideas in order to adopt others, just as the snake sheds its old skin to bask in its new multi-coloured vestment in the light of the sun.

But the sexual life of man is not easily changed. The sexual tendencies are what provide the motor behind many ideological stances and actions of man. This, today, is an unquestionable truth, without necessarily accepting the extremes of Freud who makes the libido the mother of all human activity. Sexual practices, which stem from the mysterious complexities of the organism, from the intimate dynamics of the cells, are changed with great difficulty. In any case, they cannot be altered through external imposition, by the mandates of a Catholic or Communist State, because in order to change them they have to have undergone a previous process of evolution. For this reason, the collective sexual revolution, the social liberation from the laws and dogmas which today bind sexuality, will never manage to implement the individual sexual revolution. State imposition, just as it was not able to kill off the desire for sexual liberation harboured by many, will not be able to twist the sexual destiny of those who live their love lives pleasurably although surrounded by the dominant hypocrisy...

The sexual question cannot be resolved by a revolution, at least not by a rapid, theatrical, ostentatious revolution. The sexual revolution must be begun now; it must forge itself systematically and without interruption, "unhurried, but without a pause, like a star," as Goethe said. Sexuality cannot be dominated and channelled by some hastily written decree, drawn up on the barricades of victory; it needs to be preceded by an evolutionary process.

The great revolutions were never made in a violent and sudden manner, like the marionette that pops out of the hatch in a puppet theatre, but were the mature fruit of a long evolutionary process. They have been mined as a mole digs its lair, not in a lion's leap.

To believe that a violent revolution, which falls from the sky like a thunder bolt on to society, can destroy old oppressions and create a new, liberal state of things is an act of tremendous ingenuousness. This would be to accept the old version of History, which thought of itself in the romantic mode—a history of heroes and leaders, conquests and revolutions. But if it is judged serenely, History can be seen to be a scientific process, a collective History of labour, where peoples and collectives have substituted the romantic fighters and where revolutions have been replaced by creative evolution.

It is in this evolutionary cycle, as beads on a piece of string, that revolutionary processes are woven together. By this I mean authentic revolutionary processes, full of consequences. It is these that have been preceded by long evolutionary prologues. The other revolutions, those that have not been based on firm historical preparation, those revolutions which have emerged spontaneously, without the long process of fermentation, have been violent episodes with no further historical import.

And so some norms for application to the sexual sphere become apparent. Any pretended sexual revolution is a myth if by this it is understood as a violent revolutionary change in collective sexuality. Revolutions and the sexual revolution in particular, should not be something theatrical and ostentatious, an apotheosis of revolutionary decrees imposing free love. It should be a revolution made off-stage, which is where the constructive and historical part of the revolution takes place.

The sexual revolution, the supreme liberation of collective sexuality, should be the humble silent task of a phalanx of tenacious fighters, who by means of the book, the word, the conference and personal example, create and forge that sexual culture which is the key to liberation.

That is the real Revolution, what Reclus called "revolutionary evolution," in which the historical process advancing towards sexual freedom takes place without interruption. It is a process of evolution whereby the revolution filters through to all aspects of public life; it is present in all instants and in everything, like a day to day advancement towards the Ideal.

In this profound revolution, much more profound than passing episodes of violence, violent revolutions will only come when there is an insuperable obstacle placed in the way of Humanity's route towards progress. Then the river spontaneously becomes a torrent, sweeps away the obstacle, and returns to its path once more. Revolution and evolution are thus reconciled. But this tactic, which eliminates as far as possible the use of violence, which is the weapon of the weak, demands a high awareness of the duties and responsibilities of the sexual freedom that we advocate. It is important to realize that if we are proposing to destroy a form of morality and substitute for it another, the first thing to do is to show how honourable our attitude towards love and our moral stance towards sexuality both are.

We have in our hands the soft clay of new generations, with which we need to mould the figures of new people, to blow into that clay the breath of freedom and the understanding of the duties it brings with it. It is only in this way that we shall lift love out of the mire which surrounds it today, so that it can raise itself up in elegant flight towards the bright light of freedom.

122. Lucía Sánchez Saornil: The Question of Feminism (1935)

Lucía Sánchez Saornil (1895-1970) was a Spanish poet, writer and anarchist feminist. She was active in the CNT but critical of the sexist attitudes of many male Spanish anarchists. She helped found the anarchist feminist group, Mujeres Libres, in April 1936, a confederal organization of Spanish anarchist women that played an important role in the Spanish Revolution and Civil War (1936-1939). The following excerpts are taken from her article, "The Woman

Question in Our Ranks," originally published in the CNT paper, Solidaridad Obrera, *September-October 1935 (reprinted in* "Mujeres Libres" España, 1936-1939, *Barcelona: Tusquets, 1976, ed. Mary Nash). The translation is by Paul Sharkey.*

IT IS NOT ENOUGH TO SAY: "We must target women with our propaganda and draw women into our ranks;" we have to take things further, much further than that. The vast majority of male comrades—with the exception of a half dozen right-thinking types—have minds infected by the most typical bourgeois prejudices. Even as they rail against property, they are rabidly proprietorial. Even as they rant against slavery, they are the cruellest of "masters." Even as they vent their fury on monopoly, they are the most dyed-in-the-wool monopolists. And all of this derives from the phoniest notion that humanity has ever managed to devise. The supposed "inferiority of women." A mistaken notion that may well have set civilization back by centuries

The lowliest slave, once he steps across his threshold, becomes lord and master. His merest whim becomes a binding order for the women in his household. He who, just ten minutes earlier, had to swallow the bitter pill of bourgeois humiliation, looms like a tyrant and makes these unhappy creatures swallow the bitter pill of their supposed inferiority...

Time and again I have had occasion to engage in conversation with a male comrade who struck me as rather sensible and I had always heard him stress the need for a female presence in our movement. One day, there was a talk being given at the Centre, so I asked him:

"What about your partner. How come she didn't attend the talk?"

His response left me chilled.

"My partner has her hands full looking after me and my children."

On another occasion, I was in the corridors of the court building. I was with a male comrade who holds a position of responsibility. Out of one of the rooms emerged a female lawyer, maybe the defence counsel for some proletarian. My companion threw her a sidelong glance and mumbled as a resentful smirk played on his lips: "I'd send her type packing."

How much of a sad tale is told by those two, seemingly so banal, episodes?

Above all, they tell us that we have overlooked something of great significance: that while we were focusing all our energies on agitational work, we were neglecting the educational side. That our propaganda designed to recruit women should be directed, not at the women but at our own male comrades. That we should start by banishing this notion of *superiority* from their heads. That when they are told that all human beings are equal, "human beings" means women as well, even should they be up to their necks in housework and surrounded by saucepans and domestic animals. They need to be told that women possess an intellect like their own and a lively sensitivity and yearning for improvement; that before putting society to rights, they should be putting their own households in order; that what they dream of for the future—equality and justice—they should be practicing right here and now towards the members of their household; that it is nonsense to ask woman to understand the problems facing humanity unless she is first allowed to look inside herself, unless he ensures that the woman with whom he shares his life is made aware of her individuality, unless, in short, she is first accorded the status of individual…

There are many male comrades who honestly want to see women do their bit in the struggle; but this desire is not prompted by any change in their idea of women; they seek her cooperation as a factor that may hold out the prospect of victory, as a strategic contribution, so to speak, without giving a moment's thought to female autonomy or ceasing to regard themselves as the centre of the universe…

Etched in my memory is a certain trade union propaganda rally in which I was a participant. It took place in a small provincial town. Before the meeting got under way I was accosted by a male comrade, a member of the most important Local Committee…Through his fiery enthusiasm about the "sublime calling" of woman there shone, clear and precise, the blunt argument maintained by Oken—with whom he, no doubt, was not familiar, but to whom he was connected by the invisible thread of atavism—"Woman is but the means rather than the end of nature. Nature has but one end, one object: man."

…He was complaining about something that was, as far as I could see, the main grounds for satisfaction: That women had broken with the tradition that had them as men's dependents and stepped out into the labour market in search of economic independence. This pained him and delighted me because I knew that contact with the street and with social activity would provide a stimulus that in the end would activate her consciousness of her individuality.

His complaint had been the universal complaint of a few years before when women first quit the home for factory or workshop. Could it be deduced from this that it amounted to damage done to the proletarian cause? Woman's absorption into the workforce, coinciding with the introduction of machinery into industry, merely heightened labour competition and as a result led to a discernible fall in wages.

Taking the superficial view, we would say that the male workers were right: but if, ever ready to delve into the truth, we were to explore the core of the issue we will find that the outcome could have been so different, had the male workers not let themselves be carried away by their hostility to women, based on some supposed female inferiority.

Battle was joined on the basis of this supposed inferiority and lower pay rates were countenanced and women excluded from the class organizations on the grounds that social toil was not woman's calling, and on this was built an illicit competition between the sexes. The female machine-minder fitted in well with the simplistic view of the female mind in those days and so they started to employ women who, inured down through the ages to the idea that they were inferiors, made no attempt to set limits to capitalist abuses. Men found themselves relegated to the rougher tasks and specialized skills.

If, instead of behaving like this, the male workers had offered women some quarter, awakening in her encouragement and raising her to their own level, drawing her, right from the outset, into the class organizations, imposing equal conditions for both sexes upon the bosses, the upshot would have been markedly different. Momentarily, their physical superiority would have given them the upper hand in the selection of their employer, since it would have cost him as much to employ a strong person as it would a weakling, and, as for woman, her desire for improvement would have been aroused and, united with the men in the class organizations, together they could have made great and more rapid strides along the road to liberation...

At the present time the theory of the intellectual inferiority of women has been rendered obsolete; a sizable number of women of every social condition have furnished practical proof of the falsity of that dogma, we might say, by displaying the excellent calibre of their talents in every realm of human activity...

But, just when the road ahead seemed clear, a new dogma—this time with a semblance of scientific foundation—stands in woman's way and throws up further ramparts against her progress...

In place of the dogma of intellectual inferiority, we now have that of sexual differentiation. The moot point now is no longer, as it was a century ago, whether woman is superior or inferior; the argument is that she is different. No longer is it a question of a heavier or lighter brain of greater or lesser volume, but rather of spongy organs known as secreting glands which stamp a specific character on a child, determining its sex and thereby its role in society...

As far as the theory of differentiation is concerned, woman is nothing more than a tyrannical uterus whose dark influences reach even into the deepest recesses of the brain; woman's whole psychic life is obedient to a biological process and that biological process is quite simply the process of gestation...Science has tinkered with the terms without tampering with the essence of that axiom: "Birth, gestation and death." The whole and all of the womanly prospect.

Plainly an attempt has been made to frame this conclusion in golden clouds of eulogy. "Woman's calling is the most cultivated and sublime that nature has to offer," we are told; "she is the mother, the guide, the educator of the humanity of the future." Meanwhile the talk is of directing her every move, her entire life, all her education towards that single goal: the only one consonant with her nature, it would seem.

So now we have the notions of womanhood and motherhood set alongside each other again. Because it transpires that the sages have not discovered any middle ground; down through the ages, the practice has been a mystical eulogization of motherhood; hitherto, the praises went to the prolific mother, the mother who gives birth to heroes, saints, redeemers or tyrants; from now on, the praise will be reserved for the eugenic mother, the conceiver, the gestator, the immaculate birth-mother…

I said that we had the notions of womanhood and of motherhood set beside each other, but I was wrong; we already have something worse: the notion of motherhood overshadowing that of womanhood, the function annihilating the individual.

It might be said that down through the ages the male world has wavered, in its dealings with woman, between the two extreme notions of whore and mother, from the abject to the sublime without stopping at the strictly human: woman. Woman as an individual, as a rational, thoughtful, autonomous individual…

The mother is the product of the male backlash against the whore that every woman represents to him. It is the deification of the uterus that hosted him.

But—and let no one be scandalized for we are in the company of anarchists and our essential commitment is to call things by their proper name and tear down all wrong-headed notions, no matter how prestigious these may be—the mother as an asset to society has thus far merely been the manifestation of an instinct, an instinct all the sharper because woman's life has revolved solely around it for years; but an instinct, for all that, except that in some superior women it has acquired the status of *sentiment*.

Woman, on the other hand, is an individual, a thoughtful creature, a higher entity. By focusing on the mother you seek to banish woman when you could have woman and mother, because womanhood never excludes motherhood.

You sneer at woman as a determinative factor in society, assigning her the status of a passive factor. You sneer at the direct contribution of an intelligent woman, in favour of her perhaps inept male offspring. I say again: we must call things by their proper names. That women are women before all else; only if they are women will you have the mothers you need.

What I find really shocking is that male comrades who style themselves anarchists, bedazzled, perhaps, by the scientific principle upon which the new dogma purports to rest, are capable of upholding it. At the sight of them, I am assailed by this doubt: if they are anarchists, they cannot be for real, and if they are for real, they are no anarchists.

Under the theory of differentiation, the mother is the equivalent of the worker. To an anarchist, above all else a worker is a man, and above all else the mother should be a woman. (I am speaking in a generic sense). Because, for an anarchist, the individual comes first and foremost...

Regrettable it may be, but the campaigns for greater sexual freedom have not always been properly understood by our young male comrades, and in many instances, they have attracted into our ranks a large number of youths of both sexes who could not care less about the social question and who are just on the look-out for an opening for their own amorous adventures. There are some who have construed that freedom as an invitation to over-indulgence and who look upon every woman that passes their way as a target for their appetites...

In our centres, rarely frequented by young women, I have noticed that conversations between the sexes rarely revolve around an issue, let alone a work-related matter; the moment a youth comes face to face with someone of the opposite sex, the sexual issue casts its spell and free love seems to be the sole topic of conversation. And I have seen two types of female response to this. One, instant surrender to the suggestion; in which case it is not long before the woman winds up as a plaything of masculine whims and drifts away completely from any social conscience. The other is disenchantment: whereby the woman who arrived with loftier ambitions and aspirations comes away disappointed and ends up withdrawing from our ranks. Only a few women with strength of character who have learned to gauge the worth of things for themselves manage to weather this.

As for the male response, that remains the same as ever, in spite of his vaunted sexual education and this is plain when, in various amorous entanglements with the woman he regards as a "female comrade," the Don Juan figure turns into an Othello and the woman—if not the pair of them—is lost to the movement...

It is, ultimately, my considered opinion that resolution of this problem lies solely in a proper resolution of the economic question. In revolution. And nowhere else. Anything else would merely be calling the same old slavery by a new name. (Further reading: Martha Ackelsberg, *Free Women of Spain: Anarchism and the Struggle for the Emancipation of Women*, Bloomington: Indiana University Press, 1991; 2005 reprint by AK Press)

124. The CNT: Resolutions from the Zaragoza Congress (1936)

The CNT was founded in 1910, continuing the tradition of the anti-authoritarian and federalist workers' movement in Spain that dated back to the First International (Selection 36). The CNT was consciously anti-bureaucratic and revolutionary. At the CNT's 1919 congress, the delegates adopted the following statement of principles:

> Bearing in mind that the tendency most strongly manifested in the bosom of workers' organizations in every country is the one aiming at the complete and absolute moral, economic and political liberation of mankind, and considering that this goal cannot be attained until such time as the land, means of production and exchange have been socialized and the overweening power of the state has vanished, the undersigned delegates suggest that, in accordance with the essential postulates of the First International, it declares the desired end of the CNT to be anarchist communism. (Quoted in José Peirats, The CNT in the Spanish Revolution, Vol. 1, Hastings: Meltzer Press, 2001, page 11)

The CNT, as the most militant workers' organization in Spain, suffered the consequences. Many CNT militants were murdered by the hired guns of the employers, others were executed by the Spanish authorities, and many more were imprisoned. In 1924, the CNT was suppressed by the dictatorship of Primo de Rivera, and remained underground until 1930.

The CNT quickly sprang back into action, despite internal disputes over the direction of the organization, primarily between the anarcho-syndicalists and more reformist oriented syndicalists, but also between the "pure" anarchists and various Marxist elements that had been trying to co-opt the CNT since the early 1920's. In the late 1920's, the more militant anarchists formed the Iberian Anarchist Federation (FAI), the primary purpose of which was to foment revolution, but also to keep the CNT on an anarchist path.

The CNT and the FAI were involved in a variety of unsuccessful uprisings during the 1930's, in areas such as Catalonia, Casas Viejas and the Asturias, resulting in further waves of repression.

In February 1936, a leftist Popular Front government was elected and many imprisoned CNT and anarchist militants were released. The CNT began to regroup and prepare for the coming battle with fascism. On the eve of the election, the CNT National Committee had issued this prophetic communiqué:

> Proletarians! On a war footing against the monarchist and fascist conspiracy! Day by day the suspicion is growing that rightist elements are ready to provoke military intervention… Insurrection has been deferred, pending the out-

come of the elections. They are to implement their preventive plan if there is a leftist victory at the polls. We are not the defenders of the Republic, but we will do unstinting battle with fascism, committing all of our forces to rout the historical executioners of the Spanish proletariat. Furthermore, we have no hesitation in recommending that, wherever the legionnaires of tyranny launch armed insurrection, an understanding be speedily reached with anti-fascist groups, with vigorous precautions being taken to ensure that the defensive contribution of the masses may lead to the real social revolution and libertarian communism. Let everyone be vigilant. Should the conspirators open fire and should their fascist rebellion be defeated in its first stages, then the act of opposition must be pursued to its utmost consequences without tolerating attempts by the liberal bourgeoisie and its Marxist allies to hold back the course of events. Once hostilities begin in earnest, and irrespective of who initiates them, democracy will perish between two fires because it is irrelevant and has no place on the field of battle. If, on the other hand, the battle is tough, that recommendation will be redundant, for no one will stop until such time as one side or the other has been eliminated; and during the people's victory its democratic illusions would be dispelled. Should it be otherwise, the nightmare of dictatorship will annihilate us. Either fascism or social revolution. The defeat of fascism is the duty of the whole proletariat and all lovers of freedom, weapons in hand, yet the most profound preoccupation of members of this Confederation is that the revolution should be social and libertarian. If we are to be the greatest source of inspiration of the masses, if they are to initiate libertarian practices and create an unbreachable bulwark against the authoritarian instincts of the whites and the reds alike, we must display intelligence and unity of thought and action. (Peirats, page 94)

In May 1936 the CNT held a national congress in Zaragoza, with 649 delegates representing 982 unions with a membership of over 550,000. The Spanish Revolution was to begin a few months later, on July 19, 1936. Consequently, the resolutions passed at the Zaragoza Congress are particularly important, as they set forth the CNT's stance on a number of issues on the eve of the Revolution and Civil War. The resolution on libertarian communism was largely the work of Isaac Puente, author of the widely reprinted and translated pamphlet of the same name (Sydney: Monty Miller, 1985; originally published 1932). He was killed by the fascists soon after the outbreak of the Spanish Civil War. The following extracts are taken from José Peirats, The CNT in the Spanish Revolution, Vol. 1 *(Hastings: Meltzer Press, 2001), and are reprinted with the kind permission of the publisher.*

THE CONTENTION THAT THE REVOLUTION is nothing but a violent episode through which the capitalist system is sloughed has been given undue tolerance. In fact, it is merely the phenomenon which effectively clears the way for a state of affairs which has slowly taken shape in the collective consciousness.

The revolution, therefore, has its origins in the moment when the gulf between the state of society and the individual conscience is realized, when the latter finds itself, either through instinct or through analysis, obliged to react against the former.

So, in a few words, our belief is that revolutions come about:

1. as a psychological phenomenon opposed to a given state of affairs which stands in contradiction to individual aspirations and needs;

2. as a social phenomenon, whenever that response takes collective shape and clashes with the capitalist system;

3. as organization, whenever the need is felt to create a force capable of imposing the realization of its biological objective.

In the external order, these factors deserve to be stressed:

a. breakdown of the ethic which serves as the foundation of the capitalist system;

b. the economic bankruptcy of that system;

c. failure of its political manifestations, whether the democratic system or, in its ultimate expression, state capitalism or, to all intents and purposes, authoritarian communism.

When these factors coincide at a given point and time, a violent act is needed to lead into the truly evolutionary phase of the revolution.

In the belief that we are now at the precise point when the convergence of all those factors may bring about this tantalizing possibility we deem it necessary to frame a proposition which, in broad outline, profiles the basic pillars of the future social edifice.

Constructive conception of the revolution. Our understanding is that our revolution should be organized on a strictly equitable basis.

The revolution cannot be based on mutual aid, on solidarity or on the archaic notion of charity. In any case, these three formulae, which historically have sought to compensate for the deficiencies of rudimentary social models which left the individual defenceless in the face of a concept of arbitrary law, ought to be recast and refined into the new norms of social coexistence which find their clearest expression in libertarian communism. In other words, all human needs are to be met with no limitations other than those imposed by the requirements of the new economy...

Organization of the new post-revolutionary society. The first steps of the revolution.

Once the revolution has moved beyond its violent phase, the following will be abolished: private property, the state, the principle of authority and, consequently, the classes which divide humanity into exploiters and exploited, oppressors and oppressed.

With wealth socialized, the unfettered organizations of the producers will assume charge of the direct administration of production and consumption.

Once the libertarian commune has been established in each locality, we shall set the new mechanisms of society to work. The producers of each sector or trade, organized in their unions and workplaces, will freely determine the manner in which this is to be organized.

The free commune is to confiscate whatever was formerly possessed by the bourgeoisie in the way of provisions, clothing, footwear, raw materials, work tools, etc.

Such tools and raw materials pass into the hands of the producers so that the latter may administer them directly in the interests of the collectivity.

Firstly the communes will see to it that all the inhabitants of each district are housed with as many amenities as possible, with specific attention being guaranteed to health and education.

According to the fundamental principle of libertarian communism…all able-bodied individuals must work, assisting the collectivity proportionate to their strength and capabilities. Once labour is free, work will become a true right and, in return, the commune will fulfill its obligation by meeting the needs of all.

It is necessary to explain that the initial stages of the revolution will not be easy and that each individual will need to give of their best efforts and consume only what productive capabilities can afford. Every period of construction requires sacrifice and the acceptance of individual and collective restraints geared to improving the work of social reconstruction.

The producers' organizational plan. The economic plan will be tailored to the most rigorous principles of social economy in all spheres and directly administered by the producers through their various organs of production, which are to be appointed at general assemblies of all organizations and which will be under their constant supervision.

In the workplace, the union, the commune, in every agency regulating the new society, the producer, the individual, will be the most fundamental unit, the cell and the cornerstone of all social, economic and moral creations.

The point of liaison within the commune and in the workplace will be the workshop and factory council, which will form agreements with other work centres.

The liaison organs between unions will be the statistical and production councils which will federate with one another until they comprise a network of all the producers within the Iberian Confederation.

In the rural context, the basic unit will be the producer in the commune, which will have usufruct of all the natural assets within its political and geographical boundaries. The liaison body will be the cultivation council, which, composed of technical personnel and workers from the agricultural producers' associations, will be responsible for the intensification of production by selecting the most suitable lands.

These cultivation councils are to build up the same network of liaison as the workshop, factory, production and statistical councils, thereby complementing the free federation of the commune as a political jurisdiction and geographical sub-division.

For as long as Spain remains the only country to have effected its social transformation, the industrial producers' associations and the agricultural producers' associations alike are to federate at the national level if, of course, they deem this proper for the fruitful running of the economy. There will a similar federation among those services whose characteristics require this as a means of facilitating logical and necessary liaison between libertarian communes throughout the peninsula.

It is our view that the new society will eventually equip every commune with all the agricultural and industrial accoutrements required for it to be autonomous, according to the biological principle that the individual is most free when they need least from their fellow individuals.

The libertarian communes and their operation. We must erect the political expression of our revolution upon the triple base: individual, commune and federation.

Within a scheme of activities reaching into every facet of the peninsula, the administration will be of an absolutely communal nature.

Consequently, the foundation of this administration will be the commune. These communes are to be autonomous and will be federated at regional and national levels to achieve their general goals. The right to autonomy does not preclude the duty to implement agreements regarding collective benefits.

In this way, a consumers' commune without any voluntary restrictions will undertake to adhere to whatever general norms may be agreed by majority vote after free debate. In return, those communes which reject industrialization, the naturists and nudists, for instance, may agree upon a different model of coexistence and will be entitled to an autonomous administration released from the general commitments. Since such naturist/nudist communes (or communes of some other sort) will be unable to satisfy their own needs, however limited these needs may be, their delegates to congresses of the Iberian Confederation of Autonomous Libertarian Communes will be empowered to enter into economic contacts with other agricultural and industrial communes.

In conclusion, we propose that the commune be created as a political and administrative entity and that the commune be autonomous and confederated with other communes.

Communes are to federate at county and regional levels, and set their own geographical limits, whenever it may be found convenient to group small towns, hamlets and townlands into a single commune. Amalgamated, these communes are to make up an Iberian Confederation of Autonomous Libertarian Communes.

To handle the distribution side of production and so that the communes may be better able to support themselves, supplementary agencies designed for such purposes may be set up. For instance there might be a confederal council of production and distribution with direct representation from the national federations of production and from the annual congress of communes.

The commune's mission and internal workings: the commune will have a duty to concern itself with whatever may be of interest to the individual.

It will have to oversee organizing, running and beautification of the settlement. It will see that its inhabitants are housed and that items and products are made available to them by the producers' unions or associations.

Similarly it is to concern itself with hygiene, the keeping of communal statistics and with collective requirements such as education, health services and the maintenance and improvement of local means of communication.

It will orchestrate relations with other communes and will take care to stimulate all artistic and cultural pursuits.

So that this mission may be properly fulfilled, a communal council will have to be appointed, with representatives on it from the cultivation, health, cultural, distribution and production, and statistical councils.

The procedures for choosing the communal councils are to be determined according to a system that provides for differences such as population density, taking account of the fact that metropolitan areas will be slow to decentralize politically and to form federations of communes.

None of these posts will carry any executive or bureaucratic powers. Apart from those who may perform technical or merely statistical functions, the rest will perform their role as producers coming together in session at the close of the day's work to discuss the detailed items which may not require the endorsement of communal assemblies.

Assemblies are to be summoned as often as required by communal interests, upon the request of members of the communal council or according to the wishes of the inhabitants of each commune.

Liaison and exchange of produce. As we have outlined, our organization is federalist and guarantees the freedom of the individual within the group and the commune, as well as the freedom of the communes within the federations and the federation's rights within the confederations.

So we proceed from the individual to the collective, guaranteeing all individual rights, thereby maintaining the principle of liberty.

The inhabitants of a commune are to debate among themselves their internal problems regarding production, consumption, education, hygiene and whatever may be necessary for the moral and economic growth of the commune. Federations are to deliberate over major problems affecting a county or province and all communes are to be represented at their reunions and assemblies, thereby enabling their delegates to convey the democratic viewpoint of their respective communes.

If, say, roads have to be built to link the villages of a county or any matter arises to do with transportation and exchange of produce between agricultural and industrial counties, then naturally every commune which is implicated will have the right to have its say.

On matters of a regional nature, it is the duty of the regional federation to implement agreements which will represent the sovereign will of all the region's inhabitants. So the starting point is the individual, moving on through the commune, to the federation and right on up finally to the confederation.

Similarly, discussion of all problems of a national nature will follow a like pattern, since our organisms will be complementary. The national agency will regulate international relations, making direct contact with the proletariat of other countries through their respective bodies, linked, like our own, to the IWA.

As far as the interchange of produce between communes is concerned, the communal councils are to liaise with the regional federations of communes and with the confederal council of production and distribution, applying for whatever they may need and any available surplus stocks.

By means of the network of liaisons established between the communes and the production and statistical councils set up by the national federations of producers, this problem will be resolved and simplified.

As for the communal aspect of this question, the producers' cards issued by the workshop and factory councils, which will entitle holders to acquire whatever they need to meet their requirements, will suffice. The producers' card constitutes the basis of exchange and will be subject to two conditions: firstly, that it is non-transferable; secondly, that a method be adopted whereby the card records the labour value in working units, a value which will be valid for the acquisition of products for a maximum period of one year.

Members of the non-active population are to be issued with consumer cards by the communal councils.

Naturally we will not prescribe a hard and fast norm. The autonomy of the communes ought to be respected, although they may, should they see fit, adopt some other arrangement for internal distribution, provided that these new procedures do not in any way trespass against the interests of other communes.

The individual's duties towards the collectivity and the notion of distributive justice. Libertarian communism is incompatible with any system of castigation, something which thus implies the disappearance of the current system of correctional justice and of the instruments of punishment (jails, penitentiaries, etc.).

...[S]ocial circumstances are the principal cause of so-called offences in the present state of affairs and consequently, once the causes underlying the offence have been removed, then, as a general rule, crime will cease to exist...

Thus we understand that whenever the individual fails to perform his duties, whether morally or as a producer, popular assemblies will arrive at some harmonious and just solution to the problem.

So, libertarian communism will found its "corrective action" upon medicine and pedagogy, the sole preventive measures acknowledged by modern science. Should some individual suffer from anti-social or pathological conditions, pedagogical therapy will cure any imbalance or lunatic inheritance and stimulate an ethical sense of social responsibility.

The family and relations between the sexes...The first step in the libertarian revolution consists of ensuring that all human beings, without distinction of sex, are economically independent. Thus it is understood that both sexes are to enjoy equality of rights and duties alike and the economic inferiority between man and woman will thereby disappear.

Libertarian communism proclaims free love regulated only by the wishes of the man and the woman...

The religious question. Religion, a purely subjective facet of the human being, will be acknowledged as long as it remains a matter of individual conscience, but in no instance may it be regarded as a form of public display or moral or intellectual coercion...

Concerning pedagogy, art, science and the freedom to experiment. A radical approach will have to be adopted to the question of education. Firstly there will have to be a vigorous and systematic assault upon illiteracy. It is an obligation of restorative social justice incumbent upon the revolution that learning be restored to those who have been dispossessed of it, since just as capitalism has appropriated and arrogated society's wealth to itself, so the cities have appropriated and arrogated learning and education for themselves...

We deem it a primary function of pedagogy that it should help mould men with minds of their own—and let it be clear that we use the word "men" in the generic sense—to which end it will be necessary for the teacher to cultivate every one of the child's faculties so that the child may develop every one of its capacities to the full.

In the context of the educational system which libertarian communism is to put into practice, any schedule of punishments and rewards is to be repudiated once and for all, since those two precepts are at the root of all inequality...

Apart from the merely educational aspect, libertarian communism will guarantee access to science, art and all manner of research compatible with the pursuit of the production of necessities, thereby ensuring that human nature will be balanced and healthy.

The aim is that in libertarian communist society the producers are not to be divided into toilers or intellectuals, but that they may all be simultaneously toilers and intellectuals. When individuals have completed their daily work and fulfilled their mission as a producer for the community they are to have free access to the arts and science.

There are needs of a spiritual nature which run parallel to material needs and which will become more prominent in a society in which humanity is emancipated.

Since evolution is a continuous line, the individual will always have aspirations and ambitions to get on, to outdo his parents, outstrip his fellows and improve himself.

All such drives to better oneself, to experiment, to create—be it artistically, scientifically, or in a literary way—cannot, under any circumstances, whether material or general, be cast aside by a society based upon wide freedom: it will not thwart them, as presently happens, but instead will encourage and cultivate them in the belief that humanity does not live by bread alone and that a humanity living by bread alone would be a disgrace...

Defence of the revolution...until the social revolution may have triumphed internationally, the necessary steps will be taken to defend the new regime, whether against the perils of a foreign capitalist invasion...or against counter-revolution at home. It must also be remembered that a standing army constitutes the greatest danger to the revolution, since its influence could lead to dictatorship, which would necessarily kill off the revolution...The people armed will be the best assurance against any attempt to restore the system destroyed from either within or without.

125. Diego Abad de Santillán: The Libertarian Revolution (1936)

Upon his return to Spain in 1933, Abad de Santillán took an active role in the CNT and the FAI. He advocated a kind of anarchist pluralism in economics and politics, in favour of a mixed economy and wary of some aspects of the decentralist, libertarian communist position adopted by the CNT at the Zaragoza Congress. The following excerpts are taken from his book, After the Revolution: Economic Reconstruction in Spain Today *(New York: Greenberg, 1937; originally published as* El Organismo Economico de la Revolucion, *Barcelona, 1936; republished by Jura Media, Sydney, 1996).*

WE ARE COGNIZANT OF THE FACT THAT the grade of economic development and material conditions of life influence powerfully human psychology. Faced with starvation, the individual becomes an egoist; with abundance he may become generous, friendly and socially disposed. All periods of privation and penury produce brutality, moral regression and a fierce struggle of all against all, for daily bread. Consequently, it is plain that economics influences seriously the spiritual life of the individual and his social relations. That is precisely why we are aiming to establish the best possible economic conditions, which will act as a guarantee of equal and solid relationships among men. We will not stop being anarchists, on an empty stomach, but we do not exactly like to have empty stomachs...

The ideal of well-being is shared by all social movements. What distinguishes us is our condition as anarchists, which we place even before well-being. At least as individuals, we prefer freedom with hunger to satiation alongside of slavery and subjection...

If anarchism for the anarchists can exist with abundance as well as with misery, communism must have as its basis, abundance. In communism there is a certain generosity, and this generosity in a time of want is replaced little by little by egoism, distrust, competition; in a word, the struggle for bread...

Communism will be the natural result of abundance, without which it will remain only an ideal. In each locality the degree of communism, collectivism or mutualism will depend on the conditions prevailing. Why dictate rules? We who make freedom our banner, cannot deny it in economy. Therefore there must be free experimentation, free show of initiative and suggestions, as well as the freedom of organization.

To make possible this freedom, we must insist on the prerequisite of abundance which we can attain by the thorough use of industrial technique, modern agriculture and scientific development…

We are not interested in how the workers, employees and technicians of a factory will organize themselves. That is their affair. But what is fundamental is that from the first moment of Revolution there exist a proper cohesion of all the productive and distributive forces. This means that the producers of every locality must come to an understanding with all other localities of the province and country, which must have an international direct entente between the producers of the world. This cohesion is imperious and indispensable for the very function of all the factors of production…

We believe there is a little confusion in some libertarian circles between social conviviality, group affinities and the economic function. Visions of happy Arcadias or free communes were imagined by the poets of the past; for the future, conditions appear quite different. In the factory we do not seek the affinity of friendship but the affinity of work. It is not an affinity of character, except on the basis of professional capacity and quality of work, which is the basis of conviviality in the factory. The "free commune" is the logical product of the concept of group affinity, but there are no such free communes in economy, because that would presuppose independence, and there are no independent communes.

One thing is the free commune from the political or social standpoint and quite another, from an economic point of view. In the latter, our ideal is the federated commune, integrated in the economic total network of the country or countries in revolution…Our work on the land and in the factory does not make of us individual or collective proprietors of the land or of the factory; but it makes of us contributors to the general welfare. Everything belongs to everybody and the product of all labour must be distributed as equitably as the human efforts themselves. We cannot realize our economic revolution in a local sense; for economy on a localist basis can only cause collective privation and scarcity of goods. Economy is today a vast organism and all isolation must prove detrimental…

The revolution may awake in many men the forces of liberation, held in lethargy by daily routine and by a hostile environment. But it cannot by art or magic convert the anarchist minority into an absolute social majority. And even if tomorrow we were to become a majority, there would still remain a dissident minority which would suspect and oppose our innovations, fearing our experimental audacity.

However, if today we do not renounce violence in order to fight enslaving forces, in the new economic and social order of things we can follow only the line of persuasion and practical experience. We can oppose with force those who try to subjugate us in behalf of their interests or concepts, but we cannot resort to force against those who do not share our points of view, and who do not desire to live as we attempt to. Here, our respect for liberty must encompass the liberty of our adversaries to live their own life, always on the condition that they are not aggressive and do not deny the freedom of others.

If, in the social revolution, in spite of all the obstacles, we were to become a majority, the practical work of economic reconstruction would be enormously facilitated, because we could immediately count on the good will and support of the great masses. But even so, we would have to respect the experiments of different minorities, and reach an understanding with them in the exchange of products and services. Surely, as an historical minority, we anarchists have the right of revindicating this same liberty of experimentation and to defend it with all our might against any individual party or class which would attempt to crush it. Any totalitarian solution is of fascist tailoring, even though it may be defended in the name of the proletariat and the revolution. The new mode of life is a social hypothesis, which only practical experience should evaluate...

We want, first of all, to recognize the right of free experimentation for all social tendencies in our revolution; for this reason, it will not be a new tyranny, but the entrance into a reign of freedom and well being, in which all forces can show themselves, all initiative be tried out and all progress be put in practice. Violence is justified in the destruction of the old world of violence, but it is counter-revolutionary and anti-social when it is employed as a reconstructive method.

126. Gaston Leval: Libertarian Democracy

Gaston Leval (1895-1978) was one of the CNT's delegates to the Red International in Russia in 1921, where he managed to visit Voline in prison, and helped put pressure on the Bolsheviks to release Voline, Maksimov and other imprisoned anarchists. Partly as a result of his report, the CNT rescinded its tentative affiliation with the Red International and affiliated with the IWA (Selection 114). In 1923, he left Spain for Argentina to escape the Primo de Rivera dictatorship, returning in 1936 to participate in the Spanish Revolution, recording its positive accomplishments for posterity.

On July 19, 1936, the Spanish military attempted to seize power. The militants of the CNT-FAI took to the streets, thwarting the coup in large areas of Spain, while the Republican government virtually collapsed and offered only token resistance. The people of Spain began a massive social revolution, taking over the land and the factories and creating their own di-

rectly democratic collective organizations to run their own affairs. In the following extracts from Gaston Leval's Collectives in the Spanish Revolution *(London: Freedom Press, 1975; originally published 1971), Leval describes the general principles of "libertarian democracy" and emphasizes the original nature of the Spanish collectives.*

THERE WAS, IN THE ORGANIZATION set in motion by the Spanish Revolution and by the libertarian movement, which was its mainspring, a structuring from the bottom to the top, which corresponds to a real federation and true democracy. It is true that deviations can occur at the top and at all levels; that authoritarian individuals can transform, or seek to transform, delegation into intangible authoritarian power. And nobody can affirm that this danger will never arise. But the situation was quite different from what it is or would be in a State apparatus. In the State which Marx…called a "parasitic superstructure" of society, men installed in positions of command are inaccessible to the people. They can legislate, take decisions, give orders, make the choice for everybody without consulting those who will have to undergo the consequences of their decisions: they are the masters. The freedom which they apply is their freedom to do things in the way they want, thanks to the apparatus of law, rules and repression that they control, and at the end of which there are the prisons, penal settlements, concentration camps and executions. The USSR and the satellite countries are tragic examples of this.

The non-Statist system does not allow these deviations because the controlling and coordinating *Comités*, clearly indispensable, do not go outside the organization that has chosen them, *they remain in their midst*, always controllable by and accessible to the members. If any individuals contradict by their actions their mandates, it is possible to call them to order, to reprimand them, to replace them. It is only by and in such a system that the "majority lays down the law."

…Did this mean that there were no minorities, no individuals, exerting an often decisive influence on the assembly, or in the daily life of the Syndicates, Collectives, Federations? To answer in the affirmative would be to lie and would deceive nobody. As everywhere and always, there were in those organisms militants who were better prepared, who were the first to stand in the breach, and to preach by example, risking their own skins, and who, driven by the spirit of devotion and sacrifice, were better informed on the problems, and found solutions to them more readily. The history of mankind concedes a worthy place to the minorities who have assumed the responsibility for the happiness of their contemporaries and the progress of the species. But the libertarian minority assumed that role according to anti-authoritarian principles, and by opposing the domination of man by man.

To emancipate the people it is first of all necessary to teach them, to push them to think and to want. The sizeable and enthusiastic libertarian minority sought therefore...to teach the masses to do without leaders and masters and to that end were always communicating information to them, educating them, accustoming them to understand the problems affecting them either directly or indirectly, to seek and to find satisfactory solutions. The syndical assemblies were the expression and the practice of libertarian democracy...

Normally those periodic meetings [of the assemblies] would not last more than a few hours. They dealt with concrete, precise subjects concretely and precisely. And all who had something to say could express themselves. The *Comité* presented the new problems that had arisen since the previous assembly, the results obtained by the application of such and such a resolution on the volume of production, the increase or decrease of any particular speciality, relations with other syndicates, production returns from the various workshops or factories. All this was the subject of reports and discussion. Then the assembly would nominate the commissions, the members of these commissions discussed between themselves what solutions to adopt; if there was disagreement, a majority report and a minority report would be prepared.

This took place in *all* the syndicates *throughout* Spain, in *all* trades and *all* industries, in assemblies which, in Barcelona, from the very beginnings of our movement brought together hundreds or thousands of workers depending on the strength of the organizations. So much so that the awareness of the duties, responsibilities of each spread all the time to a determining and decisive degree.

The practice of this democracy also extended to the agricultural regions. We have seen how, from the beginning of the Civil War and of the Revolution the decision to nominate a local management *Comité* for the villages was taken by general meetings of the inhabitants of villages, how the delegates in the different essential tasks which demanded an indispensable coordination of activities were proposed and elected by the whole assembled population. But it is worth adding and underlining that in all the collectivized villages and all the partially collectivized villages, in the 400 Collectives in Aragon, in the 900 in the Levante region, in the 300 in the Castilian region, to mention only the large groupings which comprised at least 60% of "republican" Spain's agriculture, the population was called together weekly, fortnightly or monthly and kept fully informed of everything concerning the commonweal.

This writer was present at a number of these assemblies in Aragon, where the reports on the various questions making up the agenda allowed the inhabitants to know, to so understand, and to feel so mentally integrated in society, to so participate in the management of public affairs, in the responsibilities, that the recriminations, the tensions which always occur when the power of decision is entrusted to a few individuals, be they democratically elected without the possibility of objecting, did not happen there. The assemblies were public, the objections, the proposals publicly discussed, everybody being free, as in the syndical assemblies, to participate in the discussions, to criticize, propose, etc. Democracy extended to the whole of social life. In most cases even the individualists could take part in the deliberations. They were given the same hearing as the collectivists.

This principle and practice were extended to the discussions in the municipal Councils in the small towns and even in sizeable ones...[W]hen, because of the exigencies of war, our comrades had joined these Councils...they secured the agreement of the other parties, who could not easily refuse, that discussions should be open to the public...And often social reforms of immediate value (building of schools, nurseries, children's playgrounds, decent conditions for the old) were snatched from the political majority which would not have been granted if the discussions had taken place behind closed doors...

One of the dominant characteristics which impresses whoever studies the Spanish Revolution is its many sidedness. This revolution was guided by certain very clear and very definite principles, which involved the general expropriation of the holders of social wealth, the seizure by the workers of the organizational structures of production and distribution, the direct administration of public services, the establishment of the libertarian communist principle. But the uniformity of these principles did not prevent a diversity in the methods for their application, so much so that one can talk of "diversity within unity" and of a surprisingly diversified federalism.

In a very short time, in the agrarian regions and especially in Aragon, a new organism appeared: the Collective. Nobody had spoken about it before. The three instruments of social reconstruction foreseen among those libertarians who had expressed themselves on a possible future were firstly the Syndicate, then the Cooperative, which did not win many supporters, and finally, on a rather large scale, the commune, or communal organization. Some foreshadowed—and this writer was among them—that a new and complementary organism could and should appear, especially in the countryside, seeing that the Syndicate had not assumed the importance it had in the towns, and the kind of life, of work and production, did not fit into an organic monolithic structure which was contrary to the multiformity of daily life.

We have seen how that Collective was born with characteristics of its own. It is not the Syndicate, for it encompasses all those who wish to join it whether they are producers in the classic economic sense or not. Then it brings them together at the complete human individual level and not just at a craft level. Within it, from the first moment, the rights and duties are the same for everybody; there are no longer professional categories in mutual opposition making the producers into privileged consumers compared with those, such as housewives, who are not producers in the classical definition of the word.

Neither is the Collective the municipal Council or what is called the Commune, the municipality. For it parts company with the political party traditions on which the commune is normally based. It encompasses at the same time the Syndicate and municipal functions. It is all-embracing. Each of its activities is organized within its organism, and the whole population takes part in its management, whether it is a question of a policy for agriculture, for the creation of new industries, for social solidarity, medical service or public education. In this general activity the Collective brings each and everybody to an awareness of life in the round, and everyone to the practical necessity of mutual understanding.

Compared with the Collective the Syndicate has simply a secondary or subordinate role. It is striking to observe how in the agricultural districts, it was more often than not spontaneously relegated, almost forgotten, in spite of the efforts that the libertarian syndicalists and the anarcho-syndicalists had previously made. The Collective replaced them. The word itself was born spontaneously and spread into all the regions of Spain where the agrarian revolution had been brought about. And the word "collectivist" was adopted just as quickly and spread with the same spontaneity.

One could advance the hypothesis that these two words—collective and collectivism—better expressed the people's moral, human, fraternal feelings than did the terms Syndicates and syndicalism. A question of euphony perhaps, and of a breadth of views, of humanism: man as something more than the producer. The need for syndicates no longer exists when there are no more employers...

Going deeply into these matters it could perhaps be said that they were developing a new concept of liberty. In the village Collectives in their natural state, and in the small towns where everybody knew one another and were interdependent, liberty did not consist in being a parasite, and not interesting oneself in anything. Liberty only existed as a function of practical activity. *To be is to do*, Bakunin wrote. To be is to *realize*, voluntarily. Liberty is secured not only when one demands the rights of the "self" against others, but when it is a natural consequence of solidarity. Men who are interdependent feel free among themselves and naturally respect each other's liberty. Furthermore so far as collective life is concerned, the freedom of each is the right to participate spontaneously with one's thought, one's heart, one's will, one's initiative to the full extent of one's capacities. A negative liberty is not liberty: it is nothingness…

On this subject we would like to make an observation to which we attach great philosophical and practical importance. The theoreticians and partisans of the liberal economy affirm that competition stimulates initiative and, consequently, the creative spirit and invention without which it remains dormant. Numerous observations made by the writer in the Collectives, factories and socialized workshops permit him to take quite the opposite view. For in a Collective, in a grouping where each individual is stimulated by the wish to be of service to his fellow beings, research, the desire for technical perfection and so on are also stimulated. But they also have as a consequence that other individuals join those who were the first to get together. Furthermore when, in present society, an individualist inventor discovers something, it is used only by the capitalist or the individual employing him, whereas in the case of an inventor living in a community not only is his discovery taken up and developed by others, but is immediately applied for the common good. I am convinced that this superiority would very soon manifest itself in a socialized society.

127. Albert Jensen: The CNT-FAI, the State and Government (1938)

Albert Jensen belonged to the Swedish section of the IWA, the SAC. The following article, "The CNT-FAI, the State and the Government," was originally published in the International, *No. 2, May 1938, the monthly review of the IWA. Jensen sets forth some of the background to the Spanish Revolution, and offers some criticisms of the conduct of the CNT-FAI, particularly its fateful decision to collaborate with the Republican government, a policy which ultimately led to the defeat of the anarchist social revolution in Spain prior to the fascist military victory in March 1939.*

THE MILITARY REVOLT OF JULY 19, 1936 and the extraordinarily swift suppression of that revolt in Barcelona and Catalonia by the workers: It was the masses and the comrades of the CNT-FAI who took the initiative. The governmental authority was absolutely passive. The workers took possession of industry, collectivizing it and putting it under the control of the syndicates. The expropriation of large farms, the collectivization of these, and also, in a certain measure, those of small rural proprietors. Land and sea transport, the post, telegraph and telephone services, schools, and public health organizations were collectivized and controlled by the syndicates. At the same time, the workers created an army of militias under the control of the syndicates. Militia Committees were founded with the collaboration of the UGT [the Socialist trade union federation] and the political parties. With the same collaboration, a Council of Economy was constituted. The Police force was cleaned out and reorganized with the organs of revolutionary control. Political and economic control was almost completely controlled by the syndicates and the organism created in collaboration with the political parties. The military camarilla was suppressed with astonishing rapidity by the commencement of the social revolution.

With the new economic life and the political activities passing into the hands of the revolutionary movement, the Catalan State started to break up. Already, the Government had no real authority. Perhaps no more than a certain nominal power. A state without institutions of coercion and violence is no more a state. The Catalan government has no more the military apparatus at its disposal. The government no longer controls the police force which put itself under the control of the revolutionary organs. The State is without authority and the government powerless. Companys [Republican politician] tried to create a new military apparatus by mobilizing the old forces with the end of forming a new state army, barracked, commanded and formed by officers devoted to the State. The various classes of men of military age in Barcelona decided against enrolment in this army and instead formed groups of militias controlled by the syndicates and the organisms of the revolutionary movements.

The Catalan Government was deprived of one function after another and was powerless with regard to the productive life by the syndicates; the control of public services and transport by the same organizations; the revolutionary control of the police force by the Workers' Patrols; the absence of military and police apparatus of its own replaced by workers' administration of the new military apparatus of the militias. The Committee of Militias and the Council of Economy had power in their hands and were working for the Revolution. Obviously the State was not liquidated completely but there remained but a rudiment of it. The liquidation of the State had begun and this would continue progressively until the end in complete agreement with anarcho-syndicalist ideas if the revolutionary movement could continue the work undertaken.

But the line of revolutionary development was broken. A new government was formed in Barcelona. Was it perhaps thought that the latter answered more to the character of a revolutionary council than to an authoritarian government? But such self-deceit could not be continued for very long by the revolutionaries. The Generalidad assumed the appearance of any other government with all its customary activities. The CNT-FAI helped to form this government and offered its representation in it. With a generosity—a little too opportune—the CNT-FAI renounced all its majority positions, which are rightfully theirs, thus working in favour of the representatives of the UGT, the partisans of Marxist dictatorship, and the bourgeois parties. And once this was an accomplished fact, it was the beginning of self-destruction and counter-revolution and, from that time on, it was stated that the CNT-FAI could not make a "totalitarian" revolution.

This was the construction given of the historic events, for the greater part by foreign comrades probably. But for us, the question is this: Was this acceptance of the State and the Government—even if it had to have a purely provisional character—in reality, the only issue? Was no other attitude possible? And if so, cannot these events be considered as a proof of the weakness of the revolutionary anarcho-syndicalist theory? If such is the case, must we not admit frankly that our movement has ideologically gone astray? And if the tactic employed was inevitable, must we not be forced to the conclusion that the State cannot be suppressed in any way?

First of all, permit me to make one observation. At the time when the question of governmental participation in Catalonia was still being discussed, the CNT-FAI was still in the position to take power unto themselves, if they had so wished. That has been affirmed many times. But this idea was repulsed because logically it was realized that that would mean a dictatorship of the CNT-FAI. And nothing is more objectionable to anarcho-syndicalism than dictatorship, not only the dictatorship of others but also its own. In place of this, a democratic solution was adopted, in all good faith by the comrades, through the acceptance of governmental collaboration.

But a government in a state of war must have recourse always to dictatorship. Let it pretend to be democratic, liberal, social democratic, or anything else it pleases, it will still be dictatorial. It governs by decrees and uses full powers. The CNT-FAI thus accepted a system of state and governmental dictatorship which is essentially counter-revolutionary, and they arrived at this in order not to be compelled to realize their own dictatorship. That was certainly noble, but is hardly loyalty to ideas.

However, can one say that this solution carried great advantages for the social revolutionary movement and the war against fascism? Probably it will be said that it was an advantage to the anti-fascist war. But there remains what I consider to be no less a fact: that one form of dictatorship was repulsed in order to accept another. If the line adopted was the only one possible then the question is raised whether the movement was or was not obliged to change its attitude regarding the taking of power and dictatorship. There are so many questions and problems that, in the name of logic, it is necessary to clarify.

I have noted already the following question: If, compulsorily, the State and the government must be accepted, and with participation in the latter, must it not be concluded that the State cannot be suppressed in any way? Whether the State is accepted as a means of dictatorship or for a slow reform of society, experience in other countries where either of these lines has been followed has proven that the State has always been the stronger. There is Russia where the path of dictatorship was pursued. The dictatorship was to be nothing more than the transition period. But dictatorship leads to the inevitable: the creation of a new master class that uses the State to maintain its position in power. The abolition of the State promised by the Bolsheviks never came. The development of dictatorship within forms into a vicious circle: first, revolution to suppress class society and gain freedom; second, the creation of the proletarian State power to achieve this end; third, the proletarian State produces a new master class (State bureaucrats, party officials, military chiefs, the Cheka, etc.); fourth, the new master class, having in its hands, the State apparatus, consolidates it and secures it in order to maintain its privileged positions; and fifth, the point is reached where a new revolution is needed to create a new proletarian State. Thus is created a circular movement for the creation of a new dominant class and another revolution, never attaining the suppression of classes or the conquest of liberty. If the State cannot be completely liquidated in the Revolution and by the Revolution, then never will we be able to be free.

In the countries where the State was accepted as an instrument of reform to achieve Socialism and for the realization, through its intermediary, of libertarian communism and by making propaganda against the phantom of the State which gradually withers away, there the reformist State has been replaced by the dictatorial State (as in Germany, for example) and there is slavery indeed. Or, in the countries where Socialism is sacrificed (as in the Scandinavian countries) for the purpose of gaining reforms within the capitalist system, the State is considered, not as something to be abolished, but, on the contrary, as the supreme expression of "liberty." In one or the other case, the only thing there is, is the absence of liberty, the essence of the State system.

But the CNT and the FAI did not enter the government for the purpose of renouncing their opposition to the State. If I understand their motives well enough, they thought that thus they would be better able to defend the interests of the revolution within the government itself. That, in principle, is accepting the social democratic point of view, and renouncing, on the other hand, methods of direct action which are an integral part of the social conceptions of anarcho-syndicalism. Such a position produces practically the obligation to accept all the theoretical political system, even to reserving direct action as a complement to parliamentary political action. And such a combination of direct action with parliamentary political action is quite in harmony with social democracy. It is worth noting one other thing proven by experience: that in this case, direct action is slowly strangled by political and parliamentary action and that all the revolutionary tendencies are exhausted and die of atrophy.

At the commencement, the CNT and the FAI did not abandon their opposition to the State. They still defended the point of view that the State must be destroyed. Logically, that is incomprehensible. How can one maintain an anti-State attitude while, at the same time, accepting what one wants to suppress? The consequences are there and these must be taken into account.

If our conception of the revolutionary process in Catalonia is relatively just, if, in effect, the Catalan State lacked power and had none of the governmental apparatus at its disposal, if the control of public, political, and productive life had passed over to the syndicates and revolutionary organisms, if all the State apparatus really collapsed like a burst balloon, there was no logic in accepting the State, thus giving it new power and a new spirit. This acceptance of the State can scarcely be described otherwise than counter-revolutionary. Wounded unto death, the State received new life thanks to the governmental participation of the CNT-FAI. The dying body of the state recovered and gained new strength. Its feeling of power reappeared. The transfusion of the fresh blood of the CNT-FAI to this cadaverous body gave it the renewed desire to govern, to be powerful, to exercise its power over the masses and to dominate them. The CNT-FAI gave new substance to this monster. The Council of Economy became a State institution. The Committee of Militias followed the same road. The renewing blood of the dominant class circulated in the veins of the State. The militias were militarized. The State began to attack the revolutionary conquests of the workers. Free trade was an offering to the profit making system of the middle-class. The State systematized its resistance by carrying several blows against the collectivist regime. Under the protection of the State, the counter-revolutionary elements of the population acquired a position that became more and more solid. The State which had never been an instrument of the revolution but on the contrary, the very being of the counter-revolution, became more established each day. At the same time that the State was being strengthened, the position of the revolutionary forces became weaker. The State created a police force sufficiently strong. Also it transformed the militias into a body under its orders and no longer controlled by the workers. While becoming stronger each day, it became more and more the enemy of the social revolution.

Naturally the situation was very much more difficult for the CNT and the FAI...In effect, the Spaniards struggled and are struggling still not only against the masters in their own country but also against international fascism which is sustained by international capitalism...In this situation, the CNT had to act in such a fashion that would prevent internal conflicts between their own forces inside the country. They continued to collaborate with, and unite all the available forces for the war against international fascism. That was, in a general way, the desperate situation to which the CNT and the FAI had to adapt their tactics and their activities.

...But despite all that, the fact must be noted that new strength was given to the State and to the enemies of the Revolution by the governmental participation of the CNT-FAI. *The enemy of the working-class was assisted to reconstruct its instrument of power called the "State"—this State which had reached irremediably the stage of concentrating the counter-revolutionary forces that were directed against the revolution for the purpose of suppressing it. Thus, the revolutionary forces themselves assisted the hangman whose purpose it was to strangle them.*

To recognize the State as an inevitable evil in a determined situation is one thing. But it is another thing to collaborate actively in the reconstruction of the counter-revolutionary power, and that seems to us, and to numerous other foreign comrades, an absolutely incomprehensible method. If it was necessary to resign itself to the existence of the State, the CNT and the FAI should have dispensed, nevertheless, with collaborating actively in the reconstruction of the same. It appears that the CNT and the FAI would have better been able to defend itself by profiting from the revolutionary achievements without the governmental power, by pressing forward, through the means of its organized forces, to its own methods, and to control over the essential part of the country—that is, over industry and agriculture.

Numerous foreign comrades are wondering if it would not have been possible, at a certain moment, to have taken the initiative in concentrating the revolutionary forces against the bourgeois State. For example, was it not possible to have created a new expression of power by convoking a representation of a Council of Workers, Peasants, and Soldiers—a power that would not fall into the hands of the counter-revolutionary bourgeoisie? Would not such an assembly have been able to mobilize the worker and peasant masses in such a fashion as would have brought forth a new form of life for all the revolutionary forces that wanted a real social change? Would not such an appeal have separated a considerable mass from the UGT and which would have continually increased? For success in such a sense, would it not have been possible to pass over the bureaucracy of the UGT and the sectarian intrigues which later prevented the revolutionary alliance? Would it not have been possible to win over particularly the peasant masses, thus creating a revolutionary basis of the masses which would have made all counter-revolutionary sabotage impossible? Would not anarcho-syndicalism have obtained, within the new power, a directing and decisive influence?

...We are told that the collaboration of the CNT-FAI for the war was necessary unconditionally. But was it necessary to collaborate with the government for that? And if that were so, why could the CNT-FAI not address a clear and firm declaration to the government stating that, after having been in the first lines of struggle, in the organization of defence, and after having obtained the first successes, they would continue to collaborate loyally for the war against fascism, but that, under no pretext, would they tolerate any attack on the revolutionary accomplishments and that they would defend these with all the necessary means? I think such an attitude would have inspired a little more respect from the bourgeois class than has governmental participation, collaboration, and manufacturing of laws with which the counter-revolution has been able to sentence to prison for more than ten years, certain of our comrades because of their revolutionary activities. In any case, it seems to me, that the theses of anarcho-syndicalism which say that the force of the working-class is not in its political representatives but in its organizations and in the capacity of action of the workers, have still some value.

128. Diego Abad de Santillán: A Return to Principle (1938)

Abad de Santillán was one of several prominent anarchists in the CNT-FAI to collaborate with the Republican government, becoming a Generalidad minister from December 1936 to March 1937. In May 1937, there was a civil war within the Civil War, the "May Days" in Barcelona, where the anarchists were forced to fight for their lives and the social revolution, attacked by Communist and Republican forces. Hundreds of anarchists were killed, including many prominent militants, such as the Italian anarchist writer, Camillo Berneri, and the Libertarian Youth leader, Alfredo Martinez, who were both murdered. Abad de Santillán ceased his collaboration with the government and later wrote the following article, "Apropos of Our Libertarian Goals," published in Timon *(Barcelona), No. 2, August 1938. In January 1939 he left Spain, was interned in various concentration camps in France, and towards the end of the Second World War returned to Latin America. The translation is by Paul Sharkey.*

NO IDEA HAS BEEN SO DISFIGURED by its own and by outsiders as the anarchist idea has been, some in order to cover up their defection to the other side, others to halt its spread through the broad masses. Has any school of thought in modern times ever been attacked with as much vitriol as has been thrown at us by those whose over-riding aim is to live off another man's labours?

But it must be conceded that no ridicule, no criticism, no underhanded tricks, no political dishonesty by our adversaries has ever done us as much harm, nor provoked us to such outrage, as the ridicule and criticism emanating from those who, having—thanks to our movement—attained a certain degree of popularity, have sought to use it as a springboard to defect to the other side where the pickings are easier and the thorns less sharp.

If they mean to tell us that they are not the stuff of which revolutionaries are made, that they have no faith in the people and that they are weary of "sacrifices," there is no need for them to throw mud at an idea that stands above such pettiness and demands no reluctant tribute from anybody.

Our anarchy's only defenders are those...whom understand it and feel for it. It does not force itself on anybody nor does it require that anyone make sacrifices for it. Be they few in number or many, anarchists are sufficient and more than sufficient unto themselves when it comes to bringing credit to their ideas, in no matter what terrain they operate. We force no one to become an anarchist and to give his life or his sweat for anarchy, but neither do we remain silent as a sublime ideal is besmirched through the malice of unscrupulous adversaries or the weariness of faithless friends.

The doors are open for anyone to join us and open for any who would leave again. But there is not an open door when it comes to turning anarchy—a perfectly clear, well-defined teaching with a clear-cut profile—into a ridiculous monstrosity just to cover up desertions. Nor is there an open door for turning basic anarchist ideas into slavish pillars of diametrically opposed principles. Might we make so bold as to argue that this is not our movement's present function?

As for those who have learned over the past two years that a change of tack is called for, let them change tack! But let them leave our colours untouched, let them not drag them through the mire, let them not disfigure them just to carry on usurping the benefits; let them flourish the colours of whichever party or organization suits them best; or let them come up with a new doctrine, a new party. We will have no quarrel with them. But we do have a quarrel if they claim that anarchy can be turned to any use; that the revolution boils down to wading through the blood of martyrs and heroes to high positions of political and economic privilege. Against such, every anarchist with any love of anarchy has a right and a duty to resist and criticize…

Anybody taking fundamental exception to our ideas is entitled to do so. We shall even afford him space in these columns so that he may do so, but we reserve the right to respond immediately. We declare that, apart from the accretions of historical evolution, which bear out rather than rebut anarchy's underlying principles, there is nothing that we would strike from our ideological baggage. We are what our predecessors were.

As for methodology, the practices whereby we implement our aspirations, there is ample room for discussion. Tactics are circumstantial and dependent upon surroundings and opportunities, the locality and the time in which we live. There is no requirement to act the same in industry as in agriculture, or in a country that displays certain features as in another where conditions are different. We facilitated the victory of the republican left in the February 1936 elections, in order to thwart fascism's taking power by a lawful route. We had a comprehensive debate then on principles and tactics, stressing the fundamental character of the former and the contingent nature of the latter. We could return to this debate now. But the upshot will always be that we agree that certain methods leave us further removed from rather than closer to our goals.

Participation in political power, say, which we thought advisable due to circumstances, in the light of the war, will demonstrate for us yet again what Kropotkin once said of the parliamentary socialists: "You mean to conquer the State, but the State will end up conquering you."

…Contrary to the experience of all the socialist and revolutionary movements in history, we in Spain have known a phenomenon that is hard to comprehend. The best trained, most prestigious, sharpest-witted avant-garde minorities have not been in the vanguard of economic and social change; these have instead proved a hindrance, a brake, a hurdle to that change.

Awaiting instructions from none, the broad masses embarked upon the realization of what they carried in their hearts, and what they carried in their hearts was an intuitive grasp of and enthusiasm for a new order, a new regimen of economic and social relations.

With all of the shortcomings of impromptu, spontaneous activity, the Spanish people laid down the course to be followed from July 1936. And, no matter how this war turns out, the achievements of that people cannot be wiped from our memories and will live on in the memories of upcoming generations as a mighty spur to action and as a reliable guide.

The avant-garde minorities, over the two turbulent and hazardous years of our war against fascism, give the impression that they were taken aback by their own daring and they have gladly retreated to older positions that the broad masses have long since left in their wake with their revolutionary creations. Fear of freedom? Fear of the unknown? Ignorance? Stuck in a rut, even though that rut be as anti-revolutionary and anti-proletarian as can be? We shall leave it to historians of the future to unravel that mystery, which may in any case be explained thus:

1. The avant-garde minorities were not equal to their task nor were their words thought through and heartfelt.

2. The broad masses were better prepared than their supposed mentors and guides when it came to revolutionary reconstruction.

It is otherwise hard to understand the ease with which those who seemed to be marching in the vanguard reconciled themselves to what they had been fighting only the day before as if it were Public Enemy Number One.

In every revolution, the vanguard minorities aim to strike as deep as possible into the territory of practice, for the destruction of the old regime and the building of new ways of life. In the Spanish Revolution those minorities facilitated, not society's advance, but its retreat. Because there has been a lot of ground lost since the early months after the July events. And that ground was lost, not at the people's instigation, but at the prompting of what appeared to be the most advanced revolutionary minorities. But those minorities were revolutionary only in appearance, for show, and the people were more revolutionary than those minorities!

History teaches us that a motley society contains a large inert mass bereft of any will of its own, readily dragged to the right or to the left, depending on whether the minority forces of progress or reaction wield the whip in hand. Events in Spain have caused us to amend that outmoded outlook: in Spain there was a huge mass yearning for revolution and some so-called leading minorities, our own among them, which not only failed to egg on, articulate and facilitate the realization of that yearning, but indeed did all they could to clip its wings. The Spanish revolution was not the doing of any organization or party, but was eminently an achievement of the people, of the greater number. The retreat was made by so-called progressive social minorities...

We commonly hear remarks that mirror unhappiness with current conditions, but which also disclose an utter ignorance of our ideas and our methods. There is all too much glib talk such as: Dictatorship for dictatorship, ours would have been the better option!

It would have been preferable for those who act out the part of dictators, but not for the producing masses, the people, the community. As far as the people are concerned, no dictatorship is to be preferred over any other; they are all equally repugnant.

The dictatorship approach, its methodology and its demands are the same, the very same, whether it is exercised by self-styled fascists or those who profess to be communists, republicans, democrats or anarchists.

Dictatorship is a reversion to the most bestial tyranny and absolutism which should have been beaten back by revolutionary social progress. It now offers itself to us in a new garb, be it fascist or communist, but totalitarian rule which is to be enforced and employed as a pre-requisite cannot help but arrive at the same destination, regardless of how it is dressed up, the name its goes under or the colours it flies.

An anarchist dictatorship would be as poisonous for Spain as a fascist or communist dictatorship. Not to mention that in practicing it, we would become the very negation of what we are and what we stand for. It is not a question of personnel, but one of systems and procedures. As government men we are no worse and no better than anybody else and we know by now that our intervention in government serves no purpose other than to bolster governmentalism and in no way upholds the rights of labour against its parasitical enemies, economic and political.

As dictators, as tyrants, we are not, and no one is, made of better stuff than any other dictator and tyrant. On the other hand there is no need for us to lend a willing hand to the doing of evil and the practice of iniquity, forging the chains of human slavery. All of this has been proceeding for centuries without our being missed. Passivity or tolerance from us is enough if we want to stray from the path of freedom and justice for all; but let us at least fight shy of active complicity.

We have already highlighted the outstanding difference in our revolution. The minorities that seemed to be leading from the front were the biggest brakes on the constructive revolutionary action of the people. Might these minorities, less daring than the broad masses, be called upon to embody the *anarchist* dictatorship?

The merest whisper and hint of the nonsensical lamentation that we should, when we had the chance, have imposed our dictatorship should not be countenanced by comrades. The "going for broke" argument is a latent expression of the craving for dictatorship that the libertarian movement has had the good sense to thwart.

Since we have proved incapable of entrenching the revolution begun by the labouring people, let no one accuse us of being the grave-diggers of that revolution or accessories to the smothering and crushing of the revolutionary movement. And our dictatorship would, like any other, have smothered and buried that revolution.

Heads everywhere, centre nowhere! We have said it over and over, a thousand times. We continue to say it. From the organizational viewpoint, our own, as well as from the politico-national point of view.

No doubt about it: we have made mistakes and had our shortcomings; but rejection of our own dictatorship was neither a mistake nor a shortcoming, for our social message consists precisely of systematic opposition to all dictatorship, on the grounds that it is anti-revolutionary and anti-human...

The grounds for our irreconcilable opposition to statism are economic, moral and intellectual in nature. Day to day experience and the lessons of history furnish unambiguous proof to support us. The State subsists, not because of any *raison d'etre*, not because it has convinced its victims to put up with it and support it, but because it has strength and, as long as it has more strength than its adversaries, it will carry on playing the lion's part in social life, carrying on with its drive to smash culture and stifle individual and social life.

Let us summarize the economic basis for our anti-statism:

1. The State is an unduly expensive parasitical organism. It performs no service that could not be performed directly by those concerned at infinitely less cost and, above all, with much more efficiency. Twelve thousand million dollars are squandered yearly in the United States on the fight against crime. Prior to the war, Spain had 55,000 men spared productive toil and engaged in so-called public order duties. And the United States has not succeeded in eradicating the usual instances of so-called crime; and in Spain, the public order authorities have never managed to guarantee any such order.

2. Starting out as an agency defending the position of the wealthy classes, the modern State has become an end in itself, a supreme master of lives and finances, at the heart of everything. Which is why its bureaucracy, police and militarism have expanded. With every passing day the costs rise and humanity is thrust into shortage and penury just so that the State can be maintained. The tastiest and finest tidbits from life's banquet are gobbled up by statism, and the economically privileged devour the rest. Leaving only crumbs for the toilers of society. All in order to preserve a redundant agency whose functions society could perform for itself through its own direct organs, at no discernible cost to the producers. The State is unduly expensive and thoroughly sterile and sterilizing. It performs no essential social function. Bureaucracy, the military and police are its very essence. Although the State had meddled in it, nothing else is essential to statism. For instance, the railways, the posts and telegraphs ser-

> vices, public education, etc. Do we need the State to get the trains running, to get the mail distributed, so that we have schools, to make the wheat sprout in the fields?
>
> 3. As the ever-expanding ramifications of the State gobble up the greater and better part of socially useful labour, its existence represents a standing offence to human life, a curtailment of the right to life and development inherent in every human being.

But in cultural terms, the State is like Attila's horse: it leaves devastation in its wake. Its centralism cannot be reconciled with thoughtfulness, because it wants to see everything subjected to its guns, its ordinances, its interests, and thought, unless it be free, is nothing or only a caricature of thought. The creative endeavours of the mind require freedom and that freedom perishes on contact with statism...

We will always falter, make mistakes and make wrong moves: that was true yesterday, just as it will be today, tomorrow and always. Our human condition and our condition as dynamic activists ever ready to give it a go, will always keep us teetering on the edge of error. But trial and error are the cornerstone of all progress, in science as well as in matters political and social. We must give it a go and risk error so that we can harvest morsels of truth from the unknown.

It is not the making of mistakes that frightens us. Given a choice between error on the one hand and passivity, indifference and a deadly coldness in the face of life's many problems on the other, we should rather make mistakes, groping in the dark, and stumble. If we fall by the wayside, let us do it in our own style, while searching for the light, a better way for humanity. More damaging than error is persisting with an error and an inability to set mistakes aright.

But what we are concerned to state as our conclusion is that whereas there is no infallible criterion for truth, there is one way of always looking truth in the face: the people. If we are with it in good times and the bad, in its successes and its failures, we may not always feel satisfied but we shall never feel that we have strayed from our course. With the people, alongside the people, interpreters of its grievances and aspirations, carrying out its mandates. That must be our unvarying position, the only sure and always worthy one.

But one cannot serve two masters at once. If we are with the people, we cannot be with the State, which is its enemy. And right now we are with the State, which is tantamount to being against the people. For the first time in history, in anarchism's name, we prize the interests of governmentalism over those of the people. And the people, which has a healthy instinct, and an intuitive feel for the truth, is beginning to see plainly, to feel disheartened and hopeless when it sees us who had always offered our lives in defence of its cause forget it for a mess of ministerial pottage.

Nearly all of you, beloved comrades, will have been stung by some spontaneous popular exclamation, the truthfulness of which you cannot gainsay: "They're all the same when they make it to the top!"

We are all the same as those who went before us in the manning of high public and government office. The people cast this up to us. And the people are right. In order to hang on to those posts, from where the only thing we can plant is decrees, fresh taxes, new impositions and burdens, we must stand up to the people's demands. And should the people tomorrow, wearying of suffering, take to the streets as they so often have when we were on its side and in its midst, it will fall to us to massacre them. And unless we want to find ourselves facing that splendid prospect, we must deploy our every organizational resource to ensure that injustice, hunger and outrage are supinely and universally borne without complaint.

For how long, comrades? This sacrifice that we have made of our revolutionary identity: can there be any other outcome to it than furnishing all too much justification for snuffing out the trust that the people had placed in us? In government we are all the same! And we cannot serve two masters. Hence our insistence that we make our minds up. With the people, or with the State? Our conclusion is that in standing with the State and thus against the people, we are not only committing an irreparable act of betrayal of the revolution, which is taken as read, but we are also betraying the war effort, because we are denying it the active support of the people, the only invincible force, provided that it and its boundless resources are properly deployed.

For the future of the revolution and the prospects of the war, comrades, we may yet be in time, if we stand always alongside the people!

Chapter 24
Epilogue And Prologue To Volume 2

129. Emma Goldman: A Life Worth Living (1934)

Emma Goldman remained active in the anarchist movement until her death in Toronto in 1940. Despite her disillusionment in Russia, the rise of fascism and the tragic defeat of anarchism in Spain, she remained committed to her anarchist ideals to the very end. The following excerpts are taken from her article, "Was My Life Worth Living," originally published in Harper's Magazine, *Vol. CLXX, in December 1934.*

I CONSIDER ANARCHISM THE MOST BEAUTIFUL and practical philosophy that has yet been thought of in its application to individual expression and the relation it establishes between the individual and society. Moreover, I am certain that Anarchism is too vital and too close to human nature ever to die. It is my conviction that dictatorship, whether to the right or to the left, can never work—that it never has worked, and that time will prove this again, as it has been proved before. When the failure of modern dictatorship and authoritarian philosophies becomes more apparent and the realization of failure more general, Anarchism will be vindicated. Considered from this point, a recrudescence of Anarchist ideas in the near future is very probable. When this occurs and takes effect, I believe that humanity will at last leave the maze in which it is now lost and will start on the path to sane living and regeneration through freedom.

There are many who deny the possibility of such regeneration on the ground that human nature cannot change. Those who insist that human nature remains the same at all times have learned nothing and forgotten nothing. They certainly have not the faintest idea of the tremendous strides that have been made in sociology and psychology, proving beyond a shadow of a doubt that human nature is plastic and can be changed. Human nature is by no means a fixed quantity. Rather, it is fluid and responsive to new conditions. If, for instance, the so-called instinct of self-preservation were as fundamental as it is supposed to be, wars would have been eliminated long ago, as would all dangerous and hazardous occupations.

Right here I want to point out that there would not be such great changes required as is commonly supposed to insure the success of a new social order, as conceived by Anarchists. I feel that our present equipment would be adequate if the artificial oppressions and inequalities and the organized force and violence supporting them were removed.

Again it is argued that if human nature can be changed, would not the love of liberty be trained out of the human heart? Love of freedom is a universal trait, and no tyranny has thus far succeeded in eradicating it. Some of the modern dictators might try it, and in fact are trying it with every means of cruelty at their command. Even if they should last long enough to carry on such a project—which is hardly conceivable—there are other difficulties. For one thing, the people whom the dictators are attempting to train would have to be cut off from every tradition in their history that might suggest to them the benefits of freedom. They would also have to isolate them from contact with any other people from whom they could get libertarian ideas. The very fact, however, that a person has a consciousness of self, of being different from others, creates a desire to act freely. The craving for liberty and self-expression is a very fundamental and dominant trait.

The fact that the Anarchist movement for which I have striven so long is to a certain extent in abeyance and overshadowed by philosophies of authority and coercion affects me with concern, but not with despair. It seems to me a point of special significance that many countries decline to admit Anarchists. All governments hold the view that while parties of the right and left may advocate social changes, still they cling to the idea of government and authority. Anarchism alone breaks with both and propagates uncompromising rebellion. In the long run, therefore, it is Anarchism which is considered deadlier to the present regime than all other social theories that are now clamoring for power.

Considered from this angle, I think my life and my work have been successful. What is generally regarded as success—acquisition of wealth, the capture of power or social prestige—I consider the most dismal failures. I hold when it is said of a man that he has arrived, it means that he is finished—his development has stopped at that point. I have always striven to remain in a state of flux and continued growth, and not to petrify in a niche of self-satisfaction. If I had my life to live over again, like anyone else, I should wish to alter minor details. But in any of my more important actions and attitudes I would repeat my life as I have lived it. Certainly I should work for Anarchism with the same devotion and confidence in its ultimate triumph.

130. Herbert Read: Poetry and Anarchism (1938)

Herbert Read (1893-1968) was an English poet, writer and art critic who declared his allegiance to anarchism at a time when it was decidedly out of favour. His writings bridge the decline of classical anarchism, with the defeat of the anarchists in the Spanish Revolution and Civil War, and the post-war development of modern anarchism, particularly in his emphasis on spontaneity, creativity and self-realization. The following extracts are taken from Poetry and Anarchism *(London: Faber and Faber, 1938; reprinted in Anarchy and Order, Boston: Beacon Press, 1971).*

TO DECLARE FOR A DOCTRINE SO REMOTE as anarchism at this stage of history will be regarded by some critics as a sign of intellectual bankruptcy; by others as a sort of treason, a desertion of the democratic front at the most acute moment of its crisis; by still others as merely poetic nonsense…

I speak of doctrine, but there is nothing I so instinctively avoid as a static system of ideas. I realize that form, pattern, and order are essential aspects of existence; but in themselves they are the attributes of death. To make life, to insure progress, to create interest and vividness, it is necessary to break form, to distort pattern, to change the nature of our civilization. In order to create it is necessary to destroy; and the agent of destruction in society is the poet. I believe that the poet is necessarily an anarchist, and that he must oppose all organized conceptions of the State, not only those which we inherit from the past, but equally those which are imposed on people in the name of the future. In this sense I make no distinction between fascism and Marxism…

I am not concerned with the practicability of a program. I am only concerned to establish truth, and to resist all forms of dictation and coercion. I shall endeavour to live as an individual, to develop my individuality; and if necessary I shall be isolated in a prison rather than submit to the indignities of war and collectivism. It is the only protest an individual can make against the mass stupidity of the modern world…

Civilization has gone from bad to worse…and there are many young artists today whose only desire is to escape to some fertile soil under a summer sky, where they may devote themselves entirely to their art free from the distractions of an insane world. But there is no escape. Apart from the practical difficulty of finding a secure refuge in this world, the truth is that modern man can never escape from himself. He carries his warped psychology about with him no less inevitably than his bodily diseases. But the worst disease is the one he creates out of his own isolation: uncriticized phantasies, personal symbols, private fetishes. For whilst it is true that the source of all art is irrational and automatic—that you cannot create a work of art by taking thought—it is equally true that the artist only acquires his significance by being a member of a society. The work of art, by processes which we have so far failed to understand, is a product of the relationship which exists between an individual and a society, and no great art is possible unless you have as corresponding and contemporary activities the spontaneous freedom of the individual and the passive coherence of a society. To escape from society (if that were possible) is to escape from the only soil fertile enough to nourish art...

Liberty is always relative to man's control over natural forces, and to the degree of mutual aid which he finds necessary to exert this control. That is why, in face of the material problems of existence, the ideal of anarchy becomes the practical organization of society known as anarcho-syndicalism. Government—that is to say, control of the individual in the interest of the community—is inevitable if two or more men combine for a common purpose; government is the embodiment of that purpose. But government in this sense is far removed from the conception of an autonomous State. When the State is divorced from its immediate functions and becomes an entity claiming to control the lives and destinies of its subjects—then liberty ceases to exist.

What might be called the tyranny of facts—the present necessity which most of us are under to struggle for our very existence, our food, our shelter, and other no less essential amenities of life—this tyranny is so severe that we ought to be prepared to consider a restriction of liberty in other directions if in this respect some release is promised. But it is no less essential to realize that this tyranny is to a large extent due to the inefficiency of our present economic system, and that liberty now and always depends on a rational organization of production and distribution...

The problem, in its broad outlines, is simple enough. On the one side we have mankind, needing for its sustenance and enjoyment a certain quantity of goods; on the other side we have the same mankind, equipped with certain tools, machines, and factories, exploiting the natural resources of the earth. There is every reason to believe that with modern mechanical power and modern methods of production, there is or could be a sufficiency of goods to satisfy all reasonable demands. It is only necessary to organize an efficient system of distribution and exchange. Why is it not done?

The only answer is that the existing inefficient system benefits a small minority of people who have accumulated sufficient power to maintain it against any opposition. That power takes various forms—the power of gold, the power of tradition, the power of inertia, the control of information—but essentially it is the power to keep other people in a state of ignorance. If the superstitious credulity of the masses could be shaken; if the fantastic dogmas of the economists could be exposed; if the problem could be seen in all its simplicity and realism by the simplest worker and peasant, the existing economic system would not last a day longer. The creation of a new economic system would take more than the following day; but it would be better to begin with a revolution, as in Spain, than to go through the slow-motion agony of a so-called "transitional period." A transitional period is merely a bureaucratic device for postponing the inevitable...

The society I desire and will and plan is a leisure society—a society giving full opportunity for the education and development of the mind. Mind only requires time and space—to differentiate itself. The worst conditions of intellectual uniformity and stupidity are created by conditions of poverty and lack of leisure. The ordinary man under our present unjust system has to have his education stopped before his mind is fully opened. From the age of fourteen he is caught up in an endless treadmill; he has neither time nor opportunity to feed his undeveloped senses—he must snatch at the diuretic pabulum of the newspapers and the radio, and as a consequence, tread the mill with more urgency...

I would define the anarchist as the man who, in his manhood, dares to resist the authority of the father; who is no longer content to be governed by a blind unconscious identification of the leader and the father and by the inhibited instincts which alone make such an identification possible. Freud...sees the origin of the heroic myth in such a longing for independence. "It was then, perhaps, that some individual, in the exigency of his longing, may have been moved to free himself from the group and take over the father's part. He who did this was the first epic poet; and the advance was achieved in his imagination. This poet disguised the truth with lies in accordance with his longing. He invented the heroic myth. The hero was a man who by himself had slain the father—the father who still appeared in the myth as a totemistic monster. Just as the father had been the boy's first ideal, so in the hero who aspires to the father's place the poet now created the first ego ideal." But the further step which the anarchist now takes is to pass from myth and imagination to reality and action. He comes of age; he disowns the father; he lives in accordance with his own ego-ideal. He becomes conscious of his individuality...

The obsessive fear of the father which is the psychological basis of tyranny is at the same time the weakness of which the tyrant takes advantage. We all know the spectacle of the bully goaded into sadistic excesses by the very docility of his victim. The tyrant or dictator acts in exactly the same way. It is not psychologically credible that he should act in any other way. The only alternative to the principle of leadership is the principle of co-operation or mutual aid; not the father-son relationship which has persisted from primitive times, but the relationship of brotherhood; in political terms, the free association of producers working for the common good. This is the essential doctrine of anarchism, and far from having been discredited by Marxian economics or the achievements of the Soviet Union, it has everywhere received overwhelming confirmation in the events of the last twenty years, until we may now claim that the realization of this principle of brotherhood is the only hope of civilization...

Outbreaks of "unofficial" strikes, strikes against the authority of the Trade Unions and against the State as employer, are now a characteristic of our time. These developments are devolutionary—revolts against centralization and bureaucratic control—and as such essentially anarchist. For the anarchist objects, not merely to the personal tyranny of a leader like Stalin, but still more to the impersonal tyranny of a bureaucratic machine.

What is wrong with bureaucracy? In the vast and extremely complicated conditions of modern civilization, is not a bureaucracy necessary merely to hold that civilization together, to adjust relationships, to administer justice and so on?

Actually, of course, in a society of rich and poor nothing is more necessary. If it is necessary to protect an unfair distribution of property, a system of taxation and speculation, a monopolist money system; if you have to prevent other nations from claiming your ill-gotten territorial gains, your closed markets, your trade routes; if as a consequence of these economic inequalities you are going to maintain pomp and ceremony, ranks and orders; if you are going to do any or all these things you will need a bureaucracy.

Such a bureaucracy consists of armed forces, police forces, and a civil service. These are largely autonomous bodies. Theoretically they are subordinate to a democratically elected Parliament, but the Army, Navy, and Air Forces are controlled by specially trained officers who from their schooldays onwards are brought up in a narrow caste tradition, and who always, in dealing with Parliament, can dominate that body by their superior technical knowledge, professional secrecy, and strategic bluff. As for the bureaucracy proper, the Civil Service, anyone who has had any experience of its inner workings knows the extent to which it controls the Cabinet, and through the Cabinet, Parliament itself. We are really ruled by a secret shadow cabinet, the heads of the Treasury, the Foreign Office, the Home Office, the Service Departments, and the Permanent Secretary to the Cabinet. Below this select club...we have a corps of willing and efficient slaves—beetle-like figures in striped trousers, black coats, winged collars, and bow ties. All these worthy servants of the State are completely out of touch with the normal life of the nation: they are ignorant of the methods and conditions of industrial production, unaware of the routine and atmosphere of proletarian life—or life of any real kind.

Every country has the bureaucracy it deserves. Ours, trained in public school and university, is efficient, unimaginative, unfeeling, dull, and honest. In other countries the bureaucracy has no such gentlemanly traditions; it is lazy, lousy, and corrupt. In any case, lazy or efficient, honest or corrupt, a bureaucracy has nothing in common with the people; it is a parasitic body, and has to be maintained by taxation and extortion. Once established (as it has been established for half a century in England and as it is newly established in Russia) it will do everything possible to consolidate its position and maintain its power. Even if you abolish all other classes and distinctions and retain a bureaucracy you are still far from the classless society, for the bureaucracy is itself the nucleus of a class whose interests are totally opposed to the people it supposedly serves...

The syndicalist—the anarchist in his practical rather than his theoretical activity—proposes to liquidate the bureaucracy first by federal devolution. Thereby he destroys the idealistic concept of the State—that nationalistic and aggressive entity which has nearly ruined Western civilization. He next destroys the money monopoly and the superstitious structure of the gold standard, and substitutes a medium of exchange based on the productive capacity of the country—so many units of exchange for so many units of production. He then hands over to the syndicates all other administrative functions—fixing of prices, transport, and distribution, health, and education. In this manner the State begins to wither away! It is true that there will remain local questions affecting the immediate interests of individuals—questions of sanitation, for example; and the syndicates will elect a local council to deal with such questions—a council of workers. And on a higher plane there will be questions of co-operation and exchange between the various productive and distributive syndicates, which will have to be dealt with by a central council of delegates—but again the delegates will be workers. Until anarchism is complete there will be questions of foreign policy and defence, which again will be dealt with by delegated workers. But no whole-time officials, no bureaucrats, no politicians, no dictators. Everywhere there will be cells of workers, working according to their abilities and receiving according to their needs...

The degeneration of political consciousness in modern democratic states is not a moral degeneration. It is due to this very process of centralization and collectivization which is taking place independently, and in spite of the particular political system we supposedly enjoy. There was a time when the relationship between the citizen and his representative in Parliament was direct and human; there was a time when the relationship between a member of Parliament and the government was direct and human; but all that has passed. We have been the victims of a process of dehumanization in our political life. Parties have become obedient regiments of mercenaries; delegates have been replaced by committees; the paid official, the omnipresent bureaucrat, stands between the citizen and his Parliament. Most departments of national life are controlled by vast and efficient bureaucratic machines which would continue to function to a large extent independently—that is to say, irrespective of political control.

Universal political franchise has been a failure—that we have to confess. Only a minority of the people is politically conscious, and the remainder only exist to have their ignorance and apathy exploited by an unscrupulous Press. But do not let us confuse universal franchise, which is a system of election, with democracy, which is a principle of social organization. Universal franchise is no more essential to democracy than divine right is to monarchy. It is a myth: a quite illusory delegation of power. Justice, equality, and freedom—these are the true principles of democracy, and it is possible—it has been amply proved by events in Italy and Germany—that the universal franchise can in no sense guarantee these principles, and may, indeed, impose a fiction of consent where in effect no liberty of choice exists.

If you go into a village and propose to introduce electric power; if you go into a city street and propose to widen it; if you raise the price of bread or curtail the hours of drinking licences—then you touch the immediate interests of the citizen. Put these questions to the voter and without any coaxing or canvassing he will run to the poll.

In short, real politics are local politics. If we can make politics local, we can make them real. For this reason the universal vote should be restricted to the local unit of government, and this local government should control all the immediate interests of the citizen. Such interests as are not controlled by the local council should be controlled by his local branch of the syndicate or soviet to which he belongs. His remoter interests—questions of co-operation, intercommunication, and foreign affairs—should be settled by councils of delegates elected by the local councils and the syndicates. Only in that way shall we ever get a democracy of vital articulation and efficient force.

It is important, however, to make one qualification without which any democratic system will fail. A delegate should always be an *ad hoc* delegate. Once a delegate separates himself from his natural productive function, once he becomes a professional delegate, then all the old trouble sets in again. The bureaucratic parasite is born; the evil principle of leadership intervenes; the lust for power begins to corrode these chosen people. They are consumed by pride.

The professional politician is an anomalous figure...He is the man who deliberately adopts politics as a career. He may incidentally be a lawyer or a trade union secretary or a journalist; but he is in politics for what he can get out of it. He means to climb to office and to power, and his motive throughout is personal ambition and megalomania. Owing to the preoccupations of the other types of parliamentary representatives, this professional politician is only too likely to succeed. It is he, in particular, who is a danger in a socialist society, for with the disappearance of the disinterested man of leisure, he becomes the predominant type of politician. Unchecked by rival types, he monopolizes all offices of power, and then, intoxicated with the exercise of this power, turns against his rivals within his own category, ruthlessly exterminates those who threaten to supplant him, and enforces the strict obedience of all who promise to serve him. Such is the process by which dictators rise and establish themselves; such is the process by which Mussolini, Stalin, and Hitler established themselves. It is a process which the social democratic state unconsciously but inevitably encourages. The only safeguard against such a process is the abolition of the professional politician as such and the return to a functional basis of representation...

Modern anarchism is a reaffirmation of...natural freedom, of...direct communion with universal truth. Anarchism rejects the man-made systems of government, which are instruments of individual and class tyranny; it seeks to recover the system of nature, of man living in accordance with the universal truth of reality. It denies the rule of kings and castes, of churches and parliaments, to affirm the rule of reason, which is the rule of God.

The rule of reason—to live according to natural laws—this is also the release of the imagination. We have two possibilities: to discover truth, and to create beauty. We make a profound mistake if we confuse these two activities, attempting to discover beauty and to create truth. If we attempt to create truth, we can only do so by imposing on our fellow-men an arbitrary and idealistic system which has no relation to reality; and if we attempt to discover beauty we look for it where it cannot be found—in reason, in logic, in experience. Truth is in reality, in the visible and tangible world of sensation; but beauty is in unreality, in the subtle and unconscious world of the imagination. If we confuse these two worlds of reality and imagination, then we breed not only national pride and religious fanaticism, but equally false philosophies and the dead art of the academies. We must surrender our minds to universal truth, but our imagination is free to dream; is as free as the dream; is the dream.

I balance anarchism with surrealism, reason with romanticism, the understanding with the imagination, function with freedom. Happiness, peace, contentment—these are all one and are due to the perfection of this balance. We may speak of these things in dialectical terms—terms of contradiction, negation, and synthesis—the meaning is the same. The world's unhappiness is caused by men who incline so much in one direction that they upset this balance, destroy this synthesis. The very delicacy and subtlety of the equilibrium is of its essence; for joy is only promised to those who strive to achieve it, and who, having achieved it, hold it lightly poised.

131. Malatesta: Toward Anarchy

By way of conclusion, I end this volume with a short extract from an article by Malatesta, "Toward Anarchy," originally published in La Questione Sociale, *New Series No. 14, December 9, 1899, an "anarcho-socialist periodical" based in Paterson, New Jersey, then a centre of Italian American anarchism. This article has previously been mistranslated into English as "Towards Anarchism," obliterating the important distinction Malatesta always drew between anarchy, the future free society, and anarchism, the doctrine in support of that ideal. It is anarchy towards which we should always be striving, not the triumph of any particular ideology.*

IT IS A COMMONLY HELD VIEW THAT WE, because we call ourselves revolutionaries, expect anarchy to come with one stroke, as the immediate result of an insurrection which violently overthrows all that which exists and replaces it with truly new institutions. And to tell the truth this idea is not lacking among some comrades who also conceive the revolution in such a manner.

This prejudice explains why so many honest opponents believe anarchy a thing impossible; and it also explains why some comrades, disgusted with the present moral condition of the people and seeing that anarchy cannot come about soon, waver between an extreme dogmatism which blinds them to the realities of life and an opportunism which practically makes them forget that they are anarchists and that for anarchy they should struggle.

Of course, the triumph of anarchy cannot be the result of a miracle and neither can it come about in contradiction to the general law (it being an axiom of evolution that nothing can happen without sufficient cause) that nothing can be done without having the strength to do it.

If we should want to substitute one government for another, that is, impose our desires upon others, it would only be necessary to combine the material forces needed to resist the actual oppressors and put ourselves in their place.

But we do not want this; we want Anarchy which is a society based on free and voluntary accord—a society in which no one can force his wishes on another and in which everyone can do as he pleases and together all will voluntarily contribute to the general well-being. But because of this anarchy will not have definitively and universally triumphed until all of humanity will not only not want to be commanded but will not want to command, and everyone will have understood the advantage of solidarity and will know how to organize a mode of social life wherein there will be no more traces of violence and imposition.

And just as conscience, will and ability gradually develop and find the occasion and means of development in the gradual modification of the environment and in the realization of desires in proportion to their being formed and becoming urgent, so also anarchy cannot come but little by little—slowly, but surely, growing in intensity and extension.

Therefore, it is not a matter of achieving anarchy today, tomorrow, or within ten centuries, but that we walk toward anarchy today, tomorrow, and always…every blow given to the institutions of private property and government, every uplifting of the popular conscience, every disruption of the present conditions, every lie unmasked, every part of human activity taken away from the control of the authorities, every augmentation of the spirit of solidarity and initiative, is a step toward anarchy.

Index

R

Books on Anarchism

1984 AND AFTER
Marsha Hewitt, Dimitrios Roussopoulos, eds
Paperback ISBN: 0-920057-29-2 $14.99
Hardcover ISBN: 0-920057-28-4 $43.99

ANARCHISM AND ECOLOGY
Graham Purchase
Paperback ISBN: 1-55164-026-0 $19.99
Hardcover ISBN: 1-55164-027-9 $48.99

ANARCHIST COLLECTIVES: Workers' Self-Management in Spain 1936-39
Sam Dolgoff, editor
Paperback ISBN: 0-919618-20-0 $16.99
Hardcover ISBN: 0-919618-21-9 $45.99

ANARCHIST AND THE DEVIL DO CABARET
Norman Nawrocki
Paperback ISBN: 1-55614-204-2 $19.99
Hardcover ISBN: 1-55164-205-0 $48.99

ANARCHISM OF JEAN GRAVE: Editor, Journalist and Militant
Louis Patsouras
Paperback ISBN: 1-55164-184-4 $24.99
Hardcover ISBN: 1-55164-185-2 $53.99

ANARCHIST ORGANISATION: The History of the F.A.I
Juan Gómez Casas, trans. by Abe Bluestein
Paperback ISBN: 0-920057-38-1 $18.99
Hardcover ISBN: 0-920057-40-3 $47.99

ANARCHIST PAPERS, revised edition
Dimitrios Roussopoulos, editor
Paperback ISBN: 1-55614-180-1 $24.99
Hardcover ISBN: 1-55164-181-X $53.99

ANARCHIST PAPERS 2
Dimitrios Roussopoulos, editor
Paperback ISBN: 0-921689-36-5 $12.99
Hardcover ISBN: 0-921689-37-3 $41.99

ANARCHIST PAPERS 3
Dimitrios Roussopoulos, editor
Paperback ISBN: 0-921689-52-7 $12.99
Hardcover ISBN: 0-921689-53-5 $41.99

ANOTHER VENICE: Ciao, Anarchici
Agnoldo Maciel, Marianne Enckell, Fabio Santin
Paperback ISBN: 0-920057-71-3 $19.99
Hardcover ISBN: 0-920057-73-X $48.99

APHRA BEHN: The English Sappho
George Woodcock
Paperback ISBN: 0-921689-40-3 $19.99
Hardcover ISBN: 0-921689-41-1 $48.99

BAKUNIN: The Philosophy of Freedom
Brian Morris
Paperback ISBN: 1-895431-66-2 $18.99
Hardcover ISBN: 1-895431-67-0 $47.99

BAKUNIN ON ANARCHISM
Sam Dolgoff, editor
Paperback ISBN: 0-919619-06-1 $18.99
Hardcover ISBN: 0-919619-05-3 $47.99

BOLSHEVIKS AND WORKERS' CONTROL
Maurice Brinton
Paperback ISBN: 0-919618-69-3 $ 7.99
Hardcover ISBN: 0-919618-70-7 $36.99

CONQUEST OF BREAD
Peter Kropotkin, Introduction by George Woodcock
Paperback ISBN: 0-921689-50-0 $24.99
Hardcover ISBN: 0-921689-51-9 $53.99

CUBAN REVOLUTION: Critical Perspective
Sam Dolgoff
Paperback ISBN: 0-919618-35-9 $15.99
Hardcover ISBN: 0-919618-36-7 $44.99

DECENTRALISM: Where It Came From—Where Is It Going?
Mildred J. Loomis
Paperback ISBN: 1-55164-248-4 $19.99
Hardcover ISBN: 1-55164-249-2 $48.99

DECENTRALIZING POWER: Paul Goodman's Social Criticism
Taylor Stoehr, editor
Paperback ISBN: 1-55164-008-2 $19.99
Hardcover ISBN: 1-55164-009-0 $48.99

DURRUTI: The People Armed
Abel Paz, translated by Nancy MacDonald
Paperback ISBN: 0-919618-74-X $16.99
Hardcover ISBN: 0-919618-73-1 $45.99

EMMA GOLDMAN: Sexuality and the Impurity of the State
Bonnie Haaland
Paperback ISBN: 1-895431-64-6 $19.99
Hardcover ISBN: 1-895431-65-4 $48.99

ETHICS: Origins and Development
Peter Kropotkin, Introduction by George Woodcock
Paperback ISBN: 1-895431-36-0 $24.99
Hardcover ISBN: 1-895431-37-9 $53.99

EVOLUTION AND ENVIRONMENT
Peter Kropotkin, Introduction by George Woodcock
Paperback ISBN: 1-895431-44-1 $24.99
Hardcover ISBN: 1-895431-45-X $53.99

from Black Rose Books

FIELDS, FACTORIES AND WORKSHOPS
Peter Kropotkin, Introduction by George Woodcock
Paperback ISBN: 1-895431-38-7 $24.99
Hardcover ISBN: 1-895431-39-5 $53.99

FINDING OUR WAY: Rethinking Eco-Feminism
Janet Biehl
Paperback ISBN: 0-921689-78-0 $19.99
Hardcover ISBN: 0-921689-79-9 $48.99

FREEDOM FIGHTERS: Anarchist Intellectuals, Workers, and Soldiers in Portugal's History
João Freire, trans. by M.F. Noronha da Costa e Sousa
Paperback ISBN: 1-55164-138-0 $24.99
Hardcover ISBN: 1-55164-139-9 $53.99

FROM THE GROUND UP: Essays on Grassroots and Workplace Democracy
C. George Benello
Paperback ISBN: 1-895431-32-8 $19.99
Hardcover ISBN: 1-895431-33-6 $48.99

FUGITIVE WRITINGS
Peter Kropotkin, Introduction by George Woodcock
Paperback ISBN: 1-895431-42-5 $24.99
Hardcover ISBN: 1-895431-43-3 $53.99

GEOGRAPHY OF FREEDOM: The Odyssey of Elisée Reclus
Marie Fleming
Paperback ISBN: 0-921689-16-0 $16.99
Hardcover ISBN: 0-921689-17-9 $45.99

GREAT FRENCH REVOLUTION
Peter Kropotkin, Introduction by George Woodcock
Paperback ISBN: 0-921689-38-1 $24.99
Hardcover ISBN: 0-921689-39-X $53.99

IN RUSSIAN AND FRENCH PRISONS
Peter Kropotkin, Introduction by George Woodcock
Paperback ISBN: 0-921689-98-5 $24.99
Hardcover ISBN: 0-921689-99-3 $53.99

IRRATIONAL IN POLITICS
Maurice Brinton
Paperback ISBN: 0-919618-24-3 $ 4.99
Hardcover ISBN: 0-919618-50-2 $33.99

LOUISE MICHEL
Edith Thomas, translated by Penelope Williams
Paperback ISBN: 0-919619-07-4 $19.99
Hardcover ISBN: 0-919619-08-2 $48.99

MEMOIRS OF A REVOLUTIONIST
Peter Kropotkin, Introduction by George Woodcock
Paperback ISBN: 0-921689-18-7 $24.99
Hardcover ISBN: 0-921689-19-5 $53.99

MODERN CRISIS
Murray Bookchin
Paperback ISBN: 0-920057-62-4 $18.99
Hardcover ISBN: 0-920057-61-6 $47.99

MODERN STATE: An Anarchist Analysis
J. Frank Harrison
Paperback ISBN: 0-920057-00-4 $13.99
Hardcover ISBN: 0-919619-18-5 $42.99

MURRAY BOOKCHIN READER
Janet Biehl, editor
Paperback ISBN: 1-55164-118-6 $24.99
Hardcover ISBN: 1-55164-119-4 $53.99

MUTUAL AID: A Factor of Evolution
Peter Kropotkin, Introduction by George Woodcock
Paperback ISBN: 0-921689-26-8 $24.99
Hardcover ISBN: 0-921689-27-6 $53.99

NATIONALISM AND CULTURE
Rudolf Rocker, translated by Ray E. Chase
Paperback ISBN: 1-55164-094-5 $28.99
Hardcover ISBN: 1-55164-095-3 $57.99

PARTICIPATORY DEMOCRACY
Dimitrios Roussopoulos, C. George Benello, eds
Paperback ISBN: 1-55164-224-7 $24.99
Hardcover ISBN: 1-55164-225-5 $53.99

PETER KROPOTKIN: From Prince to Rebel
George Woodcock, Ivan Avakumovic
Paperback ISBN: 0-921689-60-8 $24.99
Hardcover ISBN: 0-921689-61-6 $53.99

PHILOSOPHY OF SOCIAL ECOLOGY: Essays on Dialectical Naturalism
Murray Bookchin
Paperback ISBN: 1-55164-018-X $19.99
Hardcover ISBN: 1-55164-019-8 $48.99

PIERRE-JOSEPH PROUDHON: A Biography
George Woodcock
Paperback ISBN: 0-921689-08-X $19.99
Hardcover ISBN: 0-921689-09-8 $48.99

POLITICS OF INDIVIDUALISM: Liberalism, Liberal Feminism and Anarchism
L. Susan Brown
Paperback ISBN: 1-55164-202-6 $24.99
Hardcover ISBN: 1-55164-203-4 $53.99

POLITICS OF OBEDIENCE: The Discourse of Voluntary Servitude
Etienne de la Boétie, Introduction by M.N. Rothbard
Paperback ISBN: 1-55164-088-0 $15.99
Hardcover ISBN: 1-55164-089-9 $44.99

Printed by the workers of
MARC VEILLEUX IMPRIMEUR INC.
Boucherville, Québec

CPSIA information can be obtained
at www.ICGtesting.com
Printed in the USA
BVHW082336170919
558710BV00001B/62/P